Data Engineering with Google Cloud Platform

A guide to leveling up as a data engineer by building a scalable data platform with Google Cloud

Adi Wijaya

‹packt›

Data Engineering with Google Cloud Platform

Copyright © 2024 Packt Publishing

All rights reserved. No part of this book may be reproduced, stored in a retrieval system, or transmitted in any form or by any means, without the prior written permission of the publisher, except in the case of brief quotations embedded in critical articles or reviews.

Every effort has been made in the preparation of this book to ensure the accuracy of the information presented. However, the information contained in this book is sold without warranty, either express or implied. Neither the author, nor Packt Publishing or its dealers and distributors, will be held liable for any damages caused or alleged to have been caused directly or indirectly by this book.

Packt Publishing has endeavored to provide trademark information about all of the companies and products mentioned in this book by the appropriate use of capitals. However, Packt Publishing cannot guarantee the accuracy of this information.

Group Product Manager: Kaustubh Manglurkar

Publishing Product Manager: Nilesh Kowadkar

Book Project Manager: Farheen Fathima and Shambhavi Mishra

Senior Editor: Nazia Shaikh

Technical Editor: Kavyashree K S

Copy Editor: Safis Editing

Proofreader: Nazia Shaikh and Manikandan Kurup

Indexer: Pratik Shirodkar

Production Designer: Alishon Mendonca

Senior DevRel Marketing Coordinator: Nivedita Singh

First published: April 2022
Second edition: April 2024
Production reference: 1240424

Published by Packt Publishing Ltd.
Grosvenor House
11 St Paul's Square
Birmingham
B3 1RB, UK.

ISBN: 978-1-83508-011-5

www.packtpub.com

To all of you readers who have spent your time and effort following the book, and to all the readers of the first version who reached out to give amazing feedback – Samil, Pene, Siddarth, António, and many others. It always touches me to know the book is making a positive impact. I sincerely hope this book can help many more data enthusiasts reach their career goals.

Special thanks to those who supported me during the book writing process – Sylviana, Eleana, Arkan, and Toni.

– Adi Wijaya

Foreword

Several years ago, I found myself in the pursuit of enhancing my proficiency with the **Google Cloud Platform** (**GCP**) stack, so I would be able to collaborate and work on GCP data architectures.

This book served as the catalyst, empowering me to implement practical batch/streaming data pipelines alongside customers and to implement centralized data models with GCP with their business data.

The significance and utilization of Google Data Cloud have since grown, rendering expertise in the GCP stack indispensable.

To understand how BigQuery works, how to process data with Dataproc (Apache Spark) or Dataflow (Apache Beam), how to collect data in real time with Pub/Sub, or how to orchestrate DAGs to manage all pipeline dependencies with Google Cloud Composer (Apache Airflow), this is a must-read since all of this is covered by Adi within these pages.

As a data engineer, I appreciated the straightforwardness of Adi's explanations and the reproducibility of the examples within my own environment, thanks to the inclusion of commands and scripts for practical application.

This book equips you to create ETL/ELT pipelines using GCP; collect, transform, and visualize data from multiple source types (batch/streaming); and learn about tools that will be very important in your data engineer career. Abundant exercises throughout will facilitate your journey toward mastery.

With this book, you too can emerge as an esteemed data engineer, proficient in harnessing the full potential of the Google Cloud Platform stack. Highly recommended!

Print ("This GCP book is awesome!!!")

António Vilares,

Data Platform Technical Manager at Viator, Tripadvisor

Contributors

About the author

Adi Wijaya is a strategic cloud data engineer at Google, with over a decade of global experience as an engineer and a consultant working with dozens of organizations. He brings his expertise to the pages of this book. Throughout his career, Adi has successfully built scalable data pipelines and optimized data processing workflows for various industries. Valuing the importance of sharing, Adi is also a dedicated educator and mentor. He has conducted numerous workshops and training sessions, empowering aspiring data talent with the skills and knowledge required to excel. Based on the recognition of the first edition, Adi aims to further empower readers and provide them with the tools they need to thrive in the dynamic world of this field.

About the reviewers

Raghava Satya SaiKrishna Dittakavi, a cloud computing specialist focused on cost optimization, is crucial at a leading SAAS company in Boston. With a master's from the University of Massachusetts Lowell and over a decade in the field, his strategies enhance cloud efficiency and reduce costs. Raghava's innovations in technology have earned him recognition as a cloud technology leader. He's an influential voice in cloud computing, contributing to platforms such as DZone and HackerNoon. Raghava, a member of IEEE, BCS, and ACM, also mentors upcoming professionals. His achievements have been honored with awards such as the Titan and Globee awards, marking his impact on cloud computing and DevOps.

Ankit Virmani is a senior cloud and machine learning leader, with over a decade of work experience in MLOps, data operations, and data engineering. Having worked for companies such as Google, Amazon, CVS, and Deloitte, he has both the strategies and hands-on experience to design and productionize data and machine learning platforms at a petabyte scale. He is a Forbes Technology Council member and evangelizes the use of ethical AI with thought leadership articles. He also works at multiple non-profit organizations to make them successful in grant writing, campaign management, and other operations using AI.

Table of Contents

Preface　　　　　　　　　　　　　　　　　　　　　　　　　　　　　xv

Part 1: Getting Started with Data Engineering with GCP

1

Fundamentals of Data Engineering　　　　　　　　　　　　　　　　3

Understanding the data life cycle	4	The difference between ETL and ELT	14
Understanding the need for a data warehouse	4	What is not big data?	15
Start with knowing the roles of a data engineer	9	A quick look at how big data technologies store data	16
A data engineer versus a data scientist	10	A quick look at how to process multiple files using MapReduce	17
The focus of data engineers	11	Summary	19
Going through the foundational concepts for data engineering	13	Exercise	20
ETL concept in data engineering	13	Further Reading	20

2

Big Data Capabilities on GCP　　　　　　　　　　　　　　　　　　21

Technical requirements	22	Getting started with GCP	23
Understanding what the cloud is	22	Introduction to the GCP console	25
The difference between the cloud and non-cloud era	22	Practicing pinning services	26
The on-demand nature of the cloud	23	A quick overview of GCP services for data engineering	32

Understanding the GCP serverless service	33	User account versus service account	39
Service mapping and prioritization	35	**Summary**	**40**
The concept of quotas on GCP services	38		

Part 2: Build Solutions with GCP Components

3

Building a Data Warehouse in BigQuery 43

Technical requirements	**44**	Step 3 – Initializing the gcloud init command	57
Introduction to GCS and BigQuery	**44**	Step 4 – Downloading example data from Git	57
BigQuery data location	45	Step 5 – Uploading data to GCS from Git	58
Introduction to the BigQuery console	**46**	**Practicing developing a data warehouse**	**59**
Creating a dataset in BigQuery using the console	48	Data warehouse in BigQuery – Requirements for scenario 1	60
Loading the local CSV file into the BigQuery table	49	Steps and planning for handling scenario 1	61
Using public data in BigQuery	51	Data warehouse in BigQuery – Requirements for scenario 2	72
Data types in BigQuery compared to other databases	53	Using the GCP console versus the code-based approach	72
Timestamp data in BigQuery compared to other databases	55	Steps and planning for handling scenario 2	73
Preparing the prerequisites before developing our data warehouse	**56**	**BigQuery's useful features**	**99**
		BigQuery console sub-menu options	100
Step 1 – Accessing Cloud Shell	56	BigQuery partitioned table	103
Step 2 – Checking the current setup using the command line	56	**Summary**	**105**
		Exercise – Scenario 3	**106**
		See also	**107**

4

Building Workflows for Batch Data Loading Using Cloud Composer 109

Technical requirements	**110**	Cloud Composer 1 vs Cloud Composer 2	113
Introduction to Cloud Composer	**110**	**Provisioning Cloud Composer in a GCP project**	**113**
Understanding the working of Airflow	**111**		

Introducing the Airflow web UI	115	Level 2 DAG – scheduling a pipeline from	
Cloud Composer bucket directories	118	Cloud SQL to GCS and BigQuery datasets	126
		Level 3 DAG – parameterized variables	133
Exercise – build data pipeline orchestration using Cloud Composer	**119**	Level 4 DAG – Guaranteeing task idempotency in Cloud Composer	146
		Level 5 DAG – handling DAG dependency using an Airflow dataset	150
Level 1 DAG – creating dummy workflows	120		
Deploying the DAG file into Cloud Composer	123	**Summary**	**158**

5

Building a Data Lake Using Dataproc 159

Technical requirements	**160**	**Exercise – Creating and running jobs on a Dataproc cluster**	**177**
Introduction to Dataproc	**160**		
A brief history of the data lake and Hadoop ecosystem	160	Preparing log data in GCS and HDFS	178
A deeper look into Hadoop components	161	Developing a Spark ETL job from HDFS to HDFS	178
How much Hadoop-related knowledge do you need on GCP?	163	Developing a Spark ETL job from GCS to GCS	182
Introducing the Spark RDD and DataFrame concepts	163	Developing a Spark ETL job from GCS to BigQuery	184
Introducing the data lake concept	164	**Understanding the concept of an ephemeral cluster**	**185**
Hadoop and Dataproc positioning on GCP	166		
Introduction to Dataproc Serverless	167	Practicing using a workflow template on Dataproc	187
Exercise – Building a data lake on a Dataproc cluster	**167**	Building an ephemeral cluster using Dataproc and Cloud Composer	190
Creating a Dataproc cluster on GCP	167	Submitting a Spark ETL job from GCS to BigQuery using Dataproc Serverless	192
Using GCS as an underlying Dataproc filesystem	169	**Summary**	**194**

6

Processing Streaming Data with Pub/Sub and Dataflow 195

Technical requirements	195	Introduction to CDC	
Processing streaming data	196	and Datastream	225
Introduction to Pub/Sub	199	What is Datastream?	225
Introduction to Dataflow	200	Exercise – Datastream ETL streaming	
Exercise – publishing event streams to Pub/Sub	201	to BigQuery	226
Creating a Pub/Sub topic	202	Step 1 – create a CloudSQL MySQL table	226
Creating and running a Pub/Sub publisher using Python	203	Step 2 – create a GCS bucket	227
Creating a Pub/Sub subscription	206	Step 3 – create a GCS notification to the Pub/Sub topic and subscription	227
Exercise – using Dataflow to stream data from Pub/Sub to GCS	210	Step 4 – create a BigQuery dataset	228
		Step 5 – configure a Datastream job	228
Creating a HelloWorld application using Apache Beam	210	Step 6 – run a Dataflow job from the Dataflow template	231
Creating a Dataflow streaming job without aggregation	217	Step 7 – insert a value in MySQL and check the result in BigQuery	231
Creating a streaming job with aggregation	222	Summary	232

7

Visualizing Data to Make Data-Driven Decisions with Looker Studio 233

Technical requirements	234	Exercise – creating a Looker Studio report using data from a bike-sharing data warehouse	241
Unlocking the power of your data with Looker Studio	234		
Don't confuse Looker Studio with Looker	235	Understanding how Looker Studio can impact the cost of BigQuery	250
From data to metrics in minutes with an Illustrative use case	235	What kind of table could be 1 TB in size?	251
Understanding what BigQuery INFORMATION_SCHEMA is	236	How can a table be accessed 10,000 times in a month?	251
Exercise – accessing the BigQuery INFORMATION_SCHEMA table using Looker Studio	237	Creating Materialized Views and understanding how BI Engine works	252
		Understanding BI Engine	255
		Summary	258

8

Building Machine Learning Solutions on GCP — 259

Technical requirements	260	Exercise – using GCP in AutoML to train an ML model	276
A quick look at ML	260		
Exercise – practicing ML code using Python	262	Exercise – deploying a dummy workflow with Vertex AI Pipelines	281
Preparing the ML dataset by using a table from the BigQuery public dataset	262	Creating a dedicated regional GCS bucket	282
		Developing the pipeline on Python	283
Training the ML model using Random Forest in Python	264	Monitoring the pipeline on the Vertex AI Pipelines console	286
Creating a batch prediction using the training dataset's output	266	Exercise – deploying a scikit-learn model pipeline with Vertex AI	287
The MLOps landscape in GCP	268	Creating the first pipeline, which will result in an ML model file in GCS	288
Understanding the basic principles of MLOps	268		
Introducing GCP services related to MLOps	269	Running the first pipeline in Vertex AI Pipelines	291
Exercise – leveraging pre-built GCP models as a service	272	Creating the second pipeline, which will use the model file from the prediction results as a CSV file in GCS	292
Uploading the image to a GCS bucket	272		
Creating a detect text function in Python	274	Running the second pipeline in Vertex AI Pipelines	293
		Summary	294

Part 3: Key Strategies for Architecting Top-Notch Solutions

9

User and Project Management in GCP — 297

Technical requirements	298	Deciding how many projects we should have in a GCP organization	305
Understanding IAM in GCP	298		
Planning a GCP project structure	301	Controlling user access to our data warehouse	307
Understanding the GCP organization, folder, and project hierarchy	303	Use-case scenario – planning BigQuery ACLs on an eCommerce organization	308

| Practicing the concept of IaC using Terraform | 311 | Self-exercise – managing a GCP project and resources using Terraform | 317 |
| Exercise – creating and running basic Terraform scripts | 311 | Summary | 317 |

10

Data Governance in GCP 319

Technical requirements	320	A deeper understanding of being accountable	345
Introduction to data governance	320	Clear traceability	346
A deeper understanding of data usability	322	Clear data ownership	347
		Data lineage	348
Exercise – implementing metadata tagging using Dataplex	324	Clear data quality process	349
A deeper understanding of data security	329	Exercise – practicing data quality using Dataform	351
Example – BigQuery data masking	337		
Exercise – finding PII using SDP	339	Summary	366

11

Cost Strategy in GCP 369

Technical requirements	369	Tips to optimize BigQuery using partitioned and clustered tables	384
Estimating the cost of your end-to-end data solution in GCP	369	Partitioned tables	384
		Clustered tables	387
Comparing BigQuery on-demand and editions	371	An exercise – optimizing BigQuery on-demand cost	390
An example – an estimating data engineering use case	377	Summary	391

12

CI/CD on GCP for Data Engineers 393

Technical requirements	393	Understanding CI/CD components with GCP services	396
An introduction to CI/CD	394		
Understanding the data engineer's relationship with CI/CD practices	394	Exercise – implementing CI using Cloud Build	398

Creating a GitHub repository using a Cloud Source Repository	398	Preparing the cloudbuild.yaml configuration file	408
Developing the code and Cloud Build scripts	400	Pushing the DAG to our GitHub repository	411
Creating a Cloud Build trigger	403	Checking the CI/CD result in the GCS bucket and Cloud Composer	411
Pushing the code to the GitHub repository	404		

Exercise – deploying Cloud Composer jobs using Cloud Build	407	CI/CD best practices in data engineering	414
Preparing the CI/CD environment	408	Summary	416
		Further reading	417

13

Boosting Your Confidence as a Data Engineer — 419

Overviewing the Google Cloud certification	419	Answers	431
Exam preparation tips	420	The past, present, and future of data engineering	432
Extra GCP service materials	422	Boosting your confidence and final thoughts	434
Quiz – reviewing all the concepts you've learned about	426	Summary	435
Questions	426		

Index — 437

Other Books You May Enjoy — 452

Preface

There is too much information – too many options and plans. Things are complicated. We live in a world where there is more and more information, which can be as problematic as too little information, and I'm aware that this condition applies when people want to start doing data engineering in the cloud, specifically **Google Cloud Platform** (**GCP**) in this book.

When people want to embark on a career in data, there are so many different roles whose definitions sometimes vary from one company to the next.

When someone chooses to be a data engineer, there are many technology options – cloud versus non-cloud, a big data database versus a transactional database, a self-managed service versus a managed service, and so on.

Upon deciding to use the cloud on GCP, you will find that the public documentation contains a wide variety of product options and tutorials.

In this book, instead of adding further dimensions to the data engineering and GCP products, the main goal is to help you narrow down the information. This book will help you focus on all the important concepts and components from the vast array of information available on the internet.

The guidance and exercises are based on the writer's experience in the field. By reading the book and following exercises, you will learn the most relevant and clear path to start and boost your career in data engineering using GCP.

Readers of the first edition have consistently reported using the book to successfully achieve GCP certification and launch careers as GCP data engineers. Building on this proven approach, in this second edition, we've updated all information to reflect the latest GCP landscape, while preserving the book's successful format.

Who this book is for

This book is intended for anyone involved in the data and analytics space, including IT developers, data analysts, data scientists, or any other relevant role that an individual wants to jump into in the data engineering field.

This book is also intended for data engineers who want to start using GCP, prepare for certification, and get practical examples based on real-world scenarios.

Finally, this book will be of interest to anyone who wants to know the thought process, have practical guidance, and have a clear path to run through the technology components to be able to start, achieve the certification, and gain a practical perspective in data engineering with GCP.

What this book covers

This book is divided into 3 parts and 13 chapters. Each part is a collection of independent chapters that have one objective.

Chapter 1, *Fundamentals of Data Engineering*, explains the role of data engineers and how data engineering relates to GCP.

Chapter 2, *Big Data Capabilities on GCP*, introduces the relevant GCP services related to data engineering.

Chapter 3, *Building a Data Warehouse in BigQuery*, covers the data warehouse concepts using BigQuery.

Chapter 4, *Building Workflows for Batch Data Loading Using Cloud Composer*, explains data orchestration using Cloud Composer.

Chapter 5, *Building a Data Lake Using Dataproc*, details the data lake concept with Hadoop using Dataproc.

Chapter 6, *Processing Streaming Data with Pub/Sub and Dataflow*, explains the concept of streaming data using Pub/Sub and Dataflow.

Chapter 7, *Visualizing Data to Make Data-Driven Decisions with Looker Studio*, covers how to utilize data from BigQuery to visualize it as charts in Looker Studio.

Chapter 8, *Building Machine Learning Solutions on GCP*, sets out the concepts of MLOps using Vertex AI.

Chapter 9, *User and Project Management in GCP*, explains the fundamentals of GCP identity and access management as well as GCP project structures.

Chapter 10, *Data Governance in GCP*, explains the concept of data governance and how to utilize Dataplex and Dataform to implement some of the foundations.

Chapter 11, *Cost Strategy in GCP*, covers how to estimate an overall data solution using GCP.

Chapter 12, *CI/CD on GCP for Data Engineers*, explains the concept of CI/CD and its relevance to data engineers.

Chapter 13, *Boosting Your Confidence as a Data Engineer*, prepares you for the GCP certification and offers some final thoughts in terms of summarizing what's been learned in this book.

To get the most out of this book

To successfully follow the examples in this book, you need a GCP account and project. If, at this point, you don't have a GCP account and project, don't worry. We will cover that as part of the exercises in this book.

Occasionally, we will use the free tier from GCP for practice, but be aware that some products might not have free tiers. Notes will be provided if this is the case.

All the exercises in this book can be completed without any additional software installation. The exercises will be done in the GCP console, which you can open from any operating system using your favorite browser.

You should be familiar with basic programming languages. In this book, I will focus on utilizing Python and the Linux command line.

If you are using the digital version of this book, we advise you to type the code yourself or access the code from the book's GitHub repository (a link is available in the next section). Doing so will help you avoid any potential errors related to the copying and pasting of code.

Always remember that this book is not positioned to replace GCP public documentation. Hence, comprehensive information on every single feature of GCP services might not be available in this book. We also won't use all the GCP services that are available. For such information, you can always check the public documentation.

Remember that the main goal of this book is to help you narrow down information. Use this book as your step-by-step guide to build solutions to common challenges facing data engineers. Follow the patterns from the exercises, the relationship between concepts, important GCP services, and best practices. Always use the hands-on exercises so that you can experience working with GCP.

Download the example code files

You can download the example code files for this book from GitHub at https://github.com/PacktPublishing/Data-Engineering-with-Google-Cloud-Platform-Second-Edition. If there's an update to the code, it will be updated in the GitHub repository.

We also have other code bundles from our rich catalog of books and videos available at https://github.com/PacktPublishing/. Check them out!

Conventions used

There are a number of text conventions used throughout this book.

`Code in text`: Indicates code words in text, database table names, folder names, filenames, file extensions, pathnames, dummy URLs, user input, and Twitter handles. Here is an example: "To do that, find the `credit_card_default` table in the `bigquery-public-data` project, under the `ml_datasets` dataset."

A block of code is set as follows:

```
random_forest_classifier = RandomForestClassifier(n_estimators=100)
random_forest_classifier.fit(X_train,y_train)
```

Any command-line input or output is written as follows:

```
$ pip install -r requirements
```

Bold: Indicates a new term, an important word, or words that you see on screen. For instance, words in menus or dialog boxes appear in **bold**. Here is an example: "First, you must create a Vertex AI notebook – either **Colab Enterprise** or **Workbench**."

> Tips or important notes
> Appear like this.

Get in touch

Feedback from our readers is always welcome.

General feedback: If you have questions about any aspect of this book, email us at `customercare@packtpub.com` and mention the book title in the subject of your message.

Errata: Although we have taken every care to ensure the accuracy of our content, mistakes do happen. If you have found a mistake in this book, we would be grateful if you would report this to us. Please visit `www.packtpub.com/support/errata` and fill in the form.

Piracy: If you come across any illegal copies of our works in any form on the internet, we would be grateful if you would provide us with the location address or website name. Please contact us at `copyright@packt.com` with a link to the material.

If you are interested in becoming an author: If there is a topic that you have expertise in and you are interested in either writing or contributing to a book, please visit `authors.packtpub.com`.

Share Your Thoughts

Once you've read *Data Engineering With Google Cloud Platform*, we'd love to hear your thoughts! Scan the QR code below to go straight to the Amazon review page for this book and share your feedback.

https://packt.link/r/1-835-08011-1

Your review is important to us and the tech community and will help us make sure we're delivering excellent quality content.

Download a free PDF copy of this book

Thanks for purchasing this book!

Do you like to read on the go but are unable to carry your print books everywhere?

Is your eBook purchase not compatible with the device of your choice?

Don't worry, now with every Packt book you get a DRM-free PDF version of that book at no cost.

Read anywhere, any place, on any device. Search, copy, and paste code from your favorite technical books directly into your application.

The perks don't stop there, you can get exclusive access to discounts, newsletters, and great free content in your inbox daily

Follow these simple steps to get the benefits:

1. Scan the QR code or visit the link below

https://packt.link/free-ebook/9781835080115

2. Submit your proof of purchase
3. That's it! We'll send your free PDF and other benefits to your email directly

Part 1: Getting Started with Data Engineering with GCP

This part will talk about the purpose, value, and concepts of big data and cloud computing and how **Google Cloud platform** (**GCP**) products are relevant for data engineering. You will learn about a data engineer's core responsibilities, how they differ from data scientists, and how to facilitate the flow of data through an organization to derive insights.

This part has the following chapters:

- *Chapter 1, Fundamentals of Data Engineering*
- *Chapter 2, Big Data Capabilities on GCP*

1
Fundamentals of Data Engineering

Years ago, when I initially entered the world of **data analytics**, I used to think data was clean – clean in terms of readiness and neatly organized. I was so excited to experiment with **machine learning** models, find unusual patterns in data, and play around with clean data. But after years of experience working with data, I realized that data analytics in big organizations isn't straightforward.

Most of the effort goes into collecting, cleaning, and transforming the data. If you have had any experience in working with data, I am sure you've noticed something similar. But the good news is that we know that all processes can be automated using proper planning, designing, and engineering skills. That was the point where I realized that data engineering would be the most critical role in the future of the data science world.

To develop a successful data ecosystem in any organization, the most crucial part is how they design the **data architecture**. If the organization fails to make the best decision on the data architecture, the future process will be painful. Here are some common examples: the system is not scalable, querying data is slow, business users don't trust your data, the infrastructure cost is very high, and data is leaked. There is so much more that can go wrong without proper **data engineering** practice.

In this chapter, we are going to acquire the fundamental knowledge behind data engineering. The goal is to introduce you to common terminologies that are often used in this field and will be mentioned in the later chapters.

In particular, we will be covering the following topics:

- Understanding the data life cycle
- Starting with knowing the roles of a data engineer
- Going through the foundational concepts of data engineering

Understanding the data life cycle

Understanding the data life cycle is the first principle in becoming a data engineer. If you've worked with data, you must know that data doesn't stay in one place; it moves from one storage to another, from one database to another database. Understanding the data life cycle means you need to be able to answer these sorts of questions if you want to display information to your end user:

- Who will consume the data?
- What data sources should I use?
- Where should I store the data?
- When should the data arrive?
- Why does the data need to be stored in this place?
- How should the data be processed?

To answer all those questions, we'll start by looking back a little bit at the history of data technologies.

Understanding the need for a data warehouse

Data warehouse is not a new concept; I believe you've at least heard of it. In fact, this terminology is no longer appealing. In my experience, no one got excited when talking about data warehouses in the 2020s, especially when compared to terminologies such as **big data**, **cloud computing**, and **artificial intelligence**.

So, why do we need to know about data warehouses? The answer to that is that almost every single data engineering challenge from the old times to the modern day is conceptually the same. The challenges are always about moving data from the data source to other environments so the business can use it to get information. The difference from time to time is only about the evolution of better approaches along with newer technologies. If we understand why people needed data warehouses in historical times, we will have a better foundation to understand the data engineering space and, more specifically, the data life cycle.

Data warehouses were first developed in the 1980s to transform data from operational systems to decision-making support systems. The key principle of a data warehouse is combining data from many different sources into a single location and then transforming it into a format the data warehouse can process and store.

For example, in the financial industry, say a bank wants to know how many credit card customers also have mortgages. It is a simple enough question, yet it's not that easy to answer. Why?

Most traditional banks that I have worked with had different operating systems for each of their products, including a specific system for credit cards and specific systems for mortgages, saving products, websites, customer service, and many other systems. So, to answer the question, data from multiple systems need to be stored in one place first.

See the following diagram on how each department is independent:

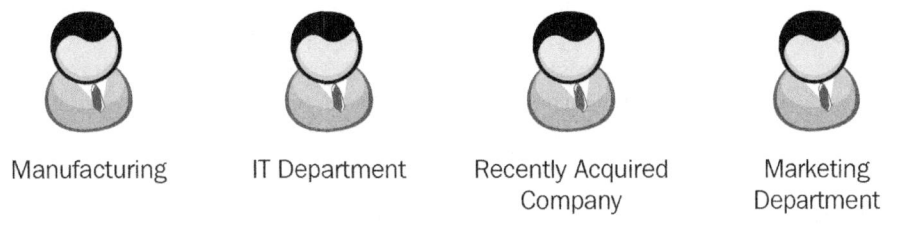

Manufacturing   IT Department   Recently Acquired Company   Marketing Department

Figure 1.1 – Data silos

Often, independence not only applies to the organization structure but also to the data. When data is located in different places, it's called **data silos**. This is quite common in large organizations where each department has different goals, responsibilities, and priorities.

In summary, what we need to understand from the data warehouse concept is the following:

- Data silos have always occurred in large organizations, even back in the 1980s.
- Data comes from many different source systems.
- To get the full benefit of the data, we need to store the data from different systems in one central place or storage.

What does a typical data warehouse stack look like?

This diagram represents the four logical building blocks in a data warehouse, which are **Storage**, **Compute**, **Schema**, and **SQL Interface**:

| SQL Interface |
| Schema |
| Compute |
| Storage |

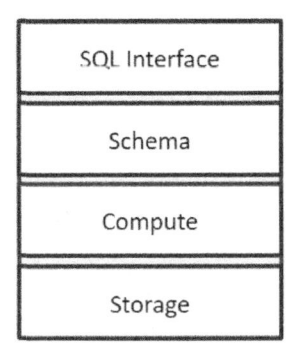

Figure 1.2 – Main components of a data warehouse

Data warehouse products are mostly able to store and process data seamlessly and the user can use the SQL language to access the data in tables with a structured schema format. It is basic knowledge, but an important point to be aware of is that the four logical building blocks in the data warehouse are designed as one single software that evolved over the later years and was the start of the **data lake**.

Getting familiar with the differences between a data warehouse and a data lake

Fast forward to 2008, when an open-source data technology named **Hadoop** was first released, and people started to use the data lake terminology. If you try to find the definition of a data lake on the internet, it will mostly be described as a centralized repository that allows you to store all your structured and unstructured data.

So, what is the difference between a data lake and a data warehouse? Both have the same idea of storing data in centralized storage. Is it simply that a data lake stores unstructured data and a data warehouse doesn't?

What if I say some data warehouse products can now store and process unstructured data? Does the data warehouse become a data lake? The answer is *no*.

One of the key differences from a technical perspective is that data lake technologies separate most of the building blocks, in particular, the storage and computation, and other blocks on top of that, such as schema, governance, SQL interfaces, machine learning, and many other components.

This evolves the concept of a single software into a modern and modular platform consisting of separated components, as illustrated in the following diagram:

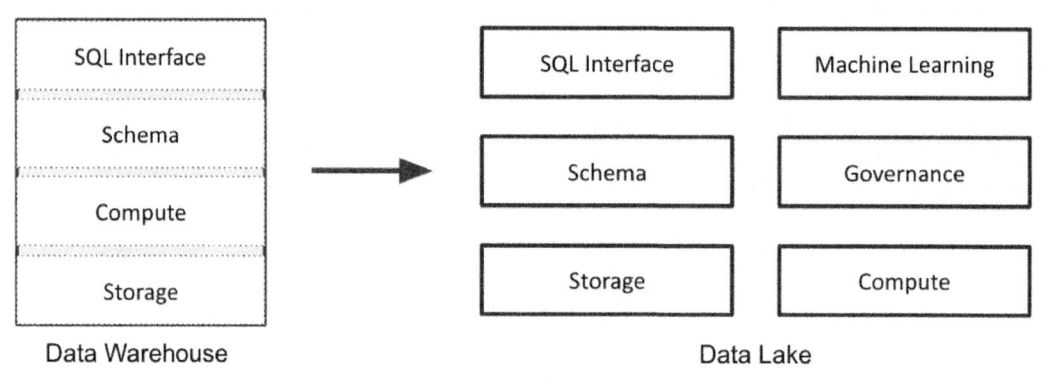

Figure 1.3 – Data warehouse versus data lake components

For example, in a data warehouse, you insert data by calling SQL statements and query the data through SQL tables, and there is nothing you can do as a user to change that pattern.

In a data lake, you can access the underlying storage directly, for example, by storing a text file, choosing your own computation engine, and choosing not to have a schema.

There are many impacts of this concept, but I'll summarize it in three differences:

Data Warehouse	Data Lake
Schema is essential	Schema is not essential
All access through SQL. Users doesn't have much control over on how to compute and store the data.	Very common to use different computation for different purpose, using the same underlying storage.
The first focus is on business data model. The mindset is to store data when it has clear relevance to the business.	The first focus is to store data as much as possible. Business relevancy and data model are defined later.

Table 1.1 – Table comparing data lakes and data warehouses

Large organizations start to store any data in the data lake system for two reasons: **high scalability** and **cheap storage**. In modern data architecture, both data lakes and data warehouses complete each other, rather than replacing each other.

We will dive deeper and carry out some practical examples throughout the book, such as trying to build a sample in *Chapter 3, Building a Data Warehouse in BigQuery*, and *Chapter 5, Building a Data Lake Using Dataproc*.

The data life cycle

Based on our understanding of the history of the data warehouse, now we know that data does not stay in one place. As an analogy, data is very similar to water; it flows from upstream to downstream. Later in this book, both terminologies, upstream and downstream, will be used often since they are common terminologies in data engineering.

One example of a water flow is a waterfall; the water falls freely without any obstacles.

Another example in different circumstances is a water pipeline; upstream is the water reservoir and downstream is your kitchen sink. In this case, you can imagine the different pipes, filters, branches, and knobs in the middle of the process.

Data is very much like water flows. There are scenarios where you just need to copy data from one storage to another storage, or in more complex scenarios, you may need to filter, join, and split multiple steps downstream before the data can be consumed by the end users.

As illustrated in the following diagram, the data life cycle mostly starts from frontend applications and flows up to the end for data users as information in the dashboard or ad hoc queries:

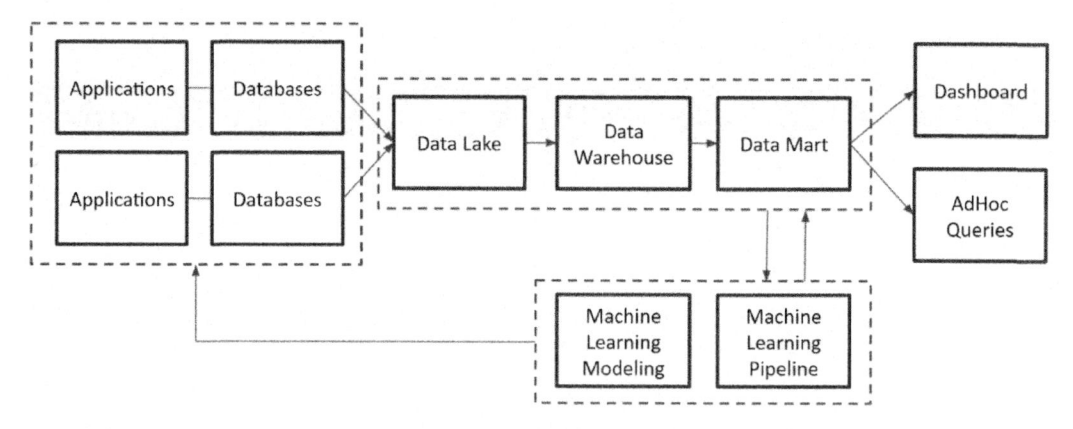

Figure 1.4 – Data life cycle diagram

Let's now look at the elements of the data life cycle in detail:

- **Apps and databases**: The application is the interface from the human to the machine. The frontend application in most cases acts as the first data upstream. Data at this level are designed to serve application transactions as fast as possible.

- **Data lake**: Data from multiple databases needs to be stored in one place. The data lake concept and technologies suit the needs. The data lake stores data in a file format such as a CSV file, Avro, or Parquet.

    The advantage of storing data in a file format is that it can accept any data sources; for example, a MySQL Database can export the data to CSV files, image data can be stored as JPEG files, and IoT device data can be stored as JSON files. Another advantage of storing data in a data lake is it doesn't require a schema at this stage.

- **Data warehouse**: When you know any data in a data lake is valuable, you need to start thinking about the following:

    - What is the schema?
    - How do you query the data?
    - What is the best data model for the data?

    Data in a data warehouse is usually modeled based on business requirements. With this, one of the key requirements to build the data warehouse is that you need to know the relevance of the data to your business and the expected information that you want to generate from the data.

- **Data mart**: A data mart is an area for storing data that serves specific user groups. At this stage, you need to start thinking about the final downstream of data and who the end user is. Each data mart is usually under the control of each department within an organization. For example, a data mart for a finance team will consist of finance-related tables, while a data mart for data scientists might consist of tables with machine learning features.

- **Data end consumer**: The last stage of data will be back to humans as information. The end user of data can have various ways to use the data but at a very high level, these are the three most common usages:
  - Reporting and dashboard
  - Ad hoc query
  - Machine learning model

Are all data life cycles like this? No. Like the analogy of water flowing upstream and downstream, in different circumstances, it will require different data life cycles, and that's where data engineers need to be able to design the data pipeline architecture. However, the preceding data life cycle is a very common pattern.

Throughout my career, I have worked with many business industries, including finance, government, telecommunication, and e-commerce. Most of the companies that I worked with followed this pattern or were at least going in that direction.

As an overall summary of this section, we've learned that since historical times, data is mostly in silos, and it drives the needs of the data warehouse and data lake. The data will move from one system to others as specific needs have specific technologies and, in this section, we've learned about a very common pattern in data engineering. In the next section, we'll try to understand the role of a data engineer and who should be responsible for this.

Start with knowing the roles of a data engineer

In the later chapters, we will spend much of our time doing practical exercises to understand data engineering concepts. But before that, let's quickly take a look at the data engineer role.

The job role is getting more and more popular now, but the terminology itself is relatively new compared to well-established job roles, such as accountant, lawyer, and doctor. The impact is that sometimes there is still a debate about what a data engineer should and shouldn't do.

For example, if you came to a hospital and met a doctor, you know for sure that the doctor would do the following:

1. Examine your condition.
2. Make a diagnosis of your health issues.
3. Prescribe medicine.

The doctor wouldn't do the following:

1. Clean the hospital.
2. Make the medicine.
3. Manage hospital administration.

It's clear, and it applies to most well-established job roles. But how about data engineers? The expectation is sometimes unclear.

This is just a very short list of examples of what data engineers should or shouldn't be responsible for:

- Handling all big data infrastructures and software installation
- Handling application databases
- Designing the data warehouse data model
- Analyzing big data to transform raw data into meaningful information
- Creating a data pipeline for machine learning

The unclear condition is unavoidable since it's a new role and I believe it will be more and more established following the maturity of the modern data analytics world. In this section, let's try to understand what a data engineer is and, despite many combinations of responsibilities, what you should focus on as a data engineer.

A data engineer versus a data scientist

A data engineer is someone who designs and builds data pipelines.

The definition is that simple, but the question about the difference between a data engineer and a data scientist is still one of the most frequently asked questions when someone wants to start their data career. The hype of "data scientists" on the internet is one of the drivers; for example, up until today, people still like to quote the following:

Data scientist: the sexiest job of the 21st century

– Harvard Business Review

The data scientist role was originally invented to refer to groups of people who are highly curious and able to utilize big data technologies for business purposes back in 2008. But since the technologies are maturing and becoming more complex, people have started to realize that it's overwhelming. It's very rare for a company to hire someone who knows how to do all of the following:

- How to handle big data infrastructure
- How to properly design and build **Extract, Transform, and Load** (**ETL**) pipelines
- How to train machine learning models
- Understand deeply about the company's business

Not that it's impossible, some people do have this knowledge, but from a company's point of view, it's not practical.

These days, for better focus and scalability, the data scientist role can be split into many different roles, for example, data analyst, machine learning engineer, and business analyst. But one of the most popular and realized to be very important roles is a data engineer.

The focus of data engineers

Let's map the data engineer role to our data life cycle diagram (*Figure 1.4*) from the previous section.

In the diagram, I added two underlying components:

- **Job Orchestrator**: This designs and builds a job dependency and scheduler that runs data movement from upstream to downstream.
- **Infrastructure**: Provisions of the necessary data infrastructure to support the execution of data pipelines.

    On each step, I added numbers from 1 to 3. The numbers will help you to identify which components are the data engineer's main responsibility. This diagram works together with *Figure 1.6*, a data engineer-focused diagram to map the numbering. First, let's check this data life cycle diagram that we've discussed before with the numbering on it:

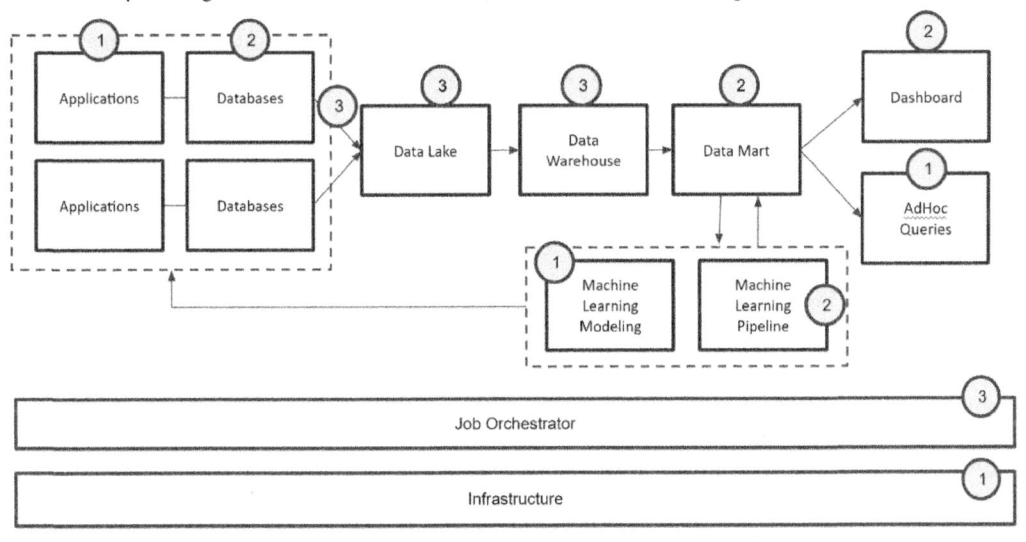

Figure 1.5 – Data life cycle flows with focus numbering

After seeing the numbering on the data life cycle, check out this diagram that illustrates the focus points of a data engineer:

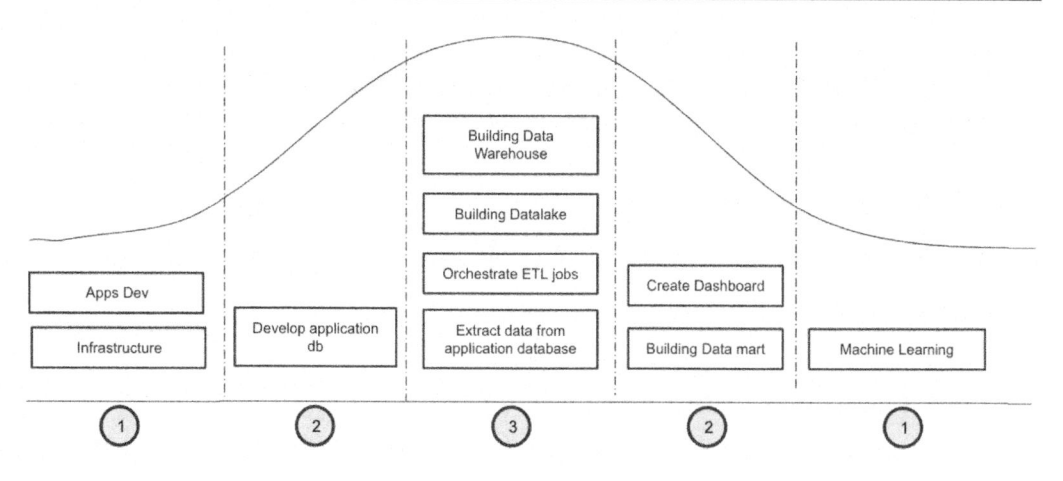

Figure 1.6 – Data engineer-focused diagram

The diagram shows the distribution of the knowledge area from the end-to-end data life cycle. At the center of the diagram (number 3) are the jobs that are the key focus of data engineers, and I will call it the core.

Those numbered "2" are the "good-to-have" areas. For example, it's still common in small organizations that data engineers need to build a data mart for business users.

> **Note**
> Designing and building a data mart is not as simple as creating tables in a database. Someone who builds a data mart needs to be able to talk to business people and gather requirements to serve tables from a business perspective, which is one of the reasons it's not part of the core.

While knowing how to collect data to a data lake is part of the data engineer's responsibility, exporting data from operational application databases is often done by the application development team, for example, by dumping MySQL tables as CSV in staging storage.

Those numbered 1 are "good-to-know" areas. For example, it's rare that a data engineer needs to be responsible for building application databases, developing machine learning models, maintaining infrastructure, and creating dashboards. It is possible, but less likely. The discipline requires knowledge that is a little bit too far from the core.

After learning about the three areas of focus, let's now review our understanding and vision of data engineers. Study the diagram carefully and answer the following questions:

- What are your current focus areas as an individual?
- What are your current job role's focus areas (or, if you are a student, your study areas)?
- What is your future goal in the data science world?

Depending on your individual answers, check with the diagram from *Figure 1.6* – do you have all the necessary skills at the core? Does your current job give you experience in the core? Would you be excited if you could master all subjects at the core soon?

From my experience, what is important to data engineers is the core. Even though there are a variety of data engineers' expectations, responsibilities, and job descriptions on the market, if you are new to the role, then the most important thing is to understand what the core of a data engineer is.

The diagram gives you guidance on what type of data engineer you are or will be. The closer you are to the core, the more of a data engineer you are. You are on the right track and in the right environment to be a good data engineer.

In scenarios where you are at the core, plus other areas beside it, then you are closer to a full-stack data expert; as long as you have a strong core, if you are able to expand your expertise to the "good-to-have" and "good-to-know" areas, you will have a good advantage in your data engineering career. But if you focus on other non-core areas, I suggest you find a way to master the core first.

In this section, we learned about the role of a data engineer. If you are not familiar with the cores, the next section will be your guidance on the fundamental concepts in data engineering.

Going through the foundational concepts for data engineering

Even though there are many data engineering concepts that we will learn throughout the book by using **Google Cloud Platform** (**GCP**), there are some basic concepts that you need to know as data engineers. In my experience of interviewing in data companies, I discovered that these foundational concepts are often asked to assess how much you know about data engineering. Take the following examples:

- What is ETL?
- What's the difference between ETL and **Extract, Load, and Transform** (**ELT**)?
- What is big data?
- How do you handle large volumes of data?

These questions are quite common, yet particularly important to deeply understand the concepts since they may affect our decisions on architecting our data life cycles.

ETL concept in data engineering

ETL is the key foundation of data engineering. Everything in the data life cycle is ETL; any part that happens from upstream to downstream is ETL. Let's take a look at the upstream to downstream flows that have an ETL process in between here:

Upstream → Extract → Transform → Load → Downstream

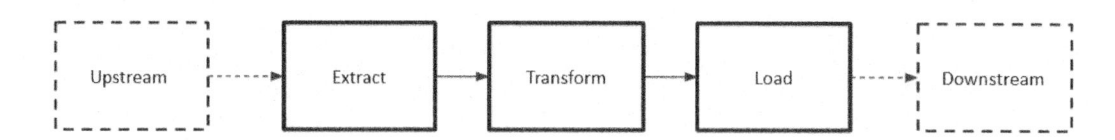

Figure 1.7 – ETL illustration

ETL consists of three actual steps that you need to follow to move your data:

- **Extract**: This is the step to get the data from the upstream system. For example, if the upstream system is a **Relational Database Management System (RDBMS)**, then the extract step will be dumping or exporting data from the RDBMS.
- **Transform**: This is the step where you apply any transformation to the extracted data. For example, the file from the RDBMS needs to be joined with a static CSV file, then the transform step will process the extracted data, load the CSV file, and finally, join both pieces of information together in an intermediary system.
- **Load**: This is the step to put the transformed data into the downstream system. For example, if the downstream system is BigQuery, then the load step will call the BigQuery load job to store the data in BigQuery's table.

Back in *Figure 1.4*, each of the individual steps may have a different ETL process. For example, at the application database to data lake step, the upstream is the application database and the data lake is the downstream. But at the data lake to data warehouse step, the data lake becomes the upstream and the data warehouse as its downstream. So, you need to think about how you want to do the ETL process in every data life cycle step.

The difference between ETL and ELT

From the acronym itself, the difference between ETL and ELT is only the ordering of the letters "T" and "L." Should you transform first and then load the data downstream or load the data downstream first and then transform the data inside the downstream system?

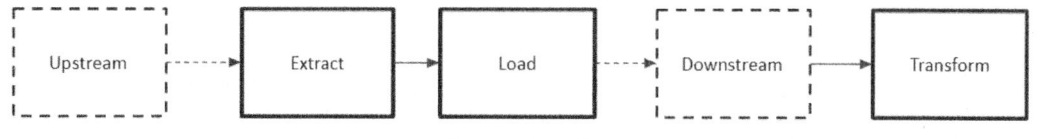

Upstream → Extract → Load → Downstream → Transform

Figure 1.8 – ELT

Easy! What's the big deal?

Even though it's quite a simple difference in the acronym, deciding on the method can really affect your choice of technology products, system performance, scalability, and cost. For example, not all downstream systems are powerful enough to transform large volumes of data; in this case, ETL is preferred since using the ELT pattern will introduce issues in your downstream system.

In other cases, the downstream system is a lot more powerful compared to any intermediary system, so you want to choose the ELT pattern. This mostly happens after the data lake era where the downstream are products such as Hadoop, BigQuery, or other scalable data processing products. But this is not the absolute answer; depending on your available choice of technology, you may change your ETL or ELT strategy.

You will understand this better after running through the content of this book with a lot of ETL and ELT examples, but at this point, the important thing to keep in mind is, as a data engineer, you have two options of where to transform your data: in an intermediary system or the target system.

What is not big data?

After learning about ETL and ELT, the other most common bit of terminology is **big data**. Since big data is still one of the highly correlated concepts close to data engineering, it is important to how you interpret the terminology as a data engineer. Note that the word "big data" itself refers to two different subjects:

- The data itself is big
- Big data technology

With so much hype in the media about the words, both in the context of data getting bigger and big data technology, I don't think I need to tell you the definition of the word big data. Instead, I will focus on eliminating the non-relevant definitions of big data for data engineers. Here are some definitions in media or from people that I have met personally:

- All people already use social media; the data in social media is huge, and we can use social media data for our organization. That's big data.
- My company doesn't have data. Big data is a way to use data from the public internet to start my data journey. That's big data.
- The five Vs of data: volume, variety, velocity, veracity, and value. That's big data.

All the preceding definitions are correct but not very helpful to us as data engineers. So, instead of seeing big data as general use cases, we need to focus on the *how* questions and think about what actually works under the hood. Take the following examples:

- How do you store 1 PB of data in storage, while the size of common hard drives is in TBs?
- How do you average a list of numbers when the data is stored on multiple computers?
- How can you continuously extract data from the upstream system and implement aggregation as a streaming process?

These kinds of questions are what are important for data engineers. Data engineers need to know when a condition (the data itself is big) should be managed using big data or non-big data technology.

A quick look at how big data technologies store data

Knowing that answering the *how* question is what is important to understanding big data, the first thing we need to address is how it stores the data. What makes it different from non-big data storage?

The word "big" in big data is relative. For example, say you analyze Twitter data and then download the data as JSON files with a size of 5 GB, and your laptop storage is 1 TB with 16 GB memory.

I don't think that's big data. However, if the Twitter data is 5 PB, then it becomes big data because you need a special way to store it and a special way to process it. So, the key is not about whether it is social media data or not, or unstructured or not, which sometimes many people still get confused by. It's more about the size of the data relative to your system.

Big data technology needs to be able to distribute the data to multiple servers. The common term for multiple servers working together is a **cluster**. I'll give an illustration to show you how a very large file can be distributed into multiple chunks of file parts on multiple machines:

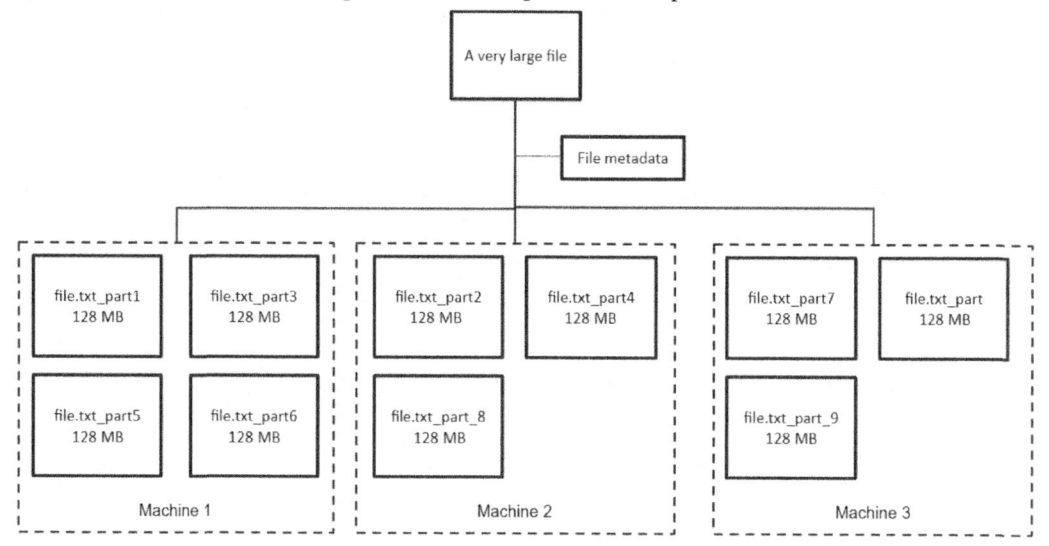

Figure 1.9 – Distributed filesystem

In a distributed filesystem, a large file will be split into multiple small parts. In the preceding example, it is split into nine parts, and each file is a small 128 MB file. Then, the multiple file parts are distributed into three machines randomly. On top of the file parts, there will be metadata to store information about how the file parts formed the original file, for example, a large file is a combination of file.txt_part1, located in Machine 1, file.txt_part2, located in Machine 2, and more.

The distributed parts can be stored in any format that isn't necessarily a file format; for example, it can be in the form of data blocks, byte arrays in memory, or some other data format. But for simplicity, what you need to be aware of is that in a big data system, data can be stored in multiple machines and to optimize performance, sometimes you need to think about how you want to distribute the parts.

After we know data can be split into small parts on different machines, it leads to further questions:

- How do I process the files?
- What if I want to aggregate some numbers from the files?
- How does each part know the value of the records from other parts while it is stored in different machines?

There are many approaches to answering these three questions, but one of the most famous concepts is **MapReduce**.

A quick look at how to process multiple files using MapReduce

Historically speaking, MapReduce is a framework that was published as a white paper by Google and is widely used in the Hadoop ecosystem. There is an actual open-source project called MapReduce mainly written in Java that still has a large user base, but slowly people have started to change to other distributed processing engine alternatives, such as **Spark**, **Tez**, and **Dataflow**. But MapReduce as a concept itself is still relevant regardless of the technology.

In a brief summary, the word "MapReduce" can refer to two definitions:

- MapReduce as a technology
- MapReduce as a concept

What is important for us to understand is MapReduce as a concept. MapReduce is a combination of two words: map and reduce.

Let's take a look at an example if you have a file that's divided into three file parts:

Banana
Apple

Part 1

Melon
Apple
Banana

Part 2

Apple

Part 3

Figure 1.10 – File parts

Each of the parts contains one or more words, which in this example are fruits. The file part is stored in different machines. So, each machine will have these three file parts:

- **Part 1** contains two words: **Banana and Apple**.
- **Part 2** contains three words: **Melon, Apple, and Banana**.
- **Part 3** contains one word: **Apple**.

Consider how you would write a program to calculate a word count that produces these results:

- **Apple** = 3
- **Banana** = 2
- **Melon** = 1

Since the file parts are separated into different machines, we cannot just count the words directly. We need MapReduce. Let's take a look at the following diagram, where file parts are mapped, shuffled, and, lastly, reduced to get the final result:

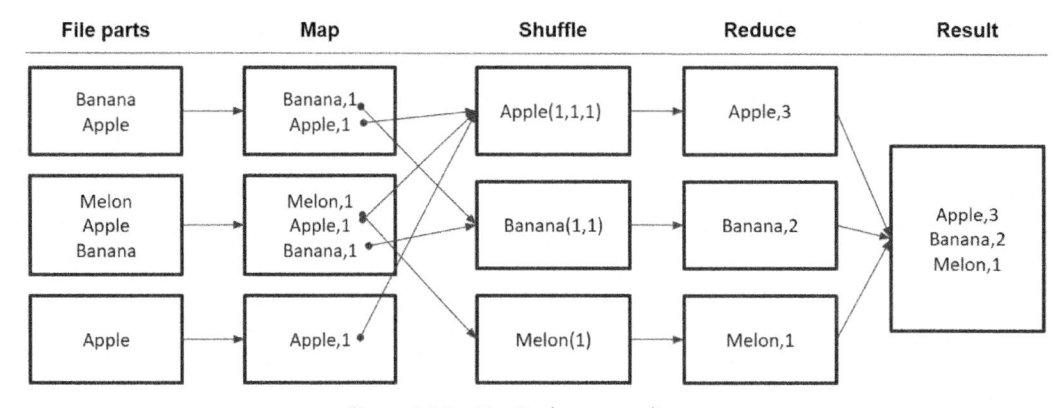

Figure 1.11 – MapReduce step diagram

There are four main steps in the diagram:

1. **Map**: Add to each individual record a static value of 1. This will transform the word into a key-value pair where the value is always 1.
2. **Shuffle**: At this point, we need to move the fruit words between machines. We want to group each word and store it in the same machine for each group.
3. **Reduce**: Because each fruit group is already in the same machine, we can count them together. The Reduce step will sum up the 1 static value to produce the count results.
4. **Result**: Store the final results back in a single machine.

The key idea here is to process any possible process in a distributed manner. Looking back at the diagram, you can imagine each box on each step is a different machine.

Each step, Map, Shuffle, and Reduce, always maintains three parallel boxes. What does this mean? It means that the processes happened in parallel on three machines. This paradigm is different from calculating all processes in a single machine. For example, we can simply download all the file parts into a pandas DataFrame in Python and do a count using the pandas DataFrame. In this case, the process will happen in one machine.

MapReduce is a complex concept. The concept is explained in a 13-page-long document by Google. You can find the document easily on the internet, but here is a link: `https://static.googleusercontent.com/media/research.google.com/en//archive/mapreduce-osdi04.pdf`. In this book, I haven't added a much deeper explanation of MapReduce. In most cases, you don't need to really think about it; for example, if in a later chapter, you use BigQuery to process 1 PB of data, you will only need to run an SQL query and BigQuery will process it in a distributed manner in the background.

In fact, all technologies in GCP that we will use in this book are highly scalable and without question able to handle big data out of the box. But understanding the underlying concepts helps you as a data engineer in many ways, for example, choosing the right technologies, designing data pipeline architecture, troubleshooting, and improving performance.

Summary

As a summary of the first chapter, we've learned the fundamental knowledge we need as data engineers. Here are some key takeaways from this chapter. First, data doesn't stay in one place. Data moves from one place to another, called the data life cycle. We also understand that data in a big organization is mostly in silos, and we can solve these data silos using the concepts of a data warehouse and data lake.

As someone who has started to look into data engineer roles, you may be a little bit lost. The role of data engineers may vary. The key takeaway is not to be confused about the broad expectations in the market. First, you should focus on the core and then expand as you get more experience from the core. In this chapter, we've learned what the core of a data engineer is. At the end of the chapter, we learned some of the key concepts. There are three key concepts as a data engineer that you need to be familiar with. These concepts are ETL, big data, and distributed systems.

In the next chapter, we will visit GCP, a cloud platform provided by Google that has a lot of services to help us as data engineers. We want to understand its position, what the services are that are relevant to big data, and lastly, we will start using the GCP console.

Now, let's put the knowledge from this chapter into practice.

Exercise

You are a data engineer at a book publishing company and your product manager has asked you to build a dashboard to show the total revenue and customer satisfaction index in a single dashboard.

Your company doesn't have any data infrastructure yet, but you know that your company has these three applications that contain TBs of data:

- The company website
- A book sales application using MongoDB to store sales transactions, including transactions, book IDs, and author IDs
- An author portal application using a MySQL Database to store authors' personal information, including age

Do the following:

1. List down important follow-up questions for your manager
2. List down your technical thinking process of how to do it at a high level
3. Draw a data pipeline architecture

There is no right or wrong answer to this practice. The important thing is that you can imagine how the data flows from upstream to downstream, how it should be processed at each step, and finally, how you want to serve the information to end users.

Further Reading

You can visit the following links to explore more about the topics discussed in this chapter:

- Understand more about Hadoop and its distributed filesystem: `https://hadoop.apache.org/docs/r1.2.1/hdfs_design.pdf`
- Understand more about how MapReduce works: `https://static.googleusercontent.com/media/research.google.com/en//archive/mapreduce-osdi04.pdf`
- Key facts about data engineers and why the role was becoming more popular than the data scientist role in 2021: `https://www.kdnuggets.com/2021/02/dont-need-data-scientists-need-data-engineers.html`

2
Big Data Capabilities on GCP

When people first dive into **Google Cloud Platform** (**GCP**), it's common for them to find themselves amid a wealth of exciting products and services. Yet, this excitement can occasionally give way to a sense of being overwhelmed.

GCP offers a broad range of services for multiple disciplines, such as application development, microservices, security, AI, and of course, **big data**. But even for big data products, there are multiple options from which you can choose.

As an analogy, GCP is like a supermarket. A supermarket has everything that you need to support your daily life. For example, if you plan to cook pasta and come to a supermarket to buy the ingredients, no one will tell you what ingredients you should buy; or even if you know which ingredients you want to buy, you will still be offered the ingredients by different brands, price tags, and producers. If you fail to make the right decision, you will end up cooking bad pasta. In GCP, it's the same – you need to be able to choose your products or services. It is also important to show how each service depends on the others. It's impossible to build a solution using only a single service.

In this chapter, we will learn about the products and services of GCP. But instead of explaining every single service, which you can do by accessing public documentation, we will help you narrow down the available options. To do so, we will map the services into categories and priorities. After this chapter, you will know exactly what services you need to start your journey.

On top of that, we will start using GCP! We will kick off our hands-on practice with fundamental knowledge of the GCP console.

By the end of the chapter, you will understand the positioning of GCP services related to big data, be able to start using the GCP console and be able to plan what services you should focus on as a data engineer.

Here is the list of topics we will discuss in this chapter:

- Understanding what the cloud is
- Getting started with GCP
- A quick overview of GCP services for data engineering

Technical requirements

In this chapter's exercise, we will start using the GCP console, **Cloud Shell**, and **Cloud Editor**. All these tools can be opened using any internet browser.

To use the GCP console, we need to register using a Google account (Gmail). You'll also require a payment method. Please check out the available payment methods to make sure you are successfully registered.

Understanding what the cloud is

Renting someone else's server. This definition of the **cloud** is my favorite as it's quite a simple definition of what the cloud really is.

It means that so long as you don't need to buy your own machine to store and process data, you are using the cloud.

But increasingly, due to some leading cloud providers, such as Google Cloud, gaining more traction and technology maturity, the terminology is becoming representative of sets of architecture, managed services, and highly scalable environments that define how we build solutions.

For data engineering, that means building data products using collections of services and APIs. We trust the underlying infrastructure of the cloud provider one hundred percent.

The difference between the cloud and non-cloud era

If we want to compare the cloud with the non-cloud era from a data engineering perspective, we will find that all the data engineering principles are the same. But from a technological perspective, there is a lot of evolution in the cloud.

In the cloud, computation and storage are configured as services, not hardware. This means that as engineers, we can control them using code and configuration. We can also only request them whenever we need them (on demand).

If you're starting your data journey directly with cloud services, maybe it's a bit difficult for you to imagine what non-cloud looks like. As an illustrative example of a non-cloud experience, I once helped a company implement a **data warehouse** before the cloud era.

The customer had data in **Oracle** databases and wanted to store the data in an on-premises data warehouse. How long do you think it took before I could store my first table in the data warehouse? 4 months!

We needed to wait for the physical server to be shipped from the manufacturer's continent to our continent. After the server arrived, we waited for the network engineer to plug in cables, routers, power, software installation, and more, which again took months before the data engineers could access the software and store our first table in it.

But how long do you need to store your file in a table in **BigQuery**? Less than 1 minute.

The on-demand nature of the cloud

Another important aspect of the cloud is the ability to *turn on*, *turn off*, *create*, and *delete* services based on your actual usage.

For example, it's common for organizations to have different infrastructure environments. Common examples are production, development, and testing. Imagine that, in the cloud, you can only create the testing environment when testing occurs. After the testing is done, we can delete the services.

In a non-cloud environment, that approach would be like selling the entire machine to other companies and then repurchasing it when you need it. This never happens.

Another example involves a Hadoop pattern. The usual Hadoop usage on-premises is to have a giant cluster that consists of tens to thousands of server nodes to store data in the **Hadoop File System** (**HDFS**) and process thousands of jobs in Spark. In GCP, it's common to create a **Spark cluster** for each job.

Since it's quite easy and fast to create a Hadoop cluster in GCP, a common practice is to create a dedicated cluster to run one Spark job at a time and delete the cluster after the job is finished. The reason? Dedicated resources – you only want to pay for the cluster when the job runs. If you don't use it, you don't need to pay for the idle nodes. This concept is called an **ephemeral cluster** and something we'll cover in more detail in *Chapter 5, Building a Data Lake Using Dataproc*.

Getting started with GCP

OK, let's get started by taking our first steps and trying out GCP.

Chances are you already registered or created a project in GCP before reading this book. But in case you haven't, the following steps are mandatory:

1. Access the GCP console by going to `https://console.cloud.google.com` in any browser.
2. Login with your Google account (for example, Gmail).
3. Register for GCP using your Google account.

At this point, I won't write many step-by-step instructions since it's a straightforward registration process. Check out `https://cloud.google.com/docs/get-started` if you have doubts about any step.

A common question at this point is, do I have to pay for this? The answer is no, but you need to register with a payment method.

When you initially register for GCP, you will be asked for a payment method, but you won't be charged for anything at that point.

When will you be charged?

You will be charged after you do any of the following:

- Using any services
- Using the service more than the free tier allows
- Using GCP for longer than the free trial

I'll explain. You will be charged after you use a service, but not until you pass the free tier limits. Some products have free tiers, some do not.

For example, when you use BigQuery, you won't be charged when you store less than 10 GB of data a month or perform less than 1 TB of queries per month. If your usage in BigQuery is less than that, your bill will be zero.

An example of a service that doesn't have a free tier is Cloud Composer. When you use Cloud Composer, you will be charged when you start Cloud Composer instances.

Check out the GCP pricing calculator if you are interested in simulating costs: `https://cloud.google.com/products/calculator`.

At this point, it may not be crystal clear about the cost aspect because every single service at GCP has a pricing mechanism. On the cloud, the cost is one of the major factors to be considered and needs to be strategized, so we will have a special section dedicated to that in *Chapter 11, Cost Strategy in GCP*.

My suggestion is not to think about it for now. It's better to focus on the *how-to* aspect of the services; we will learn about the pricing mechanisms while learning about the services.

In later chapters, when we take on some hands-on exercises, I will always warn you if cost is unavoidable. You may choose to continue the exercise or not.

Another question that might pop up in your mind is whether there are any free trials.

Yes – if you are a new GCP customer, then you will get a free $300 to try any services within 90 days. This $300 is applied on top of the free tiers of each product.

Introduction to the GCP console

Once you've finished registering, you will be directed to the GCP console. GCP centralizes every single user interaction in this console, as shown in the following screenshot:

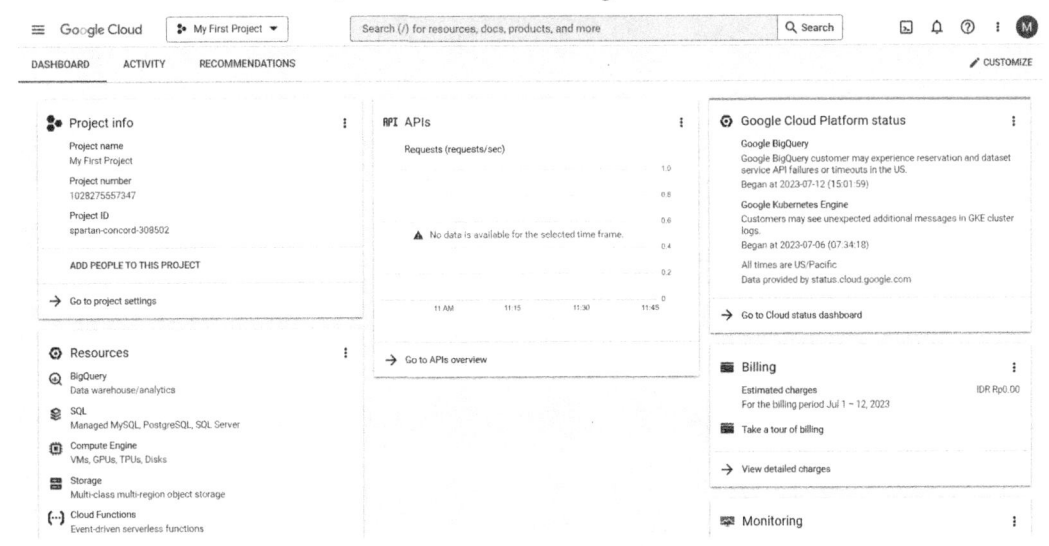

Figure 2.1 – The GCP console's main page

From enabling services, configuring user access, monitoring billing, checking logs, and much more, you can even build an entire end-to-end data ecosystem without leaving the console. So, the GCP console is very powerful. Let's take a closer look:

1. We'll start by clicking the navigation menu (the hamburger button) at the top left of our screen:

Figure 2.2 – Navigation button in the GCP console

2. After the menu has expanded, you should see the list of services available on GCP in the navigation menu.
3. Scroll down and click **MORE PRODUCTS**.
4. You will see what services are available there. Check out how GCP categorizes products – for example, **COMPUTE**, **STORAGE**, **DATABASES**, and many others:

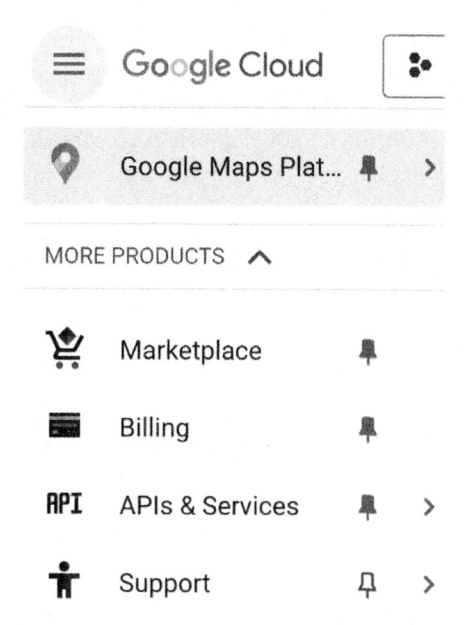

Figure 2.3 – Navigation menu in the GCP console

You will see a lengthy list of services in the navigation menu. The list covers all the services that you can use in GCP.

Practicing pinning services

You will be a little bit overwhelmed at first since there are so many services to choose from. Let's make this simpler by pinning products that are relevant to us.

As an example, let's pin BigQuery:

1. At the very bottom of the navigation menu, click on **MORE PRODUCTS**
2. Find **BigQuery** under the **ANALYTICS** section.
3. Find the pin button to the right of **BigQuery** and click it.
4. Back at the very top of the navigation menu, **BigQuery** will be pinned there:

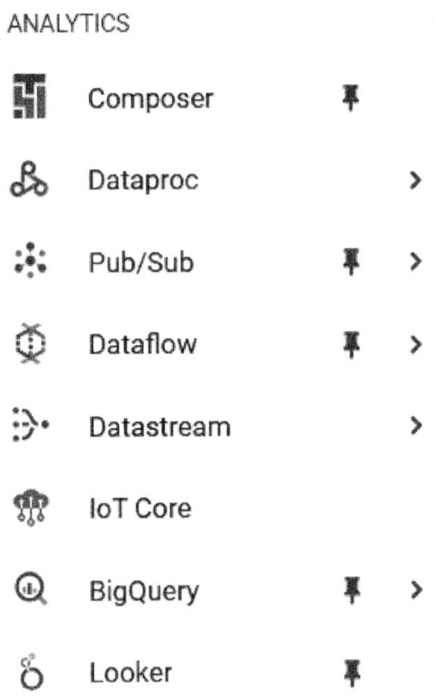

ANALYTICS

⊞	Composer	📌	
⋔	Dataproc		>
⋮⋮⋮	Pub/Sub	📌	>
⊕	Dataflow	📌	>
⋮⋗	Datastream		>
⋔	IoT Core		
⊕	BigQuery	📌	>
⊗	Looker	📌	

Figure 2.4 – Pinning the BigQuery service

Now, practice this by pinning the following services:

- **IAM & Admin (PRODUCTS)**
- **Cloud Storage (STORAGE)**
- **SQL (DATABASES)**
- **Composer (ANALYTICS)**
- **Dataproc (ANALYTICS)**
- **Pub/Sub (ANALYTICS)**
- **Dataflow (ANALYTICS)**
- **BigQuery (ANALYTICS)**
- **Dataplex (ANALYTICS)**
- **Vertex AI (ANALYTICS)**

Once you've done this, you will have all these services at the top of your navigation menu.

Creating your first GCP project

As a first hands-on step, we will start by creating a GCP project. You will use this GCP project for all the exercises in this book. Please follow these steps to create your first GCP project:

1. On the top bar, you will see **My First Project**. This is your project's name. We want to change this default project name to a new one. So, click the **My First Project** text. I will call this button the project menu for simplicity in later steps:

Figure 2.5 – Top bar

2. Once you are in the project menu, click **NEW PROJECT** at the top right:

Figure 2.6 – The NEW PROJECT button

3. After that, you will find a form that you can fill in with the project details. Enter your new project name in the form. There are two pieces of project information in GCP:

   - **Project Name**: A user-friendly name – it doesn't need to be unique.
   - **Project ID**: This needs to be unique globally, which means you cannot use a project ID that's already being used by other users. If you need to change your project ID, click **EDIT** under the **Project Name** form.

   The project name can be the same as the project ID, so long as it's globally unique.

   I usually use the initial of my name or my company in front of the project name, followed by the project's purpose. Most of the time, this will help with uniqueness and standardization.

   For example, I could use the following:

   - **Project Name**: `packt-gcp-data-eng`
   - **Project ID**: `wired-apex-392509` (auto-generated – this needs to be unique globally)

   If **Project ID** is already in use by another user, GCP will automatically generate a unique **Project ID** value for you. You can check this under the **Project name** form.

4. After deciding on your new project name, click **CREATE**:

Project name *
packt-data-eng-on-gcp

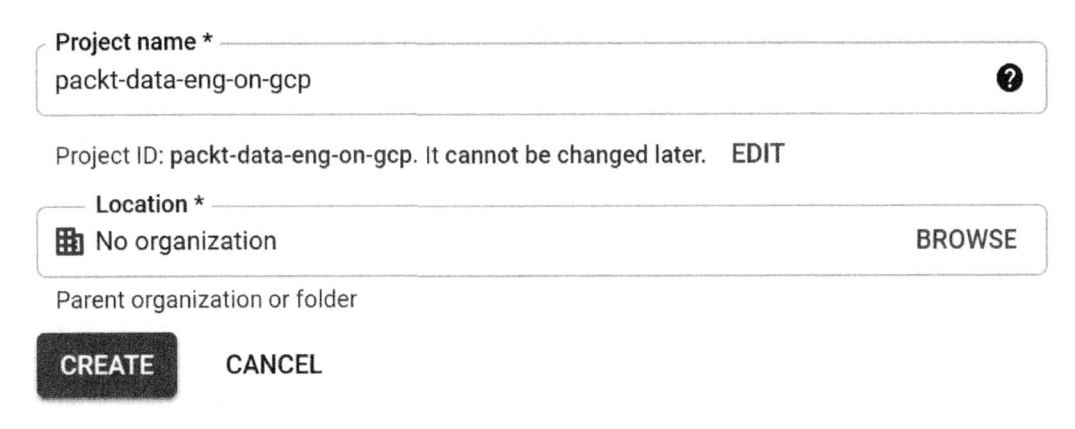

Project ID: **packt-data-eng-on-gcp**. It cannot be changed later.   EDIT

Location *
🏢 No organization   BROWSE

Parent organization or folder

CREATE   CANCEL

Figure 2.7 – Creating a new project

5. After successfully creating your project, click on the **Project** menu again and do the following:

   A. Search for your newly created project.

   B. Click your project name from the list.

This way, you will be working on your own project, not the default **My First Project**:

Select a project   🔧 NEW PROJECT

Search projects and folders
🔍

RECENT	STARRED	ALL

	Name	ID
✓ ☆ :•	packt-gcp-data-eng ❓	wired-apex-392509
☆ :•	My First Project ❓	responsive-seat-392505

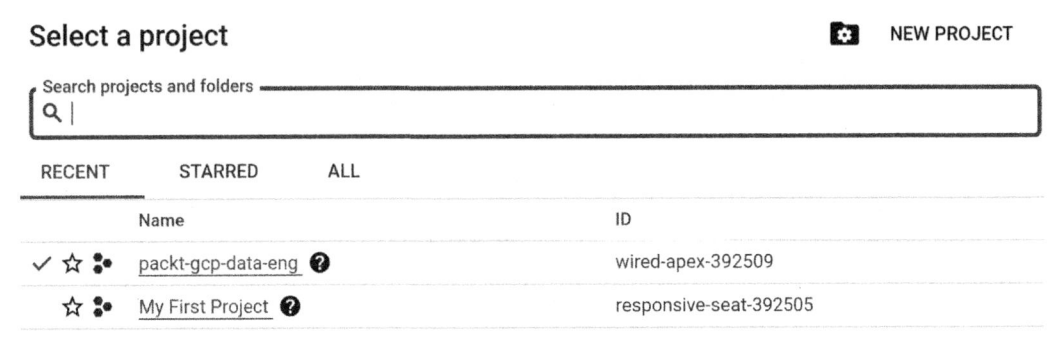

Figure 2.8 – Choosing the new project

The project is an important aspect of GCP that you need to design and strategize to answer these kinds of questions:

- How many projects should I create?
- When should I create a new project?
- Can I use one project for all my tasks?

We will learn about projects later, in *Chapter 9, User and Project Management in GCP*. But at this stage, let's not worry much about this and focus on how to use individual services first.

Using GCP Cloud Shell

I want to introduce one important feature in GCP that will help a lot with our practice later, which is the terminal and editor tool. You can access a Linux terminal in the GCP console. This is a standard Linux environment that comes preinstalled with all the necessary libraries – for example, the `gcloud` command. Let's try to use it:

1. Open the terminal by clicking the top-right button in the GCP console:

Figure 2.9 – The Cloud Shell button at the top right

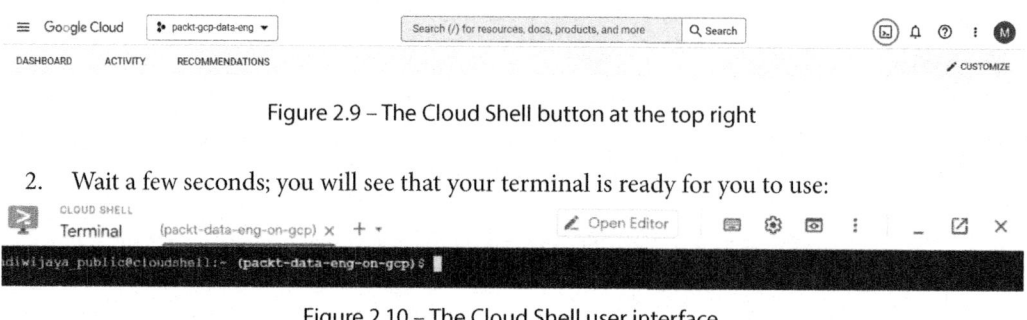

2. Wait a few seconds; you will see that your terminal is ready for you to use:

Figure 2.10 – The Cloud Shell user interface

3. Still in the terminal, if you check out the bar at the top, you will see the **Open Editor** button. Let's try using it:

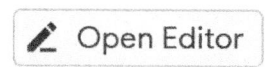

Figure 2.11 – The Open Editor button at the top right

4. The terminal will change into a simple text editor. The text editor is not designed to replace an IDE such as **IntelliJ** or **Eclipse**, but this is good enough to edit your code in the Linux system:

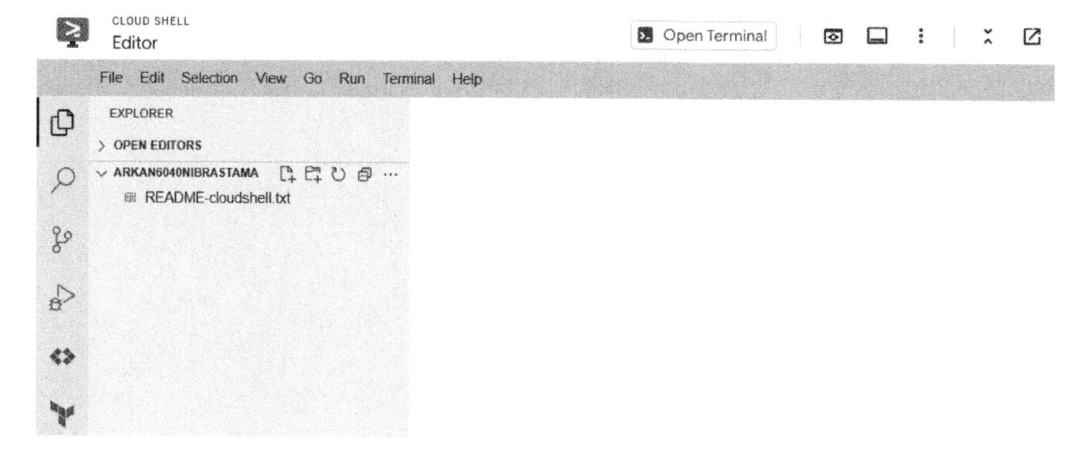

Figure 2.12 – The cloud editor user interface

Now that the system is ready for us to write some commands, let's warm up by creating a `Hello world` Python script:

1. Go to **File** | **New File** and name the file `hello_world.py`.
2. In the editor, add the following command:

   ```
   print ("Hello world")
   ```

   At this point, your cloud editor should look like this:

   Figure 2.13 – Using the cloud editor for Python code

   The editor will automatically save your file, so you don't need to click a save button.

3. Now, let's run the Python script from the terminal by clicking the **Open Terminal** button and running the following Python command:

   ```
   $ python hello_world.py
   ```

   Your Cloud Shell should look like this:

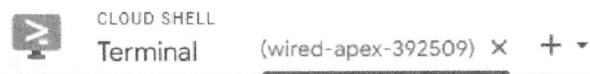

   Figure 2.14 – Running the "Hello World" script in Cloud Shell

The terminal will show you the **Hello World** text from the Python file, and that's it.

Let's summarize what we've done so far. Here, we've learned how to use the GCP console and how to create and use a new project. In this section, we learned how to use Cloud Shell. We will use this tool a lot in this book to run `gcloud` commands, as well as write and run Python scripts.

Starting from the next chapter, *Chapter 3, Building a Data Warehouse in BigQuery*, we will be a lot more hands-on with practical use cases using the services that we introduced in this chapter to build data solutions. So, make sure you set up the GCP console properly in this exercise.

In the next section, we will learn what services are available in GCP and how to focus on specific services for data engineering use cases.

A quick overview of GCP services for data engineering

As shown in the GCP console's navigation bar, there are a lot of services in GCP. These services are not only limited to data and analytics – there are other areas, such as application development, machine learning, networks, source repositories, and many more. As a data engineer working on GCP, you will face situations where you need to decide which services you need to use for your organization.

You might be wondering, who in an organization should decide on the services to use? Is it the CTO, IT manager, solution architect, or data engineer? The answer depends on their experience of using GCP. But most of the time, data engineers need to be involved in the decision.

So, how should we decide? In my experience, there are three important decision factors:

- Choose serverless services
- Understand the mapping between the service and the data engineering areas
- If there is more than one option in one area, choose the most popular service on the market

Choosing a serverless service or, to use another common term, a fully managed service, **Software-as-a-Service** (**SaaS**) can also mean choosing services that are the easiest. The easiest in terms of Google manages everything for us, so we can just use the tool.

On top of that, to choose the right service, you need to be able to understand the service positioning in data engineering areas. You can go back to *Chapter 1, Fundamentals of Data Engineering, The focus of the data engineer* section, to learn more. Each service in GCP can be mapped to the data flow diagram in that section.

Lastly, if there are multiple options in the same area, I suggest that you choose the most popular one. Not because of **fear of missing out** (**FOMO**), but because this is often a good indicator to choose a product in the IT industry. There are a couple of good reasons for this, such as you know that the products or services will still be there in the long run, the support from both Google and the community will be a lot better, and lastly, from the company's perspective, you will be able to hire an expert more easily compared to less popular products.

Let's discuss these three factors in more detail.

Understanding the GCP serverless service

Before diving into **serverless services** or **fully managed services**, if this is the first time you have heard of a managed service, it is a term for products that are managed – in other words, they are configured and maintained by the service provider.

This was a breakthrough in the IT industry in the early 2010s. Before that era, if you wanted to use an IT product, you needed to buy a computer, install an operating system, install the software, configure the software, and use it.

In the managed service era, if you want to use an IT product, you just simply use it. And that's the new normal in the IT industry. But the question is, how easy is it to simply use it?

This varies widely, depending on the service provider, and even in Google Cloud, it varies depending on the services. Some services are a lot easier to use compared to others.

To simplify this, I will introduce three approaches to using managed services in GCP. In general, there are three groups of services in GCP:

- **VM-based**
- **Managed services**
- **Serverless**

VM-based means you, as a user, use a Google-managed **virtual machine** (**VM**) (in GCP, this service is called **Google Compute Engine** (**GCE**). You don't need to buy a machine and install an operating system, but you need to install the software yourself. This is still an option because not all software is available in GCP.

As an example, from my own experience, Google doesn't have a managed service for the Elasticsearch database, so what I need to do is create VMs in GCE and install Elasticsearch on top of the VMs.

Managed service means Google manages the software for you. Not only do you not need to install an operating system but you don't need to install software dependencies either or carry out maintenance.

As another real example, the first time I used GCP was because I wanted to use Hadoop on the cloud. At the time, I took the VM-based approach. I installed Hadoop from an open-source installer on some VMs until I realized that was not the best practice. The best practice, if you want to use Hadoop on GCP, is to use **Dataproc**, which is a Hadoop-managed service on GCP.

Using Dataproc, you don't need to install Hadoop yourself; Google manages this for you. But since it's a managed service, you still need to configure the machine size, choose the networks, and other configurations.

A serverless service means simply using it. You just use the software instantly. You don't need to set up anything to use the software, such as BigQuery. In BigQuery, we can instantly create tables and trigger SQL queries without configuring anything.

n the other hand, we also have zero visibility of the underlying infrastructure. We will discuss this in more detail in *Chapter 3, Building a Data Warehouse in BigQuery*.

The following table shows the key differences between the three groups and on-premises for comparison:

	Manage physical infrastructure	Manage Virtual Machines (VMs)	Manage application service	Develop solution on top of the service
On-premise (Non cloud)	O	O	O	O
VM based	X	O	O	O
Managed service	X	X	O	O
Serverless	X	X	X	O

Figure 2.15 – Comparison metrics for managed services

Let's see what **X** and **O** in the preceding table mean:

- (**X**): You, as an engineer, don't need to do it. Google manages it for you.
- (**O**): You, as an engineer, need to do it. Google gives you flexibility.

Let's take a look at a practical example: As a GCP data engineer, you are requested to store and process CSV data. The file size is 1 TB, and your end user wants to access it in table format using SQL. How do you solve the request?

You need a big data service to handle this amount of data, and there are three possible scenarios.

Scenario 1 – VM-based:

1. Provision multiple VM instances in GCP using Compute Engine. Then, configure the VM networks, operating system, packages, and any infrastructure requirements.
2. Install the Hadoop cluster on top of the Compute Engine instances. You can choose any Hadoop version that you like.
3. Store data in HDFS and create a hive table on top of the Hadoop cluster.

Scenario 2 – managed service:

1. Provision a Hadoop-managed service cluster (Dataproc).
2. Store data in HDFS and create a hive table on top of the Hadoop cluster.

Scenario 3 – serverless:

1. Store data in a BigQuery table, which is a fully managed service for a data warehouse.

Scenario 3 only has one step; it shows you that serverless services, in general, are the best choice for simplicity since you can jumpstart the development stage without worrying about setting up the infrastructure and software installation.

What is the drawback? Flexibility. In scenario 1, you can install any software version you like; you have full control of your infrastructure, but you need to take care of its scalability, availability, logging, and other management stuff yourself.

In scenario 2, when using Dataproc, you don't need to create each VM instance manually; Google will set the underlying Hadoop infrastructure for you, but you need to choose the available version.

In general, use serverless services if one is available and suits your needs. Unless you have compatibility issues, have specific feature requirements, or the cost doesn't meet your budget, then you may consider scenarios 1 and 2.

Service mapping and prioritization

Given that there are many services in GCP, let's narrow things down.

There are two aspects that I use to decide what we should focus on:

- How close is the service to the core of data engineering? (Check out *Chapter 1*, *Fundamentals of Data Engineering*, *The focus of data engineers* section.)
- The number of adoptions by companies across industries

To understand service categorization in GCP, let's take a look at the following figure:

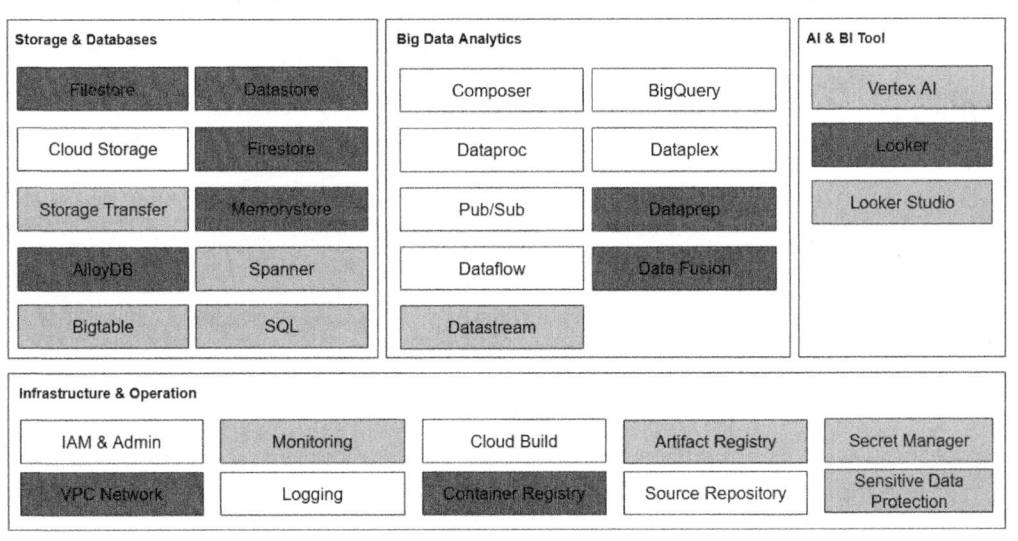

Figure 2.16 – Big data service mapping and priority

The GCP services are mapped to their main categories. Four main categories are relevant to data engineers. In each category, there are service options that are represented by three different box colors:

- **White**: Priority 1
- **Light gray**: Priority 2
- **Dark gray**: Priority 3

Take your time while checking out each service in this figure and its priority. The reason we want to use the two aspects to decide on our first focus is that we want to make sure we start with the data engineer's main responsibility, as discussed in *Chapter 1, Fundamentals of Data Engineering*.

On top of that, if there are options in the same category, I would prefer to start with services that have been adopted the most by GCP customers.

When many GCP customers use their services, it gives us confidence that the services are proven both in terms of scalability and maturity. On top of that, the service will be highly supported by the product team at Google in the long-term future, and this is a particularly important aspect of choosing products.

Another reason is the community and the expertise available. The more well-known a service is, the easier you will find the experts that can help you use the service.

Why are there so many services? The answer is that each service is meant for a specific purpose. Unlike most traditional IT products, which try to provide full-stack services as one bundled product, in GCP, each service usually has one specific purpose. And as data engineers, we need to combine them to build solutions.

Now that we know the categorization of each prioritized product from the previous section, we want to quickly look at each product's main position in data engineering.

Analytics

Here is the list of services under **analytics**:

- **Cloud Composer**: An Airflow-managed service. Airflow is a Python-based job orchestration tool.
- **Dataproc**: A Hadoop-managed service that includes HDFS, MapReduce, Spark, Presto, and more.
- **Pub/Sub**: A serverless messaging system that's used to publish and subscribe data. It's comparable to Kafka, even though they are not the same.
- **Dataflow**: A serverless distributed processing framework service that's suitable for streaming jobs. The technology is comparable with Spark, even though they're not the same.
- **Datastream**: A serverless **change data capture** (**CDC**) that's used to capture record changes in OLTP databases. The record changes can then be streamed to other environments, such as GCS or BigQuery.
- **BigQuery**: A serverless data warehouse service.

- **Dataplex**: A serverless data governance tool for managing data on GCP.
- **Dataprep**: A UI-based data wrangling tool. While data wrangling is like the ETL process in general, Dataprep has unique features, including checking data distribution in histograms and checking missing values. Dataprep is managed by a third party, **Trifacta**, which means that GCP customers need to have separate legal agreements with Trifacta.
- **Data Fusion**: A UI-based orchestration tool to run Hadoop jobs on Dataproc.

Storage and database

Here is the list of services under **storage and database**:

- **Filestore**: A serverless file storage that offers extremely low latency. Compared to Cloud Storage, this service is more suitable for backend storage for web and application files.
- **Cloud Storage**: A serverless object storage for storing large files. Compared to Filestore, this service is more suitable for storing large files. The common use case is for the staging layer, temporary files, and data lakes.
- **Storage Transfer**: A serverless service to transfer files between objects and file storage
- **AlloyDB**: A serverless PostgreSQL-compatible database
- **Bigtable**: A serverless NoSQL database service. The technology is comparable with Hbase in the Hadoop ecosystem
- **Datastore**: A serverless NoSQL document database service for web and applications. This product is a predecessor of Firestore
- **Firestore**: A serverless NoSQL document database service for web and applications. This product is the successor of Datastore
- **Memorystore**: A serverless memory store based on Redis
- **Spanner**: A serverless SQL database that offers exceedingly high scalability and availability
- **SQL**: A managed service for application databases – for example, MySQL, PostgreSQL, and SQL Server

Identity and management tools

Here is the list of services under **Identity and management tools**:

- **IAM & Admin**: User and project management for all GCP services
- **Monitoring**: A serverless monitoring system with dashboards driven by data from Cloud Logging
- **Logging**: A serverless logging system for all GCP services
- **Cloud Build**: A serverless CI/CD tool for managing the deployment pipeline

- **Container Registry**: A serverless artifacts registry for storing Docker images, for example. This service is a predecessor of Artifact Registry
- **Artifact Registry**: The next generation of Container Registry
- **Source Repository**: A serverless git repository

Machine learning and BI tools

Here is the list of services under **machine learning and BI tools**:

- **Vertex AI**: All the tools that you need to build machine learning and MLOps – for example, notebooks, pipelines, a model store, and other Machine learning-related services
- **Looker**: A full-fledged BI tool to visualize data in reports and dashboards
- **Looker Studio**: A simple visualization tool to visualize data

Security

Here is the list of services under **security**:

- **Sensitive Data Protection**: For detecting sensitive data in BigQuery and GCS storage
- **Secret Manager**: For storing sensitive information such as keys and passwords

At this point, I have only added truly short and simple descriptions for each service. At this stage, we only need to know the services' positioning. A detailed explanation of each service can be found on the internet. You can start by going to `https://cloud.google.com/products#section-7`.

The GCP services that I have listed in this chapter are the ones that are related to data analytics. However, GCP also offers other services, such as Compute Engine, Cloud Functions, GKE, and many more. The motivation is for us to focus on the most important services. When needed, you will find that you will understand the other services naturally.

In this book, we will try all the priority 1 services and some of the priority 2 services with hands-on exercises. By the end of this book, you will understand the benefits of using them.

The concept of quotas on GCP services

Another fundamental terminology that we need to be aware of is **quotas**. When we talk about limitations in the cloud ecosystem, one of the most common boundaries that people usually think of is cost. It's quite common to think that, so long as you have an unlimited budget, then you can store and process any amount of data you need.

That is partially true, but there is another important boundary, which is quotas. Quotas are sets of limitations on each GCP service as a default rule that applies to all GCP users.

For example, in BigQuery, you cannot have more than 10,000 columns in a table. Another example is that the maximum size limit of individual objects stored in Cloud Storage is 5 TB.

Each service has quotas, and the most important thing is that you are aware of this and know where to check. You can check out the Cloud Storage quotas at `https://cloud.google.com/storage/quotas` and the BigQuery quotas at `https://cloud.google.com/bigquery/quotas`.

You can check out the quotas for other products by following the same URL pattern. There are two main reasons that quotas are in place:

- To make sure services are highly available:

  Even though you don't need to worry about physical servers in GCP, the services are running on top of giant Google Cloud clusters that are shared with many customers. Quotas prevent uncontrolled usage by one customer that affects other customers.

- Quotas can function as a reminder of bad practices:

  If you develop a solution and exceed the quotas, you might need to review your solution design. For example, from the previous BigQuery example, you might need to review your table if your table has more than 10,000 columns because that indicates that, generally, that's not a common practice.

Quotas are gradually updated based on GCP customers' usage and needs. You don't need to remember all the quotas; the important takeaway from this section is that you need to be aware of what a quota is and where you can check out the different ones.

User account versus service account

The last terminologies that we need to be aware of before we continue with the hands-on exercises in the following chapters are **user account** and **service account**:

- A user account is your personal account as a human user
- A service account is an account that will be used by non-humans

What are non-humans? In many cases, we want to automate our solutions, and to do that, we want machines to complete certain tasks – for example, triggering jobs, building Docker images, running Python scripts, and much more. We need service accounts for this instead of personal user accounts.

For example, if an organization has an email address of `domain@company.com` and has three employees called Arkan, Toni, and Sylvi, then the typical user accounts would be as follows:

- `arkan@company.com`
- `toni@company.com`
- `sylvi@company.com`

The company uses **Cloud Composer** to orchestrate an ETL load from GCS to BigQuery. Using one of the employee user accounts is not a clever idea at all! Imagine if the person left the company – the whole ETL in Cloud Composer would not be accessible.

What they need is a service account for Cloud Composer – for example, `service-composer@company.iam.gserviceaccount.com`.

This Cloud Composer service account will have access to the GCS bucket and BigQuery datasets.

In this case, the company doesn't need to use one of the employee's emails to run these automated jobs. This way, the company also has the flexibility to limit the employees' access to sensitive datasets and let the service account manage the jobs.

Understanding the difference between a user and a service account is particularly important in GCP. We will use both a user account and a service account in our exercises. By doing so, you will get more of an idea of how to use them properly.

Summary

We've learned a lot of new things in this chapter about the cloud and GCP. We started by accessing the GCP console for the first time. Then, we narrowed things down to find our priority GCP services for data engineers to focus on.

We closed this chapter by familiarizing ourselves with notable features and terminologies, such as quotas and service accounts.

In the next chapter, we will start by practicing developing a data warehouse. As we've learned in this chapter, the cloud data warehouse in GCP is BigQuery. We will start by learning about this incredibly famous GCP service – and the most important – for GCP data engineers.

Part 2: Build Solutions with GCP Components

This part will talk about leveraging GCP products to support storage systems, pipelines, and infrastructure in a production environment. It will also cover common operations such as data ingestion, data cleansing, transformation, and integrating data with other sources. By the end of this part, you will have acquired practical knowledge to build efficient **Extract, Transform, and Load** (**ETL**) data pipelines over GCP.

This part has the following chapters:

- *Chapter 3, Building a Data Warehouse in BigQuery*
- *Chapter 4, Building Workflows for Batch Data Loading Using Cloud Composer*
- *Chapter 5, Building a Data Lake Using Dataproc*
- *Chapter 6, Processing Streaming Data with Pub/Sub and Dataflow*
- *Chapter 7, Visualizing Data to Make Data-Driven Decisions with Looker Studio*
- *Chapter 8, Building Machine Learning Solutions on GCP*

3
Building a Data Warehouse in BigQuery

The power of a **data warehouse** is that organizations can combine multiple sources of information into a single place that becomes a single source of truth. The dream of data analytics is the time when every single business aspect of an organization relies on data. That condition can be met when all business decision-makers know how to access data, trust the data, and can make decisions based on it.

Unfortunately, most of the time, dreams are far removed from reality. There are many challenges along the way. Based on my experience, there are three main challenges – *technology bottlenecks*, *data consistency*, and the *ability to serve multiple business purposes*.

The preceding challenges are natural when we build a data warehouse. They're not limited to certain technologies and organizations. In this chapter, we will learn about those challenges through two hands-on scenarios. We will mainly use **BigQuery** as the GCP data warehouse cloud service. Along with that, we will also use **Google Cloud Storage** (**GCS**) and **CloudSQL** to demonstrate their dependencies.

I will tell you in advance that this book will not offer the most complete explanation of BigQuery or data warehouse theory. The BigQuery public documentation on the internet is the best place to find the most complete detailed documentation, and there are books out there that explain data warehouse theory in great detail. So, what are we going to do in this chapter?

In this chapter, rather than explaining all the detailed features one by one, we will learn how to build a data warehouse by doing so using BigQuery. And by doing it, you will learn the exact path and order of importance for both the technology and the principles.

We will begin the chapter by introducing three services: BigQuery, GCS, and CloudSQL. In the *Practicing developing a data warehouse* section, we will utilize two scenarios to design and build a data warehouse.

After finishing this chapter, you will be familiar with how to use BigQuery and GCS, how to load data to BigQuery, and the principle of data modeling in BigQuery.

In particular, we will cover the following topics in this chapter:

- Introduction to GCS and BigQuery
- Introduction to the BigQuery console
- Preparing the prerequisites before developing our data warehouse
- Practicing developing a data warehouse

Technical requirements

In this chapter's exercises, we will use the following GCP services: **BigQuery** and **GCS**. If you have never opened any of these services in your GCP console, open them and enable the API.

Make sure you have your **GCP console**, **Cloud Shell**, and **Cloud Editor** ready.

Before starting, you must have a basic knowledge of Python programming, SQL, Linux commands, and Git.

All the example Python scripts are developed using Python 3. Make sure you run the Python commands using Python 3 instead of Python (Python 2) from Cloud Shell.

Download the example code and the dataset here: `https://github.com/PacktPublishing/Data-Engineering-with-Google-Cloud-Platform-Second-Edition/tree/main/chapter-3`

Introduction to GCS and BigQuery

GCS is an object storage service. It's a serverless service that is fully managed by GCP, which means we don't need to think about any underlying infrastructure of GCS. For example, we don't need to think about pre-sizing the storage, network bandwidth, number of nodes, or any other infrastructure-related stuff.

What is object storage? **Object storage** is a highly scalable data storage architecture that can store very large amounts of data in any format.

Because the technology can store data in almost any size and format, GCS is often used by developers to store large files, for example, images, videos, and large CSV data. But, from the data engineering perspective, we will often use GCS to store files, for example, as dump storage from databases, for exporting historical data from **BigQuery**, for storing machine learning model files, and for any other purpose related to storing files.

BigQuery is a serverless data warehouse in the cloud. BigQuery allows users to store and analyze data immediately without needing to think about infrastructure.

On top of that, using BigQuery gives you a high degree of confidence regarding scalability in terms of both storage and processing power. BigQuery is able to store and process petabytes of data in many organizations around the world.

Going a little bit deeper into what is under the hood of BigQuery, BigQuery consists of four data warehouse main parts, as discussed in *Chapter 1, Fundamentals of Data Engineering*:

- SQL interface
- Schema
- Compute
- Storage

BigQuery *stores* data in a distributed filesystem called **Google Colossus**, in columnar storage format. Colossus is the successor to Google File System, which is the inspiration for **Hadoop Distributed File System** (**HDFS**). As users, we can't access Google Colossus directly. We access the data using tables (metadata) and the **SQL interface** to process the data.

BigQuery *processes* data in a distributed **SQL execution engine** inspired by **Dremel SQL**. Dremel SQL is a Google internal SQL analytics tool. The main purpose of Dremel is to interactively query large datasets. But BigQuery is a product in its own right. Many improvements and adjustments have been made to BigQuery compared to Dremel. The reason is, of course, to serve broader GCP customer requirements around the world. By way of a simple example, the SQL language is different in Dremel (Legacy SQL) to BigQuery (Standard SQL).

As BigQuery users, we don't need to know what happens under the hood (**Colossus** and **Dremel**). However, as a GCP data engineer, it's good to be aware of this. We sometimes encounter situations when we need to improve the performance of BigQuery, troubleshoot table issues, or fix any other issues. Knowing Colossus and Dremel SQL at a high level might help. You can read in more detail about how both technologies work in their whitepapers on the internet.

One final topic before we go to the exercise is *data location*. When people start using cloud technologies, sometimes they may wonder where the data is stored. Is the data stored in a private place? Is it going to meet certain data locality regulations? We will discuss this in the next section.

BigQuery data location

BigQuery is physically located in different countries and cities. The different locations are grouped into regions, and each region has different zones. For example, in the country where I live, the closest region is *asia-southeast*. There are two zones in the region: *Singapore* and *Jakarta*. When I choose *Singapore* as the BigQuery dataset region, the data will be stored and processed in Google Cloud *Singapore's* clusters.

The data is stored in a GCP cluster in the specified region, and no user, including Google's internal users, can access the data. You can decide for yourself whether this satisfies your organization's regulations.

At the same time, as a data engineer who, most of the time, is responsible for creating BigQuery objects, you need to pay attention to the location configuration for each GCP service (not only BigQuery) to make sure you choose the correct location. As an additional note, not every GCP service is available in every region, so you need to check the public documentation regarding availability.

BigQuery is very good at storing large volumes of data and performing analysis and processing immediately using the SQL interface. On top of that, there are two main features that I think excel compared to other similar products in the market, which are **streaming** and **machine learning**. BigQuery allows you to insert streaming data. BigQuery also allows you to perform machine learning using BigQuery SQL directly in the console at scale. This is very useful for organizations that need to quickly gain access to machine learning capability.

Given all the advantages of BigQuery, keep in mind that BigQuery is not a transactional database. BigQuery is not designed for millisecond query latency. It can process 1 TB of data in 5 seconds, but this doesn't mean you can process 1 MB of data in 0.0005 seconds. It is simply not designed for that purpose.

Having got to grips with the basic principles of BigQuery, in the next section, let's start using it from the BigQuery console.

Introduction to the BigQuery console

The best way to understand BigQuery is by using it, so let's start with a simple exercise. This first exercise will focus on understanding the BigQuery console. The BigQuery console is your main user interface for developing and using BigQuery. In this exercise, we will create a dataset and table and query the table using the BigQuery console.

Let's start our exercise by opening the BigQuery console from our browser:

1. Open your GCP console.
2. Go to the navigation bar and choose **BigQuery**. This is the BigQuery main page, called the BigQuery console:

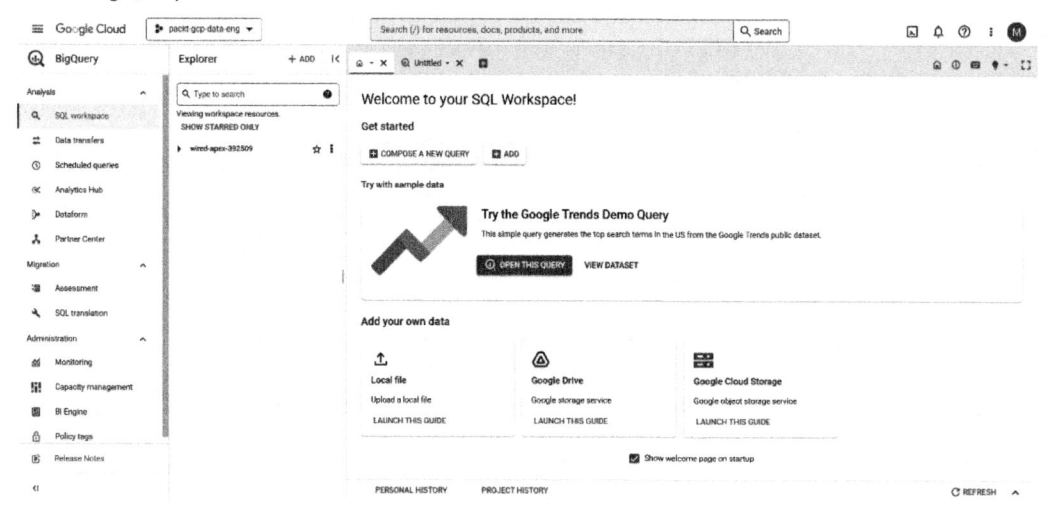

Figure 3.1 – BigQuery console

3. As you can see, there are many buttons and panels in the BigQuery console. There are three main sections on the page. On the left-hand side, there is the BigQuery menu bar, where you can see **SQL Workspace**, **Data Transfers**, **Scheduled Queries**, and the other menus. The second section is the **Explorer** section, and the third section is the query panel section.

   I recommend that you quickly scan through the console to familiarize yourself with the menus.

Now let's look at **Explorer**. You can find your project ID in **Explorer** as a default, as shown in the following screenshot, but later you can add datasets, tables, views, and any other BigQuery objects under **Explorer**.

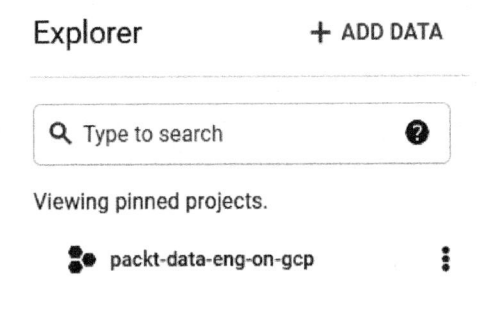

Figure 3.2 – BigQuery Explorer section

In the center panel, there will be a welcome message.

Find and click the **COMPOSE A NEW QUERY** button. You will see the query editor, where you can write your query here and run it either using the **RUN** button or using keyboard shortcuts. I recommend you use the latter option for agility.

Check the shortcuts button and look for the **Run Queries** and **Run selected queries** shortcuts, as these will be helpful for us. On Windows, for example, this will be *Ctrl + E*.

Please follow these steps to run your query in BigQuery:

1. First, we want to simply write a `hello world` query by typing the following into the editor:

   ```
   SELECT 'hello world';
   ```

   Then, click on the **RUN** button.

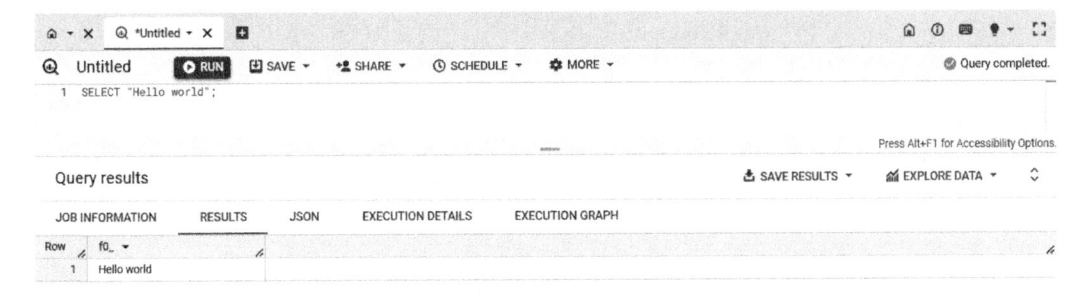

Figure 3.3 – Running a BigQuery query in the Editor section

2. After running the query, you can see the results shown at the bottom as tables, and there are five other sections: **JOB INFORMATION**, **RESULTS**, **JSON**, **EXECUTION DETAILS**, and **EXECUTION GRAPH**. At the very bottom of the page, you can also see two tabs, **PERSONAL HISTORY**, and **PROJECT HISTORY**, where you can check your query job logs.

Take a look at all of them and become familiar with how to read the information there. In the next section, we will learn how to create a dataset in BigQuery.

Creating a dataset in BigQuery using the console

The term *dataset* in BigQuery is used to abstract groups of tables. By calling it a dataset, BigQuery tries to influence users to create meaningful data groups compared to only thinking about technical purposes.

For example, if we have data from banking systems, we can name our datasets as follows:

- `Layer_1`
- `Layer_2`
- `Reference data`

Or, we can name our datasets as follows:

- `Customer saving`
- `Website logs`
- `Customer loan`

Which one do you think is better? For me, the latter is far more meaningful for humans.

Some other data technologies often use the term *database* for the table group abstractions, which often leads data engineers to group tables for technical purposes. On the other hand, the term *datasets* is often used by data scientists, which drives one's thinking to design the table groupings based on business representation, so try to think from the business perspective when you design your datasets.

Let's now try to create our first BigQuery dataset:

1. Click the action button. The action button is an icon alongside the project name, like this:

▶ wired-apex-392509   ☆ ⋮

Figure 3.4 – Action button

2. After clicking on the **Create dataset** button, proceed to the next step.

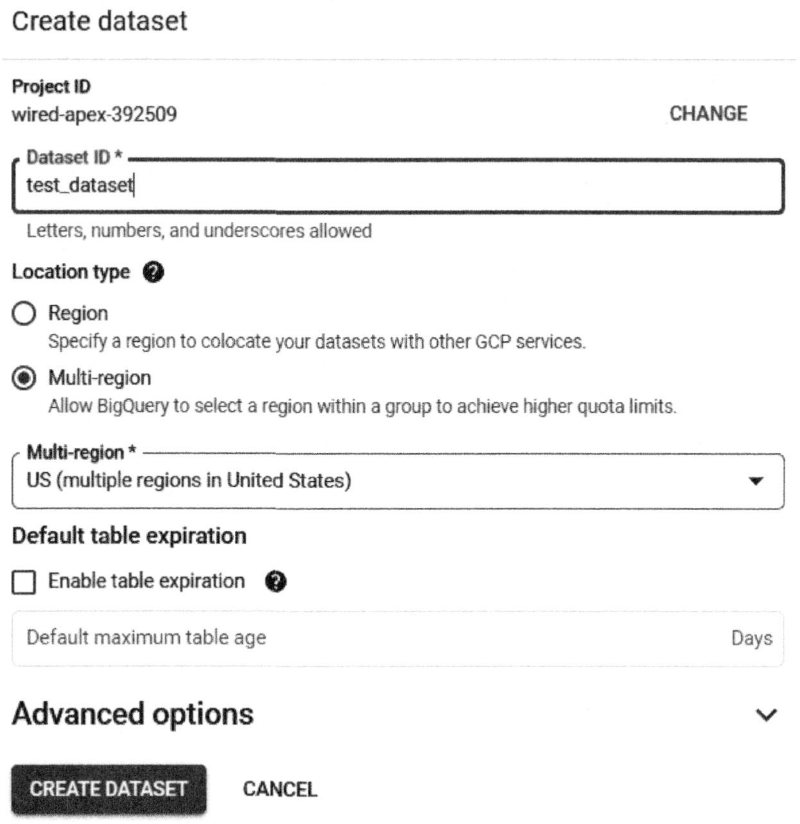

Create dataset

Project ID
wired-apex-392509   CHANGE

Dataset ID *
test_dataset

Letters, numbers, and underscores allowed

Location type

○ Region
    Specify a region to colocate your datasets with other GCP services.

● Multi-region
    Allow BigQuery to select a region within a group to achieve higher quota limits.

Multi-region *
US (multiple regions in United States)

Default table expiration

☐ Enable table expiration

Default maximum table age   Days

Advanced options

CREATE DATASET   CANCEL

Figure 3.5 – Creating a BigQuery dataset using the console

3. Choose a name for the dataset. Any name will do.
4. Choose the data location. You can choose any location, but to ensure the continuity of this book's exercise, let's choose the default one, which is **US Multi-region**.
5. Set everything else as the default settings for now and then click **CREATE DATASET**.

After finishing, you can see your dataset under the project name in the **Explorer** panel. In the next section, we want to create a table from a CSV file using the BigQuery console.

Loading the local CSV file into the BigQuery table

There are many ways to load data into BigQuery, and one of the simplest and most user-friendly for early users is to use the BigQuery console.

Do that by clicking the action button alongside the dataset name. This differs from the previous section. The action button is situated next to the dataset name, and not the project name, like this:

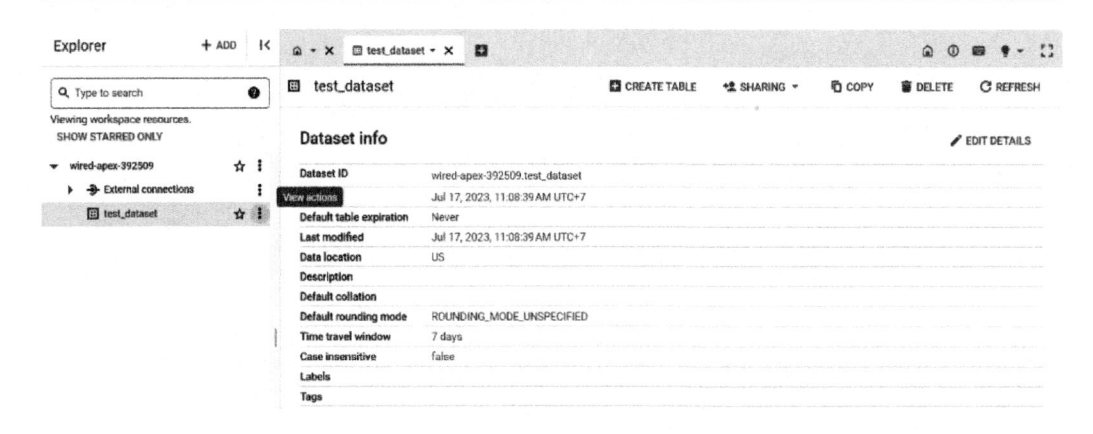

Figure 3.6 – Finding the dataset action button alongside the dataset name

You can find the **CREATE TABLE** button in the top-right corner of the screen. Let's create a table as demonstrated in the following screenshot:

Figure 3.7 – Creating a BigQuery table from the console

After completing the steps, you can see your table under the dataset. Then, you can access the table using the `SELECT` statement in the editor or choose **PREVIEW** after clicking the table name in **Explorer**.

We have now completed the first example of loading data into BigQuery using local files, so you can delete your table and the dataset. We will create new ones for later sections. In the next section, we will try to use public data from BigQuery.

Using public data in BigQuery

The easiest approach to loading data into BigQuery, as shown in the previous section, is to upload a local file directly into the BigQuery table. This is straightforward when it comes to experimentation as an early user.

If we are talking about the most common approach, loading data from local files is not the most common data engineering practice. The most common is to load data from GCS files or use Dataflow into BigQuery, which we will do in *Practicing developing a data warehouse*.

However, if you are new to BigQuery, sometimes you will be wondering what data you can use for practice. In my experience, looking for public data to learn data engineering on the internet is difficult. You can find a lot of *data*, but most of it is ready-made data and not representative of an actual database schema, which should consist of multiple tables, inconsistent values, unclear column names, and other real challenges that always happen in databases.

A good resource for finding such data is BigQuery public datasets. BigQuery comes up with a lot of example data in the public datasets. Even though there is also a lot of small data there, they provide some real raw datasets. For example, later you can check the dataset names, such as `stackoverflow`, `crypto_ethereum`, and `github_repos`, that are pretty good at representing real databases.

Let's try to access one of them by following these steps:

1. From **Explorer** in the BigQuery console, click the **+ADD** button.
2. Scroll down a little bit, and under **Additional sources**, find the **Public Datasets** button.
3. In the **Marketplace** screen, you can explore the available dataset descriptions. You can choose anything here, but as a start, choose **Encyclopedic** for **Category**.
4. Find a dataset named **MLB 2016 Pitch-by-Pitch**, and click it.
5. And lastly, click the **VIEW DATASET** button.

Now you can see that `bigquery-public-data` is pinned under **Explorer**, and you can access the baseball dataset and any table under this `bigquery-public-data` project, as shown in the following screenshot:

Building a Data Warehouse in BigQuery

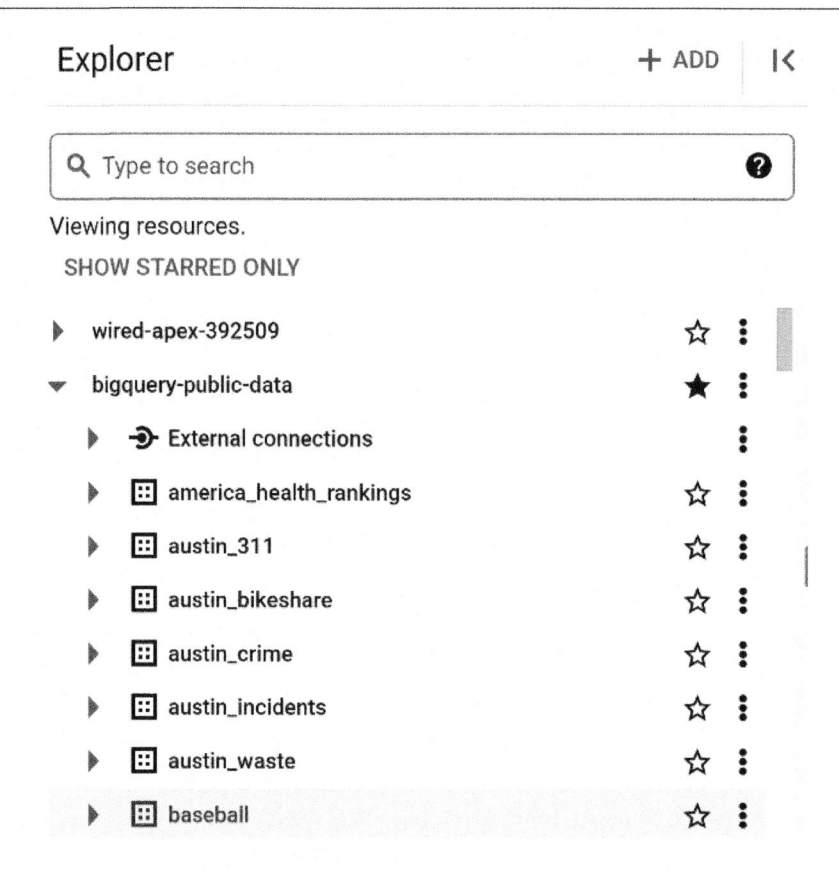

Figure 3.8 – bigquery-public-data pinned in Explorer

For this exercise, find a table named `schedules`.

> **Important note**
> Please be mindful of the table size of public datasets. If you want to explore data in public data, always check the table size first before querying it. As a rule of thumb, as long as the table is under 1 GB in size, in general, there is no risk of unexpectedly high costs. Remember that the free tier is 1 TB query size per month.

Quickly check the baseball schedules' table size, and perform the following steps:

1. Click on the table name: **schedules**.
2. Four option bars will appear: **SCHEMA**, **DETAILS**, **PREVIEW**, and **LINEAGE**.
3. Click on **DETAILS**.

Following the preceding steps will show you the table details, which is where you can see the table.

For example, as regards the `baseball.schedules` table, the size is **569.15 KB**, as shown in this screenshot:

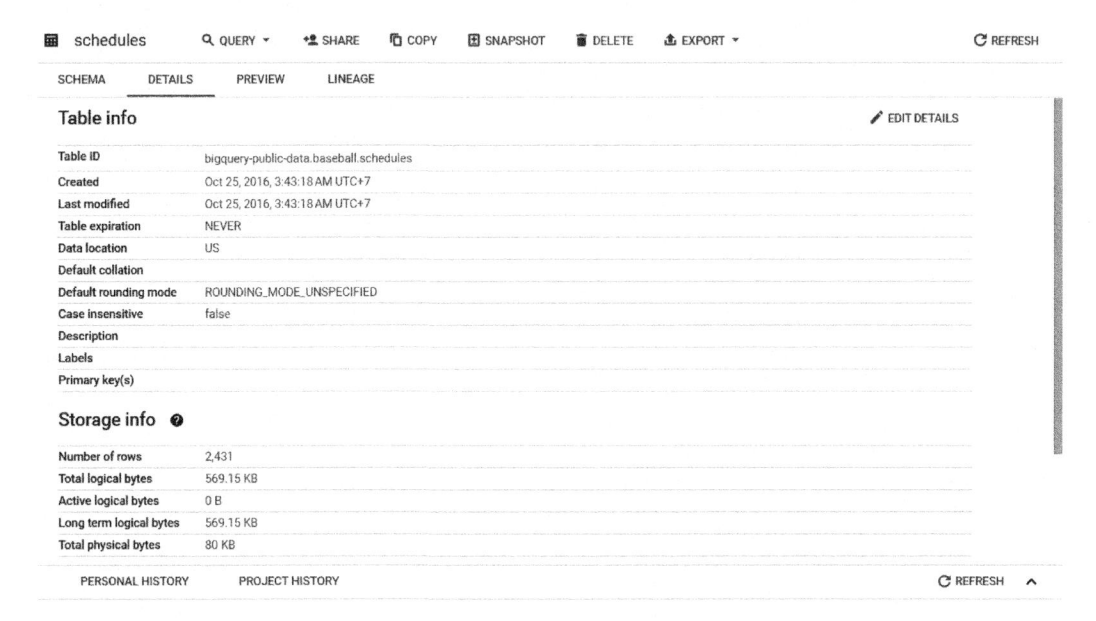

Figure 3.9 – BigQuery table info

Given the small table size, it's good for our first practice. Therefore, let's access this table: `baseball.schedules`.

Run the query in Editor:

```
SELECT * FROM `bigquery-public-data.baseball.schedules` LIMIT 1000;
```

You will see the query result under the **QUERY** panel. Take your time to play around with other tables and other functionalities in the BigQuery console. Following the exercises, let's spend time understanding some of the principles and features of BigQuery.

Data types in BigQuery compared to other databases

One of the things that you can check regarding the table metadata is data types. For example, try to click the `baseball.schedules` table and check the **SCHEMA** pane. You can see the field data types there:

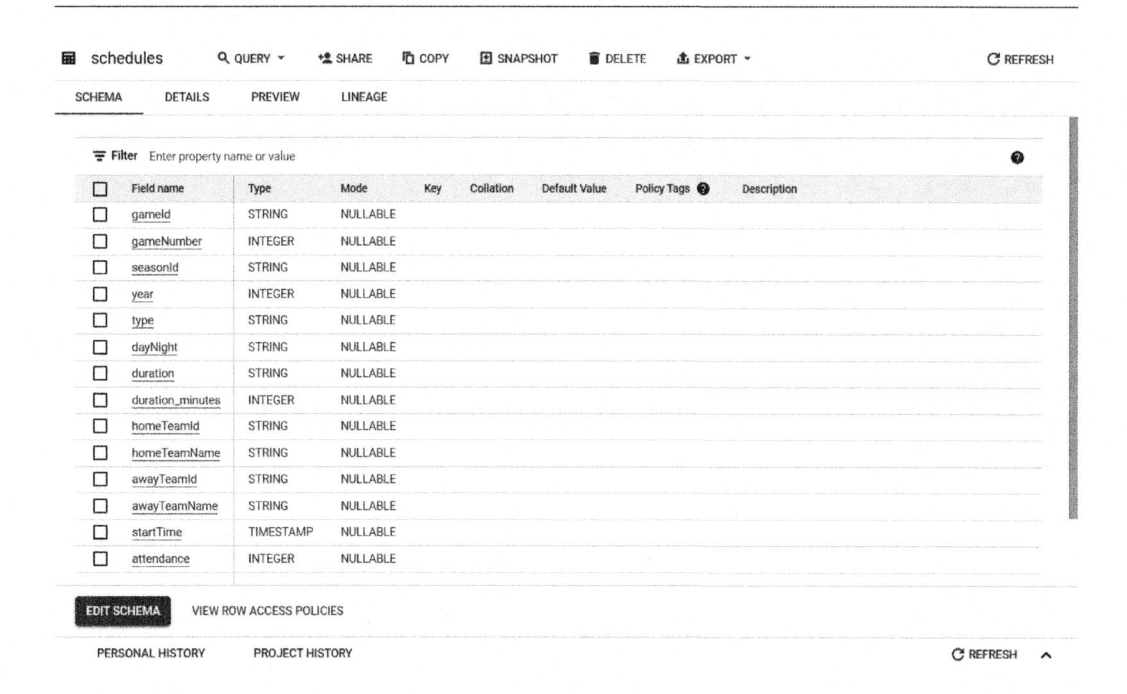

Figure 3.10 – BigQuery table schema

One of the most common attributes in every database is data type. In principle, data types in BigQuery are similar to any other database. However, I want to highlight something about data types in this section.

BigQuery has a very simple list of data types. For example, to store text in BigQuery, you simply use the `STRING` data type, while to store numbers, you simply use `INTEGER`. This might seem odd if your background is in other database technologies. In traditional data warehouse systems such as Teradata, Oracle, or perhaps a simple PostgreSQL database, you need to think about the expected data size. For example, for text columns, you might need to choose between `char`, `varchar`, `text`, and `varchar(n)`. If you want to store numbers, you also need to choose between `smallint`, `int`, `int8`, `int32`, and `int64`, but in BigQuery, all round numbers are `INTEGER`.

There are, of course, other data types, including `numeric`, `timestamp`, `date`, `boolean`, and other data types that you can check in the following public documentation: `https://cloud.google.com/bigquery/docs/reference/standard-sql/data-types`.

As you can see from the documentation, the list is very short and simple, but don't be confused by the simplicity in BigQuery. As the user, you don't need to think about the data type memory and efficiency in BigQuery. BigQuery will handle all of that under the hood. For example, when storing one character, *I*, or some long text, *I really enjoy reading books almost all the time*, in the `STRING` BigQuery, both have the exact same efficiency.

After learning about BigQuery data types, in the next section, we will take a look specifically at the timestamp data type.

Timestamp data in BigQuery compared to other databases

The last, but by no means least, fundamental aspect of BigQuery that I want to highlight is timestamp data. Timestamp data stores information about the date and time hours in detail. For example, take a look at the `baseball.games_wide` table, specifically at the `startTime` column.

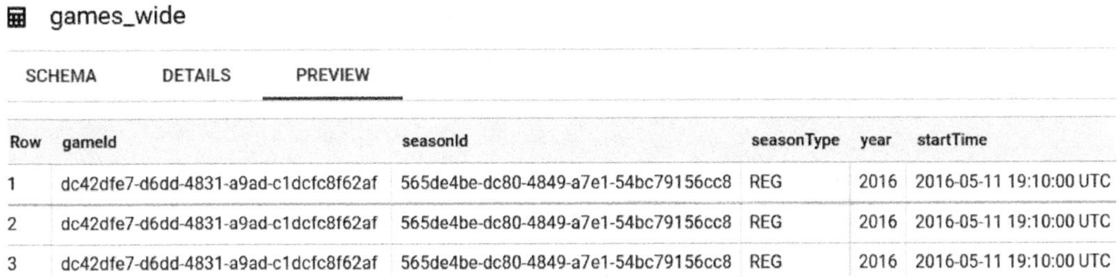

Row	gameId	seasonId	seasonType	year	startTime
1	dc42dfe7-d6dd-4831-a9ad-c1dcfc8f62af	565de4be-dc80-4849-a7e1-54bc79156cc8	REG	2016	2016-05-11 19:10:00 UTC
2	dc42dfe7-d6dd-4831-a9ad-c1dcfc8f62af	565de4be-dc80-4849-a7e1-54bc79156cc8	REG	2016	2016-05-11 19:10:00 UTC
3	dc42dfe7-d6dd-4831-a9ad-c1dcfc8f62af	565de4be-dc80-4849-a7e1-54bc79156cc8	REG	2016	2016-05-11 19:10:00 UTC

Figure 3.11 – The startTime column contains timestamp data

You will notice according to the timestamp postfix that the time is stored in UTC format. In BigQuery, you can't store timestamp data in non-UTC format. BigQuery wants you to always store timestamps in UTC format. The reason for this is data consistency. This is very useful for organizations that conduct business in multiple countries or regions that have time differences. Using the UTC-only format, the data engineer will be forced to transform the local time format to UTC before loading it to BigQuery.

As a user, if you need to convert back to your local timezone in your query, you can always use the time function, as follows:

```
SELECT DATETIME(startTime,"America/Los_Angeles") as startTime 
FROM `bigquery-public-data.baseball.games_wide`;
```

This query will give you the `startTime` column data in the `Los Angeles` timezone.

To summarize our first BigQuery exercise, what we've done up to this point is as follows:

- We've learned that in BigQuery, we can group tables into datasets
- One method for loading data to BigQuery is by uploading a file from your local machine
- For experimentation purposes, BigQuery came up with a public dataset that we can use and access from your project
- BigQuery has unique prepositions pertaining to data types

This is the most basic information that you need to know to start using BigQuery. However, using BigQuery doesn't mean we are creating a data warehouse. In the next section, we will practice creating our simple data warehouse and, more importantly, go through the thinking process for designing one.

But before that, we need to set out some prerequisites for preparing our credentials using `gcloud` commands.

Preparing the prerequisites before developing our data warehouse

Before starting our practice exercise, let's carry out these small but important steps for authentication purposes. In this section, we will do the following:

1. Accessing Cloud Shell.
2. Checking our credentials using `gcloud info`.
3. Initializing our credentials using `gcloud init`.
4. Downloading example codes and datasets from `git`.
5. Uploading data to GCS from `git`.

Let's look at each of these steps in detail.

Step 1 – Accessing Cloud Shell

Revisit *Chapter 2, Big Data Capabilities on GCP*, specifically the *Using GCP Cloud Shell* section, if you haven't accessed your Cloud Shell in the GCP console.

Step 2 – Checking the current setup using the command line

We want to check our current setup in Cloud Shell. To do that in Cloud Shell, type the following:

```
$ gcloud info
```

Click **Authorize** if prompted to.

This command will give you information about installed components, Python versions, directories, and much more information. But what we want to check for now are the account and project, written in this format:

```
Account : [your email]
Project : [your project]
```

Check the account and project. Make sure it's your email and the project you created.

Step 3 – Initializing the gcloud init command

After checking the environment, we want to configure a new environment using the `gcloud init` command. In Cloud Shell, run the following command:

```
$ gcloud init
```

This command will show lists of configurations that have been created, but we want to try to create a new one, so choose the following option:

```
[2] Create a new configuration
```

Then, give this configuration a name, for example, `personal-config`. Choose one of the options to use the existing email:

```
[1] your email
```

Alternatively, if you need to log in with other emails, choose the following option:

```
[2] Login in with a new account
```

Lastly, choose your project number. You can see the number alongside your project ID:

```
[number] project id.
```

The last option relates to configuring the default region and zone. Just choose n (no).

You can check using `gcloud info` again to confirm that the `gcloud init` steps work; for example, check whether the project name and your email are as intended.

Step 4 – Downloading example data from Git

The final prerequisite is to download the example codes and dataset from Packt's Git repository.

To do that, in Cloud Shell, clone the Git repository from your GitHub repository: https://github.com/PacktPublishing/Data-Engineering-with-Google-Cloud-Platform-Second-Edition

For example, use this command to clone the repository:

```
$ git clone https://github.com/PacktPublishing/Data-Engineering-with-Google-Cloud-Platform-Second-Edition
```

Each chapter will contain its code and datasets. Make sure the repository is properly cloned to Cloud Shell since we will use all code and datasets throughout the book.

Step 5 – Uploading data to GCS from Git

After having our dataset in Cloud Shell, let's upload the file to our GCS bucket using the GCP console.

There are three steps involved in this:

1. Creating a GCS bucket.
2. Entering the bucket information.
3. Uploading a local file to the GCS bucket using `gcloud`.

Let's look at each of these in detail.

Creating a GCS bucket

Go to the **Navigation** menu and choose **Cloud Storage**. You will see the GCS console:

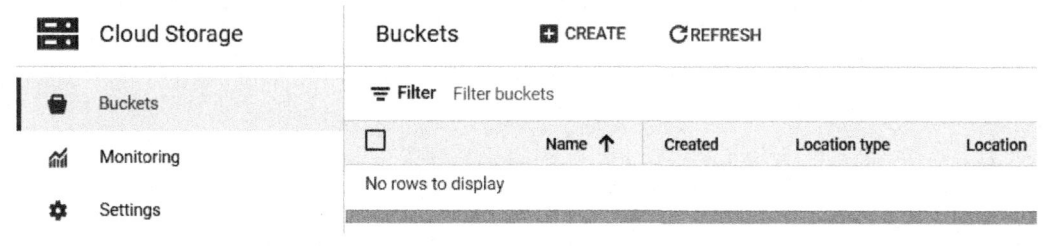

Cloud Storage	Buckets	CREATE	REFRESH		
Buckets	Filter Filter buckets				
Monitoring	☐ Name ↑		Created	Location type	Location
Settings	No rows to display				

Figure 3.12 – GCS main page

Click on the **CREATE** button.

Entering the bucket information

Fill in the bucket name: `[your own project id]-data-bucket`.

Keep in mind that the bucket name in GCS should be unique globally, so using your project ID as a prefix is a way to ensure uniqueness.

You may notice that you can choose the location for the GCS bucket on the page, but for this practice exercise, we will use **Default** to make sure that we don't have a location issue when loading data to BigQuery.

> **Important note**
> Loading data from GCS to BigQuery requires data to be stored in the same location. For example, files in a GCS bucket located in the **asia-southeast2** region can't be loaded to the BigQuery dataset's `us-central1` location. By using **Default**, this means that we store the data in the multi-region US location.

Finally, click on the **CREATE** button at the bottom. If there is a pop-up message saying **Public access will be prevented**, just click on **CONFIRM**; this means you want to keep your bucket private.

Uploading a local file to the GCS bucket using gcloud

Now, let's upload our files to the newly created GCS bucket using the `gcloud` command.

In Cloud Shell, enter the following commands:

```
$ export DESTINATION_BUCKET_NAME=[your own project id]-data-bucket
$ gcloud storage cp -r Data-Engineering-with-Google-Cloud-Platform/*
gs://$DESTINATION_BUCKET_NAME/from-git/
```

Please check in your bucket by going to the `/from-git/chapter-3/dataset` directory. You will see the three dataset folders there, `regions/`, `stations/`, and `trips/`, as in the following screenshot:

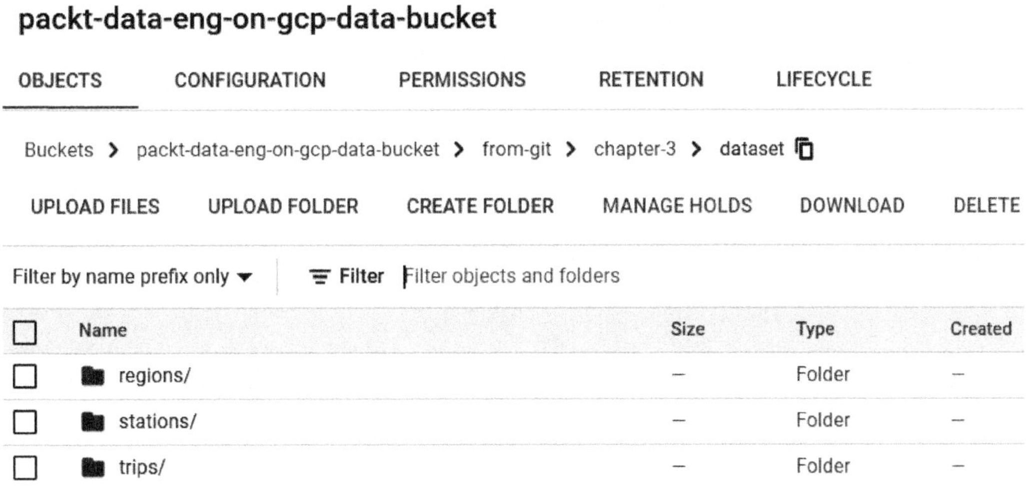

Figure 3.13 – The three folders should be in the GCS bucket

We will use these datasets and code for our practice exercise in the next sections.

Practicing developing a data warehouse

Now we are set and ready to build our first data warehouse. We will proceed with the help of two scenarios. Each scenario will have different learning purposes.

In the first scenario, we are going to focus on how to use the tools. After understanding the tools, in the second scenario, we will focus on the practice. Practice here means learning how to build a solution, not only learning how to use the tools.

We understand that even though we know how to use the tools, there are many possibilities for using them. But when it comes to practice, usually we learn from common best practices, patterns, and different theories from practitioners.

We will use the San Francisco bike-sharing dataset. The dataset relates to a bike-sharing company. The company records the trip data of its members. Each bike trip contains information about the stations, and each station is located in certain regions. This dataset is very simple compared to a real-world data warehouse, but for practice purposes, this is a good representation of real database tables from application databases.

In each scenario, the starting point is *requirements* and *business questions*. In a real-world scenario, it's the same. You will satisfy end-user requirements and business questions, and these two aspects are the ingredients for designing and building a data warehouse.

The second step is the *thinking process*. After reading the requirements and business questions, I suggest you think for yourself first in terms of how you want to do it. However, I will also share my thoughts on the steps and planning, so you can compare them with yours. After that, we will build the *solutions* in BigQuery. Follow the steps in the next section.

Data warehouse in BigQuery – Requirements for scenario 1

In this scenario 1, we met with business users, and here are the requirements:

1. As a regional manager user, I want to know the top two region IDs, ordered by the total capacity of the stations in that region.
2. As a regional manager, I want to download the answers to my questions and download them as CSV files to my local computer.
3. The data source table is the `stations` table, which is located in the `CloudSQL-MySQL` database.
4. There will be more data sources in the future besides the `stations` table, coming from other application systems.

Given the requirements, I suggest you take a moment to imagine yourself in this situation:

- What will you do?
- What GCP services will you use?
- How will you do it?

> **Important note**
> By way of a reminder, CloudSQL is a managed service for application databases, for example, MySQL, PostgreSQL, and SQL Server. As a managed service, you don't need to worry about VM creation and software installation. However, you will still need to decide the VM machine type, software versions, and other configurations that you can find when you create an instance.

In the next section, we will use the requirements to plan and decide how we want to build our solution.

Steps and planning for handling scenario 1

Given the first and second statements, we understand that the business user wants to be able to download the results as a CSV file from a very specific business question.

Here are some high-level ideas:

1. Since there is a very specific business rule, we need some transformation. The rule seems doable in SQL, and BigQuery is a good system for handling such jobs.
2. The BigQuery table can easily be downloaded into CSV files from the console. So, storing the results as a BigQuery table or view will be great.

From the second and third requirements, we learned that the source data is in the MySQL database and potentially from another database in the future.

Here is the plan based on the preceding ideas: since the data sources come from multiple systems, this is a data warehouse situation.

The data is in the `CloudSQL-MySQL` database, so we need to find a way to extract the `station` table from the MySQL database and load it into BigQuery.

There are options for doing the extract and load from MySQL to BigQuery. For standardization and scalability, we will use GCS as our staging layer from MySQL. This extraction method applies to almost any data source. On top of that, GCS is also very scalable when it comes to handling incoming data in terms of volume, variety, and velocity.

Loading data from GCS to BigQuery is very straightforward, and we can use the BigQuery console for this.

So, here are the overall steps:

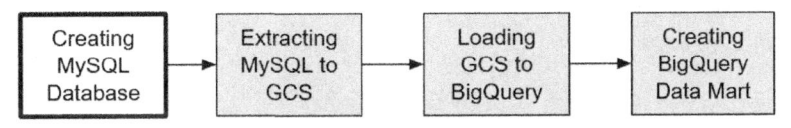

Figure 3.14 – The four steps of our data pipeline

Note that in this exercise, we don't want to learn about the MySQL database in depth, but we will still try to create a CloudSQL instance for MySQL. The goal is for us to try to understand what the *extract* in *ETL* really means, and how to achieve it.

Let us understand each of these steps in the following sections.

Step 1 – Creating a MySQL database in CloudSQL

The first step is to prepare our CloudSQL-MySQL environment. This step is not part of building a data warehouse. However, simulating table extraction from application databases to GCS will be very helpful. So, let's start by creating the CloudSQL instance. Here are the steps:

1. Creating a CloudSQL instance.
2. Connecting to the MySQL instance.
3. Creating a MySQL database.
4. Creating a table in the MySQL database.
5. Importing CSV data into the MySQL database.

Let's look at each of the steps in detail in the following sections.

Creating a CloudSQL instance

You can create a CloudSQL instance from the GCP console by choosing **SQL** under the database section in the navigation bar. You can follow the **Create Instance** steps, but for simplicity, we will run it using the `gcloud` command in Cloud Shell.

Run the following command in Cloud Shell:

```
$ gcloud sql instances create mysql-instance-source \
--database-version=MYSQL_8_0 \
--tier=db-g1-small \
--region=us-central1 \
--root-password=packt123 \
--availability-type=zonal \
--storage-size=10GB \
--storage-type=HDD
```

> **Warning**
>
> Is it going to cost us? Yes. CloudSQL instances will cost us, based on instance hours. However, since we will be using the smallest instance tier for development (db-g1-small) across a short period, the cost will be $0.035/hour. If you still have a $300 free tier, then you don't need to pay the costs but don't forget to delete the instance after this practice exercise.

Wait for around five minutes. After it's finished, refresh your browser or go back to your Cloud SQL home page and you will see that your MySQL instance is ready.

Connecting to the MySQL instance

Return to Cloud Shell and run this `gcloud` command to connect to your `mysql` instance using a MySQL shell:

```
$ gcloud sql connect mysql-instance-source --user=root
```

When prompted for a password, the password is `packt123`. This is stated in the `gcloud` command in the *Creating a CloudSQL instance* step. However, if you have changed the password, use your password to log in. After successfully logging in, you will see the MySQL shell.

Creating a MySQL database

Let's create a MySQL database named `apps_db`.

Run this script in the MySQL shell:

```
mysql > CREATE DATABASE apps_db;
```

After creating the database, you can check whether your database has already been created by running the following command:

```
mysql > SHOW DATABASES;
```

Creating a table in the MySQL database

While still in the `mysql` shell, we need to create the table using a **Data Definition Language (DDL)** statement.

You can create the table by running the following DDL:

```
mysql > CREATE TABLE apps_db.stations(
station_id varchar(255),
name varchar(255),
region_id varchar(10),
capacity integer
);
```

The `create table` script will create the `stations` table in `apps_db`. Next, we want to import data using a CSV file.

Importing CSV data into the MySQL database

In the real-life scenario, the tables will be used by applications, and the data will be inserted based on user interactions with the database. We will not go back too far to build a sample application that writes records to our table. We will just load CSV files to our tables from GCS.

In a later section, *Step 2 – Extracting MySQL to GCS*, we will export the MySQL table back to GCS, and you may be wondering why. The reason why we are doing this is to simplify the data generation to the MySQL database. But for the later steps, given that the MySQL database is a genuine example of a data source, we will use it for simulating the *extraction* step in an ETL process.

To import the CSV data from GCS to MySQL, we can use the Cloud SQL console.

Don't close the MySQL shell yet, since we want to check our imported data later using the `SELECT` statement. Just minimize Cloud Shell if necessary.

To upload the data, go to the Cloud SQL console and perform the following steps:

1. Click on the created `mysql-instance` source, and then find and click on the **Import** button.
2. Choose `bucket/file name` from our GCS bucket: `gs://[your project id]-data-bucket/from-git/chapter-3/dataset/stations/stations.csv`.
3. Change the **File format** option to **CSV**.
4. Input the destination database, `apps_db`, and the table name, `stations`.
5. The configuration will be as shown in the following screenshot:

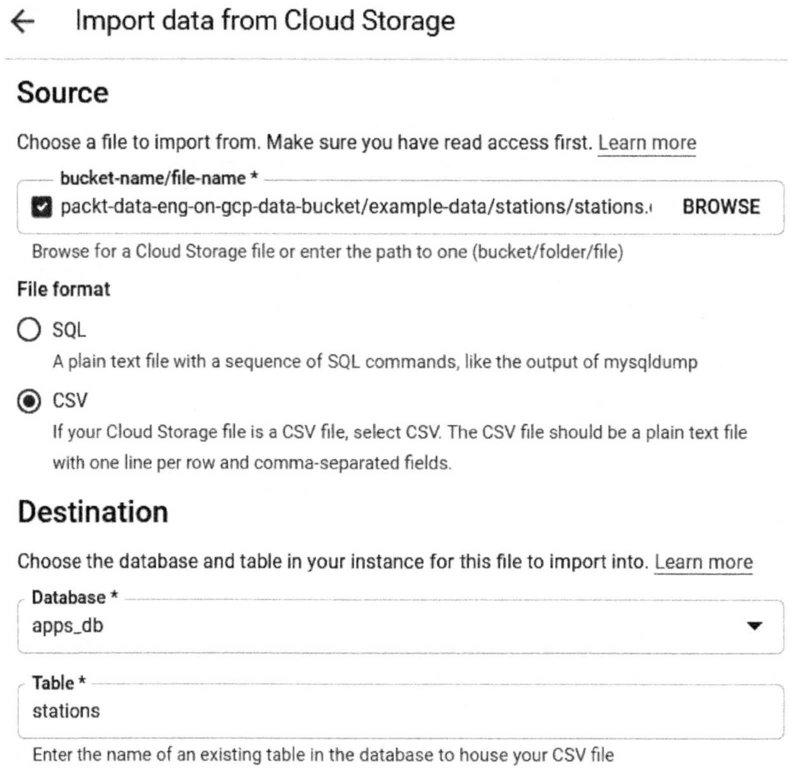

Figure 3.15 – Import data from Cloud Storage

6. Once everything is complete, click on the **Import** button.
7. Now we will return to Cloud Shell and try to access the `stations` table. In the MySQL shell, run the following query:

```
mysql> SELECT * FROM apps_db.stations LIMIT 10;
```

Make sure you see some data there. Repeat the process if you can't see any records. If successful, exit from the MySQL shell by typing `exit`, as shown in the following code:

```
mysql > exit
```

Now we have a simulation MySQL database as our data source. In the next section, we will do the extraction from MySQL to GCS.

Step 2 – Extracting MySQL to GCS

In *step 2*, we want to extract data from the MySQL database to GCS.

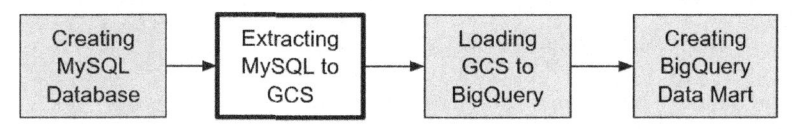

Figure 3.16 – Step 2: extracting MySQL to GCS

Since we are using CloudSQL, we can use the `gcloud` command to dump tables into GCS files, but you can do the same thing in self-managed MySQL without using the `gcloud` command.

First of all, we need to handle **Identity and Access Management (IAM)**. We need to assign the **CloudSQL service account** a **Storage Object admin** role first. This step will be a little bit confusing if you are new to IAM, but it's a good starting point for understanding IAM without going into too much depth.

IAM is a broad concept by itself, and GCP uses IAM to manage all user authentication and authorization for all services. IAM needs to be viewed holistically organization-wide, across projects, services, groups, and users. So, we will have a dedicated chapter later to talk about this in more detail.

At this point, let's break down what we need just for this scenario. CloudSQL automatically generated one service account to operate. You can find the service account in your CloudSQL console.

From the CloudSQL console, go to your MySQL instance, for example, **mysql-instance-source**, and click on it.

Scroll down a little bit, and you can find the service account somewhere in the middle, like this:

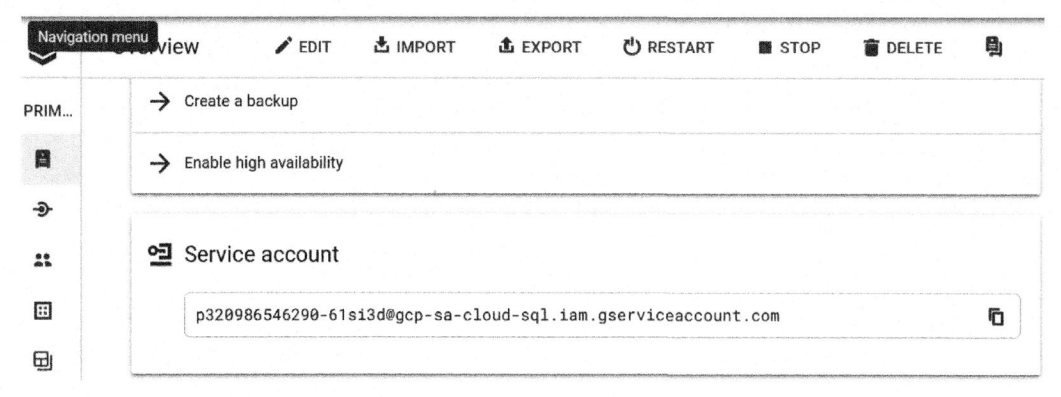

Figure 3.17 – Copying the service account from the CloudSQL console

The service account will be in this format:

```
[any text]@gcp-sa-cloud-sql.iam.gserviceaccount.com
```

Your service account will be different from what's shown in the preceding code. The service account is autogenerated and different each time you create a CloudSQL instance.

Copy that service account to any text editor because we want to add that to an IAM role.

To add the new role to the service account, follow these steps:

1. Go to the navigation bar.
2. Choose **IAM & Admin | IAM**.
3. Select **GRANT ACCESS**.
4. Paste the CloudSQL service account into **New principals**.
5. Then, select a role.
6. Type `gcs object` and you will be able to choose **Storage Object Admin** (not **Storage Admin**).

The screen will look like this:

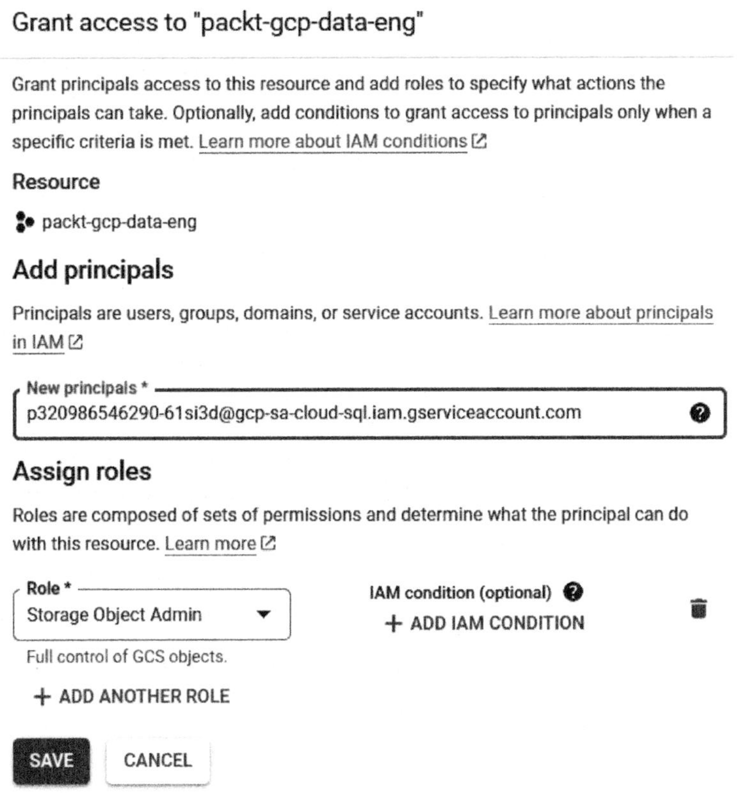

Figure 3.18 – Finding the Storage Object Admin role in IAM

After finishing the process, your CloudSQL service account will have permission to write and delete file objects in all GCS buckets in your project.

To summarize, the preceding steps are necessary to grant the CloudSQL service account the **Storage Object Admin** role. The role is to allow the service account to load data to your GCS bucket. Next, we want to load it.

Access your Cloud Shell again and trigger a `gcloud` command to export the MySQL query results to a CSV file using a shell script from our Git repository.

The file is available here: `Data-Engineering-with-Google-Cloud-Platform-Second-Edition/chapter-3/code/gcloud_export_cloudsql_to_gcs.sh`.

We need to edit some variables, so open the file using **Cloud Editor**. To refresh your memory, Cloud Editor is a simple text editor that you can access from Cloud Shell. Click on the **Open Editor** button in the top-right corner.

Find " the file and then change the `bucket_name` variable to that of your variable; remove the brackets:

```
bucket_name=[YOUR BUCKET'S NAME]
gcloud sql export csv mysql-instance-source \
gs://$bucket_name/mysql_export/stations/20180101/stations.csv \
--database=apps_db \
--offload \
--query='SELECT * FROM stations WHERE station_id <= 200;'
gcloud sql export csv mysql-instance-source \
gs://$bucket_name/mysql_export/stations/20180102/stations.csv \
--database=apps_db \
--offload \
--query='SELECT * FROM stations WHERE station_id <=400;'
```

Once finished, return to Cloud Shell and run the script by running this command:

```
$ sh Data-Engineering-with-Google-Cloud-Platform-Second-Edition/
chapter-3/code/gcloud_export_cloudsql_to_gcs.sh
```

The script will export the `stations` table twice. Each of the exports will be stored in two different directories. Notice the difference between `/20180101` and `/20180102`. The latter (`/20180102`) is for our second data warehouse exercise scenario.

For each `export` command, wait around five minutes for completion.

Once finished, you can check in your GCS bucket under the `mysql_export` folder. Your station CSV file should be there. If not, recheck every step.

In a real-world scenario, most of the time, the extractions happen from the clone instance. Application databases usually have a clone instance to provide high availability. Hence, it's good to extract data from there. That way, we won't interrupt the production database.

Summarizing this step regarding CloudSQL to GCS, it is designed to demonstrate the *E* in *ETL*, which is to extract data from a data source into a GCS bucket. The method is pretty much the same for other database types, but each database might have a different command for dumping (exporting) table data to files.

For the next exercises throughout this chapter, we will assume that the data is already in the GCS bucket. You can delete the MySQL instance for now.

You can delete the MySQL instance by running the following command and typing Y (for *yes*):

```
$ gcloud sql instances delete mysql-instance-source
```

Check the CloudSQL home page to ensure that the instance is deleted.

Step 3 – Loading GCS to BigQuery

In *step 3*, we will load data from GCS to BigQuery using the BigQuery console.

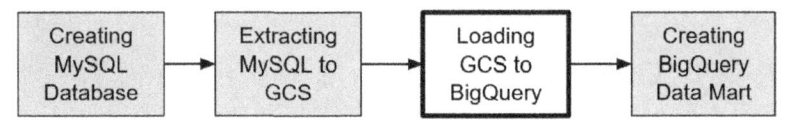

Figure 3.19 – Step 3: Loading GCS to BigQuery

Let's go back to the BigQuery console.

Create a new dataset named `raw_bikesharing`.

Just as a reminder, for this exercise, let's use the default (multi-region US) dataset location. Later, in scenario 2, we will want to use some tables from public datasets that are located in the US.

In the `raw_bikesharing` dataset, let's create a new table from the BigQuery console:

1. Click on the create-table icon (+).
2. In the **Create table form** option, choose **Google Cloud Storage**:
3. Browse to **Select file** in the GCS bucket:

    [your bucket name]/mysql_export/stations/20180101/stations.csv

4. For **Table name**, select `stations`. Note that the BigQuery table name is case-sensitive. We use lowercase letters in this instance.
5. In the **Schema** option, choose **Edit as text**.
6. Write the following to the **schema** textbox:

    station_id:STRING,name:STRING,region_id:STRING,capacity:INTEGER

7. Click on **Create table**.

> **Important note**
> There is another alternative for defining the schema. You can try to enter your field names yourself. However, don't use the autodetect schema since the CSV file from the `mysql` export doesn't provide headers.

You can check the `stations` table and see that the data is already in the BigQuery table. We have four columns as shown here: `station_id`, `name`, `region_id`, and `capacity`.

station_id	name	region_id	capacity
6	The Embarcadero at Sansome St	3	0
64	5th St at Brannan St	3	0
133	Valencia St at 22nd St	3	0
79	7th St at Brannan St	3	3

Figure 3.20 – The stations table in BigQuery

If you can see the preceding table, we are good to go regarding the final step of this scenario.

Step 4 – Creating a BigQuery data mart

Depending on company regulations, most companies don't allow business users to access raw tables directly. Business users usually access data from data marts.

Technically, you can use BigQuery or other databases as the data mart. In this example, we will use BigQuery as our data mart, which is a very common practice.

Let's create a new dataset with the name `dm_regional_manager`.

Now, at this point, let's revisit what the business question is.

As a business user, I want to know the top two region IDs, ordered by the total stations' capacity in that region.

As the final step, we want to create a table or view in our BigQuery data mart based on the query result:

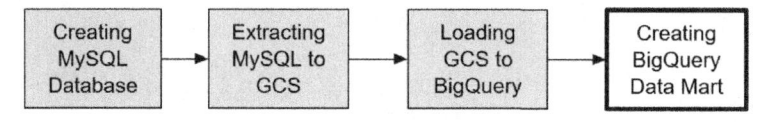

Figure 3.21 – Step 4: creating a BigQuery data mart

Now we have two options for the query results:

- Create a table
- Create a view

Both tables and views have advantages and disadvantages. There are two advantages to using a view. First, the view costs no additional storage. If you create a view, the data won't be stored anywhere; it will just save the SQL formula. The second advantage is real time; if you access the view, then every time the underlying table changes, the view will get the latest update.

However, there are reasons as to why you would want to avoid using too many views physicalized into a new table. Sometimes, views can be heavy, and when the underlying tables are large and there are many joins and aggregations in the view's query, you can end up having very heavy processing.

> **Important note**
> A physicalized table means using the query result to create a new table.

Imagine you have five tables, each 1 PB in size, as upstream raw tables, and your downstream consists of 1,000 views accessing the five tables. You may end up processing the PBs of data repeatedly, and that's bad in terms of both cost and performance.

In this scenario, however, since the `stations` table is small, we will use a view in the data mart.

Create a view based on the query using this SQL script:

```
CREATE VIEW `[your project id].dm_regional_manager.top_2_region_by_capacity`
AS
SELECT region_id, SUM(capacity) as total_capacity
FROM `[your project id].raw_bikesharing.stations`
WHERE region_id != ''
GROUP BY region_id
ORDER BY total_capacity desc
LIMIT 2;
```

And that's it. You can access your view by submitting the following query:

```
SELECT * FROM `[your project id].dm_regional_manager.top_2_region_by_capacity`;
```

This will produce results such as this:

Row	region_id	total_capacity
1	3	2903
2	12	849

Figure 3.22 – The query result

After checking the results, let's carry out the final steps:

1. Try to click **SAVE RESULTS**.
2. Take a moment to see what the available export options are.
3. Finally, choose `CSV` (local file).

Done! We've practiced running an end-to-end ELT process on GCP. We extracted data from MySQL into a GCS bucket, loaded it into BigQuery, and transformed the table into a data mart table. The key takeaway from this scenario is a hands-on experience using all the important components. But this is not yet a data warehouse, since we are only using one table, and we haven't thought much about what we should do with the data model. In scenario 2, we will try to load transaction data and start thinking about how we should reload and model the tables.

Data warehouse in BigQuery – Requirements for scenario 2

In the second scenario, we are going to load two more tables – bike trips and regions. In this scenario, we want to simulate how to handle new data loading and think about data modeling.

Here are some requirements:

1. As an operational business user, I need to access the following information:

    I. How many bike trips take place daily?

    II. What is the daily average trip duration?

    III. The top five starting station names that have the longest trip duration.

    IV. The top five region names that have the shortest total trip durations.

2. The bike trips data is in the GCS bucket, and each bucket folder contains daily data.
3. The regions data is from the BigQuery public dataset.
4. New data will be updated daily in the GCS bucket for the `stations` and `trips` tables.

Similar to scenario 1, I suggest you take a moment to imagine yourself in the situation:

- What will you do?
- What services will you use?
- How will you do it?

Make sure you've got the whole idea from what we've learned so far in scenario 1, before we continue.

Using the GCP console versus the code-based approach

I want to use this small sub-section to emphasize this practice. As a data engineer working in a cloud environment, it's very important that you are comfortable with code. On top of that, always use code whenever possible compared to using the console or the user interface.

In the next scenario, we will start using the **Python** API instead of using the GCP console. Using the GCP console is still the best way to start learning GCP services, but it's not scalable from an engineering perspective; for example, when you need to create multiple ETL pipelines, it's better to have a loop in the pipelines using code rather than clicking buttons one by one by hand.

For example, code can be useful for managing infrastructure (infrastructure as code), managing pipelines, managing objects such as BigQuery tables, and managing testing deployment (CI/CD pipeline).

Using code makes you and your whole organization team able to implement proper testing and deployment. This practice will greatly reduce the amount of human error that occurs, which is often very costly. So, we will perform all the steps in the next scenario using Python code.

Steps and planning for handling scenario 2

Now, the business users have more complex business questions. To answer the questions, we need to use the `JOIN` operation from multiple tables in our queries.

Here are some initial thoughts and planning:

- Since the user is interested in daily measurements, we may create a layer to provide daily aggregation to the user.
- There will be new data daily, so we need to plan how to handle the incoming data from GCS directories.
- If you consider the real-life corollaries of our three main tables, `stations`, `regions`, and `trips`, they are different entities. Stations and regions are static objects, while trips are events. We will get clearer information after checking the data later, but at this point, we should think about how to handle both types of information differently.
- The data mart is similar to scenario 1. We can use the same BigQuery datasets to store the table results there.

So, here are the overall steps:

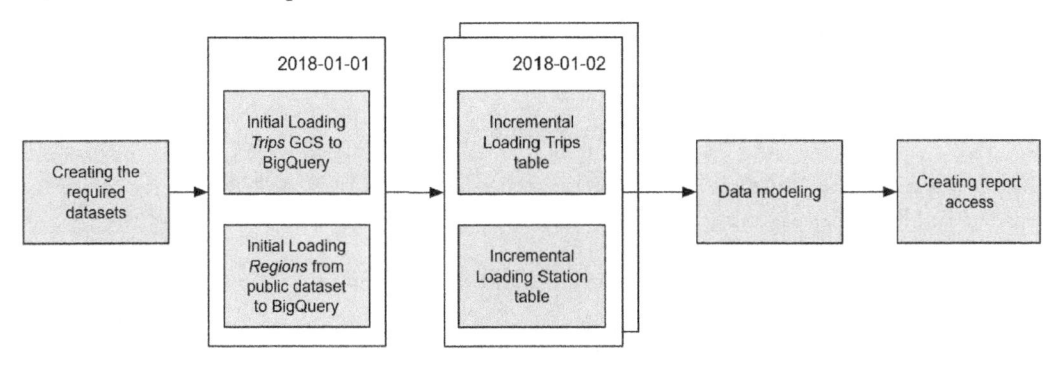

Figure 3.23 – The overall steps for scenario 2

There are five principal steps involved here:

1. Create the required datasets.
2. Initially load the trips and region tables to BigQuery:
    - Trips from GCS
    - Regions from the BigQuery public dataset
3. Handle the daily batch data loading:
    - For the `trips` table
    - For the `stations` table
4. Design data modeling for BigQuery.
5. Store the business question results in tables.

There are two dates for our experiment. The initial load is using 2018-01-01, and we need to be able to handle the new data from 2018-01-02 and the upcoming days without any issues, for example, duplication.

Step 1 – Creating the datasets using Python

Let's create our datasets using Python. We want to add a new dataset called `dwh_bikesharing`. But since it is code-based, it's very easy to add the other datasets. So, we'll also add `raw_bikesharing` and `dm_bikesharing` to the list just to make sure you don't miss the datasets from scenario 1.

> **Important note**
> You can run the Python script from your local computer if you have already installed a Python Google Cloud SDK or use Cloud Shell. I recommend using Cloud Shell for simplicity.

To do that, check our code example from our repository.

The file is located here: `Data-Engineering-with-Google-Cloud-Platform-Second-Edition/chapter-3/code/bigquery_scenario_2_step_0_create_datasets.py`.

The file contains Python code that will create our required datasets:

1. Let's look at the code example. First, we will use the `bigquery` Python client line as follows:

    ```
    from google.cloud import bigquery
    client = bigquery.Client()
    ```

2. The BigQuery Python library is installed by default in Cloud Shell, so you don't need to install it manually. We will loop the `datasets_name` list to check whether the datasets exist. If they don't, create new ones:

   ```
   datasets_name = ['raw_bikesharing',........
                    'dm_ regional_manager'.....]
   ```

   You don't need to change anything in the code. Let's run it using Cloud Shell.

3. Go to the `chapter 3` directory:

   ```
   $ cd Data-Engineering-with-Google-Cloud-Platform-Second-Edition/
   chapter-3/code
   ```

4. Then, run the Python script using the `python3` command, like this:

   ```
   $ python3 bigquery_scenario_2_step_0_create_datasets.py
   ```

After running the code, check your BigQuery console and make sure the three datasets have been created in your project. Note that BigQuery Explorer won't refresh automatically, so you need to refresh your internet browser to view the changes.

Step 2a – Initial loading of the trips table into BigQuery

The first step is to load the initial `trips` data from GCS into BigQuery.

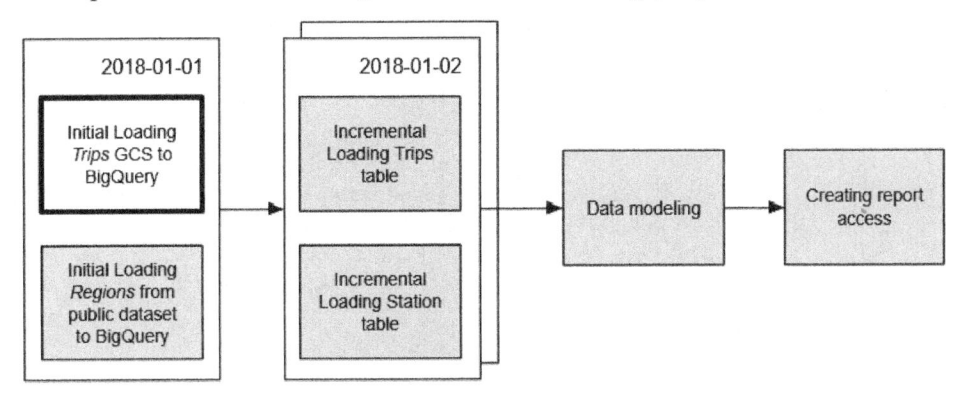

Figure 3.24 – Load the event table from GCS to BigQuery

The dataset is in our GCS bucket, inside this directory: `packt-data-eng-on-gcp-data-bucket/from-git/chapter-3/dataset/trips`.

Notice that there are two folders there with the date information. This is a common directory format for storing daily batch data in GCS.

To load to BigQuery, let's look at the code in our repository. The filename is as follows:

```
$ bigquery_scenario_2_step_1a_load_trips_data.py
```

The script will load `trips` data from `gcs` to BigQuery. There are a few things that you need to pay attention to in the code.

The GCS file path contains date information, for example, `20180101`. We will use the folder name in our `gcs` file path like this:

```
gcs_uri = f"gs://{project_id}-data-bucket/from-git/chapter-3/dataset/trips/20180101/*.json"
```

The data stored in `NEWLINE DELIMITED JSON` is compressed in `gzip` files. The BigQuery load job config accepts the `NEWLINE_DELIMITED_JSON` file format, and not the standard JSON file. If you have standard JSON file formats, you need to transform the file first to the correct JSON format. In the code, we need to define the format like this:

```
source_format=bigquery.SourceFormat.NEWLINE_DELIMITED_JSON,
```

The write disposition is `WRITE_APPEND`. This won't matter during the initial load, but is an important configuration for handling new data. We will revisit this later in the next steps:

```
write_disposition = 'WRITE_APPEND'
```

You will need to change the `PROJECT_ID` variable to that of your `PROJECT_ID` variable since you want to load data from your own GCS bucket. Refer to the following line:

```
PROJECT_ID = "packt-data-eng-on-gcp"
```

Run the Python script from Cloud Editor using this command:

```
$ python3 bigquery_scenario_2_step_1a_load_trips_data.py
```

After running the Python script, you will see that the new table has been created in your `raw_bikesharing` dataset. Check the table preview to familiarize yourself with the data:

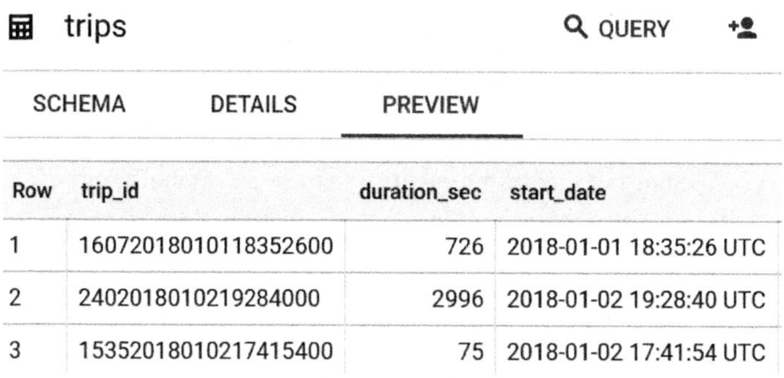

Row	trip_id	duration_sec	start_date
1	16072018010118352600	726	2018-01-01 18:35:26 UTC
2	24022018010219284000	2996	2018-01-02 19:28:40 UTC
3	15352018010217415400	75	2018-01-02 17:41:54 UTC

Figure 3.25 – BigQuery table PREVIEW feature

Check your `trips` table in the **PREVIEW** table. We will load another table in the next section.

Step 2b – Initial loading of the regions table into BigQuery

Still, in *step 2*, we want to load another table, the `regions` table, from the BigQuery public dataset. This is to illustrate the nature of the data warehouse, where you can combine data from different data sources.

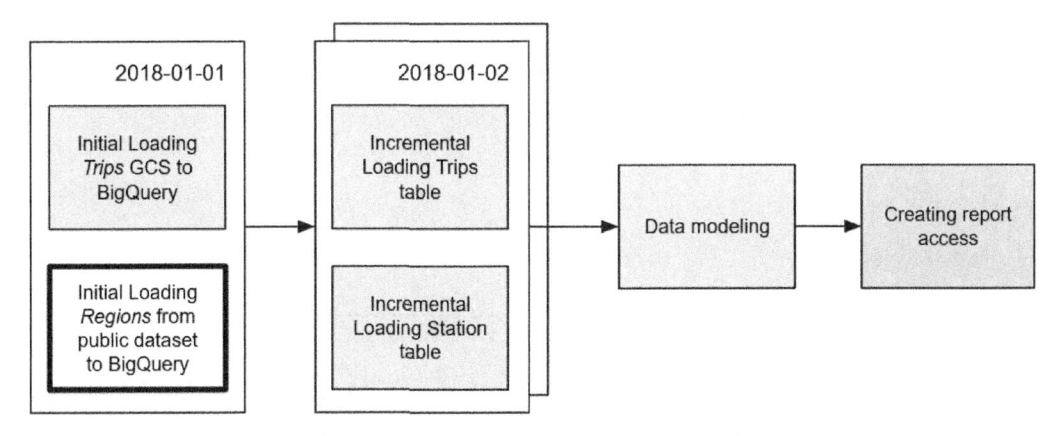

Figure 3.26 – Load table from the BigQuery public dataset

To do that, let's look at the code example:

```
bigquery_scenario_2_step_1b_load_regions_data.py
```

The script will run a query to access data from the `bigquery-public-data` dataset:

```
public_table_id = "bigquery-public-data.san_francisco_bikeshare.bikeshare_regions"
sql = f"SELECT * FROM `{public_table_id}`;"
```

But instead of showing the result, the query will create a table in our project. Take a look at this particular line:

```
job_config = bigquery.QueryJobConfig(destination=target_table_id)
```

Run the Python script using the `python3` command:

```
$ python3 bigquery_scenario_2_step_1b_load_regions_data.py
```

After running the script, the `regions` table will be available in your `raw_bikesharing` dataset.

78 Building a Data Warehouse in BigQuery

Row	region_id	name
1	12	Oakland
2	14	Berkeley
3	3	San Francisco

Figure 3.27 – Example results from the regions table

As a summary of *step 2*, we added two new tables to our `raw_bikesharing` dataset. The next step is to load additional data into our existing tables and make sure that the loading doesn't mess with the existing data.

Step 3a – Handling the daily batch data loading for the trips table

In *step 3*, we will add new records to our existing tables:

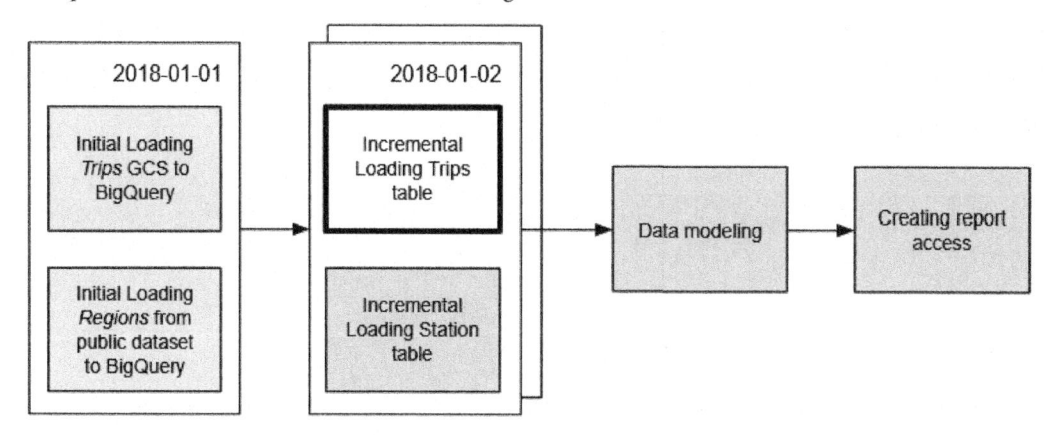

Figure 3.28 – Loading data for the next date

We will load data from the same bucket, but a different date directory, for example, `20180102`.

How about the code? You can use the same code as in *Step 2a – Initial loading of the trips table into BigQuery*:

```
File : bigquery_scenario_2_step_1a_load_trips_data.py
```

But we need to change the code a little bit. Let's adjust the date by changing this line:

```
gcs_uri = f"gs://{project_id}-data-bucket/example-data/
trips/20180101/*.json"
```

Change it to the following:

```
gcs_uri = f"gs://{project_id}-data-bucket/example-data/
trips/20180102/*.json"
```

Or, as an alternative, you can use the code that has already been modified:

```
File : bigquery_scenario_2_step_1a_load_trips_data_20180102.py
```

Before running the script, let's understand first what will happen with our data.

The code will append new records to the `trips` table. This kind of data is called event data. In event data, every new record is a new event, which won't affect any existing data. The nature of an event, once it happens, can't be updated and deleted. This is similar to the real world; you can't change something that has happened.

Technically, BigQuery has three `write_disposition` variables. This configuration is to determine what the intended data writing behavior is. Here are the three options:

- WRITE_APPEND: If the table exists, BigQuery appends the data to the table
- WRITE_EMPTY: Only write to the table when the table exists and contains no data
- WRITE_TRUNCATE: If the table exists, BigQuery overwrites the table data

For event data, we can use WRITE_APPEND to keep appending new records to the table. In our case, the trip records from 2018-01-02 will be appended to the existing 2018-01-01 record.

> **Important note**
> In *Chapter 4, Building Workflows for Batch Data Loading Using Cloud Composer*, we will revisit this matter for data orchestration purposes, but for now, WRITE_APPEND is a natural way to load event data.

Now, after changing the date in our Python variable, let's run the Python script and do some checking. Run the Python script as usual:

```
$ python3 bigquery_scenario_2_step_1a_load_trips_data.py
```

Let's check whether we have data from both 2018-01-01 and 2018-01-02 by using this SQL query in the BigQuery console:

```
SELECT distinct(date(start_date))
FROM `[your project id].raw_bikesharing.trips`;
```

The query should produce two records:

- 2018-01-01
- 2018-01-02

And finally, we want to make sure that no records have been duplicated by using this SQL query:

```
SELECT count(*) cnt_trip_id, trip_id
FROM `[your project id].raw_bikesharing.trips`
GROUP BY trip_id
HAVING cnt_trip_id > 1;
```

The query will return no records. Retry and review the overall steps if your results are incorrect.

Step 3b – Handling the daily batch data loading for the stations table

In this section, we want to simulate loading data for our `stations` table. We will load data from 2018-01-02.

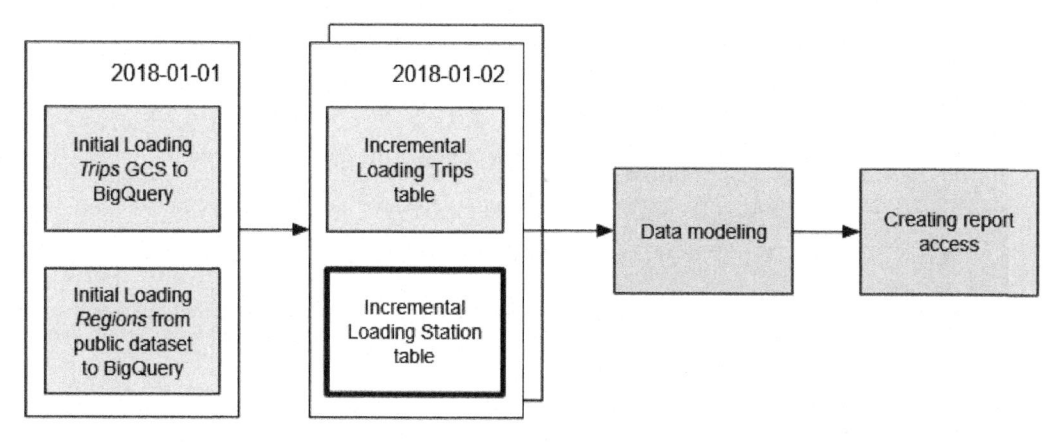

Figure 3.29 – Loading stations data for the next date

For the `stations` table, the approach will be different compared to the `trips` table. This kind of table may have new records (`INSERT`), updated records (`UPDATE`), and removed records (`DELETE`). Imagine a real-world bike station: a new bike station can be demolished, capacities or the station name may change, or a new station may be established in the region. So, this kind of data is called a **snapshot**. Snapshot data is not event data. Snapshot data is an object or entity in the real world; it doesn't happen, it's just there.

Let's use an illustration by way of example in our `stations` table. Just for illustration, we will use the **DAY 1** and **DAY 2** data.

The **DAY 1** data has two records, `station_1` and `station_2`, as shown in the following table. But for **DAY 2**, for a variety of business reasons, `station_1` gets additional capacity (`UPDATE`), `station_2` no longer exists (`DELETE`), and there is a new station, `station_3` (`INSERT`).

DAY 1

station_id	name	region_id	capacity
501	station_1	3	10
504	station_2	5	10

DAY 2

station_id	name	region_id	capacity
501	station_1	3	20
505	station_3	5	15

Figure 3.30 – stations table illustration

Then, if you use `WRITE_APPEND`, after loading the **DAY 2** data, the table will look like this:

station_id	name	region_id	capacity
501	station_1	3	10
504	station_2	5	10
501	station_1	3	20
505	station_3	5	15

Figure 3.31 – stations table after WRITE_APPEND

This is invalid because there are duplications for `station_1`, and `station_2` should no longer be in the table. If the end user wants to count how many stations are in the table, `SELECT count(*) FROM stations` won't give the correct answer.

There are several approaches for handling this condition, so let's start with the easiest one, by using the `write_disposition` variable: `WRITE_TRUNCATE`. Look at the following code example:

`bigquery_scenario_2_step_2b_load_stations_data.py`

As you may have noticed, the `write_disposition` variable is `WRITE_TRUNCATE`:

`write_disposition = 'WRITE_TRUNCATE'`

Before running it, make sure you change the `project_id` variable. After that, run the following Python script:

```
$ python3 bigquery_scenario_2_step_2b_load_stations_data.py
```

If the script results in an error because it can't find the file, review the *Extracting MySQL to GCS* section in scenario 1.

The `bucket/mysql_export/stations` GCS directory should look like this:

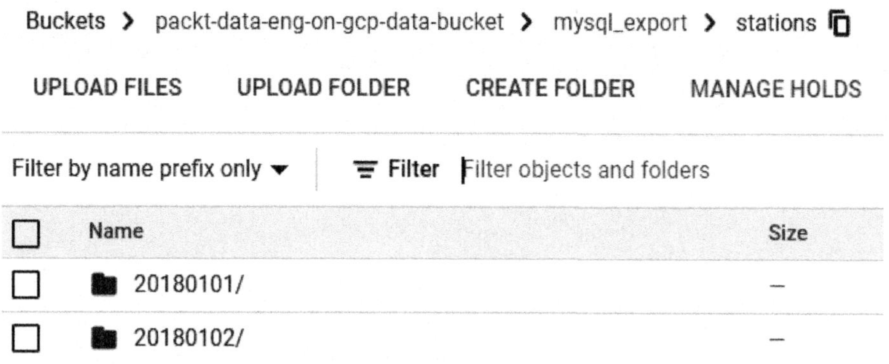

Figure 3.32 – Inside the GCS bucket stations folder

Now, let's check whether there are any duplicated records by using a SQL query:

```
SELECT
station_id, count(*) AS cnt_station
FROM `[your project id].raw_bikesharing.stations`
GROUP BY station_id
HAVING cnt_station > 1;
```

The query should give you no records, which means there are no duplicated stations in our records, and that is good enough. In some cases, however, you may want to keep your historical data. Using the preceding method, you will lose your historical information. That means if you want to know how many stations existed in the last month, or compare station names from today with yesterday's, you can't.

In the next section, we will learn how to keep historical records while maintaining valid information.

Handling loads using snapshots

Since, in our scenario, there is no requirement for maintaining historical data, we won't do this section as part of our exercise, but let's quickly get an idea of how to do it conceptually by looking at this figure:

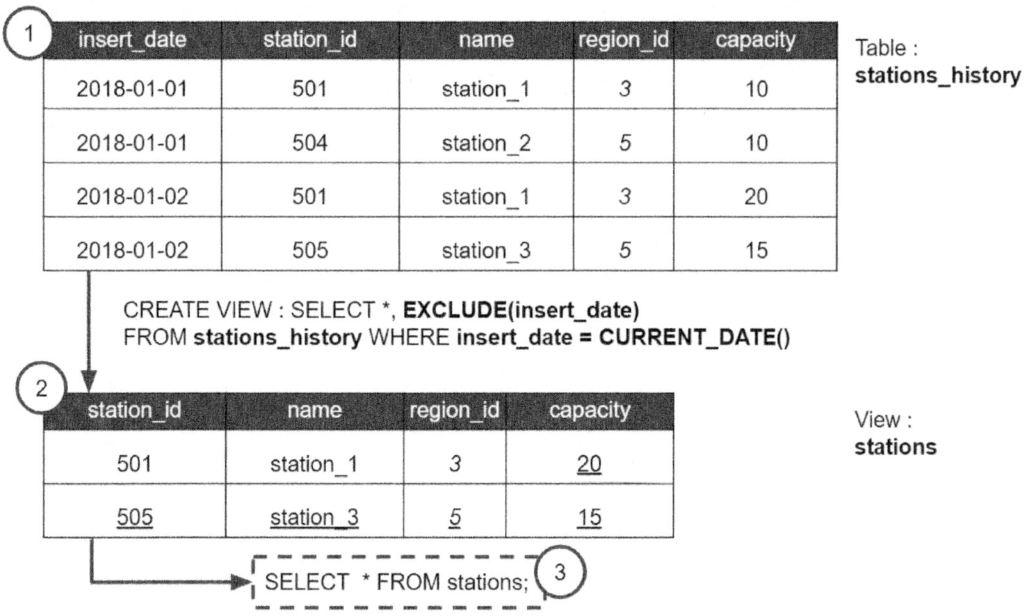

Practicing developing a data warehouse

insert_date	station_id	name	region_id	capacity
2018-01-01	501	station_1	3	10
2018-01-01	504	station_2	5	10
2018-01-02	501	station_1	3	20
2018-01-02	505	station_3	5	15

Table: **stations_history**

CREATE VIEW : SELECT *, **EXCLUDE(insert_date)** FROM **stations_history** WHERE **insert_date = CURRENT_DATE()**

station_id	name	region_id	capacity
501	station_1	3	20
505	station_3	5	15

View: **stations**

SELECT * FROM stations;

Figure 3.33 – General concept of the snapshot table

There are three additional steps compared to simply using the `WRITE_TRUNCATE` approach:

1. After loading to our table in `raw_bikesharing`, we will create another table that adds an `insert_date` column (or you can add it as an ETL process, before loading to BigQuery). The table will keep appending the new data daily. There will be duplication at the `station_id` level, but since we have the `insert_date` column, we can use the date information to get just the latest data snapshot.
2. Create a view that excludes the `insert_date` column and filter `insert_date` using the `CURRENT_DATE()` function, which returns today's date.
3. The final user will access the view instead of the raw or historical tables. The user experience will still be the same since they can use common query `SELECT * FROM stations` and obtain just today's station version.

With this mechanism, any time business users have requests for data from historical periods, you can always access the `stations_history` table.

What is the drawback? Naturally, it will affect storage and performance. That's why it always goes back to the requirements.

There are two other common approaches that I will not cover in this book, but I suggest you research these concepts on the internet:

- **Incremental load using the MERGE BigQuery**: MERGE is a unique operation in BigQuery. It's a combination of INSERT if it does not exist, and UPDATE if there are changes.
- **Slowly Changing Dimensions (SCDs)**: SCDs are methods that you can follow to handle dimension data. Dimension data is equal to snapshot data in our context here, but I chose not to use dimension data since it's tightly related to data modeling techniques that we will visit in the next section.

Let's summarize our overall progress so far by checking our three tables. Now your tables should have these amounts of records:

- regions: 6 records
- stations: 342 records
- trips: 4,627 records

If you don't have the same result, I suggest the following options:

1. Revisit all the previous steps.
2. If there are tables with zero records, I strongly suggest revisiting all the previous steps.
3. If all the tables have records, but they have different numbers of records, you may continue to *step 4*. You might miss some small detail steps, but this won't prevent you from continuing the practice exercise.

Step 4 – Designing data modeling for BigQuery

In this section, we want to start thinking about whether there are any better ways to reshape our table's schema to better represent our business user needs. Just to summarize, this is the second-to-last step in the following plan.

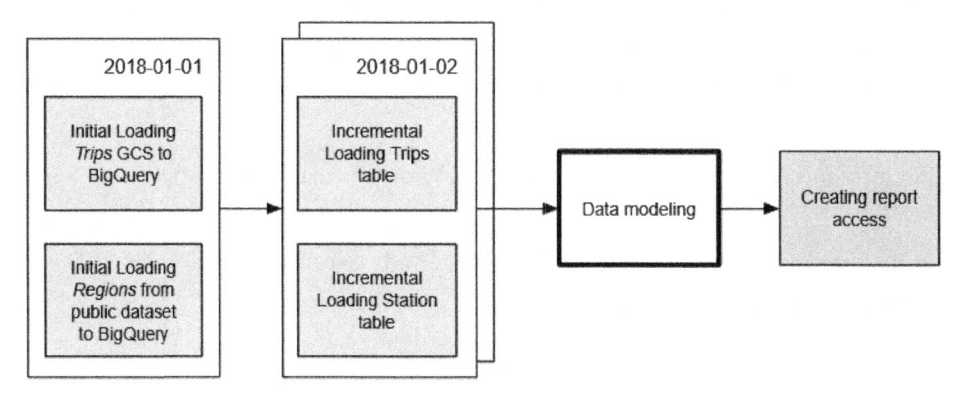

Figure 3.34 – The data modeling step

I will give you a heads-up here before we continue our practice exercise: we will spend more time in this section learning some theory and principles compared to the other steps.

When this book was written, I felt there was a big gap between how far data technology has come and how far data theory has come, such as data warehouse modeling. For example, the storage size and computational power of today's data warehouses differ enormously from what they were 30 years ago, yet the data warehouse modeling principles that we often use today are based on theories from the 1990s.

There are two concerns here. The first one is that some of the old design principles that used to handle storage and process efficiency may no longer be relevant in modern technologies. Secondly, since modern data engineers realize the irrelevance of the old principles and, at the same time, the demand for being able to insert any data into a data warehouse is growing tremendously, they tend to skip the data modeling steps, and that's bad. Skipping the data warehouse principles means ignoring the fact that we need to maintain data consistency. This fact may lead to some bad results. Take the following common example:

- Data is duplicated in many locations
- Some values are not consistent across different users and reports
- The cost of processing is highly inefficient
- The end user doesn't understand how to use the data warehouse objects
- The business doesn't trust the data

In my opinion, a modern data warehouse is still a data warehouse, regardless of the tools and technologies. The objective of a data warehouse is to build a centralized and trustworthy data storage solution that can be used for business. Data engineers need to take more time to do proper data modeling in data warehouses rather than data lakes in order to meet their objectives.

Introducing data modeling

What is data modeling? **Data modeling** is a process for representing database objects from a business perspective. Objects in BigQuery can be datasets, tables, or views. Representing the objects as close as possible to the real world is important because the end users of the data are human. Some of the most common end users are business analysts, data analysts, data scientists, BI users, and any other roles that require access to data for business purposes.

This is the main difference between designing a data model in a data warehouse and designing an **Online Transaction Processing (OLTP)** database (transactional database) for applications. In the application database, the end users of the database are applications, not humans. In the data warehouse, you serve humans. So, as data engineers, we need to think from their perspective.

Let's look at this example. We want to represent people in a table object. Which of the following two tables, A or B, do you think better represents people? Here is `People` table A:

name	age	hair color	gender
Mona	20	black	Female
Oscar	35	black	Male
Adam	56	white	Male
Barb	34	red	Male
Hazel	25	brown	Female

Figure 3.35 – People table A

Try and compare this with `People` table B:

name	gender	postal code	wealthy
Mona	Female	111111	yes
Oscar	Male	232323	no
Adam	Man	423333	no
Barb	Man	NULL	yes
Hazel	Woman	452222	yes

Figure 3.36 – People Table B

If we look back at the objective, we want to represent people. I think we can all agree that `People` table A is better at representing people because this table represents people clearly. It's very natural to imagine people having names, ages, hair colors, and genders. A good data model is self-explanatory, like `People` table A. This means that even without anyone explaining to you how to read the table, you know what the table is about.

Now, why is Person Table B bad? There are a few reasons:

- The lists of attributes don't really represent people, for example, `postal code`. Even though we know people may have houses and houses have postal codes, it's difficult to imagine people as entities having a postal code as part of them.

- What is `NULL` in relation to `postal code`? Does that mean Barb doesn't have a house? Or maybe he forgot his postal code? Or perhaps this is just a bug. The table can't really tell you that.

- Still on the subject of the postal code, how about if one of the people here has more than one house? Should we add new records to this table? It can become complicated.

- Gender is inconsistent. `Female` and `Woman`, or `Male` and `Man`, might have the same meaning, or they might not.

- The `wealthy` column has `yes` and `no` values. What does this mean? How can this column be justified?

It is not that the information is wrong; it's often the case that we need to store this kind of information. The question is, can we store the same information but with a better data model?

Let's take another example. Perhaps this better represents the real world for the required information:

Salary

name	Salary
Mona	1000000
Oscar	2000
Adam	3000
Barb	100000
Hazel	100000

People

name	gender
Mona	Female
Oscar	Male
Adam	Male
Barb	Male
Hazel	Female

Address

name	postal code
Mona	111111
Oscar	232323
Adam	423333
Hazel	452222

Figure 3.37 – Alternative C, using multiple tables

Maybe this *Alternative C* is better. We still have the `People` table, but only with people-related attributes, such as `gender`. Then, `postal code` is part of the `Address` table. We may have other address information, but in this example, we will keep it simple with just the postal code. And if someone such as `Barb` doesn't have a postal code, then we don't need to put the `NULL` record there. Lastly, we may assume that wealth is driven by salary (just for example purposes), so we had better just store the salary information, and later use queries to put the `wealthy` logic on top of the salary information. This is closer to the real world.

What could happen with a bad data model? It is often the case that the end user will end up too dependent on the data engineering team. Unable to understand the table shapes, end users would need to keep posing the following questions to the data engineering team:

- What does `NULL` mean?
- How should I join the tables?
- Why are there duplications?
- Why do some records have the attribute *X* while others don't?

In the worst-case scenario, the end user doesn't trust the data in the data warehouse, and the goal of using the data for a business impact is not achieved.

In the best-case scenario, the end user doesn't need to put any questions to the data engineering team. They can answer any business questions just by looking at the table structures, and they trust the data 100%. That's our goal as data engineers.

But, at the end of the day, it's very difficult to design a perfect data model because there are other aspects that a data engineer needs to think about when designing a data model.

Other purposes of the data model

Besides representing data, there are three other reasons that we require a data model in a data warehouse:

- **Data consistency**
- **Query performance**
- **Storage efficiency**

Let's start with the last reason first: *storage efficiency*. How can we improve storage efficiency using a data model?

Take a look at this example again. Which one is more storage-efficient? Perhaps a table with `name` and `gender`, where `gender` is written in a string data type as `Female` or `Male`:

People

name	gender
Mona	Female
Oscar	Male
Adam	Man
Barb	Man
Hazel	Woman

Figure 3.38 – Storage efficiency option A

Or perhaps option B: we could create a gender reference table, and the main table will only store one character, `gender_id`, as a reference. The user can later join both tables for the same result as option A.

People

name	gender_id
Mona	1
Oscar	2
Adam	2
Barb	2
Hazel	1

Gender

gender_id	gender
1	Female
2	Male

Figure 3.39 – Storage efficiency option B

Option B is definitely better, as we don't need to repeat storing `Female` and `Male` strings in our storage. It looks small, but the same technique applies to all categorical string attributes, and that can have a significant impact.

Using the same technique, we can also improve data consistency. For example, we can use the gender reference table for other tables, as in the following example user table:

People

name	gender_id
Mona	1
Oscar	2
Adam	2
Barb	2
Hazel	1

Gender

gender_id	gender
1	Female
2	Male

User

user_id	gender_id
10002	2
10003	2
10004	1
10005	1
10006	1

Figure 3.40 – Storage efficiency option B with an additional table

With that, we avoid data inconsistency; for example, the `People` table uses `Female/Male`, and the `User` table uses `Man/Woman`. This is a very common practice; the terminology used to refer to this kind of differentiation in the data warehouse world is **normalized** and **denormalized**.

Storage efficiency option A is a denormalized table, while storage efficiency option B is a normalized table.

Last but not least, one reason why we need a data model is to query performance. In a big data system where data is stored in distributed storage, there is a rule of thumb regarding which operation is the most resource-intensive, which is `JOIN`. Now, `JOIN` in general is a very expensive operation, especially when we need to join multiple large-volume tables. If you look back at the normalized and denormalized approaches, you will realize that even normalized data is good for storage efficiency and data consistency, but it's bad for performance because you require a lot of `JOIN` operations.

At the end of the day, we need to find a balance between all the factors. There will be no right or wrong answer for a data model in a complex data warehouse. A complex data warehouse might involve thousands or even millions of tables. So, everyone will have a different approach to designing a data model. However, there are some theories that we can refer to when deciding what is best for BigQuery.

Inmon versus the Kimball data model

If you look online, there will be many references to data modeling, but two of the most famous approaches are the **Inmon** method (data-driven) and the **Kimball** method (user-driven).

We will take a quick look at these methods, but we won't spend much time or go into too much detail in this book since there are so many details to explain regarding the framework. I suggest you do some more in-depth research from other resources regarding these two methods to better understand the step-by-step approaches involved. What we want to learn about them are the differences and the thought process.

At a very high level, the Inmon method focuses on building a central data warehouse or single source of truth. To achieve that, the data model must be highly normalized to the lowest level, so the data can be highly consistent. The Inmon data model follows a top-down approach, which means the data warehouse is built as the central data source for all the downstream data marts, sometimes referred to as the **enterprise data warehouse**. The downstream data marts need to follow the rules from the data warehouse, as in this figure. Imagine the gray boxes are tables.

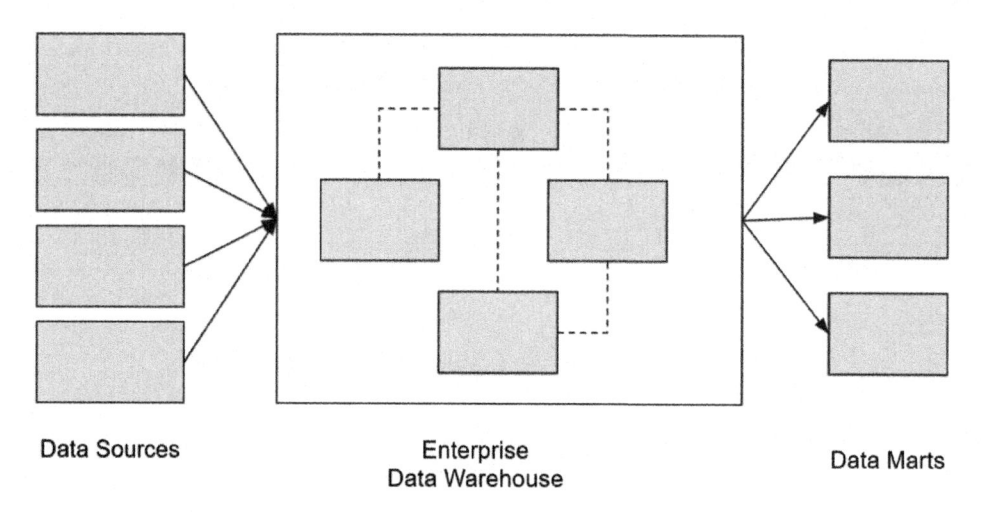

Figure 3.41 – Inmon data model illustration

Compared to the Inmon method, the Kimball method focuses on answering user questions and so follows a bottom-up approach. This method keeps end user questions in mind and uses the questions as a basis to build necessary tables. The goal is to ease end user accessibility and provide a high level of performance improvement.

The tables may contain the entity's basic information and its measurements. This is what are now known as fact and dimension tables. A **fact table** is a collection of measurements or metrics in a predefined granularity. A **dimension table** is a collection of entity attributes that support the fact tables. This collection of fact and dimension tables will later be the data warehouse.

Here is an example of a fact table. The fact table has two measurements that measure customers in daily granularity:

Date	Customer Id	Number of clicks	Number of purchase
2021-01-01	1	100	4
2021-01-01	2	10	2
2021-01-02	1	200	10
2021-01-01	2	50	4

Figure 3.42 – Customer fact table in daily granularity

Here is an example of a dimension table with `Customer ID` as the primary key and the attributes:

Customer Id	Name	Age
1	Agnes	34
2	Bony	23
1	Charlie	54
2	Darwin	12

Figure 3.43 – Customer dimension table

As you can see from the examples, the facts and dimension tables are different. So, how do they relate together as a data model?

One of the most well-known data models for the Kimball method is the star schema. The star schema follows the fact and dimension table relations. There is a rule of thumb regarding the star schema that a dimension table can't have parent tables, which means the dimension is a denormalized table. Check the following diagram, which provides a high-level illustration of a data warehouse using the Kimball approach. Imagine that all the gray boxes are tables:

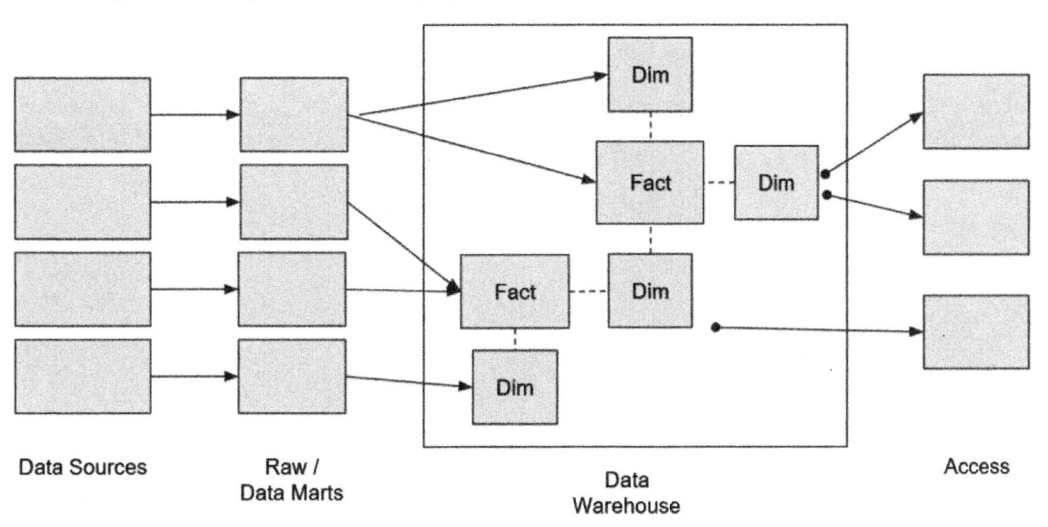

Figure 3.44 – Illustration of the Kimball data model

The pros and cons of both methods are summarized as follows:

	Inmon	Kimball
Data warehouse scope	Enterprise-wide.	Business areas.
Development time	Longer initial design and implementation time.	Shorter time for initial design and implementation.
Normalized data model	Highly normalized.	Low normalization.
Computation performance	Highly computation expensive. Involves many join operations.	Lower computation cost. Information already denormalized in dimensional tables.
Consistency	Highly consistent and highly regulated.	Often a lot of redundant information and is subject to revision.

Figure 3.45 – Inmon versus the Kimball method

Use the preceding comparison as a reference when deciding between the Inmon and Kimball methods. This is usually not a straightforward and quick decision to make. It's a difficult decision because choosing one of them means your entire organization needs to commit to the data model for the long term. An experienced data modeler is usually the best person to decide this. In the next section, we will try to figure out which data model is best in BigQuery.

The best data model for BigQuery

Since both approaches are quite old, the common question is, which data model is better for BigQuery?

But before answering the question about which data model is best for BigQuery, let's summarize what we've learned so far in terms of which aspects we need to think about when deciding on the data model approach.

A data model needs to do the following:

- Represent the real-world scenario for the end user
- Have high data consistency
- Perform well in the chosen database (query speed)
- Demonstrate efficiency when storing data

The complication we've learned, however, is that the four aspects can't all be perfect at the same time; each point is a trade-off in relation to the other points.

Repeating the example from the previous section, there are cases when we need to sacrifice consistency and efficient storage for better performance and better real-world representation. Or, in other cases, we may sacrifice performance for high consistency.

Now, let's talk about the technological evolution following the Hadoop era. Modern data technologies are increasingly friendly in terms of storage costs, including in BigQuery. Storing data used to be very expensive in days gone by, but it's no longer true in BigQuery (at least compared to non-cloud technologies). For example, in BigQuery, the cost of storing 1 TB of data is $20/month. Compare this to the old days, when companies needed to pay thousands of dollars to store the same amount of data on-premises.

The other aspect that has evolved is computation performance. In the Hadoop technology, data engineers were very cautious of `JOIN` operations. A join is highly resource-intensive, especially in the original Java MapReduce technology. However, this is no longer true in BigQuery,

Look at my query result in the following screenshot. I did a full table join on 587 GB of data, and the query finished in `23.4` seconds:

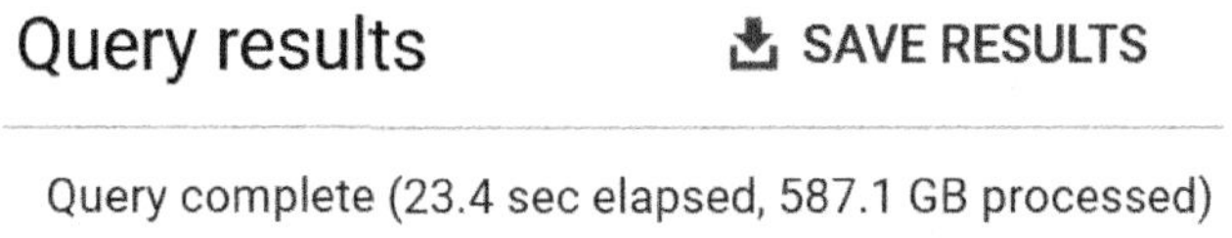

Query results   ⬇ SAVE RESULTS

Query complete (23.4 sec elapsed, 587.1 GB processed)

Figure 3.46 – Query time for aggregating 587 GB of data

If you are wondering about the preceding query cost, that query cost is around $3 in BigQuery. (In on-demand, the processing cost is $5 per 1 TB., so a 587 GB query will cost around $3.)

Given the preceding facts about storage and computation, in BigQuery, we can stipulate these two aspects as lower-level priorities. Just to be clear, we are not ignoring these aspects entirely, but if we find ourselves in a situation where we need to sacrifice some aspects, then we may choose to sacrifice storage and computation efficiency over data consistency and better representation of the real world (for user friendliness).

Now let's get back to the main question: should we use the Inmon method or the Kimball method? My answer is both. You should use either depending on the circumstances.

Let's use a real example. Imagine you are a data engineer. You are working for the finance department as your business user. They have asked for financial statement reports. You might consider using the Inmon method for three reasons:

- You need high-level consistency for a financial report; you cannot make any mistakes with this kind of report.
- A financial statement usually requires minimum data source changes.
- The initial development time is not as important as highly accurate data.

However, the decision will be different in other cases. In the big data era, we may expect data to arrive more quickly and in greater variety. Organizations tend to store almost all possible data. The main reason is agility in analytics and data science. New data sources, tables, and columns will appear every single day. In this case, if you follow the Inmon method, you may fail to catch up in terms of agility. The Kimball method is a better way to handle such a situation owing to the **user-driven** mindset. If business users are happy with the data and able to make business decisions based using it, then it's good enough even if there are inconsistencies and inefficiencies here and there.

To summarize this long section regarding data models, in the traditional data warehouse era, people chose which data model to use based on technological capabilities and constraints. By using BigQuery as our data warehouse, we are in a situation that has never been seen before. We choose how we want to model the data based on the business use case.

Creating fact and dimension tables

Let's get back to our bike-sharing datasets. Since, in scenario 2, we already have clear questions from business users and we don't require high consistency, we will use Kimball's star schema for our data warehouse. Our table schema will look like this:

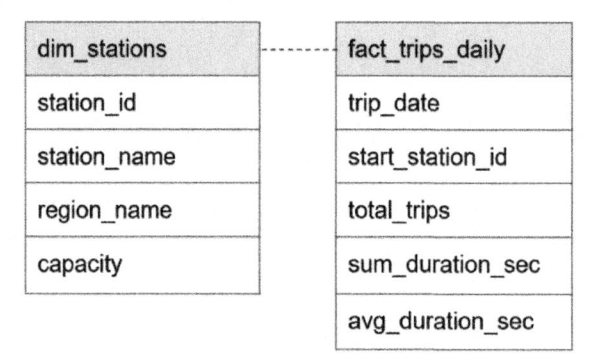

dim_stations		fact_trips_daily
station_id	———	trip_date
station_name		start_station_id
region_name		total_trips
capacity		sum_duration_sec
		avg_duration_sec

Figure 3.47 – Target table for the fact and dimension tables

These two tables are good examples of fact and dimension tables. The fact table represents measurements for the station ID by date; the granularity is daily. The dimension table represents stations. You can easily imagine a station in the real world given the attributes. A station has a name and indicates where the region is and what the capacity is. This table format will be easier for our user, who, in scenario 2, is an operational business user. Accessing these two tables is a lot easier compared to the raw tables.

Now, let's create our `fact_trips_daily` table by running the Python script in our repository:

```
bigquery_scenario_2_step_3_create_fact_table_daily_trips.py
```

Open the script in Cloud Editor and change the project ID to your project, as we did in the other preceding steps.

After that, check this line in the code:

```
load_date = sys.argv[1] # date format : yyyy-mm-dd
```

This script requires a date parameter in the format `yyyy-mm-dd`. So, you need to provide one when calling the Python command, like this:

```
$ python bigquery_scenario_2_step_3_create_fact_table_daily_trips.py
2018-01-01
```

Run it again to load the next day's data:

```
$ python bigquery_scenario_2_step_3_create_fact_table_daily_trips.py
2018-01-02
```

If successful, the script will create the `fact_trips_daily` table in the `dwh_bikesharing` dataset. Check in the BigQuery console whether the table looks like this:

fact_trips_daily

SCHEMA DETAILS PREVIEW

Row	trip_date	start_station_id	total_trips	sum_duration_sec	avg_duration_sec
401	2018-01-02	109	15	6837	455.8
402	2018-01-02	77	15	13869	924.59999999999991
403	2018-01-02	36	15	7826	521.73333333333335
404	2018-01-02	53	15	60898	4059.8666666666668

Figure 3.48 – The fact_trips_daily table

For the `dim_stations` table, run the Python script in this location:

```
Chapter-3\code\bigquery_scenario_2_step_3_create_dim_table_stations.py
```

Change the `project_id` variable in the script and run it. If successful, you will see the `dim_stations` table created like this:

dim_stations

SCHEMA DETAILS PREVIEW

Row	station_id	station_name	region_name	capacity
1	222	10th Ave at E 15th St	Oakland	3
2	167	College Ave at Harwood Ave	Oakland	7
3	18	Telegraph Ave at Alcatraz Ave	Oakland	11
4	46	San Antonio Park	Oakland	15

Figure 3.49 – The dim_stations table

After successfully generating the two tables, we can continue to the next step. But before that, let's quickly look at an alternative for our tables using one of the features in BigQuery called nested data types.

Alternative data model using nested data types

There is one alternative that we may consider in data modeling with BigQuery, which is nested data types. If we return to the debate regarding normalized versus denormalized tables, one of the reasons why people use normalized tables is for storage efficiency, while one of the advantages of using denormalized tables is ease of use, since we don't need to join tables.

Can we achieve both advantages in a single solution? The answer is yes. You can achieve that in BigQuery using nested data types.

For example, let's look at our bike-sharing `regions` and `stations` tables. In the raw dataset, the original data is denormalized.

Row	region_id	name
1	14	Berkeley
2	5	San Jose
3	12	Oakland
4	13	Emeryville
5	23	8D
6	3	San Francisco

Figure 3.50 – Raw regions table

And in our `stations` table, each region has one or more stations.

station_id	name	region_id	capacity
64	5th St at Brannan St	3	0
133	Valencia St at 22nd St	3	0
79	7th St at Brannan St	3	3
102	Irwin St at 8th St	3	4

Figure 3.51 – Raw stations table

Looking at our dimension table in the dwh dataset, we decided to denormalize the table to meet the star schema rule. The rule is that you can't have parent tables for a dimension table, or, in other words, you can't join dimension tables to other dimension tables:

station_id	station_name	region_name	capacity
222	10th Ave at E 15th St	Oakland	3
167	College Ave at Harwood Ave	Oakland	7
18	Telegraph Ave at Alcatraz Ave	Oakland	11
46	San Antonio Park	Oakland	15

Figure 3.52 – The dim_stations table

Since one region can have one or many stations, we can store the stations as nested information under regions. This may be hard to imagine, so let's just try to create one by running this query in the BigQuery console. The query will create a region and station as one table:

```
CREATE OR REPLACE TABLE `dwh_bikesharing.dim_stations_nested`
AS
SELECT
  regions.region_id,
  regions.name as region_name,
  ARRAY_AGG(stations) as stations
FROM `packt-data-eng-on-gcp.raw_bikesharing.regions` regions
JOIN `packt-data-eng-on-gcp.raw_bikesharing.stations` stations
ON CAST(regions.region_id AS STRING) = stations.region_id
GROUP BY regions.region_id, regions.name;
```

Take a look at the `dim_stations_nested` table schema:

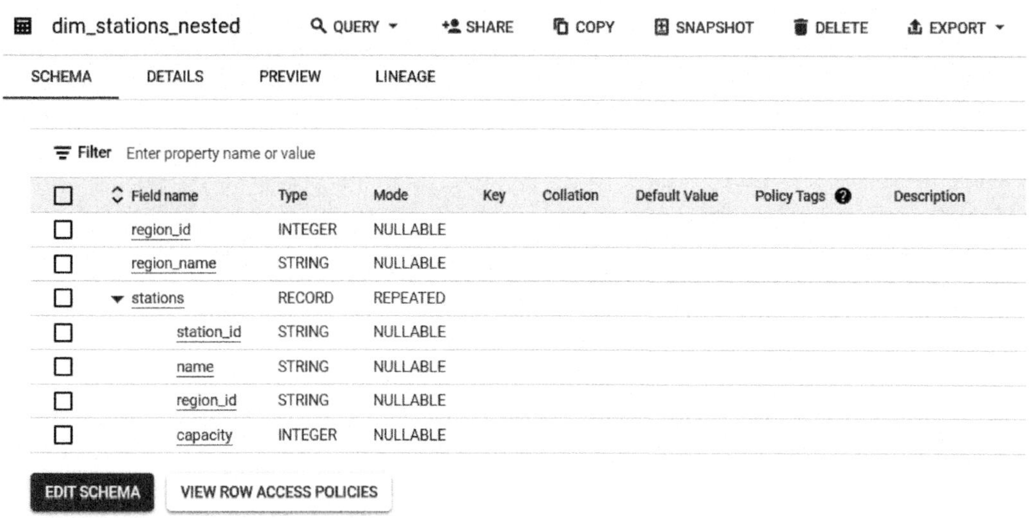

98   Building a Data Warehouse in BigQuery

Figure 3.53 – Nested table schema in the SCHEMA tab

You will see that the stations are part of the regions as repeated columns. If you query the data, you will see that `region_id` and `region_name` are only stored once even though there are multiple station records.

Row	region_id	region_name	stations.station_id	stations.name
1	3	San Francisco	64	5th St at Brannan St
			133	Valencia St at 22nd St
			79	7th St at Brannan St

Figure 3.54 – Nested table content example

The downside of using nested tables is that it's not easy to digest for common SQL users. Business users who are familiar with SQL might get confused by it the first time around. But the feature is there, and you can always use it when you need it.

Next, we will move on to the final step to create our reports.

Step 5 – Storing the business questions result in tables

The final step is to answer the business questions with our fact and dimension tables. This is going to be straightforward. So, let's look at each question and answer with SQL statements:

1. How many bike trips take place daily?

   ```
   CREATE VIEW dm_operational.bike_trips_daily
   AS
   SELECT trip_date, SUM(total_trips) as total_trips_daily
   ```

```
        FROM dwh_bikesharing.fact_trips_daily
        GROUP BY trip_date;
```

2. What is the daily average trip duration?

```
        CREATE VIEW dm_operational.daily_avg_trip_duration
        AS
        SELECT trip_date, ROUND(AVG(avg_duration_sec)) as daily_average_
        duration_sec
        FROM dwh_bikesharing.fact_trips_daily
        GROUP BY trip_date;
```

3. What are the top five starting station names with the longest trip duration?

```
        CREATE VIEW dm_operational.top_5_station_by_longest_duration
        AS
        SELECT trip_date, station_name, sum_duration_sec
        FROM dwh_bikesharing.fact_trips_daily
        JOIN dwh_bikesharing.dim_stations
        ON start_station_id = station_id
        WHERE trip_date = '2018-01-02'
        ORDER BY sum_duration_sec desc
        LIMIT 5;
```

4. What are the top three region names that have the shortest total trip durations?

```
        CREATE VIEW dm_operational.top_3_region_by_shortest_duration
        AS
        SELECT trip_date, region_name,
        SUM(sum_duration_sec) as total_sum_duration_sec
        FROM dwh_bikesharing.fact_trips_daily
        JOIN dwh_bikesharing.dim_stations
        ON start_station_id = station_id
        WHERE trip_date = '2018-01-02'
        GROUP BY trip_date, region_name
        ORDER BY total_sum_duration_sec asc
        LIMIT 3;
```

And that's it. Congratulations on finishing all the steps! Now as an addition, let's take a look at other functionalities on top of BigQuery.

BigQuery's useful features

Having completed the exercise from the previous section, where we used BigQuery in a practical scenario where we were developing a data warehouse, in this last section of the chapter, let's bring back our perspective to see BigQuery as a tool.

BigQuery is an integral tool in the GCP data engineering ecosystem, so even though BigQuery at its core is a database, on top of that, there are many more features, such as ones for machine learning, transferring data, and scheduling queries.

I will use this section to guide you quickly through the important additional BigQuery features that you might use in the future. As usual, I will focus on helping you narrow down what is important to you as a data engineer.

As a reminder, the best source for detailed information about each feature is the GCP public documentation. This book will only give a high-level description of features so that you can understand when certain features are relevant to your use case.

BigQuery console sub-menu options

First, let's go back to our GCP console and look at what sub-menu options are available other than the SQL workspace.

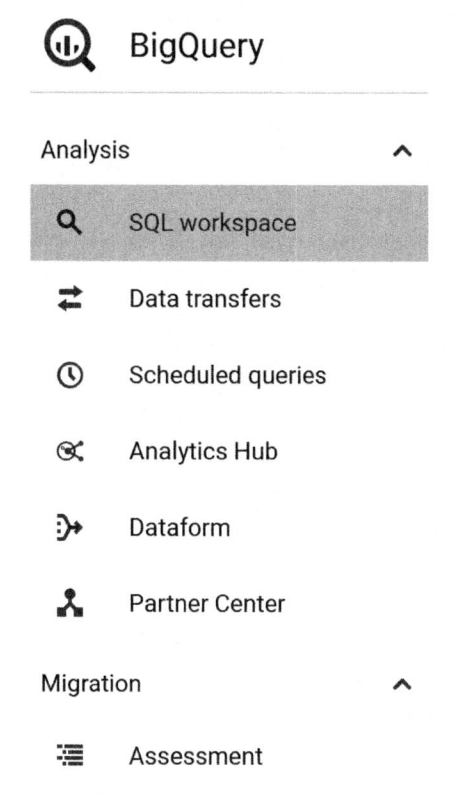

Figure 3.55 – The BigQuery console sub-menu options

Let's start with the first option after **SQL workspace**.

Data transfers

This is a link to **Data Transfer Service (DTS)**. This tool is for extracting and loading data to BigQuery from data sources such as Amazon S3, Google Ads, and YouTube.

This feature is helpful when you are transferring data from specific data sources. It will simplify your development process and turn it into only a configuration-based setup process. You will only find it useful when the source of data matches your use case. Beyond that, you can skip this option.

Here is a link to the public documentation: `https://cloud.google.com/bigquery/docs/dts-introduction`

Scheduled queries

This feature will help users to schedule queries. If you click on the **Create new scheduled query** button, you will be redirected to the Query Editor page. Don't worry, this is an expected behavior (when this book was written, in 2023). For you to create a scheduled query, write it in the BigQuery Editor and click on the **SCHEDULE** button:

```
1  SELECT trip_date, region_name, SUM(sum_duration_sec) as
2  FROM dwh_bikesharing.fact_trips_daily
3  JOIN dwh_bikesharing.dim_stations
4  ON start_station_id = station_id
5  WHERE trip_date = '2018-01-02'
6  GROUP BY trip_date, region_name
7  ORDER BY total_sum_duration_sec asc
8  LIMIT 3;
9
```

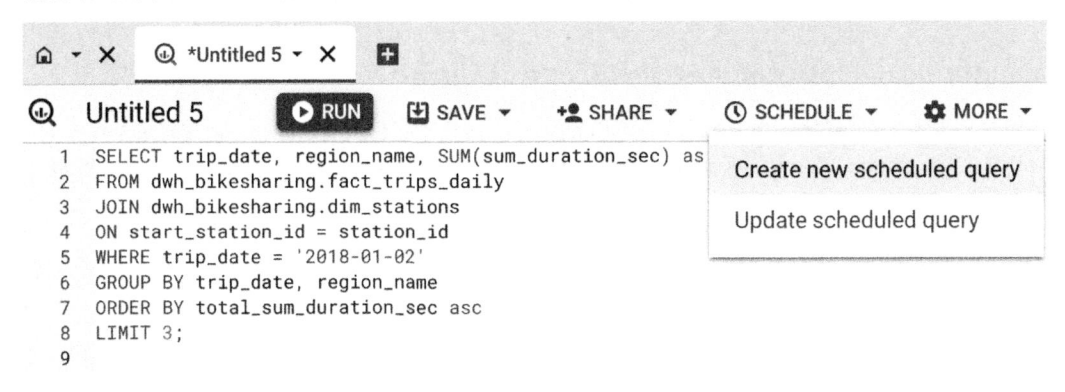

Figure 3.56 – The Create new scheduled query button

After that, you will be prompted on how you want to schedule your query.

This feature is useful for end users such as data analysts and business analysts who are not familiar with scripting code and need to schedule their queries to create BigQuery tables.

In general, as a data engineer, you should avoid using this tool. As a data engineer, you should know that scheduling table creation is part of ETL pipelines. This tool will not help much with tasks that are essential for creating ETL pipelines. It's better to use tools such as Cloud Composer for scheduling.

Analytics Hub

Analytics Hub is a tool for data exchange. This helps the business process of data sharing become seamless with the user interface. This is relevant to you if you plan to share your data with other organizations or teams using publishing and subscribing mechanisms.

Here is a link to the public documentation: https://cloud.google.com/bigquery/docs/analytics-hub-introduction

Dataform

Dataform is a sophisticated tool for data transformation. This will be covered in more detail in *Chapter 10, Data Governance in GCP*.

Migration | Assessment

This is only relevant if you are planning on migrating a data warehouse from Teradata to BigQuery. This tool will help assess the Teradata environment.

There may be more options in the future for the type of technology covered.

SQL translation

This is helpful when you need to translate your SQL queries from other dialects to BigQuery SQL, such as HiveQL, Netezza, and Redshift.

Monitoring, Capacity Management, and BI Engine

These features are needed for managing BigQuery costs and slots for the enterprise. BigQuery pricing will be covered in the *Comparing BigQuery on-demand and Edition* section of *Chapter 11, Cost Strategy in GCP*.

Policy Tags

This menu option will refer you to the Data Catalog API. If you have enabled the API, you will get access to Policy Tags features in BigQuery, which are useful for data governance.

BigQuery routines

The next set of features is the functions under BigQuery routines. This is not available in the BigQuery console. You can create a BigQuery routine by scripting it in the BigQuery Editor.

There are three types of BigQuery routine:

- **Stored Procedure**: This is useful when you have chains of queries that you need to run in sequence. This feature also allows you to define variables in the statement.

    Note that you shouldn't overuse this function to replate ETL pipelines. It's always better to use ETL tools such as Cloud Composer to manage query dependencies. Overusing it will make your data pipeline difficult to understand and debug when needed.

    Here is a link to the public documentation: https://cloud.google.com/bigquery/docs/procedures

- **User-Defined Function** (**UDF**): This allows you to create a custom function in a BigQuery statement. The function can be created by using an SQL expression or JavaScript.

  The example use case is for calculating mathematical formulas for a business context. For example, a function called `NewMetrics`, when the formula is variable X multiplied by 1.345, is as follows:

  ```
  CREATE TEMP FUNCTION NewMetrics(X INT64)
  RETURNS FLOAT64
  AS (X * 1.345);
  ```

  There is a benefit of creating UDFs instead of embedding the formula in a query such as this:

  ```
  SELECT 100 * 1.345 as new_metrics
  FROM …;
  ```

  The benefit is that the UDF can be re-used multiple times by many users. This allows consistency across organizations. For example, when a new user with minimal business understanding wants to calculate the `new_metrics` value, they just need to use the UDF. Utilizing UDFs is quite common in data engineering practice.

  Here is a link to the public documentation: `https://cloud.google.com/bigquery/docs/user-defined-functions`

- **Table functions**: These are similar to UDFs, but the output of these functions results in a table. This means that you can use a table function to join with other BigQuery tables.

  Here is a link to the public documentation: `https://cloud.google.com/bigquery/docs/table-functions`

- **Remote functions**: This is a unique feature in BigQuery for transforming BigQuery table records in other environments, for example, Cloud Run. This is useful when you need functions that are not supported by SQL or JavaScript.

  An example case would be when you need to do record transformation using a Java-specific library, such as performing specific encryption tasks.

  Typically, this function is needed to cover edge cases. Only use this approach if other alternatives are not possible because this approach requires more complicated architecture to run.

  Here is a link to the public documentation: `https://cloud.google.com/bigquery/docs/remote-functions`

BigQuery partitioned table

In this sub-section, we will cover one of the most important features in BigQuery: **partitioned tables**. This feature is important for performance and cost aspects in BigQuery, and it is important to understand before we move on to *Chapter 4, Building Workflows for Batch Data Loading Using Cloud Composer*.

When you create a BigQuery table and configure it as a partitioned table, BigQuery will logically divide the data by partitioning it into segments using your selected column.

There are three partition column options:

- **Time-unit columns**: Based on a column containing a TIMESTAMP, DATE, or DATETIME value
- **Ingestion time**: Based on the timestamp of when BigQuery ingests data to the table
- **Integer range**: Based on a column containing the integer value

The most common scenario is to use either a time-unit column or ingestion time. Note that even though you can partition down to an hourly level of granularity, the most common scenario is still partitioning at a daily level.

This feature will benefit you mainly in terms of cost and performance optimization, but other than those two factors, using BigQuery partitioned tables can help manage ETL loads, which we will cover in *Chapter 4, Building Workflows for Batch Data Loading Using Cloud Composer*.

Take a look at the next example.

We create a table with PARTITION BY (column name), as follows:

```
CREATE TABLE example_table
(
  val1 INT64,
  val2 STRING,
  date DATE,
)
PARTITION BY (date);
```

Under the hood of BigQuery storage, the `example_table` table will be divided based on the Date column, like this:

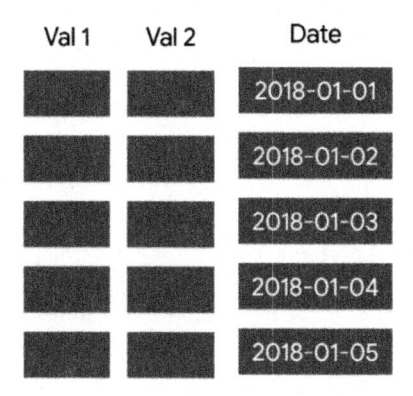

Figure 3.57 – BigQuery rows and columns example

Every table record will be stored in a separate storage location. With this, it's theoretically the same as having multiple tables with the same schemas. But you don't need to worry about this, as BigQuery will handle it seamlessly.

What you can do as a user is access the table and filter it using the `partition` column, like this:

```
SELECT val1
FROM example_table
WHERE date = '2018-01-03';
```

The query will only access a partial amount of data from the table, which is the `val1` column at `2018-01-03`. Please see the following figure:

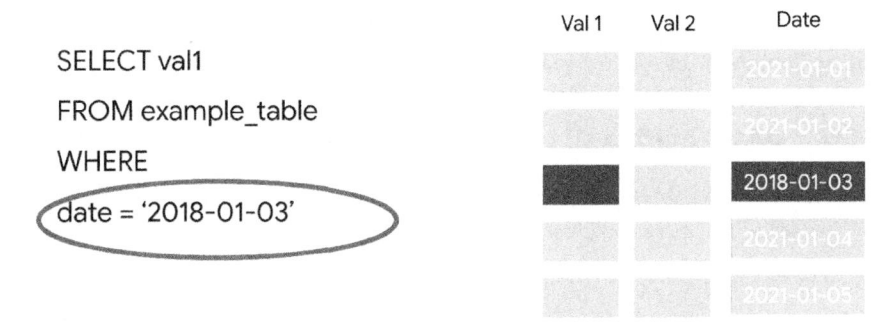

Figure 3.58 – Illustration of how a BigQuery partitioned table works

As mentioned before, one of the main reasons that people use partitioned tables in BigQuery is for cost optimization. We will discuss more on this subject from a cost strategy point of view later in *Chapter 11, Cost Strategy in GCP*, when we focus on the subject of GCP costs.

Summary

In this chapter, we've practiced using BigQuery to build a data warehouse. In general, we've covered the three main aspects of how to use the tools, how to load the data to BigQuery, and the data modeling aspect of a data warehouse.

After following all the steps in this chapter, you will have a better understanding of the data life cycle and you will understand that data moves from place to place. We also practiced the ELT process in this chapter, extracting data from a MySQL database, loading it to BigQuery, and doing some transformations to answer business questions. And on top of that, we did it all on a fully managed service in the cloud, spending zero time worrying about any infrastructure aspects.

By way of a footnote for this chapter, I want to remind you that, even though we have covered the common practices of using BigQuery, we haven't covered all of its features. There are a lot of other features in BigQuery that are worth checking out, such as partitioned tables, clustered tables, materialized views, the `WITH` query statement, the streaming insert, machine learning, and many other cool features.

We will cover some of these in later chapters, but not all of them. If you are new to BigQuery, I recommend you focus on the practice, not the features and capabilities.

Why? In my experience, the best way to learn is to face the issues and find solutions for them. To be able to face the issue, you need to practice more, rather than spending time learning all the features without any context.

This chapter is the foundation of data engineering in GCP. GCS and BigQuery are the most important services in GCP. Both products are easy to learn, but understanding how to use them properly by means of extensive practice is very important.

In later chapters, we will almost always use GCS and BigQuery as our underlying storage. For example, in the next chapter, we will start thinking about how to automate our data loading. In this chapter, we used a Python script and manually triggered the script to load the daily data. In the next chapter, we will use Cloud Composer, an Airflow-managed service to automate those processes.

Exercise – Scenario 3

As a final activity in this chapter, you can do a self-exercise to solve an additional business question from business users. Our operational user from scenario 2 wants to ask this additional question:

Show me the top three regions that have the most female riders as of the most recent date (2018-01-02).

Because the gender of members is not yet included in our fact and dimension table, you need to create a different fact and dimension table.

Remember that the data model is subjective, especially in the Kimball method. There is no right or wrong answer to the question. As we've discussed in this chapter, people can use different data models to represent the real world.

Try to solve it yourself and compare it to the solution in the Git code example:

- https://github.com/PacktPublishing/Data-Engineering-with-Google-Cloud-Platform-Second-Edition/blob/main/chapter-3/code/bigquery_self_excercise_create_dim_table_regions.py
- https://github.com/PacktPublishing/Data-Engineering-with-Google-Cloud-Platform-Second-Edition/blob/main/chapter-3/code/bigquery_self_excercise_create_fact_table_daily_by_gender_region.py
- https://github.com/PacktPublishing/Data-Engineering-with-Google-Cloud-Platform-Second-Edition/blob/main/chapter-3/code/bigquery_self_excercise_query_answer.sql

See also

- Kimball data model: `https://www.kimballgroup.com/data-warehouse-business-intelligence-resources/kimball-techniques/dimensional-modeling-techniques/`
- BigQuery features: `https://cloud.google.com/bigquery#section-10`

4
Building Workflows for Batch Data Loading Using Cloud Composer

In data engineering, the definition of a *workflow* is a set of configurations to automate tasks, jobs, and their dependencies. If we are talking about database workflow, we talk about how to automate the table creation process.

The main objects in any database system are tables, and one of the main differences between an application database and a data warehouse is the creation of tables. Compared to tables in application databases, where tables are mostly static and created to support frontend applications, tables in data warehouses are dynamic. The table is the main product as it is a collection of business logic, and data flows.

In this chapter, we will learn how to create the workflow for our data warehouse tables from *Chapter 3, Building a Data Warehouse in BigQuery*. We will learn how to automate the table creations using a **Google Cloud Platform** (**GCP**) service called **Cloud Composer**. This will include how to create a new Cloud Composer environment, how it works, and what are the best practices to develop workflows using it.

Learning Cloud Composer is relatively easy, and you may find out that you can already create an automatic scheduler for our tables in BigQuery in the early pages of this chapter, but the challenge is how we can improve our orchestration jobs to handle common data pipeline issues. Issues that usually happen are data duplication, handling task dependencies, managing connections, handling late data, and many other issues that we will discuss in this chapter.

The approach of this chapter is different from *Chapter 3, Building a Data Warehouse in BigQuery*. Instead of using multiple scenarios, we will do multiple levels of exercises. The goal is for you to understand step by step the maturity of workflows. This means that we won't jump to complex workflows directly from the beginning, because it may be very confusing. Instead, we will start from the very basics, and little by little improve the code to apply common best practices in Cloud Composer. These are the main topics in this chapter:

- Introduction to Cloud Composer
- Understanding the working of Airflow

- Provisioning Cloud Composer in a GCP project
- Exercise: Build data pipeline orchestration using Cloud Composer

Technical requirements

For this chapter's exercises, we will need the following:

- A Cloud Composer environment
- A Cloud SQL instance
- A **Google Cloud Storage (GCS)** bucket
- BigQuery datasets
- Cloud Shell
- A cloud editor
- Example code and data from `https://github.com/PacktPublishing/Data-Engineering-with-Google-Cloud-Platform-Second-Edition`
- Steps on how to access, create, or configure the technical requirements will be provided later in each exercise.

Introduction to Cloud Composer

Cloud Composer is an Airflow-managed service in GCP. Using Cloud Composer, we don't need to think about the infrastructure, installation, and software management for the Airflow environment. With this, we can focus only on the development and deployment of our data pipeline.

From the perspective of a data engineer, there is almost no difference between Cloud Composer and Airflow. When we learn how to use Cloud Composer, basically we learn how Airflow works.

Now, what is Airflow? Airflow is an open source workflow management tool. It comes with many features to support workflows, including monitoring, logging, a user interface, backfilling, and metadata management. What is unique in Airflow is that we use a Python script to manage our workflows, which is very friendly for data engineers in general.

There are some elements that we need to look at in the previous statement. Let's break down the statement into more detail. When talking about a workflow management tool, there are three main components:

- Handling task dependencies
- Scheduler
- System integration

As a workflow management tool, Airflow will connect to systems (integration), handle the chain of tasks (dependencies), and run it as a scheduled batch process (scheduler).

To illustrate, let's take a kitchen workflow as an example. If we want to cook pasta, here are the tasks:

1. Prepare the ingredients.
2. Cook the pasta.
3. Serve it on plates.

Each task has a specific output and each task depends on the others, forming a chain of tasks. In Airflow, tasks work in the same way—each task will have a specific output and may have dependencies on the other tasks that we need to manage.

The second element is the scheduler. If we really love pasta, we might want to cook it every day for breakfast. Then, for example, the order of tasks can be scheduled every day at 5:00 A.M. It's the same thing in Airflow—each task's dependencies can be scheduled, and Airflow is built for this purpose. Every Airflow feature is made for scheduled tasks rather than one-time jobs. Back to the kitchen example, it's not about a one-time experimental cooking experience—it's about cooking routines every day.

The third element is system integration. Each task might need integration with tools. Here's an example:

1. Preparing ingredients needs integration with a set of knives.
2. Cooking pasta requires a stove and pans.
3. Serving the pasta requires plates.

In Airflow, each task can be integrated into specific tools to run. Tools can be **GCS**, **BigQuery**, **Python**, **Bash scripts**, **an email application programming interface (API)**, and any other services. In the next section, we will learn much more about these tools and how Airflow works.

Understanding the working of Airflow

Airflow handles all three of the preceding elements using Python scripts. As data engineers, what we need to do is to create code in Python for handling task dependencies, scheduling our jobs, and integrating with other systems. This is different from traditional **extract, transform, load** (**ETL**) tools. If you have ever heard of or used tools such as **Control-M**, **Informatica**, **Talend**, or many other ETL tools, Airflow has the same positioning as these tools. The difference is that Airflow is not a **user interface** (**UI**)-based drag and drop tool. Airflow is designed for you to write the workflow using code.

There are a couple of good reasons why managing the workflow using code is a better idea than using drag-and-drop tools. Here's why we should do this:

- Using code, you can automate a lot of development and deployment processes
- Using code, it's easier for you to enable good testing practices
- All the configurations can be managed in a Git repository for versioning

Let's take a look at this example Airflow Python script:

```
dag = DAG('packt_dag', start_date=datetime(2023, 6, 12))
first_task = DummyOperator(task_id='task_1')
second_task = DummyOperator(task_id='task_2')
third_task = DummyOperator(task_id='task_3')

task_1>> task_2>> task_3
```

This is a very simple example of how we will define the three main workflow components.

Every single workflow in Airflow is called a **directed acyclic graph** (**DAG**). A DAG is a collection of tasks that are chained together with their dependencies.

In the first line of the preceding code snippet, you can see that we define a DAG in Python code, named `packt_dag`. The `packt_dag` DAG will run starting from June 6, 2023, and this is a part of how we schedule the DAG later.

In the second to fourth lines, you can see we define three `DummyOperator` tasks. This is the **system integration** part of our workflow. Airflow uses operators as interfaces to other systems; for example, later, we will use the GCS and BigQuery operators. This is not only for GCP-related products; Airflow, as an open source product, also has operators for other systems, such as MySQL, PostgreSQL, Oracle, email **Simple Mail Transfer Protocol** (**SMTP**), and many more. This is one of the main advantages of using Airflow: it has a lot of operators compared to other similar tools.

Now, in the last line, we can see unique Python syntax in Airflow called **bitshift operators**. This is the **jobs** or **tasks dependencies** part of our workflow. The `>>` syntax indicates the task directions; in the code example, it means task_1 will start first, followed by `task_2`, and then `task_3`.

The preceding piece of code is the core of what we need to understand in Airflow, and we will learn more about this through practice in the later sections.

Before we continue, I want to quickly introduce you to a glossary of some Airflow terms. We will use the glossary presented here in our later discussions, so it's good to get an idea of what those terms are:

- **DAG**: Airflow term for a job configuration. A job configuration contains a collection of tasks, scheduling information, and dependencies.
- **DAG Run**: A DAG Run is a term for when a DAG is running. When you trigger or schedule a DAG to run, it will be called a DAG Run.
- **Operator**: Operators are collections of connections to different systems. Airflow uses operators to define tasks.

We will repeat these three terms in throughout the book with a lot of examples, but at this point, it's good to know about them.

Cloud Composer 1 vs Cloud Composer 2

Currently, there are two main Cloud Composer versions, Cloud **Composer 1** and **Composer 2**. Don't be mistaken for the Airflow version, Airflow also has their versioning from the open-source. For example, currently, the latest Airflow version is 2.5.3.

What is the main difference between the two major Cloud Composer versions? There are some aspects that make Cloud Composer 1 and 2 different. But one of the most significant aspects is how the Airflow managed service works. In Cloud Composer 1, the number of Airflow workers is pre-defined for each environment. Cloud Composer 2 introduces the auto-scaling capability for the number of Airflow workers.

For example, in Cloud Composer 1, you need to choose the number of workers when you create the environment, let's say three workers. This environment will always occupy three virtual machines for the environment, with or without workloads running on top of it. In other cases, if there are too many workloads running, the whole environment may slow down.

For Cloud Composer 2, it can go to zero workers if there are no workloads running, up to the number of maximum workers that we specified. This five-minute video explains the advantages of using Cloud Composer 2: `https://www.youtube.com/watch?v=gi-uP_S2FEw`. Please check the video in case you need a deeper explanation.

In general, choose Cloud Composer 2 because it's the newer architecture and has better scalability. For learning purposes, it doesn't make much difference which version you use because what's important is the Airflow version. For this exercise, we will use Cloud Composer 2.3.2 with Airflow version 2.5.1, which is the latest available when this book is being written.

For a comparison of Composer 1 and Composer 2, please check the public documentation: `https://cloud.google.com/composer/docs/composer-2/composer-versioning-overview`

Now, let's create our Cloud Composer 2 environment.

Provisioning Cloud Composer in a GCP project

In order to develop our Airflow code, we will need a Cloud Composer environment. In this section, we will create our first Cloud Composer environment using the GCP console.

Follow these steps to create our environment:

1. Go to the **GCP Console** navigation bar.
2. Find and click on **Composer** in the pinned services, or if you haven't, find it in the **ANALYTICS** section, as illustrated in the following screenshot:

114　Building Workflows for Batch Data Loading Using Cloud Composer

        Dataflow　　>

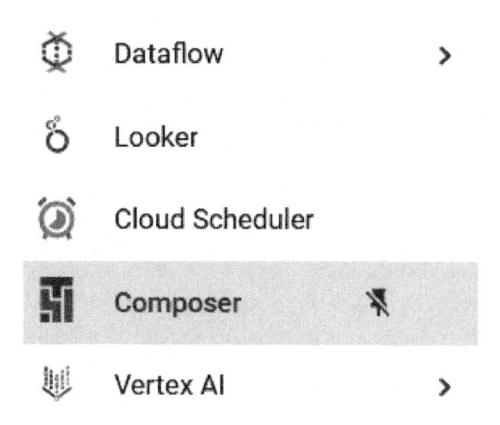

        Looker

        Cloud Scheduler

        Composer

        Vertex AI　　>

Figure 4.1 – Composer button in the navigation bar

3. After clicking on Composer in the navigation bar, you may be asked to enable the API (if you have already enabled it, you can ignore this). After enabling the API, you will be on a new web page. We will call this web page **Cloud Composer Console**. Let's continue our steps.
4. Click **CREATE ENVIRONMENT – Composer 2** on the **Cloud Composer Console** web page.
5. Choose your **Composer Environment** name.
6. Choose `us-central1` for the location. You can choose any location, but as the default in this book, we will use the `us-central1` region.

> **Important note**
> You don't need to use Cloud Composer in the same regions as with BigQuery and GCS, but for networking reasons, it's a lot better if you do.

7. Choose `composer-2.3.2-airflow-2.5.1` for the **Image version** option.

> **Important note**
> The **Image version** option may or may not be there when you read this book. Google might update the version and this version might no longer be there. In that case, `composer-2.x.x-airflow-2.5.X` is generally better for ensuring compatibility with the examples in this book.

8. In the **Service account** field, choose any service account that you see in the option. That is your project's default service account.
9. If this is the first time you have created a Cloud Composer instance, there will be a statement in the screen saying: **GRANT REQUIRED PERMISSIONS TO CLOUD COMPOSER SERVICE ACCOUNT**, just check the checkbox and click on **GRANT**.

10. Keep the other options as the defaults.
11. Before clicking **CREATE**, let's talk about the expected cost for this environment.

The Cloud Composer cost is based on the cluster hours, which means that if you create an environment for 7 hours for 1 day, you will be billed for those 7 hours; If you create an environment for 1 year, the cost will be 365 days multiplied by 24 hours. Cloud Composer is not billed based on individual usage—for example, you won't be billed by the number of DAGs or tasks that you have in a day.

So, in our exercise, it depends on how fast you can finish your exercises in this chapter. Let's take an example—if you think that you will finish this chapter in 7 days, then it means the cost is 7 days * cost/24 hours. Cost/24 hours is around 2 **United States dollars** (**USD**).

So, this means that the total Cloud Composer cost for 7 days is $14. I strongly suggest you create a cluster for the exercise in this chapter, and if you are still using the $300 GCP free tier, the total cost is totally reasonable.

This cost mechanism is a simplified calculation for Cloud Composer 1. Cloud Composer 2 has a more complex calculation. Even though the cost mechanism are different for Cloud Composer 1 and Cloud Composer 2, principally, it's the same as explained here. Both are billed for as long as the environment exists.

Now, back to the GCP console, and let's create our Cloud Composer environment by clicking the **CREATE** button. If this is successful, your Airflow environment will be ready for you. In the next section, we will learn how to run through the Airflow UI.

Introducing the Airflow web UI

Let's learn about the Airflow web UI. You can access the Airflow web UI from the **Cloud Composer Console** web page. If you click the environment, you can see **MONITORING, LOGS, DAGS, ENVIRONMENT CONFIGURATION**, and the other menus. However the more complete UI is found by accessing the Airflow UI. To do that, click **Open Airflow UI** in the top menu, as shown in the following screenshot:

Figure 4.2 – Finding the Airflow UI button in the top menu

116   Building Workflows for Batch Data Loading Using Cloud Composer

Clicking the button will open a new browser tab opening the Airflow web UI. In the UI, you will see a pretty simple and blank web page. The page will list down all of our DAGs on the main page, and as an example, it will come up with one example DAG called `airflow_monitoring`, as follows:

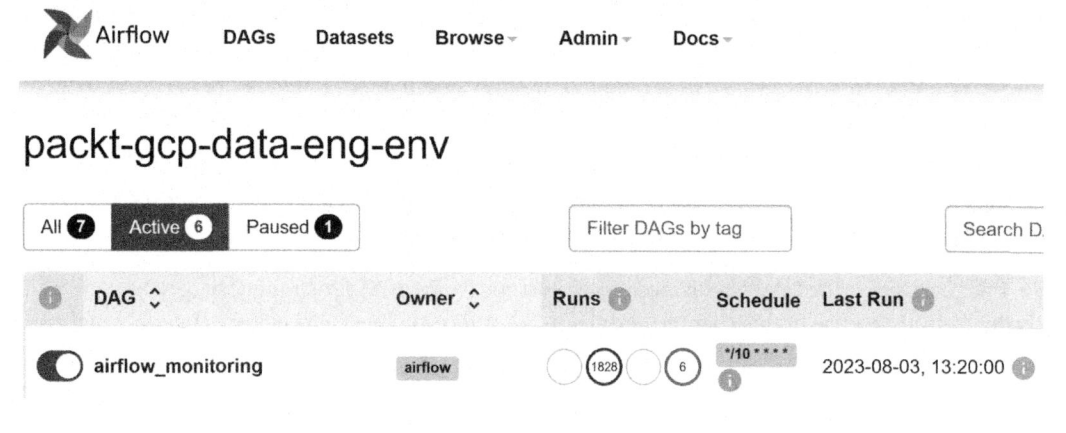

Figure 4.3 – Airflow main UI

As our first step, let's click the `airflow_monitoring` DAG. This will bring up the following DAG page:

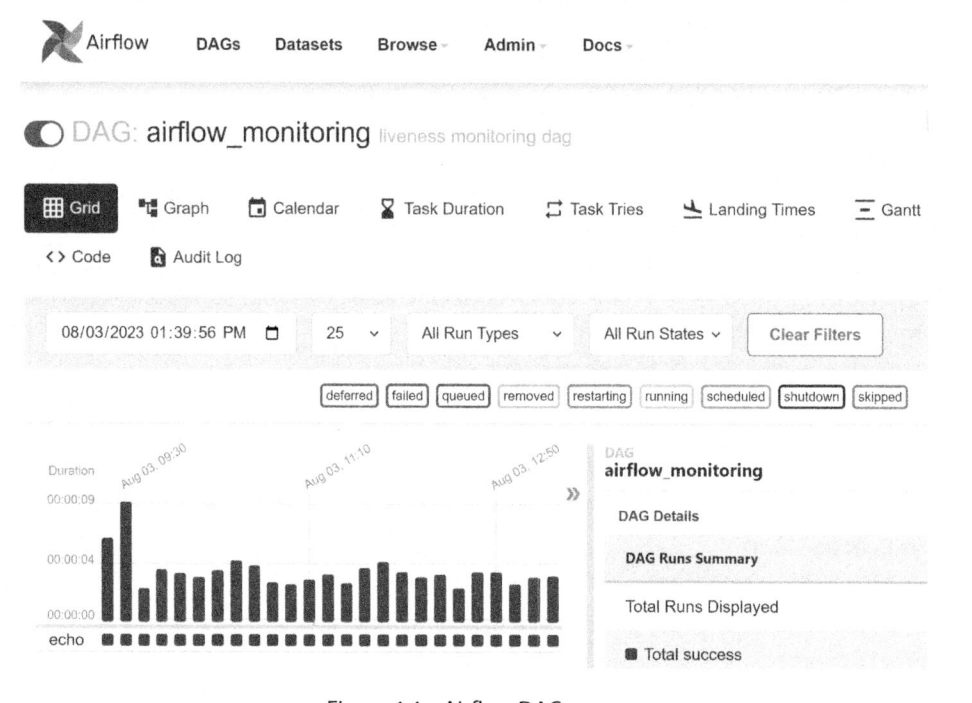

Figure 4.4 – Airflow DAG page

Provisioning Cloud Composer in a GCP project   117

The page is a dashboard with many components in it. I have to say that it may be confusing for a first-time user to see this page. This DAG page will show you many useful buttons.

Let's try to generalize it into three main information categories, as follows:

- Task dependencies
- DAG Runs
- DAG code

To check task dependencies, you can choose **Graph**. Since the `airflow_monitoring` DAG only has one task, it won't show you any dependencies, but later, in the *Exercise – build data pipeline orchestration using Cloud Composer* section, your task dependencies will look like this in **Graph**:

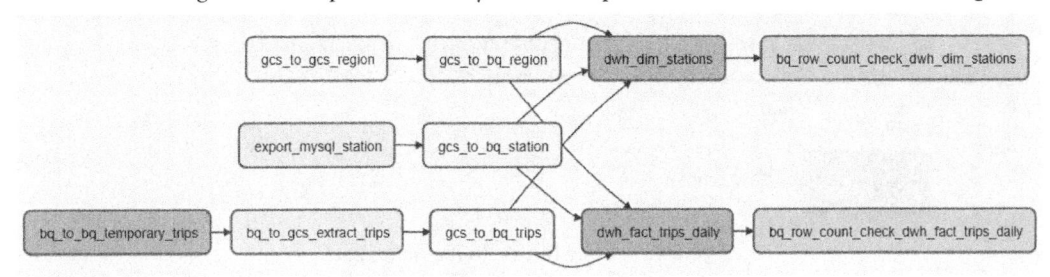

Figure 4.5 – DAG dependencies in Graph

Now, on the **Grid** page, you will see something like this on the left of your screen. It's a combination of bars on top of many squares, duration, and date times:

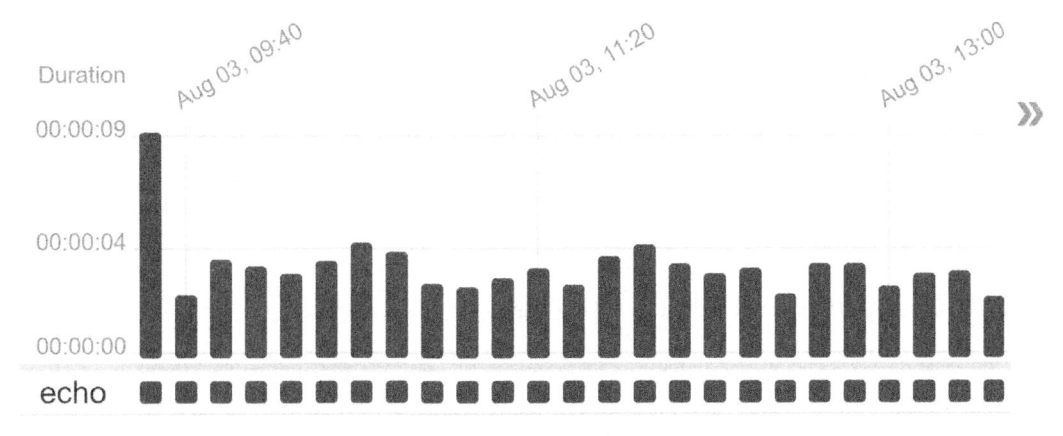

Figure 4.6 – DAG Run indicators

This is unique to Airflow and is a very important feature. One bar represents one DAG Run at a specific time, and it will be listed horizontally for the other DAG Runs ordered by execution time.

At the bottom of the bars, there are rows of squares ordered vertically. One box represents a single task in a DAG Run.

For each bar and boxes, there will be colors. The colors will tell you the status, which can be **Running**, **Success**, **Failed**, or other statuses that you can check out in the legend. Initially, you will see most of them are green, which means they are all successful.

Last but not least is the DAG code. You can click the **Code** button in the menu bar. Here, you can see the DAG code for a particular DAG.

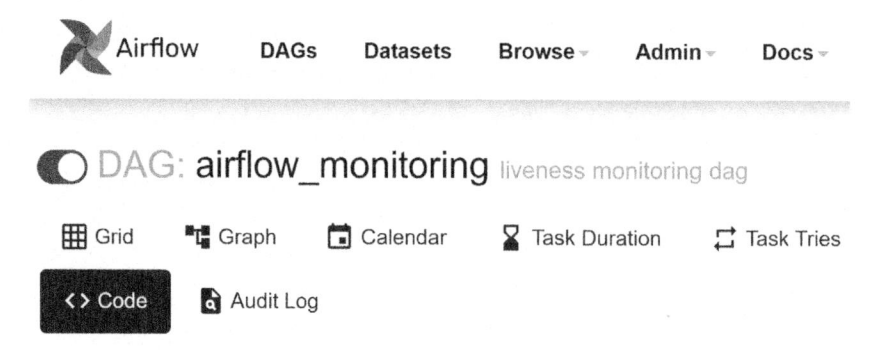

Figure 4.7 – Code button in the menu bar

This is important for checking quickly what the DAG is doing without needing to go to the source code repository, and sometimes I use this after updating the DAG code to check whether the DAG is running the correct code version in case it hasn't been updated properly.

After seeing the task flows, you might be wondering: *Can we create a DAG using the UI?* The answer is no. Airflow is not built as a drag-and-drop tool. As we've discussed in the previous sections, we will use Python to create a DAG.

To create a DAG using code, we won't use the Airflow UI either. We will need to code in our own environment and submit the DAG to Cloud Composer. We will do that in our exercise, but before that, there is one final thing that you need to know about Cloud Composer, which is the GCS directory structure.

Cloud Composer bucket directories

Cloud Composer has specific folders in the GCS bucket for Airflow management—for example, all of our DAG code is the result of a Python file in the `gs://{composer-bucket}/dags` directory. If you open this directory, you will find the `airflow_monitoring.py` file.

That `/dags` directory is very important for our development. In practice, you can develop your Airflow DAG in any environment—for example, from your laptop using your favorite **integrated development environment** (**IDE**) or using Cloud Editor. But at the end of the day, the Python file needs to be stored in this directory. By uploading the correct DAG file to this directory, Airflow will automatically schedule and run your DAG based on your configuration, and you can see the DAG in the UI.

To summarize, your Airflow web UI will only be your monitoring dashboard, but the actual code will be in the Cloud Composer GCS bucket. Here is a list of important GCS bucket directories for our development:

GCS directories	Mapped local directory	Usage
`gs://{composer-bucket}/dags`	`/home/airflow/gcs/dags`	DAGs
`gs://{composer-bucket}/plugins`	`/home/airflow/gcs/plugins`	Airflow plugins
`gs://{composer-bucket}/data`	`/home/airflow/gcs/data`	Workflow-related data
`gs://{composer-bucket}/logs`	`/home/airflow/gcs/logs`	Airflow task logs

Figure 4.8 – Table of GCS directories used by Cloud Composer

Here are the high-level explanations of GCS bucket directories:

- The `/dags` directory contains all the Python DAG files.
- The `/plugins` directory contains Airflow plugins for example Macro functions.
- The `/data` directory contains all side-files data that you need to use in the DAG. For example, we can put table schema files in this directory.
- The `/logs` directory contains Airflow logs.

Keep all this information in mind for now. You might have missed some of the concepts, terms, and ideas at this point, and that is fine. We will learn all of the important aspects when doing the exercises. So, make sure you've created your Cloud Composer environment so that we can start the exercise.

Exercise – build data pipeline orchestration using Cloud Composer

We will continue our bike-sharing scenario from *Chapter 3, Building a Data Warehouse in BigQuery*. Please finish *Chapter 3* before going through this exercise.

This Cloud Composer exercise will be divided into five different DAG levels. Each DAG level will have specific learning objectives, as follows:

- **Level 1**: Learn how to create a DAG and submit it to Cloud Composer
- **Level 2**: Learn how to use operators
- **Level 3**: Learn how to use variables
- **Level 4**: Learn how to apply task idempotency
- **Level 5**: Handling DAG dependencies using an Airflow dataset

It's important for you to understand that learning Airflow is as easy as Level 1 DAG. But as we go through each of the levels, you will see the challenges and opportunities we may have in practicing it.

In reality, you can choose to follow all of the best practices or none at all—Airflow won't forbid you from doing that. Using this leveling approach, you can learn step by step from the simplest to the most complicated way of configuring a DAG. At the end of the chapter, you can choose which level you want to follow for your data engineering journey. And for that, let's start at Level 1.

Level 1 DAG – creating dummy workflows

The main goal of Level 1 DAG is for us to understand how to create a DAG using Python, how timing in Airflow works, and how to handle task dependencies.

Please clone or download the example code here: `https://github.com/PacktPublishing/Data-Engineering-with-Google-Cloud-Platform-Second-Edition`. If you haven't cloned the repository from *Chapter 3, Building a Data Warehouse in BigQuery*, please clone the repository from your Cloud Shell and check out the code in the `chapter-4` directory.

For the Level 1 DAG example, please check out the code in this file: `https://github.com/PacktPublishing/Data-Engineering-with-Google-Cloud-Platform-Second-Edition/blob/main/chapter-4/code/level_1_dag.py`.

Now, let's create our first DAG using a Python file. As a first step, we want to declare our DAG. The DAG will have information about the following:

- DAG **identifier (ID)**
- DAG owner
- Schedule
- Start date

The DAG code looks like this in Python:

```
args = {
    'owner': ' packt-developer '

packt-developer will be inside single quatations

'owner': ' packt-developer ' ,
}
with DAG(
    dag_id='hello_world_airflow',
    default_args=args,
    schedule ='0 5 * * *',
    start_date=days_ago(1),
) as dag:
```

This is a very common DAG declaration in Airflow. Do remember that a DAG has three important pieces of information: the DAG ID, the time you want to start the DAG, and the schedule—in other words, how you want to schedule the DAG. As a note, the DAG ID needs to be unique for the entire Airflow environment.

`schedule` follows the `CronJob` or `Preset` scheduling format. `Preset` is the simpler version with annotations such as `@daily` and `@weekly`, and the other options that are listed here: https://airflow.apache.org/docs/apache-airflow/1.10.1/scheduler.html#dag-runs.

`CronJob` format is a bit trickier to understand, but very common if you are familiar with Linux. It looks like this: * * * * *.

`CronJob` uses five numerical values that represent the following: minute, hour, day(month), month, and day(week). An asterisk (*) means *every*. For example, * * * * * means the DAG will run every minute, while 0 1 * * * means the DAG will run every day at 1:00 A.M.

You don't need to memorize this; you can check this website if you want to generate a `CronJob` format for your scheduled time: https://crontab.guru/.

The tricky part of the DAG is `start_date`. It's a little bit counter-intuitive if you use Airflow for the first time, so let's get an illustration of this.

Today is **January 1, 2023**, and I want to create a DAG that runs immediately today.

I want it to be scheduled every day at midnight (0 0 * * *).

What should I put as `start_date` in Airflow?

This is not the answer:

```
start_date=datetime(2023, 1, 1)
```

The correct answer is shown here:

```
start_date=datetime(2022, 12, 31)
```

Why? Airflow DAG runtime is a combination of `start_date` and `schedule`. So, if the start date is **January 1** and it is scheduled at **midnight**, Airflow will know that **midnight** on **January 1** has already passed, and will start the scheduler tomorrow, on **January 2** at **midnight**.

The same with our illustration—if we want the DAG to start immediately on **January 1**, we need to tell Airflow that the start_date value is supposed to be **December 31, 2022**, or the current day -1.

In the following code example, instead of using the exact date, we will use the `days_ago()` function:

```
days_ago(1)
```

This simply means that if you submit the DAG today for our exercise, the DAG will immediately run.

The other parameters in the DAG declaration are optional—for example, the DAG owner, handling task errors, and other parameters. We will skip these for now, but you can find out more about them in the Airflow public documentation.

After learning about DAGs, we will learn about **tasks** and **operators**. A DAG consists of one or many tasks. A task is declared using operators. As in our example code, we will use two `BashOperator` instances, and both operators will print words.

The first task will print `Hello` and the second task will print `World`, like this:

```
print_hello = BashOperator(
    task_id='print_hello',
    bash_command='echo Hello',
)
print_world= BashOperator(
    task_id='print_world',
    bash_command='echo World',
)
```

`BashOperator` is one of many operators that are available for Airflow. `BashOperator` is a simple operator for you to run Linux commands.

> **Important note**
> Do not overuse `BashOperator`. If one day you do something too complicated using `BashOperator`, review and check the available native operator.

Every operator has a task ID and other parameters, and the parameters are different for each operator. You need to check two things to use operators: first, what are the available parameters; and second, how to import the operator.

The Python library directory is not always in the same repository, so you need to check out the public documentation on how to import them. For example, for `BashOperator`, you need to import like this:

```
from airflow.operators.bash import BashOperator
```

Lastly, for the dependency, we will use a bitwise operator. Bitwise operators use `>>` to indicate task dependencies, like this:

```
print_hello >> print_world
```

A task can be dependent on more than one task—for example, if you want `task_three` to run after `task_one` and `task_two` have finished, you can do something like this:

```
[task_one, task_two] >> task_three
```

You can also add a label to the task edges, like this:

```
from airflow.utils.edgemodifier import Label
print_hello >> Label("Label 1") >> print_world
```

The label will look like this:

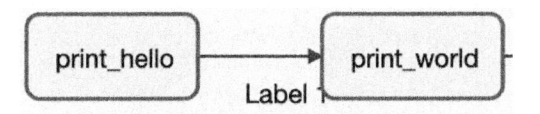

Figure 4.9 – Label in the task edge

That's it—we've learned about DAGs, tasks, and dependencies. Check out the full code example in the GitHub repository.

Now, let's deploy our DAG file into Cloud Composer.

Deploying the DAG file into Cloud Composer

To deploy our DAG Python file into Cloud Composer, we need to call the `gcloud` command from Cloud Shell, as follows:

1. Go to Cloud Shell.
2. From Cloud Shell, go to your Python file directory that contains the DAG Python file. Run the following command:

   ```
   $ cd Data-Engineering-with-Google-Cloud-Platform-Second-Edition/chapter-4/code
   ```

3. Run the following `gcloud` command:

   ```
   $ gcloud composer environments storage dags import --environment
   [Your Cloud composer environment name] --location [Your Cloud
   composer region] --source [DAG Python file].py
   ```

   As an example, this is my `gcloud` command:

   ```
   $ gcloud composer environments storage dags import --environment
   packt-composer-dev --location us-central1 --source level_1_dag.
   py
   ```

4. With that, you can check back to the Airflow web UI. A DAG called `hello_world_airflow` will be shown in the UI, as illustrated here:

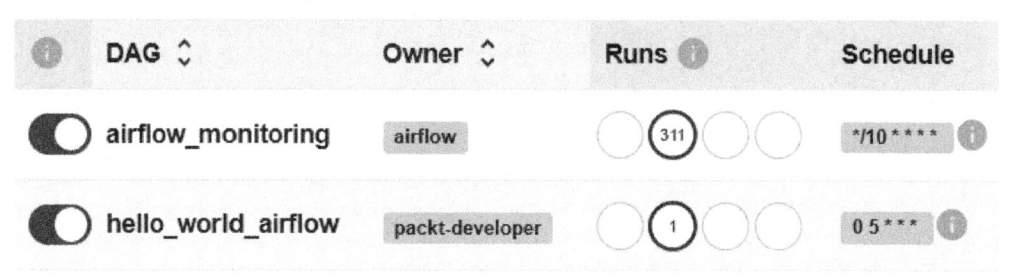

DAG	Owner	Runs	Schedule
airflow_monitoring	airflow	311	*/10 * * * *
hello_world_airflow	packt-developer	1	0 5 * * *

Figure 4.10 – Checking hello_world_airflow DAG

You can also check in your GCS bucket by checking the folder:

```
gs://[your cloud composer GCS bucket]/dags/
```

Your DAG Python file is automatically stored in the directory. Every DAG Python file in this bucket directory will be automatically deployed as Airflow DAG and shown in the web UI by Airflow.

"Automatically" here means that Airflow has a heartbeat checking for this directory. Airflow will detect any file changes in this directory and will affect the DAG without any additional steps needed.

This also applies to deletion. If you somehow delete a file inside this directory, your DAG will also be deleted, so don't do that. Instead, to delete a DAG properly, we will use the following `gcloud` command:

```
gcloud composer environments storage dags delete
    --environment [Your Cloud composer environment name]
    --location [Your Cloud composer region]
    [DAG Python file].py
```

After learning about deleting DAGs, we now want to learn some of the Airflow important buttons. To do that, let's carry out the following steps:

1. Go back to your Airflow web UI.
2. Click your `hello_world_airflow` DAG.

Exercise – build data pipeline orchestration using Cloud Composer | 125

In our DAG Run indicator buttons, remember that we will have bar and square symbols. Notice that your indicators may be different from what's shown here because of the number of successful or failed runs, and that's fine. They'll be different because your DAG run date will depend on the time you spend running this exercise. For me, the indicators look like this:

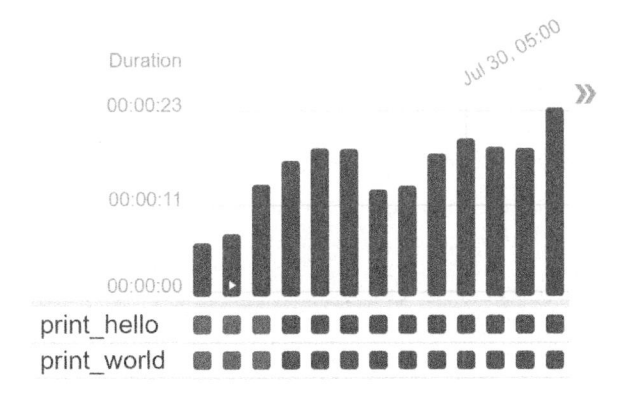

Figure 4.11 – Example DAG Run indicators

1. Now, let's click one of the bar buttons. Bar buttons are the green bars on top of the squares.

After clicking it, see the right panel, one of the most important options here is the **Clear existing tasks** button. If you click it, you will notice the green color will turn to a brighter green. This simply means your DAG will rerun. In Airflow, you can rerun a task or multiple tasks by clearing it.

If you click one of the square buttons (any one of the squares below the bar buttons), there will be two submenus: **Details** and **Logs**. Choose **Details** and you will see some options there:

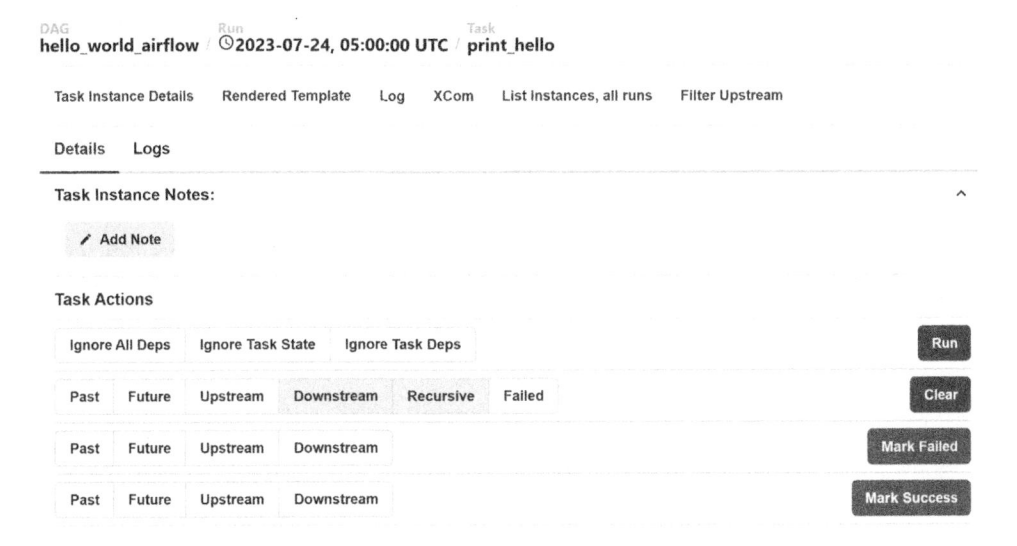

Figure 4.12 – Finding the Clear button on the task page

If you click the **Clear** button from here, your DAG will be retried or re-run in the task level, not the DAG level. It will be useful if you want to retry only one task from a whole DAG.

Another important button on this task-level page is the **Logs** button. This will show you application-level logs from each independent task. This is very important, and you will need this a lot for the development and debugging of your code.

The log is independent for each task and DAG Run level, which means that if you already have more than one DAG Run and an error occurs on a specific date, you can check a specific log on that date in a particular task to see the error message.

If, later, you find an error and need to change your DAG Python file, what you need to do is the same as when creating a new DAG using the `gcloud` command.

And since there is no DAG versioning in the latest version of Airflow, the best practice in a production environment is to label the DAG name with versions—for example, `hello_world_dag_v1`. This way, if you need to update your DAG, you will always create a new one labeled with a new version, and then delete the old one after the new version is stable.

Let's summarize what we've learned in this Level 1 exercise. In this exercise, we've learned about the basic features of Airflow. We've learned how to create a DAG with its tasks and dependencies. We deployed the DAG to Cloud Composer, and our `level_1` DAG will run on schedule, starting today. In the next exercise, we will learn how to use GCP native operators to do ELT from Cloud SQL to BigQuery.

Level 2 DAG – scheduling a pipeline from Cloud SQL to GCS and BigQuery datasets

The main goal of Level 2 DAG is for us to understand how to create a DAG specifically for doing ELT from the data source to GCS and BigQuery. GCP comes with its own native operators and is pre-installed in Cloud Composer.

In this exercise, we will create a DAG that extracts data from Cloud SQL to our GCS bucket, and from the GCS bucket to BigQuery tables. We will use the bike-sharing tables similar to our exercise in *Chapter 3, Building a Data Warehouse in BigQuery*.

Please check out the example code here: `https://github.com/PacktPublishing/Data-Engineering-with-Google-Cloud-Platform-Second-Edition/blob/main/chapter-4/code/level_2_dag.py`

In this exercise, we will need a Cloud SQL instance to demonstrate extraction using Airflow. The Cloud SQL instance and table that we need are the same as in *Chapter 3, Building a Data Warehouse in BigQuery*. So, if you haven't deleted Cloud SQL, you can skip this step. But if you have already deleted the instance, please revisit *Chapter 3* and go to the *Creating a MySQL database on Cloud SQL* section.

As a summary, this is what we need to do in the section:

1. Create a Cloud SQL instance.
2. Configure the Cloud SQL service account **identity and access management** (**IAM**) permission as `GCS Object Admin`.
3. Create a `stations` table from the MySQL console.
4. Import the `stations` table data from a **comma-separated values** (**CSV**) file.

   To check if you are ready with the instance, run this query from your MySQL console:

   ```
   SELECT * FROM apps_db.stations LIMIT 10;
   ```

   The table should be accessible and contain data, as illustrated in the following screenshot:

```
mysql> SELECT * FROM apps_db.stations LIMIT 10;
+------------+-------------------------------------------------+-----------+----------+
| station_id | name                                            | region_id | capacity |
+------------+-------------------------------------------------+-----------+----------+
| 501        | Balboa Park (San Jose Ave at Sgt. John V. Young Ln |           | 0        |
| 504        | Onondaga Ave at Alemany Blvd                    |           | 0        |
| 505        | Geneva Ave at Moscow St                         |           | 0        |
```

Figure 4.13 – Expected result from MySQL table

If you are already in this state, you are good to go to the next steps. The next steps are given here:

- Using a Cloud SQL operator to extract data to a GCS bucket
- Using GCS storage for a BigQuery operator
- Using `BigQueryOperator` for data transformation

In the next step, we will use an operator to extract data from our Cloud SQL database.

Using a Cloud SQL operator to extract data to a GCS bucket

In the Level 1 DAG exercise, we used `BashOperator`; in this Level 2 DAG, we will use GCP-specific operators. And to extract data from Cloud SQL, we can use `CloudSQLExportInstanceOperator`.

We can import the operator in Python like this:

```
from airflow.providers.google.cloud.operators.cloud_sql import CloudSQLExportInstanceOperator
```

To declare the task, the code will look like this. The operator has a few parameters that we need to provide—the Cloud SQL project ID, the Cloud SQL instance name, and the body:

```
    sql_export_task = CloudSQLExportInstanceOperator(
        task_id='sql_export_task'
        project_id=GCP_PROJECT_ID,
```

```
            body=export_body,
            instance=INSTANCE_NAME
    )
```

The body will contain information about how you want to extract your data. We can define the body using **JavaScript Object Notation (JSON)**. In this exercise, we will export the CSV file to our GCS bucket directory. The code looks like this:

```
EXPORT_URI = 'gs://[your GCS bucket]/mysql_export/from_composer/
stations/stations.csv'

SQL_QUERY = "SELECT * FROM apps_db.stations"

export_body = {
    "exportContext": {
        "fileType": "csv",
        "uri": EXPORT_URI,
        "csvExportOptions":{
            "selectQuery": SQL_QUERY
        }
    }
}
```

The operator parameters are pretty straightforward. If later we run the DAG, this task will export data from your Cloud SQL operator to the GCS bucket. Let's continue to the next step: loading data from GCS to BigQuery.

Using GCS storage for a BigQuery operator

To load data from a GCS bucket to a BigQuery table, we will use `GCSToBigQueryOperator`. You can import the operator in Python like this:

```
from airflow.providers.google.cloud.transfers.gcs_to_bigquery import
GCSToBigQueryOperator
```

This operator has some parameters that we need to provide, but if you look at it, you will notice that the parameters are actually similar to the BigQuery Python API that we worked with in *Chapter 3*, *Building a Data Warehouse in BigQuery*.

You need to define the source bucket, source objects, the table schema, write disposition, and other parameters that are available in the BigQuery Python API.

So, to load our `stations` table into BigQuery, we can define a task like this:

```
gcs_to_bq_example = GCSToBigQueryOperator(
    task_id="gcs_to_bq_example",
```

```
        bucket='{}-data-bucket'.format(GCP_PROJECT_ID),
        source_objects=
            ['mysql_export/from_composer/stations/stations.csv'],

        destination_project_dataset_table='raw_bikesharing.stations',
        schema_fields=[
            {'name': 'station_id', 'type': 'STRING',
             'mode':'NULLABLE'},
            {'name': 'name', 'type': 'STRING', 'mode': 'NULLABLE'},
            {'name': 'region_id', 'type': 'STRING',
             'mode':'NULLABLE'},
            {'name': 'capacity', 'type': 'INTEGER',
             'mode':'NULLABLE'}
        ],
        write_disposition='WRITE_TRUNCATE'
)
```

The output of this task is that a BigQuery table will be created in the target dataset with the station data in it. With this, we covered the EL part of the ELT. Next, we want to do some transformation inside BigQuery using `BigQueryInsertJobOperator`.

Using BigQueryOperator for data transformation

To transform our table, we will use `BigQueryInsertJobOperator`. Using `BigQueryInsertJobOperator`, you can trigger a query and load it to a target table. You can import the operator in Python, like this:

```
from airflow.providers.google.cloud.operators.bigquery import
BigQueryInsertJobOperator
```

As an example, do a very simple aggregation to our `stations` table. We will count the number of records in our `stations` table from the `raw_bikesharing` dataset and store it in the `dwh_bikesharing.temporary_stations_count` table. The code will look like this:

```
bq_to_bq = BigQueryInsertJobOperator(
    task_id="bq_to_bq",
    configuration={
        "query": {
            "query": "SELECT count(*) as count
                     FROM `raw_bikesharing.stations`",
            "useLegacySql": False,
            "destinationTable": {
                "projectId": GCP_PROJECT_ID,
                "datasetId": "dwh_bikesharing",
```

```
                "tableId": "temporary_stations_count"
            },
            "createDisposition": 'CREATE_IF_NEEDED',
            "writeDisposition": 'WRITE_TRUNCATE',
            "priority": "BATCH",
        }
    }
)
```

The full configuration options can be found in this public documentation: `https://cloud.google.com/bigquery/docs/reference/rest/v2/Job#JobConfigurationQuery`

I want to highlight three points in this task. The first is the `use_legacy_sql` parameter. The `use_legacy_sql` parameter by default will be set to `True`, so you need to always state `use_legacy_sql = False` to use `BigQueryInsertJobOperator`. If you are not familiar with BigQuery Legacy SQL, it's literally just a legacy language in BigQuery that you shouldn't use today. What we use today and going forward is called *standard SQL*. So, make sure to set `legacy_sql` to `False` in this operator.

The second point is the priority—the priority default value is `INTERACTIVE`. This is quite risky for our pipeline. If you check out the quota page in the BigQuery public documentation (`https://cloud.google.com/bigquery/quotas`), it states *Concurrent rate limit for interactive queries — 100 concurrent queries*.

> **Important note**
> The 100 concurrent queries quota for interactive queries will be updated with a new concept in the near future with a queuing mechanism. When you read this book, most probably the new concept has been applicable. But the idea is still the same, we should use `BATCH` for our Airflow jobs since it's the nature of our batch jobs.

Interactive query is also literally meant for interactive queries—or in other words, ad hoc queries by humans from the BigQuery console. Your ETL jobs will face issues when you have more than 100 DAG Runs running BigQuery operators at a time, but it won't happen using BATCH priority, so always set the priority value to `BATCH`.

The third point is the `query` parameter. The `query` parameter in `BigQueryInsertJobOperator` widely opens many possibilities. Notice that you can write any **Structured Query Language** (**SQL**) statement in this operator, such as `CREATE TABLE`, `UPDATE`, `INSERT`, `DELETE`, `CREATE VIEW`, and any other SQL operations. Even if you can, my suggestion is don't. The common usage pattern for this operator is to declare the transformation logic in the `query` parameter and load the data to the destination table.

Using this pattern will handle the table creation and data insertion. The configuration can be seen in `createDisposition` and `writeDisposition`, which, in our example, are configuring the jobs to create the table if needed (`CREATE_IF_NEEDED`) and write the records to the table; when records exist, they truncate the table first (`WRITE_TRUNCATE`).

If you want to delete the table, there will be a specific operator for that: `BigQueryDeleteTableOperator`.

After running the preceding task in our DAG, we will have a new `dwh_bikesharing.temporary_stations_count` table.

And with that, we will have a complete ELT process from data source to BigQuery with transformation. To chain the task dependencies, let's use the bitwise operator by writing it in our DAG Python file, as follows:

```
sql_export_task >> gcs_to_bq_example >> bq_to_bq
```

Try to construct the code as a DAG Python file and check with the full example in our GitHub repository: https://github.com/PacktPublishing/Data-Engineering-with-Google-Cloud-Platform-Second-Edition/blob/main/chapter-4/code/level_2_dag.py.

Deploy the DAG to Cloud Composer and check if the DAG is running successfully. As an example, this is the `gcloud` command that I call from Cloud Shell:

```
$ cd Data-Engineering-with-Google-Cloud-Platform-Second-Edition/chapter-4/code
$ gcloud composer environments storage dags import --environment packt-gcp-data-eng-env --location us-central1 --source level_2_dag.py
```

If there are some errors, you can check the red indicators in DAG or task level, check the logs, and review the steps in this section.

Sometimes, the Cloud SQL extract task will fail because of parallel tasks running at the same time. If you find that issue, try to rerun the failed DAG Run. Remember that you just need to click the red bar indicator, then find the **Clear existing tasks** button. The entire DAG Run will be rerun after that.

Things to be avoided in BigQuery DAG

In this Level 2 DAG exercise, you might already have a good understanding of how to use Airflow for BigQuery. You can use Airflow for loading, transforming, or maybe later exporting BigQuery data to other storage.

Even though the code is simple and straightforward, using Python as a configuration file is very risky in the sense that you can do literally anything in the Airflow DAG using Python.

An extreme case would be to call a **machine learning** (**ML**) library or `matplotlib` in the DAG Python file and run it in the DAG as a Python application. This doesn't make sense since it's an extreme example.

But, surprisingly, I found out there are common bad practices that people do on using Python for Airflow DAG. Let's talk about that next.

Avoid using the BigQuery Python library

In the DAG Python file, you can import the BigQuery Python library to load data to BigQuery—for example, like this:

```
from google.cloud import bigquery
client = bigquery.Client()
. . .
query_job = client.query(sql, job_config=job_config)
```

Even if you can, don't. Always use the BigQuery native operators in Airflow for any BigQuery actions whenever possible, even though under the hood, both using Airflow operators and using BigQuery Python clients calling the same BigQuery API.

There are three main benefits of only using the operators, outlined as follows:

- Your code will be simpler, standardized, and easy to read as a configuration
- The operators handle the BigQuery client connections for you
- The operators will handle the logging for you

Remember that in Airflow, we use Python for DAG configuration, not to code applications. In this case, standardization and simplicity are very important.

If there are edge cases that you need to perform in Airflow, it's also common to use `PythonOperator`. Similarly, in general, don't overuse this operator when there is a native operator alternative. While using it is very common and doable, it leads to bad practice risks, such as downloading unnecessary data, which we will cover next.

Avoid downloading data to Cloud Composer

Using Python, you can download data from any database or storage. For our example in this exercise, you can download data from a MySQL database, GCS files, and BigQuery. For example, in the DAG Python code, if you ignore the previous recommendation, you can call the GCS client and download files like this:

```
from google.cloud import storage
storage_client = storage.Client()
. . .
blob.download_to_filename(destination_file_name)
```

The same thing can happen for MySQL and BigQuery. Even if you can, don't.

You don't want to download the files to Cloud Composer workers in general. Cloud Composer and Airflow are not storage systems. If you download files in the DAG Python script, it will download to the underlying **virtual machine** (**VM**) hard disks, which is limited, and you don't want that.

Another common example is to load a BigQuery table to a pandas DataFrame in Python. Even though it's not downloading the data to a hard disk, loading data to pandas means your code will download the table to the workers' memories. In both scenarios, you may have a Cloud Composer issue such as out-of-memory or hard disk full errors for all of your DAGs.

Avoid processing data in Python

Airflow is a workflow management tool or **orchestrator**. The main responsibility of an orchestration tool is to trigger jobs and let other systems process the job. This is a special case of using Airflow for orchestrating big data.

What does this mean? Similar to the previous recommendation, one bad practice that might happen is to process big data in Cloud Composer workers. For example, you might be tempted to process data from BigQuery or GCS quickly using pandas because of its simplicity, and an Airflow DAG allows you to do that.

But never do that for big data. The Cloud Composer workers won't be powerful enough to process the data volume.

In this exercise, we learned how to do a proper ELT process using GCP native operators. We've learned that every GCP service has native operators in Airflow, and for each service, there are specific operators for each task operation. For example, in BigQuery, you can use `GCStoBigQueryOperator` to load data, `BigQueryInsertJobOperator` to transform tables, and `BigQueryDeleteTableOperator` to delete tables.

Using the native operators will help you simplify your DAG Python code, and on top of that, you will avoid carrying out bad practices that may happen in Airflow.

At this point, you can use the Level 2 DAG code to do any data loading to BigQuery for your needs, but we can improve the code for implementing more best practices on data loading to BigQuery. So, let's move on to Level 3 DAG.

Level 3 DAG – parameterized variables

The main goal of Level 3 DAG is for us to load the more tables from our bike-sharing data. When loading more than one table, we might realize there are variables that we can parameterize to improve our DAG code. Also, in this exercise, we need to start paying more attention to the table's time values, since we will load trip data that has time information in it.

Please check out the example code here: `https://github.com/PacktPublishing/Data-Engineering-with-Google-Cloud-Platform-Second-Edition/blob/main/chapter-4/code/level_3_dag.py`

In addition, we will also use JSON schema files for our BigQuery tables, which you can obtain from here: `https://github.com/PacktPublishing/Data-Engineering-with-Google-Cloud-Platform-Second-Edition/tree/main/chapter-4/code/schema`

You can check the `level_3_dag.py` code to get familiar with it, but at this point, you don't need to deploy the DAG because before continuing the practice, we will learn some fundamental concepts and Cloud Composer features in the next section.

Understanding types of variables in Cloud Composer

In the Level 2 DAG exercise, we have some variables that are hardcoded in the DAG script—for example, `GCP_PROJECT_ID`, `INSTANCE_NAME`, `EXPORT_URI`, and `SQL_QUERY`.

Imagine a scenario where you already have a pipeline running in your current Cloud Composer project. Your infrastructure team says that you need to migrate your Cloud Composer cluster to another project for some reason. What do you need to do?

You will need to move all the DAG code from the GCS bucket to the new project. But don't forget that because the variable is hardcoded, you need to change all the `GCP_PROJECT_ID` variables manually one by one for each script.

Are there any better ways to do that? Yes—using variables.

We have three options for declaring variables, as follows:

- DAG variables
- Airflow variables
- Environment variables

> **Important note**
> There is a fourth way to declare variables for sensitive information, by using GCP Secret Manager. This approach is very useful to prevent leaving sensitive variables unprotected, for example, for declaring keys or passwords. But this approach will not be covered in this book to prevent too much configuration and complexity for learning Airflow. The public documentation for this approach is well documented here: https://cloud.google.com/composer/docs/composer-2/configure-secret-manager.

The first option, DAG variables are variables that we have already used in our Level 1 and Level 2 exercises. The variables live in the DAG script and are applicable only to the DAG.

The higher-level variables are Airflow variables. You can call Airflow variables from all of your DAG.

Let's create one by following these steps:

1. Go to the Airflow web UI.
2. In the top menu bar, find and click on **Admin | Variables**, as illustrated in the following screenshot:

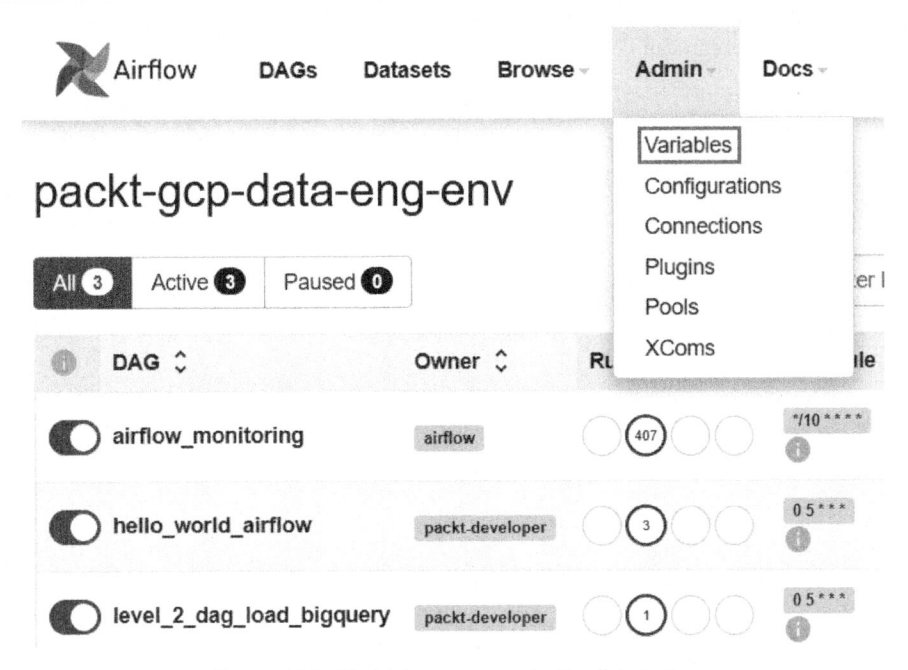

Exercise – build data pipeline orchestration using Cloud Composer 135

Figure 4.14 – Variables menu under the Admin bar

3. On the Airflow **Variables** page, let's create a new variable by clicking the + button.
4. The variable is a key-value pair. In the key, input `level_3_dag_settings`.
5. In the **Val** value, input the following:

   ```
   {"gcs_source_data_bucket":"[YOUR GCP PROJECT ID]-data-bucket",
   "bq_raw_dataset":"raw_bikesharing", "bq_dwh_dataset":"dwh_
   bikesharing" }
   ```

6. And finally, click the **Save** button.

In the example, we want to parameterize the GCS bucket name and BigQuery datasets. These variables might be helpful for other DAGs in the future, so defining them as Airflow variables is a better practice than using DAG variables.

Notice that the value is defined as a JSON string. This is the recommendation, rather than declaring each parameter as individual Airflow variables—for example, key: `bq_dwh_dataset`; value: `dwh_bikesharing`. It is not mandatory to follow this pattern, but it's better for Airflow performance.

In the backend, Airflow has an internal application database. Every Airflow variable needs an independent database connection when we call it from a DAG. If we have too many variables, then we might open too many database connections for each DAG. If we are using JSON, as we are in this example, we will only open one database connection for each DAG.

Now, in your DAG, you can call the variables like this:

```
from airflow.models import Variable

# Airflow Variables
settings = Variable.get("level_3_dag_settings", deserialize_json=True)

# DAG Variables
gcs_source_data_bucket = settings['gcs_source_data_bucket']
bq_raw_dataset = settings['bq_raw_dataset']
bq_dwh_dataset = settings['bq_dwh_dataset']
```

The code will call the Airflow variables and get the value for our three DAG variables. This way, if the GCS bucket needs to change or the BigQuery dataset is renamed, we just need to change the Airflow variable.

The last and broadest-level variables are environment variables. You can set an environment variable in the Cloud Composer UI. Follow this step to add one:

1. Go to the **Cloud Composer Console** web page.
2. Choose your Cloud Composer environment—for example, mine is `packt-gcp-data-eng-env`.
3. Find the **ENVIRONMENT VARIABLES** button and click it.
4. Click **Edit**.
5. On the **Environment variables** page, click **ADD ENVIRONMENT VARIABLE**.
6. For **Input Name**, insert `MYSQL_INSTANCE_NAME` (all in uppercase).
7. For **Input Value**, insert `mysql-instance` (your Cloud SQL instance name).
8. Click **Save**.

Wait a couple of minutes. After finishing, the environment variables will be available for you. For illustration, this is the **Environment variables** page:

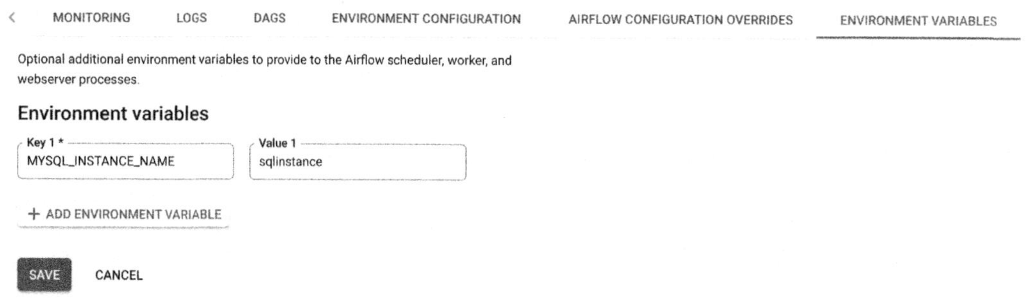

Figure 4.15 – Add Environment variables from Cloud Composer

To use it in your DAG, you can load the variables like this:

```
import os
# Environment Variables
gcp_project_id = os.environ.get('GCP_PROJECT')
instance_name  = os.environ.get('MYSQL_INSTANCE_NAME')
```

> **Important note**
>
> Setting the environment variable in Cloud Composer may take time after we click the **Save** button. It may take 10-15 minutes.
>
> On rare occasions, setting environment variables in Cloud Composer 2 may fail. Please try again if that happens. If it still fails, for the purpose of the exercise, you can hardcode `gcp_project_id` and `instance_name` manually in the code.

We use `MYSQL_INSTANCE_NAME` and `GCP_PROJECT` as variables. You will notice that you never added `GCP_PROJECT` in the previous step. This is because Cloud Composer already provides some default environment variables, and one of them is `GCP_PROJECT`. The variable will return the gcp project ID where the Cloud Composer environment is located.

For the list of predefined environment variables from Cloud Composer, please check out the public documentation: https://cloud.google.com/composer/docs/how-to/managing/environment-variables.

You will get the benefit of using environment variables when you need to declare the parameter with the DAG deployment. For example, in our `gcloud` command, you can input an environment variable as one of the arguments, like this:

```
gcloud beta composer environments create --env-variables=['MYSQL_INSTANCE_NAME'='mysql_instance']
```

This way, you can adjust the variable each time you deploy a DAG.

In the next section, we will add macro variables, which are different from environment variables.

Introducing Airflow macro variables

Airflow macro variables are variables that return information about the DAG Run. For example, you can get the execution date, DAG ID, and task ID. You can see a full list of macros in the Airflow public documentation at the following link: https://airflow.apache.org/docs/apache-airflow/stable/macros-ref.html

One variable that is essential for our data pipeline is the execution date. This is a very important and useful variable that you should use to build your data pipeline. To use the execution date in a DAG, you can use this code:

```
# Macros
logical_date = '{{ ds }}'
```

`{{ ds }}` is an Airflow macro. When you use that format in your DAG, Airflow will render into a value such as `'2023-08-04'`.

Now, let's understand better what the logical date is. In Airflow, remember that in a DAG, you declare two pieces of time information: `start_date` and `schedule`. The start date doesn't always mean the current date; the start date is the time when you expect the DAG to be run the first time. You can choose to use dates in the past, and that means Airflow will run the DAG from past dates.

For example, today is `2023-08-04`.

You define the `start_date` value in the DAG as `2023-08-01`.

Then, there are two different dates that you need to differentiate, as follows:

- The real human world time at which the DAG runs
- The expected time when you need the DAG to be run

The first one will be called the DAG start date, and the second one will be called the logical date.

If we set the schedule interval to run daily, starting from today, you will see in your DAG that your DAG start date is `2023-08-01`, there will be four DAG Runs with four execution dates from `2023-08-01` to `2023-08-04`.

Back to the `ds` macro, in your DAG, you can use this variable to get your expected date value rather than today's date, which is very helpful for loading data from the past.

In my own experience, I found that this concept is hard to digest the first time without really practicing it. So, at this point, just be aware that you will see in the example code that we will use Airflow macros such as `{{ }}`, and that means we want to use the DAG Run information for our operator parameters.

Loading bike-sharing tables using Airflow

After learning some new concepts, let's continue our code development. In the previous exercise, we created our tasks for loading the `stations` table. Next, we will create tasks for loading `regions` and `trips` tables.

The `regions` table will be loaded from a GCS bucket, and for the `trips` table, we will extract from the BigQuery public dataset this time. The DAG will look like this:

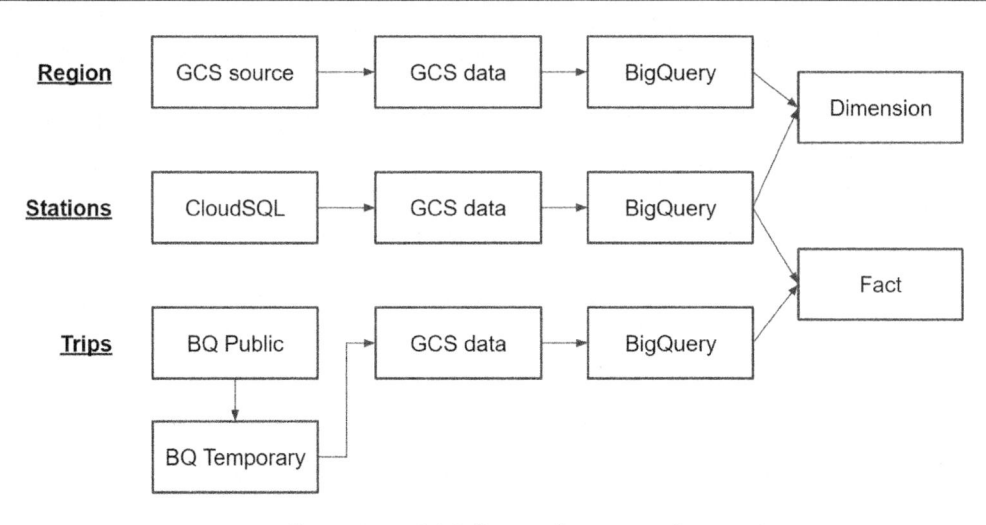

Exercise – build data pipeline orchestration using Cloud Composer

Figure 4.16 – DAG diagram for our exercise

To load region data from GCS, we will use `GCSToGCSOperator`. The code looks like this:

```
### Load Region Table ###
gcs_to_gcs_region = GCSToGCSOperator(
        task_id = 'gcs_to_gcs_region',
        source_bucket = gcs_source_data_bucket,
        source_object = gcs_regions_source_object,
        destination_bucket = gcs_source_data_bucket,
        destination_object = gcs_regions_target_object
)
```

The code will transfer data from one source to the destination object. The rest of the code is the same as for the `stations` table. Check the example code in the repository to review your code.

For the `trips` table, the case will be a little bit non-realistic here. We will load data from BigQuery to BigQuery, from the public dataset to our `raw_bikesharing` dataset. In reality, we can simply use `BigQueryInsertJobOperator` to load the data in a single task. But for the purpose of our practice, we will see the BigQuery public dataset as an external database. So, we will extract the table from the public dataset to the GCS bucket and load data from the GCS bucket to our BigQuery dataset. The idea is that you can reuse this pattern if the data source is not BigQuery. You can apply the same pattern to data from different databases such as **Cloud SQL**, **Oracle**, **Hadoop**, or any other data source.

To do that, we will create a temporary BigQuery dataset to store `trips` daily data using the `bq` command. Follow these steps:

1. Open Cloud Shell.

2. Run this command in Cloud Shell:

```
bq --location=us mk \
--dataset \
[your gcp project id]:temporary_staging
```

3. In our DAG, we will add `BigQueryInsertJobOperator` to extract the table to this temporary dataset, as follows:

```
### Load Trips Table ###
    bq_to_bq_temporary_trips = BigQueryInsertJobOperator(
      task_id='bq_to_bq_temporary_trips',
      configuration={
        "query": {
          "query": f"""SELECT * FROM `bigquery-public-data.san_
            francisco_bikeshare.bikeshare_trips`
            WHERE DATE(start_date) = DATE('{logical_date}')""",
          "useLegacySql": False,
          "destinationTable": {
              "projectId": gcp_project_id,
              "datasetId": bq_temporary_extract_dataset_
                name,
              "tableId": f"{bq_temporary_extract_table_
                name}_{logical_date_nodash}"
          },
          "createDisposition": 'CREATE_IF_NEEDED',
          "writeDisposition": 'WRITE_TRUNCATE',
          "priority": "BATCH",
        }
      }
    )
```

4. Notice that in the SQL query, we use the `{ logical_date }` variable. That's the variable from this line of code:

```
logical_date = '{{ ds }}'
```

5. The task will create a table in the `raw_bikesharing` dataset.

6. Lastly, we will store the temporary table in a GCS bucket, as follows:

```
bq_to_gcs_extract_trips = BigQueryToGCSOperator(
    task_id='bq_to_gcs_extract_trips',
    source_project_dataset_table=bq_temporary_table_id,
    destination_cloud_storage_uris=[gcs_trips_source_uri],
```

```
                    force_rerun=True,
                    print_header=False,
                    export_format='CSV')
```

After this task, you will have your `trips` data in the GCS bucket, and the rest of the steps are similar to the other tables.

The other improvement that we can make in this Level 3 DAG example is to centralize our BigQuery schema in the GCS bucket. For example, in the Level 2 DAG example, we hardcoded `schema_fields` in the DAG code.

In the Level 3 DAG example, the schema is loaded from JSON files. In order to do that, follow these steps:

1. Check the table schema files from this directory:

    `/chapter-4/code/schema/*`

2. Upload all the files into GCS in this specific bucket:

    `[Cloud Composer Bucket]/data/schema/*`

    For example, after making sure you are in `chapter-4/code/` directory, you can use the `gcloud` command from Cloud Shell like this:

    `$ gcloud storage cp -r /chapter-4/code/schema/* gs://[Cloud Composer Bucket]/data/schema/`

    The command will copy the schema files from the Cloud Shell environment to the GCS bucket. If there is an error in your environment, check if you called the command in the correct directory. You should call the command from your `git` folder.

3. In the DAG code, we need to read the JSON file—for example, using the self-defined `read_json_schema` function. This function can be found in the `level_3_dag.py` example code.

4. Lastly, the schema in the DAG can be defined like this:

    ```
    bq_trips_table_schema = read_json_schema("/home/airflow/gcs/
    data/schema/trips_schema.json")
    ```

With this improvement, we learned two things. First, we learned that we can store files in the `gs://[Cloud Composer Bucket]/data` directory and we can read the files from our DAG. Second, we can manage the schema better outside of the code, so in case we want to change the table schema, we can update the JSON files instead of the DAG files.

Try to continue the code development yourself and check out the example code in the GitHub repository.

Lastly, try to continue the tasks to the transformation step by creating `fact_trips_daily` and `dim_stations` tables. The explanation and the SQL queries of both tables can be found in *Chapter 3, Building a Data Warehouse in BigQuery*, in the *Creating fact and dimension tables* section. For the DAG, as we've discussed, you can use `BigQueryInsertJobOperator` to handle these tasks.

There is one more thing that I want to introduce in this Level 3 DAG example, which is `BigQueryCheckOperator`. `BigQueryCheckOperator` is an operator that will check whether a condition is met by the query result or not. For example, we want to know if our `fact_trips_daily` table contains any records or not. We can add the operator like this:

```
bq_row_count_check_dwh_fact_trips_daily = BigQueryCheckOperator(
task_id='bq_row_count_check_dwh_fact_trips_daily',
sql=f"""
select count(*) from `{bq_fact_trips_daily_table_id}`
""",
use_legacy_sql=False)
```

The operator will trigger a query to BigQuery and check the result from the query `count(*)` to the table. If the result is 0, the task will fail, and your DAG will be marked as failed. This is very simple checking but is helpful for making sure your ELT process is successful downstream.

In the code, try to do the same thing with the `dim_stations` table. So, at the end of the DAG, we will have two checkers to make sure the table is loaded with records.

Handling dependencies for our bike-sharing tasks

To handle the task dependencies, we will use bitwise operators, as usual. But since our tasks are a lot more complicated than the Level 2 DAG example, we will review how we should do that. Firstly, take a look at the full task dependency code:

```
export_mysql_station >> gcs_to_bq_station
gcs_to_gcs_region >> gcs_to_bq_region
bq_to_bq_temporary_trips >> bq_to_gcs_extract_trips >> gcs_to_bq_trips

[gcs_to_bq_station,gcs_to_bq_region,gcs_to_bq_trips] >> dwh_fact_
trips_daily >> bq_row_count_check_dwh_fact_trips_daily

[gcs_to_bq_station,gcs_to_bq_region,gcs_to_bq_trips] >> dwh_dim_
stations >> bq_row_count_check_dwh_dim_stations
```

Our sets of tasks and the preceding bitwise instructions will generate this DAG:

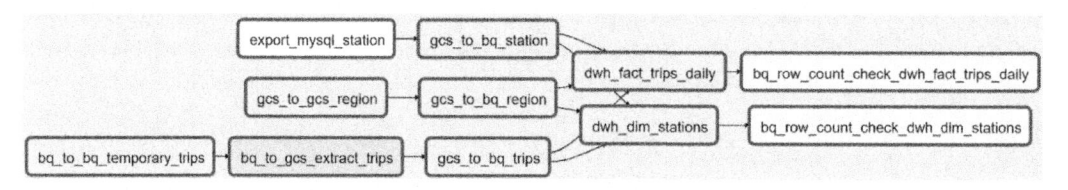

Figure 4.17 – DAG graph view for trips and stations data

Notice that we introduce multiple task dependencies here. For example, `dwh_fact_trips_daily` and `dwh_dim_stations` will only start when all the `gcs_to_bq` tasks are finished. To do that, we use brackets, like this:

```
[gcs_to_bq_station,gcs_to_bq_region,gcs_to_bq_trips] >> dwh_fact_
trips_daily
```

This bitwise operator means that `dwh_fact_trips_daily` will only run after the three tasks in the bracket are finished.

In this exercise, we improved our DAG by utilizing variables. Variables are a very important element in Airflow. You will find using variables more and more important after creating many DAGs, tasks, and dependencies. Using variables allows you to think about automation. It's a very common practice to create DAG templates and think that you only need to change the variables, so this will be very helpful in speeding up your development time. Before continuing to our Level 4 DAG example, we need to understand the three Airflow features.

Understanding Airflow backfilling, rerun, and catchup

In a data pipeline, we often need to handle data from the past. This is a very common scenario in data engineering. Most of the time, applications as data sources are created before a data lake or data warehouse, so we need to load data from the past. There are three main terms relating to this.

The first one is **backfilling**. Backfilling happens when you need to load data from the past.

For illustration, imagine in a real-life scenario you already run a data pipeline for *7 days* starting from 2023-01-10, without any issue. For some reason, your end user asked you to also load data from 2023-01-03. This is a backfilling scenario. In this case, you need to load the historical data without changing or disturbing your running data pipeline, as illustrated in the following diagram:

Figure 4.18 – Backfill illustration

In Cloud Composer, you can run backfilling using the `gcloud` command, like this:

```
gcloud composer environments run \ ${your_composer_environment_name} \
--location [your composer environment region] \
dags backfill -- -s [your backfill start date] \
-e [your backfill end date] [your dag id]
```

144 Building Workflows for Batch Data Loading Using Cloud Composer

If you run the preceding command, Airflow will trigger DAG Runs for the given date. Remember our section about using Airflow macros for getting the `logical_date` variable? The `logical_date` variable will return the backfill date.

The second one is a **rerun**. A rerun happens when you need to reload data from the past. The difference between a rerun and a backfill is that a rerun works for a DAG or tasks that have run before. The scenario of using a rerun is when a DAG or tasks have failed, so you need to rerun them, as illustrated in the following diagram:

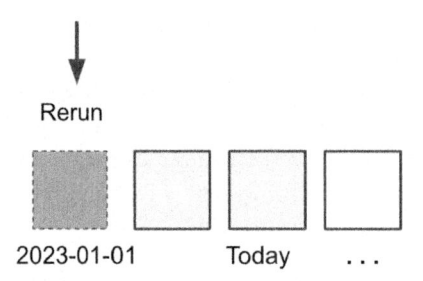

Figure 4.19 – Rerun illustration

You can trigger a rerun from the Airflow web UI. In the web UI, if you click **Clear** in either the DAG or task indicator (in the DAG **Grid View**), the DAG or task will retry, and that's what we call a rerun. A second option is using the `gcloud` command, like this:

```
gcloud composer environments run \
[your composer environment name] \
   --location [your composer environment region] \
dags clear -- [your dag id] \
-t [your tasks id or regex] \
-s [your start date] -d [your end date]
```

The command will trigger a rerun of the specific DAG and tasks.

The third one is a **catchup**. A catchup happens when you deploy a DAG for the first time. A catchup is a process when Airflow automatically triggers multiple DAG Runs to load all expected date data. It's similar to a backfill, but the trigger happens automatically as intended, as illustrated in the following diagram:

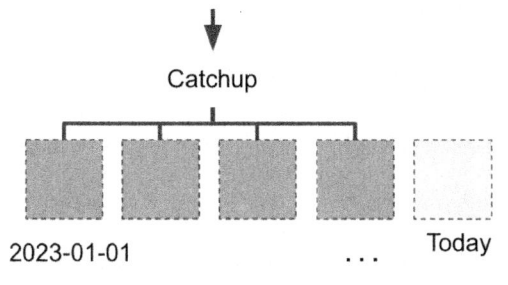

Figure 4.20 – Catchup illustration

For example, today is 2023-01-07.

You declare the `start_date` value of a DAG is 2023-01-01.

When you deploy the first time, there will be seven DAG Runs automatically running: 2023-01-01 to 2023-01-07. These DAG runs are the catchups.

The preceding scenario is by default how Airflow works for your DAG, but you can disable that behavior. You can set the catchup to `False` in your DAG declaration—for example, like this:

```
with DAG(
    dag_id='example_dag',
    start_date=datetime(2023, 1, 1),
    catchup=False
) as dag:
```

If you set the `catchup` parameter to `False` in your DAG, the catchup won't run.

These three Airflow features are very important and highly relevant to real-world scenarios. Whether you are in the development phase or in production mode, you will use these features.

Back to our Level 3 DAG exercise, if a rerun happens to our DAG, that will be an issue with the current code. Why?

Take a look at our GCS to BigQuery task for the `trips` table:

```
gcs_to_bq_trips = GCSToBigQueryOperator(
. . .
destination_project_dataset_table = bq_trips_table_id,
schema_fields = bq_trips_table_schema,
write_disposition = 'WRITE_APPEND'
)
```

See that in our `write_disposition` parameter, the task will append the target table with data from the source every time the DAG runs. This is fine only if the DAG runs once for every `logical_date` parameter. What will happen if we rerun the DAG at any date? The data will be duplicated.

A good task in a DAG is a task that can run and produce the same result every time it runs, and there is a term for this: **task idempotency**.

For illustration, imagine you have five empty glasses, and you are filling them with water one at a time.

First, you pour the first glass, the second glass, and the third glass. Someone stopped you and said, there is dirt in the first glass and you need to refill it. How will you do that?

If you do the exact same action as the first time, which is pouring the water in the filled first glass, it will be overflown. This example illustrates a task that is not idempotent, meaning that if you perform the same task on the glass, the end result of doing the exact same action is different.

An idempotent task will always empty the glass before pouring and filling the water. We will learn how to make sure the task in our DAG code is idempotent for the Level 4 DAG exercise.

Level 4 DAG – Guaranteeing task idempotency in Cloud Composer

The main goal of Level 4 DAG is for us to make sure that our tasks are idempotent. More specifically, we will modify our tasks for loading `trips` tables, to make sure there will be no duplication when we rerun the DAG.

Please download the example code from here: https://github.com/PacktPublishing/Data-Engineering-with-Google-Cloud-Platform-Second-Edition/blob/main/chapter-4/code/level_4_dag.py

Understanding what task idempotency means

Let's understand more about the task idempotency by way of illustration in the BigQuery table.

Let's say we have a DAG; the DAG will load an `event` table from GCS to BigQuery.

The expected start date is `2023-01-01`. The current date is `2023-01-03`.

The schedule interval is `daily`. In this scenario, if we use the `WRITE_APPEND` method, the files from GCS bucket directories will be loaded to BigQuery tables. For an illustration of this, check out the following diagram:

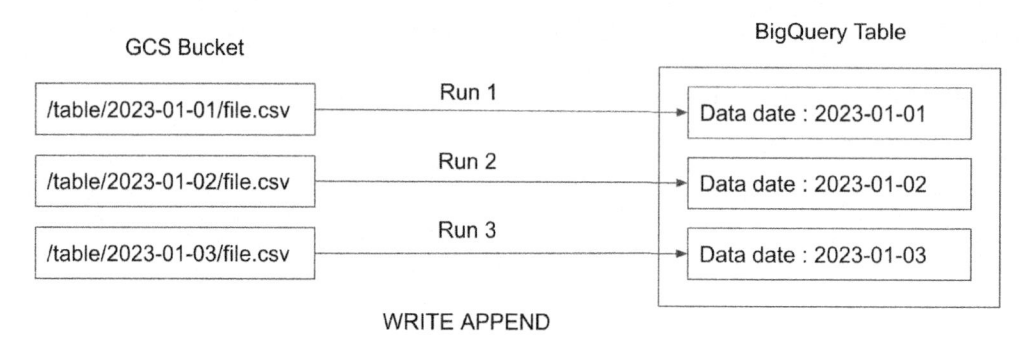

Figure 4.21 – WRITE_APPEND method illustration

Now, if the DAG needs to be rerun for `2023-01-02`, then the data loading task from that date will run for a second time. The problem is that, because the method is `WRITE_APPEND`, then the data from GCS will be appended to the BigQuery table, and the date will be duplicated on the second run, like this:

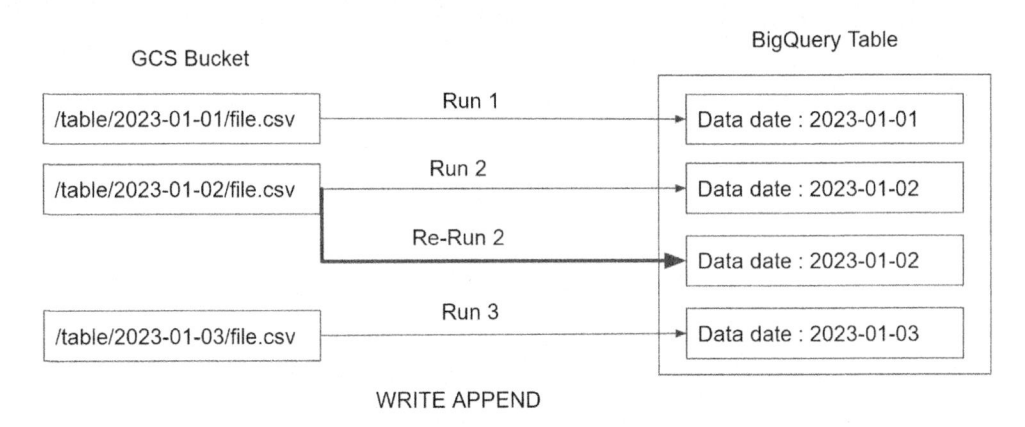

Figure 4.22 – WRITE_APPEND method with rerun illustration

The solution is using `WRITE_TRUNCATE` instead of `WRITE_APPEND` for the write disposition parameter. Using `WRITE_TRUNCATE` and changing the GCS directory source using a wildcard will load every file from the GCS bucket in the /table/ directory to the BigQuery table, and every time there is a new DAG Run, the BigQuery table will be reloaded without duplication.

As an illustration, this diagram shows data being loaded from the GCS bucket to the BigQuery table using a wildcard (*):

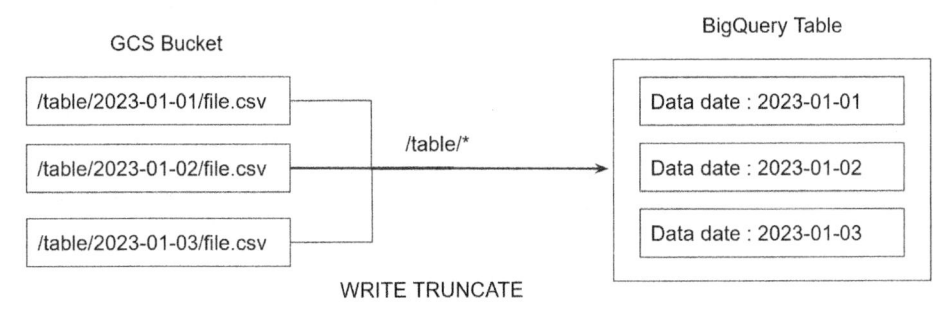

Figure 4.23 – WRITE_TRUNCATE method illustration

If you implement the `WRITE TRUNCATE` method, your task will be idempotent, which means that every time there is a rerun for any date, the data in BigQuery will be truncated first before writing the records. This will make sure the table always is correct without duplication. The BigQuery table won't have repeated data since the records will be reloaded on each DAG Run. But is this a best practice? The answer is: *not yet*.

This is not yet the best practice. Using this approach, you will notice that the BigQuery table will be rewritten over and over again for the whole table. If you have a table that's 1 **terabyte** (**TB**) in size and the DAG already runs for 1 year, Airflow will rewrite 1 TB of data 365 times. We don't want that—we need the BigQuery partition tables to improve this approach.

Refreshing the concept of BigQuery partitioning and its relevance to Airflow DAG

Back to *Chapter 3, Building a Data Warehouse in BigQuery*. We've learned about BigQuery partitioning, where we can configure BigQuery to store data partitioned by date.

Under the hood of BigQuery storage, a table can be divided based on a `Date` column, like this:

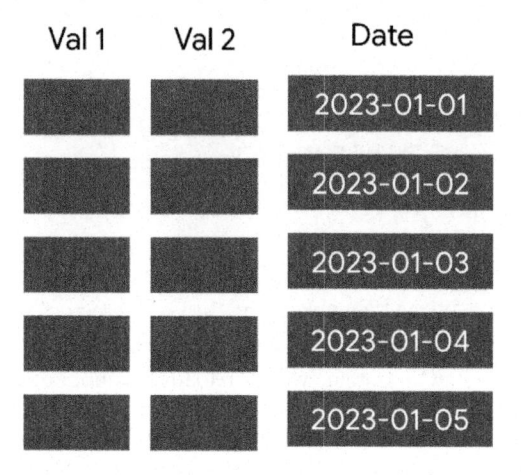

Figure 4.24 – BigQuery rows and columns example

Every table record will be stored in a separate storage location. This is theoretically the same as having multiple tables with the same schemas. But you don't need to worry about this as BigQuery will handle it seamlessly.

What you can do as a user is to access the table, and filter the table using the `partition` column, like this:

```
SELECT val1
FROM example_table
WHERE date = '2023-01-03';
```

The query will only access a partial amount of data from the table, which is the `val1` column at `2023-01-03`.

Back to our exercise—at this point, we will use the BigQuery partitioned table to help us optimize the `WRITE_TRUNCATE` issue. We will still use `WRITE_TRUNCATE` rather than `WRITE_APPEND` disposition, but we will only write and truncate the table for a specific partition. This way, we don't need to rewrite the entire table every time the DAG runs.

In the next section, we will use what we've learned about BigQuery partitioned tables and the `WRITE_TRUNCATE` method in our DAG.

Airflow jobs that follow task idempotency for incremental load

Please take a look at our example code and check the difference between the `level_3_dag.py` and `level_4_dag.py` files.

First, we want to use the Airflow macro that returns the logical date but with no dash like this: `20230101`. The macro is `ds_nodash`, as illustrated here:

```
logical_date_nodash = '{{ ds_nodash }}'
```

Now, in the `trips` table, notice that `bq_trips_table_id` has a postfix in the `level_4_dag.py` file:

```
destination_project_dataset_table = bq_trips_table_id + f"${logical_date_nodash}",
```

With this, the destination table ID will look like this:

```
project.raw_bikesharing.trips$20230101
```

The $ postfix followed by the date means that you are targeting a specific table partitioned to load your data. In the preceding example, you will load data to the `trips` table at the `2023-01-01` partition.

In the `gcs` source object, we also want to use this extracted date information to get the daily data from a specific GCS directory, like this:

```
gcs_trips_source_object = f"chapter-4/trips/{logical_date_nodash}/*.csv"
```

Finally, in `GCSToBigQueryOperator`, we will modify the parameters a little bit. We add the `time_partitioning` parameter by `DAY` on the `start_date` field, as follows:

```
time_partitioning = {'time_partitioning_type':'DAY',
                     'field': 'start_date'}
```

This means that our `trips` table will be partitioned using a time-unit column, which is the `start_date` column, and the granularity of the partition is `DAY`.

Now this is our full task code, we will keep `write_disposition` set to `WRITE_TRUNCATE`, as follows:

```
gcs_to_bq_trips = GCSToBigQueryOperator(
        task_id="gcs_to_bq_trips",
        bucket=gcs_source_data_bucket,
        source_objects=[gcs_trips_source_object],
        destination_project_dataset_table=bq_trips_table_id +
            f"${logical_date_nodash}",
        schema_fields=bq_trips_table_schema,
```

```
        time_partitioning={
            'time_partitioning_type': 'DAY', 'field': 'start_date'},
        write_disposition='WRITE_TRUNCATE',
        create_disposition='CREATE_IF_NEEDED',
        force_rerun=True
    )
```

With this, every time there is a rerun on a particular date, the table partition will be rewritten, but again, only on a specific partition date, as illustrated in the following diagram:

```
         GCS Bucket                                BigQuery Table
                                                     Partitions

   /table/2023-01-01/file.csv    ───────▶   Data date : 2023-01-01

   /table/2023-01-02/file.csv    ───────▶   Data date : 2023-01-02

   /table/2023-01-03/file.csv    ───────▶   Data date : 2023-01-03

                              WRITE TRUNCATE
```

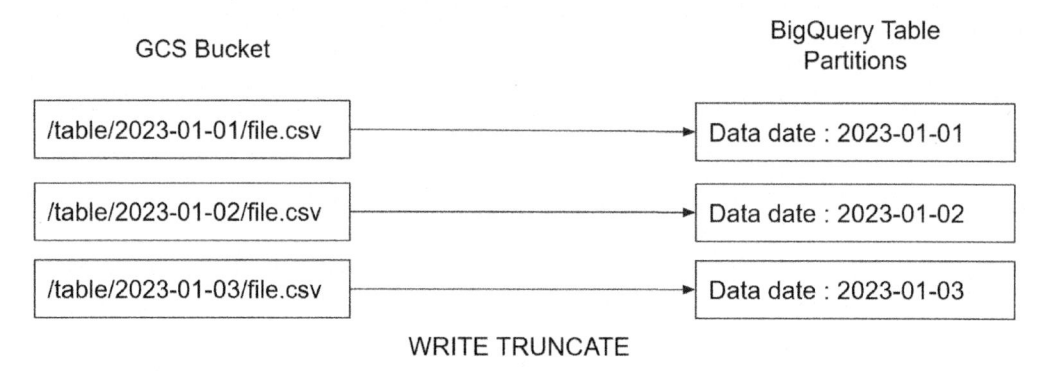

Figure 4.25 – WRITE_TRUNCATE method with BigQuery partitioned table illustration

With this, your DAG and all tasks are idempotent. Imagine that you want to retry any tasks on any expected day—in that case, you do not need to worry. The tasks are safe to rerun and there will be no data duplication, thanks to the `WRITE_TRUNCATE` method. And also, for the `partitioned_by` date, the table will only rewrite the records on the rerun execution day.

Level 5 DAG – handling DAG dependency using an Airflow dataset

The main goal of Level 5 DAG is for us to understand DAG dependencies or data-aware scheduling. It means being able to create a flexible DAG runtime depending on the upstream data arrival.

In this exercise, we will use one of the Airflow features called dataset. Don't be confused by the name, because the feature does not actually refer to any sets of data. For example, it has nothing to do with the BigQuery dataset.

This feature is relatively new, released in Airflow 2.4. The feature is a successor to sensors in the earlier versions. Both features are helpful for constructing a group of DAGs that depend on each other, and also for handling late data.

First, let's understand that in practice an organization may have more than one DAG to run an end-to-end data pipeline. For example, let's say we have a data architecture such as this:

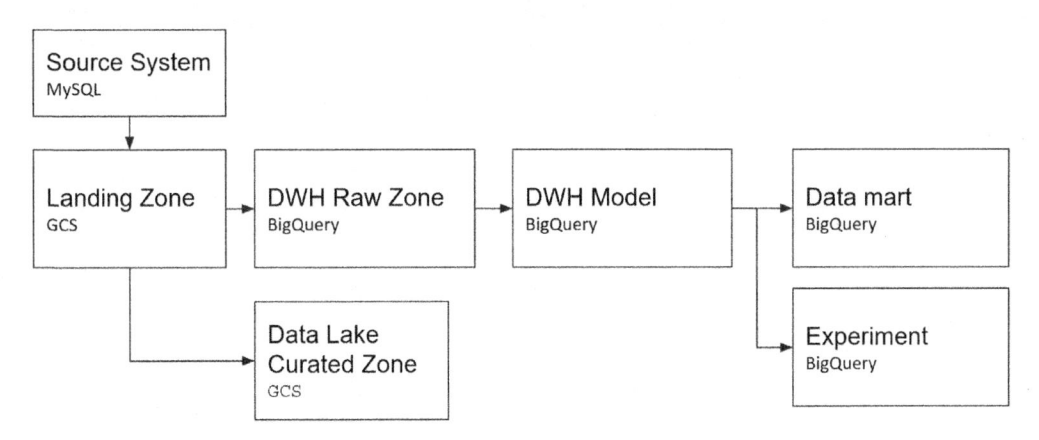

Exercise – build data pipeline orchestration using Cloud Composer

Figure 4.26 – End-to-end data architecture example

Technically speaking, all data movement from the source system to the downstream systems is manageable in one DAG. But realistically, depending on how big an organization is, the team that is managing each step may be different. Some teams may not have visibility of the entire data architecture.

For example, a team of data scientists may need to create a DAG to schedule a batch data transformation from the DWH model to the Experiment zone. They usually don't have the visibility to extract data from the data source to the landing zone.

If you put the team role and responsibilities in the data architecture, it's more likely that the DAG structure will look like this, where the **Data Engineering** (**DE**) team can be divided into multiple teams, such as **Data Warehouse** (**DWH**) and Data Lake teams, and **Business Intelligence** (**BI**) and **Data Scientists** (**DS**) team:

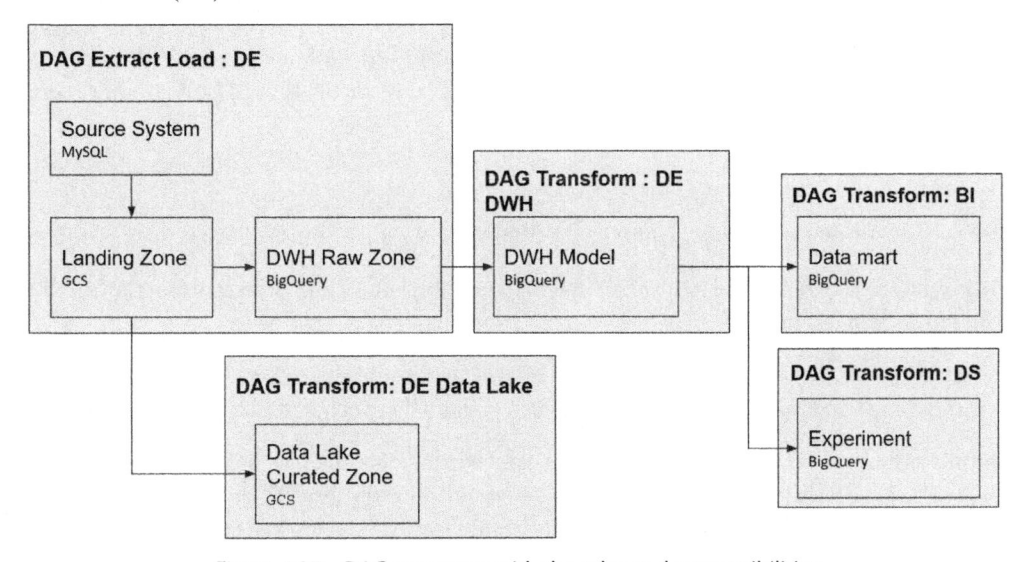

Figure 4.27 – DAG structures with the roles and responsibilities

When there are multiple teams working in different departments to build an end-to-end data pipeline, it's a bad idea to manage everything in one single DAG because it will be difficult to maintain the Python code. Thus, multiple DAG dependencies are needed.

Let's back to our main topic in this subsection: why it's important to have data-aware scheduling. Imagine you have two DAGs. The first DAG loads data from GCS to a BigQuery raw table and to a modeling layer, as follows:

```
GCS → BigQuery raw table → BigQuery modeling tables
```

The second DAG will load data from the BigQuery raw table to a data mart table, as follows:

```
BigQuery modeling tables → BigQuery data mart
```

Here are the two scenarios:

- The data sources from GCS are ready at 5:00 A.M.
- The requirement is to have a data mart table ready by 6:00 A.M.

What can go wrong in this scenario? To answer that, let's do some pseudocode for handling the requirements, as follows:

1. The data is ready by 5:00 A.M. For a time buffer, let's add 10 minutes, which means that we can create a scheduler that runs at 5:10 A.M. every day for the first DAG. In our DAG, we can define the following:

    ```
    schedule = 10 5 * * *
    ```

2. The second DAG is dependent on the first DAG. Let's assume the first DAG will be finished after 30 minutes or at 5:40 A.M.. For a time buffer, let's add 5 minutes on top of that. Then, we can create a scheduler that runs at 5:45 A.M. every day for the second DAG. In our second DAG, we can define the following:

    ```
    schedule = 45 5 * * *
    ```

Sounds good? Yes—for most cases, assuming that the first DAG will be finished in less than 35 minutes.

Now, imagine what will happen if the first DAG is 10 minutes late, or—in other words—the first DAG finishes in 45 minutes rather than 30 minutes.

If the first DAG finishes late, then the second DAG will start blindly. *Blindly* means that the DAG will run without knowing that the upstream data is not actually there yet, and that is very bad.

In a real-world scenario, DAG dependencies are everywhere—there can be tens to hundreds (or even more) of DAG dependencies in a day. If one DAG is late, imagine the implication to all the downstream DAGs. All your daily data will be corrupted just because some DAGs are late by a couple of minutes. How should we avoid that? The answer is by using Airflow sensors.

Introducing Airflow sensors

In the earlier version, Airflow came up with a feature called a **sensor**. A sensor is a mechanism that checks some conditions before starting a DAG Run.

The question now is: *what are the conditions?* There are many sensor operators that we can use. One of the most common in the GCP pipeline is using an operator called `GCSObjectExistenceSensor`.

Let's see the example code. Note that the code in this subsection is not included in the repository as an exercise. We will only go through this as an example so that you get the idea of sensor operators. What is important is to be familiar with the concept and the terminology. Understanding this predecessor feature is needed before we continue our exercise in the next section, *Introducing Airflow datasets*.

Pay attention to the parameters here:

```
data_input_sensor = GCSObjectExistenceSensor(
    object=f'dir/{execution_date_nodash}/_SUCCESS',
    poke_interval=60
)
```

There are two important parameters here: `object` and `poke_interval`. When you have `GCSObjectExistenceSensor` in your DAG, this operator will watch over the GCS object in the given directory. The operator will check the existence of the file in that specific directory.

If the object doesn't exist in the directory, the operator will wait. It will wait and keep checking every 60 seconds, and that's what you set in the `poke_interval` parameter. This will be very useful for our DAG dependencies, in that the downstream DAG can wait before it runs the other tasks.

To give you an illustration, I will get back to our scenario and change the pseudocode using a standard sensor. Just a reminder, you don't need to change your code; what's important is that you got the idea. The example is as follows:

1. The data is ready by 5:00 A.M. I can create a scheduler that runs at 5:00 A.M. every day for the first DAG without any time buffer. In our DAG, I can define the following:

   ```
   schedule = 0 5 * * *
   ```

   The first task will start with the sensor, like this:

   ```
   data_source_sensor = GCSObjectExistenceSensor(
       . . .
       object=f'data_source/{{ ds }}/data.csv',
       poke_interval=60
   )
   ```

As an additional step, at the end of the task, I will write a file to GCS as a signal. Here's an example of this:

```
success = GCSToGCSOperator(
...
destination_object=f'dag_success/first_dag/{{ ds }}/_SUCCESS'
)
```

2. For the second DAG, I will no longer assume anything from the first DAG. I don't assume how long the first DAG will be finished. The first DAG can finish in 1 minute, 5 minutes, or 1 hour—I don't need to assume. Rather, I will start the schedule at the same time as the first DAG, which is 5:00 A.M; and what I will do is to put a sensor to the signal directory from the first DAG. So, the logic will look like this:

```
schedule = 0 5 * * *
```

And as the first task in our DAG, I will use the sensor, like this:

```
upstream_sensor = GCSObjectExistenceSensor(
...
object=f'dag_success/first_dag/{{ ds }}/_SUCCESS'
poke_interval=60)
```

And that's it—that's how the sensor operator works, the first DAG will send a signal file into a directory in the GCS bucket, and later, the downstream DAGs can use this signal to automatically start or wait for the DAG to run.

The Sensor operators in Airflow are still there and, in some conditions, we still need to use this approach compared to the new approach. In case it's needed, I have the example code from the book's first edition, here is the link to the repository: https://github.com/PacktPublishing/Data-Engineering-with-Google-Cloud-Platform-Second-Edition/blob/main/chapter-4/code/level_5_dag.py

Now, let's continue to learn how to use sensors using Airflow datasets in the next section.

Introducing Airflow datasets

In the previous subsection, we learned the concept of Airflow sensors. It's important to understand the concept because, from my understanding of the Airflow open source community, the feature will be replaced with new alternatives.

Understanding the standard Sensor will help you to understand the alternatives because the basic concept is still the same. The advancements are there to improve resource efficiency.

If you think about the Sensor example, the poke mechanism will consume a lot of computation resources accumulatively. And this is concerning because computation resources will affect infrastructure costs.

Because of that, a lot of advancements happen, and it may be difficult to know when to use which one. Here, I will try to explain the differences between these features:

- **Airflow Sensor**: The original concept of DAG dependencies. The function can still be used in the latest Airflow version (2.x), but should be deprecated in the near future.

- **Airflow Smart Sensor**: Because of the infrastructure cost concerns, there is a feature starting in Airflow 2.0 to improve the underlying architecture. This feature is again deprecated in Airflow 2.4 and has been replaced by Deferrable. Avoid using this feature at all.

- **Airflow Deferrable**: This is similar to the first two predecessors, but the main difference is it introduces `Triggerer` class. Please check out the public documentation for the full explanation of the concept: https://airflow.apache.org/docs/apache-airflow/stable/authoring-and-scheduling/deferring.html

  There are some GCP operators that are compatible with this new feature, but not all. For that reason we will not use this feature in our exercise; instead, we will use an even newer alternative, which is the **Airflow Dataset**.

- **Airflow Dataset**: Airflow Dataset was released in Airflow version 2.4. This is similar to the standard Sensor concept, but instead of using actual files for triggers and sensors, the feature will do it for us in memory.

In Airflow Dataset, the sensor mechanism can be applied like this:

```
# DAG 1 Upstream
from airflow.datasets import Dataset
task=Operator(
...
outlets=[Dataset("example_table_a")]
)
```

And a downstream DAG can use the `example.csv` file as the signal like this:

```
# DAG 2 Downstream
with DAG(
    dag_id="multiple_datasets_example",
    schedule=[example_table_a],
...,
```

DAG 1 will send a signal called `example_table_a`, and DAG 2 will start when the signal is sent by DAG 1.

Don't be confused by the naming of the *Dataset*. It isn't actually related to any kind of storage or dataset, see it as metadata labels or tags.

In summary, you will need an Airflow sensor or the newer alternatives for better DAG dependencies compared to relying on a fixed schedule time.

Now, as the final exercise in this chapter, let's add the Airflow dataset to our DAG code. The idea is that we want to create a new DAG. The new DAG will write BigQuery data mart tables using data from our bike-sharing fact table. We want this DAG to run only after the fact table is successfully loaded.

Please download the example code for Level 5 DAG and Level 5 DAG downstream from the following links:

- `https://github.com/PacktPublishing/Data-Engineering-with-Google-Cloud-Platform-Second-Edition/blob/main/chapter-4/code/level_5_dag.py`

- `https://github.com/PacktPublishing/Data-Engineering-with-Google-Cloud-Platform-Second-Edition/blob/main/chapter-4/code/level_5_downstream_dag.py`

Let's create a new DAG called `level_5_downstream_dag.py` for our downstream DAG. These are the steps:

1. In our upstream DAG (`level_5_dag.py`), we will send signals or in Airflow the parameter is called: `outlets`, from the last tasks. For example, the code is like this:

```
bq_row_count_check_dwh_dim_stations = BigQueryCheckOperator(
    task_id='bq_row_count_check_dwh_dim_stations',
    sql=f"""select count(*)
        from `{bq_dim_stations_table_id}`""",
    use_legacy_sql=False,
    # Send signal for downstream dag
    outlets=[Dataset("dwh_dim_stations")]
)
```

2. In the downstream DAG (`level_5_downstream.py`), we changed the schedule to this:

```
with DAG(
    dag_id='level_5_downstream_dag',
    default_args=args,
    schedule=[
        Dataset("dwh_fact_trips_daily"),
        Dataset("dwh_dim_stations")
    ],
    start_date=datetime(2018, 1, 1)
```

This is again to tell Airflow to start the DAG not at any fixed scheduled time, but by waiting for signals from `dwh_fact_trips_daily` and `dwh_dim_stations`.

When triggered, `level_5_downstream` will run another BigQuery job to create a data mart table and store it in the `dm_bikesharing` dataset.

If successful, the Airflow Dataset will also generate a graph that you can access from **Datasets** in the top bar menu.

Figure 4.28 – Datasets button

And the following graph will show you the DAG dependencies, which look like this:

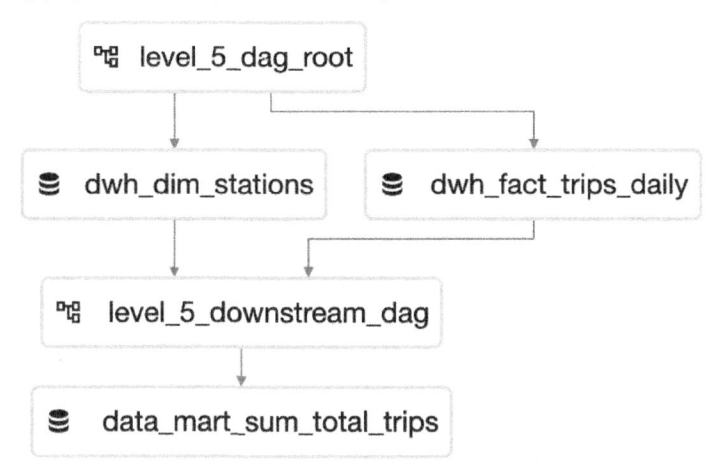

Figure 4.29. Datasets graph visualization

That's it—with this setup, your second DAG will start only if `level_5_dag` successfully runs. Please check the full code in the example code. Try to build a solution yourself first and try to compare the example code.

Before we summarize the chapter, don't forget to delete both the Cloud Composer and Cloud SQL instances. Both services are billed by the number of hours running, so make sure you delete both of the instances after you've finished the exercises. You can delete them from the GCP console with the **Delete** button, or you can run `gcloud` commands.

For Cloud SQL, delete the instance by running the following command:

```
$ gcloud sql instances delete [CLOUDSQL INSTANCE NAME]
```

For Cloud Composer, delete the environment by running the following command:

```
$ gcloud composer environments delete [CLOUD COMPOSER ENVIRONMENT_
NAME] --location [LOCATION]
```

Let's close this chapter with a summary.

Summary

In this chapter, we learned about Cloud Composer. Having learned about Cloud Composer, we then needed to know how to work with Airflow. We realized that as an open source tool, Airflow has a wide range of features. We focused on how to use Airflow to help us build a data pipeline for our BigQuery data warehouse. There are a lot more features and capabilities in Airflow that are not covered in this book. You can always expand your skills in this area, but you will already have a good foundation after finishing this chapter.

As a tool, Airflow is fairly simple. You just need to know how to write a Python script to define DAGs. We've learned in the Level 1 DAG exercise that you just need to write simple code to build your first DAG, but a complication arises when it comes to best practices, as there are a lot of best practices that you can follow. At the same time, there are also a lot of potential bad practices that Airflow developers can make.

By learning the examples in different code levels in this chapter, you learned that the DAG code decision can lead to potential data issues, and as data engineers, it's our job to make sure we know which best practice we should apply. Every organization may have different conditions, and every condition may lead to different use cases. Understanding the potential risk and understanding Airflow's best practices are key to building the best orchestrator for your data pipelines.

In the next chapter, we will go back to storage and processing components, but we will use **Dataproc** as an alternative approach to BigQuery. Just as we compared Cloud Composer and Airflow, with Dataproc you will learn about Hadoop because they are correlated tightly. We will learn about both Dataproc and Hadoop to build our data lake.

5
Building a Data Lake Using Dataproc

A data lake shares similarities with a data warehouse, yet its fundamental distinction lies in the nature of stored content. Unlike a data warehouse, a data lake is designed to manage extensive raw data, agnostic to its eventual value or purpose. This pivotal divergence reshapes approaches to data storage and retrieval within a data lake, setting it apart from the principles that we learned in *Chapter 3, Building a Data Warehouse in BigQuery*.

This chapter helps you understand how to build a data lake using **Dataproc**, which is a managed Hadoop cluster in **Google Cloud Platform** (**GCP**). But, more importantly, it helps you understand the key benefit of using a data lake in the cloud, which is allowing the use of ephemeral clusters.

Here is a high-level outline of this chapter:

- Introduction to Dataproc
- Exercise – Building a data lake on a Dataproc cluster
- Exercise – Creating and running jobs on a Dataproc cluster
- Understanding the concept of an ephemeral cluster
- Building an ephemeral cluster using Dataproc and Cloud Composer

Technical requirements

Before we begin to learn in this chapter, make sure you have the following prerequisites ready.

In this chapter's exercises, the GCP services that we will use are Dataproc, **Google Cloud Storage** (**GCS**), BigQuery, and Cloud Composer. If you have never opened any of these services in your GCP console, open them and enable the APIs.

Make sure you have your GCP console, Cloud Shell, and Cloud Shell Editor ready.

Download the example code and the dataset from `https://github.com/PacktPublishing/Data-Engineering-with-Google-Cloud-Platform-Second-Edition/tree/main/chapter-5`.

Be aware of costs you might incur from Dataproc and the Cloud Composer cluster. Make sure you delete all the environments after the exercises to prevent any unexpected costs.

Introduction to Dataproc

Dataproc is a Google-managed service for Hadoop environments. It manages the underlying **virtual machines** (**VMs**), operating systems, and Hadoop software installations. Using Dataproc, Hadoop developers can focus on developing jobs and submitting them to Dataproc.

From a data engineering perspective, understanding Dataproc is equal to understanding Hadoop and the data lake concept. If you are not familiar with Hadoop, let's learn about it in the next section.

A brief history of the data lake and Hadoop ecosystem

The popularity of the data lake rose in the 2010s. Companies started to talk about this concept a lot more, compared to the data warehouse, which is similar but different in principle. The concept of storing data as files in a centralized system makes a lot of sense in the modern era, compared to the old days when companies stored and processed data typically for regular reporting. In the modern era, people use data for exploration from many data sources. Exploration can mean anything, including answering hypothetical questions about customer behavior, finding potential fraud, A/B testing, and doing **machine learning** (**ML**).

The concept of storing and processing huge amounts of data is actually nothing new. Google was the first pioneer of this in the early 2000s. Their ambitious goal of storing all the web page information in the world on their server was where the story began. In their use case, there were no other options; they couldn't store the web pages in common database tables. They needed to store their data as unstructured data and distribute it across multiple machines for scalability.

The great success of the technology behind it and how the world saw Google becoming a very successful data-driven company made a lot of companies want to do the same thing. Unfortunately, not all companies were able to do that in those years. The storage costs didn't make sense, and no technology was popular enough to support that – not until 2003, when Google published how their technology works with **Google File System** (**GFS**) and MapReduce. In 2006, the open source Hadoop was published, inspired by the two technologies. As a result, all companies around the world started to adopt it, and the rest is history.

A deeper look into Hadoop components

In my experience, understanding Hadoop is not only good for adding our knowledge to the ETL landscape. Understanding Hadoop can help you understand the principle of parallel processing in big data and why it's different from common database technologies.

Essentially, Hadoop consists of three main components:

- A **distributed file system** (**DFS**) or, as it is called in the Hadoop environment, **Hadoop Distributed File System** (**HDFS**): This is the concept that a system will automatically split your files into multiple parts. The goal is for you to be able to store terabytes to petabytes of data on multiple physical hard disks.
- **MapReduce**: This is the concept that defines how to process data parallelly. The goal is for you to be able to process data using multiple CPUs, hard disks, and memory at the same time. In recent years, Spark has become a more popular framework for doing parallel processing, but as a concept, Spark still uses the MapReduce concept.
- **YARN**: This is a resource management tool in Hadoop. YARN is an important part of Hadoop for allocating resources, in terms of how much CPU and memory are available in the cluster and how much it should allocate to each individual job.

These are the three main components of Hadoop. But nowadays, you can see Hadoop as an ecosystem rather than just these three main components. Hadoop is well known because of how active and big the community is; for example, you might have heard the following:

- Hadoop can do real-time streaming
- Hadoop can do ML
- In Hadoop, you can create a data warehouse

All of these statements are correct, but Hadoop needs more than just the three core components. For example, for streaming, you might need Kafka, Flume, and Spark Streaming. For creating a data warehouse, you might need Hive or Impala. In summary, Hadoop is an ecosystem; it's a collection of many open source projects that are compatible with each other.

Let's take a quick look at the simplified Hadoop components in this diagram, where the starting point is the servers:

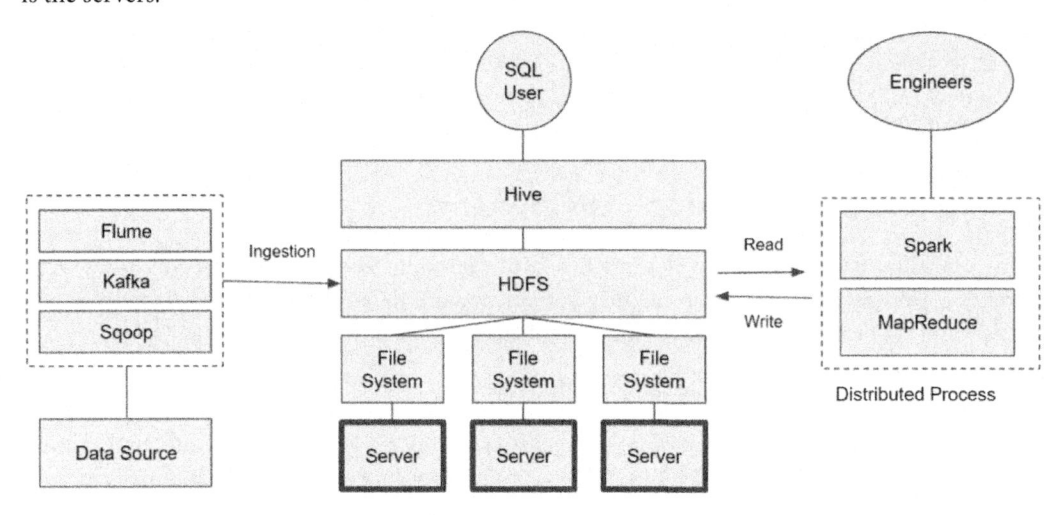

Figure 5.1 – Hadoop high-level architecture

Hadoop runs on top of multiple servers or nodes, which is called a **Hadoop cluster**. It has one-to-many working servers or, in Hadoop terms, **worker nodes**. The worker nodes are simply computers with a filesystem where you can store files. HDFS sits on top of these multiple filesystems; when you store data in HDFS, Hadoop seamlessly distributes the files to these filesystems. You can create a table structure on top of the files using Hive, so SQL users can access the data using the SQL. The other option is to process it using distributed processing frameworks such as Spark or MapReduce. These kinds of frameworks can read and write files directly to HDFS.

There are tools that are usually used to ingest data to HDFS; for example, Flume, Kafka, and Sqoop. *Figure 5.1* is just a very simplified summary of the Hadoop ecosystem; in the marketplace, there are a lot of other alternatives for each component. If this is the first time you have learned about Hadoop, don't fall into a trap where you think you need to understand all of the products and their alternatives. Instead, focus on understanding how HDFS works and how Spark or MapReduce can process data in HDFS. The other components will come naturally with time when you understand HDFS and the processing framework.

At this point, you may already have a high-level understanding of what Hadoop is. To continue our learning about data engineering on GCP, we need to also think about how much Hadoop knowledge is required if you are working in a GCP environment.

The answer depends on how new Hadoop is for you and what your organizational direction is in using Hadoop. But assume that you are new to both Hadoop and GCP, and your organization has no strong opinion on Hadoop. It's best to focus your Hadoop understanding on it being a data processing framework.

How much Hadoop-related knowledge do you need on GCP?

Since most functionalities of open source products have native alternatives in GCP, it's recommended to avoid using unmanaged open source products and to use managed services. For example, Hive is an open source product for creating tables on top of HDFS. On GCP, we will avoid using it because BigQuery is a much better alternative for creating table structures. As another example, HDFS as a storage system for a data lake is also not really relevant in GCP since it's replaceable by a serverless service, GCS. Even though they are not identical, they serve the same purpose.

The most common Hadoop use case in GCP is for a data processing framework such as MapReduce or Spark. A lot of data engineers really love Spark because of its simplicity, and it has a big community following. Because of this and many other reasons, data engineers prefer processing big data using Spark. And if we want to compare it to MapReduce, Spark is a much more popular and robust framework. Let's take a deeper look at what Spark is and some of its key terms.

Introducing the Spark RDD and DataFrame concepts

Spark is a framework for distributed processing. With Spark, we can create programs or applications to extract, transform, and load data in a distributed manner. Note that Spark is a framework that was built using Scala, and by default, Scala is the preferred language to develop Spark programs. But there is an alternative you can use – a Spark Python API called **PySpark**. We will use PySpark consistently with the Python programming language throughout the exercises in the book.

Spark is a framework on its own; there are many features and concepts in Spark. In this book, we will focus only on the core concepts. With Spark, you can process ETL in a distributed manner, all thanks to the **resilient distributed dataset** (**RDD**) concept. An RDD is a unique concept in Spark. It distributes your data between multiple machines. And as for the word *resilient*, it means the dataset is fault-tolerant. For example, imagine you run a Spark job where the RDD stores data on multiple machines, but then one machine turns off for some reason. The resiliency in Spark will ensure your job is still running and smart enough to get a replacement from other machines.

You can think of an RDD as arrays or lists in Python. For example, in Python, you can define a list like this:

```
this_is_a_list = [1,2,3,4,5]
```

In Spark, you can define an RDD using the Python list like this:

```
this_is_RDD = spark_context.parallelize(this_is_a_list)
```

Using the previous code, the `this_is_RDD` variable is an RDD. As an illustration of how it differs from other variables, you can't print an RDD like this:

```
print(this_is_RDD)
```

You can't print an RDD as you would print list variables. Later, we will try it, in the *Exercise – Building a data lake on a Dataproc cluster* section.

An RDD is an abstract dataset. When you define an RDD from a list, the list becomes distributed. The previous example won't really make sense because it only contains five data units (1-5). But if you have a list that contains millions of pieces of data, the RDD will distribute the data between multiple memories, such as **random-access memory** (**RAM**) across different machines (servers). We will practice using RDD later, in the *Exercise – Building a data lake on a Dataproc cluster* section; for now, let's just keep RDDs in mind.

On top of an RDD, there is another abstraction layer called a **Spark DataFrame**. You can think of a Spark DataFrame like `pandas` in Python. Like the relationship between a Python list and a Spark RDD, a Spark DataFrame is similar to `pandas` but distributed. With a Spark DataFrame, we can give a schema to our files on the fly. On top of that, we can use SQL to transform the data in an RDD. As a best practice, always transform all RDDs into a Spark DataFrame when possible. A Spark DataFrame is better than using an RDD because it provides more optimization in the process. Use an RDD only when you don't have a clear schema or delimiter. We will learn how to use both in the exercise, but to summarize, in Spark, there are two important glossaries – an RDD and a Spark DataFrame.

Introducing the data lake concept

When talking about Hadoop, it's inevitable that we talk about data lakes. Hadoop and data lakes are inseparable. The popularity of Hadoop made the world invent the data lake terminology.

To refresh your learning about what the difference is between a data lake and a data warehouse, please review *Chapter 1, Fundamentals of Data Engineering*, in the *What makes a data lake different from a data warehouse?* section.

Three main factors make a data lake unique as a system. Let's look at each of these in detail.

The ability to store any kind of data

A data lake system needs to be able to store any kind of data. To clarify the word *any*, we can break it down into three different categories:

- Structured (table)
- Semi-structured (CSV, JSON, or XML)
- Unstructured data (image, audio, or logs)

But in my experience, these three categorizations won't really help you other than as an introduction. It's a great way to introduce the capabilities of a data lake to new people, but at the end of the day, what you see as a data engineer are files.

If the technology you use is meant for data lake storage (such as GCS), you don't actually need to do anything. There is no additional configuration that you need to do to prepare structured, semi-structured, or unstructured data; it's all the same – files.

So, the keyword here is *any*. It means that in a data lake, the system should be able to store data in a file format rather than in a database table. For me, it's a lot simpler to think in this way.

The ability to process files in a distributed manner

A data lake should be able to handle files regardless of the format and size. We've talked about the format previously; the key is that the system needs to be able to read files.

But size is another key differentiator here. A data lake needs to be able to distribute data processes. A distributed process means that the system is able to break down data processes into smaller chunks and run them in parallel on more than one machine (computer).

The other terminology for this is being able to *scale out*. If data in the data lake keeps getting bigger and bigger, the solution is not to *scale up* the machine but to *scale out*. Scaling up means upgrading the server specification, and scaling out means adding more servers. Scaling up is limited, and scaling out is limitless.

As an example, to read data from a file, you can actually use any programming language, such as Python. You can read data from files in Python and then load the file content into variables or a `pandas` DataFrame and process the data. But Python by itself won't distribute the process between multiple machines; it needs different frameworks to do that. The most well-known distributed processing frameworks are MapReduce and Spark. But there are others, such as Flink, Dataflow, and Dremel. So, the key here is that a data lake needs to be able to process data in a distributed manner.

The ability to focus on loading the data first

The third factor is a development mindset. A data engineer who builds a data lake needs to know that the focus of building it is to store data first; the business logic and structure come later. This means that the mindset is to store as many files as possible from multiple data sources in the data lake and let other teams or departments figure out the value of the data. The other teams could be data scientists, data analysts, or business analysts.

There are cases when organizations try to adopt a data lake by purchasing data lake technology, but the mindset is not adjusted in terms of data being costly, not clean, useless, or unstructured. In this case, the organization will have endless debates about what the difference is between a data lake and a data warehouse. So, the key here is to **focus on loading the data first**.

> **Important note**
>
> A new term arose in the late 2010s – the **data lakehouse**. Please don't be confused by this terminology. This started when companies started to realize that the majority of use cases in the data lake were using structured data.
>
> That is then supported by advancement in the technology side, where there are better technologies that support better metadata governance on data lakes and a more optimized SQL engine.
>
> The two combinations of practical use cases and the technology bring a new architecture, where companies are already used to the data lake architecture but willing to practice more data warehousing.
>
> For the purpose of learning, we can ignore this since there are no fundamental changes in the underlying principles. If we understand *data lake* and *data warehouse*, understanding why the term *data lakehouse* occurred will be natural.

If we take a look back at what Hadoop is, all three data lake factors fit into the Hadoop ecosystem:

- Hadoop stores data in HDFS as files
- Hadoop processes data in a distributed manner using MapReduce or Spark
- Hadoop engineers know that the majority of their job is to develop, maintain, and manage data loading jobs from data sources to HDFS and is less about data modeling

Now, how does Hadoop fit into the GCP ecosystem? Since there are a lot of overlapping components from open source Hadoop to GCP components, we need to better understand the Hadoop positioning on GCP.

Hadoop and Dataproc positioning on GCP

Based on my experience working with organizations that use Dataproc on GCP, one of the common reasons they are using Dataproc is that they were already using the Hadoop ecosystem before moving to GCP. This means that the organization has already invested a lot of time and effort in scripting ETL code and has a lot of developers who are very familiar with Hadoop. In this case, it's best to move everything as is from GCP to Dataproc without many changes.

In this case, Dataproc will save the organization a lot of time and infrastructure effort to provision a Hadoop cluster. Creating a Hadoop cluster using Dataproc will take around 5 minutes. Compare this to the efforts needed to create a Hadoop cluster ourselves, including installing the operating system, installing Hadoop, and configuring the Hadoop configurations, which might take days to finish.

In addition, with the new Dataproc feature called Dataproc Serverless, a data engineer will no longer need to think about the Hadoop cluster at all. We will see what this feature means to Dataproc in the next subsection, *Introduction to Dataproc Serverless*.

One of the biggest user experience changes from traditional Hadoop compared to Dataproc is the storage layer. Although HDFS and GCS are very similar in nature (both can store files and are accessible by Dataproc seamlessly), the best practice is to use GCS compared to HDFS because it's serverless.

And for further implementation, it's a lot better; compared to HDFS, data in GCS is compatible with almost all other GCP services, such as BigQuery, Vertex AI, and Cloud SQL. We will talk more about this in the *Using GCS as an underlying Dataproc filesystem* section and try both storing and accessing data in HDFS and GCS.

Introduction to Dataproc Serverless

Dataproc has undergone continuous evolution since its initial introduction as a managed Hadoop service on GCP. Among the recent advancements, a particularly noteworthy stride is the release of Dataproc Serverless!

Using this service, you can submit Hadoop jobs without creating and managing Hadoop clusters. This will make all infrastructure-related efforts become zero.

Currently, Dataproc Serverless supports Spark jobs. Thus, in some documentation, it will be called Spark Serverless. This serverless mechanism is supported with the Autoscaling feature by default, which again means that you, as a data engineer, no longer need to think about the machine scales and can focus on the code quality.

Please keep in mind that the release of this feature doesn't mean the core Dataproc as a Hadoop-managed service is removed. There are still many cases where an organization still prefers the Dataproc-managed service. In this book's exercises, we will practice both.

There are a lot of concepts and key terms that we've learned so far in this chapter. Before learning about the other Dataproc features and concepts, let's start our exercise in this chapter.

Exercise – Building a data lake on a Dataproc cluster

In this exercise, we will use Dataproc to store and process log data. Log data is a good representation of unstructured data. Organizations often need to analyze log data to understand their users' behavior.

In the exercise, we will learn how to use HDFS and PySpark using different methods. In the beginning, we will use Cloud Shell to get a basic understanding of the technologies. In the later sections, we will use Cloud Shell Editor and submit jobs to Dataproc. But for the first step, let's create our Dataproc cluster.

Creating a Dataproc cluster on GCP

To create a Dataproc cluster, access your navigation menu and find **Dataproc**. If this is the first time you're accessing this page, please click the **Enable API** button. After that, you will find the **CREATE CLUSTER** button. There are two options, **Cluster on Compute Engine** and **Cluster on GKE**. Choose **Cluster on Compute Engine**, which leads to this **Create a cluster** page:

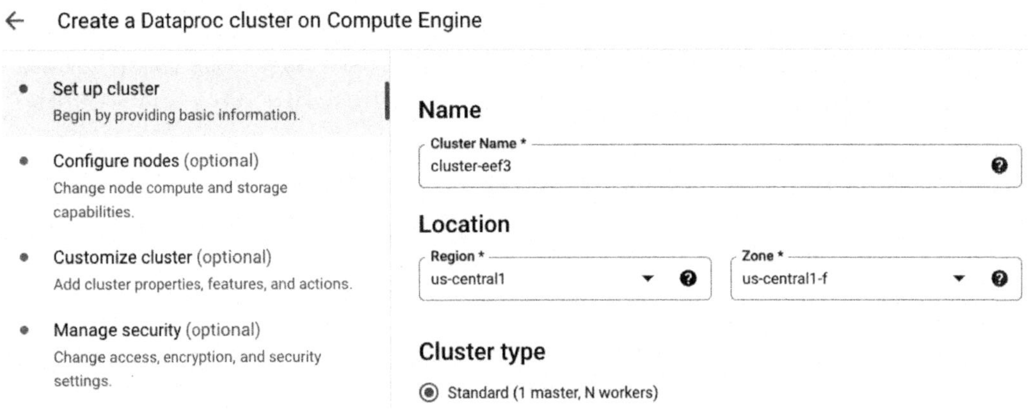

Building a Data Lake Using Dataproc

← Create a Dataproc cluster on Compute Engine

- **Set up cluster**
  Begin by providing basic information.

- **Configure nodes** (optional)
  Change node compute and storage capabilities.

- **Customize cluster** (optional)
  Add cluster properties, features, and actions.

- **Manage security** (optional)
  Change access, encryption, and security settings.

Name
Cluster Name *: cluster-eef3

Location
Region *: us-central1
Zone *: us-central1-f

Cluster type
◉ Standard (1 master, N workers)

Figure 5.2 – Creating a cluster page

There are many configurations in Dataproc. We don't need to set everything. Most of them are optional. For your first cluster, follow this setup:

- **Cluster Name**: Choose your cluster name.
- **Location**: `us-central1`
- **Cluster type: Single Node (1 master, 0 workers)**
- **Versioning**: The versioning options can be different from time to time since Google updates versions. Choose any version; for example, in my case, the latest is 2.1 (Debian 11, Hadoop 3.3, Spark 3.3).
- **Component Gateway**: Enable Component Gateway.

Move to the **Configure nodes** section. We will set the minimum specifications for our machines:

- **Series**: N2
- **Machine type**: `n2-standard-8`
- **Primary disk size**: 30 GB

If all is set, find and click the **CREATE** button. If you are lost, the equivalent `gcloud` command is this:

```
gcloud dataproc clusters create cluster-431d --enable-component-
gateway --region us-central1 --zone us-central1-a --single-node
--master-machine-type n2-standard-8 --master-boot-disk-size 30
--image-version 2.1-debian11 --project YOUR_PROJECT_ID
```

If all steps are correct, it will start provisioning the Dataproc cluster. It will take around 2–5 minutes until it is finished.

> **Important note**
>
> When we are using the Google Cloud free tier, the default CPU quota for a region is 8 cores.
>
> For this reason, we can only create a Dataproc cluster with a single node. In the real world, a Hadoop cluster ideally has three master nodes and many workers.
>
> In production, you can increase the CPU quota. Please check the public documentation for this: https://cloud.google.com/compute/resource-usage.

While waiting, let's familiarize ourselves with some of the options that we skipped during configuration. These options are very useful features in Dataproc, mostly for optimization. All of these are optional, so they're good to know at this point:

- **Autoscaling**: Autoscaling is a feature in Dataproc to automatically scale up and scale down the number of worker nodes. The scaling is based on resource availability in YARN.

- **Initialization actions**: This feature is for when you need to run any actions after Hadoop is installed on machines. A common example is to install some dependency libraries.

- **Custom Image**: You can choose the base image for your underlying Hadoop cluster. This will be useful, for example, when you have specific requirements for the OS version.

- **Component Gateway**: In the Hadoop ecosystem, there are many open source projects that have a web UI; for example, Jupyter Notebook and Zeppelin. Enabling Component Gateway will give you access to those web UIs seamlessly. Google will manage the web proxies. Without this enabled, you'll need to configure the access to the web UI yourself.

- **Secondary worker nodes**: Dataproc allows secondary workers in a Hadoop cluster. Secondary workers are sets of machines that will be dedicated to processing only, not storing data. The most common use case is to use secondary workers in preemptible mode. With this, overall, jobs are faster and cheaper compared to having fewer workers or using non-secondary workers. But the trade-off is stability. Preemptible secondary worker nodes have a higher chance of being dropped internally by GCP. The best practice is to use preemptible secondary workers for less than 50% of the total number of workers.

As these configurations are optional, use them only when you need them. In other words, only consider using them when you find potential optimization in your Hadoop workloads. As always, focus on implementation first and optimization later.

Check that your Dataproc cluster has been created successfully. In the next section, we will use it to try storing data in HDFS and process it using Spark.

Using GCS as an underlying Dataproc filesystem

Now our Hadoop cluster is ready, we can start using the core Hadoop components. The first component that we will try using is the HDFS component.

Building a Data Lake Using Dataproc

These are the steps we will perform in this section:

1. Accessing HDFS from the Hadoop node shell
2. Loading data from GCS to HDFS
3. Creating a Hive table on top of HDFS
4. Accessing an HDFS file from PySpark
5. Accessing a GCS file from PySpark

Let's look at each of these steps in detail.

Accessing HDFS from the Hadoop node shell

One way to access HDFS in our Hadoop cluster is by accessing the Linux command line from the master node. To do that, follow these steps:

1. Go to the Dataproc console and select your cluster name.
2. On the **Cluster details** page, find the **VM INSTANCES** tab.
3. You will see three VM instances there, and one of them will have the **Master** role.
4. Click on the **SSH** button, which you will find on the right of the **Master** node VM:

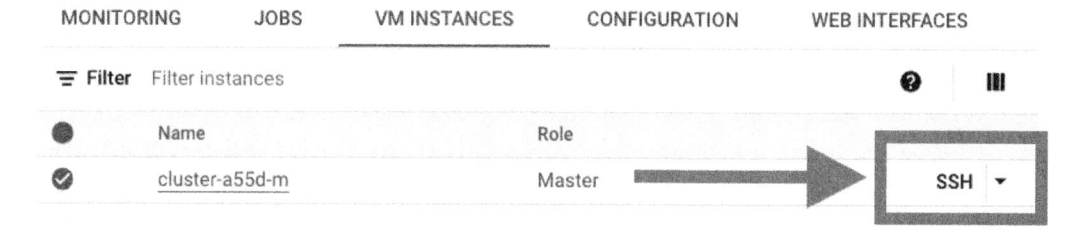

Figure 5.3 – The SSH button on the right of the screen

5. Wait for around 1 minute until the command line appears as follows:

Figure 5.4 – Command line for the Hadoop master node instance

Note that this is not Cloud Shell; this is the Linux Hadoop master node. We can access the HDFS from here using the command line. Let's try that by typing the following:

```
$ hdfs dfs -ls ../
```

The command will give you the list of folders inside HDFS like this:

```
adiwijaya@cluster-a55d-m:~$ hdfs dfs -ls ../
Found 12 items
drwxrwxrwt   - hdfs hadoop          0 2023-08-29 11:56 ../adiwijaya
drwxrwxrwt   - hdfs hadoop          0 2023-08-29 11:56 ../dataproc
drwxrwxrwt   - hdfs hadoop          0 2023-08-29 11:56 ../hbase
drwxrwxrwt   - hdfs hadoop          0 2023-08-29 11:56 ../hdfs
drwxrwxrwt   - hdfs hadoop          0 2023-08-29 11:56 ../hive
drwxrwxrwt   - hdfs hadoop          0 2023-08-29 11:56 ../mapred
drwxrwxrwt   - hdfs hadoop          0 2023-08-29 11:56 ../pig
drwxrwxrwt   - hdfs hadoop          0 2023-08-29 11:56 ../solr
drwxrwxrwt   - hdfs hadoop          0 2023-08-29 11:56 ../spark
drwxrwxrwt   - hdfs hadoop          0 2023-08-29 11:56 ../yarn
drwxrwxrwt   - hdfs hadoop          0 2023-08-29 11:56 ../zeppelin
drwxrwxrwt   - hdfs hadoop          0 2023-08-29 11:56 ../zookeeper
```

Figure 5.5 – HDFS file list output example

The 10 folders are not stored in the OS-level filesystem; they're in HDFS. To verify that, you can run ls in the shell, and you won't see those 10 folders in the Linux filesystem. This might sound abstract at this point, but it will get clearer and clearer after some practice.

Loading data from GCS to HDFS

In this step, we want to load data from a file in the master node to HDFS. To illustrate that, let's try to load the file from our Git repository at https://github.com/PacktPublishing/Data-Engineering-with-Google-Cloud-Platform-Second-Edition.

Copy all the folders from chapter-5 to your GCS bucket if you haven't done so in the previous chapters. For example, you can use the gcloud storage cp command like this from **Cloud Shell**:

```
$ cd Data-Engineering-with-Google-Cloud-Platform
$ gcloud storage cp -r chapter-5 gs://[BUCKET NAME]/from-git
```

If the data is already in GCS, we now can load it to our master node. Go to the **Dataproc master node shell** and use the gcloud storage cp command like this:

```
$ gcloud storage cp gs://[BUCKET NAME]/from-git/chapter-5/dataset/simple_file.csv ./
```

Try to run the ls command, and you can see simple_file.csv is now in your master node.

To explain more about what we were doing, we just prepared our exercise to load data to HDFS. It can be done as long as the data is in the master node; for example, you can transfer data to the master node using FTP or download any data from the internet. The key is that we want to have a file in the master node.

Any data in the master node can be loaded to HDFS using the command line like this:

```
$ hdfs dfs -mkdir ../../data
$ hdfs dfs -mkdir ../../data/simple_file
$ hdfs dfs -put simple_file.csv ../../data/simple_file/
```

The command will load data from the Linux filesystem to HDFS. With that, you can see the file in HDFS using the following command:

```
$ hdfs dfs -ls ../../data/simple_file/
```

You will see `simple_file.csv` shown in HDFS under the `data` folder.

Creating a Hive table on top of HDFS

One alternative for accessing the file is using Hive. Hive is a tool to give a schema to your file. To do that, let's access Hive Shell from our command line by typing `hive` in our master node shell, like this:

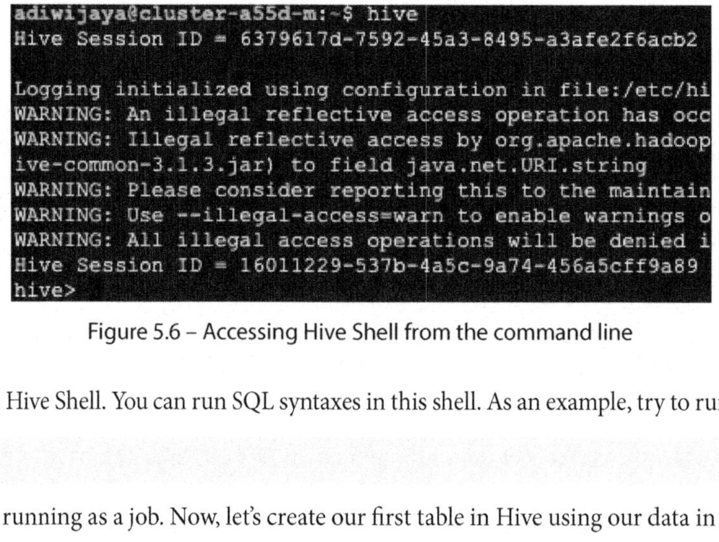

Figure 5.6 – Accessing Hive Shell from the command line

Now, you are in Hive Shell. You can run SQL syntaxes in this shell. As an example, try to run the following:

```
SELECT 1;
```

You will see it's running as a job. Now, let's create our first table in Hive using our data in HDFS like this:

```
CREATE EXTERNAL TABLE simple_table(
        col_1 STRING,
        col_2 STRING,
        col_3 STRING)
ROW FORMAT DELIMITED FIELDS TERMINATED BY ','
STORED AS TEXTFILE
```

```
location '/data/simple_file'
TBLPROPERTIES ("skip.header.line.count"="1")
;
```

The CREATE EXTERNAL TABLE statement will create a table called simple_table using data from the file directory in HDFS. If the table is successfully created, you can access it using the following:

```
SELECT * FROM simple_table;
```

The table results will show like this:

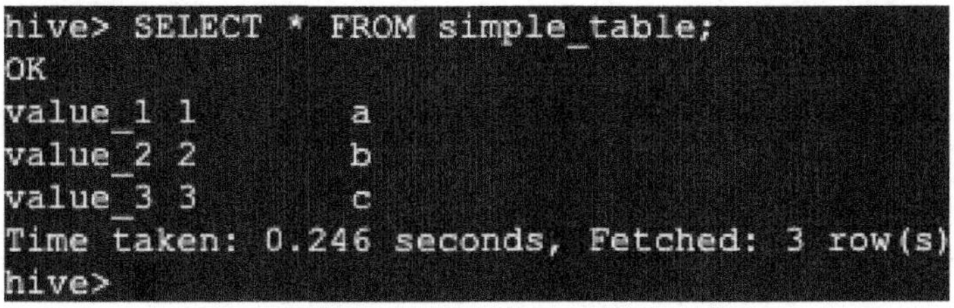

```
hive> SELECT * FROM simple_table;
OK
value_1    1       a
value_2    2       b
value_3    3       c
Time taken: 0.246 seconds, Fetched: 3 row(s)
hive>
```

Figure 5.7 – Example Hive table result

To exit, in Hive Shell, type the following:

```
exit;
```

You will be back at the master node. As you can see, with Hive, you can access CSV files using SQL. This fundamental concept of processing data directly from a file is the key differentiator between data lake technology and databases.

Accessing an HDFS file from PySpark

The second alternative for processing data in HDFS is using PySpark. You can access PySpark using the Spark shell. To do that, type pyspark in the master node like this:

```
adiwijaya@cluster-eef3-m:~$ pyspark
```

Figure 5.8 – Accessing PySpark from the command line

With that command, you will be directed to the Spark shell, as shown in the following figure:

Figure 5.9 – Spark shell example

The Spark shell is a good tool for practice and doing simple tests. In reality, we will develop Spark applications in our IDE or Cloud Editor. We will do that later, in the next exercise, but as a starter, let's use the Spark shell.

The Spark shell actually works as a Python shell, and you can use any Python code in here. For example, you can use these common Python syntaxes:

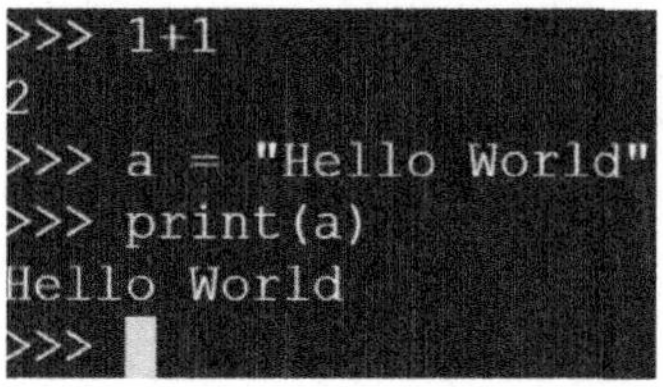

Figure 5.10 – Example Spark shell similar to Python

But the difference is, in the Spark shell, you can use `SparkContext` or `SparkSession` directly without configuring it in the script.

`SparkContext` or `SparkSession`, which are different but essentially the same, are connections from our code to the Spark cluster. See them as an entry point to use Spark whenever you need it from a code.

In this exercise, I will use `SparkSession` terminology for referring to both `SparkContext` and `SparkSession`. In practice, you should use `SparkSession`, because it's newer and contains more complete sets of interfaces – for example, Spark DataFrame and Datasets.

Let's use `SparkSession` to load our data from HDFS. We will access the file in HDFS from the master node, which is named `cluster-a55d-m`.

To do that, use this node, and don't forget to change the master node name to yours:

```
simple_file_from_hdfs = sc.textFile('hdfs://[YOUR-MASTER-NODE-NAME]/
data/simple_file/simple_file.csv')
simple_file.collect()
```

For example, my HDFS path looks like this: `hdfs://cluster-a55d-m-m/data/simple_file/simple_file.csv`.

The code will print out the file contents as an array:

```
['col_1,col_2,col3', 'value_1,1,a', 'value_2,2,b', 'value_3,3,c']
```

If this is the first time you have used Spark, congratulations! You just experienced using one of the most popular big data processing frameworks in the world.

Spark is a very widely used framework for processing big data. I have found that a lot of companies include Spark as a job requirement and in the interview process for data engineer roles. So, knowing about the Spark concept will be very beneficial in your data engineering journey.

So, what really happens? What actually is the `simple_file` variable?

When we call `sc.textFile` to the `simple_file` variable, the `simple_file` variable will become an RDD. Try typing `type(simple_file)`, like this:

```
>>> type(simple_file)
<class 'pyspark.rdd.RDD'>
>>>
```

Figure 5.11 – Checking the RDD file type

You will see the variable type is RDD. To refresh our memory about RDDs, you can review the *Introducing the Spark RDD and DataFrame concepts* section.

Note that we accessed the HDFS files by pointing to the master node instead of the data nodes. That is the default mechanism in Hadoop. Even though the master node doesn't store the real files, the master node has the index to all files in the data nodes. This means that even if you have many data nodes in your Hadoop cluster, you don't need to know where files are actually stored in the data nodes; you just need to access the files from the master node. It will automatically read the required files from the data nodes.

Understanding RDDs in PySpark

An interesting feature of RDDs is the concept of lazy computation. Lazy computation processes instructions only when they're needed. For example, let's define this in Python code:

```
variable_a = 10
variable_b = variable_a * 10
variable_c = variable_b * variable_a
print(variable_c)
```

If you run the previous code in Python, it will execute each variable and store the results in memory for each variable. So, if we print `variable_c`, what actually happens in Python is it stores three different pieces of data in memory for each variable.

The same principle cannot be applied to big data. It's wasteful to store data in `variable_a` and `variable_b` since both variables are essentially just formulas. In the lazy computation concept, we will only process all the formulas when we call `print(variable_c)`.

Back to our exercise. Let's sum up the number in `col_2`. We use this RDD:

```
['col_1,col_2,col3', 'value_1,1,a', 'value_2,2,b', 'value_3,3,c']
```

We expect the result to be 6:

```
6 = 1 + 2 + 3
```

Let's use the following PySpark syntax and understand it step by step:

1. Since the value still contains the CSV headers, we want to filter out any value that contains `'col'`:

   ```
   rdd_without_header = simple_file_from_hdfs.filter(lambda row: 'col' not in row)
   ```

2. The values are delimited by commas, so we need to split them using the Python `split` method. But instead of using a `for` loop, we will use the map function. Using the map function in Spark will distribute the process:

   ```
   split = rdd_without_header.map(lambda row:    row.split(','))
   ```

3. We will get the `col_2` value and convert it into an integer:

   ```
   rdd_col_2 = split.map(lambda row: int(row[1]))
   ```

4. Finally, we will sum the values and print them:

   ```
   sum = rdd_col_2.sum()
   print(sum)
   ```

If all is correct, the code will print 6. To try lazy computation, try printing any variable other than the sum variable. You won't see any data from other variables. rdd_without_header, split, and rdd_col_2 are variables that store the formula (logic). They won't compute or store any data before we call the sum() method. Imagine you have 1 billion records in your .csv file. You will save all unnecessary memory stores to all variables that only contain formulas.

Accessing a GCS file from PySpark

In the previous section, we stored and accessed data in HDFS. This time, we want to see how easy it is to change the file storage from HDFS to GCS.

To do that, check that simple_file.csv is already in your GCS bucket. We did this in the previous section, using the gcloud storage cp command. For example, in my environment, it's located here:

```
gs://[YOUR-BUCKET-NAME]/chapter-5/dataset/simple_file.csv
```

Now, back to the PySpark shell, type this:

```
simple_file_from_gcs = sc.textFile('gs://[YOUR-BUCKET-NAME]/from-git/chapter-5/dataset/simple_file.csv')
```

The code is exactly the same as when we accessed data from HDFS. To compare, remember this line from the previous section:

```
simple_file_from_hdfs = sc.textFile('hdfs://[YOUR-MASTER-NODE-NAME]/data/simple_file/simple_file.csv')
```

The difference is only in the file location. Spark can access data in GCS seamlessly even though the file is not stored in the Hadoop cluster. And with that, you can continue the rest of the code exactly the same. For example, you can use this same syntax:

```
rdd_without_header = simple_file.filter(lambda row: 'col' not in row)
```

To quit the PySpark shell, use quit().

As a summary of this section, we've seen that there is no difference in the development effort using HDFS or GCS. The trade-off of using HDFS or GCS is in the I/O latency versus compatibility and maintenance. You can optimize the I/O latency by using SSD in HDFS on Hadoop cluster VMs. That's the fastest possible option. But for compatibility with other GCP services and less maintenance effort, GCS is the clear winner. In the next section, we will start the hands-on practice. We will try different approaches to using Dataproc. As a starter, let's begin the exercise by creating a Dataproc job.

Exercise – Creating and running jobs on a Dataproc cluster

In this exercise, we will try three different methods to submit a Dataproc job: running on a permanent Dataproc cluster, running on an ephemeral cluster, and running on Dataproc Serverless.

In the previous exercise, we used the Spark shell to run our Spark syntax, which is common when practicing but not common in real development. Usually, we would only use the Spark shell for initial checking or testing simple things. In this exercise, we will code Spark jobs in editors and submit them as jobs.

Here are the scenarios that we want to try:

- Preparing log data in GCS and HDFS
- Developing a Spark ETL job from HDFS to HDFS
- Developing a Spark ETL job from GCS to GCS
- Developing a Spark ETL job from GCS to BigQuery

Let's look at each of these scenarios in detail.

Preparing log data in GCS and HDFS

The log data is in our GitHub repository, located here: `https://github.com/PacktPublishing/Data-Engineering-with-Google-Cloud-Platform-Second-Edition/tree/main/chapter-5/dataset/logs_example`

If you haven't cloned the repository, clone it to your Cloud Shell environment.

Clone the syntax from Cloud Shell and copy the log file folders into `gcs`:

```
$ cd chapter-5/dataset
$ gcloud storage cp -r logs_example/* gs://[YOUR-BUCKET-NAME]/chapter-5/dataset/logs_example/
```

Now, go to the Hadoop master node shell, copy our folder there, and use the HDFS put command to load the files into HDFS, like this:

```
$ gcloud storage cp -r gs://[YOUR-BUCKET-NAME]/from-git/chapter-5/dataset/logs_example .
$ hdfs dfs -copyFromLocal logs_example ../../data
```

With the preceding command, the logs will be ready in HDFS.

Developing a Spark ETL job from HDFS to HDFS

If we look at the log file, the records are like this:

```
97.116.185.190 - - [17/May/2015:11:05:59 +0000] "GET /articles/dynamic-dns-with-dhcp/ HTTP/1.1" 200 18848
"http://ubuntuforums.org/showthread.php?t=2003644" "Mozilla/5.0 (Windows NT 5.2; WOW64) AppleWebKit/537.36 (KHTML, like Gecko) Chrome/32.0.1700.107 Safari/537.36"
```

This is common Apache web log data. The data contains some information: the user IP that accesses the website, the access time, HTTP GET access information, and all other information.

For our exercise, we want to use HTTP GET access information to provide two metrics.

We want to calculate how many user requests each article has. Take these three records as an example:

```
/articles/dynamic-dns-with-dhcp
/articles/ssh-security
/articles/ssh-security
```

We expect an output file that contains this information:

```
dynamic-dns-with-dhcp,1
ssh-security,2
```

The challenge is that the records are not structured data. You can't load the files to a BigQuery table to run a SQL query. This is an unstructured data condition, which is the best case for PySpark. So, let's create a PySpark application to handle this. Our first application will read data from HDFS and store the output back in HDFS.

To do that, open Cloud Shell Editor and create a new working folder and a file named pyspark_job.py.

In the code, let's import SparkSession:

```
from pyspark.sql import SparkSession
```

Declare the SparkSession like this:

```
spark = SparkSession.builder \
    .appName('spark_hdfs_to_hdfs') \
        .getOrCreate()
sc = spark.sparkContext
```

As mentioned before, SparkSession and SparkContext are what make a Python file have a Spark connection to the Hadoop cluster. We will use SparkContext to declare an RDD, run map, run reduce, and create a Spark DataFrame.

First, let's load our data from HDFS:

```
MASTER_NODE_INSTANCE_NAME="[Your Master Node instance name]"
log_files_rdd = sc.textFile('hdfs://{}/data/logs_example/*'.
format(MASTER_NODE_INSTANCE_NAME))
```

This is similar to the exercise using the Spark shell when we declared an RDD that connected data to an HDFS directory. This time, we specify the file location in our logs directory.

The next step is to split the logs with the " " delimiter space; this code line will split each record so that we can access the records such as arrays:

```
splitted_rdd = log_files_rdd.map(lambda x: x.split(" "))
```

We can access the array like this:

```
selected_col_rdd = splitted_rdd.map(lambda x: (x[0], x[3], x[5], x[6]))
```

The previous code snippet highlights the following:

- x[0] will give you the 97.116.185.190 IP
- x[3] will give you the [17/May/2015:11:05:59 access time
- x[5] will give you the GET method
- x[6] will give you the /articles/dynamic-dns-with-dhcp/ URL

At this point, our data is already structured; we can create a Spark DataFrame using the RDD, like this:

```
columns = ["ip","date","method","url"]
logs_df = selected_col_rdd.toDF(columns)
logs_df.createOrReplaceTempView('logs_df')
```

We can tell Spark to structure the RDD into a DataFrame with .toDF(columns). And so that we can access the DataFrame later in an SQL statement, we should use the logs_df.createOrReplaceTempView('logs_df') syntax.

When we declare a Spark DataFrame, we can access the DataFrame using SQL in Spark, like this:

```
sql = f"""
    SELECT
    url,
    count(*) as count
    FROM logs_df
    WHERE url LIKE '%/article%'
    GROUP BY url
    """
article_count_df = spark.sql(sql)
print(" ##$ Get only articles and blogs records ##$ ")
article_count_df.show(5)
```

In the previous code, notice that you use SQL to access a table named logs_df. Remember that that is not a table anywhere in any database. Instead, that is our Spark DataFrame that we declared in the previous statement. The SQL is answering our question about which article the user accesses.

The last step is to store the result back in HDFS. To do that, use this code:

```
article_count_df.write.save('hdfs://{}/data/article_count_df'.
format(MASTER_NODE_INSTANCE_NAME), format='csv', mode='overwrite')
```

That will write the result from our SQL to HDFS as CSV files. And that's it – you have your Spark application ready to run in Dataproc. To make sure your code is correct, check it against the complete code in the code repository: https://github.com/PacktPublishing/Data-Engineering-with-Google-Cloud-Platform-Second-Edition/blob/main/chapter-5/code/pyspark_hdfs_to_hdfs.py

As an example, here is my Cloud Shell Editor with the PySpark code (ignore the error warning):

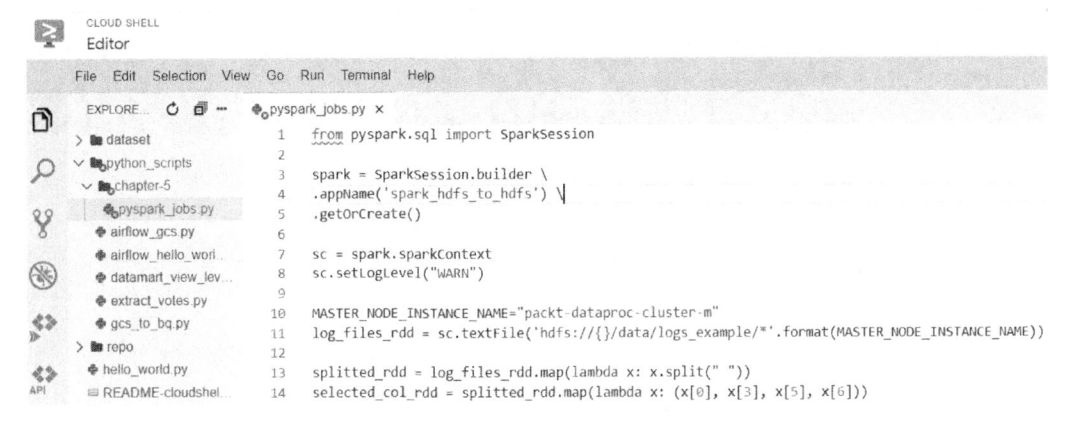

Figure 5.12 – PySpark code in Cloud Shell Editor

To run it in your Dataproc cluster, you need to upload the code to GCS. You can do that from GCS or by using `gcloud storage cp`, like this:

```
$ gcloud storage cp pyspark_job.py gs://[BUCKET NAME]/chapter-5/code/
```

Finally, you can submit it as a job to Dataproc using the Dataproc console in the `job` section or by using the `gcloud` command from Cloud Shell, like this:

```
$ gcloud dataproc jobs submit pyspark --cluster=[YOUR CLUSTER NAME]
--region=us-central1 gs://[BUCKET NAME]/chapter-5/code/pyspark_job.py
```

If all is correct, then the job will start, and you can check it in the console. As an example, here are my jobs, showing **Failed** and **Succeeded** jobs:

Figure 5.13 – Example Spark jobs on Dataproc

To check whether the output file is already in HDFS, from the Dataproc shell, use the HDFS `dfs -ls` command or, as an alternative, access it using Hive or the PySpark shell. For example, it will look like this:

```
adiwijaya@cluster-a55d-m:~$ hdfs dfs -ls ../../data/article_count_df
Found 2 items
-rw-r--r--   1 root hadoop          0 2023-08-29 12:24 ../../data/article_count_df/_SUCCESS
-rw-r--r--   1 root hadoop       1069 2023-08-29 12:24 ../../data/article_count_df/part-00000-8ad4f96c-0e29-43a9-ad65-f9846fae96cd-c000.csv
```

Figure 5.14 – Example output from the job

As you can see, the job has successfully generated the result into a file folder in the directory. The filename is `part-00000.csv`. There is only one file because the output of this job is small; if the output results in large data, then there will be multiple file parts.

Developing a Spark ETL job from GCS to GCS

As we discussed before, we can use either HDFS or GCS seamlessly from PySpark. In this section, let's try to change our code to read and write to GCS instead of HDFS.

To do that, we just need to make a simple modification to our code. More specifically, check your PySpark code when it's reading data from an RDD. Change it to access GCS, like this:

```
BUCKET_NAME="[Your GCS Bucket name]"
log_files_rdd = sc.textFile('gs://{}/from-git/chapter-5/dataset/logs_
example/*'.format(BUCKET_NAME))
```

And finally, here's the line where we write to another GCS directory:

```
article_count_df.write.save('gs://{}/chapter-5/job-result/article_
count_df'.format(BUCKET_NAME), format='csv', mode='overwrite')
```

To submit the job, we can perform the exact same step as in the previous section by copying the Python file into GCS and running it using the `gcloud` command. Try it yourself, and if you have any issues, revisit the previous section; all the steps should be the same.

The commands are as follows:

```
$ gcloud storage cp pyspark_job.py gs://[BUCKET NAME]/chapter-5/code/
$ gcloud dataproc jobs submit pyspark --cluster=[Your Cluster name]
--region=us-central1 gs://[BUCKET NAME]/chapter-5/code/pyspark_job.py
```

If successful, check your GCS bucket directory; your output file should be in the GCS target directory now. Here is an example from my bucket. You will notice that there are multiple file parts in the output folder, like this:

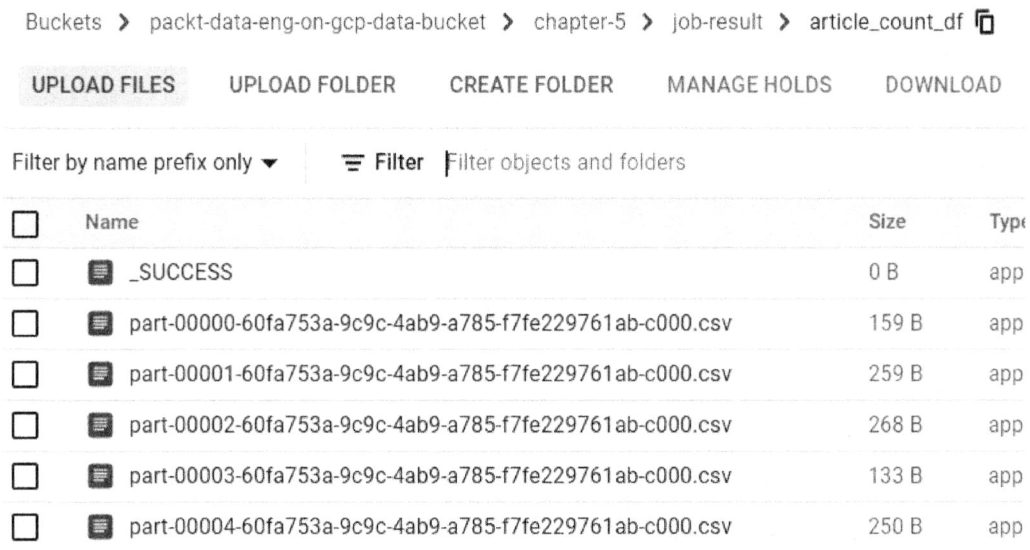

Buckets > packt-data-eng-on-gcp-data-bucket > chapter-5 > job-result > article_count_df
UPLOAD FILES
UPLOAD FOLDER
CREATE FOLDER
MANAGE HOLDS
DOWNLOAD
Filter by name prefix only
Filter
Filter objects and folders
Name
Size
Typ
_SUCCESS 0 B app
part-00000-60fa753a-9c9c-4ab9-a785-f7fe229761ab-c000.csv 159 B app
part-00001-60fa753a-9c9c-4ab9-a785-f7fe229761ab-c000.csv 259 B app
part-00002-60fa753a-9c9c-4ab9-a785-f7fe229761ab-c000.csv 268 B app
part-00003-60fa753a-9c9c-4ab9-a785-f7fe229761ab-c000.csv 133 B app
part-00004-60fa753a-9c9c-4ab9-a785-f7fe229761ab-c000.csv 250 B app

Figure 5.15 – Checking multiple file partitions from the job's output

If you open those files, each file contains partial records from the output. This is another good perspective on what's called a distributed filesystem and processing. In this case, there are five file parts (`part-00000` to `part-00004`); you may find yours are different. In the background of our Spark job, it parallelizes the execution into five streams, and each stream produces individual output files. And for downstream usage, it doesn't matter how many file parts are there. All you need to do is access the `/article_count_df/*.csv` directory.

As another possible extension to your exercise, remember that you can also create a BigQuery external table to access output files. With this, you will get a clear picture of how a data lake works to process unstructured data to produce output for downstream users.

At the end of the day, as data engineers, we would like to process unstructured data into structured data so that more users can gain information from the data. From our example case, not many people in an organization know how to process log data to gain information. It is a data engineer's responsibility to be able to process unstructured information into more meaningful information for other users.

Developing a Spark ETL job from GCS to BigQuery

The last alternative that we have is to read and write data directly from BigQuery using PySpark. In the previous exercise, you may have used the BigQuery external table to access data from the GCS output file. Another option is to store the output directly to BigQuery as a native table.

To do that, let's jump to the section where we stored our output to GCS and change it to BigQuery, like this:

```
article_count_df.write.format('bigquery') \
.option('temporaryGcsBucket', BUCKET_NAME) \
.option('table', 'dwh_bikesharing.article_count_df') \
.mode('overwrite') \
.save()
```

And for the job submission, after copying the code to your GCS bucket, you need to add the BigQuery `jars` connector, like this:

```
$ gcloud storage cp pyspark_job.py gs://[BUCKET NAME]/chapter-5/code/
$ gcloud dataproc jobs submit pyspark --cluster=[Your Cluster name]
--region=us-central1 gs://[BUCKET NAME]/chapter-5/code/pyspark_job.
py  --jars gs://spark-lib/bigquery/spark-bigquery-latest_2.12.jar
```

Note that the `gs://spark-lib/bigquery/spark-bigquery-latest_2.12.jar` library is from a public GCS bucket named `spark-lib`; do not change that bucket name.

The preceding code will make our PySpark job write the Spark DataFrame into a BigQuery table. As an example, I put the table into the `dwh_bikesharing` dataset with a table named `article_count_df`.

You can check in the BigQuery console, under the `dwh_bikesharing` dataset; the result will look like this:

Row	url	count
1	/articles/ssh-security	1
2	/blog/articles/week-of-unix-too...	1
3	/articles/dy	1
4	/articles/ppp-over-ssh	1
5	/blog/articles/ppp-over-ssh/m...	1
6	/blog/articles/dynamic-dns-wit...	1

Figure 5.16 – The article_count_df table result

All the other lines of code are the same. As you can see from these three I/O alternatives, you have the flexibility to read and write data from HDFS, GCS, or BigQuery from a Dataproc cluster.

You may choose to store the data directly in a native BigQuery table if you are working with structured data that has a clear table schema.

In general, accessing data from HDFS is faster than GCS, and GCS is faster than BigQuery. But this is a general rule of thumb; how much faster still depends on the data volume. A lot of times, the time difference is not significant compared to the ease of using a slower storage connection.

With that in mind, focus on the use case; if your use case uses all structured data, then use BigQuery as your underlying storage. If you need more flexibility to store all of your data in files, use GCS. And if the processing time is critical, use HDFS on the SSD.

This is the end of the exercise for which we needed a permanent Dataproc cluster. Please delete the Dataproc cluster if you have finished the exercise.

Understanding the concept of an ephemeral cluster

After running the previous exercises, you may notice that Spark is very useful for processing data, but it has little to no dependence on HDFS. It's very convenient to use data as is from GCS or BigQuery compared to using HDFS.

What does this mean? It means that we may choose not to store any data in the Hadoop cluster (more specifically, in HDFS) and only use the cluster to run jobs. For cost efficiency, we can smartly turn on and off the cluster only when a job is running.

Furthermore, we can destroy the entire Hadoop cluster when the job is finished and create a new one when we submit a new job. This concept is what's called an ephemeral cluster.

An **ephemeral cluster** means the cluster is not permanent. A cluster will only exist when it's running jobs. There are two main advantages to using this approach:

- **Highly efficient infrastructure cost**: With this approach, you don't need to have a giant Hadoop cluster with hundreds of workers hanging and waiting for jobs. It's typical for organizations that adopt Hadoop on-premises to have this giant cluster model. However, since we have the flexibility to destroy and create clusters easily in the cloud, we can reduce all unnecessary costs from idle clusters and worker machines.

- **Dedicated resource for isolated jobs**: With this approach, every set of jobs can run in a dedicated cluster. A dedicated cluster means you can specify the following:
  - The OS version
  - Hadoop versions
  - Dependency libraries
  - Cluster specs

This will remove all common issues in Spark about resource allocation and dependency conflicts. When jobs are isolated, you know exactly the expected job completion time given a specific cluster spec.

Understanding the ephemeral cluster concept, you will realize that this process is even simpler when using Dataproc Serverless, where create and delete cluster tasks are handled by GCP in the background. However, understanding this ephemeral cluster concept is still important to handle edge cases and will be a common topic if you are pursuing certification.

In general, use Dataproc Serverless whenever possible. Use an ephemeral cluster model when you need a certain level of custom configuration that can't be handled by Dataproc Serverless; for example, software versions or using frameworks other than Spark.

Compared to a permanent cluster, an ephemeral cluster is recommended. Only use a permanent Dataproc cluster model in the following scenarios:

- You need to use HDFS and Hive as your underlying data storage for the data lake
- You need to use the UI on the Hadoop cluster; for example, Hue, Jupyter Notebook, or Zeppelin
- You are sure about the cost of the permanent cluster in the long run

Remember that in the ephemeral model, your cluster literally will be deleted. The data in the cluster machines will also be gone after each job. In the preceding case, using a permanent Dataproc approach is the only option.

If we decide to use the ephemeral cluster approach, then a question may come up – how do we sync cluster creation and deletion with a job?

There are many ways; you can do it manually and automatically. One automatic option is using a Dataproc workflow template. Let's practice using it to understand the next section.

Practicing using a workflow template on Dataproc

A workflow template is a feature in Dataproc that can help you manage simple job dependencies. Using a workflow template, you can also define an ephemeral cluster as a part of jobs. This means that if you run jobs using a workflow template, it will automatically create a new Dataproc cluster, run the jobs, and drop the cluster after it finishes.

To create a workflow template, go to the Dataproc console. In the left sidebar, find **Workflows**, like this:

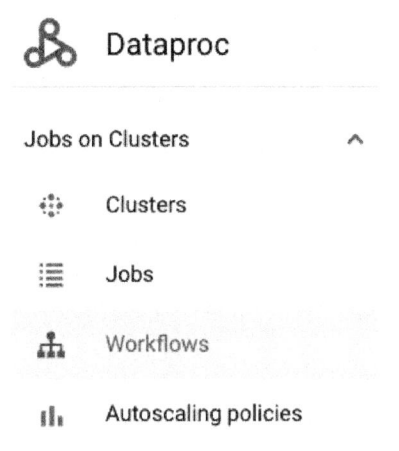

Figure 5.17 – The Workflows menu in the Dataproc console

Find and click the **CREATE WORKFLOW TEMPLATE** button and configure some important options:

- **Template ID**: `run_pyspark_job`
- **Region**: `us-central1`
- **Time to Live**: Enable
- **Duration**: `30 minutes`

Click **Next**.

On the next page, click **CONFIGURE MANAGED CLUSTER**, which will be similar to the options we have when creating a Dataproc cluster. This time, we can use the **Single Node** cluster type:

Building a Data Lake Using Dataproc

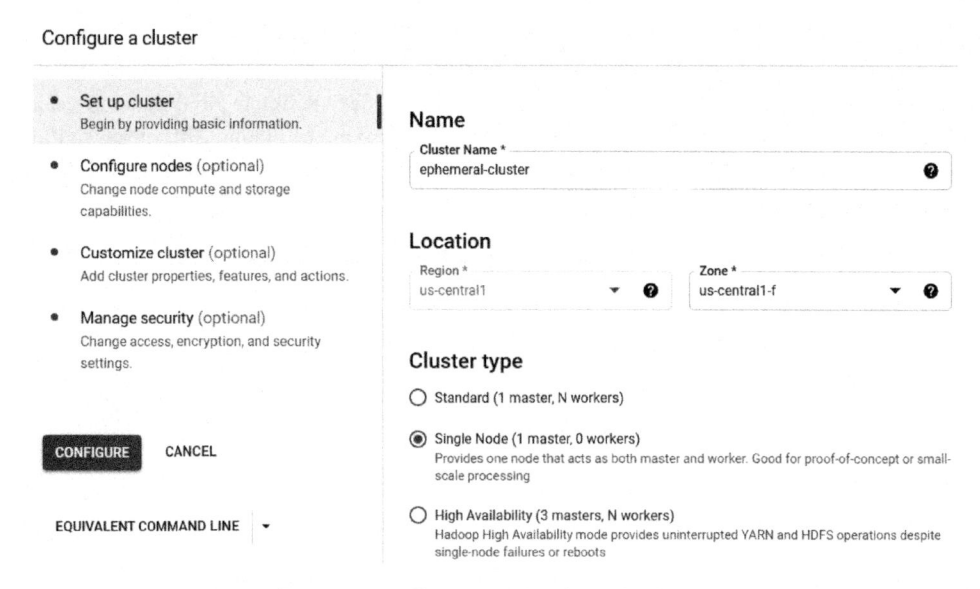

Figure 5.18 – Choosing a Single Node cluster

Don't forget to configure the node to use n2-standard-2 machines with 30 GB storage. This will save a little bit on costs. Then, click CONFIGURE.

If finished, click **Next**. You will be on the **Job config** page; find and click the **ADD JOB** button. This is to add our PySpark job; we need to provide the code location in GCS and the required JAR files. In our case, we need the BigQuery connector library:

Figure 5.19 – Example job configuration

Scroll down and click the **ADD** button. If finished, find the **CREATE** button at the bottom of the screen. You should see your workflow template is there. Click **RUN** to try it:

	Template ID	Region	Creation time ↓	Cluster type	Total jobs	Action
☐	run_pyspark_job	us-central1	Aug 28, 2023, 8:10:25 PM	Auto managed cluster	1	RUN

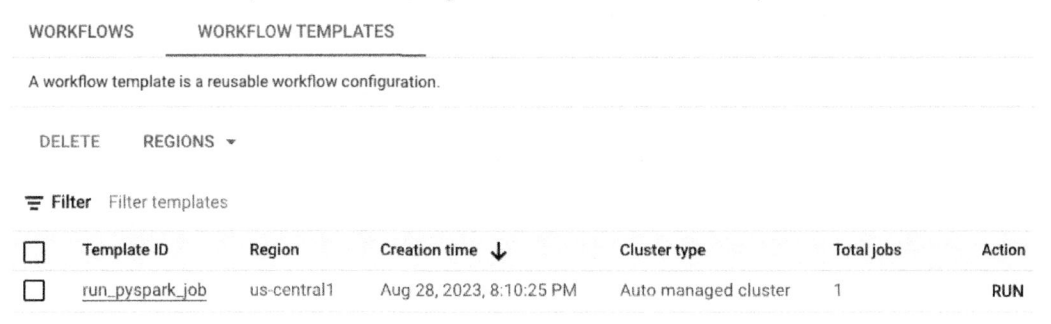

Figure 5.20 – A Dataproc workflow template

While running, we can check three different menus to see what really happens:

1. In the **WORKFLOWS** tab, you can see the workflow template is running:

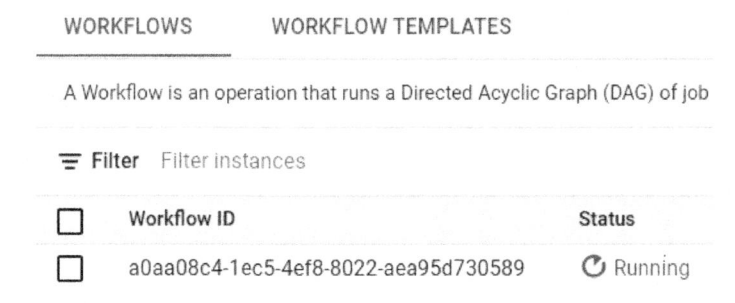

	Workflow ID	Status
☐	a0aa08c4-1ec5-4ef8-8022-aea95d730589	Running

Figure 5.21 – A workflow template is running

2. In the Dataproc **Clusters** menu, you can see a newly created cluster:

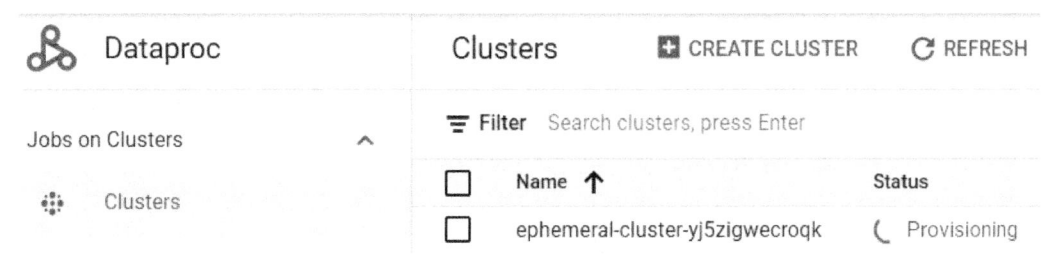

	Name ↑	Status
☐	ephemeral-cluster-yj5zigwecroqk	Provisioning

Figure 5.22 – A Dataproc cluster is provisioned

3. After the cluster is successfully provisioned, you can see the job is running in the **Jobs** menu.
4. Wait for around 5 minutes after the job has finished; you should then see that the cluster has gone.

What we've looked at here is a Dataproc ephemeral cluster to run a PySpark job. As you can see, the cluster lives only when running a job; after that, it will automatically be destroyed. If you want to rerun the job, you can go back to the **WORKFLOW TEMPLATES** menu and run it again.

In this exercise, we only run one job in the template. The workflow template can also run multiple jobs as a **directed acyclic graph** (**DAG**), with job dependencies that you can configure while creating the template.

Building an ephemeral cluster using Dataproc and Cloud Composer

Another option to manage ephemeral clusters is using Cloud Composer. We learned about Airflow in the previous chapter to orchestrate BigQuery data loading. But as we've already learned, Airflow has many operators, and one of them is, of course, Dataproc.

You should use this approach compared to a workflow template if your jobs are complex, in terms of developing a pipeline that contains many branches, backfilling logic, and dependencies to other services, since workflow templates can't handle these complexities.

For this exercise, if your Cloud Composer environment is no longer available, you don't need to execute it. Simply go through the following example code. Once you've completed *Chapter 4, Building Workflows for Batch Data Loading Using Cloud Composer*, you'll understand the complete concept.

In the following example exercise, we will use Airflow to create a Dataproc cluster, submit a PySpark job, and delete the cluster when finished.

Check the full code in the GitHub repository of the book: `https://github.com/PacktPublishing/Data-Engineering-with-Google-Cloud-Platform-Second-Edition`

To use Dataproc operators in Airflow, we need to import the operators, like this:

```
from airflow.providers.google.cloud.operators.dataproc import (
    ClusterGenerator,
    DataprocCreateClusterOperator,
    DataprocDeleteClusterOperator,
    DataprocSubmitJobOperator,
)
```

After importing the three Dataproc operators, we can create a cluster, delete a cluster, and submit a job using an Airflow DAG. If you don't remember how to create and submit a DAG to Cloud Composer, please revisit the *Level 1 DAG – Creating dummy workflows* section of *Chapter 4, Building Workflows for Batch Data Loading Using Cloud Composer*.

Building an ephemeral cluster using Dataproc and Cloud Composer 191

The first operator is `DataprocCreateClusterOperator`; this operator will create a Dataproc cluster. You can specify the cluster configuration using a JSON string, like this:

```
CLUSTER_NAME = 'ephemeral-spark-cluster-{{ ds_nodash }}'
cluster_config = ClusterGenerator(
project_id=PROJECT_ID,
master_machine_type="n1-standard-4",
num_workers=0,
idle_delete_ttl=600).make()
create_cluster = DataprocCreateClusterOperator(
        task_id="create_cluster",
        project_id=PROJECT_ID,
        cluster_config=cluster_config,
        region=REGION,
        cluster_name=CLUSTER_NAME)
```

In the preceding example, we configured the number of workers to be two. There are many other configurations that we can specify; a full list can be found in this public documentation: https://cloud.google.com/dataproc/docs/reference/rest/v1/ClusterConfig.

The other thing that we specify is the `idle_delete_ttl` value to be 600 seconds. This means that if the DAG fails for any reason, the cluster will automatically be deleted after 600 seconds. Lastly, another trick is to add a postfix to our cluster name; for this example, we use the date from the Airflow **macro** variable. Using this date as the cluster name will prevent a collision between jobs with different execution dates. This will be useful if the DAG is running multiple backfills.

Next, we want to add a task for submitting a `pyspark` job. To do that, we need the job's code URI, and in our example, because we need to use the BigQuery connector, we can specify the JAR file in the PySpark job configuration, like this:

```
PYSPARK_URI = 'gs://[BUCKET NAME]/chapter-5/code/pyspark_gcs_to_bq.py'
PYSPARK_JOB = {
    "reference": {"project_id": PROJECT_ID},
    "placement": {"cluster_name": CLUSTER_NAME},
    "pyspark_job": {"main_python_file_uri": PYSPARK_URI,
    "jar_file_uris":
        ["gs://spark-lib/bigquery/spark-bigquerylatest_2.12.jar"]
    }
}
pyspark_task = DataprocSubmitJobOperator(
    task_id="pyspark_task", job=PYSPARK_JOB, region=REGION,
    project_id=PROJECT_ID
)
```

In the preceding example, we only have one job. Remember that you can add as many PySpark job tasks as needed. And lastly, after the jobs are finished, we want the cluster to be deleted. It's a simple task, like this:

```
delete_cluster = DataprocDeleteClusterOperator(
        task_id="delete_cluster", project_id=PROJECT_ID,
            cluster_name=CLUSTER_NAME, region=REGION
)
```

The DAG dependency is very simple, like this:

```
create_cluster >> pyspark_task >> delete_cluster
```

As a summary, remember that if you want to develop Spark jobs using an ephemeral cluster, you have two options, as follows:

- A workflow template
- Cloud Composer

Use the first option if jobs are simple, but it's very common for data engineers to choose Cloud Composer so that they can combine all the best practices from Cloud Composer with Dataproc, BigQuery, and GCS.

Submitting a Spark ETL job from GCS to BigQuery using Dataproc Serverless

In this last section, we will try the latest Dataproc feature, which is Dataproc Serverless. To create a Dataproc Serverless job, go to the Dataproc console. In the left sidebar, find **Serverless** | **Batches**, like this:

Figure 5.23 – Finding the Dataproc Serverless menu

To submit a job, you can use the console by clicking the **CREATE** button. The menu is straightforward, and we can also use the `gcloud` command to submit the job. For example, the command will look like this:

```
$ gcloud dataproc batches submit --project [YOUR PROJECT NAME]
--region us-central1 pyspark --batch [ANY NAME] gs://[YOUR BUCKET
NAME]/chapter-5/code/pyspark_job.py --version 2.1 --jars gs://spark-
lib/bigquery/spark-bigquery-latest_2.12.jar --subnet default
```

Unfortunately, at this point, if you are using the Google Cloud free tier, you can't try this feature because of the CPU quota. For using Dataproc Serverless, it will need at least 12 cores. The default CPU quota for the free tier doesn't meet the requirement. Don't worry about it – the result is the same as for a regular Dataproc job.

To give you an illustration, if finished, the job will look like this in Dataproc Serverless:

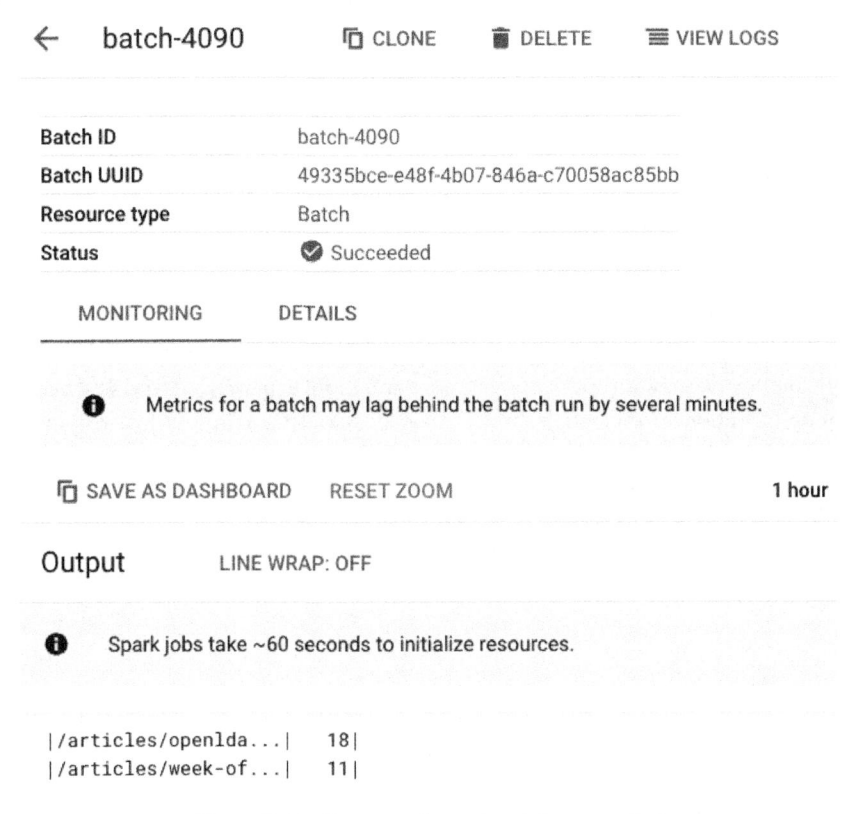

```
← batch-4090        CLONE    DELETE    VIEW LOGS

Batch ID           batch-4090
Batch UUID         49335bce-e48f-4b07-846a-c70058ac85bb
Resource type      Batch
Status             ✓ Succeeded

MONITORING    DETAILS

  ⓘ  Metrics for a batch may lag behind the batch run by several minutes.

  SAVE AS DASHBOARD    RESET ZOOM                               1 hour

Output        LINE WRAP: OFF

  ⓘ  Spark jobs take ~60 seconds to initialize resources.

|/articles/openlda...|   18|
|/articles/week-of...|   11|
```

Figure 5.24 – Dataproc Serverless job succeeded

The job will result in exactly the same output as our previous exercises. But notice that to submit a Spark job using Dataproc Serverless, you only need the code and can submit it with the `gcloud` command! You don't even need to create any Dataproc cluster.

The Dataproc backend will create all the required infrastructure in the background, starting from two worker nodes. If needed it will be auto-scaled up to 2,000 worker nodes.

This is a huge improvement to our development and production experience. Try to use the Dataproc Serverless approach whenever possible for simplicity. But as you can also see in the configuration, there are a limited number of options that we can choose from; for example, the Spark version. If the Spark version doesn't meet your requirements, then use the regular Dataproc.

Before wrapping up, as a reminder, please don't forget to delete your Dataproc cluster from the exercise if you no longer need it. To really clean it up, after the cluster is deleted, go to the GCS console; you will see some buckets created for Dataproc temporary and staging files – delete those buckets. With that, we are clean and ready to continue to the next chapter.

Summary

This chapter covered one component of GCP that allows you to build a data lake, called Dataproc. As we've learned in this chapter, learning about Dataproc means learning about Hadoop. We learned about and practiced the core and most popular Hadoop components, HDFS and Spark.

By combining the nature of Hadoop with all the benefits of using the cloud, we also learned about new concepts. A Hadoop ephemeral cluster is relatively new and is only possible because of cloud technology. In a traditional on-premises Hadoop cluster, this highly efficient concept is never an option.

In this chapter, we focused on the core concepts of Spark. We learned about using RDDs and Spark DataFrames. These two concepts are the first entry point before learning about other features such as Spark ML and Spark Streaming. As you get more and more experienced, you will need to start to think about optimization – for example, how to manage parallelism, how to fasten-join, and how to maximize resource allocation.

In the next chapter, we will learn about another data processing framework, **Dataflow**. Dataflow is a serverless service that processes structured and unstructured data, but we will focus on using Dataflow for streaming a data pipeline.

6
Processing Streaming Data with Pub/Sub and Dataflow

Processing streaming data is becoming increasingly popular since this enables businesses to get real-time metrics on business operations. In this chapter, we will understand which paradigm should be used – and when – for streaming data. We will also learn how to apply transformations to streaming data using Cloud Dataflow, as well as how to store processed records in BigQuery for analysis.

Learning about streaming data is easier when we do it, so we will complete some exercises where we will create a streaming data pipeline on **Google Cloud Platform** (**GCP**). We will use two GCP services, **Pub/Sub** and **Dataflow**. Both services are essential in creating a streaming data pipeline. At the end of this chapter, we will compare how similar and different streaming is to the batch approach that we learned about in *Chapter 5, Building a Data Lake Using Dataproc*.

Here are the topics that we will discuss in this chapter:

- Processing streaming data
- Exercise – publishing event streams to Pub/Sub
- Exercise – using Dataflow to stream data from Pub/Sub to BigQuery

Let's get started!

Technical requirements

Before we begin this chapter, you must have a few prerequisites ready.

In this chapter's exercises, we will use **Dataflow**, **Pub/Sub**, **Google Cloud Storage** (**GCS**), and **BigQuery**. If you've never opened any of these services in your GCP console, you can open them now and enable their **application programming interfaces** (**APIs**).

Also, make sure you have your **GCP console**, **Cloud Shell**, and **Cloud Shell Editor** ready.

You can download the example code and the dataset from here: `https://github.com/PacktPublishing/Data-Engineering-with-Google-Cloud-Platform-Second-Edition/tree/main/chapter-6`.

Be aware of the cost that might arise from **Dataflow streaming**. Make sure you delete all the environments after executing the exercises in this chapter to prevent unexpected charges.

This chapter will use the same data from *Chapter 5, Building a Data Lake Using Dataproc*. You can choose to use the same data or prepare new data from the preceding GitHub repository.

Processing streaming data

In the big data era, people like to correlate big data with real-time data. Some people say that if the data is not real time, then it's not big data. This statement is partially true. In reality, the majority of data pipelines in the world use the batch approach, and that's why it's still very important for data engineers to understand the batch data pipeline. From *Chapter 3, Building a Data Warehouse on BigQuery*, to *Chapter 5, Building a Data Lake Using Dataproc*, we focused on handling batch data pipelines.

However, real-time capabilities in the big data era are something that many data engineers need to start to rethink in terms of data architecture. To understand more about architecture, we need to have a clear definition of what real-time data is.

From the end user perspective, real-time data can mean anything – from faster access to data, more frequent data refresh, and detecting events as soon as they happen. From a data engineer perspective, what we need to know is *how* to make it happen. For example, if you search any keyword in Google Search, you will get an immediate result in real time. As another example, if you open any social media page, you can find your account statistics and the number of friends, visitors, and other information in real time.

But if you think about it, you may notice that there is nothing new in either of these examples. As an end user, you can get fast access to this data because of the backend database; this is a common practice dating from the 1990s. In big data, what's new is *real time* in terms of incoming data and processing. This specific real-time aspect is called **streaming data**. For example, you need to detect fraud as soon as an event happens. In most cases, detecting fraud needs many parameters from multiple data sources, which are impossible to handle in the application database. If fraud has no relevance to your company, you can think of other use cases, such as real-time marketing campaigns and real-time dashboards for sales reporting. Both use cases may require a large volume of data from multiple data sources. In these kinds of cases, being able to handle data in streams may come in handy.

Streaming data for data engineers

Streaming data in data engineering means a data pipeline that flows data from upstream to downstream as soon as the data is created. In nature, all data is created in real time, so processing data in batches is a way to simplify the process.

What does this mean?

If you think about how every piece of data is created, it's always in real time – for example, a user registered to a mobile application. The moment the user registered, data was created in the database. Another example is data being input into a spreadsheet. The moment the data entry is written in the spreadsheet, data is created in the sheet. Looking at these examples, you can see that data always has a value and we know the time when it's created. Processing streaming data means we process the data as soon as the data is inputted into a system.

Take a look at the following diagram. Here, there are two databases: **Source Database** and **Target Database**. For streaming data, every time a new record is inserted into the source database (illustrated as boxes with numbers), the record is immediately processed as an event and inserted into the target database. These events happen continuously, which makes the data in the target database real-time compared to the source database:

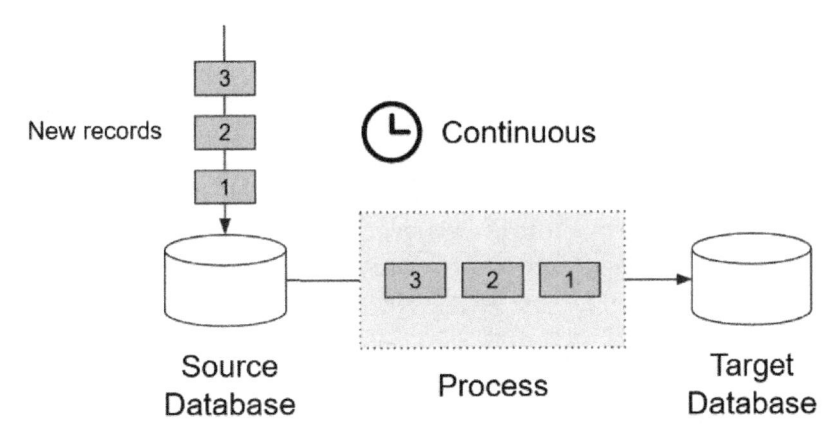

Figure 6.1 – Streaming data

In data engineering, the antonym for *stream* is *batch*. Batching is a very common approach for data engineers to process data. Even though we know data is real-time in nature, it's a lot easier to process data in a set time. For example, if your **chief executive officer** (**CEO**) wants to know about the company's revenue, it's a lot easier to populate the purchase history in a month and calculate the revenue, rather than build a system that continuously calculates the purchase transactions. Or, on a more granular level, a batch is commonly done on a weekly, daily, or hourly basis. The batch approach is a widely used practice in the data engineering world; I can say 90% of the data pipeline is a batch.

Take a look at the following diagram. Here, the two databases are the same as in *Figure 6.1*. The nature of how data is inserted into the source database is also the same – it's always real-time from the source database perspective. The difference is in the processing step, where the records are grouped into batches. Every batch is scheduled individually to be loaded to the target database:

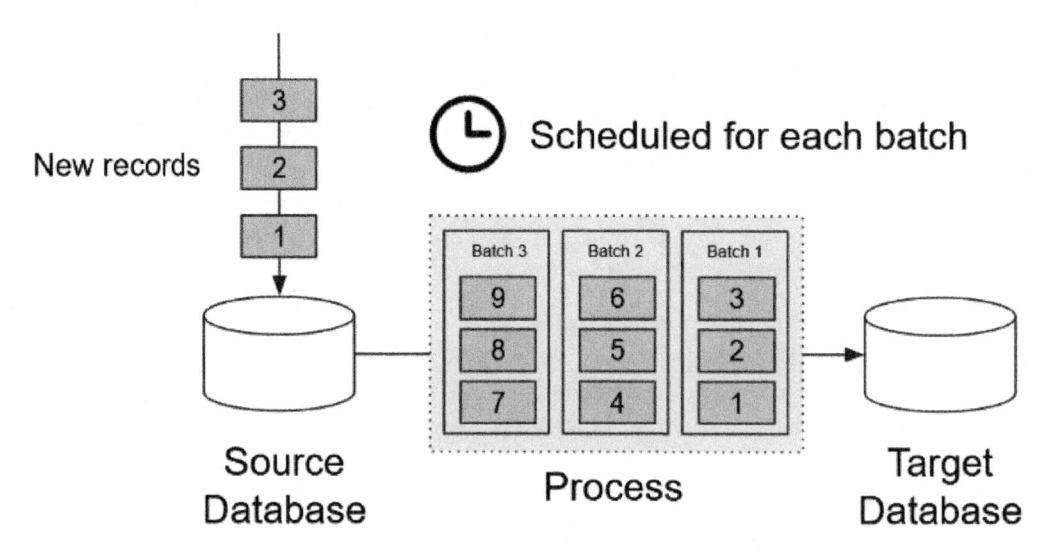

Figure 6.2 – Batch data

There are two major reasons why processing data in batches is more popular compared to streams. The first is because of the data user's needs. The data user, who is usually called a **decision maker**, naturally asks for information over a certain period. As we've discussed in the previous example, common questions are *How much X in a day?* Or how *many X in a month?* It's very rare to have a question such as *How much X this second compared to the last second?*

The second reason is the complexity of technology. Batching is easier than streaming because you can control a lot of things in a batch – for example, you can control how you want to schedule data pipeline jobs. This doesn't apply to stream processing. A streaming process is one job; once it runs, it will process all the incoming data and it never ends. To handle all the complexities, we need specific sets of technologies.

In GCP, the common technology stack uses Pub/Sub and Dataflow. The following diagram shows the most common pattern for processing streaming data from data sources to BigQuery tables:

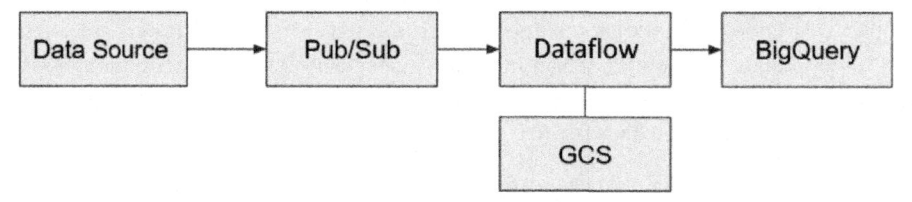

Figure 6.3 – High-level data streaming pattern

We will need Pub/Sub to control the incoming and outgoing data streams as messages. The next step is to set up Dataflow jobs that accept the messages to process the data as a streaming process. Dataflow will process the data in a distributed manner, and since Dataflow is a serverless service, we don't need to think about the servers. Dataflow will need GCS to store data temporarily if needed, and as the final process, it will stream the data to BigQuery tables. There will be no scheduler in the picture; all processes are long-running jobs, and we will learn how to run them in the *Exercise – using Dataflow to stream data from Pub/Sub to GCS* section. For now, let's learn the basics of Pub/Sub and Dataflow.

Introduction to Pub/Sub

Pub/Sub is a messaging system. What messaging systems do is receive messages from multiple systems and distribute them to multiple systems. The key here is *multiple systems*. A messaging system needs to be able to act as a bridge or middleware to many different systems.

The following diagram provides a high-level picture of Pub/Sub:

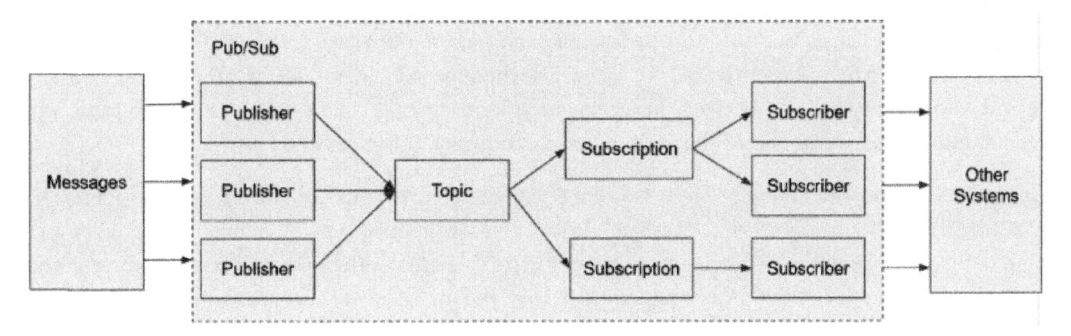

Figure 6.4 – Pub/Sub terminologies and flows

To understand how to use Pub/Sub, we need to understand the four main terminologies inside Pub/Sub, as follows:

- **Publisher**

    The entry point of Pub/Sub is the publisher. Pub/Sub uses the publisher to control incoming messages. Users can write code to publish messages from their applications using programming languages such as Java, Python, Go, C++, C#, **Hypertext Preprocessor** (**PHP**), and Ruby. Pub/Sub will store the messages in topics.

- **Topic**

    The central point of Pub/Sub is the topic. Pub/Sub stores messages in its internal storage. The sets of messages that are stored in Pub/Sub are called topics. As an analogy, Pub/Sub topics are similar to tables in a database – and using that analogy, Pub/Sub messages are similar, with rows or records in the tables.

- **Subscription**

    At the other end, each topic can have one or many subscriptions. Subscriptions are entities that have an interest in receiving messages from the topic. For example, for one topic that has two subscriptions, the two subscriptions will get identical messages from the topic.

- **Subscriber**

    A subscriber is different from a subscription. Each subscription can have one or many subscribers. The idea of having multiple subscribers in a subscription is to split the loads. For example, for one subscription that has two subscribers, the two subscribers will get partial messages from the subscription.

In addition to those four main terminologies, there is one more important term, which is **acknowledge** (**ack**). Note that ack is not a component or object in Pub/Sub, which is why I didn't include it in the preceding terminologies.

Back to our last point about subscribers – after messages are delivered to the subscriber, the subscriber will acknowledge them. In Pub/Sub, this is called **ack**. When a message is *ack-ed*, the topic will stop sending the message to the subscriber. In scenarios when the subscriber can't *ack* the message for any reason – for example, a code error, a server overload, or any other reason – the Pub/Sub topic will retry sending the message up until it's either successfully ack-ed or expired.

An analogy for understanding *ack* is by thinking of a pizza delivery service. The pizza chef (publisher) will store the pizzas on the pizza shelf (topic). When you are ordering a pizza (subscriber), the delivery man (subscription) will try to deliver the pizza to you. Whenever the pizza is delivered to you, you need to acknowledge it, by signing a paper. With that, the pizza delivery will consider the job is done and won't send you another pizza. The moment you sign the paper is the *ack* in Pub/Sub.

This bunch of terminologies might sound abstract to you at this point, but it's a good start to be familiar with common terms. The easiest way to understand Pub/Sub is by using it. We will practice Pub/Sub in the next section, but before that, let's get familiar with Dataflow.

Introduction to Dataflow

Dataflow is a data processing engine that can handle both batch and streaming data pipelines. If we want to compare with technologies that we already learned about in this book, Dataflow is comparable with Spark – in terms of positioning, both technologies can process big data. Both technologies process data in parallel and can handle almost any kind of data or file.

But in terms of underlying technologies, they are different. From the user perspective, the main difference is the serverless nature of Dataflow. Using Dataflow, we don't need to set up any cluster. We just submit jobs to Dataflow, and the data pipeline will run automatically on the cloud. How we write the data pipeline is by using Apache Beam.

If you have finished reading *Chapter 5*, *Building a Data Lake Using Dataproc*, you will know that Dataproc is also available with Spark Serverless. At the time of writing, this feature is relatively new compared to Dataflow. There are still many limitations regarding Spark Serverless, including that it can't support Spark Streaming and there is no UI for checking the task flow. But as it's getting more and more mature, the difference between using Spark Serverless and Dataflow Serverless will become narrow. This also depends on your **software development kit** (**SDK**) preference between Spark or Apache Beam.

Apache Beam is an open source tool that's used to define data pipelines, but instead of executing them, Apache Beam will send the data pipelines to an execution engine such as Dataflow. Not only Dataflow – Apache Beam can run data pipelines on Direct Runner, Apache Flink, Nemo, Samza, and other engines. But the key here is the relationship between Apache Beam and Dataflow – we write code using the Apache Beam SDK, and Apache Beam will run the data pipeline using Dataflow. Later, we will learn about Apache Beam and run it using Direct Runner and Dataflow. In the next section, we will start the exercises in this chapter by creating our first Pub/Sub topic.

Exercise – publishing event streams to Pub/Sub

In this exercise, we will try to stream data from Pub/Sub publishers. The goal is to create a data pipeline that can stream the data to a BigQuery table, but instead of using a scheduler (as we did in *Chapter 4*, *Building Workflows for Batch Data Loading Using Cloud Composer*), we will submit a Dataflow job that will run as an application to flow data from Pub/Sub to a BigQuery table. In the exercise, we will use the bike-sharing dataset we used in *Chapter 3*, *Building a Data Warehouse in BigQuery*. Here are the overall steps we will cover:

1. Creating a Pub/Sub topic.
2. Creating and running a Pub/Sub publisher using Python.
3. Creating a Pub/Sub subscription.

We'll start by creating a Pub/Sub topic.

Creating a Pub/Sub topic

We can create Pub/Sub topics using many approaches – for example, using the GCP console, the `gcloud` command, or through code. As a starter, let's use the GCP console. Proceed as follows:

1. Open the console and find **Pub/Sub** in the navigation bar, as illustrated in the following screenshot:

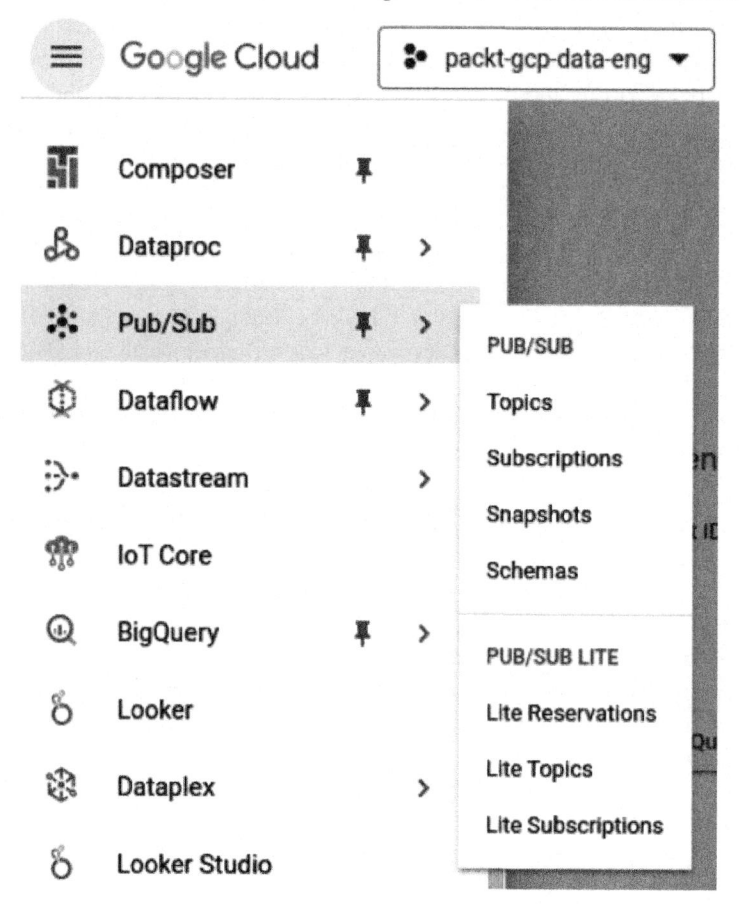

Figure 6.5 – The Pub/Sub menu in the navigation bar

If this is the first time you have accessed Pub/Sub, you will be asked to enable the API. Do that by clicking the **ENABLE Pub/Sub API** button.

2. On the **Topics** page, find the **CREATE TOPIC** button. It looks like this:

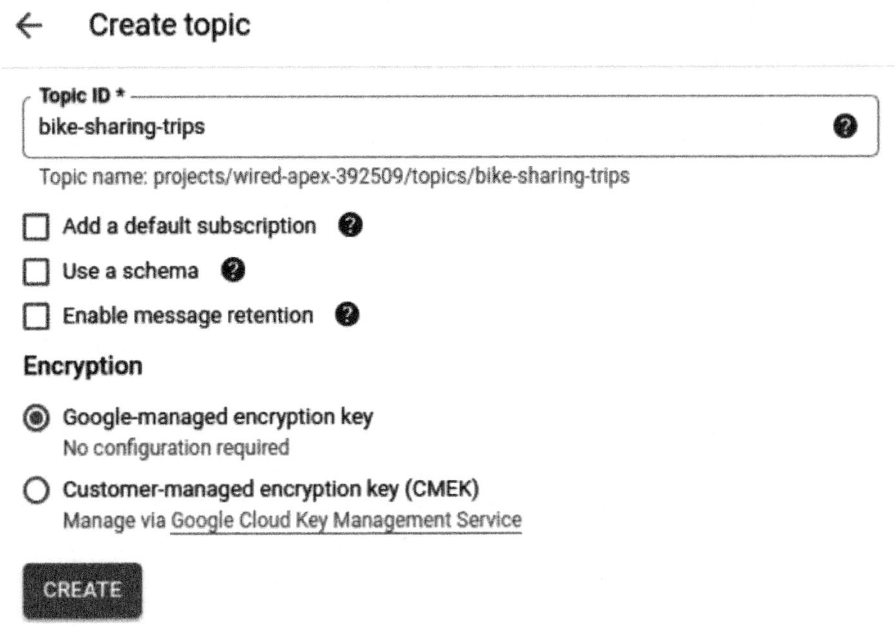

Figure 6.6 – Example of topic creation in Pub/Sub

In the **Topic ID** field, I will use `bike-sharing-trips` as the topic name or **identifier** (**ID**) to store our bike-sharing messages. Remember that a topic name is similar to a table name in BigQuery – it needs to be unique and representative of the message later. But also remember that in databases, we have higher-level groups, such as `dataset`, where you can group tables in a dataset. In Pub/Sub, there is no higher-level object, so be mindful when naming your topic – it needs to be as informative as possible. In this exercise, I'm using `bike-sharing` to describe what the dataset group is and `trips` to represent the content.

There will be three checkboxes – uncheck all of them and leave the **Encryption** option to the default Google-managed encryption key. We will create our subscription manually later to understand Pub/Sub subscription better. Once you're done, finish the process by clicking **CREATE TOPIC**.

3. Check your topic by clicking it. You will see an empty topic without messages. We will start sending messages using a publisher in the next section.

Creating and running a Pub/Sub publisher using Python

To send messages using a publisher, we should write code. As a standard in this book, we will use Python, but there are many other programming languages you can use that you can check out in the *Pub/Sub public documentation*.

Let's start by opening our Cloud Shell environment. The example code can be found in this book's GitHub repository: https://github.com/PacktPublishing/Data-Engineering-with-Google-Cloud-Platform-Second-Edition.

If you've already cloned the repository from previous chapters, open the chapter-6/code/pubsub_publisher.py file. Then, proceed as follows:

1. First, we need a Python function. This Python function will return a **JavaScript Object Notation (JSON)** record containing bike-sharing trip data. To simplify this example, we will generate five columns – trip_id, start_date, start_station_id, bike_number, and duration_sec. The Python function code looks like this:

    ```
    def create_random_message():
        trip_id = randint(10000,99999)
        start_date = str(datetime.utcnow())
        start_station_id = randint(200,205)
        bike_number = randint(100,999)
        duration_sec = randint(1000,9999)

        message_json = {'trip_id': trip_id,
                        'start_date': start_date,
                        'start_station_id': start_station_id,
                        'bike_number':bike_number,
                        'duration_sec':duration_sec
                        }
        return message_json
    ```

    As you can see, this is a simple function that randomizes some integers for our example message. Messages in Pub/Sub can be anything – they can be free text, for example – but in this example, we will send messages in JSON format.

2. For the Pub/Sub publisher, we will call PublisherClient from the Python package, like this:

    ```
    project_id = "packt-data-eng-on-gcp"
    topic_id = "bike-sharing-trips"

    publisher = pubsub_v1.PublisherClient()
    topic_path = publisher.topic_path(project_id, topic_id)
    ```

    This is straightforward Python code to call the client. Remember to change the project_id value to your GCP project ID.

3. Now, we need to send the message. To do this, we will simply loop 10 times to send exactly 10 messages. You can change the number as you like. Here is the code:

   ```
   for i in range(10):
       message_json = create_random_message()
       data = json.dumps(message_json)
       publish_future = publisher.publish(topic_path, \
           data.encode("utf-8"))
       publish_future.add_done_callback \
           (get_callback(publish_future, data))
       publish_futures.append(publish_future)
   ```

   These lines of code will call the `create_random_message()` function to get a JSON value and convert it into a string using `json.dumps()`. The message will be published using the `publisher.publish()` method.

4. Then, to make sure the message is successfully published and can handle errors when we fail to send it, we must define it in the callback function. The callback function looks like this:

   ```
   def get_callback(publish_future, data):
       def callback(publish_future):
           try:
               # Wait 60 seconds for the publish call to succeed.
               print(publish_future.result(timeout=60))
           except futures.TimeoutError:
               print(f"Publishing {data} timed out.")

       return callback
   ```

   The callback will wait for 60 seconds before it returns an exception.

5. Finally, insert the following code:

   ```
   futures.wait(publish_futures, return_when=futures.ALL_COMPLETED)
   print(f"Published messages with error handler to {topic_path}.")
   ```

   The line will instruct our application to wait until all records are done and will print out all the message IDs.

6. Go back to Cloud Shell and try to run the Python code using the following Python command:

   $ python3 pubsub_publisher.py

   If there is an issue with the `pubsub` Python library, make sure you have installed the `google-cloud-pubsub` library in your Cloud Shell environment before running the Python code using the `pip` command, like this:

   $ pip3 install google-cloud-pubsub

If the Python script is successful, it will look like this:

Figure 6.7 – Example pubsub_publisher application's output

7. Now, go back to your Pub/Sub console. You will see that the graphs show some activity in the topics, as illustrated here:

Figure 6.8 – Monitoring topic activity with a graph

If you can't see the line in the graph, don't worry – it takes around 5 minutes before the graph refreshes. To read the messages, we need a subscription. We will create one in the next section.

Creating a Pub/Sub subscription

In this section, we will create a Pub/Sub subscription. We will try creating one using the console. To do that, follow these steps:

1. From the **Pub/Sub topic** page, find and click the **CREATE SUBSCRIPTION** button at the bottom of the page. This button is under the **SUBSCRIPTIONS** tab, as shown in the following screenshot:

| SUBSCRIPTIONS | SNAPSHOTS | METRICS | DETAILS | MESSAGES |

Only subscriptions attached to this topic are displayed. A subscription captures the stream of subscription from a Cloud Dataflow job. Learn more

CREATE SUBSCRIPTION   **EXPORT**

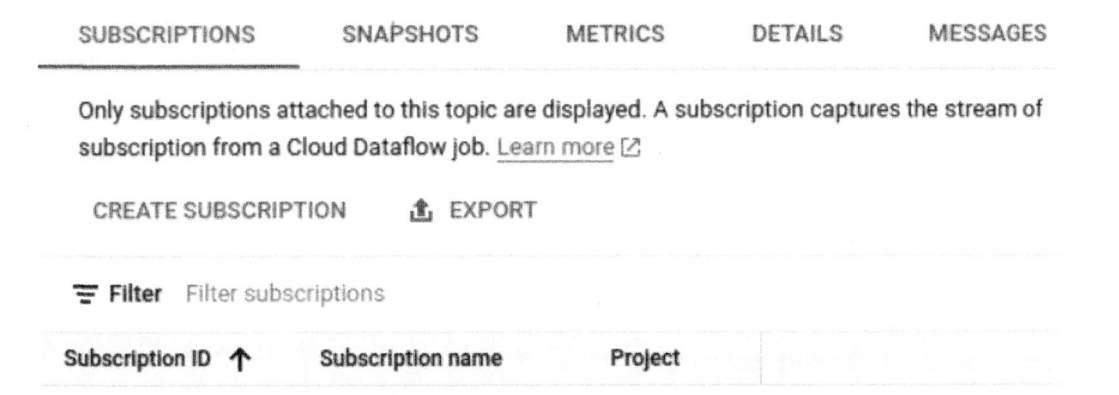

Filter   Filter subscriptions

| Subscription ID ↑ | Subscription name | Project |

Figure 6.9 – Finding the CREATE SUBSCRIPTION button

On the **CREATE SUBSCRIPTIONS** page, there are some options that you can choose. As you may recall, there was a checkbox for adding a default subscription when creating a topic – this is one of the reasons we didn't check it. We want to create one manually so that we can learn about the options and some of their concepts.

2. Define a **Subscription ID** value – feel free to choose any name. For example, I'm using `bike-sharing-trips-subs-1`.

3. The second option is **Delivery Type**; we have two options here: `pull` and `push`. In general, the `pull` option is recommended for the data pipeline use case. In the data pipeline, the subscriber can call the Pub/Sub client to pull the data from the subscription topic – for example, Dataflow can pull from a subscription topic. In that case, we use the `pull` method. The `push` method is used if the subscriber can't use the Pub/Sub client. The `push` method will provide a **HyperText Transfer Protocol** (**HTTP**) endpoint to deliver the message continuously. Neither method affects the throughput; both can provide high throughput, but the `push` method has a smaller throughput quota. As a comparison, the pull-to-push throughput difference is around 30:1; you can check the exact quota in the public documentation at `https://cloud.google.com/pubsub/quotas#quotas`.

4. The third option is **Message Retention Duration**. This is used to set up how long we want to keep unacknowledged (unacked) messages. An unacked message is a message that is sent by Pub/Sub Subscription but the downstream application fails to ack the message because of bugs, network errors, or any other reasons.

   The consideration is cost versus risk. If we keep unacked messages longer, the risk of losing the messages is lower, which means we need to pay for stored messages.

5. The **Expiration period** field is straightforward. If there is no subscriber activity in the **Subscription** field, the subscription will be deleted automatically after the expiration period.

6. The last option that we will talk about is **Acknowledgement deadline**. This is used to set up how many seconds you expect it will take for the subscription to resend the message if the message is not ack-ed. This is related to how much the subscriber can handle the message. If the process in the subscriber is light and the throughput is low, you can set the deadline lower. If the process is heavy, you can set the deadline longer so that the subscriber won't get overwhelmed by messages.

As for this exercise, I will set the message retention duration to **10 minutes** and the expiration period to **1 day**.

There are other options on the form, but we will ignore these for now; you can always revisit this later. Once you're done, click **CREATE**.

Now, we want to check our messages. You can find the **MESSAGES** tab beside the **SUBSCRIPTIONS** tab – go there and click the **VIEW MESSAGES** button.

This is a way for us to check the messages on a topic. We only use this menu in the development phase. In reality, the publishers are applications. We can imagine this process as a subscriber – to do that, find and click the **PULL** button. You won't see any messages yet, as shown in the following screenshot:

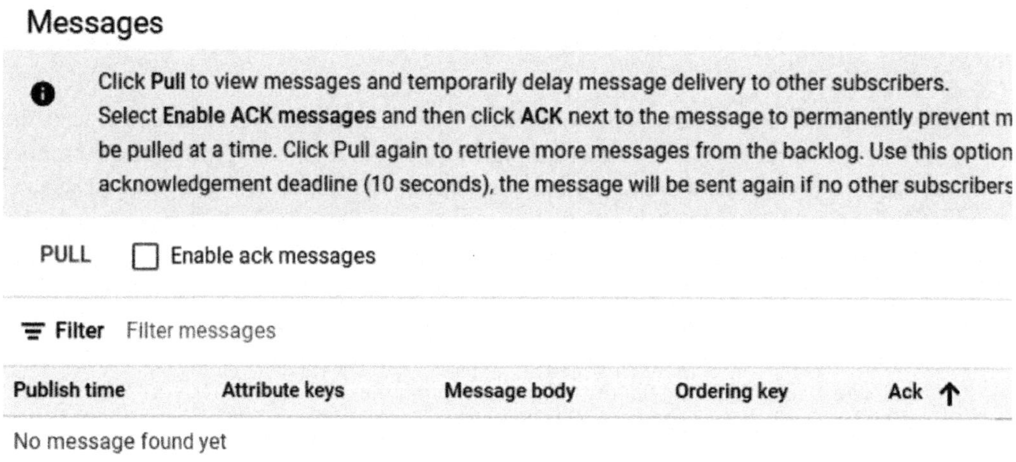

Messages

Click **Pull** to view messages and temporarily delay message delivery to other subscribers. Select **Enable ACK messages** and then click **ACK** next to the message to permanently prevent m be pulled at a time. Click Pull again to retrieve more messages from the backlog. Use this option acknowledgement deadline (10 seconds), the message will be sent again if no other subscribers

PULL   ☐ Enable ack messages

≡ Filter   Filter messages

Publish time	Attribute keys	Message body	Ordering key	Ack ↑

No message found yet

Figure 6.10 – Example blank messages screen

Now, we want to publish some messages on our topic using Python code. Please follow these steps:

1. Go back to Cloud Shell and run our `pubsub_publisher.py` Python code again. You can run this more than once to publish more than 10 messages. For example, I will run it twice in Cloud Shell, like this:

Exercise – publishing event streams to Pub/Sub   209

Figure 6.11 – Running the pubsub_publisher apps twice

2. Go back to the **Pub/Sub View Message** page and click the **PULL** button again – you will see exactly 20 messages, as well as the publish time and the message body, as illustrated in the following screenshot:

Publish time	Attribute keys	Message body	Ack ↑
Aug 3, 2021, 9:37:18 PM	–	{"trip_id": 64569, "start_date": "2021-08-03 13:37:18.339846", "start_station_id":	Deadline exceeded
Aug 3, 2021, 9:37:18 PM	–	{"trip_id": 10769, "start_date": "2021-08-03 13:37:18.340442", "start_station_id":	Deadline exceeded
Aug 3, 2021, 9:37:18 PM	–	{"trip_id": 94581, "start_date": "2021-08-03 13:37:18.340581", "start_station_id":	Deadline exceeded

Figure 6.12 – The messages are shown after being pulled

Another option is to check the **Enable ack messages** option. The **ACK** button will appear on the right-hand side – if you click it, the message will disappear:

Publish time	Attribute keys	Message body	Ack ↑
Aug 3, 2021, 9:39:42 PM	–	{"trip_id": 71687, "start_date": "2021-08-03 13:39:42.151272", "start_station_id": 203,	ACK
Aug 3, 2021, 9:39:42 PM	–	{"trip_id": 80913, "start_date": "2021-08-03 13:39:42.151783", "start_station_id": 202,	ACK

Figure 6.13 – Finding the ACK button on the screen

That's the nature of Pub/Sub. A Pub/Sub publisher is an application that sends a message to a topic. A topic can have multiple subscriptions, and when a subscriber successfully processes the topic's message, it will be ack. When a message is ack, then the message will be deleted because it's been delivered successfully. The process from publisher to subscriber happens in milliseconds, and Pub/Sub can handle multiple publishers and subscribers without scalability issues, which is why Pub/Sub is essential when creating a streaming process.

In the next section, we will use Dataflow as the subscriber. Dataflow will subscribe to our topic, transform the data, and store the data in BigQuery.

Exercise – using Dataflow to stream data from Pub/Sub to GCS

In this exercise, we will learn how to develop Beam code in Python to create data pipelines. Learning Beam will be challenging at first as you will need to get used to the specific coding pattern. So, in this exercise, we will start with some `HelloWorld` code. But the benefit of using Beam is it's a general framework. Generally, you can create a batch or streaming pipeline with similar code. You can also run using different runners. In this exercise, we will use Direct Runner and Dataflow. As a summary, here are the steps:

1. Creating a `HelloWorld` application using Apache Beam.
2. Creating a Dataflow streaming job without aggregation.
3. Creating a Dataflow streaming job with aggregation.

To get started, check out the code for this exercise:

https://github.com/PacktPublishing/Data-Engineering-with-Google-Cloud-Platform-Second-Edition/blob/main/chapter-6/code/beam_helloworld.py

Creating a HelloWorld application using Apache Beam

The application that we want to create will read the `logs_example.txt` file from GCS, do some transformation steps, and store the output back in GCS. We will run this application as a batch data pipeline. If you haven't stored the `logs_example.txt` file in GCS, store it anywhere in your bucket. Let's start our code – you can create code in Cloud Editor and run the application later using Cloud Shell. Proceed as follows:

1. First, let's import the necessary libraries, like this:

    ```
    import apache_beam as beam
    import argparse
    import logging
    ```

Exercise – using Dataflow to stream data from Pub/Sub to GCS 211

```
from apache_beam.transforms.combiners import Sample
from apache_beam.options.pipeline_options import PipelineOptions
```

2. We're going to read data from a GCS file and write the output back to GCS, so let's create variables to store the path. Here's an example; change the bucket and path based on where you store your file:

```
INPUT_FILE = 'gs://[YOUR BUCKET]/from-git/chapter-6/dataset/
logs_example.txt'
OUTPUT_PATH = 'gs://[YOUR BUCKET]/chapter-6/dataflow/output/
output_file_'
```

3. Now, we'll define our data pipeline – this is the basic code for Beam. First, the main Python application runs the `run()` function. In the `run()` function, we declare the Beam pipeline. In the pipeline, we can declare the necessary steps. The code pattern is unique to Beam. A step is formatted like this:

```
| 'step name' >> Beam step
```

Every step can be declared using the pipe symbol. We can define names for each step – this is optional, but it's recommended to always put the step's name. Later, when we use Dataflow, the step's name will be useful for monitoring. The last part is anything after >> - that is, the Beam steps. This can be anything from declaring **input and output (I/O)**, a Map function, a `print` value, and many other possibilities.

4. In our `HelloWorld` application, we'll start with three steps, as follows:

    A. Reading the file from GCS

    B. Sampling 10 records

    C. Printing the records as logs

You can use the following code to declare the pipeline and steps:

```
def run():
    with beam.Pipeline(options=beam_options) as p: (
        p
        | 'Read' >> beam.io.textio.ReadFromText(INPUT_FILE)
        | 'Sample' >> Sample.FixedSizeGlobally(10)
        | 'Print' >> beam.Map(print)
    )

if __name__ == '__main__':
    logging.getLogger().setLevel(logging.INFO)
    run()
```

There are a couple of things that you need to be aware of regarding this short code example. Notice that at the end of our pipeline, we print the records using `beam.Map(print)`. This is a very useful function to know what's happening to our data at each step, but this is not something you should do in the actual data pipeline – this is only for development and debugging purposes. Second, data from the `'Read'` step might be very big, so don't forget to sample the data before printing to avoid your application printing too many rows, which can break your terminal.

Now, to run the data pipeline, follow these steps:

1. Open Cloud Shell and install the Apache Beam package.

   We need to set up Cloud Shell so that it can run the Beam application. We can install the Beam package using the `pip install` command, but if you install it in Cloud Shell, you may get an installation error. Therefore, we need a **virtual environment** (**venv**). If you are not familiar with venv in Python, you can check out the Python public documentation about it: `https://docs.python.org/3/tutorial/venv.html`.

2. Install the Python `venv`.

   In any of your Cloud Shell folders, create a new folder called `venv`, install the `venv` package, and activate it. Here's the code you'll need for this:

   ```
   mkdir venv
   cd venv
   python3 -m venv beam-env
   source beam-env/bin/activate
   ```

   After running these commands, Python will use the dedicated environment for our Beam program.

3. Install the `apache-beam` package.

   To install the `apache-beam` package in the environment, run these commands:

   ```
   pip install --upgrade pip
   pip install wheel
   pip install 'apache-beam[gcp]==2.49.0'
   cd [your hello world python code directory]
   ```

   After running the preceding commands, you will be able to import the package from your Python code.

Make sure you activate `venv` (`beam-env`) so that you can Beam applications. For example, if you close Cloud Shell or your browser, when you go back to Cloud Shell, your environment will no longer use the `beam-env` environment. In that case, you need to reactivate `venv` (`beam-env`) on your terminal.

If you need to exit `venv`, call `deactivate` from the command line, like this:

```
$ deactivate
```

If you deactivate the environment, you will not be able to call apache-beam from the Python code.

Now that we've created the required code and installed the necessary package, let's learn how to run it. Follow these steps to run the Beam application:

1. Still in Cloud Shell, declare two environment variables, project_id and region, as follows:

    ```
    export PROJECT_ID=[YOUR PROJECT ID]
    export REGION=us-central1
    export BUCKET_NAME=[YOUR BUCKET]
    ```

2. Run the Beam application as a typical Python function in the command line. Here's an example:

    ```
    python3 beam_helloworld.py \
      --project=$PROJECT_ID \
      --region=$REGION \
      --runner=DirectRunner \
      --temp_location=gs://$BUCKET_NAME/chapter-6/dataflow/temp
    ```

Notice that in the preceding command, we declare the runner and temp_location parameters. You can choose any GCS path in your bucket for the temp_location parameter. For the runner, we will choose Direct Runner for now. Direct Runner means the application will run on your local machine. In this case, Beam will run the code in the Cloud Shell environment – in other words, this is not a Dataflow application yet. Later, we will just need to change the runner to run Dataflow jobs.

If successful, the application will look like this:

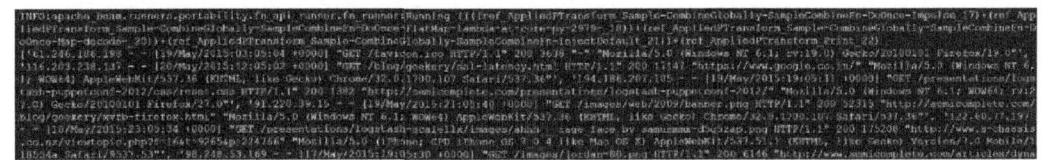

Figure 6.14 – Example output after running Dataflow using Direct Runner

The application will print out the records from the example logs. Next, we will transform and store the records in a GCS bucket. But before that, I'll summarize what you've done so far in this section:

1. You've created a very simple Beam code in Python for printing out the records from a file that is stored in a GCS bucket.

2. You've activated a Python venv and installed the apache-beam[gcp] package in that environment.

3. You've run the Beam application using Direct Runner from the command line in Cloud Shell. If successful, the program will print out the records in Cloud Shell.

Finally, we will go back to our Beam code and change the code a little bit to perform data transformation. Once we've done this, we will load the result in GCS instead of printing it to Cloud Shell. Follow these steps:

1. Let's go back to our code and try to split the records by space. The idea is to get the **Internet Protocol** (**IP**) address, date, HTTP method, and the **Uniform Resource Locator** (**URL**). We will do this using the Map function. To do that, we must prepare a new Python function that will process each input; the output is an object that provides four pieces of information. The code is illustrated here:

   ```
   def split_map(records):
       rows = records.split(" ")
       return {
           'ip': str(rows[0]),
           'date': str(rows[3]),
           'method': str(rows[5]),
           'url': str(rows[6]),
       }
   ```

2. Declare the split_map() function in our pipeline using the Map() function, like this:

   ```
   def run():
       with beam.Pipeline() as p:(
           p
           | 'Read' >> beam.io.textio.ReadFromText(INPUT_FILE)
           | 'Split' >> beam.Map(split_map)
           | 'Sample' >> Sample.FixedSizeGlobally(10)
           | 'Print' >> beam.Map(print)
       )
   ```

   Notice that it is similar to Spark code, which we learned about in *Chapter 5*, *Building a Data Lake Using Dataproc*. But as you can see, the Map function comes from the Beam package (beam.Map). When you read data from the text file, it will be stored in a parallel data structure called PCollection. The PCollection Map function and the process will result in another PCollection. As another comparison to Spark code, PCollection is comparable to a **Resilient Distributed Dataset** (**RDD**).

   PCollections are unique to Beam. Another feature of Beam is **Parallel Do** (ParDo). You can use ParDo to transform PCollection. Back to our previous example, as an alternative, we can also use ParDo to split our data, instead of using the Map function. The key difference between ParDo and the Map function in Beam is that Map always returns one row at a time, while ParDo is more flexible – it can return one to many rows per process. When it comes to splitting records, both approaches can work.

3. As a practice exercise, let's try using `ParDo`. For `ParDo`, we need to follow the format by declaring the `Split` function as a Python class. In the `Split` class, we need a process function that accepts elements Notice that the function returns an array instead of a single object. Check out these lines of code to see the standard Python format that will be used by `ParDo` in Beam:

   ```python
   class Split(beam.DoFn):
       def process(self, element):
           rows = element.split(" ")
           return [{
               'ip': str(rows[0]),
               'date': str(rows[3]),
               'method': str(rows[5]),
               'url': str(rows[6]),
           }]
   ```

4. Now, let's go back to the Beam pipeline step and change the `Map` line to `ParDo`.

   Change this line:

   ```python
   | 'Split' >> beam.Map(split_map)
   ```

   The line should now look like this:

   ```python
   | 'Split' >> beam.ParDo(Split())
   ```

5. Let's try to aggregate the URL by counting it and writing it to the output path in GCS. Our final Beam pipeline code will look like this:

   ```python
   def run():
       with beam.Pipeline() as p:(
           p
           | 'Read' >> beam.io.textio.ReadFromText(INPUT_FILE)
           #| 'Split' >> beam.Map(split_map)
           | 'Split' >> beam.ParDo(Split())
           | 'Get URL' >> beam.Map(lambda s: (s['url'], 1))
           | 'Count per Key' >> beam.combiners.Count.PerKey()
           #| 'Sample' >> Sample.FixedSizeGlobally(10)
           #| 'Print' >> beam.Map(print)
           | 'Write' >> beam.io.textio.WriteToText(OUTPUT_PATH)
   ```

6. Now, go back to Cloud Shell and run the new pipeline using Direct Runner. If successful, the application will write the output to the GCS output path that you defined in the `OUTPUT_PATH` variable.

7. Check the output in the GCS bucket. The file should contain values in the following array string format:

   ```
   [('/blog/geekery/field-extraction-tool-fex-release.html', 1)]
   ```

   The values might be different in your file, but the format should be the same.

   Since we are now sure that the application is working perfectly, let's run it as a Dataflow job. To do that, follow these simple steps:

8. In the command line, when running the Beam application, change the runner from `DirectRunner` to `DataflowRunner`.

   Change this line:

   ```
   --runner=DirectRunner \
   ```

   The line should now look like this:

   ```
   --runner=DataflowRunner \
   ```

9. Run the Beam application from your Cloud Shell environment. But before that, make sure you have enabled the Dataflow API.

10. After running it from Cloud Shell, go to the **Dataflow** page in your GCP console. Check if your job is running and that its status is **Succeeded**, as illustrated in the following screenshot:

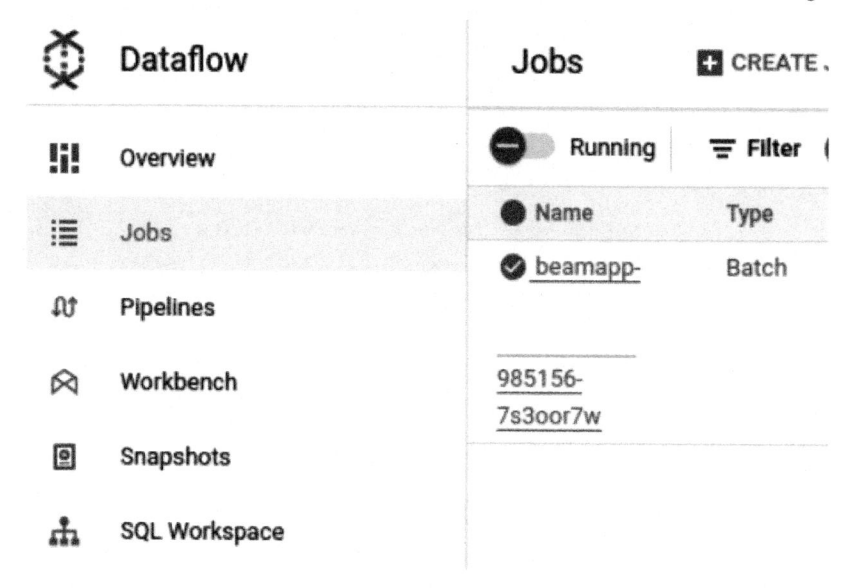

Figure 6.15 – Example of a successful job in Dataflow console

When you open the job, you will see that our steps are there as a graph, as illustrated in the following screenshot:

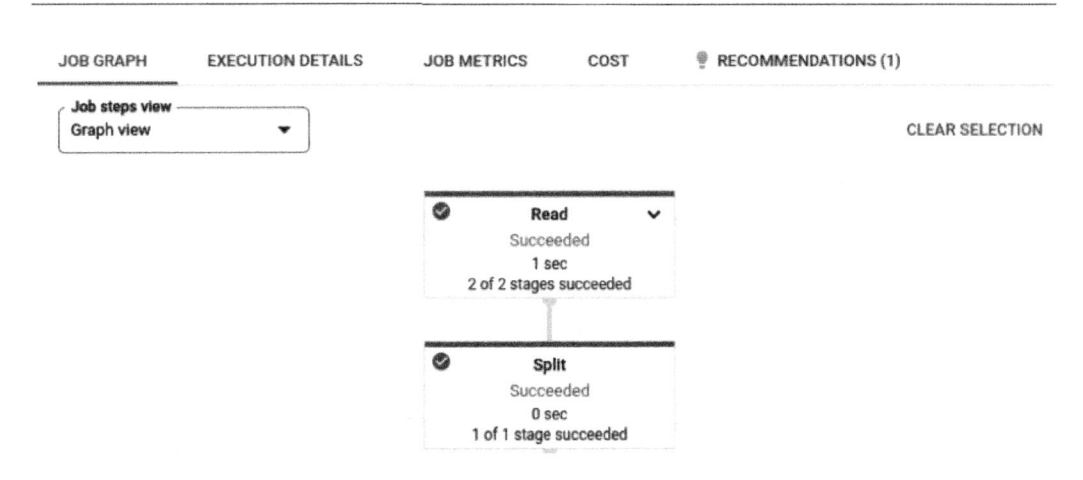

Figure 6.16 – Example of successful steps in the Dataflow console

With this, you have successfully created your first Dataflow job. The job was created using Beam in batch mode. Remember that you can develop a Dataflow job using Apache Beam. In the development phase, you should use `DirectRunner` instead of `DataflowRunner`. Compared to `DataflowRunner`, the deployment time of `DirectRunner` is faster because it runs on the local machine. But in terms of scalability, monitoring, and production standards, `DataflowRunner` is the right option.

In the next section, we will learn how to deploy a streaming job in Dataflow. We will use the Pub/Sub topic that we created from previous sections. The Dataflow streaming application will stream the messages from Pub/Sub to a BigQuery table.

Creating a Dataflow streaming job without aggregation

In this section, you will see how simple it is to change a batch application to a streaming application in Beam and Dataflow. In this section, we will use the Pub/Sub topic that we created before. To start using our code, you can create a new Python file or use the `HelloWorld` application from the previous section.

You can also check out the code in this book's GitHub repository: https://github.com/PacktPublishing/Data-Engineering-with-Google-Cloud-Platform-Second-Edition/blob/main/chapter-6/code/beam_stream_bikesharing.py.

Follow these steps to start this exercise:

1. Open the Beam code in your Cloud Editor environment.
2. Compared to the batch example, in this example, the variables are the Pub/Sub subscription ID and the BigQuery `table_id` output:

    ```
    INPUT_SUBSCRIPTION= 'projects/packt-data-eng-on-gcp/subscriptions/bike-sharing-trips-subs-1'
    ```

Here's the BigQuery table ID in the `output_table` variable:

```
OUTPUT_TABLE = 'packt-data-eng-on-gcp:raw_bikesharing.bike_trips_streaming'
```

3. Don't forget to adjust the project's name, Pub/Sub topic, and the BigQuery table ID based on your environment. In the Beam pipeline, we read from the Pub/Sub subscription. The code looks like this:

```
parser = argparse.ArgumentParser()
args, beam_args = parser.parse_known_args()
beam_options = PipelineOptions(beam_args, streaming=True)
def run():
    with beam.Pipeline(options=beam_options) as p:(
        p
        | "Read from Pub/Sub" >> beam.io.ReadFromPubSub(subscription=input_subscription    )
```

4. There are two options – **From Topic** and **From Subscription**. If you're using a topic, a subscription will be created automatically, but since we know there are many options in a subscription, it's better to manually create a subscription to make sure we know what's happening. Also, notice that we define the streaming parameter as `True` in the `PipelineOptions`. Message output from Pub/Sub. As this is in byte format, we need to convert it, as follows:

```
| 'Decode' >> beam.Map(lambda x: x.decode('utf-8'))
| "Parse JSON" >> beam.Map(json.loads)
```

5. The message from Pub/Sub is in the form of JSON strings, so we need to decode this to `utf-8` format and parse the JSON. The last step is to write to the BigQuery table, as follows:

```
| 'Write to Table' >> beam.io.WriteToBigQuery( OUTPUT_TABLE, \
    schema='trip_id:STRING,start_date:TIMESTAMP,start_station_id:STRING,bike_number:STRING,duration_sec:INTEGER', \
    write_disposition=beam.io.BigQueryDisposition.WRITE_APPEND)
)
```

In the preceding code, we defined a table schema and wrote a disposition parameter. That's it – with this code, you can now start streaming data to your Pub/Sub topic, and the data will be loaded to BigQuery in real time.

Testing if the streaming application works is going to be a bit tricky. To do that, we need some setups. We need to open three environments, as follows:

- One Cloud Shell tab to run the beam_stream_bikesharing code
- The BigQuery console to check if the records have been loaded
- Another Cloud Shell tab to run Pub/Sub publisher code

The first environment is a tab in Cloud Shell to run this command. Don't forget to adjust the `temp_location` parameter based on your path if necessary. The code is illustrated in the following snippet:

```
python3 beam_stream_bikesharing.py \
  --project=$PROJECT_ID \
  --region=$REGION \
  --runner=DirectRunner \
  --temp_location=gs://$BUCKET_NAME/chapter-6/dataflow/temp
```

When you run the `beam_stream_bikesharing` code from the command line, your Beam code will start and wait for incoming data streams. As an example, here is the first environment in Cloud Shell that you will have:

Figure 6.17 – The first environment is running the Dataflow application

For the second environment, we need a BigQuery console, but we need to do that in a different browser tab.

Open a new browser tab and go to the BigQuery console. In the BigQuery editor, write a **Structured Query Language** (**SQL**) query to read data from our streaming table. You can see an example query here:

```
SELECT * FROM `raw_bikesharing.bike_trips_streaming`
    ORDER BY start_date DESC:
```

In summary, in the first environment, you have the Beam streaming application running. The application waits for new data streams from the upstream environment. In the second environment, you have the BigQuery editor. You will use this query to check the incoming data. As an example, here's our second environment:

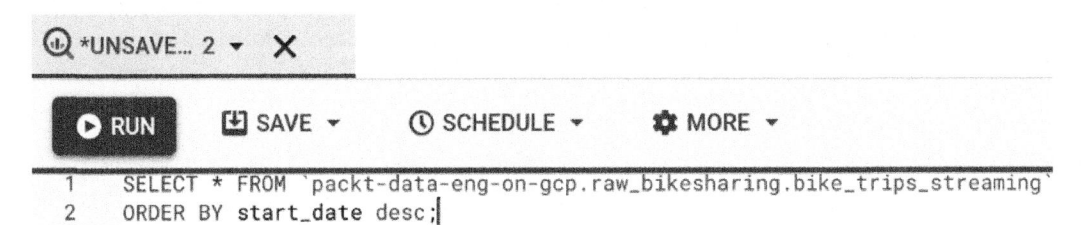

Figure 6.18 – The second environment in accessing BigQuery

In the third environment, you will need a new Cloud Shell tab. We will need this terminal to run our `pubsub_publisher` Python code.

To do that, you can add a new tab by clicking the plus (+) icon in the Cloud Shell terminal. In this new tab, go to the Pub/Sub publisher Python code. As an example, here is your third environment:

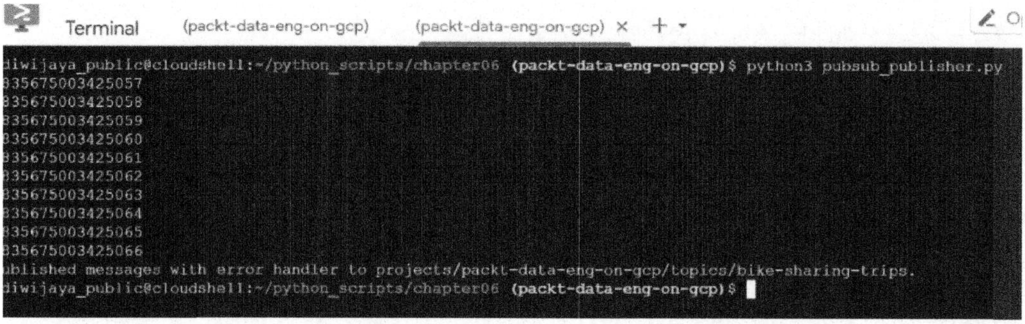

Figure 6.19 – The third environment is running pubsub_publisher

Once you have these three environments, follow these steps:

1. Make sure you've run the first environment, which is the Beam streaming code.
2. Go to the third environment and run the `pubsub_publisher.py` code in Python. The code will send 10 messages to the Pub/Sub topic.
3. Finally, go to the BigQuery console, run the query, and check if the table is there and new records are coming in. You can run the publisher code as many times as you like, and check if the BigQuery table contains new records immediately after you run the publisher.

If successful, when you query the BigQuery table, you will see new records immediately after you publish messages to Pub/Sub. To end this exercise, close the Beam streaming application from the first environment using this command:

```
$ ctrl+c
```

If you find any errors, try to recheck everything. If everything is successful, we can continue to run the streaming apps on Dataflow now. Do that by changing the runner to `DataflowRunner`, as we've done before, in the last step of the *Creating a HelloWorld application using Apache Beam* section.

We need to be aware of what's happening at this point. When you run the Beam streaming pipeline using Dataflow, the job won't be finished unless we cancel the job. To check that, go to the **Dataflow** page in the GCP console. The following screenshot shows that your streaming application is on, with a job type of **Streaming**:

Name	Type	End time	Elapsed time
beamapp-adiwijayapublic-0809061506-043357	Streaming		2 min 3 sec

Figure 6.20 – Example of a Dataflow streaming job running

Open the job and, in your other environment, try to run the Pub/Sub publisher code again. In the Dataflow job, in the right panel, you will see some statistics – for example, the number of elements added. In my case, I ran the publisher three times so that the **Elements added** field displays 30 messages, as illustrated in the following screenshot:

Output collections

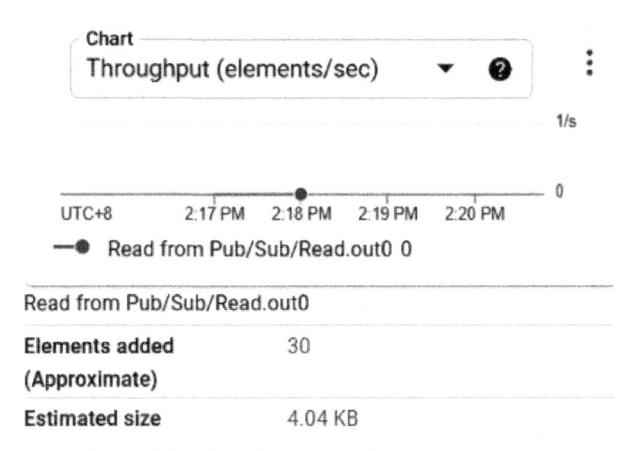

Chart: Throughput (elements/sec)

Read from Pub/Sub/Read.out0

Elements added (Approximate)	30
Estimated size	4.04 KB

Figure 6.21 – Checking streaming output metrics

With that, you've successfully created a streaming data pipeline on Dataflow that is serverless and requires less maintenance.

In terms of cost, Dataflow is billed by the number of worker hours. For example, in Dataflow, the minimum worker is one. One worker means one **virtual machine** (**VM**) is created; if the streaming runs for 24 hours, then the cost is *1 x 24 x the VM cost* (depending on the size). The number of workers can expand automatically when the data volume increases, but we can also set the maximum number of workers to prevent surprising costs. For now, take your time to understand the Dataflow job console, logs, and graphs. After that, you should stop the Dataflow job. You can do that by clicking the **STOP** button. There are three options – you can read a description about the difference between **Cancel**, **Drain**, and **Force Cancel** in the public documentation as it's pretty well described there: https://cloud.google.com/dataflow/docs/guides/stopping-a-pipeline. For now, let's choose the **Cancel** option and make sure the job is canceled.

In this section, we streamed data from raw messages to raw records in BigQuery, which is an ELT approach. We loaded data to BigQuery and let any downstream transformation happen in BigQuery. In the next and last exercise in this chapter, we will try to transform the data by aggregating `PCollection` before storing it in BigQuery.

Creating a streaming job with aggregation

In this final section, we want to aggregate the streaming data. For example, we'll sum up the duration seconds from the bike trip data for each starting station ID. Looking back to the exercise in *Chapter 4, Building Workflows for Batch Data Loading Using Cloud Composer*, we created a data mart that calculates the same metric, but daily. The following screenshot provides a reminder of our data mart table:

facts_trips_daily

This is a partitioned table. Learn more

SCHEMA	DETAILS	**PREVIEW**

Row	trip_date	start_station_id	total_trips	sum_duration_sec	avg_duration_sec
1	2018-01-01	277	1	1224	1224.0
2	2018-01-01	178	1	179	179.0
3	2018-01-01	270	1	424	424.0

Figure 6.22 – Preview of the facts_trips_daily table in BigQuery

In this section, we will create a table that contains `start_station_id` and `sum_duration_sec` information that will be appended in near real time.

Why near real time? Because if you think about aggregation in streaming data, you need to think about time windows. For example, even if the data is streamed in real time, we want to sum up the duration in seconds for each time window. Let's look at an example.

You can find a code example for this at `https://github.com/PacktPublishing/Data-Engineering-with-Google-Cloud-Platform-Second-Edition/blob/main/chapter-6/code/beam_stream_aggr.py`.

You can use the `beam_stream_aggr.py` code example to check out the final code. Continue by trying to do this yourself. Here are the steps:

1. Go back to your Beam streaming pipeline code. Go to the `Parse JSON` step. This time, we want to define a fixed time window of 60 seconds. Later, we will sum up the `duration_sec` value. Given the 60-second window, this means the result will calculate the value every 60

seconds. You can change the window's duration – for example, to 1 second or 1 hour. See the following `UseFixedWindow` step:

```
| "Parse JSON" >> beam.Map(json.loads)
| "UseFixedWindow" >> beam.WindowInto(beam.window.
FixedWindows(60))
```

The next step is to group the messages.

2. To group the message for each `start_station_id` parameter, we will use `Map` and a Lambda function to create a key-value pair. The key is `start_station_id` and the value is `duration_sec`. The step is followed by the sum operation per key. The code is illustrated here:

```
| 'Group By User ID' >> beam.Map(lambda elem: (elem['start_
station_id'], elem['duration_sec']))
| 'Sum' >> beam.CombinePerKey(sum)
```

At this point, `PCollection` from the `Sum` step will result in the sum from each `start_station_id` parameter. Imagine each new result appended to the BigQuery table – you will lose information about the time. Since the data will keep appending, you need the time information, so we will add an `AddWindowEndTimestamp` step. This time, we will create a `BuildRecordFn` `ParDo` function that will add the window time to our records, as follows:

```
| 'AddWindowEndTimestamp' >> (beam.ParDo(BuildRecordFn()))
```

Here is the `BuildRecordFn` class:

```
class BuildRecordFn(beam.DoFn):
    def process(self, element,  window=beam.DoFn.WindowParam):
        window_start = 
            window.start.to_utc_datetime().isoformat()
        return [element + (window_start,)]
```

That's all for the aggregation part. Remember that aggregating data in streams compared to batches is a little bit different as you need to be aware of the times. Data is always coming in streams, so the concept of using scheduling times, as we usually do in batch pipelines, is no longer relevant in streaming pipelines.

3. The final step is to add a schema and write the result to BigQuery. To load data to BigQuery, one of the options is to use the JSON format. We can do that using `Map` and a Lambda function, as follows:

```
| 'Parse to JSON' >> beam.Map(lambda x : {'start_station_id':
x[0],'sum_duration_sec':x[1],'window_timestamp':x[2]})
```

When writing to the BigQuery table, you can change `OUTPUT_TABLE` to a new target table. Here's an example of this:

```
OUTPUT_TABLE = 'packt-data-eng-on-gcp:dwh_bikesharing.bike_
trips_streaming_sum_aggr'
```

Here's how you can do this:

```
| 'Write to Table' >> beam.io.WriteToBigQuery(OUTPUT_TABLE, \
    schema='start_station_id:STRING,sum_duration_
sec:INTEGER,window_timestamp:TIMESTAMP', \
    create_disposition=beam.io.BigQueryDisposition.CREATE_IF_
NEEDED, \
    write_disposition=beam.io.BigQueryDisposition.WRITE_APPEND)
```

That's all for the code.

You can check your code against the code provided in this book's GitHub repository. Similar to the previous exercise, run the code using both `DirectRunner` and `DataflowRunner`. Publish some messages using the Pub/Sub publisher code. If all goes well, you will see a BigQuery result like this:

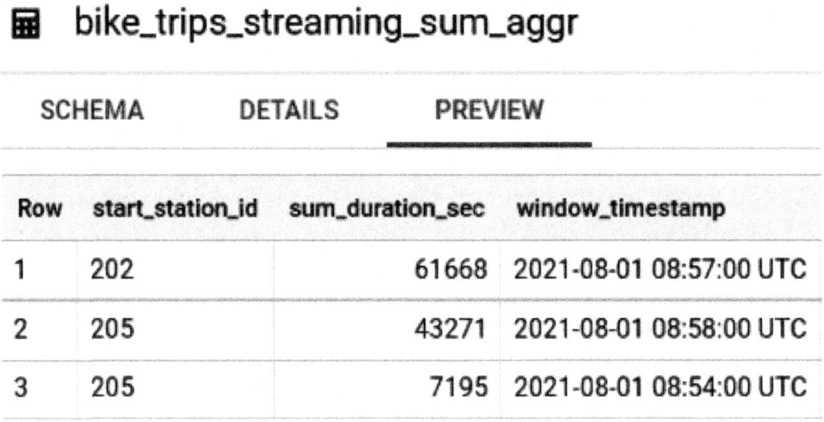

bike_trips_streaming_sum_aggr

Row	start_station_id	sum_duration_sec	window_timestamp
1	202	61668	2021-08-01 08:57:00 UTC
2	205	43271	2021-08-01 08:58:00 UTC
3	205	7195	2021-08-01 08:54:00 UTC

Figure 6.23 – A BigQuery table containing data from our stream job

You will see that each `start_station_id` value will have the `sum_duration_sec` value for every 60 seconds. If needed, you can create a view on top of the table to sum up the `sum_duration_sec` value for each `start_station_id` value, like this:

```
CREATE VIEW raw_bikesharing.bike_trips_realtime
AS
SELECT start_station_id, SUM(sum_duration_sec) as sum_duration_sec
FROM `YOUR-PROJECT-ID.bike_trips_streaming_sum_aggr`
GROUP BY start_station_id;
```

Don't forget to cancel the Dataflow job by clicking the **STOP** button in the Dataflow job console.

In the next section, we will continue learning about streaming data pipelines by using CDC technology.

Introduction to CDC and Datastream

Now that we've learned about Pub/Sub Dataflow streaming, let's get a better idea of how the data starts being pushed from the source system to BigQuery. Unfortunately, in the real world, there are many cases in which you can't change the source system code at all. This means that you can't add a Pub/Sub publisher to publish the records for streaming.

This may happen for many reasons – for example, in an organization such as banking. The core application is usually a monolith product that is developed by third-party vendors. Even if it's developed internally, the complexity of the banking core system makes it difficult to change the code to add a Pub/Sub publisher in every data point. How can we solve this?

Back to our learning batch pipeline, we must extract data from tables in databases. We export the database's table into files and load it to BigQuery. Can we do the same for streaming?

Unfortunately, no. We can't use the same extraction technique by exporting tables to files because the exported table will only contain snapshots instead of new records. And it's especially difficult to export dimension tables where `UPDATE` and `DELETE` operations are possible in the table.

Imagine exporting the preceding customer table into streaming. That isn't doable. We only need the changed records. This will only work if we can intelligently export records that are changing, including newly inserted, updated, and deleted records.

That's where the terminology came from – **Change Data Capture**, also known as **CDC**!

CDC technology is software that taps into an OLTP database. This software will access a database's internal logs and capture the changed record events. After getting the changed record events, it will store the records in destination storage.

What is Datastream?

In GCP, the serverless CDC service is Datastream. Datastream allows you to capture changed records from several databases, including MySQL, PostgreSQL, AlloyDB, and Oracle. The destinations are BigQuery, Cloud SQL, Cloud Storage, and Cloud Spanner.

For data analytics, this means that if your organization has source systems that use those OLTP databases in the backend system, you can stream the changed records to BigQuery and Cloud Storage.

In terms of the destination, should you use BigQuery or Cloud Storage? To decide this, we must back to our discussion of ETL versus ELT. If you need to do any kind of pre-aggregation before storing the code in our data warehouse, you can store it in Cloud Storage. If you prefer to transform everything in BigQuery, you should store it in BigQuery. In general, similar to batch, choose ELT over ETL. This saves both cost and performance – that is, the cost of GCS storage and the cost of loading data from GCS to BigQuery using Dataflow streaming.

The cons of using ELT using Datastream is that the BigQuery table schema is fixed, and you can't change it. If you find that this doesn't match your needs, then use the ETL approach.

Since this chapter is about Dataflow streaming, in the next exercise, we will practice using the ETL streaming approach using Datastream.

Exercise – Datastream ETL streaming to BigQuery

In this exercise, we will walk through the process of setting up a streaming process using Datastream. The pipeline will involve creating and configuring various GCP components to move and transform data from a CloudSQL MySQL table to a BigQuery dataset.

This exercise will be heavy on configurations and will use many different GCP components. I suggest that you open six browser tabs, one for each of the GCP components. To guide you, please use the following diagram as your checklist to make sure all the components are configured correctly:

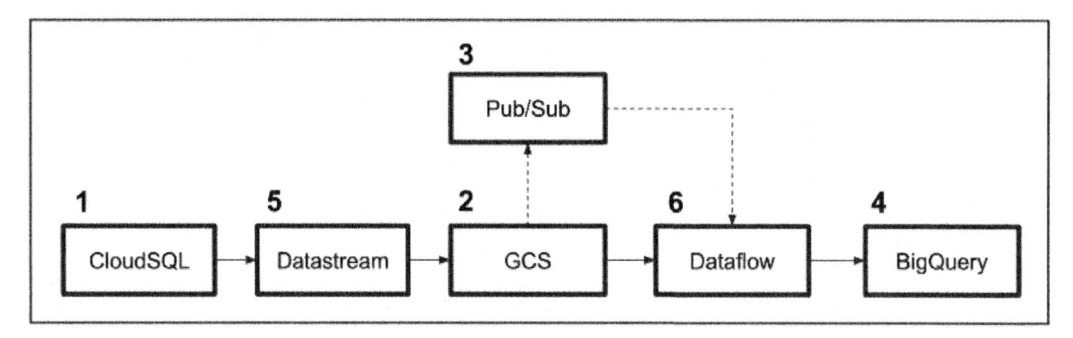

Figure 6.24 – Datastream end-to-end steps

Most of the steps other than Datastream and Dataflow were covered in this chapter or previous ones. I will not go through every step in too much detail. This is a good chance for you to review your understanding of what we've learned so far. Let's start with the first step.

Step 1 – create a CloudSQL MySQL table

First, if you have deleted our CloudSQL MySQL instance, you can recreate it by running the following command from Cloud Shell:

```
$ export PROJECT_ID=[your project id]
$ export PASSWORD=[any password]
$ sh create_cloud_sql_instance.sh
```

Access the CloudSQL Shell and run these MySQL commands to create a new table named `trips`:

```
> CREATE DATABASE apps_db;
> CREATE TABLE apps_db.trips(
trip_id varchar(255),
start_date TIMESTAMP,
start_station_id varchar(255),
bike_number integer,
duration_sec integer,
PRIMARY KEY (trip_id)
);
```

Now that the table has been created, we can insert sample records.

Step 2 – create a GCS bucket

Next, let's create a new GCS bucket for Datastream output:

```
$ gcloud storage buckets create gs://$PROJECT_ID-datastream-output
```

Double-check the GCS bucket from the GCP console.

Step 3 – create a GCS notification to the Pub/Sub topic and subscription

We need to create a Pub/Sub topic and subscription. The Pub/Sub topic will be a notification trigger whenever new files are coming to the GCS bucket. This will be used to tell the Dataflow streaming job to load the files from the GCS bucket to BigQuery.

To create the topic, use this command:

```
$ gsutil notification create -t datastream_notifs -f json -p
datastream-output/ gs://$PROJECT_ID-datastream-output
```

Then, we must create the subscription for the topic using the command line:

```
$ gcloud pubsub subscriptions create datastream_notifs_subs
--topic=datastream_notifs
```

Please open your Pub/Sub console to check if the topic and subscription have been created.

Step 4 – create a BigQuery dataset

Next, simply create a new BigQuery dataset for the destination tables:

```
$ bq --location=US mk -d datastream_output
```

Please check the BigQuery console for the newly created dataset.

Step 5 – configure a Datastream job

At this point, we are ready to create our Datastream job. First, go to the Datastream console and enable the API. Alternatively, you can use the following command to enable it:

```
$ gcloud services enable datastream.googleapis.com
```

To make it work, we need to make sure the Datastream job can read data from CloudSQL and write it to the GCS bucket. In Datastream, it's called **Connection**.

When creating a Datastream job using the console, the menu will guide you step-by-step to set up all the requirements. Please follow all the required menus. Here are the parameter values:

- **Stream name**: mysql-to-gcs-stream
- **Source type**: MySQL
- **Destination type**: Cloud Storage

When prompted to review the prerequisites for the MySQL source and Cloud Storage destination, please read carefully. I'll summarize what's important:

1. Go to the **MySQL source prerequisites** section by clicking the **OPEN** button. Choose **Cloud SQL for MySQL**. Don't worry about **Enable binary logging** – we did that in our CloudSQL instance creation command by adding these two parameters:

   ```
   --backup --enable-point-in-time-recovery
   ```

   The important part is **Create Datastream User**. Copy and paste the script and run it from the CloudSQL Shell using the MySQL command:

   ```
   CREATE USER 'datastream'@'%' IDENTIFIED BY '[YOUR_PASSWORD]';
   GRANT REPLICATION SLAVE, SELECT, RELOAD, REPLICATION CLIENT,
   LOCK TABLES, EXECUTE ON *.* TO 'datastream'@'%';
   FLUSH PRIVILEGES;
   ```

2. The next important part is when you need to create a MySQL Connection. Fill in the hostname using the IP address shown in the CloudSQL instance home page, under **Public IP address**. Use your **root** username and password.

   Go to **Define connectivity method**; you can read the description there about the best practices, but for the simplicity of this exercise, choose **IP allowlisting**. You will be prompted with five IP addresses. You need to copy each of them to your CloudSQL instance. To do that, go to your Cloud SQL instance and click the **Edit** button at the top. Find the **Connections** section. In the **Authorized networks** section, add all five addresses from **Datastream Connection**. It will look like this:

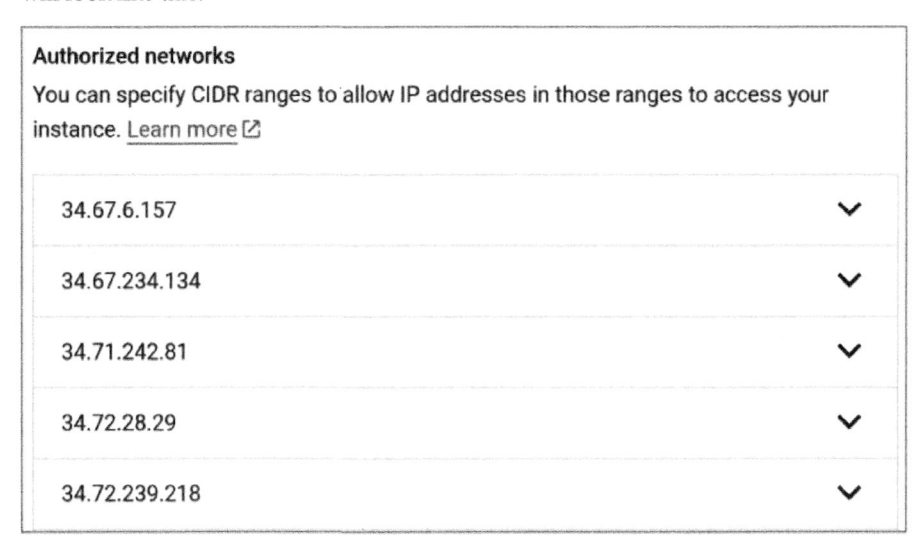

   Authorized networks
   You can specify CIDR ranges to allow IP addresses in those ranges to access your instance. Learn more

34.67.6.157	∨
34.67.234.134	∨
34.71.242.81	∨
34.72.28.29	∨
34.72.239.218	∨

   Figure 6.25 – Authorized networks in the CloudSQL console

   Now, go back to the Datastream console and click **RUN TEST**. Make sure it's successful.

   On the next page, make sure you only choose the `trips` table from under the `apps_db` database using the checkbox.

3. Lastly, in the GCS bucket connection, choose our new bucket, `[PROJECT_ID]-datastream-output`. Insert this prefix in the Connection profile path's prefix form: `/datastream-output`.

Ensure the rest of the parameters use the default value. This is my example summary:

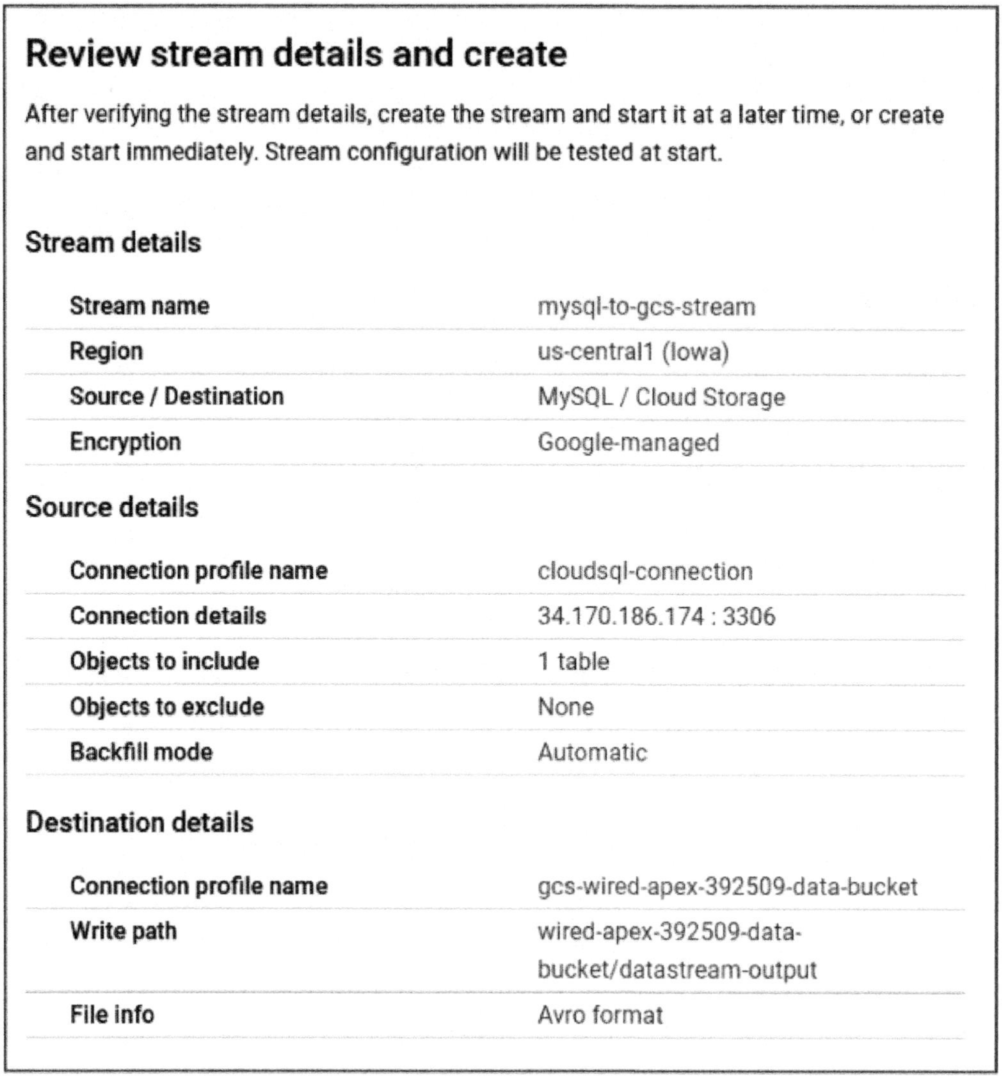

Review stream details and create

After verifying the stream details, create the stream and start it at a later time, or create and start immediately. Stream configuration will be tested at start.

Stream details

Stream name	mysql-to-gcs-stream
Region	us-central1 (Iowa)
Source / Destination	MySQL / Cloud Storage
Encryption	Google-managed

Source details

Connection profile name	cloudsql-connection
Connection details	34.170.186.174 : 3306
Objects to include	1 table
Objects to exclude	None
Backfill mode	Automatic

Destination details

Connection profile name	gcs-wired-apex-392509-data-bucket
Write path	wired-apex-392509-data-bucket/datastream-output
File info	Avro format

Figure 6.26 – Reviewing the configuration

4. Now, click **CREATE AND START**. This will start the stream from our CloudSQL to the GCS bucket.

Step 6 – run a Dataflow job from the Dataflow template

At this stage, we want to create our Dataflow job. However, rather than developing it from scratch, luckily, there is a Dataflow template that we can use. Dataflow templates can be accessed from the Dataflow console when you create a new job. There are many predefined templates that you can use. Alternatively, you can create a job using a Dataflow template via the `gcloud` command – this is what we will do in this exercise. You can read the command to learn the parameters and run it like this:

```
$ sh dataflow_command.sh
```

From all the parameters in the command, the most important line is this one:

```
$ --template-file-gcs-location gs://dataflow-templates-us-central1/latest/flex/Cloud_Datastream_to_BigQuery \
```

The preceding line refers to a Google public GCS bucket where the template is located. Note that you can create your own template whenever needed. For more information, please read the tutorial provided in the public documentation: https://cloud.google.com/dataflow/docs/guides/templates/using-flex-templates.

The `gcloud` Dataflow command will take around 5 minutes to run. When it runs, it will start reading files from the GCS bucket and load them into BigQuery tables.

Step 7 – insert a value in MySQL and check the result in BigQuery

At this point, we can insert sample records into the MySQL database. To do that, simply go to the CloudSQL shell and run the following `INSERT` queries:

```
INSERT INTO apps_db.trips VALUES
    (1,'2023-09-10 06:00:00','20','3178',10000);
INSERT INTO apps_db.trips VALUES
    (2,'2023-09-10 07:00:00','20','3178',20000);
INSERT INTO apps_db.trips VALUES
    (3,'2023-09-10 08:00:00','20','3178',30000);
INSERT INTO apps_db.trips VALUES
    (4,'2023-09-10 09:00:00','20','3178',40000);
INSERT INTO apps_db.trips VALUES
    (5,'2023-09-10 10:00:00','20','3178',50000);
```

If this was successful, you will start to see the Datastream and Dataflow jobs are reading and writing data. Finally, you can check out the BigQuery dataset: `datastream_output`. New records will start flowing into the `trips_logs` and `trips` tables! `trips_logs` will contain the CDC logs row by row, while `trips` will contain the distinct values that mimic the latest table state from the MySQL database.

Summary

In this chapter, we learned about streaming data and how to handle incoming data as soon as it is created. Data is created using the Pub/Sub publisher client. In practice, you can use this approach by requesting the application developer to send messages to Pub/Sub as the data source, though a second option is to use a CDC tool. In GCP, you can use the Google-provided tool for CDC called Datastream. CDC tools can be attached to the backend database such as CloudSQL to publish data changes such as insert, update, and delete operations.

The second part of streaming data is how to process the data. In this chapter, we learned how to use Dataflow to handle continuously incoming data from Pub/Sub to aggregate it on the fly and store it in BigQuery tables. Keep in mind that you can also handle data from Pub/Sub using Dataflow in a batch manner.

With experience in creating streaming data pipelines on GCP, you will realize how easy it is to start creating one from an infrastructure aspect. You don't need to think about any VM, software installation, capacities, or other infrastructure stuff. You can just focus on the code and configurations.

Most of the code is in Beam. As you've experienced in this chapter, learning about Beam needs time. Some concepts and features are unique to Beam and streaming, but this is simply because Beam is very powerful and flexible, and it can run on top of different runners. Beam can handle batch and streaming data pipelines with very few modifications. Take the time to learn how to use it, and as always, focus on your use case. Learning all the syntaxes and features of Beam in one go isn't practical – expand your skills and knowledge of this tool with what you need from your use case.

This chapter has given you a strong foundation in data engineering. I can say that the concepts and skills that you've learned from *Chapter 1, Fundamentals of Data Engineering* to this one already cover 70% of data engineering practices. The last 30% will expand your knowledge of other areas in data, development practice, and the GCP foundation.

In the next chapter, we will expand our knowledge of data visualization. Most of the time, data visualization is the best way to show other people how valuable data is. It's the end of data downstreaming that many people and businesses can appreciate the most. We will learn how to visualize data using a free GCP tool called Looker Studio (formerly Google Data Studio). With Looker Studio, you can visualize data from BigQuery via a drag-and-drop experience.

7
Visualizing Data to Make Data-Driven Decisions with Looker Studio

Visualizing data helps business stakeholders concentrate on important KPIs and empowers them to make data-driven decisions. Data engineers need to analyze the underlying structure of the data and curate custom reporting layers on top to enable the development of dashboards and reports.

In this chapter, we will discuss the dashboarding product **Looker Studio** in detail, which can be leveraged to visualize data coming from different sources, including **BigQuery**, to build compelling reports. On top of that, we will learn what a data engineer should see from a **data visualization** point of view.

At a high level, here is a list of content that will be covered in this chapter:

- Unlocking the power of your data with Looker Studio
- From data to metrics in minutes with an illustrative use case
- Understanding how Looker Studio can impact the cost of BigQuery
- Creating Materialized Views and understanding how BI Engine works

After finishing this chapter, you will understand the positioning of Looker Studio and how to use it to create a visualization dashboard using data from BigQuery. Let's get started!

Technical requirements

Before we begin this chapter, make sure you have the following prerequisites ready. In this chapter's exercises, we will use two **Google Cloud Platform (GCP)** services – **Looker Studio** and **BigQuery**.

We will use the data output from the exercises in *Chapter 3, Building a Data Warehouse in BigQuery*, or *Chapter 4, Building Workflows for Batch Data Loading Using Cloud Composer*. In both chapters, we produced a BigQuery dataset called `dwh_bikesharing`. Make sure you've finished the exercises in those chapters.

Unlocking the power of your data with Looker Studio

Looker Studio is a tool for you to visualize your data fully on the cloud. There are two main reasons why we need data visualization; the first is exploration, while the second is reporting:

- AqaaAAQ

    As a data engineer, even though visualizing data is not your main responsibility, there are times when visualizing data may help in your job. For example, at times when you need to optimize your data pipeline, you may need to analyze a query job's performance. Visualizing the job's data will help you get more information. If you have a data science background, you may be familiar with tools such as Jupyter Notebook. It is a fully-fledged tool for data analytics, including visualization for exploration. But in our case, we may only need to quickly visualize a bar chart from a BigQuery table, for example. In that case, Looker Studio is the best option due to its simplicity and seamless connectivity to BigQuery.

- **Data visualization for reporting**

    The second reason for visualization is reporting. If the reporting visualization is interactive and contains filters and slice and dice, it is called a **dashboard**. For simplicity, in this chapter, we will use the term *report* for both.

> **Important note**
>
> I intentionally use the term report in this chapter so that you are used to this term, which is also used by Looker Studio. Looker Studio uses the term report when you create visualization charts. Different tools sometimes use different terminologies for this aspect. The department that is in charge of creating reports is usually a team called the **Business Intelligence (BI)** team, comprising business users, data analysts, or business analysts. Each organization has its preferences as to how it names its divisions.

Data engineers don't usually need to be responsible for reports, but understanding the nature of reports is important for us since this is the last downstream of our whole work as data engineers. A lot of the time, the success of data engineering teams can be measured by looking at how satisfied these end users are.

Before we begin our exercise, let's understand the positioning of Looker Studio in the data visualization space. As mentioned earlier in this section, Looker Studio is a fully managed tool on the cloud. This means that you can start developing your report, visualizing charts, sharing the report, and more without leaving your browser. Another advantage of using Looker Studio is its simplicity as a tool. For example, later, in the *Exercise – exploring the BigQuery INFORMATION_SCHEMA table using Looker Studio* section, you will experience visualizing your data in less than 10 clicks from a BigQuery table.

But Looker Studio is not positioned to be a replacement for fully fledged BI tools such as **Tableau**, **Looker**, and **Power BI**. These tools have much wider functionalities. I will use Looker as an example since it's comparable directly with Looker Studio as a Google product, but the other BI tools are similar.

Using Looker as an example, users can have a permission hierarchy to both manage dashboards and access them. Another thing in Looker is that you can have version control, which manages your dashboards. Looker Studio doesn't have those capabilities; it is a lot more straightforward to use.

Don't confuse Looker Studio with Looker

Looker Studio and Looker are two different products. Even though they share common names, both products are independent.

Looker Studio is a re-branding product from **Data Studio**. Two types of licenses are available for Looker Studio: **Free** and **Looker Studio Pro**.

Looker Studio Pro is the paid version of Looker Studio. The benefit is that you will get enterprise support and be able to use the complete features. The full features of Looker Studio Pro can be found on their website: `https://support.google.com/looker-studio/answer/12671821`.

It's easy to be mistaken that Looker Studio Pro is equal to Looker. Looker is a paid product, and there is no free version of it.

Looker is a full-fledged BI tool that is a lot more advanced in terms of BI features compared to Looker Studio. This also means that dedicated experts are required to manage this tool. For example, you will need Looker developers and Looker admins, and they are usually not data engineers or GCP admins.

Looker Studio is a lot simpler yet a very easy tool to start with, especially to integrate with BigQuery results. Thus, in this book, to learn about data visualization, we will use Looker Studio. We'll start going through some exercises in the next section.

From data to metrics in minutes with an Illustrative use case

Now let's start our exercise – we will try to use data visualization for exploration and reporting. You will only need Looker Studio and BigQuery as the data sources for the exercise in this chapter.

We'll perform two main tasks in this section:

- Exploring the BigQuery INFORMATION_SCHEMA table using Looker Studio
- Creating a Looker Studio report using data from a bike-sharing data warehouse

Before trying out Looker Studio, let's become familiar with **INFORMATION_SCHEMA** in BigQuery.

Understanding what BigQuery INFORMATION_SCHEMA is

INFORMATION_SCHEMA is a collection of tables in BigQuery that stores your BigQuery metadata. For example, if you want to know how many tables exist in your project, you can use the table INFORMATION_SCHEMA view. The other common example is that you might be wondering how much a query costs per job, day, or month. For that, you can access the jobs INFORMATION_SCHEMA view. You can find the full list of available INFORMATION_SCHEMA views here: https://cloud.google.com/bigquery/docs/information-schema-intro.

We'll try out the jobs INFORMATION_SCHEMA view for our example. We will access it and use it for quick exploration in the *Exercise – exploring the BigQuery INFORMATION_SCHEMA table using Looker Studio* section.

To access INFORMATION_SCHEMA, follow these steps:

1. Go to the BigQuery page in the GCP console.
2. In the **Editor** tab, write the following query:

    ```
    SELECT *
    FROM `region-us`.INFORMATION_SCHEMA.JOBS_BY_PROJECT;
    ```

3. Run the query and check the result. The result of the query should be as follows:

creation_time	project_id	project_number
2021-05-29 07:49:18.377 UTC	packt-data-eng-on-gcp	320986546290

Figure 7.1 – Example result from INFORMATION_SCHEMA

There will be many other columns that you can check. Scan through all the columns and try to become familiar with them. This information is very helpful for debugging and monitoring purposes. For example, I found that one of the most interesting columns for users is total_bytes_billed. This column gives an estimation of how many bytes were read from the query. With this number, you can calculate the cost for each query for on-demand pricing users.

For example, in one of my job queries, the `total_bytes_billed` value is `10485760`. Remember that it is in bytes; if we convert it into terabytes, it will be `0.00001 TB`. If we use the US region, the on-demand cost will be $5 per TB. So, the cost for this query is as follows:

```
Query cost = $5 * 0.00001 TB
Query cost = $0.00005
```

With this knowledge, you can explore many things about your BigQuery costs – for example, how much you spend on BigQuery every day. We'll do that in Looker Studio in the next section.

In the next section, we will begin our exercise. Make sure your GCP console is open in your browser.

> **Important note**
> You can find the pricing for other regions at `https://cloud.google.com/bigquery/pricing`.

Exercise – accessing the BigQuery INFORMATION_SCHEMA table using Looker Studio

In this exercise, we will use BigQuery query results to be shown in Looker Studio. We will explore the basic functionalities in Looker Studio using the `INFORMATION_SCHEMA` table as an example use case.

Here are the high-level steps to create the visualization in Looker Studio using the `INFORMATION_SCHEMA` table:

1. Run a query in the BigQuery editor.
2. Explore the result using Looker Studio.
3. Show the time series chart for visualizing daily billed bytes.

Let's start with the first step:

1. Run a query in the BigQuery editor. Open your BigQuery editor and run the following query:

    ```
    SELECT
    EXTRACT(DATE FROM creation_time) AS creation_date,
    SUM(total_bytes_billed) AS sum_total_bytes_billed
    FROM `region-us`.INFORMATION_SCHEMA.JOBS_BY_PROJECT
    GROUP BY EXTRACT(DATE FROM creation_time);
    ```

    The query accesses the same `INFORMATION_SCHEMA` table as in the previous section. But this time, we aggregate it using the `creation_date` column to sum up the `total_bytes_billed` value.

2. Access the result using Looker Studio.

   After the results are shown, click the **EXPLORE DATA** button. This button will be in the middle of your screen, as shown in the following figure:

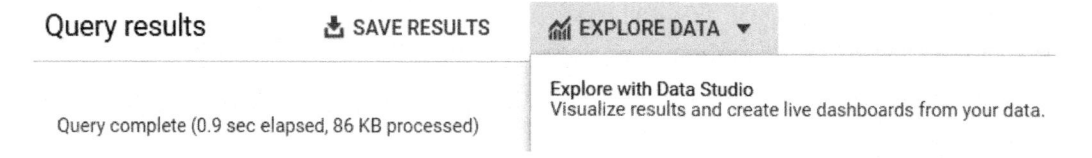

   Figure 7.2 – EXPLORE DATA within Looker Studio

   You will be redirected to a new browser tab, opening the **Looker Studio Report** page. An authorization popup will appear if this is the first time you have opened Looker Studio. The page will show your data using two pre-defined visualizations – a table and a bar chart – as shown in the following figure:

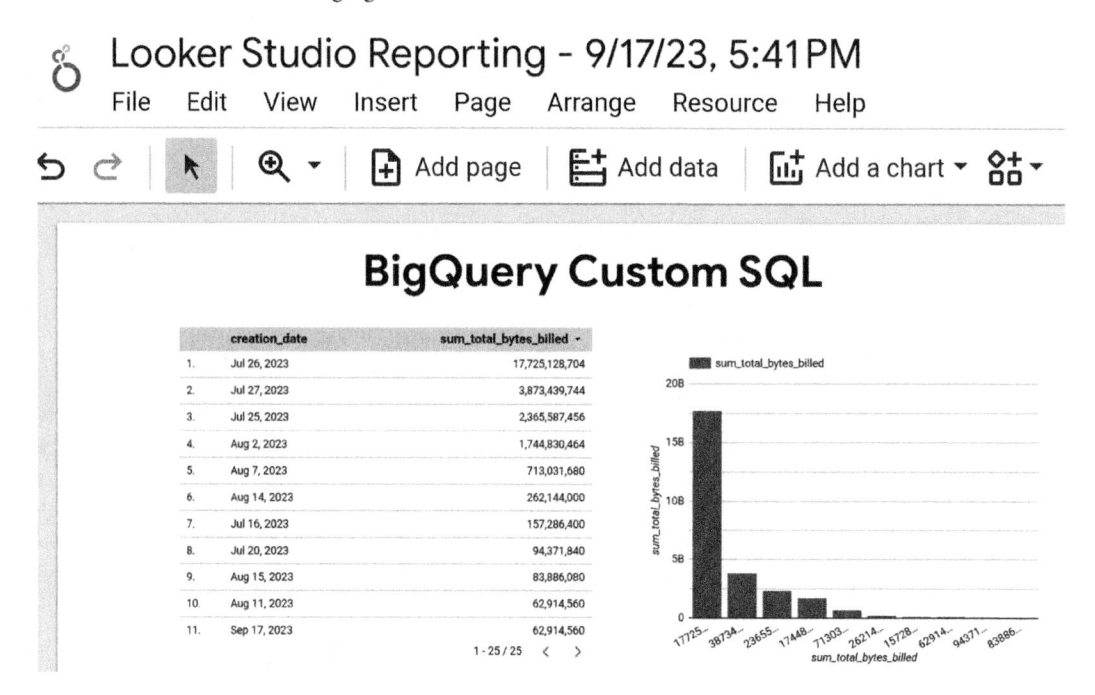

   Figure 7.3 – Example of the Looker Studio reporting page

For the first step in the **Reporting** page, let's change the **Report** title to `Report - BigQuery Information Schema`. You can do that by clicking the title, as shown in the following figure:

Report - BigQuery Information Schema
File   Edit   View   Insert   Page   Arrange   Resource   Help

Figure 7.4 – Looker Studio title bar

1. Now, we need to show a time series chart for visualizing daily billed bytes.

    Next, click **Add a chart** in the menu bar and choose the **Time series** chart:

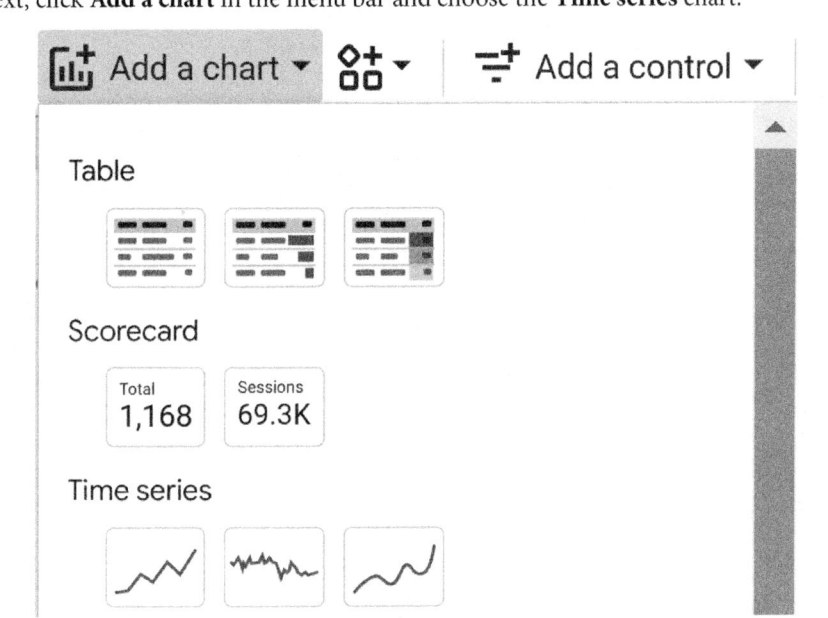

Figure 7.5 – Finding the time series icon

There are many chart types that you can use; every type requires a different number of dimensions and metric data.

In the right panel, you will see the chart's **SETUP**. Note that Looker Studio will try to automatically pick the dimension (column) for you. This may or may not be the dimensions that you want to visualize. Whenever needed, you need to set the correct input for the charts. For our use case, make sure you choose `creation_date` as **Dimension** and `sum_total_bytes_billed` with the **SUM** aggregation type as **Metric**. Here are the inputs that you can follow:

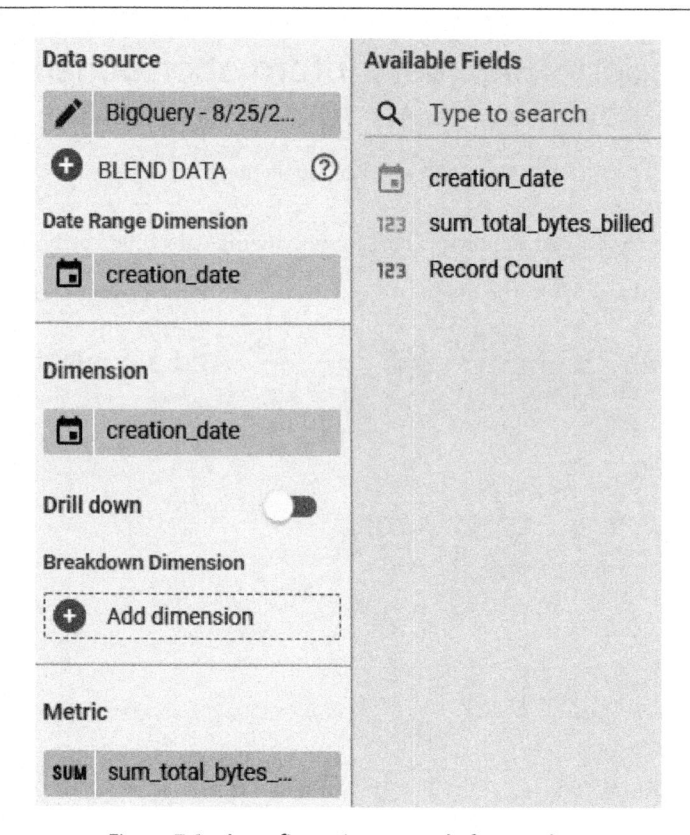

Figure 7.6 – A configuration example for our chart

After choosing the correct input, your time series chart will be shown properly. Note that your result will be different from my example. The chart in Looker Studio shows your real `total_bytes_billed` value from your historical queries in BigQuery. As an example, here's what it looks like in my chart:

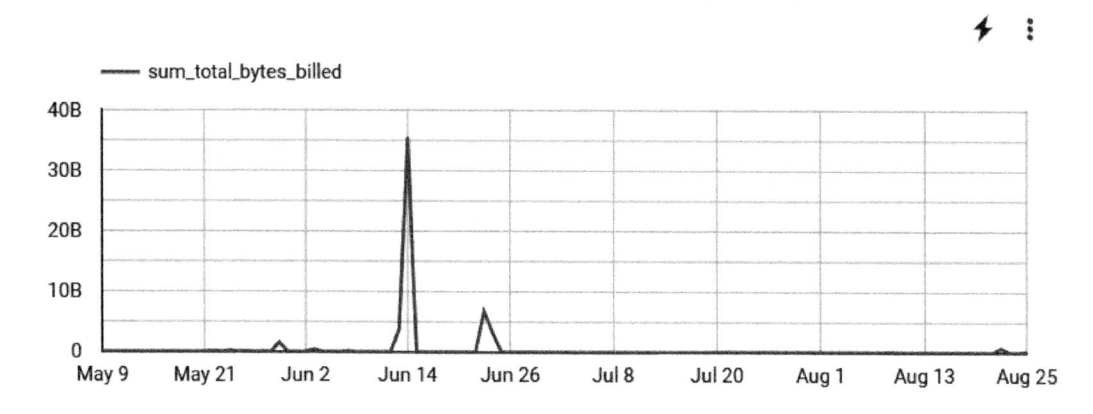

Figure 7.7 – Output from the time series chart

Note that when you click **EXPLORE DATA** in the BigQuery console, you will be directed to the **Looker Studio Reporting** page, not the **Explorer** page.

If you want to try out the Explorer user experience, you can click the home menu icon:

Figure 7.8 – Looker Studio home menu icon

You will be redirected to the Looker Studio home page. Upon clicking the **Create** button, you will find the **Explorer** button:

Figure 7.9 – The Create and Explorer buttons on the home page

Please feel free to explore the features and see the differences compared to the Report user experience. In summary, both are very similar, but Explorer focuses on finding one answer for your own using visualization, while Report is for creating a report for other users.

As you have seen in this section, showing BigQuery results using charts on a report is only a few clicks away. This is one of the reasons Looker Studio is one of the best tools for visualizing BigQuery data. The connection is seamless and there are almost no prerequisites to start using Looker Studio. In the next section, we will try to create a report in Looker Studio using our *bike-sharing* data.

Exercise – creating a Looker Studio report using data from a bike-sharing data warehouse

In this exercise, we will create another report. From the definition, the difference between a report and an exploration is clear. Exploration is a phase or activity that you do on an ad hoc basis to find answers from your data. A report is a collection of information that is created from data for other people's benefit. When creating reports, people should think about how the end users use that information and how they access it. In Looker Studio, creating exploration and creating reports consist of very similar steps. There are two additional steps when creating reports:

1. Managing the report layout.
2. Sharing the report with other users.

We will perform both these steps in this exercise, and as an additional step, we want to practice *loading data sources from a BigQuery table*. Remember that in the previous exercise, we used the BigQuery query's *result*, not the table.

For the data and use case, we will use the bike-sharing data from the data warehouse dataset we created in *Chapter 3, Building a Data Warehouse in BigQuery*, in the *Creating a fact and dimension table* section. To refresh our memory, in that section, we created two tables in the `dwh_bikesharing` dataset called `facts_trips_daily` and `dim_stations`. If you haven't done that, please revisit the chapter or use any other table. If you want to use other tables, you can use tables from BigQuery's public dataset. If you do that, focus only on Looker Studio's capability in this exercise without worrying about the use case.

At a high level, here are the steps that we will complete in this exercise:

1. Add the `facts_trips_daily` data source to the report.
2. Add and blend the `dim_stations` data source.
3. Answer the questions using charts.
4. Manage the report's layout.
5. Share the report.

Let's start with the first step:

1. Add the `facts_trips_daily` data source to the report.

    From any of your Looker Studio pages, click the Looker Studio home icon in the top left of your screen. It will redirect you to the Looker Studio home page. On the home page, find the **Create** button in the top left and click **Report**.

    You will be redirected to add data to a report form. In this form, take a moment to look at what options you can choose from. You will see that Looker Studio is not only able to use data from BigQuery; there are also hundreds of other connectivity options that you can use. For our exercise, let's choose **BigQuery**, under the **Google Connectors** section. Click the **AUTHORIZE** button if prompted.

The next step is to select the table; for that, choose your project, dataset, and, finally, the table name. At this stage, your screen should look as follows:

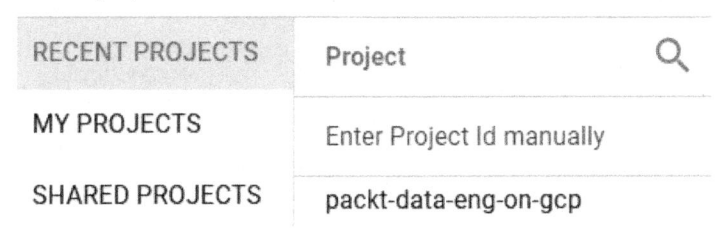

RECENT PROJECTS	Project
MY PROJECTS	Enter Project Id manually
SHARED PROJECTS	packt-data-eng-on-gcp

Figure 7.10 – Finding and choosing your GCP project

After finding your `facts_trips_daily` table, click **Add** and then **ADD TO REPORT**. Once again, you will be redirected to the report editor page, as shown in the following figure:

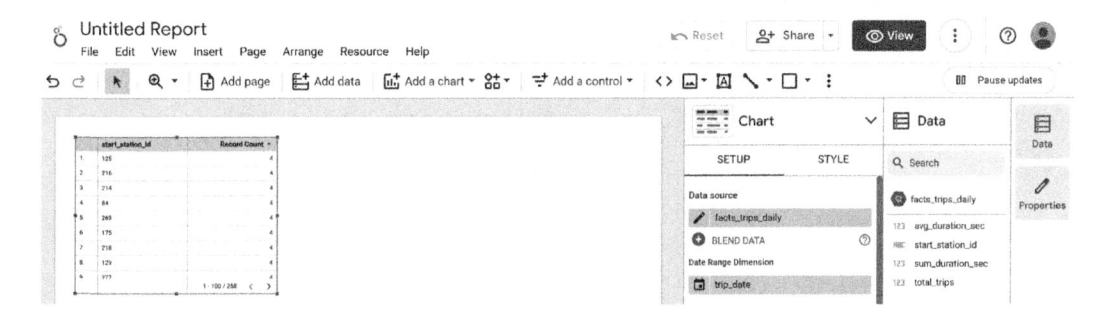

Figure 7.11 – An example of the output after adding new data

Notice that **Data source** under the **SETUP** tab on the right panel shows your table's name. If you compare this with our previous exercise, the previous exercise didn't point to any table in the data source.

2. Add and blend the `dim_stations` data source.

   The next step is to add another table, which is our `dim_stations` dimension table. To do that, in the menu bar, click **Resource** | **Manage added data source**.

   After clicking the button, you will be on the **SELECT DATASOURCE** page. Here, click **ADD A DATA SOURCE**.

   The next few steps are similar to what we did in *Step 1*. Follow those steps but this time, choose the `dim_stations` table.

   Back on the report editor page, find the **BLEND DATA** button. It's located under the **SETUP**| **Data source** section.

244　Visualizing Data to Make Data-Driven Decisions with Looker Studio

Just in case your right panel shows **Theme** and **Layout** instead of **SETUP** and **STYLE**, click the table in the editor pane:

Figure 7.12 – Make sure the table is selected

Your right panel should show the **SETUP** and **STYLE** options. Under **SETUP**, you can find the **BLEND DATA** button; click it.

On the **Blend Data** page, you will see `facts_trips_daily` shown as your data source, at which point you can click **Join another table**. You will see that `dim_stations` will be available for you to choose, as shown in the following screenshot:

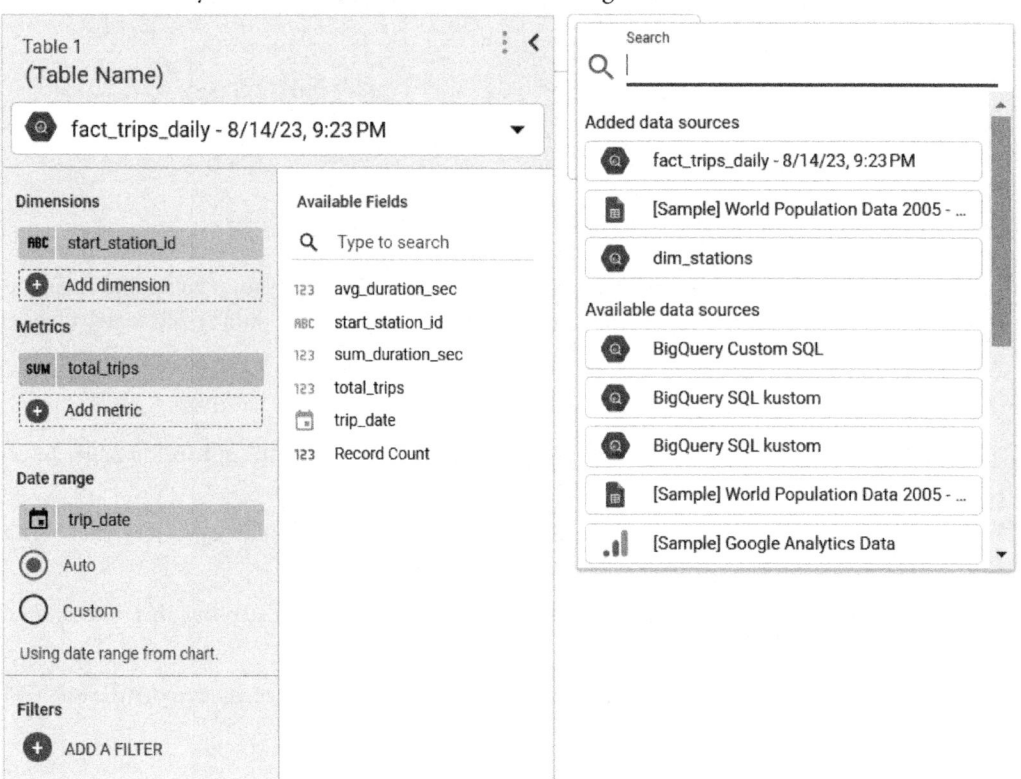

Figure 7.13 – Selecting a data source page

After clicking it, you will see that we need to input some information in the panel. First, click on **Configure join**, then choose the join operator. For this exercise, we choose the **Inner join**. Under the **Join conditions** section, add a key. Select `start_station_id` as the key in table 1 and `station_id` as the key in table 2, then click **Save**.

After that, we need to correctly define **Dimensions** and **Metrics** for both `facts_trips_daily` and `dim_stations`.

For `facts_trips_daily`, here are the configurations:

- **Dimensions**: Join key (`start_station_id`)
- **Metrics**:
  - **SUM** | `sum_duration_sec`
  - **AVG** | `avg_duration_sec`

For `dim_stations`, here are the configurations:

- **Dimensions**: Join key (`station_id`), `station_name`
- **Metrics**:
  - **SUM** | `capacity`

Ensure that your input looks as follows:

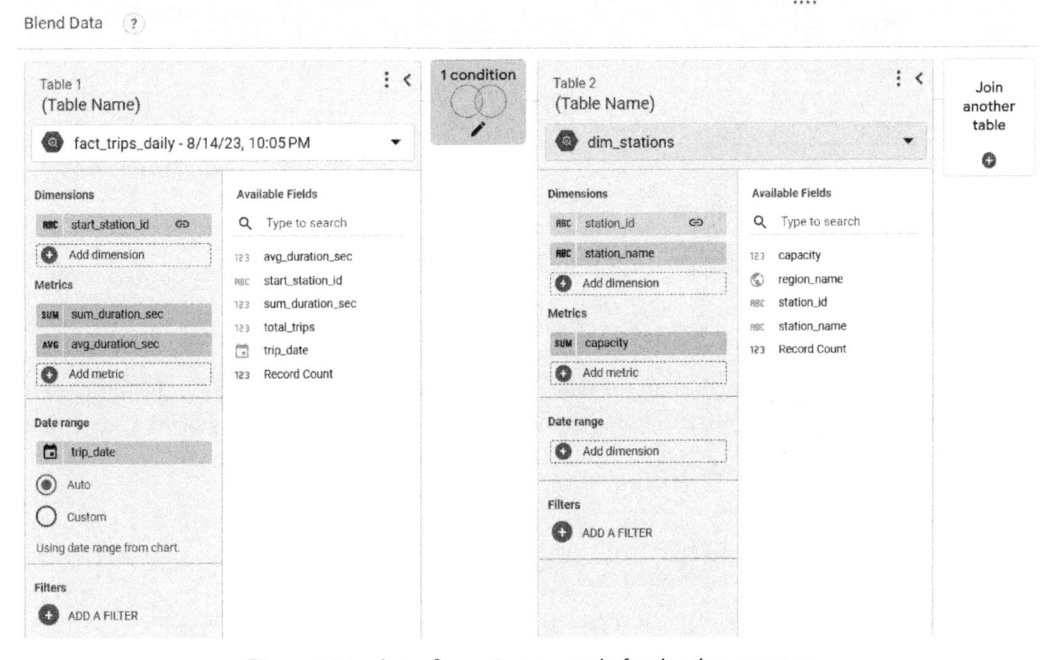

Figure 7.14 – A configuration example for the data sources

246 Visualizing Data to Make Data-Driven Decisions with Looker Studio

After choosing all the correct inputs, click **SAVE**.

3. Answer the questions using charts. For the first chart, we'll use the **Bar** chart to show the *top 5 stations by total duration*.

To do that, click the table on the editor pane so that you can choose the chart type. To open the chart options, click the top-right panel that reads **Chart**. After clicking the panel, the chart options will be shown. Choose the **Bar** chart:

Figure 7.15 – Finding the bar chart icon

After changing to a **Bar** chart, in the data panel, choose `station_name` for the dimension. In both the **Metric** and **Sort** sections, choose `sum_duration_sec` using **SUM** aggregation:

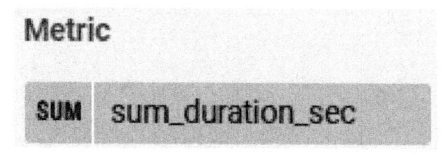

Figure 7.16 – Choosing sum_duration_sec in the Metric section

If successful, your column chart will look like this:

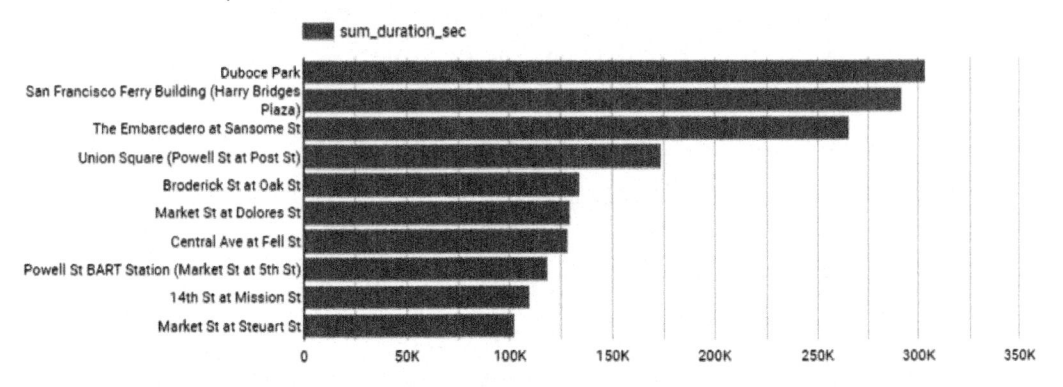

Figure 7.17 – Column chart result

To only show the top five, go to the **STYLE** panel and input 5 in the **Bars** option:

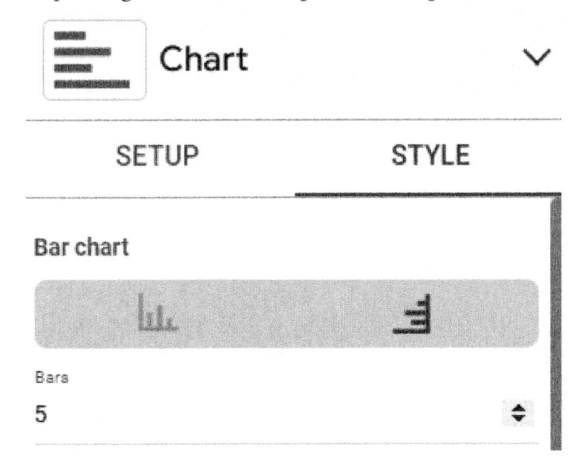

Figure 7.18 – Finding the Bars option under the STYLE section

To add the second chart, click **Add a chart** at the top of your screen, as shown in the following screenshot:

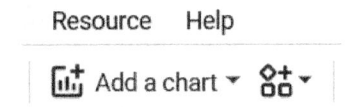

Figure 7.19 – Finding the Add a chart button

For the second chart, let's show the *top 10 stations by average duration*. For this, we'll choose the **Treemap** chart.

For **Metrics**, choose **AVG** | `avg_duration_sec`. Finally, we want to limit the number of boxes in the treemap to only 10 boxes. To do that, still in the **SETUP** tab, find a section called **Total rows**. The default is **500** rows; change it to **10**.

If successful, the chart will look like this:

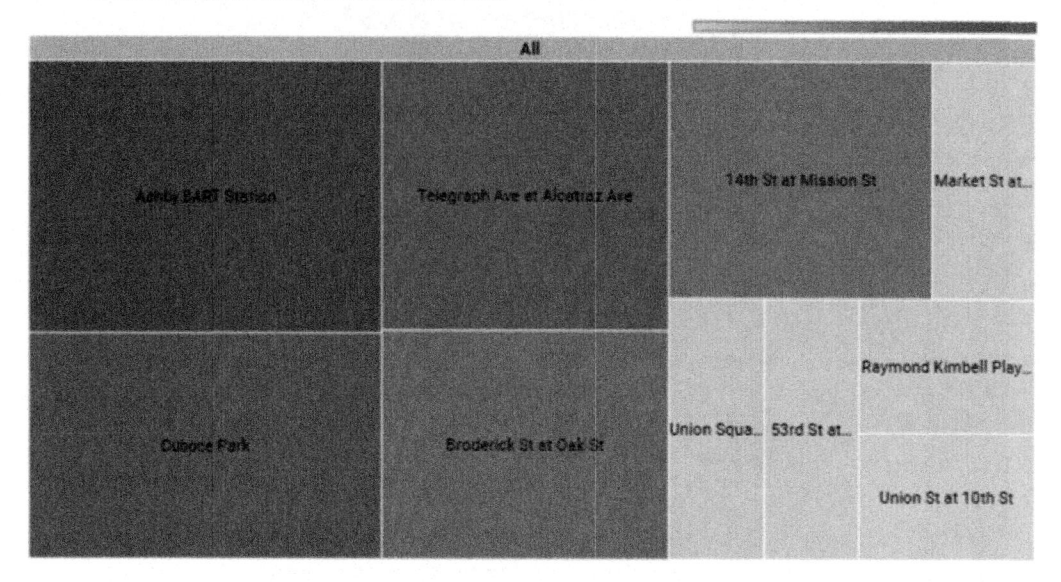

Figure 7.20 – The treemap chart's output

Lastly, add another chart; this time, choose the table chart. For the dimension, choose `station_name` and change the metrics to **SUM** | `sum_duration_sec`, **AVG** | `avg_duration_sec`, and **SUM** | `capacity`. If successful, the table chart will look like this:

	station_name	sum_duration_sec ▾	avg_duration_sec	capacity
1.	Duboce Park	303,146	11,734.23	19
2.	San Francisco Ferry Building (Harry Br...	291,525	2,381.09	38
3.	The Embarcadero at Sansome St	265,561	2,328.99	23
4.	Union Square (Powell St at Post St)	173,967	3,590.34	27
5.	Broderick St at Oak St	134,174	9,583.86	27
6.	Market St at Dolores St	129,315	3,078.93	19
7.	Central Ave at Fell St	128,288	2,547.41	31
8.	Powell St BART Station (Market St at ...	118,484	3,075.72	35
9.	14th St at Mission St	109,622	9,064.93	19
10.	Market St at Steuart St	101,803	1,453.38	25

1 - 100 / 248

Figure 7.21 – The table chart's output

4. Manage the report's layout.

    At this point, I'm sure you are already comfortable with creating a report. Play around with other buttons and functionalities. For example, you can add static text, a changing layout, and many other options. Remember that in report creation, you are creating the report for someone else, so be mindful of how you lay out the charts. If you are done, you can click the **VIEW** button at the top right of your screen and see your report there. As an example, here's mine; you don't need to follow every single detail here:

BIKE SHARING REPORT

Top 5 Station by Total Duration

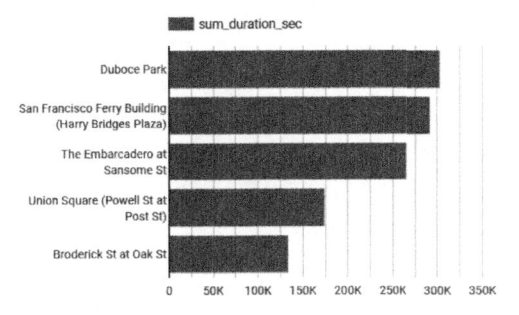

Top 10 Station by Average Duration

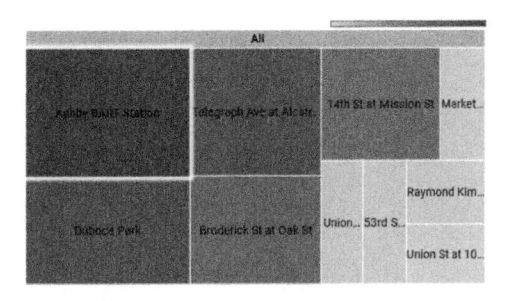

Table Detail

	station_name	sum_duration_sec ▼	avg_duration_sec	capacity
1.	Duboce Park	303,146	11,734.23	19
2.	San Francisco Ferry Building (Harry Bridges Plaza)	291,525	2,381.09	38
3.	The Embarcadero at Sansome St	265,561	2,328.99	23
4.	Union Square (Powell St at Post St)	173,967	3,590.34	27
5.	Broderick St at Oak St	134,174	9,583.86	27
6.	Market St at Dolores St	129,315	3,078.93	19
7.	Central Ave at Fell St	128,288	2,547.41	31
8.	Powell St BART Station (Market St at 5th St)	118,484	3,075.72	35
9.	14th St at Mission St	109,622	9,064.93	19
10.	Market St at Steuart St	101,803	1,453.38	25

1 - 100 / 248

Figure 7.22 – A full-screen example of the bike-sharing report

5. Share the report.

    As a final step, let's share the report with other people by email. You can do that by clicking the **Share** button. The form looks like this:

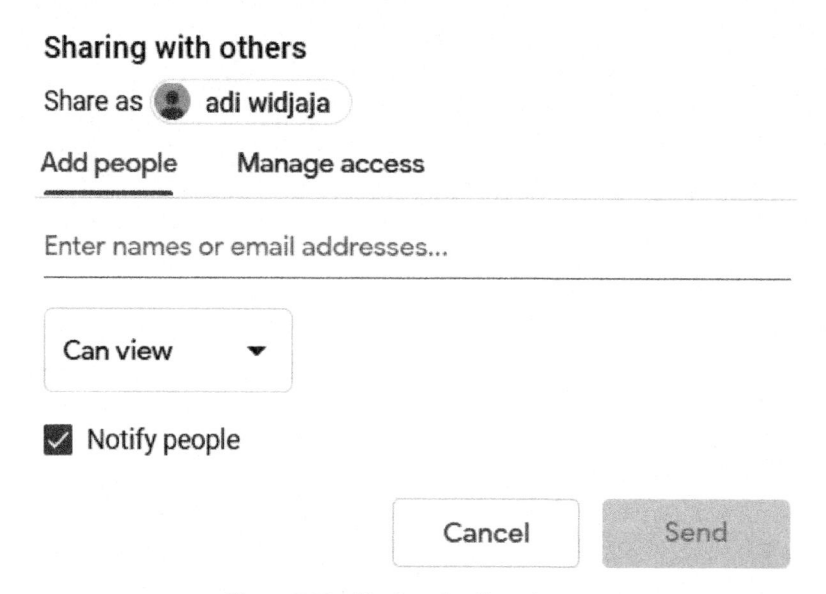

Figure 7.23 – Finding the Share button

When sharing a report with other users, the user can access the report without needing BigQuery viewer permission to the underlying table. The permission to the BigQuery table depends on your email as the data source owner.

To summarize our two exercises, we've practiced showing both the BigQuery table and the BigQuery query's results in Looker Studio. As you can see, Looker Studio is an easy tool for both exploration and creating reports. On top of that, Looker Studio has a license that allows you to use it for free. But as a data engineer, you need to be aware of how it impacts the cost of BigQuery. When you share your report with other users, the usage of the underlying BigQuery table will increase. It will increase either linearly or exponentially with the number of users. We will discuss this in the next section.

Understanding how Looker Studio can impact the cost of BigQuery

At a very high level, the total BigQuery cost is driven by *how big your data is* and *the amount of usage*. Both factors work as multipliers. For example, if you have a table that's 1 TB in size and you access the table 10,000 times in a month, it means the BigQuery cost will be *1 TB x 10,000 x $5 = $50,000 / month*.

Whether $50,000 is expensive or not depends on your organization. But we will ignore the context and focus on the cost driver aspects, so let's say $50,000 is expensive. Now, the questions are, *what kind of table could be 1 TB in size?* and *how can a table be accessed 10,000 times in a month?* We'll discuss these questions in the following sections.

What kind of table could be 1 TB in size?

To answer this, let's take a look at our data warehouse diagram from *Chapter 3, Building a Data Warehouse in BigQuery*:

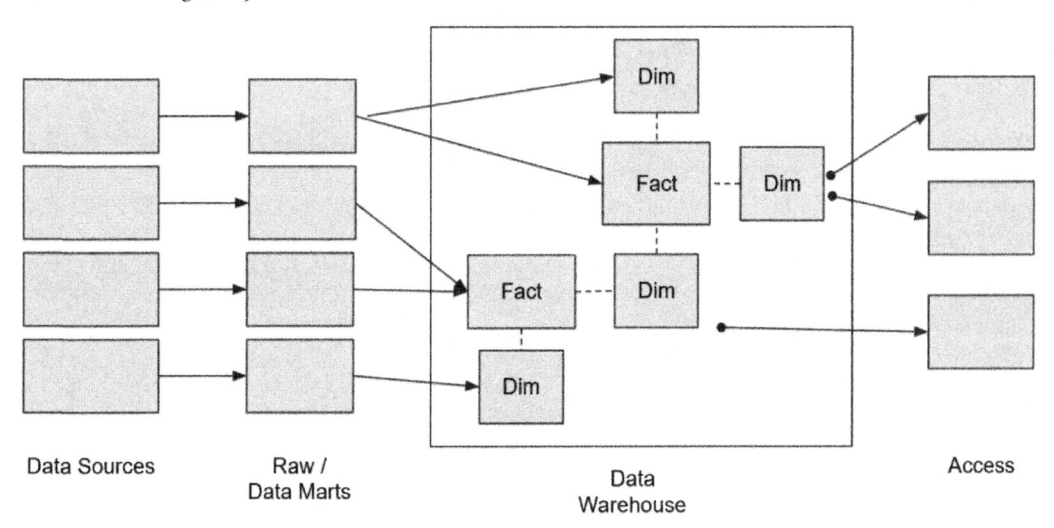

Figure 7.24 – High-level data layers

When looking at the diagram, remember that most data in the **Access** layer is already specifically created for reports. This means that it's already been filtered and aggregated, so the data in the **Access** layer is less likely to be big. Big tables more commonly come from a *transactional table in the* **Raw** *layer* and *fact tables are in the data warehouse*. But the *fact table* in the data warehouse can also be shrunk down in size if it is aggregated at a lower time granularity. For example, in our exercise, we created `facts_daily_trips`, which only had daily-level granularity. That's why modeling your data correctly is important for both performance and cost.

How can a table be accessed 10,000 times in a month?

Two main factors can drive the numbers:

- Number of users using the table per month (#user)
- How many times each user accesses the table per month (#user access)

For example, say a table is very popular and is accessed by 10 unique users in a month. Each day, every user needs to schedule a report based on the table for every half an hour; or, in other words, there will be 48 queries per user per day, which is 1,440 queries per user per month. In this case, the total queries will be as follows:

10 unique users x 1,440 users/month = 14,400 queries/month

Now, what does this have to do with Looker Studio? First, Looker Studio is a very good way for data engineers to share data adoption with non-data people across organizations. But at the same time, it means more users will be accessing BigQuery data. As mentioned previously, when a user accesses data from a Looker Studio report or Explorer, the queries are triggered in BigQuery. This factor drives `#user` up.

Every time a user changes the data filter or chart order, refreshes data, and many other actions, that will drive up `#user access`.

Looking back at our calculation example, first, it might sound like a lot to have 10,000 queries. But looking at the number, it is pretty normal to have 10 users in an organization and each user needs to refresh the data every half an hour. If the underlying BigQuery table is 1 TB, then $50,000 would indeed be the expected cost per month.

Can we avoid that number? Yes. The general rule of thumb is to avoid having the two big multiplier numbers at the same time. What does that mean?

Avoid scenarios where big tables are accessed by the reporting tool, such as Looker Studio. Even if it's a thing to be avoided, it's a very common practice that happens in the real world. For simplicity, organizations sometimes don't spend much time thinking about data architecture or modeling and use any raw data to be used by Looker Studio. The end users may not notice if they are querying TB of data because BigQuery simply may give the results in seconds. This is very likely given the power of BigQuery. Remember that BigQuery is a very powerful processing engine.

This may lead to the two big multiplier numbers at the same time scenario when large tables are queried many times by tens or hundreds of end users.

But all scenarios other than that are fine; for example, if you have large tables that are accessed by only a few users in a month, that's fine. In other cases, a lot of users accessing several small tables in a given month is also totally fine. Try to calculate things yourself with the given formula.

So, the key here is trying to be mindful of both of the multipliers. Since Looker Studio is a very easy-to-use tool and BigQuery is a very powerful query engine, both of the combinations sometimes make organizations forget to design a proper data architecture. A proper data model, as we discussed previously, is when data is divided into a raw layer, a data warehouse, and an access layer. This practice will improve your cost optimization for BigQuery.

Another thing that we can do is think about caching. There are two unique cache features in BigQuery called **Materialized Views** and **BI Engine**; both features are there to improve BigQuery caching. We will learn about the features in the next section.

Creating Materialized Views and understanding how BI Engine works

BigQuery has a feature called **Materialized Views**. It's not a table, nor a view; it's a materialized view. To understand it, let's go back to what a table is compared to a view. One of the reasons you create tables is that you want to store transformation results to be used for downstream usage. The reason you create a view instead of a table is that you need the data in real time, but with a view, you always pre-compute all the processes. A materialized view is somewhere in between. With Materialized Views, you can have real-time access, but the processes aren't pre-computed.

It's easier to understand by trying it in practice, so let's set up a scenario:

1. Create an aggregation query in the BigQuery console.

   Let's use our `facts_trip_daily` table and run this query from the BigQuery console:

   ```
   SELECT trip_date, sum(sum_duration_sec) AS sum_duration_sec
   FROM `packt-data-eng-on-gcp.dwh_bikesharing.facts_trips_daily`
   GROUP BY trip_date;
   ```

   The query will output the sum of the duration by the trip date. To continue the experiment, we need to disable the BigQuery default cache. To do that, click **MORE | Query Settings**. This button is shown in the following screenshot:

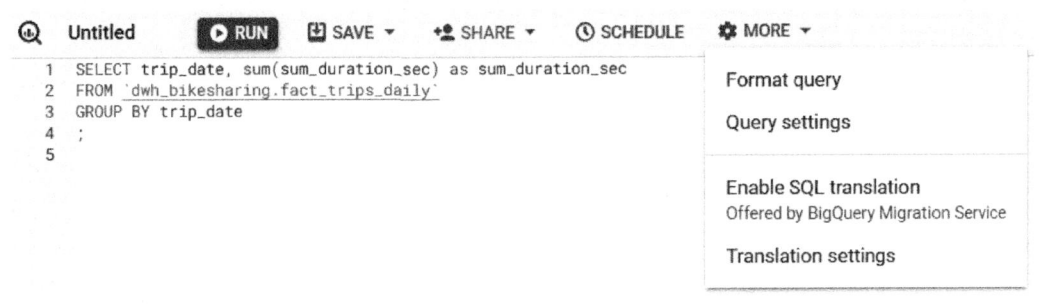

   Figure 7.25 – Finding the Query Settings button under MORE

   The **Query Settings** page will open; find the **Use cached results** checkbox under **Resource Management**. Uncheck this box and click **Save**.

   Now, run the query and check the bytes that have been processed at the top of the **Results** query:

   Figure 7.26 – Example query result in BigQuery

For example, my experiment shows that 14.9 KB was processed. Now, if you rerun the query, BigQuery will process the same amount of bytes.

If you create a view on top of that query, you can get the real-time result, but the bytes processed will still be the same. Remember that in on-demand BigQuery pricing, the total bytes processed determines the cost.

2. Create a materialized view using SQL query.

   Now, try to create a materialized view by running this query:

   ```
   CREATE MATERIALIZED
   VIEW `dwh_bikesharing.facts_trips_daily_sum_duration_sec`
   AS
   SELECT trip_date, sum(sum_duration_sec) AS sum_duration_sec
   FROM `dwh_bikesharing.facts_trips_daily`
   GROUP BY trip_date;
   ```

   After running the query, you will see that your materialized view has been created in your dataset:

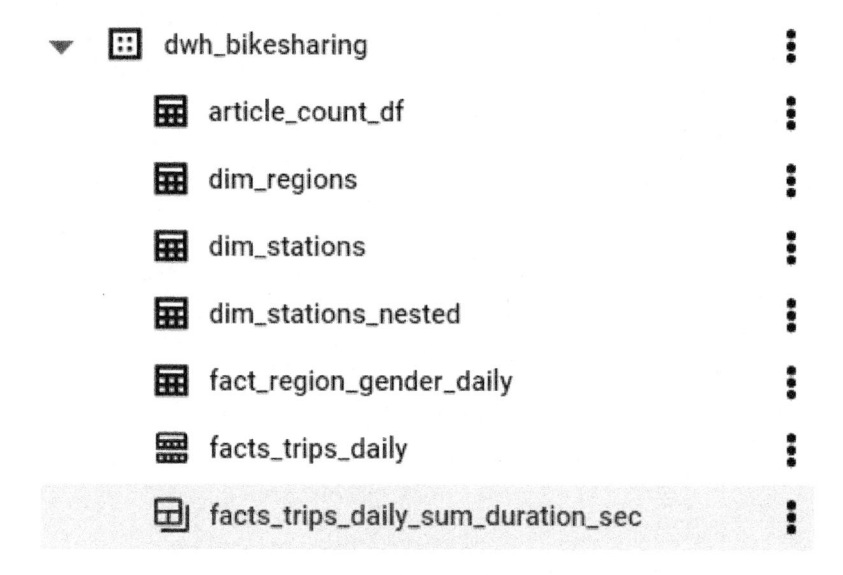

   Figure 7.27 – A materialized view example from the table list

   After successfully creating it, try to rerun the query:

   ```
   SELECT trip_date, sum(sum_duration_sec) AS sum_duration_sec
   FROM `packt-data-eng-on-gcp.dwh_bikesharing.facts_trips_daily`
   GROUP BY trip_date;
   ```

After running this twice, the bytes processed will be reduced significantly. In my case, it is 64 B compared to 14 KB from the previous run:

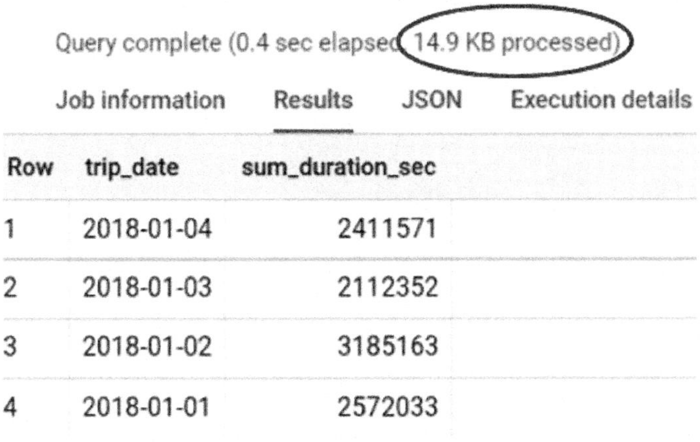
Query complete (0.4 sec elapsed, 14.9 KB processed)
Job information
Results
JSON
Execution details
Row
trip_date
sum_duration_sec
1
2018-01-04
2411571
2
2018-01-03
2112352
3
2018-01-02
3185163
4
2018-01-01
2572033

Figure 7.28 – Example query result

This can significantly reduce your BigQuery costs, especially if the underlying table is often used in a Looker Studio report and the aggregation occurs often.

Notice that you don't need to call the materialized view using a query such as this:

```
SELECT * FROM `dwh_bikesharing.facts_trips_daily_sum_duration_sec`
```

Materialized Views works as a cache in BigQuery; the goal is to provide real-time tables and, at the same time, reduce processing. But to use it, you need to know all the capabilities and limitations. At the time of writing, which is 2023, Materialized Views has matured but is still a relatively new feature. You can check out the list of its limitations in the public documentation: `https://cloud.google.com/bigquery/docs/materialized-views-intro#limitations`.

It's recommended to use Materialized Views whenever needed for cost optimization. Having Materialized Views in your BigQuery dataset will automatically reduce background processing and costs. Your Looker Studio end users don't need to change anything from their side.

Another caching mechanism that is available in BigQuery and is exclusively for BI tools such as Looker Studio is **BI Engine**; we will talk about that in the next section.

Understanding BI Engine

BI Engine is an in-memory caching mechanism in BigQuery that is commonly used by BI tools such as Looker Studio. BI Engine helps you cache very hot data that is accessed very frequently.

Unlike Materialized Views, **BI Engine** is a feature that only needs to be enabled. This means that it's a black box feature where you, as a user, don't need to create any objects to implement BI Engine.

Another difference between BI Engine and Materialized Views is that BI Engine caches almost every query result, whereas Materialized Views only caches aggregated, filtered, or inner-join results. The only limitation of BI Engine is that the cache size is small. So, as long as the total query result size per project is under 100 GB in memory, your query with Looker Studio is free.

To enable BI Engine, you just need to go to the **BigQuery** navigation menu, as shown in the following screenshot:

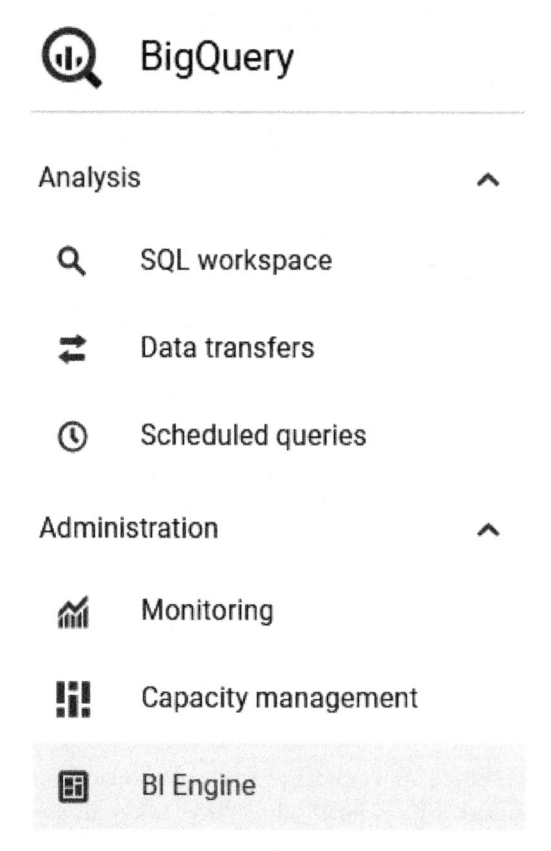

Figure 7.29 – Finding the BI Engine button under the BigQuery Administration menu

After enabling the **Reservation API**, you will be directed to the **Reservation** page. The first option is **Configure**:

1 Configure

BI Engine reservation will be assigned to your current project.

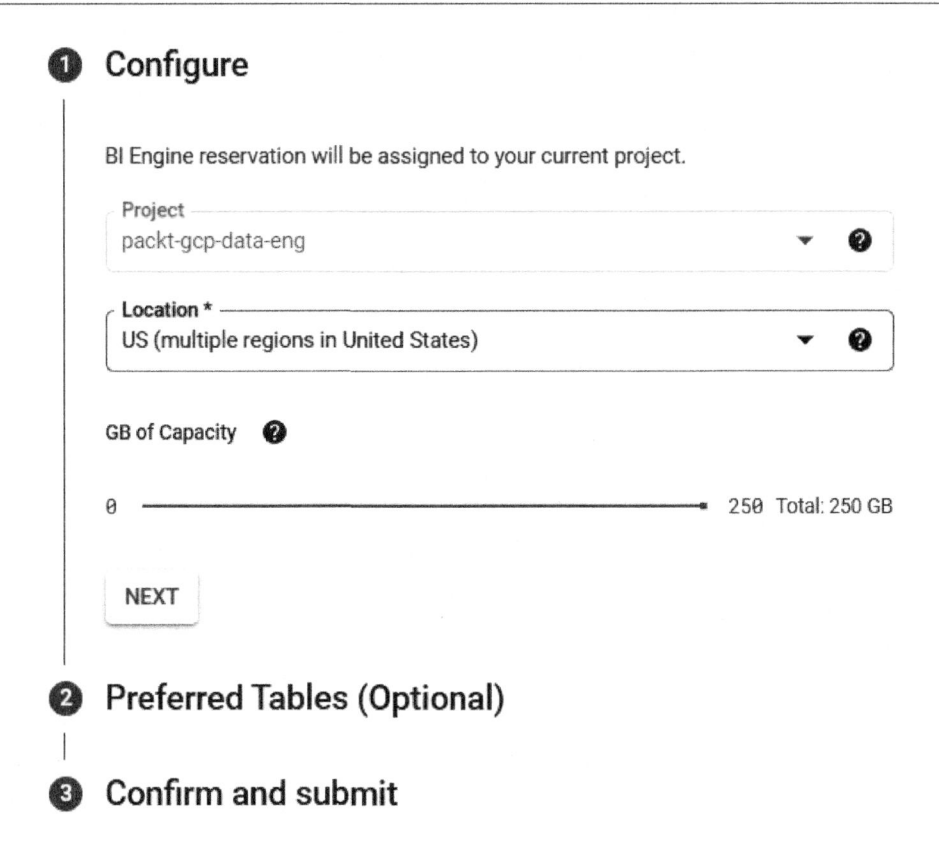

Project
packt-gcp-data-eng

Location *
US (multiple regions in United States)

GB of Capacity

0 ——————————————————— 250   Total: 250 GB

NEXT

2 Preferred Tables (Optional)

3 Confirm and submit

Figure 7.30 – An example of the BI Engine configuration menu

> **Warning**
> For this exercise, you don't need to create the BI Engine reservation at an unnecessary cost! There are no other steps that require BI Engine in this book. Use BI Engine when you use BigQuery and Looker Studio for production.

To activate BI Engine, you just need to fill in the **Location** field and its capacity. What you need to understand at this point is that BI Engine works according to memory capacity. So long as your query fits your memory capacity, you can optimize your BigQuery costs in general.

If you are on the BI Engine page, you can close it now. Don't confirm or create the reservation here because it's very expensive, if only for practice.

Lastly, if you want to check whether your Looker Studio chart utilizes BI Engine, you may notice there is a lightning icon at the top right of every chart, as shown here:

trip_date ▼	start_statio...	avg_durati...	sum_durati...
1... Jan 2, 2018	324	2,731.33	196,656
2... Jan 2, 2018	71	1,174.57	16,444

Figure 7.31 – The top-right lightning icon

If the lightning icon appears like that, it means the Looker Studio chart uses BI Engine; if the icon has a cross through it, the table's size means it doesn't fit within BI Engine's limitations.

With that, you now know the two optimization approaches that you can use to optimize BigQuery costs that might occur from Looker Studio usage. The key point is to be mindful.

As a data engineer, you always need to be aware of the implications of your end users' data usage. It doesn't mean that Looker Studio will always affect BigQuery costs significantly. Knowing how to optimize is the key message.

Summary

In this chapter, we learned how to use Looker Studio using BigQuery as the data source. We learned how to connect the data and create charts and reports for sharing it with other users.

Throughout the exercises in this chapter, we learned not only about how to create charts but also the point of view of our end users. In the exercises, we realized how important it is to create a proper data model in our datasets. Imagine if our tables didn't have proper naming conventions, weren't aggregated properly, or followed any other bad practices that can happen in a data warehouse. Since we already learned all the good data engineering practices and code from the previous chapters, it's now very easy for us to use our example tables to visualize things in Looker Studio.

And lastly, as data engineers, we need to be the ones who understand and are aware of the cost implications in our data ecosystem. In this chapter, we learned about BigQuery INFORMATION_SCHEMA, Materialized Views, and BI Engine. Knowledge of these is not only applicable to Looker Studio but to BigQuery as a whole.

In the next chapter, once again, we will visit an area that is not core to the data engineer's role – **machine learning**. Even though machine learning is more related to the role of the data scientist, understanding it is important for data engineers. We will learn about machine learning terminologies and how to build a machine learning pipeline in GCP.

8
Building Machine Learning Solutions on GCP

The first **machine learning** (**ML**) solution came from the 1950s era. And I believe most of you know that in recent years, it's become immensely popular. It's undeniable that the discussion of **artificial intelligence** (**AI**) and ML is one of the hottest topics of the 21st century. There are two main drivers of this. One is the advancement in the infrastructure, while the second is data. This second driver brings us, as data engineers, into the ML area.

In my experience of discussing ML with data engineers, there are two different reactions – either extremely excited or totally against it. Before you lose interest in finishing this chapter, I want to be clear about what we are going to cover.

We are not going to learn about ML from any historical stories and the mathematical aspects of it. Instead, I am going to prepare you, as data engineers, for potential ML involvement in your GCP environment.

As we learn about the full picture of ML in this chapter, you will realize how close this subject is to data engineering roles. In any organization, it is likely for us data engineers to be involved in ML discussions or projects. On top of that, GCP has a lot of unique services that we can utilize to create end-to-end ML projects.

After reading and completing the exercises in this chapter, you will be able to understand the different stages of the ML pipeline and how it varies from generic ETL pipelines. You will get hands-on experience setting up different GCP products and services to build ML pipelines. You will also be able to gain insights using pre-trained models with services such as Vision API, Cloud Natural Language, and more.

The following high-level topics will be covered in this chapter:

- A quick look at ML
- Exercise – practicing ML code using Python
- The MLOps landscape in GCP

- Exercise – leveraging pre-built GCP models as a service
- Exercise – using GCP in AutoML to train an ML model
- Exercise – deploying a dummy workflow with Vertex AI Pipelines
- Exercise – deploying a scikit-learn model pipeline with Vertex AI

Let's look at the prerequisites for this chapter.

Technical requirements

For this chapter's exercises, we will use the following GCP services:

- BigQuery
- GCS
- Vertex AI Pipelines
- Vertex AI AutoML
- Google Cloud Vision AI
- Google Cloud Translate

If you have never opened any of these services in your GCP console, try to open them and enable the respective API if required.

Also, make sure you have your GCP console, Cloud Shell, and Cloud Editor ready.

Finally, download the example code and the dataset from https://github.com/PacktPublishing/Data-Engineering-with-Google-Cloud-Platform-Second-Edition/tree/main/chapter-8.

Now, let's get started!

A quick look at ML

First, let's understand what ML is from a data engineering perspective. ML is a data process that uses data as input. The output of the process is a generalized formula for one specific objective, which is called the **ML model**.

As an illustration, let's imagine some of the real-world use cases that use ML. The first example is a recommendation system from an eCommerce platform. This eCommerce platform may use ML to use the customer's purchase history as input data. This data can be processed to calculate how likely each customer will purchase other items in the future. Another example is a cancer predictor that uses X-ray images from the health industry. A collection of X-ray images with cancer and without cancer can be used as input data and be used to predict unidentified X-ray images.

I believe you've heard about those kinds of ML use cases and many other real-world use cases. Even in the latest hype surrounding generative AI, the pattern is the same. The inputs are tons of images or text, while the output is a generalized formula for one specific objective – for example, a formula to calculate what are the most appropriate words following the prior words, which construct sentences.

For data engineers, it's important to notice that ML is not that different compared to data processes – it needs data as input and output. One of the key differences is the *generalized formula*, which is the key point in ML. The *generalized formula* is where some mathematical formulas come in. For example, you might have heard of regression, decision trees, neural networks, and k-means, which are called **ML models**.

We will use one ML model later called **Random Forest**. With the Random Forest model, you can create an application that learns from historical data and predicts new data. But we won't talk about this any further – our focus will be to use it as a Python package and understand its position in an end-to-end ML pipeline.

Another big aspect of ML is the terminologies. Interestingly, some terminologies are specifically used in ML (usually by data scientists) and are used by data engineers to refer to similar things. As an analogy, some people say mobile phone, while other people say cell phone, which refers to the same thing. Let's learn about some of the important terminologies:

- **Dataset**: This is data that will be used for ML input. It can be in any data format, but typically, it's stored in a database table or files. Compared to what data engineers expect from raw data, a dataset in the ML space usually expects a cleaner version of data.

    For example, a dataset in table format has three columns:

    - **Rain/No Rain**
    - **Humidity**
    - **Temperature**

- **Features**: Features are a set of information in the dataset that will be used for the ML training process. From a data engineering perspective, features are collections of columns in a table or CSV file that contain values for predicting. For example, the features from the previous example are **Humidity** and **Temperature**.

- **Target**: Target is the information that we want to predict in the future. For example, the target from the previous example is **Rain/No Rain**.

- **Accuracy/model performance**: Metrics or measurements that are used to calculate how good the ML model is – for example, 90% of the predictions correctly predict rain.

- **Hyperparameter**: When you're creating an ML model, there are certain parameters that you can provide as input. Many of them need trial and error to find the best input parameter, such as the number of trees in the Random Forest model.

- **Batch prediction**: This is used for predicting the future using new data in bulk. For example, you can predict next week's **Rain/No Rain** forecast from Monday to Sunday based on this week's **Humidity** and **Temperature** values.

- **Online prediction**: You can use this to predict the future using new data in real time. The most common practice is using an API – for example, an API that accepts input for two values, **Humidity** and **Temperature**. The output is either **Rain** or **No Rain**.

Knowing the terminologies will help us communicate better with data scientists. We'll get some real experience in using them in the next section.

Exercise – practicing ML code using Python

In this section, we will use some of the terminologies we provided in the previous section and practice creating a quite simple ML solution using Python. The focus is for us to understand the steps and start using the correct terminologies.

For this exercise, we will be using Cloud Editor and Cloud Shell. I believe you either know of or have heard that the most common tool for creating ML models for data scientists is Jupyter Notebook. There are two reasons I choose to use the editor style. One, not many data engineers are used to the notebook coding style. Second, using the editor will make it easier to port the files to pipelines.

For our example use case, we will predict if a credit card customer fails to pay their credit card bill next month. I will name the use case **credit card default**. The dataset is available in the BigQuery public dataset. Let's get started.

Here are the steps that you will complete in this exercise:

1. Preparing the ML dataset by using a table from the BigQuery public dataset.
2. Training the ML model using Random Forest in Python.
3. Creating a batch prediction using the training dataset's output.

As a primary step, go to your **BigQuery** console and create a new dataset called `ml_dataset` in the US multi-region.

Preparing the ML dataset by using a table from the BigQuery public dataset

We want to copy the table from the BigQuery public data to our newly created dataset. To do that, find the `credit_card_default` table in the `bigquery-public-data` project, under the `ml_dataset` dataset. If you haven't pinned the `bigquery-public-data` project to your project, please revisit *Chapter 3, Building a Data Warehouse in BigQuery*.

After finding the `credit_card_default` table, click it. You will see, the **COPY** button, as shown here:

🗐 COPY

Figure 8.1 – The Copy button in the BigQuery console

Set the destination for your project and dataset. Name its `credit_card_default`, as shown in the following screenshot:

Copy table

Source

Project name	Dataset	Table name
bigquery-public-data	ml_datasets	credit_card_default

Destination

Project
packt-data-eng-on-gcp   BROWSE

Dataset ID *
ml_dataset

Table name *
credit_card_default

Figure 8.2 – Copy table configuration

After clicking **COPY**, the table will appear in your dataset.

> **Note**
> We will use this table in this chapter and the rest of the exercises in this book. So, make sure that you complete this set correctly.

Back to our terminologies, we can call this table the ML dataset. There are a lot of ML features here, such as `limit_balance`, `sex`, `education_level`, and many more. The target column should be `default_payment_next_month`. As usual, you can check the table's content by clicking **PREVIEW** on the BigQuery table, as shown here:

264　Building Machine Learning Solutions on GCP

Row	id	limit_balance	sex	education_level	marital_status	age
1	27502.0	80000.0	1	6	1	54.0
2	26879.0	200000.0	1	4	1	49.0
3	18340.0	20000.0	2	6	2	22.0

Figure 8.3 – credit_card_default table preview

At this point, feel free to take your time. You might need some time to understand the table's content. Once you're done, we can start coding our ML code. You can check out the full example code in this book's GitHub repository: https://github.com/PacktPublishing/Data-Engineering-with-Google-Cloud-Platform-Second-Edition/blob/main/chapter-8/code/credit-card-default-ml.py.

You should develop the exercise as Python code using Cloud Editor and run the script in Cloud Shell. Don't forget to install the requirements by running the following command:

```
$ pip install -r requirements
```

In the next section, we will try to train the ML model using data from the BigQuery table.

Training the ML model using Random Forest in Python

To train the ML model, there are six main steps, as follows:

1. Import the necessary library and define the variables.

    First, we need to import the ML package. In our example, we will use `RandomForestClassifier` from `sklearn`:

    ```
    from google.cloud import bigquery
    from sklearn.ensemble import RandomForestClassifier
    from sklearn.model_selection import train_test_split
    from sklearn import metrics
    import joblib
    import json
    import pandas as pd
    # TODO : Change to your project id
    project_id = "packt-data-eng-on-gcp"
    ```

    Don't forget to change `project_id` to your project's ID.

2. Load the data from BigQuery into a pandas DataFrame and select the necessary features.

   The second step is to load our dataset into pandas. A pandas DataFrame is an acceptable input for the `RandomForestClassifier` package. To do that, we must call the BigQuery client and convert it into a pandas DataFrame:

   ```
   client = bigquery.Client()
   dataset_table_id="ml_dataset.credit_card_default"
   sql = f"""
   SELECT limit_balance, education_level, age,
      default_payment_next_month FROM `{dataset_table_id}`;
   """
   dataframe = (client.query(sql).result().to_dataframe())
   ```

   For simplicity, we will only use three features – `limit_balance`, `education_level`, and `age`. The target will be `default_payment_next_month`.

3. Split the data into train and test datasets.

   The third step is to split the pandas DataFrame into four train and test datasets:

   ```
   labels = dataframe["default_payment_next_month"]
   features = dataframe.drop("default_payment_next_month",
      axis = 1)
   X_train, X_test, y_train, y_test = train_test_split(features,
      labels, test_size=0.3)
   ```

   The train and test step is a quite common step when it comes to creating an ML model. The goal of this step is to have different datasets for checking the accuracy later. `test_size` is `0.3`, which means that 70% of the data will be used for training and that the rest of it (30%) can be used for checking its accuracy.

4. Perform ML training using `RandomForestClassifier`.

   The next step is to train the model. First, we need to define a `RandomForestClassifier` class. Later, we will call the `fit()` method to train the model:

   ```
   random_forest_classifier = RandomForestClassifier(
      n_estimators=100)
   random_forest_classifier.fit(X_train,y_train)
   ```

   The training process happens when we trigger the `fit` method. Notice that there is a variable there called `n_estimators = 100`. This is one example of a hyperparameter. `n_estimators` define how many trees will be used in the Random Forest model. No one knows what the best number we should put here is, and that's part of the hyperparameter. To get the best possible hyperparameter, usually, data scientists will try many combinations, get the model accuracies, and determine the best hyperparameter. This activity is called **hyperparameter tuning**.

5. Predict the test data and calculate the model's accuracy.

    The next step is to calculate the model's accuracy. We will use the `random_forest_classifier` variable to predict the testing data:

    ```
    y_pred=random_forest_classifier.predict(X_test)

    print("Accuracy:",metrics.accuracy_score(y_test, y_pred))
    ```

    In this step, this is not what's called batch or online prediction. Even though we are using the `predict` method in this step, the goal of this step is only to calculate the accuracy score. At the end of this step, you will know the accuracy of the model.

6. Save the model as a file.

    Finally, our model should be stored as a file. Do this by calling the `joblib.dump()` function:

    ```
    joblib.dump(random_forest_classifier, "cc_default_rf_model.sav")
    ```

    This step will write a `.joblib` file in your local filesystem.

    At this point, you should have an ML file that you can use to predict future credit card default datasets.

Creating a batch prediction using the training dataset's output

In the same Python file, let's look at the `predict_batch` function:

1. Load the new dataset for batch prediction.

    Similar to the training model step, we must load the data from the BigQuery table, as follows:

    ```
    client = bigquery.Client()
    sql = f"""SELECT limit_balance, education_level, age
        FROM `{dataset_table_id}` LIMIT 10;"""
    dataframe = (client.query(sql).result().to_dataframe())
    ```

    For simplicity, we will use the same table but select only the feature columns and limit it to only 10 rows. In reality, the table for prediction should be taken from a different table. The table should contain sets of data that have no target column.

2. Use the ML model to predict the batch dataset.

    The next step is simply predicting the data. To do that, we need to load the model from our previous step:

    ```
    loaded_model = joblib.load("cc_default_rf_model.sav")
    prediction= loaded_model.predict(dataframe)
    print(prediction)
    ```

    The function will print its prediction to the 10 unlabeled records with values of 0 or 1, which represent credit card default. This can result in a correct or incorrect prediction. And that's the nature of ML – it can give both right and wrong answers.

If it's successful, congratulations! You just performed ML training and batch prediction. In GCP, we can simplify the batch prediction process using **Vertex AI batch predictions**.

3. Use the ML model to predict online data.

   For online prediction, you can use the `predict_online()` function. The following is a very simplified example of online prediction:

   ```
   limit_balance = 1000
   education_level = 1
   age = 25
   feature_json = json.dumps([[limit_balance,
                               education_level, age]])
   predict_online(feature_json)
   ```

   As you can see, the nature of online prediction is giving a single input so that a function will return the result in real time. In reality, this simplified function needs to serve as a web API. The `limit_balance`, `education_level`, and `age` features are the API parameters that will be used as inputs for prediction. Web developers typically do this part, so we will not cover this topic in this book. In GCP, we can also serve the ML model as an online prediction using **Vertex AI online prediction**. The service will create the online prediction API and serve it as **endpoints**.

Now, let's summarize what we've done. Even though the given example is quite a simple use case, we've learned about the steps that are required in ML and its terminologies. At this point, we have an ML pipeline. Here are the steps we followed:

1. Loading the required ML libraries.
2. Data loading.
3. Feature selection.
4. Data splitting.
5. Model training.
6. Model evaluation.
7. Model deployment.
8. Batch prediction.
9. Simulating an online prediction.

We will learn how to manage an ML pipeline in GCP later in the *Deploying a dummy workflow with Vertex AI Pipelines* section. But before we use the GCP service, we need to understand what services in GCP are related to ML. And to learn about service positioning, we need to understand what MLOps is. We will discuss this in the next section.

The MLOps landscape in GCP

In this section, we'll learn what GCP services are related to MLOps. But before that, let's understand what MLOps is.

Understanding the basic principles of MLOps

When we created the ML model in the previous section, we created some ML code, which included creating features, models, and predictions. I found that much ML content and its discussion on the public internet is about creating and improving ML models. Some examples of typical topics include how to create a Random Forest model, ML regression versus classification, boosting ML accuracy with hyperparameters, and many more.

All of the example topics mentioned previously are part of creating ML code. In reality, ML in a real production system needs a lot more than that. Take a look at the following diagram for the other aspects:

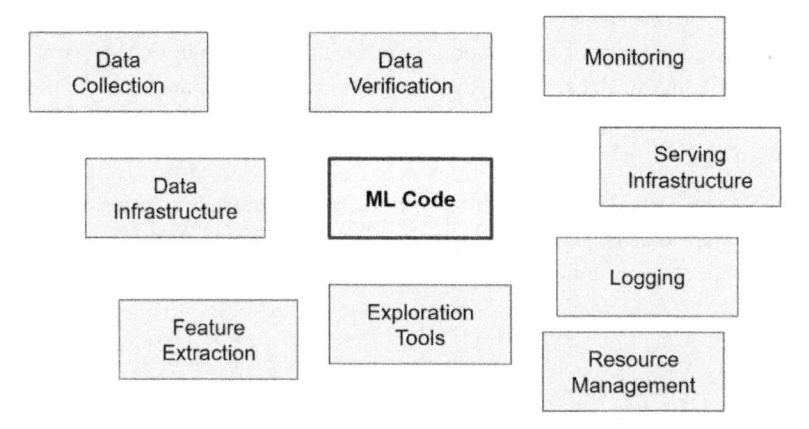

Figure 8.4 – Various ML aspects that ML code is only a small part of

As you can see, it's logical to have the other aspects in an ML environment. For example, in our previous exercise, the credit card data had already been formed, was clean, and was ready for our training step. As a data engineer, you can imagine the effort needed before that, so it's logical to have data collection, data verification, and feature extraction processes.

Another aspect to think of is the infrastructure. Where should the training process happen? In our local machine (laptop) or a **virtual machine** (**VM**)? How about the dependencies? Combined with all the other aspects, this usually takes 90% of the effort compared to the ML code.

The practice of building and maintaining all of these aspects in ML is what's called **MLOps**. Understanding all the aspects of MLOps requires us to understand several different areas of expertise, including ML models, data, orchestration, containerization (Docker), web services, monitoring, and much more. This is why ML is a broad topic and, most of the time, requires more than one team or expert to handle the entirety of MLOps.

If you start everything from scratch, it will probably take months, if not years, to complete all the stacks. Are there any ways to simplify this? Yes. In GCP, most of the stacks are available as managed services.

Is this process going to be easy? No – not in terms of the learning journey. Understanding and creating MLOps won't be as easy as creating a table and querying it in BigQuery. MLOps has many components, and the topics are extremely broad. However, managed services help reduce the development time a lot. In the next section, we'll look at the landscape of MLOps in GCP.

Introducing GCP services related to MLOps

In GCP, you can find almost all you need for MLOps. First, let's start by looking at what is available in our GCP console. In your GCP console, open Vertex AI in the **GCP** navigation menu, under **Vertex AI**. You will see that there are many services:

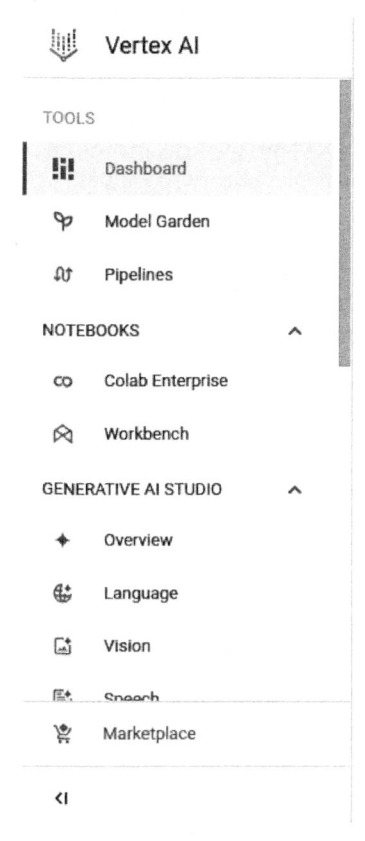

Figure 8. 5 – List of Vertex AI services in the GCP navigation menu

You can open each service and read their descriptions to know their positioning. I'll quickly highlight the flow of each service using a scenario where you would want to build an ML model.

You have some raw data in BigQuery. So, what services should you use and when?

First, you must create a Vertex AI notebook – either **Colab Enterprise** or **Workbench**. Colab Enterprise is the easiest, so we will use it here. Using a notebook, you can play around with the BigQuery data to create experimental ML models. The ML models can also be called **ML code**.

Once you're satisfied with the ML code, to automate the code, you can automate the process using Vertex AI's **Pipelines** option, which will automate all the steps.

These steps may include creating Vertex AI **Datasets**, a Vertex AI **Feature Store**, Vertex AI **Labeling tasks**, and a Vertex AI **Training service**. The **Training** step will store an ML model in Vertex AI's **Model Registry**. Later, the model can be used for Vertex AI **Batch predictions** and/or to start Vertex AI **Online predictions**. Finally, you can store any metadata from any steps in Vertex AI's **Metadata service**, such as the model's accuracy. These are the main services under Vertex AI that you need for developing and managing your ML models.

You may also notice the other options related to generative AI, the latest and emerging field in AI. They are fun features! However, I will not cover them in this book because most of them are user-friendly features that you can try and use as a ready-made product with minimum development effort. Feel free to read the documentation and explore their capabilities.

Back to our previous section's exercises, you can see that every service under Vertex AI can be used for an end-to-end ML scenario. There are two things to note here. First, you still need other GCP services outside Vertex AI, such as GCS, BigQuery, IAM, and others. Vertex AI services are specifically used to handle ML operations, but other GCP services are still needed.

Second, Vertex AI services are modular. This means that all Vertex AI services are optional. As a user, you can utilize all services or only some of them. For example, you can decide to only use Vertex AI Pipelines for orchestration but store the models as files in GCS and not use Vertex AI Models. Or, as another example, you could just use the Training service to use the AutoML feature; none of the others would be required. There are many things you must consider when you're to use all or some of these services, such as cost, regional availability, and the learning curve.

Before diving into the exercises, I want to highlight two other things about the ML services in GCP – the evolution of these ML services in GCP and the ML model training approaches.

ML services on GCP evolve rapidly. This may lead to some confusion when you start looking for examples and tutorials on the public internet. For example, at the time of writing, there are two options in GCP for creating an ML pipeline. From the navigation menu, you will see that one option is under **AI Platform Pipelines**; the second option is to use Vertex AI. This is because some services are older than others. For instance, Vertex AI is the successor of AI Platform. If this is still the case when you are reading this book, hopefully, this explanation can clear up any confusion. If this is no longer the case, you will still see some old yet valuable articles on the public internet that mention different service names.

For the ML model training process, there are four main approaches that you can utilize on GCP:

- A custom model in a custom environment
- Google pre-built models
- Vertex AI AutoML
- BigQuery ML

These approaches are there as options for three-dimensional decision points: development time, the amount of expertise, and the cost. What does this mean?

An ideal condition for a data science team in a company when building ML is having a lot of *experienced* data scientists. In terms of time, the data scientists have *a lot of time* to experiment, find the best model for each use case, and ensure that the infrastructure *costs as little as possible*. In this ideal case, creating a custom model in a custom environment is the best approach. But not every condition is ideal – some companies don't have data scientists, some need to model as soon as possible, and some have limited budgets. At that time, we should be able to decide what other options are available.

The pre-built model is a group of trained ML models provided by Google Cloud. The lists of models are continuing to grow, but as an example, at the time of writing, there are models for detecting image-to-text, translating languages, eCommerce item recommendations, and others that you can check in your GCP console under the **Artificial Intelligence** section via the navigation menu. This approach requires almost zero ML expertise and experiment time. As a user, you just need to call the API using the client library and you can make the predictions immediately. The downside is that the model is limited to what's been provided, so you can't handle edge cases. And the cost is relatively more expensive for heavy users because it's charged by the number of API calls.

AutoML is a term in ML where you, as an ML code developer, no longer need to decide what ML algorithm is the best for your model. AutoML will automatically try many possibilities and parameters. The number of trials is based on time. As a developer, you just need to tell AutoML how much time you want to give, and AutoML will return the best possible model in that given time. This approach can handle your edge cases, needs a small number of data scientists, and needs almost zero experiment time. The downside is the cost of the infrastructure. It's relatively more expensive compared to building a custom model. The upside, besides the development time, is the accuracy, since AutoML has proven to be more accurate than self-built custom models.

The last option is BigQuery ML. BigQuery ML is an approach for training ML models using SQL queries. This approach allows you to create custom ML models with any available algorithm provided by BigQuery. This approach is suitable when you want to train ML models, but you are more comfortable using SQL compared to programming languages such as Python or R, plus with libraries such as TensorFlow and scikit-learn.

Different scenarios need different approaches. In general, if we only look at the development and experimentation time, then here's what you should use, from the least to the most time-consuming:

- Pre-built model
- AutoML
- BigQuery ML
- A custom model in a custom environment

In the next section, we will start our exercise. There, we will start by using the pre-built model while using the Python API to detect text in images, using AutoML from the GCP console, and building a custom model using scikit-learn using a Vertex AI pipeline.

> **Note**
> We will not be using BigQuery ML here. The steps are straightforward and relatively easy if you already know how to use BigQuery. Go back to *Chapter 3, Building a Data Warehouse in BigQuery*, and *Chapter 4, Building Workflows for Batch Data Loading using Cloud Composer*, for the steps on creating an ML pipeline; they are similar to those for creating a data pipeline.

Exercise – leveraging pre-built GCP models as a service

In this exercise, we will use a GCP service called Google Cloud Vision. Google Cloud Vision is one of many pre-built models in GCP. In pre-built models, we only need to call the API from our application. This means that we don't need to create an ML model.

In this exercise, we will create a Python application that can read an image with handwritten text and convert it into a Python string.

The following are the steps for this exercise:

1. Upload the image to a GCS bucket.
2. Install the required Python packages.
3. Create a detect text function in Python.

Let's start by uploading the image.

Uploading the image to a GCS bucket

In the GCS console, go to the bucket that you created in the previous chapters. For example, my bucket is `wired-apex-392509-data-bucket`.

Inside the bucket, create a new folder called `chapter-8`. This is an example from my console:

wired-apex-392509-data-bucket

Location	Storage class	Public access	Protection
us (multiple regions in United States)	Standard	Not public	None

OBJECTS   CONFIGURATION   PERMISSIONS   PROTECTION   LIFECYCLE

Buckets > wired-apex-392509-data-bucket > chapter-8

Figure 8.6 – Example GCS bucket folder for storing the image file

We want to upload the image file into this folder. You can upload any image that contains text, or you can use the example provided at https://github.com/PacktPublishing/Data-Engineering-with-Google-Cloud-Platform-Second-Edition/blob/main/chapter-8/dataset/chapter-8-example-text.jpg.

The image that we want to upload looks like this:

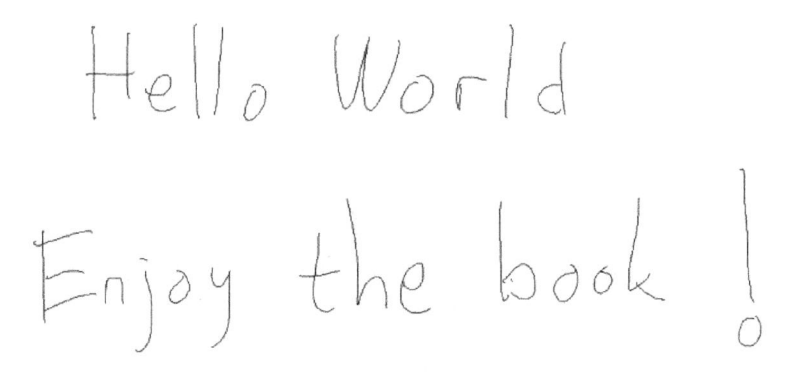

Figure 8.7 – The image that we will process using the Google Cloud Vision AI

This image is of handwritten text with no format. I have intentionally used my handwritten text as an example to show that Google Cloud Vision can convert any text – it's not limited to computer-generated fonts. After downloading the file to your local computer, upload it to GCS in your newly created folder.

Next, we want to install the necessary packages. Go to your Cloud Shell and install the following two Python packages:

```
$ pip install google-cloud-vision
$ pip install google-cloud-translate
```

Google Cloud Vision and Google Cloud Translate will be installed. We will use the Translate package to detect what language is used in the text and to illustrate how to use two pre-built models in one application.

Creating a detect text function in Python

Now, go to your Cloud Shell and Cloud Editor. Here, we will start writing the code for our application. You can find the full code example in this book's GitHub repository: https://github.com/PacktPublishing/Data-Engineering-with-Google-Cloud-Platform-Second-Edition/blob/main/chapter-8/code/pre-built-vision-ai.py.

You can enable all of the required Google APIs by using `gcloud` commands.

First, we may need to set up `auth` login using this command:

```
$ gcloud auth application-default login
```

Try this out in your Cloud Shell – run the command and follow the instructions. The instructions are pretty straightforward, so I won't go through them here. As a summary, here are the steps:

1. After running the command, you will be asked a yes or no confirmation question. Choose **yes**.
2. After confirming, a URL link will be shown in Cloud Shell. Open the link in any browser.
3. In your browser, log in with your Google account.
4. At this point, you will get a verification code. Copy and paste this code into Cloud Shell. Here is an example:

```
Enter verification code: 4/xxxxxxxxxx
```

After completing all these steps, you will get a message saying that the credential can be used for any library:

These credentials will be used by any library that requests **Application Default Credentials** (**ADCs**).

Then, we can run the following commands:

```
$ gcloud services enable aiplatform.googleapis.com
$ gcloud services enable vision.googleapis.com
$ gcloud services enable translate.googleapis.com
```

Now, let's start looking at the example code. First, we need to import the Vision and Translate APIs from the `google.cloud` package:

```
from google.cloud import vision
from google.cloud import translate_v2 as translate
```

Make sure that you change the project ID, bucket name, and folders according to your environment:

```
# TODO: Change to your project id and your gcs file uri
project_id = "packt-data-eng-on-gcp"
gcs_uri = "gs://packt-data-eng-on-gcp-data-bucket/chapter-8/chapter-8-
example-text.jpg"
```

You need to define the clients to call both APIs:

```
vision_client = vision.ImageAnnotatorClient()
translate_client = translate.Client()
```

The following is the main function for our `detect_text`:

```
def detect_text(gcs_uri: str):
    print("Looking for text from image in GCS: {}".format(gcs_uri))

    image = vision.Image(
        source=vision.ImageSource(gcs_image_uri=gcs_uri)
    )

    text_detection_response =
        vision_client.text_detection(image=image)
    annotations = text_detection_response.text_annotations
    if len(annotations) > 0:
        text = annotations[0].description
    else:
        text = ""
    print("Extracted text : \n{}".format(text))

    detect_language_response = translate_client.detect_language(text)
    src_lang = detect_language_response["language"]
    print("Detected language {}".format(src_lang))

detect_text(gcs_uri)
```

This function uses the `text_detection()` method from `vision_client` to read the image and output the text. The output is stored in a text variable that will be used in the Translate API. The Translate API uses the `detect_language()` method and will detect what language is in the image. For further usage, you can use the Translate API to translate the text into other languages.

To finish this exercise, run the Python code from Cloud Shell, like so:

```
$ python3 pre-built-vision-ai.py
```

The preceding code will print the extracted text – *Hello World Enjoy the book!*

And that's it – that is how easy it is to implement ML using pre-built models in GCP! What's good about pre-built models is that you can immediately predict new datasets without thinking about training the ML model. So long as the API is suitable for your needs, you can use it immediately. But there are cases where we need to create an ML model, and that is quite common. One way to do this with very minimum effort is by using AutoML. In the next section, we will learn how to use AutoML in GCP.

Exercise – using GCP in AutoML to train an ML model

As we learned earlier in this chapter, AutoML is an automated way for you to build an ML model. It will handle model selection, hyperparameter tuning, and various data preparation steps.

Note that for the data preparation part, it will not be smart enough to transform data from very raw tables, aggregate based on business context, and automatically clean all data to create features. Those activities are still the responsibilities of data engineers and data scientists.

What AutoML will do, however, is perform simple data preparation tasks, such as detecting numeric, binary, categorical, and text features, and then apply the required transformation to be used in the ML training process. Let's learn how to do this. Here are the steps that you will complete in this exercise:

1. Create a Vertex AI dataset.
2. Train the ML model using AutoML.
3. Choose the compute and budget for AutoML.

For the use case and dataset, we will use the credit card default dataset from our previous exercise. First, go to your GCP console and find and click **Vertex AI**. If you haven't enabled the API, there will be a button to enable **Vertex API**, so click it to enable it.

First, we will create **Datasets**, which is a requirement for using AutoML. These are not the same as BigQuery datasets. You can load data from a BigQuery table, but this is a different feature than the one in BigQuery. You can learn more about this at https://cloud.google.com/vertex-ai/docs/training/using-managed-datasets.

To do that, under the **Vertex AI** console, go to the **Datasets** menu:

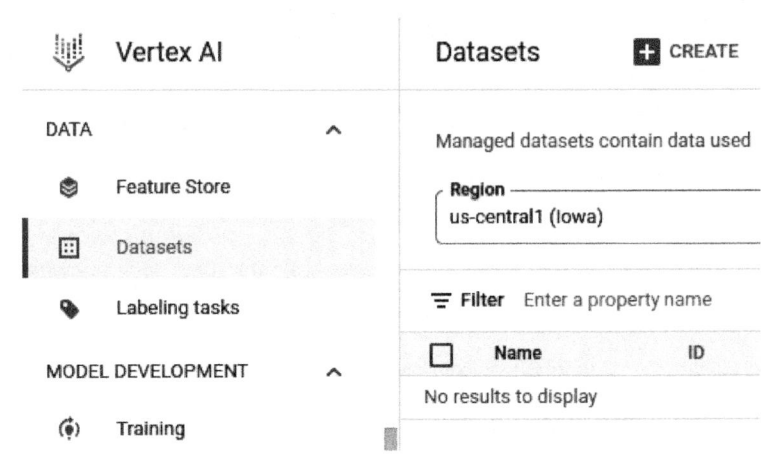

Figure 8.8 – Finding the Vertex AI Datasets menu from the GCP navigation menu

Now let's start using AutoML:

1. Create a Vertex AI dataset.

    I. Find the **CREATE** button at the top of the page and click it.

    II. Set the dataset's name to `credit_card_default`.

    III. In the **Select a data type and objective** section, choose **TABULAR Regression/classification**. This is an important selection that will be used by AutoML:

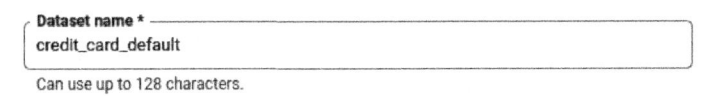

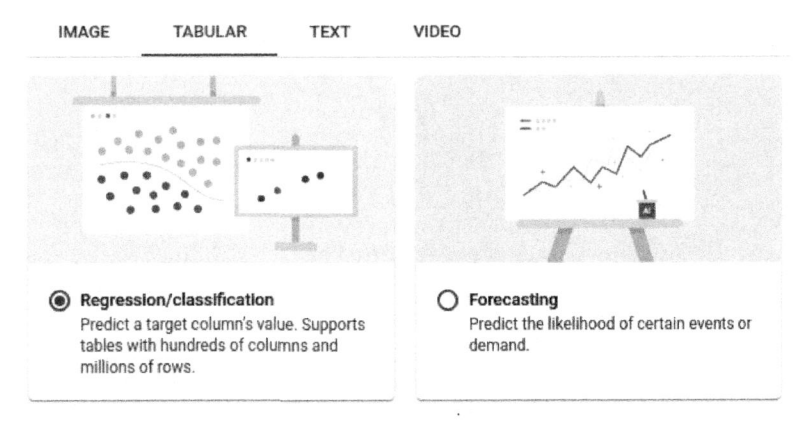

Figure 8.9 – Choosing the Regression/classification option

IV. After choosing this option, click the **CREATE** button. It will take around 5 seconds to complete, at which point you will be redirected to the data source selection page.

V. Under **Select a data source**, choose **Select a table or view from BigQuery**.

VI. Find your `credit_card_default` table in your project. Then, click **CONTINUE**. Here is the example BigQuery path from my project; you need to find yours:

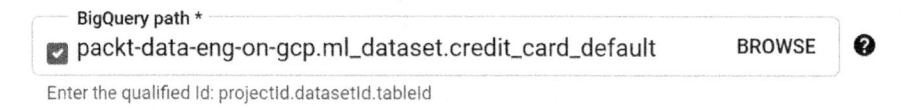

```
BigQuery path *
☑ packt-data-eng-on-gcp.ml_dataset.credit_card_default    BROWSE    ❓
Enter the qualified Id: projectId.datasetId.tableId
```

Figure 8.10 – Example BigQuery path format

At this point, you will be directed to a page where you will see some useful information about your datasets. In the next step, we will train an ML model using the dataset that we created in this step.

2. Train the ML model using AutoML.

   I. Still on the same page, at the top right, you will see the **TRAIN NEW MODEL** button – click it and select **AutoML on Pipeline**.

   II. You will be redirected to the **Pipelines** page. There are five configuration pages. For this exercise, we will keep most of the default values.

   III. On the **Runtime configuration** page, you will be prompted to set **Output directory** under **Cloud Storage Location**. You can use the existing GCS bucket with a new folder, like this: `gs://[YOUR PROJECT ID]-data-bucket/chapter-8/automl_output/`.

   IV. For **Training method**, set the objective to **Classification** and set **Target column** to `default_payment_next_month`.

   V. Under **Training options**, you can choose to set each column as **Categorical** or **Numerical** under **Transformation** or set everything to **Automatic**. The important thing now is to exclude unwanted features. We can do that by clicking the delete icon to the right of each column. The icon looks like this:

⊖

Figure 8.11 – Delete icon

Make sure that you only include `age`, `education_level`, and `limit_balance`. The other columns should be excluded. Here's what you should see at this point:

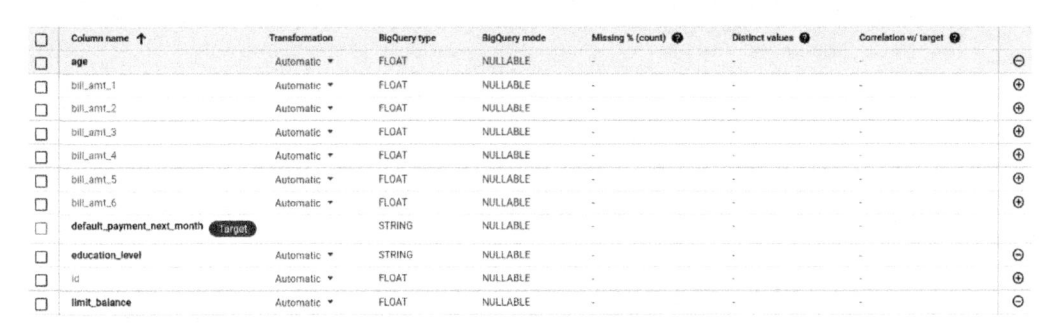

Exercise – using GCP in AutoML to train an ML model | 279

	Column name ↑	Transformation	BigQuery type	BigQuery mode	Missing % (count)	Distinct values	Correlation w/ target	
☐	age	Automatic ▼	FLOAT	NULLABLE	-	-	-	⊖
☐	bill_amt_1	Automatic ▼	FLOAT	NULLABLE	-	-	-	⊕
☐	bill_amt_2	Automatic ▼	FLOAT	NULLABLE	-	-	-	⊕
☐	bill_amt_3	Automatic ▼	FLOAT	NULLABLE	-	-	-	⊕
☐	bill_amt_4	Automatic ▼	FLOAT	NULLABLE	-	-	-	⊕
☐	bill_amt_5	Automatic ▼	FLOAT	NULLABLE	-	-	-	⊕
☐	bill_amt_6	Automatic ▼	FLOAT	NULLABLE	-	-	-	⊕
☐	default_payment_next_month (Target)		STRING	NULLABLE				
☐	education_level	Automatic ▼	STRING	NULLABLE	-	-	-	⊖
☐	id	Automatic ▼	FLOAT	NULLABLE	-	-	-	⊕
☐	limit_balance	Automatic ▼	FLOAT	NULLABLE	-	-	-	⊖

Figure 8.12 – Choosing columns

Once you're satisfied with the features you've selected, click **CONTINUE**.

3. Choose the compute and budget for AutoML.

   After clicking **CONTINUE** in the previous step, you will see the **Compute and Pricing** option. This is an option that you need to pay attention to. With this option, you can choose how much time you want AutoML to spend trying to find the best model. At this point, don't continue to the next step before reading through these pricing considerations.

   The link to the pricing guide is provided on that page, under **Pricing guide**. Check out this guide to decide if you want to continue with the process or not. The minimum cost is around $21 for AutoML models, tabular data, and 1 training node hour. If you don't have much of your free trial budget left ($300), you can stop the AutoML exercise here. If you want to try running it and don't have issues with the cost, click **SUBMIT**.

   This step will trigger a training job that you can monitor in Vertex AI's **Pipelines** menu. The `credit_card_default` job will be shown there:

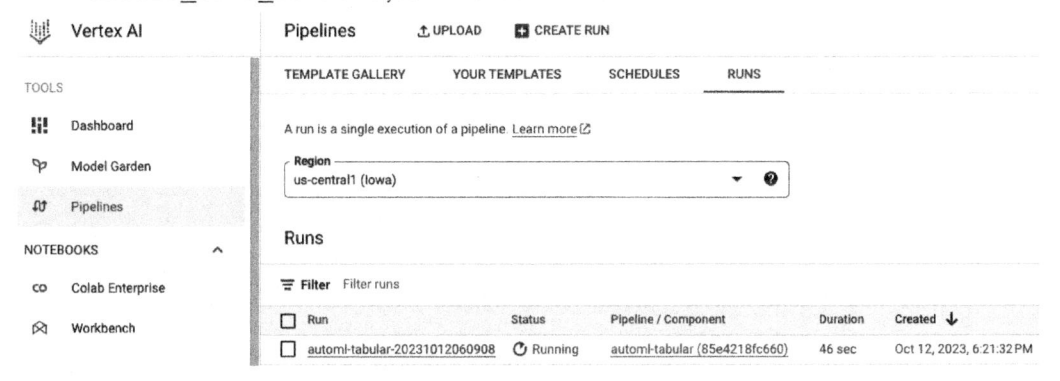

Figure 8.13 – The training job is running

This process will take a maximum of 1 hour, but it can be faster if AutoML can no longer improve its accuracy.

Once you're done, you can check the Vertex AI **Model Registry** menu under the **DEPLOY AND USE** section.

When you open the model menu, you will see a lot of interesting model metrics here, such as **F1 score**, **Precision**, **Recall**, and **ROC AUC**:

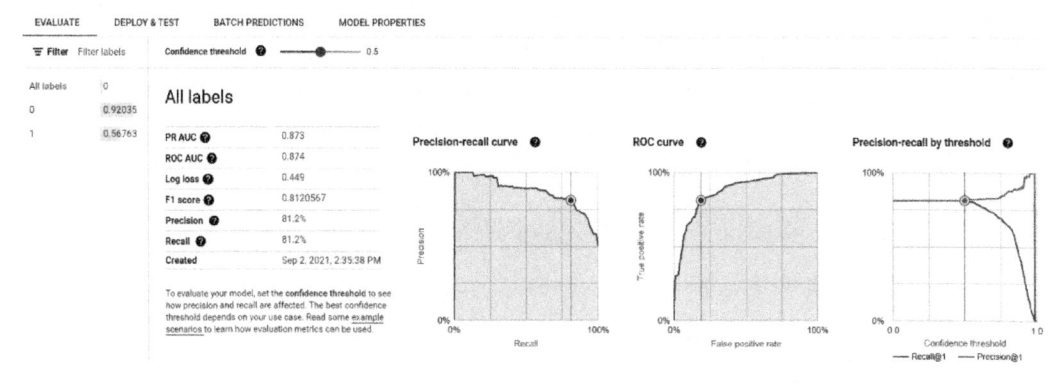

Figure 8.14 – Model labels and metrics under the EVALUATE tab

If you are not familiar with all of these metrics, don't worry – we won't be using them. These metrics are important information that is usually used by data scientists to determine if it's a good model or not. In quite simple terms, all these numbers show ML model accuracy.

Once you're satisfied with the model, there are two common next steps. First, you can deploy the model as an API for online prediction. In Vertex AI, you can click the **DEPLOY & TEST** menu and get the API up and running. The second option is performing batch prediction – for example, by using another table in BigQuery to predict the user's defaults. To do this, you can click **BATCH PREDICTIONS**. Both options are very straightforward, so we won't look at them in this exercise.

At this point, you will have an ML model that you can use to predict credit card defaults. The model was built using AutoML from Vertex AI. As you have experienced, there are three things that you don't need to do when using AutoML:

1. You don't need to code.
2. You don't need to know about any ML algorithms.
3. You don't need to worry about the infrastructure.

The whole process typically takes less than 1 hour, which can reduce a lot of time and effort when you're building an ML model. But there are scenarios where we will want to create an ML model, which is possible. On top of that, if you want to automate the steps and process, we can use Vertex AI Pipelines.

In the next exercise, we will learn about Vertex AI Pipelines. We will use it to create a custom ML model using the same code from the *Exercise – practicing ML code using Python* section.

Exercise – deploying a dummy workflow with Vertex AI Pipelines

Before we continue with the hands-on exercise, let's understand what Vertex AI Pipelines is. Vertex AI Pipelines is a tool for orchestrating ML workflows. Under the hood, it uses an open source tool called Kubeflow Pipeline. Like the relationship between Airflow and Cloud Composer or Hadoop and Dataproc, to understand Vertex AI Pipelines, we need to be familiar with Kubeflow Pipelines.

Kubeflow Pipelines is a platform for building and deploying portable, scalable ML workflows based on Docker containers. Using containers for ML workflows is particularly important compared to data workflows. For example, in data workflows, it's typical to load the BigQuery, GCS, and pandas libraries for all the steps. Those libraries will be used in the upstream to downstream steps. In ML, the upstream process is data loading; the other step is building models that need specific libraries, such as TensorFlow or scikit-learn, while the final step is to calculate the accuracy. And on top of that, each process needs different machine specifications. Implementing each step on containers is helpful for ML workloads.

This idea is great, but in reality, it is difficult to achieve without tools such as Kubeflow. Imagine that you need to understand the principles of Docker, Kubernetes, data engineering, and ML models at the same time. The Docker and Kubernetes part is usually not something that data scientists are familiar with. And that's where Kubeflow Pipelines fills in the gap. With Kubeflow Pipelines, data scientists can simplify the containerization code, yet all the pipelines will be running in containers. With Vertex AI Pipelines, you're not only simplifying the code but also the infrastructure. Using it, you don't need to think about Kubernetes clusters, networking, or installing Kubeflow. You just need to understand how to use the SDKs (`kfp` and `google-cloud-pipeline-components`). We will learn how to use these SDKs in the next section.

In this exercise, we will create a dummy workload. This dummy workload has nothing to do with ML – we will just print text. What we are going to focus on is becoming familiar with the code and how to run it on Vertex AI Pipelines.

The following are the high-level steps:

1. Install the SDKs.
2. Create a dedicated regional GCS bucket.
3. Develop the pipeline on Python.
4. Monitor the pipeline on the Vertex AI Pipelines console.

To start, let's install the required libraries in Python. To do that, go to your Cloud Shell and use the following commands to install the necessary libraries:

```
$ pip3 install kfp --upgrade
$ pip3 install -U google-cloud-pipeline-components
```

Note that there will be an error message about compatibility issues when you run the `kfp` installation. This issue is not a blocker, so we can ignore it and continue to the next section. But if it is a blocker in the future, please check the public Kubeflow documentation on how to install the Kubeflow Pipelines SDK: https://www.kubeflow.org/docs/components/pipelines/sdk/install-sdk/#install-the-kubeflow-pipelines-sdk.

Now, let's create a GCS bucket.

Creating a dedicated regional GCS bucket

We need to create a GCS bucket for this exercise. Vertex AI Pipelines will use this bucket to store temporary files, the steps, and the output. The GCS bucket's location should be the same as where Vertex AI Pipelines is located. For that reason, we need to create a new GCS bucket instead of using our existing GCS bucket from the previous chapters. To refresh our memory, our previous bucket was located in a multi-region US location, which is different from regional `us-central1`, for example.

Let's create a new GCS bucket. Go to the GCS console and create a new bucket using any bucket name. For example, my new bucket name is `packt-data-eng-on-gcp-vertex-ai-pipeline`.

As we mentioned previously, the important option that you need to be aware of is **Location type**. Choose **Region** here and set **Location** to `us-central1`:

- **Choose where to store your data**

  This permanent choice defines the geographic placement of your data and affects cost, performance, and availability. Learn more

  Location type

  ○ Multi-region
   Highest availability across largest area

  ○ Dual-region
   High availability and low latency across 2 regions

  ● Region
   Lowest latency within a single region

  Location

  us-central1 (Iowa)

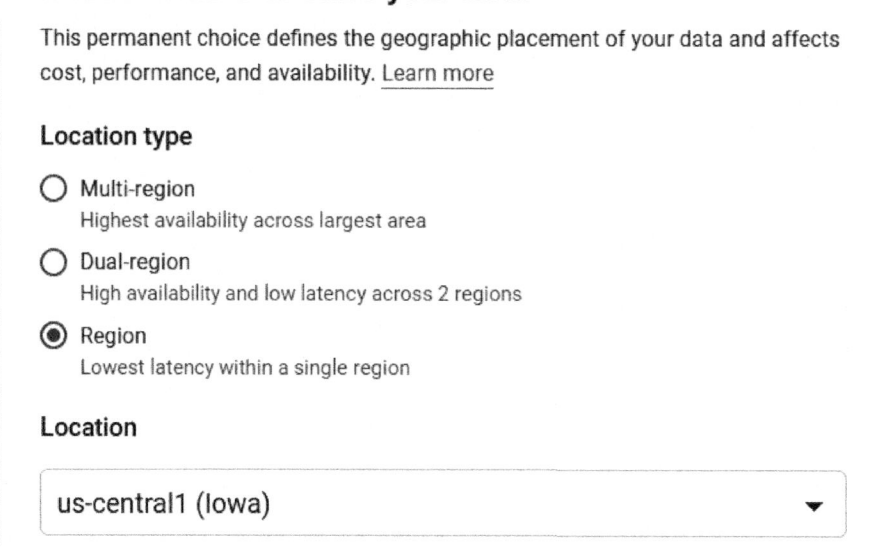

Figure 8.15 – Choosing Location type and Region values

Now that we've created the GCS bucket, we can look at the example code. In the next section, we will go through the example code for defining Vertex AI Pipelines.

Developing the pipeline on Python

In this section, we will go through the Python code that calls the Kubeflow SDK to build Vertex AI Pipelines. The code example for this chapter can be found at `https://github.com/PacktPublishing/Data-Engineering-with-Google-Cloud-Platform-Second-Edition/blob/main/chapter-8/code/practice-vertex-ai-pipeline.py`.

In this example, we will start by understanding how the SDK works and how to run the code in Vertex AI. We will not be completing any ML steps in this section. I suggest that you focus on the code part when you're defining steps, dependencies, and deployment to Vertex AI.

Let's start with the first simple step – importing the necessary libraries:

1. Declare the imports for the required libraries.

    The first step is to import the required libraries:

    ```
    from kfp.dsl import pipeline
    from kfp import compiler
    from kfp.dsl import component
    from google.cloud import aiplatform
    ```

    As you can see, we are using the `kfp` library, which is the open source Kubeflow Pipelines library that you can also use without Vertex AI. But since we will be using Vertex AI, we will need to import `aiplatform`.

    This is what I mentioned about not being confused about AIPlatform versus Vertex AI. Since AIPlatform is the predecessor of Vertex AI, the client library is still named `aiplatform` instead of `VertexAIClient`.

2. Define the Vertex AI Pipelines steps.

    Next, we want to declare the steps in our pipeline. Each step is declared using Python functions. For example, our first step will be named `step_one`. This function will print the input text and return the text's value:

    ```
    @component
    def step_one(text: str) -> str:
        print(text)
        return text
    ```

    Notice that we put `@component` in the function, which is an important step. This is the step where we can configure the container. For example, take a look at the `step_two` and `step_three` functions:

    ```
    @component(base_image="python:3.9")
    ```

We can declare the base image that we want to load for this function. The default value is Python 3.7. This means that, in the `step_one` function, it will run on top of different Python versions compared to `step_two` and `step_three`. Another option is to have the packages installed. Look at the `step_four` functions. This time, we specified `packages_to_install` with the `google-cloud-storage` package:

```
@component(packages_to_install=["google-cloud-storage"])
def step_four(text1: str, text2: str, gcs_bucket: str):
    from google.cloud import storage
    output_string = f"text1: {text1}; text2: {text2};"
    storage_client = storage.Client()
    bucket = storage_client.get_bucket(gcs_bucket)
    blob = bucket.blob(f"practice-vertex-ai-pipeline/artifacts/output.txt")
    blob.upload_from_string(output_string)
    print(output_string)
```

By defining `packages_to_install` in the component, the container will install the packages before running the code. If you are not familiar with these container concepts, then this is a good example of the benefits. Here, you can see that each step can use different images and packages. Another possibility is that you can build a Docker image and import it directly as a step instead of defining the code as functions, which will give you the benefit of portability. But we will not practice that in this book.

3. Define the Vertex AI Pipelines step's dependencies.

    The next step is to declare the pipeline and the step's dependencies. Take a look at the following code:

    ```
    @pipeline(
        name="practice-vertex-ai-pipeline",
        description="Example of Vertex AI Pipeline",
        pipeline_root=pipeline_root_path,
    )
    def pipeline(text: str = "Hello"):
        step_one_task = step_one(text=text)
        step_two_task = step_two(text=step_one_task.output)
        step_three_task = step_three(text=step_one_task.output)
        step_four_task = step_four(text1=step_two_task.output, text2=step_three_task.output,gcs_bucket=gcs_bucket)
    ```

    The step's dependencies – in other words, task chaining – are not declared explicitly. The chains are declared when the task's input is taken from other tasks' output. For example, `step_two` uses the output from `step_one` as its input. `Step_three` also uses the output from `step_one`, while `step_four` uses the outputs of `step_two` and `step_three`. The following diagram shows the expected dependencies:

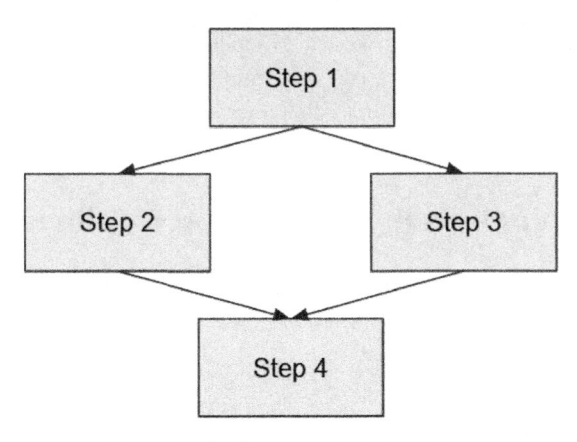

Figure 8.16 – The expected steps flow

After defining the dependencies, we expect the same pipeline when we run it in Vertex AI Pipelines.

4. Compile and submit the Vertex AI Pipelines job.

   Next, we need to export all of our code into a JSON file. This JSON file needs to be in a specific format so that Vertex AI can understand the information. To do that, use the following code:

   ```
   compiler.Compiler().compile(
       pipeline_func=pipeline, package_path=f"{pipeline_name}.json"
   )
   ```

   The compiler code will export the pipeline code into a JSON file in your local system. The next step is to submit the JSON file to Vertex AI Pipelines:

   ```
   aiplatform.init(project=project_id, location=region)
   job = aiplatform.PipelineJob(
       display_name="dp-practice-vertex-ai-pipeline",
       template_path=f"{pipeline_name}.json",
       pipeline_root=pipeline_root_path
   )
   job.submit()
   ```

And that's all that we need in our Python code. Run it as a normal Python application, like so:

```
$ python practice-vertex-ai-pipeline.py
```

Running this code will trigger the pipeline submission to Vertex AI Pipelines.

Before checking this in the GCP console, let's recap what we've done. In this section, we learned how to code Vertex AI Pipelines tasks. Tasks can be written as Python functions. These Python functions won't be run as a normal Python application in your Cloud Shell. The functions are going to be wrapped as containers with all the configurations that we declared in @component. The Python code that you ran did two things. First, it compiled the task functions and dependencies into a JSON file. Second, it submitted the JSON file to Vertex AI Pipeline. And just to repeat, the `step_one` to `step_four` Python functions won't be run on Cloud Shell or your local machine; instead, they will be run on a Vertex AI Pipelines cluster as containers. In the next section, we will check out our pipeline in the console.

Monitoring the pipeline on the Vertex AI Pipelines console

To check if our pipeline has been submitted, go to **Vertex AI Pipelines** in your GCP console. If there is no issue with your code, you will see that the pipeline is running under the **Run** list:

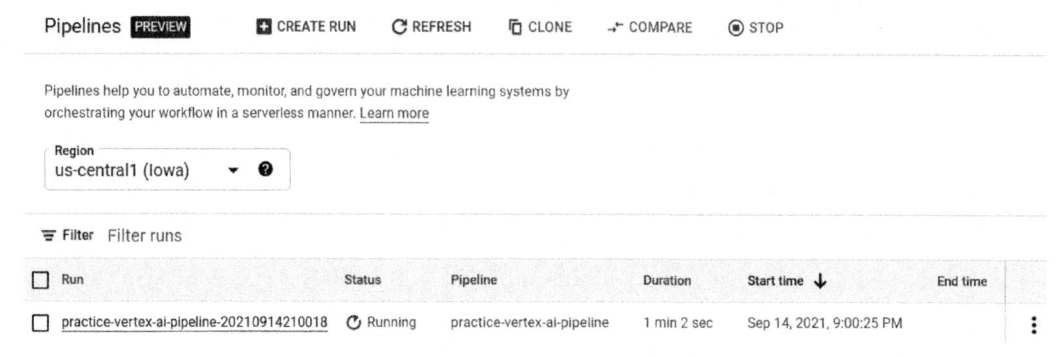

Figure 8.17 – Our pipeline is running

If you click your pipeline's name, you will see its details, as well as its steps, as expected:

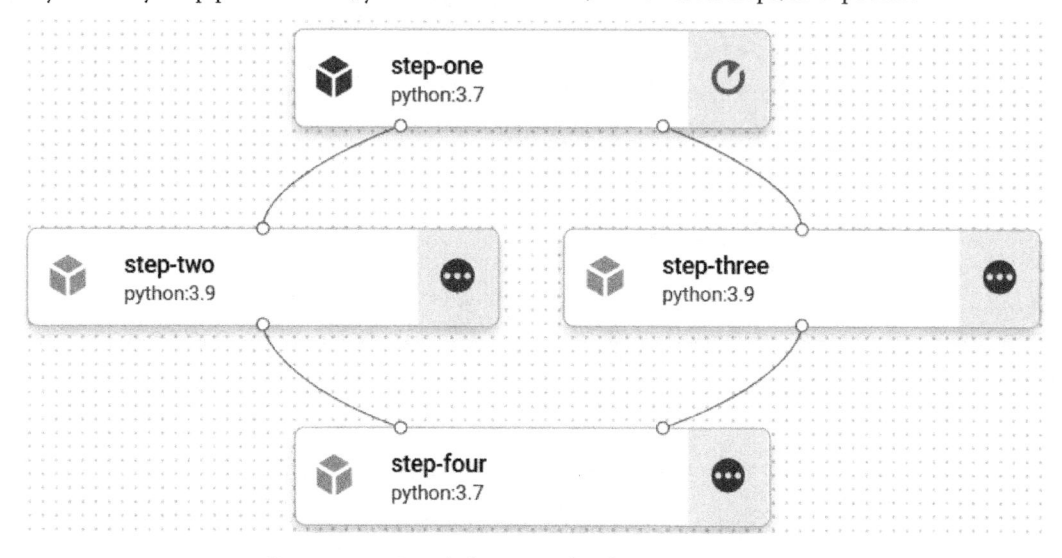

Figure 8.18 – Detailed steps under the running pipeline

step-two and **step-three** depend on **step-one**, while **step-four** depends on **step-two** and **step-three**. It will run for about 3 minutes for all the steps. If there are any errors, you can click the **VIEW LOGS** button to check the error logs in any of the steps:

Figure 8.19 – The VIEW LOGS button

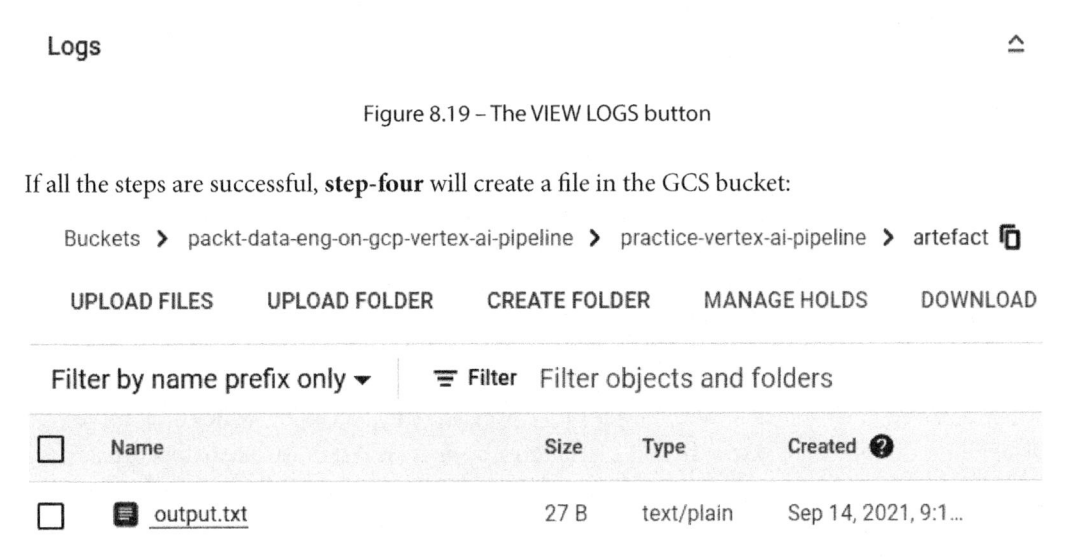

If all the steps are successful, **step-four** will create a file in the GCS bucket:

Figure 8.20 – Checking the GCS bucket to find the output file

Open the output.txt file. The output should look like this:

```
text1: Hello; text2: Hello;
```

You now have the fundamental knowledge to create a pipeline in Vertex AI Pipelines. In the next and last exercise of this chapter, we will create a pipeline that creates an ML model and a pipeline for predicting new datasets using the model.

Exercise – deploying a scikit-learn model pipeline with Vertex AI

In this exercise, we will simulate creating a pipeline for an ML model. There will be two pipelines – one to train the ML model and another to predict new data using the model from the first pipeline. We will continue using the credit card default dataset. The two pipelines will look like this:

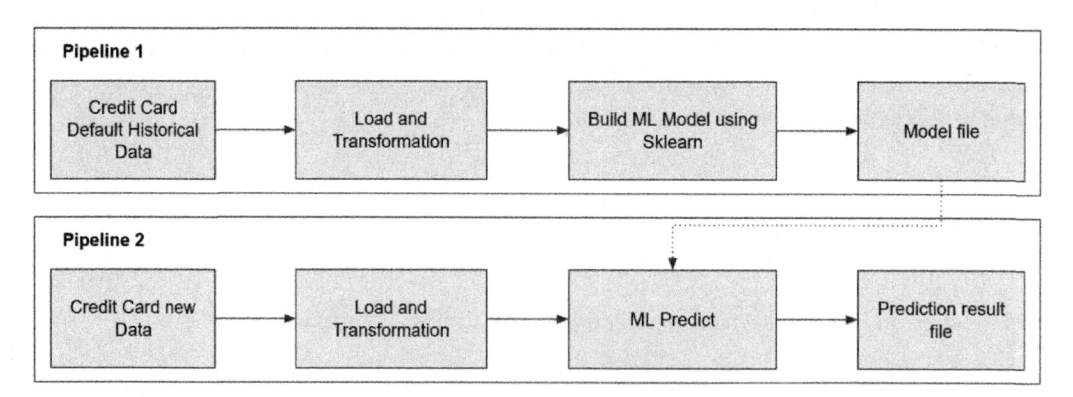

Figure 8.21 – The steps in the two pipelines

Later in this section, we will load data from BigQuery. But instead of storing the data in pandas, we will write the output to a GCS bucket. We will be doing this as we don't want to return an in-memory Python object from the function. What I mean by an in-memory Python object, in this case, is a pandas DataFrame. This also applies to other data structures, such as arrays or lists. Remember that every step in Vertex AI Pipelines will be executed in a different container – that is, in a different machine. You can't pass the pandas DataFrame from one machine to the others. What you can do, however, is store the output data in storage, such as GCS. We can pass the GCS location to the other machine to continue the downstream steps.

The following are the high-level steps for this exercise:

1. Create the first pipeline, which will result in an ML model file in GCS.
2. Run the first pipeline in Vertex AI Pipelines.
3. Create the second pipeline, which will use the model file from the prediction results as a CSV file in GCS.
4. Run the second pipeline in Vertex AI Pipelines.

In general, what you need to do is check the code example for the first and second pipelines. Make sure that you've changed all the variables as per your environment (GCP project ID, GCS bucket, and so on) and deploy the pipelines to Vertex AI ones by running the Python code from your Cloud Shell environment. Let's start with the first step.

Creating the first pipeline, which will result in an ML model file in GCS

Before I start explaining the code, please check out the code example. You can find the full code in this book's GitHub repository: https://github.com/PacktPublishing/Data-Engineering-with-Google-Cloud-Platform-Second-Edition/blob/main/chapter-8/code/ai-pipeline-credit-default-train.py.

As usual, you can use Cloud Editor and Cloud Shell to edit the code and run it. Let's go through the code. I'll explain it by breaking it down into three parts:

1. First, we must define the pipeline's first step by loading the BigQuery table into a GCS bucket.

   Let's begin by taking a look at the `load_data_from_bigquery()` function:

   ```
   @component(packages_to_install=["google-cloud-bigquery","google-cloud-storage","pandas","pyarrow","db_dtypes"])
   def load_data_from_bigquery(bigquery_table_id: str, output_gcs_bucket: str) -> str:
       from google.cloud import bigquery
       from google.cloud import storage

       project_id = "packt-data-eng-on-gcp"
       output_file = "ai-pipeline-credit-default-train/artifacts/train.csv"

       bq_client = bigquery.Client(project=project_id)
       sql = f"""SELECT limit_balance, education_level, age, default_payment_next_month FROM `{bigquery_table_id}`;"""
       dataframe = (bq_client.query(sql).result().to_dataframe())

       gcs_client = storage.Client(project=project_id)
       bucket = gcs_client.get_bucket(output_gcs_bucket)
       bucket.blob(output_file).upload_from_string(dataframe.to_csv(index=False), 'text/csv')

       return output_file
   ```

   Initially, you will notice that there are packages that we need to install. We declared the list in `packages_to_install()`. This function will call a BigQuery table. Note that in this example, the query is a quite simple `SELECT` statement. You can define any transformation process in the query. The more you can aggregate and limit the data in BigQuery, the better. Processing the data in BigQuery is a lot more scalable compared to processing the data in a pandas DataFrame. At the end of this step, we will export the pandas DataFrame to the GCS bucket. As you can see, we will only return the file location to the `return` statement.

2. Define the train model function step.

   For the next step, we want to train the model using the file that's been stored in GCS. Take a look at the following `train_model()` function – specifically, in this particular row:

   ```
   dataframe = pd.read_csv(f'gs://{gcs_bucket}/{train_file_path}')
   ```

We load the data from the GCS bucket, not directly from BigQuery or local files. This is a common practice in ML model pipelines as it keeps each step as a stateless operation. You might be wondering why we shouldn't directly access the BigQuery table and combine both the data load step and modeling step as one function. As I mentioned previously, this approach will give you flexibility regarding which packages you want to install for each step. This way, you can have high consistency for each step.

The other line of code that you might want to check is when we store the random forest classifier model as a file in GCS:

```
random_forest_classifier = RandomForestClassifier(
    n_estimators=n_estimators)
    random_forest_classifier.fit(x_train,y_train)

joblib.dump(random_forest_classifier, model_name)

bucket = storage.Client().bucket(gcs_bucket)
blob = bucket.blob(output_file)
blob.upload_from_filename(model_name)

print(f"Model saved in : {output_file}")
```

Similar to the first step, we need to store the result in GCS. This way, the output can be used by any other container or steps. In this case, we stored the .joblib file in the GCS bucket.

3. Compile and deploy the training pipeline to Vertex AI.

   As the final step in our train pipeline example, we just need to trigger a run to Vertex AI Pipelines. Take a look at the following lines:

   ```
   def pipeline():
       load_data_from_bigquery_task = load_data_from_bigquery(
           bigquery_table_id=bigquery_table_id,
           output_gcs_bucket=gcs_bucket
       )
       train_model(
           gcs_bucket=gcs_bucket,
           train_file_path=load_data_from_bigquery_task.output,
           target_column=target_column,
           n_estimators=100,
           model_name=model_name
       )
   ```

   This code is similar to the code that we looked at when we learned about the dummy pipeline. What's important is the task dependencies. Remember that the task's order is determined by the tasks' input and output. In this case, the first task's output is a string that contains a GCS file called uri. The `train_model()` function uses the output as input. This way, the pipeline will know the task's order.

The important lesson that we learned in this example code is how to implement the ML training steps in Vertex AI Pipelines. As a reminder, double-check the variables and make sure that you've changed the `project_id` and `gcs_bucket` variables. Once you're done, run the file as Python code, as we learned in the previous exercise.

For example, run the following command from Cloud Shell:

```
$ python ai-pipeline-credit-default-train.py
```

The preceding code will submit the pipeline job to Vertex AI. Now, let's continue to the next step.

Running the first pipeline in Vertex AI Pipelines

After compiling and running the code, go back to the GCP console to check out Vertex AI Pipelines. The training model steps will run. Make sure that both steps are running successfully:

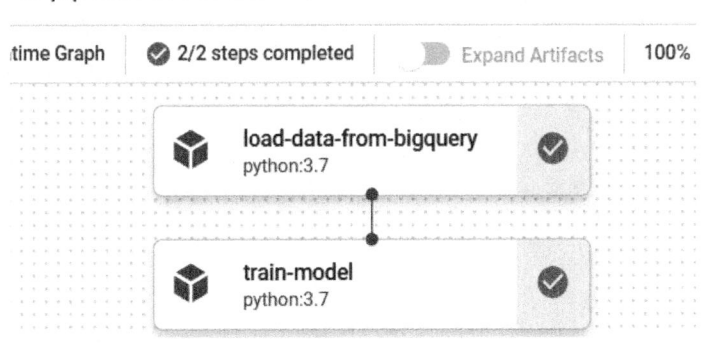

Figure 8.22 – The training pipeline's steps in the Vertex AI console

If you see any errors in any of the steps, always check the logs. If the steps are successful, they will produce the model in the GCS file. Now, you can check if the file is already in your expected GCS path:

Figure 8.23 – Checking the model file in the GCS bucket

We will use the `cc_default_rf_model.joblib` file for our second pipeline. For future consideration, you can add a model version to the model's filename. This is a common practice; the goal is for you to be able to choose which model version you want to use for prediction. In the ML world, the newest model doesn't always mean the best. Data scientists usually have some metrics as considerations for deciding which model version is the best. This is one of the reasons why the model training pipeline needs to be separate from the prediction pipeline. With this separation, the pipeline's run frequency can be different. For example, the model can refresh once every month and the prediction can run once every day.

Creating the second pipeline, which will use the model file from the prediction results as a CSV file in GCS

Now, let's continue with the second pipeline. You can find the full code in the `ai-pipeline-credit-default-predict.py` file.

Similar to the first pipeline, what you need to do is change the values of `project_id` and `gcs_bucket` to yours. Besides changing the variables, make sure you've read the example code carefully and try to understand each step.

You should already be familiar with the code. There's nothing new here – we are just combining what we've learned from the previous exercises. Let's jump to the line where we define the pipeline:

```
def pipeline():
    load_data_from_bigquery_task = load_data_from_bigquery(bigquery_
table_id=bigquery_table_id, output_gcs_bucket=gcs_bucket)
    predict_batch(gcs_bucket=gcs_bucket, 
    predict_file_path=load_data_from_bigquery_task.output,
  model_path="ai-pipeline-credit-default-train/artifacts/cc_default_
rf_model.joblib",
    output_path="ai-pipeline-credit-default-predict/artifacts/
prediction.csv" )
```

This pipeline will have two tasks – loading data from BigQuery and using both the data and the `cc_default_rf_model.joblib` file to make predictions. The output will be stored as a CSV file called `prediction.csv`.

Once you've finished looking at the example code for the second pipeline for batch prediction, run the Python code.

For example, run the following command from your Cloud Shell:

```
$ python ai-pipeline-credit-default-predict.py
```

The code will submit the pipeline job to Vertex AI. Now, let's continue to the last step.

Running the second pipeline in Vertex AI Pipelines

Finally, let's check if your pipeline is running successfully. Check that the pipeline runs on Vertex AI Pipelines; it should show the following two steps:

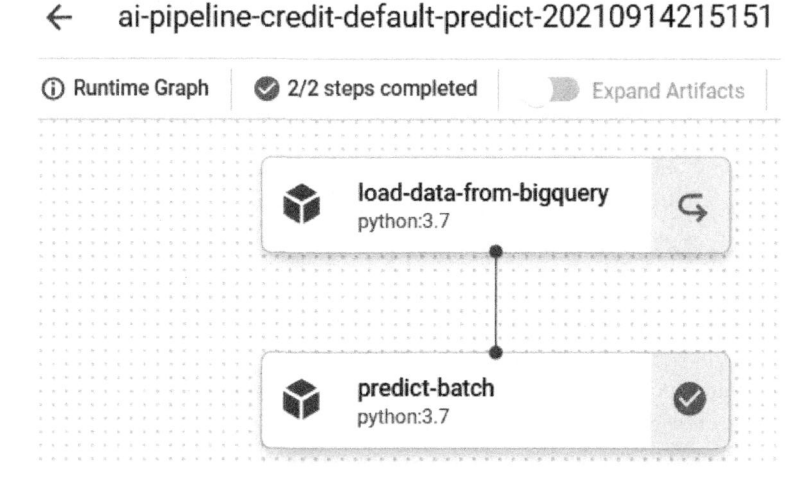

Figure 8.24 – Batch prediction pipeline steps in the Vertex AI console

If you find that the icon in any of the steps is a green arrow instead of a checked icon, this means that the step was running using a cache. If you've run a successful step more than once, then the step will run using a cache to perform faster. You can disable the cache by changing the following line of code:

```
job = aiplatform.PipelineJob(
display_name="dp-ai-pipeline-credit-default-predict",
    job_spec_path="{pipeline_name}.json",
    pipeline_root=pipeline_root_path,
    enable_caching=False
)
```

Enabling or disabling the cache will not change the result.

And with that, you've completed all the exercises in this chapter. Before summarizing this chapter, let's summarize what we've done in this exercise.

In this exercise, you learned how to create ML pipelines using Vertex AI Pipelines and define each ML step as Python functions. The steps that you've defined won't be run in your local machine or Cloud Shell. The code and the logic inside the steps will be used as instructions and will be run on containers in the Vertex AI cluster on the cloud. At the end of our first pipeline, we had the ML model file, while at the end of the second pipeline, the result was a prediction file.

Summary

In this chapter, we learned how to create an ML model. We learned that creating ML code is not that difficult and that the surrounding aspects are what makes it complex. On top of that, we learned about some basic terminologies, such as AutoML, pre-built models, and MLOps.

As I mentioned in the introduction, ML is not a core skill that a data engineer needs to have. However, understanding this topic will give a data engineer a bigger picture of the whole data architecture. This way, you can imagine and make better decisions when designing your core data pipelines.

This chapter is the end of our big section on *Building Data Solutions with GCP Components*. Starting from *Chapter 3, Building a Data Warehouse in BigQuery*, to *Chapter 8, Building Machine Learning Solutions on GCP*, we've learned about all the fundamental principles of data engineering and how to use GCP services. At this point, you are more than ready to build a data solution in GCP.

Starting from the next chapter, which is the final part of this book, we'll cover how to use the products we've mentioned so far. A good data engineer not only knows how to develop a solution but also decides on important aspects outside the solution itself. For example, creating a GCP project is easy, but how many projects should you create? What's the purpose of the projects? Should I assign one or many users to the project? These are a few of many important questions to be considered and decided to build top-notch solutions for an organization.

We will also cover the thinking process on how to decide on user and project structures, how to estimate the cost for solutions, and how to make sure the development process can be tested and deployed automatically using CI/CD concepts. After completing these remaining chapters, you will have gained far more technical knowledge. In the final chapter, we will review and summarize how to use all this new knowledge and help boost your confidence so that you can accelerate your personal goals.

Part 3: Key Strategies for Architecting Top-Notch Solutions

In the final part of this book, we will cover topics beyond how to use the GCP products for building data pipelines. A good data engineer not only knows how to develop a solution but also decides important aspects outside the solution itself – for example, creating a GCP project is easy, but how many projects should you create? What is the purpose of the project? Should you assign one or many users to the project? Those are a few of many important questions to be considered and decided in order to build top-notch solutions for organizations.

This will include what the thinking process is on how to choose a user and project structure, understanding the implementation of data governance, how to estimate the cost for the solutions, and how to make sure the development can be tested and deployed automatically using CI/CD concepts. After all the learning chapters, you should have gained much more technical knowledge, and in the final chapter, we will review and summarize how to use all this new knowledge to boost your confidence, enabling you to accelerate your personal goal after finishing the book.

This part has the following chapters:

- *Chapter 9, User and Project Management in GCP*
- *Chapter 10, Data Governance in GCP*
- *Chapter 11, Cost Strategy in GCP*
- *Chapter 12, CI/CD on GCP for Data Engineers*
- *Chapter 13, Boosting Your Confidence as a Data Engineer*

9
User and Project Management in GCP

In this chapter, we will learn how to design and structure users and projects in **Google Cloud Platform** (**GCP**). By understanding user and project management in GCP, you will learn how to turn a development solution into a production-ready one.

In a production-ready solution, it's very important to manage security by only allowing access to the right users. However, to do it efficiently, we need to understand the principle and strategy.

Managing production-ready solutions is almost impossible without understanding how a GCP project works. Understanding how to design GCP projects is another important aspect of an efficient solution.

In addition, this chapter will also include an example approach to provision GCP's services automatically using an infrastructure-building tool, Terraform.

Specifically, in this chapter, we will cover the following topics:

- Understanding **Identity and Access Management** (**IAM**) in GCP
- Planning a GCP project structure
- Controlling user access to our data warehouse
- Practicing the concept of **Infrastructure as Code** (**IaC**) using Terraform

Let's check out the technical requirements for this chapter.

Technical requirements

In this chapter's exercises, we will use the following GCP services:

- **IAM**
- **BigQuery**
- **Google Cloud Storage (GCS)**

If you've never opened any of these services in your GCP console, open them and enable the **application programming interface (API)**. We will also use an open source software called **Terraform** to help us provision the GCP services using code. It can be downloaded from their public website at https://www.terraform.io/downloads.html. The step-by-step installation will be discussed in the *Exercise – creating and running basic Terraform scripts* section.

Make sure you have your **GCP console**, **Cloud Shell**, and **Cloud Shell Editor** ready.

Download the example code and the dataset from https://github.com/PacktPublishing/Data-Engineering-with-Google-Cloud-Platform-Second-Edition/tree/main/chapter-9/code.

Understanding IAM in GCP

IAM is a central manager that manages who can access what – in other words, authorization. IAM manages all authorization within GCP. The concept is simple – you grant roles to accounts so that the accounts have the required permission to access specific GCP services. Here is a diagram for an account that needs to query a table in BigQuery:

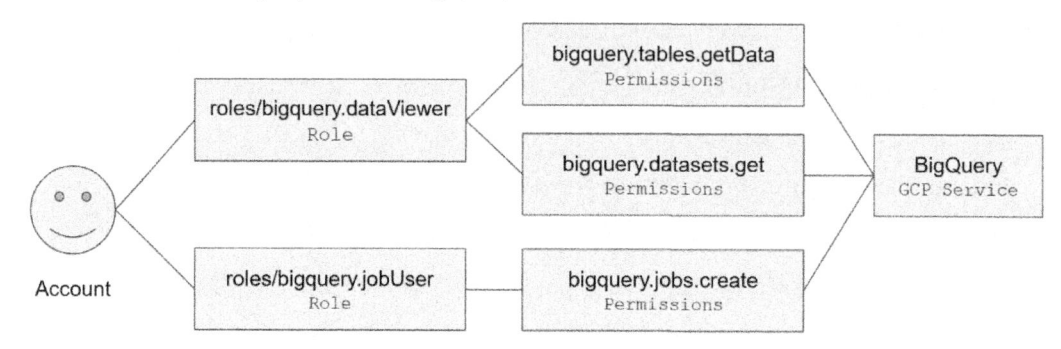

Figure 9.1 – IAM roles, permissions, and GCP service correlation

In the example shown in the preceding diagram, to access a BigQuery table, an account needs, at a minimum, two roles: *data viewer* and *job user*. These roles contain multiple permissions to specifically perform an operation in BigQuery.

Let's go through each of the important terms that we use in the IAM space:

- **Account**: An account in GCP can be divided into two – a user account and a service account:

  - **User account**: This is the user email. It can be corporate email or personal email, depending on the security requirements. A user account is meant for a human user.
  - **Service account**: A service account is a special kind of account that's used by an application or a **virtual machine** (**VM**) instance, not a person. We've experienced using service accounts in some of our exercises in the previous chapters – for example, the service account for Cloud SQL, Cloud Composer, Dataproc, and other GCP services.

  We have service accounts for running Cloud Composer, Dataflow, and Dataproc. Recall that these GCP services can access BigQuery tables. These services use service accounts to access tables instead of user accounts. If you want to check out which service account you have used, follow these steps:

  I. Open your GCP console.

  II. Go to the **IAM & Admin** page from the navigation menu.

  III. Click **Service Accounts**.

  Check out this screenshot if you can't find the options:

  Figure 9.2 – Finding the Service Accounts button from the navigation menu

  Depending on how many exercises you have followed, at a minimum, you will see a service account with the *[random number]-compute@developer.gserviceaccount.com* domain. This is called the default service account that is automatically created when a project is created. The best practice is to never use this default one – always try to create a new one with a specific purpose for your services and use cases. This way, it's better for security purposes.

- **Permission**: A permission is the most specific level of requirement to access a GCP service. For example, to query a table in BigQuery, you need at least two permissions – `bigquery.jobs.create` and `bigquery.tables.getData`.

How can you find out which permissions are required for each service? You need to check the public documentation for each service. Let's take BigQuery again as an example – a list of permissions is documented here: https://cloud.google.com/bigquery/docs/access-control#bq-permissions.

One thing to note is that you can't give permission to accounts. What you can give to accounts are roles. Permission lists are contained in the roles.

- **Role**: A role contains a set of permissions that allows you to perform specific actions on Google Cloud resources. There are three categories of roles: *basic*, *predefined*, and *custom*. You can find a full explanation in the public documentation at https://cloud.google.com/iam/docs/understanding-roles.

After reading the public documentation about understanding roles, you will start to get an idea of basic and predefined roles. For ease of understanding, I will provide some context and outline which roles should be used.

In terms of context, what you've used throughout this book is the basic role. Your user account has the **roles/owner** role in your project. The **roles/owner** role is a superuser – it has all permissions to all resources in the project. It's for this reason you don't need to add any additional roles to your user account in our exercises.

The most used role by many users in GCP is the predefined role, and I suggest that you focus on using the predefined role compared to the basic and custom roles. The reason that basic roles are not a best practice is that these roles are too permissive. As these roles are applied to all resources, this is very risky in terms of security. For example, imagine you give the **roles/editor** role to a data engineer who wants to develop a data pipeline in BigQuery. The user can access BigQuery, but at the same time, that user can access and edit all other resources, such as **Google Kubernetes Engine (GKE)**, **Google App Engine (GAE)**, and any other services to which a data engineer shouldn't have access. The better kinds of roles are predefined roles in BigQuery. You can check out predefined roles in BigQuery in the public documentation at https://cloud.google.com/bigquery/docs/access-control#bigquery.

Lastly, let's look at the **custom** role. The custom role is there in case the set of permissions in the predefined roles does not fit with your organization's needs. In that case, you can use a custom role, but remember there is an operational overhead when creating a custom role. In summary, use the predefined role if possible and only use a custom role if needed. Only use basic roles for projects that are used for practice, training, or demonstration purposes.

In more general terms, giving only the required access to the right person is the best practice, and there is a term for that: the **principle of least privilege**.

> **Note**
> The principle of least privilege is not only known in GCP, but it's a common principle that is used in computer science. The *principle* means giving a user account or processing only those permissions that are essential to perform its intended function.

In this section, we revisited common terms that we've used throughout this book. We took a deeper look at each of the terms to understand better how IAM works in GCP. There are three key things to note:

- The difference between a user account and a service account
- The relationship between account, permission, and role
- The principle of least privilege

These three points are very important to be a good data engineer in GCP. Make sure you understand them well. In the next section, we will learn how to plan a GCP project structure. Let's start getting a deeper understanding of the GCP project.

Planning a GCP project structure

After practicing a lot of exercises from the previous chapters, I believe you have become familiar with GCP. From those exercises, you've learned about GCP services, their positioning, and how to use them. In this section, we will take a step back and look at those GCP services from a higher-level point of view.

In all the previous exercises throughout this book, we used only one project. All the GCP services, including BigQuery, GCS buckets, Cloud Composer, and the other services that we used, are enabled and provisioned in one project. For me, I have a project called `packt-gcp-data-eng`. The same from your side – you must have your own project, either using the default project or a new one that we created in *Chapter 2, Big Data Capabilities on GCP*. That's a good enough starting point for learning and development, but in reality, an organization usually has more than one project. There are many scenarios and variations on how to structure projects in an organization.

Let's consider a simple example. An organization uses GCP to host its eCommerce website, and on top of that, they have a data warehouse for reporting and **machine learning** (**ML**) applications. In that case, one possible project structure is to use one dedicated project for hosting the core application and database, one project for managing data analytics in BigQuery, GCS and Cloud Composer for the data warehouse, and one other project for training the ML model using Vertex AI. Check out the following diagram for an illustration of this:

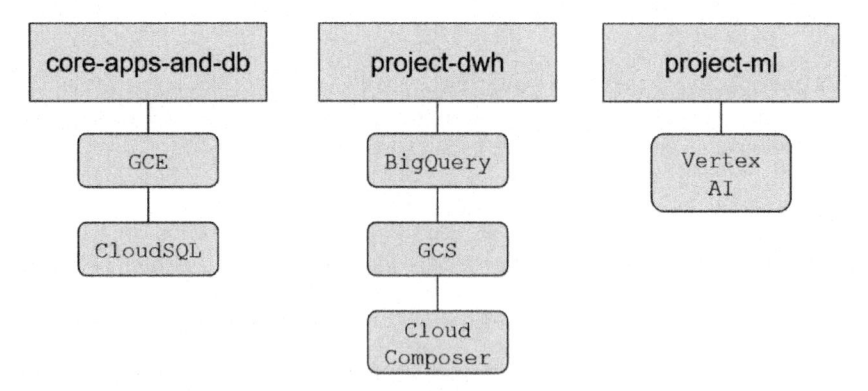

Figure 9.3 – Project structure – alternative 1

The project structure is good enough, and it makes sense to differentiate each separate workload. But why not put it all in one project? That's doable too, as illustrated here:

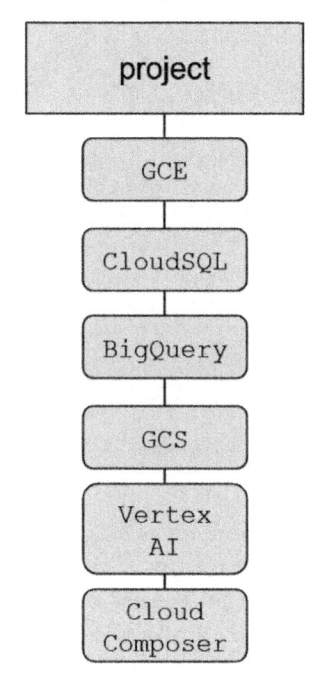

Figure 9.4 – Project structure – alternative 2

In other alternatives, you can separate each service into one specific project. That's doable too, as illustrated here:

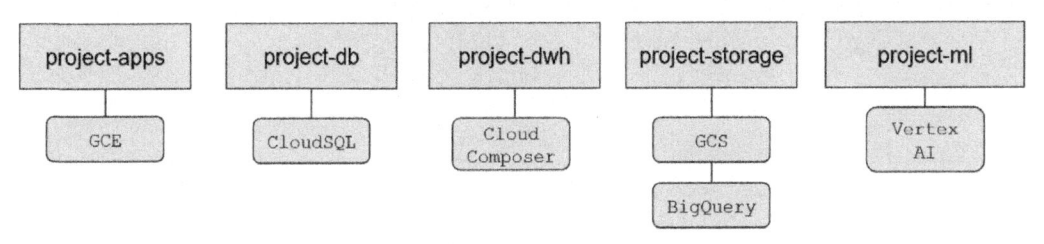

Figure 9.5 – Project structure – alternative 3

There is no right or wrong answer to choose between these three alternatives. In my experience of working with many companies, there is no single company project structure that is the same as the others. Typically, a new company will start with the second alternative, which uses one project for everything but gradually grows along with time and complexity. What's important is to understand what the considerations are.

Before continuing with the considerations, let's familiarize ourselves with the other abstraction on top of GCP projects – folders and organization.

Understanding the GCP organization, folder, and project hierarchy

A GCP project organizes all your Google Cloud resources. Resources in GCP can be services, billing, accounts, authentications, logs, and monitoring. Resources from one project can be used and accessed by other resources from other projects. So long as the permissions to resources are set correctly, there is no restriction on accessing them between projects.

For example, look at *Figure 9.3*. The cloud SQL database from the `core-apps-and-db` project can be accessed by Cloud Composer in `dwh-project`. Let's look at another example – a user account that was created in the `core-apps-and-db` project can access data from BigQuery in the data project. Note that accounts and authentications are also resources. The key point here is that resources in GCP projects are not isolated.

Now, let's talk about the GCP folder. One GCP folder can contain one to many GCP projects. GCP folders can also contain one to many other GCP folders – or, in other words, it is possible to have multiple GCP folder levels. Using GCP folders will give you the benefit of IAM permissions inheritance. The key word here is *inheritance*. Look at the following diagram, which covers an example scenario:

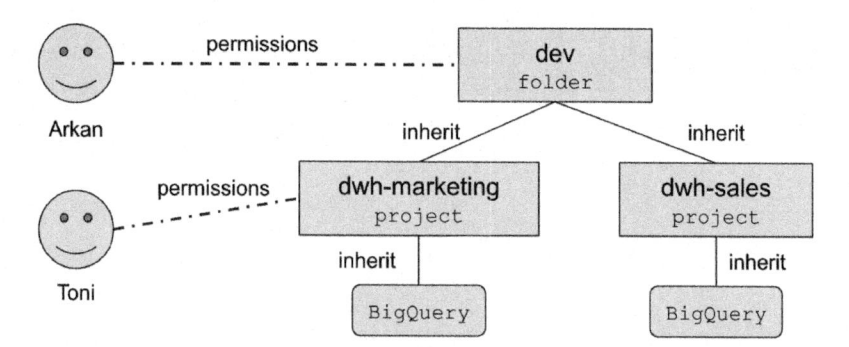

Figure 9.6 – GCP folder, project, and service inheritance

We have a GCP folder called `dev`. The `dev` folder contains two GCP projects that have BigQuery resources. There are two users. The first user, **Arkan**, needs viewer access to all BigQuery datasets under the `dev` folder. The second user is **Toni** – she is only allowed to access all the datasets in the marketing project. In that case, you can grant the BigQuery viewer role in the `dev` project to **Arkan**, and the BigQuery viewer role in the marketing project to **Toni**. **Arkan** will automatically get access to all projects under the `dev` folder – or, in other words, he can access all child projects under the `dev` folder. The `dev` folder is the parent of the product and marketing projects.

If we are talking about the folder concept in general (not within any GCP context), it's natural to think about folders to tidy up objects. For example, on your personal computer, you create a folder to tidy up your documents, images, or any other files. I've found that people use this intuition to decide on a folder and project hierarchy in GCP. Even though it's not entirely wrong, having folders without the benefit of IAM permissions inheritance is not useful. For example, let's say you have a very tall folder hierarchy such as this, but all the permissions are set individually at the project level:

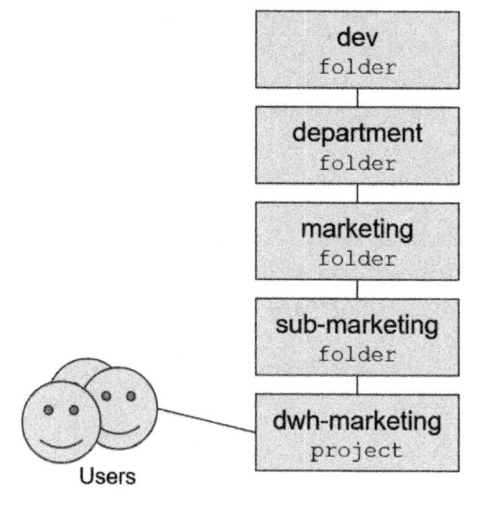

Figure 9.7 – Tall GCP folder hierarchy

The hierarchy in the previous diagram uses a top-bottom mindset. A top-bottom mindset thinks about which parent folders should be created on top and which child folders should be added at the bottom. In this case, the folders will give you almost no benefit in GCP – they will only give you more operation overhead.

Rather than doing that, it's better to think and plan from the bottom up. Think about which permissions can be grouped and inherited together from the individual projects. If you can find any user, user group, or service account that always needs access to a set of projects by default, that's a good reason to create a parent folder. With that mindset, you will have a better GCP folder hierarchy.

The key point is that using a GCP folder allows you to inherit IAM permissions to child folders and projects. Decide on the hierarchy from the bottom up instead of adopting a top-bottom approach.

The last part of the hierarchy is the GCP organization. Compared to folders and projects, deciding on how many organizations to have is simple. There is typically only one GCP organization in a company. In other words, the GCP organization is the single root of all folders and projects in GCP.

With this deeper understanding of the concepts surrounding GCP, we can decide how many projects we should have in a GCP organization.

Deciding how many projects we should have in a GCP organization

After getting a better understanding of GCP organizations, folders, and projects, we now know that deciding on the hierarchy is not based on a *tidying-up* mindset. Deciding on the hierarchy from a benefits point of view is better. I've summarized these into three main benefits that will be discussed in the following sub-sections.

IAM and GCP service requirements

Imagine that you are starting a startup company with a small team. Your team wants to start the development and release the **minimum viable product** (**MVP**) quickly to test if your product fits the market. You don't have any dedicated people yet to manage operations, and you want to minimize any operational overhead as much as possible.

In that scenario, *Figure 9.4* depicts a better approach. You can create one GCP project that is developed by your small team and use all the GCP services in that one GCP project. Splitting GCP projects based on IAM and GCP services doesn't help when you have a small development team.

In the other scenario, imagine you are starting to use GCP for a corporation. The corporation has more than one team that uses GCP for specific use cases. That's a good indication that you need different sets of IAM and GCP services or API requirements for each team. Usually, each team has different workloads, access levels, or purposes on GCP. In that case, it's good practice to separate projects based on teams when the IAM and GCP service required for each team is different.

Our previous example from *Figure 9.3* is a good example. You can see that the application team, data team, and ML team have different GCP service needs. They must also have different roles and permissions. In that case, the approach depicted in *Figure 9.3* is in general better than the one shown in *Figure 9.4*.

If we compare *Figure 9.3* to *Figure 9.5*, the question you should ask again is, *Are there any IAM and GCP service benefits?*

If your company has a specific team to manage each GCP service, then you can consider the approach in *Figure 9.5*. But talking about which are more common practices, it's more common that one team manages multiple GCP services. For example, the data engineering team that uses the data project typically needs a set of BigQuery, Cloud Composer, and GCS permissions. Separating the IAM permissions into three different projects for the same team gives no benefit at all. So, in general, the approach shown in *Figure 9.3* is better.

Project limits and quota

Each service in GCP has limits and quotas. It's a good practice to split projects to avoid hitting those limits and quotas. For example, a company uses only BigQuery on GCP. For the IAM requirements, each team requires the same set of permissions for accessing BigQuery. However, the teams are using BigQuery heavily and have more than 1,000 active users.

In the given example, if we refer back to point number one about IAM permissions' benefits, it's fine to use only one GCP project. But from a quota factor, this is a potential issue. If you check out the BigQuery public documentation about quotas (`https://cloud.google.com/bigquery/quotas#query_jobs`), you will see that one of the quotas is *Concurrent rate limit for interactive queries: 100*.

Remember that quotas are on a per-project basis, which means that one project can only handle 100 interactive queries. If the company has 1,000 active users, then there will be potential issues. In this case, it's good to split the projects.

Each service has its limits and quotas – you need to read the public documentation to be aware of them and plan the number of projects based on this factor.

Cost tracking

Another benefit of splitting projects is to track the cost distribution within an organization. You can check your billing dashboard from the GCP console. If you never opened the billing dashboard, I suggest that you try it. Go to your GCP console and go to **Billing** from the navigation menu. From the dashboard, you will see the current month and trends; one of the metrics that's available here is the cost per project. If your organization needs clear cost tracking for each different team or different initiative, you can do that by splitting the project. Note that this is only for tracking purposes – the billing will still be billed to one billing account.

In this section, you learned that using GCP in an organization or company usually needs more than one GCP project. The difficult question is, *How many projects does your organization need?* There is no right or wrong answer to this architectural question – we can use the three approaches discussed previously to decide on this. The key is to balance operational overhead and the benefits that you aim for when splitting projects.

Controlling user access to our data warehouse

Now that we've learned about user access at the organization, folder, and project levels, we will look specifically at **access control lists** (**ACLs**) in BigQuery. An ACL is the same concept as IAM, but the ACL terminology is more commonly used when talking about the data space. Planning an ACL in BigQuery means planning who can access what in BigQuery.

At a very high level, there are two main types of GCP permission in BigQuery, as follows:

- **Job permissions**: BigQuery has job-level permissions. For example, for a user to be able to run a query inside the project, they need `bigquery.jobs.create`.

   Note that being able to run a query job doesn't mean having access to the data. Access to the data is managed by the other permissions, which will be explained next.

- **Access permissions**: This one is a little bit more complicated compared to job permissions. If we talk about data access, we need to understand that the main goal of planning ACL is to secure the data as granularly as possible. As we discussed in the previous sections, we need to think about the *principle of least privilege*, meaning that you only give the right access to the right users.

In BigQuery, you can grant data access to BigQuery users on many levels. Here is a list, in order from the highest to the least granular level:

1. Project
2. Dataset
3. Table
4. Column- and row-level security

Inheritance is also applied here. If you grant a BigQuery viewer role to a user at a project level, the user will be able to access all the datasets, tables, columns, and rows under the project. At a minimum, a user needs BigQuery table-level viewer permissions to run a query on a table, and if needed, you can prevent the user from accessing certain columns and rows.

Granting access to a user in BigQuery is straightforward. You can find the **Menu** button or check out the public documentation to go through the steps.

Check out the public documentation to learn how to control access to a BigQuery dataset: `https://cloud.google.com/bigquery/docs/dataset-access-controls`.

I will cover an example scenario to explain the thinking process for planning the ACL.

Use-case scenario – planning BigQuery ACLs on an eCommerce organization

Imagine that you work for an eCommerce company. The company has four user groups, as follows:

- **Data Engineer**
- **Marketing**
- **Sales**
- **Head of Analysts**

From the data source side, the company has six tables, as follows:

- `user_profile`
- `user_address`
- `customer_checkouts`
- `customer_carts`
- `event_campaigns`
- `campaign_metrics`

After interviewing a user from each user group, these are their access requirements for the table:

- The **Data Engineers** group can create and view all tables.
- The **Head of Analysts** group can view all tables except `user_profile` and `user_address`.
- **Sales** can view data in `customer_checkouts` and `customer_carts`.
- **Marketing** can view data in `event_campaigns`, `campaign_metrics`, and `user_profile`.
- **Marketing** cannot access credit card number columns that are stored in the `user_profile` table. Managing column-level security in BigQuery requires more complex steps and an understanding of utilizing **policy tags**. This will be discussed in *Chapter 10, Data Governance in GCP*, in the *Exercise – column-level access control in BigQuery* section.

From the given scenario, take a look at this diagram for a list of our puzzle pieces:

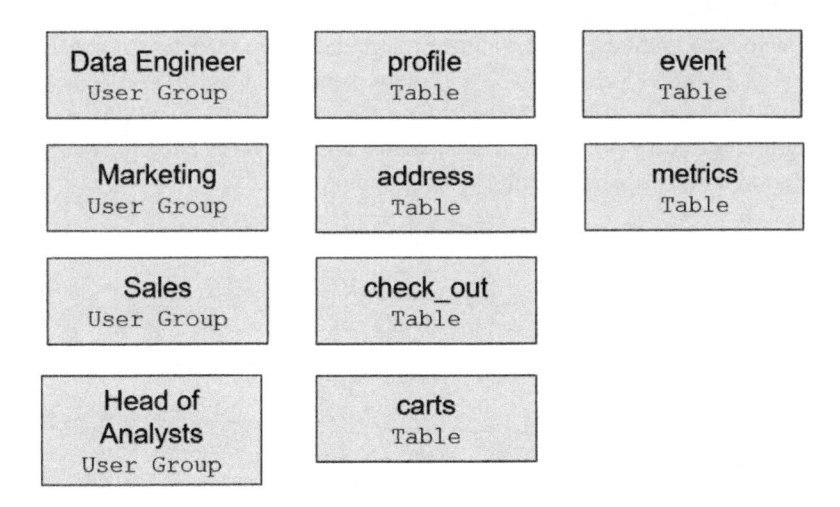

Figure 9.8 – User groups and tables

How would you grant data access to the user groups? Try to think of a solution and check it against mine.

To answer this question, we need to map the user groups to the tables based on the access requirements. As an illustration, it looks like this:

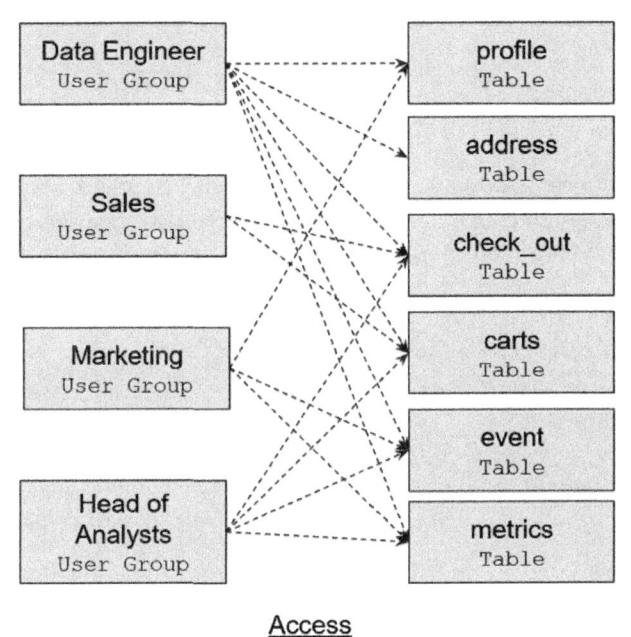

Figure 9.9 – User group-to-table mapping

Remember that you can grant data access at the project, dataset, or table level. One alternative is to grant table-level access individually based on the requirements. But that isn't scalable – for example, if you already know that a data engineer will always have access to all tables, there will be new upcoming tables in the future, and you don't want to grant access manually one by one to all tables. We need to utilize the power of inheritance by thinking about grouping.

We can group some of the tables into datasets. For example, take a look at the following diagram:

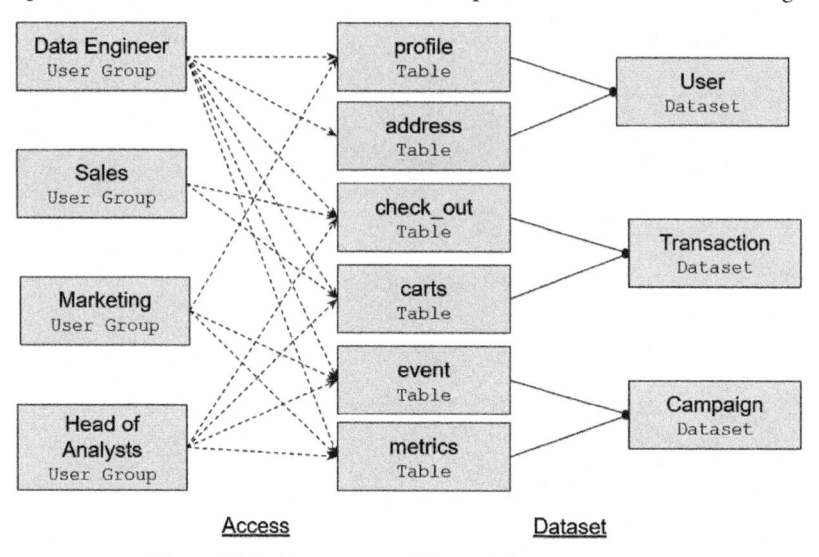

Figure 9.10 – User group, table, and dataset mapping

The idea is to create datasets based on the data access requirements. For example, since the **Sales** team needs access to two tables, `check_out` and `carts`, we can create a dataset named **Transaction**. This way, we can give the BigQuery viewer role in the **Transaction** dataset to the **Sales** team.

As a final solution, here are some possible BigQuery roles for the user groups:

User Group	Role	Resource
Data Engineer	BigQuery Data Editor roles/bigquery.dataEditor	Project level
Head of Analytics	BigQuery Data Viewer roles/bigquery.dataViewer	Transaction dataset Campaign dataset
Sales	BigQuery Data Viewer roles/bigquery.dataViewer	Transaction dataset
Marketing	BigQuery Data Viewer roles/bigquery.dataViewer	Campaign dataset user_profile table

Figure 9.11 – User group, IAM roles, and GCP resources table

We used predefined roles for the user group. With the given role, each user group will have the required permissions to each resource at either the project, dataset, or table level.

Now that we've learned about all the fundamentals of IAM, project structure, and BigQuery ACL, in the last section, we will jump a little bit into the infrastructure space. We will learn about what's called *IaC*. The concept is rarely a data engineer's responsibility, but understanding the concept and the benefits of using it will have a big impact on how we plan and design our data resources.

Practicing the concept of IaC using Terraform

IaC is the process of provisioning and managing resources using code. In our GCP case, the resources can be the GCP project, BigQuery datasets, GCS buckets, IAM, and all other resources that we've learned about throughout this book.

So far, we've created our resources using the GCP console's **user interface** (**UI**) or the `gcloud` command. Imagine that you need to do that manually one by one using the UI for hundreds to thousands of objects throughout a large organization. That can be very painful – not only from a provisioning point of view but also in terms of managing it.

The common issues without the IaC approach are missing consistency, such as naming conventions, forgetting to configure some parameters, such as location, and losing track of resources that have been created.

With an IaC approach, we can use code to provision our resources. The advantage of using code is that you can implement software engineering practices, such as utilizing templates, testing before deploying, and in-line documentation.

There are many software options for doing this, and one of the most commonly used is Terraform. **Terraform** is an open source IaC software tool. You, as the developer, declare which resources your organization needs in the Terraform scripts. The scripts can be run on any machine, from your local laptop, Cloud Shell, or VM. Note that you don't need to install Terraform as an application – what you need to do is download it from the internet. Let's learn how to do this by way of a practical example.

Exercise – creating and running basic Terraform scripts

In this exercise, we will practice running the Terraform scripts using Cloud Shell. The scripts will create a BigQuery dataset in your existing project. These are the steps:

1. Downloading Terraform to Cloud Shell.
2. Configuring the Terraform backend to a GCS bucket.
3. Using variables in Terraform.
4. Running a Terraform script using Cloud Shell.
5. Configuring a BigQuery dataset using Terraform.

Let's start by opening the Cloud Shell environment to download Terraform.

Downloading Terraform to Cloud Shell

You can find the download link for the latest version on Terraform's public website: https://www.terraform.io/downloads.html.

For example, in your Cloud Shell environment, run the following command to download the file to your Terminal:

```
$ wget https://releases.hashicorp.com/terraform/1.6.1/terraform_1.6.1_linux_amd64.zip
```

After downloading it, you will have a .zip file in your terminal. Unzip the file using the `unzip` command from the command line, as follows:

```
$ unzip terraform_1.6.1_linux_amd64.zip
```

Finally, let's move the Terraform file to the /usr/local/bin/ path so that we can call the file an application, as follows:

```
$ sudo mv terraform /usr/local/bin/
```

Now, let's try to call the Terraform command to check its version:

```
$ terraform --version
```

The command should run like this:

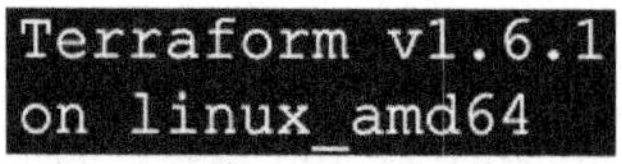

```
Terraform v1.6.1
on linux_amd64
```

Figure 9.12 – Checking Terraform's version from the command line

You will see the Terraform version that's installed on your machine. Make sure you are doing this before continuing to the next step.

Configuring the Terraform backend to a GCS bucket

In this step, we will start scripting the Terraform configurations. Open your Cloud Editor environment and create a new folder called `terraform-basic`. In that folder, create a file named `backend.tf`. The .tf format is a special file format that's used by Terraform. All files in this format will be written as configurations when we run the `terraform` command.

In the `backend.tf` file, write the following script in Cloud Editor. Don't forget to change the bucket name to your own GCS bucket:

```
terraform {
    backend "gcs" {
        bucket = "packt-data-eng-on-gcp-data-bucket"
        prefix = "terraform-backend-basic"
    }
}
```

This script will configure Terraform to use a GCS bucket to store the configuration files in the GCS bucket, in a folder that's stated in the *prefix*. In this example, this is `terraform-backend-basic`.

Using variables in Terraform

Next, we need to create a file called `main.tf`. In the file, add the following script:

```
provider "google" {
    project = var.project_id
}
```

The `provider` script tells Terraform to load all `google` (GCP) libraries. Remember that Terraform is an open source software, and it can manage many other environments outside of GCP.

Inside the `provider` configuration, we also declare the `project_id` variable, but I use a variable here instead of a static value. By calling `var.`, the value should be declared as a variable. Using variables is optional, but they are an important feature in Terraform, so we should start using them as early as possible.

To declare the variable, let's create another file named `variables.tf`. Use the following script inside the file:

```
variable "project_id" {
    type = string
}
```

The `variable` script doesn't set the `project_id` value yet – it just says that a variable named `project_id` exists. There are some options to set the variable; in this exercise, we will use a file to set the variable. To do that, create a file named `terraform.tfvars`.

In that file, set the `project_id` variable, like this. Don't forget to change the project ID from the `packt` example to your project ID:

```
project_id    = "packt-data-eng-on-gcp"
```

And that's all you need to do to run Terraform. Check out the following screenshot to see if you have the same files:

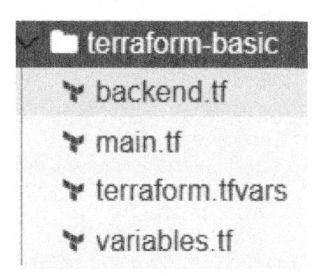

Figure 9.13 – The terraform-basic folder in Cloud Editor

If this is the first time you have practiced using Terraform, you might be wondering what you've been doing up until this point. I experienced this the first time I scripted Terraform code. That's common, and you will get the idea after running it.

In this section, you created the minimum required files and configurations to run Terraform scripts for managing GCP resources. Terraform needs the backend configuration to GCS, the provider, and – optionally – variables.

Running Terraform scripts using Cloud Shell

To run the Terraform scripts, go back to Cloud Shell. We will run Terraform's `init`, `plan`, and `apply` commands. Remember these commands in order:

1. `terraform init`.
2. `terraform plan`.
3. `terraform apply`.

That's an important order for running Terraform properly. First, let's run the `terraform init` command, inside the `terraform-basic` folder. Make sure you are inside the folder, not outside. Run this command:

```
$ terraform init
```

The following program will start running:

Practicing the concept of IaC using Terraform

```
adiwijaya_public@cloudshell:~/terraform-basic (packt-data-eng-on-gcp)$ terraform init
Initializing the backend...

Successfully configured the backend "gcs"! Terraform will automatically
use this backend unless the backend configuration changes.

Initializing provider plugins...
- Reusing previous version of hashicorp/google from the dependency lock file
- Installing hashicorp/google v3.87.0...
- Installed hashicorp/google v3.87.0 (signed by HashiCorp)

Terraform has been successfully initialized!

You may now begin working with Terraform. Try running "terraform plan" to see
any changes that are required for your infrastructure. All Terraform commands
should now work.

If you ever set or change modules or backend configuration for Terraform,
rerun this command to reinitialize your working directory. If you forget, other
commands will detect it and remind you to do so if necessary.
```

Figure 9.14 – Output from the terraform init command

The `terraform init` command will install the required library into the folder. By *install*, we mean creating a hidden folder named `.terraform`.

Next, run the `terraform plan` command, as follows:

`$ terraform plan`

The command will say that there will be no changes, as illustrated in the following screenshot:

```
adiwijaya_public@cloudshell:~/terraform-basic (packt-data-eng-on-gcp)$ terraform plan
No changes. Your infrastructure matches the configuration.
```

Figure 9.15 – Output from the terraform plan command

The `terraform plan` command is a way for you to check what Terraform will do to your GCP resources. Terraform can add, change, or destroy any resources in your project. This step ensures the list of actions is expected. In our case, this is expected to have no changes because we haven't configured any resources in the Terraform scripts.

Lastly, let's run the `terraform apply` command, as follows:

`$ terraform apply`

It will say `Apply complete! With 0 added, 0 changed, destroyed`. Again, this is expected; we will add a resource in the next step.

Configuring a BigQuery dataset using Terraform

Back in Cloud Editor, go to the `main.tf` file. Under the `provider` section, add the following `google_bigquery_dataset` resource script:

```
provider "google" {
    project = var.project_id
}
resource "google_bigquery_dataset" "new_dataset" {
    project    = var.project_id
    dataset_id = "dataset_from_terraform"
}
```

This configuration will tell Terraform to create a BigQuery dataset called `dataset_from_terraform`.

To run it, go back to Cloud Editor and run the `terraform plan` command, as follows:

```
$ terraform plan
```

Terraform will tell you, *If you run the terraform apply command later, I will create a dataset with this configuration*:

```
Terraform will perform the following actions:

  # google_bigquery_dataset.new_dataset will be created
  + resource "google_bigquery_dataset" "new_dataset" {
      + creation_time              = (known after apply)
      + dataset_id                 = "new_dataset"
      + delete_contents_on_destroy = false
      + etag                       = (known after apply)
      + id                         = (known after apply)
      + last_modified_time         = (known after apply)
      + location                   = "US"
      + project                    = "packt-data-eng-on-gcp"
      + self_link                  = (known after apply)

      + access {
          + domain         = (known after apply)
          + group_by_email = (known after apply)
          + role           = (known after apply)
          + special_group  = (known after apply)
          + user_by_email  = (known after apply)

          + view {
              + dataset_id = (known after apply)
              + project_id = (known after apply)
              + table_id   = (known after apply)
            }
        }
    }

Plan: 1 to add, 0 to change, 0 to destroy.
```

Figure 9.16 – Output of the terraform plan command showing the actions list

Since the output is as expected, let's continue by running the `terraform apply` command, as follows:

```
$ terraform apply
```

The command will ask you to type `yes` – do that and click *Enter*. Once you've done this, you can check your BigQuery console. You will find that the dataset has already been created for you.

Adding a BigQuery dataset using Terraform is just one very small example of what you can do. Almost all GCP resources can be managed by Terraform, and you can find the full list in their public documentation: https://registry.terraform.io/providers/hashicorp/google/latest/docs.

Understanding IaC will give you an idea of how GCP resources are managed in a big organization. The teams that usually handle this are **development and operations** (**DevOps**) or the infrastructure team, but it's not uncommon for data engineers to contribute to the code, especially to manage the resources that are related to data engineering.

Self-exercise – managing a GCP project and resources using Terraform

If you need more examples and experience in using Terraform to handle more complex resources, you can complete this exercise to create other resources. This self-exercise will be good practice for you to summarize all the knowledge from this chapter.

In this self-exercise, try to create Terraform scripts that meet these requirements:

- A new project with any name of your choice
- The BigQuery API is enabled
- Three BigQuery datasets named `stg_dataset`, `dwh_dataset`, and `datamart_dataset`
- A service account for handling any BigQuery workloads within the project (data owner)

If you finish this self-exercise at https://github.com/PacktPublishing/Data-Engineering-with-Google-Cloud-Platform-Second-Edition/tree/main/chapter-9/code/terraform-complete-project.

If you can finish the self-exercise, congratulations! You've experienced how to manage a GCP project with resources using code. If you can't finish it, that's fine too. You've learned a lot about all the important topics for planning GCP projects in a big organization.

Summary

In this chapter, we covered three important topics in GCP – namely, IAM, project structure, and BigQuery ACLs. Additionally, we learned about IaC.

Understanding these four topics lifts your knowledge from being a data engineer to becoming a cloud data architect. People with these skills can think not only about the data pipeline but also the higher-level architecture, which is a very important role in any organization.

Always remember the principle of least privilege, which is the foundation for architecting all the topics of IAM, project structure, and BigQuery ACLs. Always make sure you only give the right access to the right user.

In the next chapter, you'll discover how data governance using GCP services can unlock the full potential of your data, ensuring usability, security, and accountability.

10
Data Governance in GCP

In the information age, data has become essential in businesses and organizations worldwide. Having a data ecosystem that has the ability to collect, store, process, and analyze data is essential for making informed decisions, gaining a competitive edge, and achieving strategic goals. **Google Cloud Platform (GCP)**, with its powerful suite of data management and analysis tools, offers a robust foundation for harnessing the potential of data. However, as data grows in volume and complexity, ensuring its usability, security, and accountability becomes important. This is where data governance in GCP plays a pivotal role.

Data governance is the set of tools, practices, and policies that dictate how data is managed, maintained, and used within an organization. GCP encompasses a wide array of tools, processes, and best practices designed to ensure that data is accurate, secure, and compliant with regulations. Whether you're a data scientist, a data engineer, or a business executive, understanding the principles of data governance in GCP is crucial for leveraging the platform effectively and responsibly.

This chapter serves as a starting point for the broader exploration of data governance within the context of GCP. We will delve into the principles, tools, and strategies that are fundamental to data governance in GCP. We'll explore metadata tagging, managing sensitive data, auditing, and data quality processes. By the end of this chapter, you will have a solid foundation for building a data governance framework within GCP and will be better equipped to navigate the tools of data governance.

These are the main topics of this chapter:

- Introduction to data governance
- A deeper understanding of data usability
- A deeper understanding of data security
- A deeper understanding of being accountable

Technical requirements

For this chapter's exercises, we will need the following services:

- BigQuery
- Dataform
- Dataplex
- Sensitive Data Protection
- Example code from `https://github.com/PacktPublishing/Data-Engineering-with-Google-Cloud-Platform-Second-Edition/tree/main/chapter-10`

Steps on how to access, create, or configure the technical requirements will be provided later in each exercise.

Introduction to data governance

Data governance is the set of processes, policies, standards, and practices that organizations use to manage their data ecosystem.

The roles involved in data governance vary depending on the size of the organization. In some cases, when the organization is not that big, data engineers are responsible for data governance. In other cases, when the organization is very big and requires a deeper understanding of legal aspects, usually there is a dedicated team called the **data governance team**.

data governance encompasses a wide spectrum of practices and principles, much like the vast realm of big data. If we want to implement data governance, understanding the underlying motivations behind implementing it is crucial. Implementing data governance with the wrong motivation usually leads to a wasted effort.

The motivations can be defined into three primary pillars:

- Usability
- Security
- Accountability

The preceding three primary pillars can be branched out to many other aspects. I will use a mind map, *Figure 10.1*, to drill down the aspects of each pillar.

Introduction to data governance 321

> **Note**
> Keep in mind that whenever you expand your research in the data governance aspect from other resources, for example, from other books or the internet, you will always find different versions of the pillars, aspects, and approaches. This is because data governance by itself doesn't refer to one singular practice or technology. It's an umbrella term that can be interpreted differently in every organization.

Please take a look at the mind map and check every node. We will go through each node throughout the book. For example, this is how you can read the mind map: one of the motivations of data governance is data security. There are two aspects of data security: data encryption and data protection. For data protection, there are two main aspects: access control and data masking. Please take a look at the following figure.

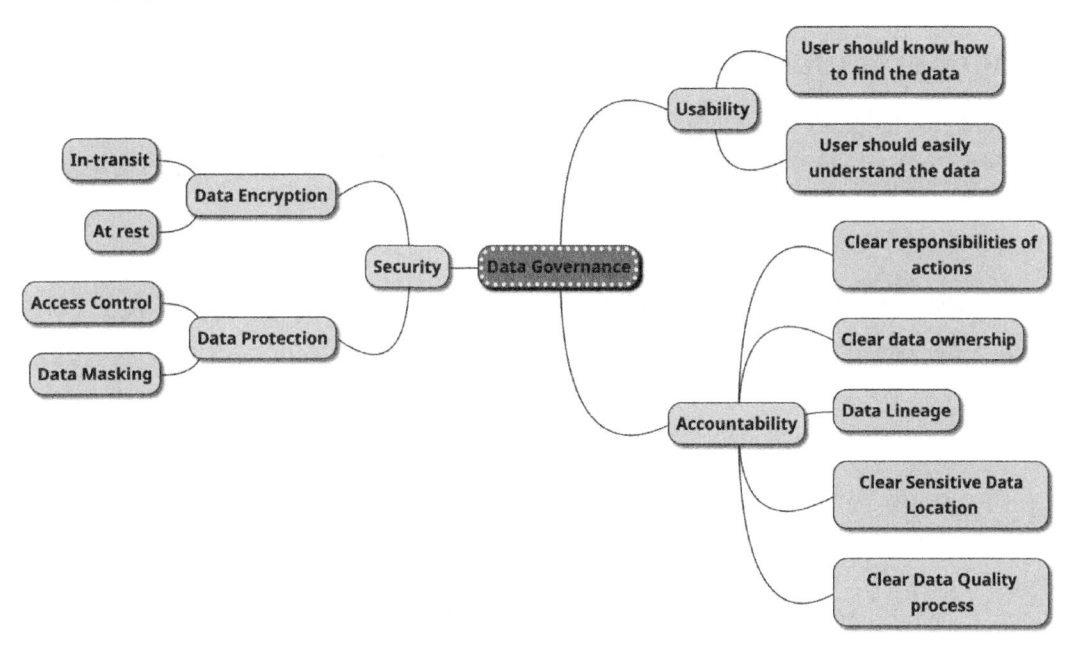

Figure 10.1 – Data governance aspects mind map

Each aspect needs both tools and practices to be able to be successful in data governance. The word *practice* here means an agreement by the users within an organization to consistently perform agreed rules.

Getting the same motivation and understanding between different users is important. As an analogy, what do you think when you hear the word *government*? You may think about sets of rules, the facilities to enable the rules, and the governors who enforce the rules. But at the end of the day, the trust of the people and the commitment to follow the rules is what makes data governance work. The same case with data governance, you always need to plan data governance implementation from both tools and practices.

For example, one of the very common data governance topics is data quality. To improve data quality, we can use **Dataform**. Dataform is a tool that can help us to implement unit testing on BigQuery, which we will learn about later, in the *Exercise – practicing data quality using Dataform* section.

But Dataform itself won't improve data quality. It requires the users to consistently write and perform proper unit testing scripts in the tool to improve data quality. Without following the best practice, the tool won't perform any function. And without the tool, some practices will be very difficult to perform. So, we need both for data governance.

To re-emphasize my statement, this is why understanding motivation is crucial. And make sure that every user in the organization that is involved in the data ecosystem understands and shares the same motivation.

Now, let's understand each motivation from the primary pillars and the aspects under it.

A deeper understanding of data usability

The first motivation for implementing data governance is that data should be usable. I think the statement alone is already very clear: we build a data platform so that it can be useful. But if we think more about it, how can data be usable by the end users?

The following are the two aspects that we should think about to improve data usability:

- Users should know how to find the data
- Users should easily understand the data

Let's discuss the first aspect, that is, the users should know how to find the data.

A data engineering team and the data governance team will be successful if only the data that they produce is used by the end users. It's nearly impossible to achieve this goal if the end users find it difficult to retrieve the data to get the information that they need.

You may think that it does not make sense that the end users can't find the data. Unfortunately, this is one of the most common problems in a big organization without proper data governance.

I will give you an example from my experience of helping a big retail company. They have a data platform that stores data in 800 GCP projects. One project may have 200,000 tables, and one table may have 200 columns. Imagine if the end users can only find the data that they need to use by the table and column names!

This can be improved with proper metadata and cataloging. Just like when we need to find information on the internet, the most efficient way to find specific objects in very large data is by using metadata tagging, content retrieval, and search engines.

On GCP we can use Dataplex Data Catalog to improve metadata management. This tool can help us have a similar experience to Google search, where the tool retrieves table and column descriptions, and we can give tags. The end users can easily search using the search box to find the tables that they need. Before going into the Dataplex exercise, let's discuss what is Dataplex in the following section.

Understanding Dataplex console for the first-time user

Dataplex is a data governance platform on GCP. When I say *platform,* it doesn't refer to any specific functionality, tools, or services. The term Dataplex is an umbrella to other services.

Inside Dataplex, you can find several services with specific functions that can be categorized into some functionalities:

- Dataplex Search and Catalog.
- Manage metadata tagging, indexing, and search. This is a successor of the Data Catalog.
- Dataplex Lakes.
- Manage the Data Lakes metastore, access control, and processes.
- Dataplex Profile.
- A tool to automatically profile BigQuery tables.
- Dataplex Data Quality.
- A tool to automatically check data quality on BigQuery tables.
- Dataplex data lineage.
- An auto-generated BigQuery table lineage based on **data definition language** (DDL) and **data manipulation language** (DML) queries. This is shown in the BigQuery console.

One thing that you need to know is that all the functionality is independent. For example, when you need to profile your data in BigQuery tables using Dataplex Profile, you don't need to create Dataplex Lakes objects or register some metadata in the Dataplex catalog. This means you can use any functionalities in Dataplex without worrying about the rest of the Dataplex services.

At the time this book was written Dataplex's first menu was the Explore sub-menu under the **Discover** menu. This is a lot of time confusing for a first-time user, because it may lead to the understanding that you need to create a **Dataproc metastore** (**DPMS**) before using all other Dataplex services in the other menus. This understanding is incorrect. The DPMS is not needed for most of the other Dataplex features. The **Explore** sub-menu is not the first step before you try the other Dataplex services on the different menus.

In summary, you need to decide first what kind of functionalities you need to perform to support your data governance.

After knowing your requirements, choose and assess the relevant Dataplex services to meet your requirements.

In our exercise, we will use the Dataplex Search and Catalog to support our users in finding the BigQuery tables that they need.

Exercise – implementing metadata tagging using Dataplex

In this exercise, we will try to create a tags template, assign tag values, and use it to search BigQuery tables.

Since this is going to be the first time you use Dataplex, let's start by opening the Dataplex console from the navigation bar. As usual, enable the API if required.

When you are in the Dataplex console, you will see many options in the Dataplex left panel, like this:

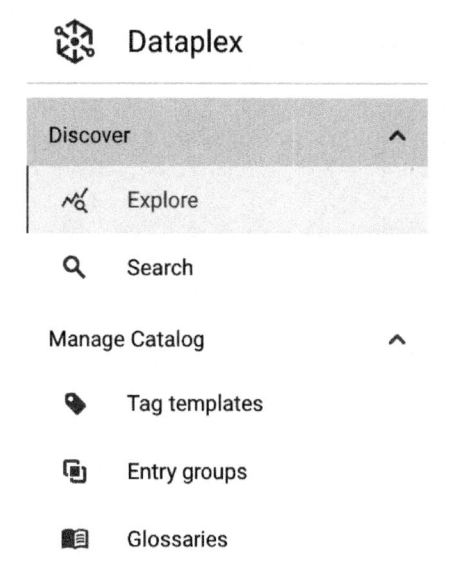

Figure 10.2 – Dataplex navigation menu

There are many options inside Dataplex. There are many sections, such as **Discovery**, **Manage Catalog**, **Manage Lakes**, and **Govern**, and all the sub-sections. They all function differently and sometimes independently.

Before continuing the exercise, let's start by explaining Dataplex to a first-time user.

Creating tag templates in Dataplex Catalog

Find the **Tag templates** menu in Dataplex, and let's create tag templates with this configuration:

- **Template display name**: data-ownership

- **Fields**:
  - `Data Owner`
  - `Business Owner`

Click the **DONE** button on each field and then click the **CREATE** button.

You will find your **Field** tags like this:

Fields

ID	Display Name	Type	Description
data_owner	Data Owner	STRING	The users who create and maintain this table
business_owner	Business Owner	STRING	The business unit team that own this information

Figure 10.3 – Dataplex search fields

After finishing the step, we need to assign the tags.

Assigning tags to BigQuery a table

Still in the Dataplex Search console, find our table named `sum_total_trips_daily`, which we created in *Chapter 4, Building Workflows for Batch Data Loading Using Cloud Composer*. If you no longer have this table, you can use any existing table. The console screen will look like the following figure:

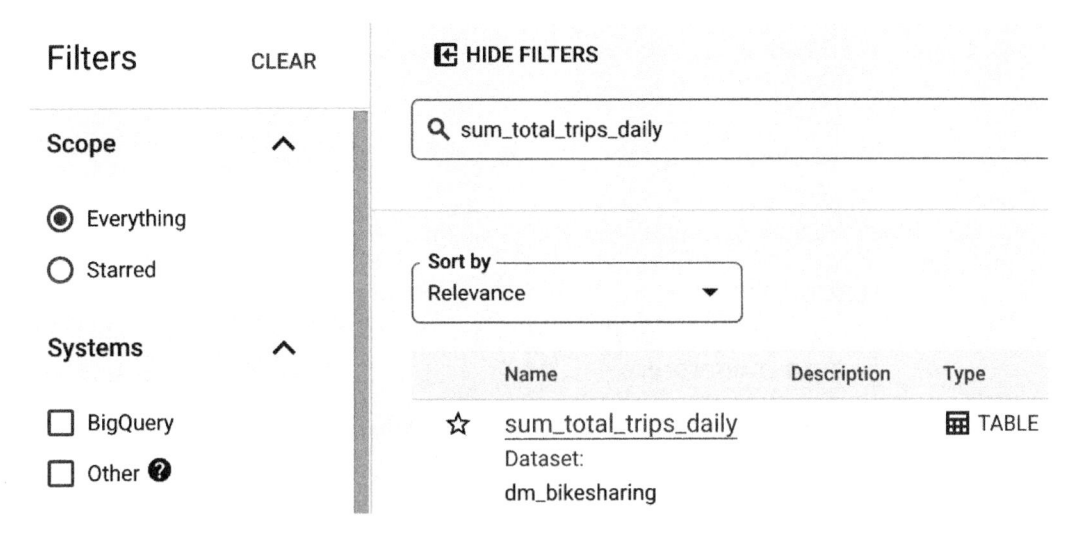

Figure 10.4 – Assigning tags to BigQuery table

Here are the steps for assigning tags:

1. Click the table's name, and you will see the BigQuery table details. Find the button **ATTACH TAGS** in the **TAGS(0)** section.
2. Now you can attach the tags to the table. Notice that you can choose to assign tags to table and column levels. For this exercise, we will tag only to the table level.
3. Choose the tags template that we created and fill in the **Data Owner** and **Business Owner** fields with any value; for example, please check out the configuration that I created from this figure:

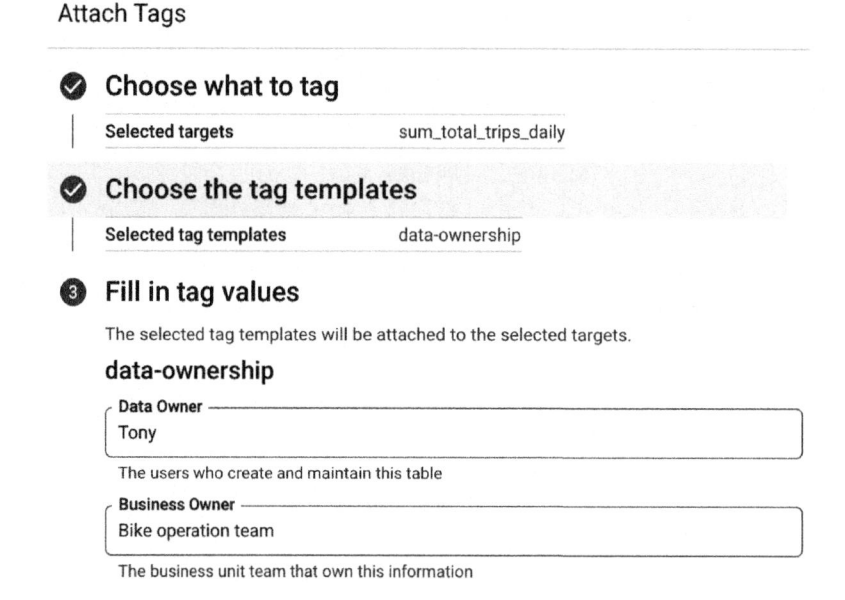

Figure 10.5 – Managing tag values to a table

4. Click **SAVE** after finishing, and you will see the tags that we have already created for this table:

Tags (1)

data-ownership

Display name	Value
Data Owner	Tony
Business Owner	Bike operation team

Figure 10.6 – The result when tags are assigned

These were all the steps to assign metadata tags in Dataplex.

Search tables using tags from Dataplex Search

Now let's see how the tags will be useful for finding tables. Now go back to the Dataplex Search:

1. On the **Filters** tab, find the **Tags** section. You can choose the **data-ownership** tag and click the button in the upper-right corner to add filters using tags. The icon and the filter forms look like this:

Figure 10.7 – Finding objects in Dataplex Search using tags

2. Click on **APPLY**, to see the table.

In this example, we learned how to create one simple tag template and assign it to one table. This sounds simple, but imagine having millions of tables with hundreds of business contexts. Practicing using tags will be very helpful to improve your data governance.

Every organization will have a different tag template. Have a look at this example to give you some idea of how you can design your tags:

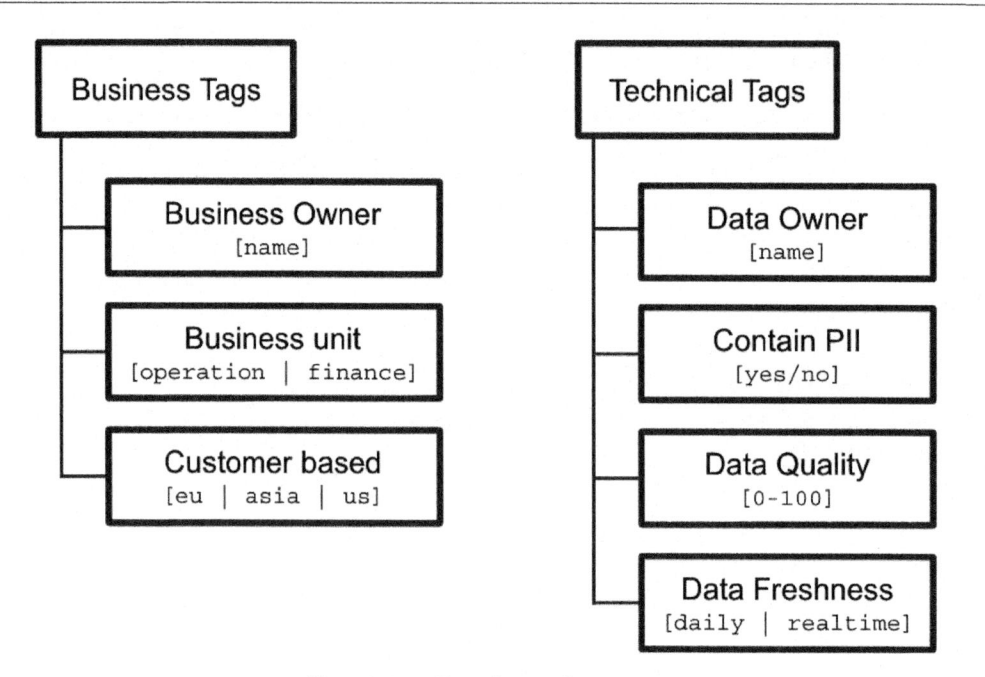

Figure 10.8 – Tags design illustration

The idea in the preceding design is to categorize tags into two major categories: **Business Tags** and **Technical Tags**. In each category, there is another tag template.

When you need to design and implement it in your organization, I recommend you define it with many other team members or stakeholders in a workshop format. This is to make sure all users who will be involved agree and understand the benefits of each tag.

In the following section, let's discuss the next aspect of data usability, which is how easily the user can understand the data.

The importance of data modeling for data usability

When a user has found the data object (table, column, file), it will be very beneficial if they can immediately understand how to use it. To improve this aspect, the first simple step and practice is to standardize the table and column descriptions.

But, as you may know, maintaining descriptions is not as easy as it sounds. It's very easy to do, yet very easy to make sure all table owners maintain a good description. One way to enforce this as a practice is by using GitOps to maintain the table and columns. We will see this in the *Exercise – practicing data quality using Dataform* section.

The second approach to make data easier to understand is to implement good data modeling. Data modeling is the process of structuring data tables to represent the business model.

Let's revisit this example from *Chapter 3, Building a Data Warehouse in BigQuery*. We want to represent people in a table object. Which of the following two tables, A or B, do you think better represents people? Here is `People Table A`:

name	age	hair color	gender
Mona	20	black	Female
Oscar	35	black	Male
Adam	56	white	Male
Barb	34	red	Male
Hazel	25	brown	Female

Figure 10.9 – People Table A

Try and compare this with `People Table B`:

name	gender	postal code	wealthy
Mona	Female	111111	yes
Oscar	Male	232323	no
Adam	Man	423333	no
Barb	Man	NULL	yes
Hazel	Woman	452222	yes

Figure 10.10 – People Table B

By maintaining a complete description and implementing good data models, the data users will naturally understand the tables.

A deeper understanding of data security

The second pillar of data governance is data security. The main motivation for data security is straightforward: any organization using data must know the implications if their data is getting leaked.

Even though the implication is clear, a lot of the time, data security is not the main priority. This is because implementing data security is often inconvenient. I'm referring to the fact that the data users often want to access and analyze the data as soon as possible. Implementing data security practices often slows down this process.

The second reason why it's common for an organization not to see this as a priority is that there is no clear tangible value when implementing it. For instance, implementing proper Data security will not generate revenue for the business.

Only when an incident happens does an organization start to panic and prioritize data security. Of course, we should know that data security is always an important aspect of the Data ecosystem before something bad happens.

The complexity of security is that incidents may happen in many different ways, on the hardware, network, and software levels. It may also happen to outsiders or insiders.

The good news is that in GCP, it's not that difficult to implement data security tools; many out-of-the-box features help us with data security. But as I mentioned at the beginning, tools aren't enough. You need practice.

To simplify data security, we can divide it into two aspects: data encryption and data protection. Let's discuss both of them.

Data encryption

Data encryption means how the data is being scrambled, and technically speaking it requires keys. Only when the system has the key does the user unscramble it. If any data is leaked, the encrypted data won't be accessible without the keys.

Encryption again can be divided into two: encryption in transit and encryption at rest. Encryption in transit means when there are data movements from one storage to another storage, the data that is being transferred through the network and in memory is encrypted. Encryption at rest means when the data is stored in permanent storage on disk.

By default, Google Cloud already handles both in-transit and at-rest encryption out of the box, including supplying and managing the keys. This is called **Google Managed Encryption Key (GMEK)**.

But if an organization has a regulation to manage their key, Google is flexible enough to allow the user to manage their key for at-rest encryption using Google **Key Management Service (KMS)**. This is called the **Customer Managed Encryption Key (CMEK)**. The menu looks like this from the BigQuery console when creating a dataset:

Advanced options

Encryption

○ Google-managed encryption key
  No configuration required

⦿ Customer-managed encryption key (CMEK)
  Manage via Google Cloud Key Management Service

Select a customer-managed key *

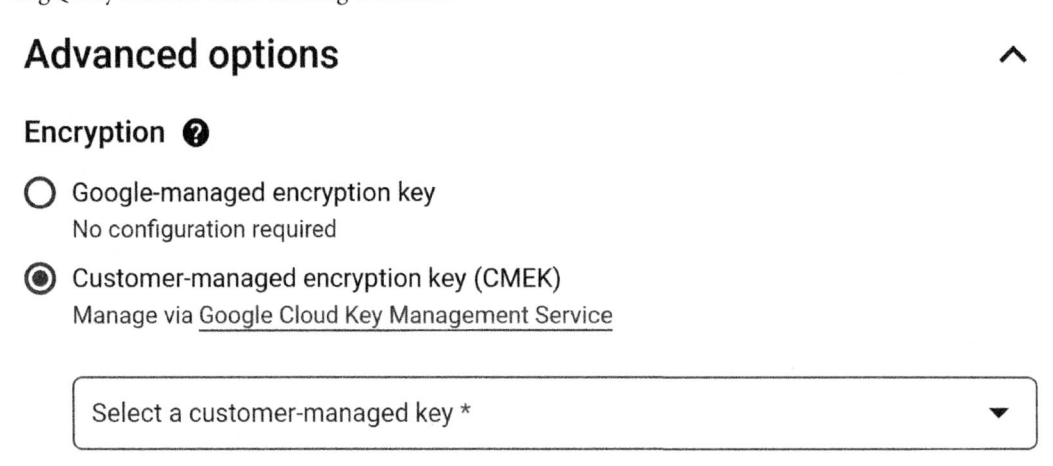

Figure 10.11 – BigQuery table CMEK encryption option

Further, if the organization needs to supply and manage its key by not using KMS, it's possible to use the **Customer Supplied Encryption Key (CSEK)**.

In general, most organizations only need GMEK. Specific industries, for example, financial or government institutions, may need to implement CMEK or CSEK, depending on the local regulations.

Data protection

Knowing all data in Google Cloud is encrypted, the question now is whether that is enough to secure the data. The answer is no.

Encryption is very helpful to protect data from outsiders, but it also needs to be mindful to protect data from insiders. The practice is called the principle of least privilege, which we covered in *Chapter 9, User and Project Management in GCP*.

Data protection here means ensuring that the data that you produce is highly protected and accessible only to the one who needs it.

There are two aspects of Data Protection, **Access Control List (ACLs)** and data masking.

ACLs

An ACL is a set of rules and configurations to control access to your data. This has been discussed in *Chapter 9, User and Project Management in GCP*, where we learned that BigQuery access can be controlled from the project, dataset, and table levels using IAM.

In addition to that, you can also manage column-level access control in BigQuery. The approach will be a little bit different than configuring IAM. To explain this in detail, let's take a look at the explanation with examples in the next section.

Exercise – column-level access control in BigQuery

Setting up column-level access control in BigQuery is a little bit trickier than granting project-, dataset-, or table-level access. There are a couple of terms that you need to understand before you configure it. The terms are **taxonomy** and **policy tags**. Once you understand the concept of column-level access control in BigQuery, it will be easy and will make sense. I will explain the concept through examples.

In BigQuery, preventing a user from accessing certain columns in tables is not as straightforward as clicking a button and putting the username in a form. Instead, we need to think first about why we want to prevent those users from having access. A common reason is to prevent users from accessing **personally identifiable information (PII)** columns.

For example, you have a `customer` table in BigQuery. The `customer` table has five columns: `user_id`, `name`, `salary`, `cc_number`, and `phone_number`. In a real-life scenario, the `customer` table may have 100 columns instead of 5 columns, but in this example, we will just use these 5 columns for simplicity. Look at this BigQuery table schema for our `customer` table:

user_id	name	salary	cc_number	phone_number
1	Toni	30000	1234 5678 9	65812345678
2	James	40000	1111 2222 3	65823456789
3	Arkan	50000	2222 3333 4	65834567
4	Lily	60000	4444 5555 6	658456789

Figure 10.12 – BigQuery customer table schema

Your business users need access to the table, but you don't want them to access the credit card number column. How to do that?

One approach is to create an **extract, transform, load** (ETL) pipeline and transform the table into two tables. One table contains only the credit card number, while the other table is without the credit card number. Another common approach is to create a view on top of the table. The third possible approach is to use the BigQuery column-level access control. The motivation is that you want to holistically define PII for many columns and tables; and also, to minimize creating new objects and data transformation.

At this point, we know that we want to prevent users from accessing a column because it contains a credit card number. The credit card number can be classified as PII data. PII data can contain many other classes—for example, name, address, phone number, and any other PII data. All of those rules are the taxonomy.

The taxonomy contains those data policy classifications, and in GCP, we can define them in the **Policy tags** menu. You can access it from the BigQuery console, in the **Administration** section.

Let's take a look at the **Policy tag taxonomies** page, as shown in this screenshot:

Policy tag taxonomies   ➕ CREATE TAXONOMY

Policy tags control access to columns in BigQuery tables. Use taxonomies to create hierarchical groups of policy tags. To apply access controls to BigQuery columns, tag the columns with policy tags. Learn more

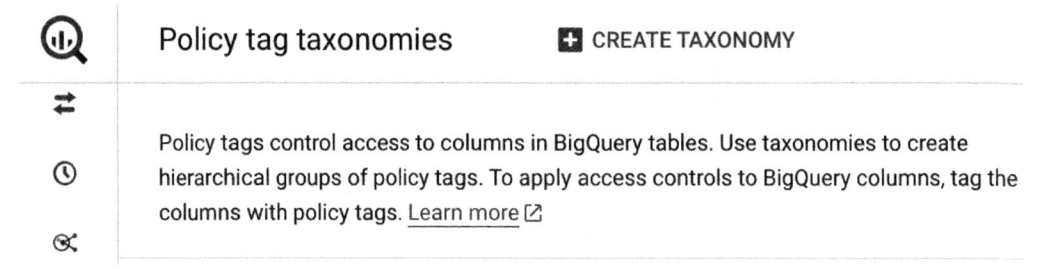

Figure 10.13 – Policy tag taxonomies page

There are three steps to apply policy tags to the BigQuery column:

1. Creating a new taxonomy.
2. Defining policy tags.
3. Adding policy tags to a BigQuery schema.

Let's go through each of the steps, as follows:

1. **Creating a new taxonomy**

    You can create a new taxonomy from the **Policy tag taxonomies** menu.

    On the taxonomy creation page, you will find the **Policy tags** form. In this form, you can define policy tags. One taxonomy can have many policy tags. As explained before, you can define your data classification in the policy tags, such as a list of PII, or other classifications—for example, departments, sensitivity level, or any other classification, depending on your organization's needs.

2. **Defining policy tags**

    Back to our example, in our taxonomy, we will set the PII tag as the parent and the credit card number as the child of PII, as illustrated in the following screenshot:

Policy tags

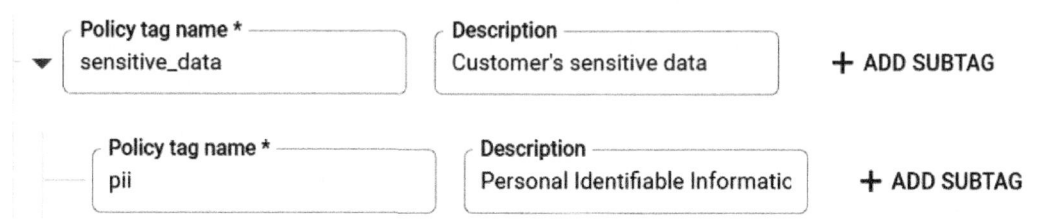

Policy tag name *	Description	
sensitive_data	Customer's sensitive data	+ ADD SUBTAG
Policy tag name *	Description	
pii	Personal Identifiable Informatic	+ ADD SUBTAG

Figure 10.14 – Policy tags page

Note that these policy tags can be used in as many columns as you need, not strictly only in our customer table.

After creating policy tags and a taxonomy, make sure to enable the **Enforce access control** toggle, as illustrated in the following screenshot. This will activate our column-level security in BigQuery when a table is using these policy tags:

✅ Enforce access control

Access to BigQuery columns tagged with the policy tags below will be restricted to users with the Fine-Grained Reader and the Masked Reader roles.

Figure 10.15 – Enforce access control toggle

That's all that we need to do in the **Policy tags** console.

3. **Adding policy tags to a BigQuery schema**

   Next, in our BigQuery table, we need to add a policy tag to our table.

   Back in our `customer` table, go to the **SCHEMA** tab. You can click **EDIT SCHEMA** and click the **ADD POLICY TAG** button on each column, as follows:

Field name	Type	Mode
user_id	STRING	NULLABLE
name	STRING	NULLABLE
salary	INTEGER	NULLABLE
cc_number	STRING	NULLABLE
phone_number	STRING	NULLABLE

   EDIT SCHEMA   VIEW ROW ACCESS POLICIES

   Figure 10.16 – Editing a schema

   In our case, we want to add the credit card number policy tag to the `cc_number` column, as illustrated in the following screenshot:

   ## Add a policy tag

   Filter — Type to filter taxonomies or policy tags

   Name ↑

   ▼ taxonomy-example
   ○ ▼ sensitive_data
   ● pii

   Figure 10.17 – Adding a policy tag to the credit card number taxonomy

   That's the last step to enable column-level security.

If a user doesn't have access to the credit card number policy tag, they will get this error when selecting the column:

Error running query

Access Denied: BigQuery BigQuery: User does not have permission to access policy tag "taxonomy-example : pii" on column packt-data-eng-on-gcp.chapter_9_dataset.users.cc_number.

Figure 10.18 – Example error message

But since the user has table-level access to the table, they can use `EXCEPT(cc_number)` to access the table, like this:

```
1  SELECT * EXCEPT(cc_number) FROM `packt-data-eng-on-gcp.chapter_10_dataset.customer` ORDER BY user_id
```

Query results

JOB INFORMATION | RESULTS | CHART PREVIEW | JSON | EXECUTION DETAILS | EXECUTION

ow	user_id	name	salary	phone_number
1	1	Toni	30000	65812345678
2	2	James	40000	65823456789
3	3	Arkan	50000	65834567
4	4	Lily	60000	658456789

Figure 10.19 – Using EXCEPT SQL syntax in BigQuery

To grant access to the user, permission needs to be granted to the policy tags in the taxonomy, not to the BigQuery column.

Using the taxonomy concept, the data access control should be defined holistically based on the organization or business needs.

Instead of thinking about the permission from users to table columns individually one by one, what you need to do is to plan the classifications. First, you need a grand plan for the taxonomy of the whole organization. This process is typically done once through a collaboration of data engineers, data governors, and the legal team. The rest of the process is about tagging each column in BigQuery using policy tags. All column-level access control will be automatically applied to all users.

Data masking

On top of ACLs, to even further protect our data, we can also implement data masking to protect PII.

Data masking functions when there are data users who have the privilege to access and analyze some data without really needing the actual PII data.

For example, a group of data scientists needs to analyze the distribution of their customers by salary. Take a look at *Figure 10.20*. Which column do you think is the PII data?

id	name	age	salary	CC number
1	Toni	34	$20,000	1234 5678 9
2	Arkan	53	$30,000	9876 5432 1

Figure 10.20 – Customer table with sensitive data

The answer is the name, age, and CC number columns. Those columns are sensitive data because they all can be used to identify a person.

To be precise, we can differentiate between PII and **Sensitive PII (SPII)**. Remember that the main point of data being sensitive is when the data can identify personal information. For example, in the preceding example, the combination of name and age usually can specifically identify a person. So, both name and age can be considered as PII. Only the age column is not PII because you can't identify a person only by age.

The SPII refers to any kind of information that when it's leaked or stolen can result in significant harm to an individual. In the preceding example, the CC number is SPII.

Back to our data scientist's case, the CC number is SPII and not needed for analysis purposes. Understanding this, we can implement the column-level access control as we practice in *Exercise – column-level access control in BigQuery*.

Further, the actual customer's name is also not necessary for the analysis. It may be needed only for grouping, filtering, or join operations. This means we can mask those sensitive values, like in *Figure 10.21*. The figure shows the name column in a masked value:

id	name	age	salary
1	e30470ae2226896865b9c6b56a0f85d5	34	$20,000
2	e14ebc2f77955df599c979adebe1a1ae	53	$30,000

Figure 10.21 – Customer table with the masked name column

If the data scientists have access to tables in that format, the risk of data leakage incidents being harmful can be significantly reduced.

In BigQuery, we can use the same approach with the column-level access control, with some additional configuration. To learn this, let's see the example from the next section.

Example – BigQuery data masking

In this example scenario, we will see how BigQuery data masking works, by continuing the previous column-level access control configuration and steps.

> **Note**
> This is only an example section, not an exercise. The reason is that at this point, adding BigQuery data masking policies can only be done if your GCP Project is managed under a GCP organization. Creating a GCP organization requires you to be in a real organization or have a dedicated web domain. The steps are very complex if only for learning or exercise purposes, thus for our learning purpose, I will show you how it works by using examples.

BigQuery data masking uses the same foundation as column-level access control, which uses **taxonomy** and **policy tags**.

The difference between a mask and column-level access control is that for masking, the end user without permission can still query the column, but only the masked data. There are many options that you can choose for masking the data, such as replacing all string characters with hash values, showing only the last four digits, and the other options that you can find in this public documentation: https://cloud.google.com/bigquery/docs/column-data-masking-intro#masking_options.

To do that, I will start by using existing or adding new policy tags in our Taxonomy. In my case, I will create a new policy tag for a person's name and phone number. The figure shows you the data policies under the **sensitive_data** tag.

MANAGE DATA POLICIES

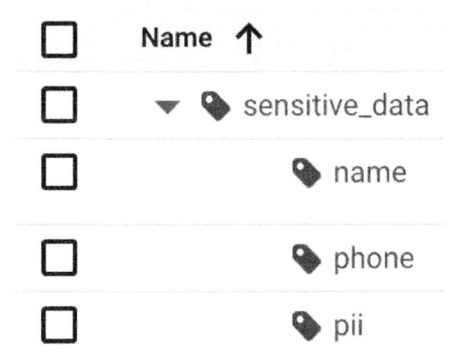

	Name ↑
☐	▼ 🏷 sensitive_data
☐	🏷 name
☐	🏷 phone
☐	🏷 pii

Figure 10.22 – Add name and phone Policy tags in the Taxonomy

To add the masking rule, I can manage it by clicking the **MANAGE DATA POLICIES** button at the bottom of the page, as shown in the following screenshot:

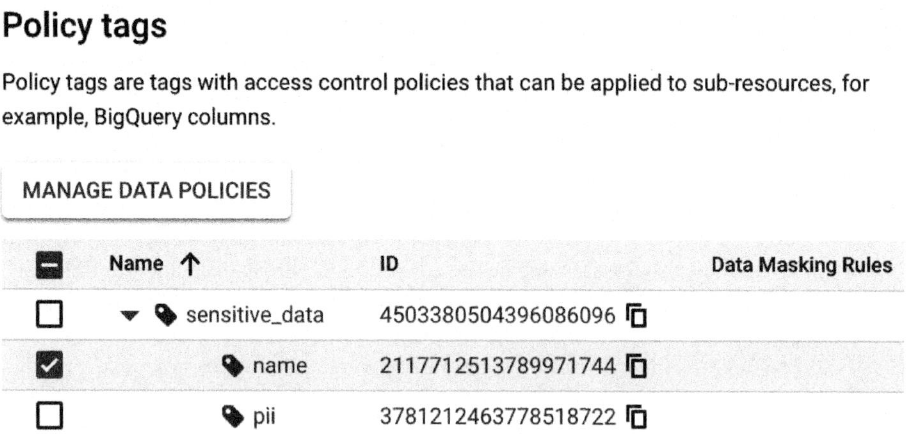

Policy tags

Policy tags are tags with access control policies that can be applied to sub-resources, for example, BigQuery columns.

	Name ↑	ID	Data Masking Rules
	▼ 🏷 sensitive_data	4503380504396086096	
✓	🏷 name	2117712513789971744	
	🏷 pii	3781212463778518722	

Figure 10.23 – Policy tags manage data policies section

After that, I can add masking rules, for example masking the name columns with the **Hash (SHA256)** rule and the phone columns with the **Last Four Characters** rule. The data masking rules will be shown like this:

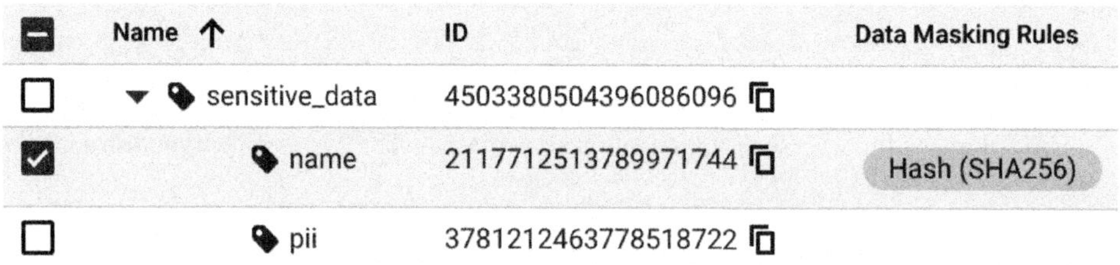

	Name ↑	ID	Data Masking Rules
	▼ 🏷 sensitive_data	4503380504396086096	
✓	🏷 name	2117712513789971744	Hash (SHA256)
	🏷 pii	3781212463778518722	

Figure 10.24 – The policy tag assigned with data masking rules

Similar to the column-level security, the final step is to assign the Policy tag to the column like this, for example:

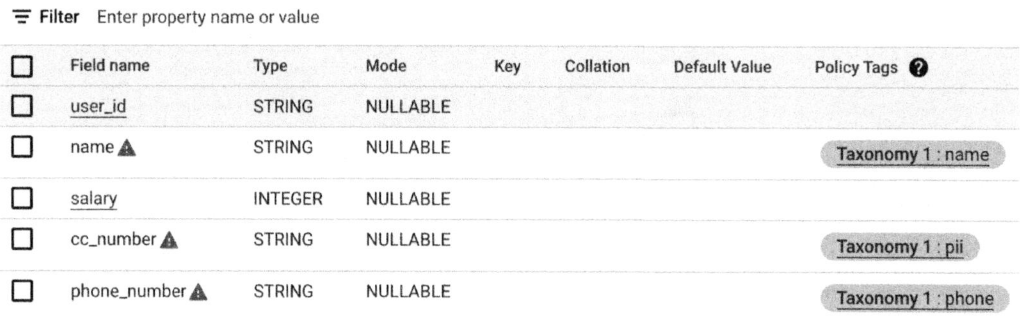

	Field name	Type	Mode	Key	Collation	Default Value	Policy Tags
	user_id	STRING	NULLABLE				
	name ⚠	STRING	NULLABLE				Taxonomy 1 : name
	salary	INTEGER	NULLABLE				
	cc_number ⚠	STRING	NULLABLE				Taxonomy 1 : pii
	phone_number ⚠	STRING	NULLABLE				Taxonomy 1 : phone

Figure 10.25 – The BigQuery table's schema with the Policy Tags assigned

With that, whenever a user doesn't have permission to access the real value, the query result will look like this:

user_id	name	salary	phone_number
1	E9FUNQpqWhw/1/eTcfMaUr0...	30000	XXXXX5678
2	k0WjWm/fF03/chkoKjrkh5eQ2...	40000	XXXXX6789
3	9O0ArjR5F7yj0BP6bt9OnFb/z...	50000	XXXXX4567
4	BZ9yesf/Xc3C+wccORAeZqnr...	60000	XXXXX6789

Figure 10.26 – Query result with masked columns

With that configuration, the data scientist team can safely access the table without worrying about the PII data. At the same time, the data engineering team only needs to maintain one single table without any ETL logic to serve the table for the end users.

After learning how to manage data protection up until the BigQuery column level, a question may arise: "How do we know if our datasets have PII or not?"

To answer that question, fortunately, GCP has come up with the **Sensitive Data Protection** (**SDP**) service. Specifically, what we need is SDP Discovery. To learn about SDP Discovery, we will complete the exercise in the next section.

Exercise – finding PII using SDP

SDP is a service that helps you discover, classify, and protect sensitive data both inside and outside GCP. This includes data in GCS buckets, BigQuery tables, Datastore, or any other data sources that can be scanned using SDP Content API.

SDP relies on two main objects called **infoTypes** and the SDP template. InfoTypes are the list of sensitive data, PII, and SPII collections that can be used to classify your data. The SDP template is a set of configurations to run the SDP services. You will learn about both of these objects in this exercise.

There are useful features in SDP, such as Inspection, Discovery, and Transformation. At a very high level, SDP Inspection scans files in GCS or individual BigQuery tables. SDP Discovery scans multiple BigQuery tables in the GCP project, folder, or organization level. SDP Transformation scans and immediately transforms the detected infoTypes into a masked value.

Note that originally SDP was named **Data Loss Prevention** (**DLP**). When this book was written, the transition was still ongoing, thus you will still see DLP in the console or API. If you find it, don't be confused. There is no difference between the two other than the name.

In this exercise, we will practice running the SDP Discovery at the GCP project level to find PII in our BigQuery tables. The steps are as follows:

1. Create a dummy table from a public dataset.
2. Create the SDP Inspect template.
3. Create the SDP Discovery configuration.

Let's start with the first step.

Step 1 – Create a dummy table from the public dataset

To start our exercise, let's first create a dummy table that contains PII data. We can do that by copying the public dataset. The steps to copy a table from a public dataset can be found in *Chapter 3, Building a Data Warehouse in BigQuery*, in the *Introduction to the BigQuery console* section.

The table ID that we will use is `bigquery-public-data.stackoverflow.comments`. The table detail looks like this screenshot:

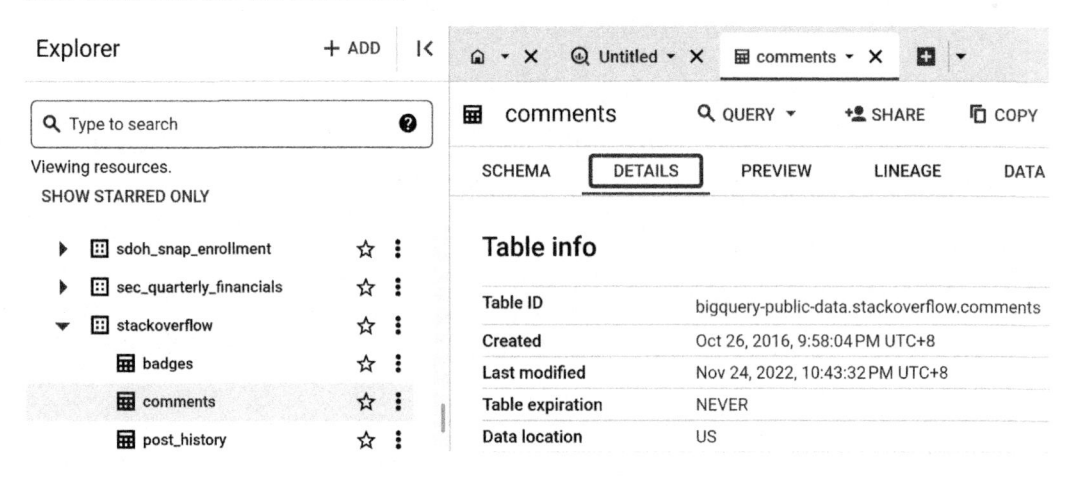

Figure 10.27 – Stack Overflow public dataset

Let's start by creating a new dataset named `stackoverflow`. From the BigQuery console, we can run this query to create the table in our project's dataset:

```
CREATE TABLE stackoverflow.comments
AS
SELECT * FROM `bigquery-public-data.stackoverflow.comments`
LIMIT 1000000;
```

After creating the first table, we will create another one to demonstrate finding name and gender PII data. Let's do that by creating a dummy table named `stackoverflow.profiles` using this SQL script:

```
CREATE TABLE stackoverflow.profiles (
    id int64,
    name string,
    gender string
);


INSERT INTO stackoverflow.profiles VALUES (1,"toni","male");
INSERT INTO stackoverflow.profiles VALUES  (2,"maria","female");
INSERT INTO stackoverflow.profiles VALUES  (3,"oliver","male");
INSERT INTO stackoverflow.profiles VALUES  (4,"jane","female");
INSERT INTO stackoverflow.profiles VALUES  (5,"james","male");
```

We will use these two tables as examples to be scanned by SDP Discovery.

Step 2 – create the SDP Inspect template

The next step is to create the SDP Inspect template.

To do that, from the GCP console find the SDP menu.

From the GCP navigation menu, find the SDP service in the **Security** > **DATA PROTECTION** section.

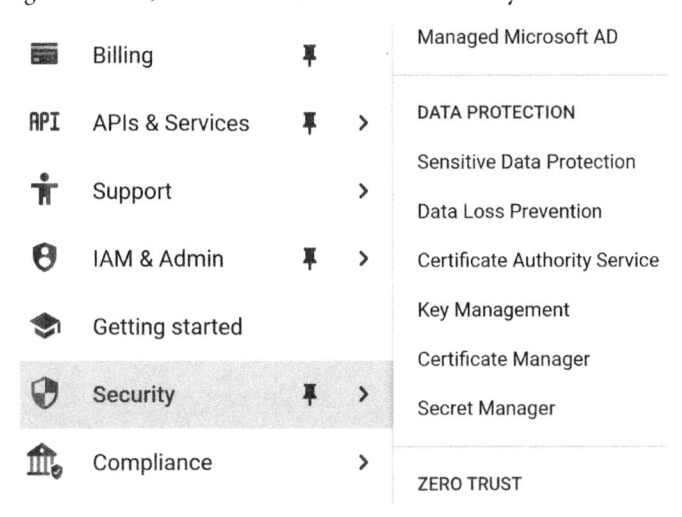

Figure 10.28 – Finding the Sensitive Data Protection menu

The SDP service is a little bit hidden in the navigation menu. If you can't find it, you can search it using the search bar by simply typing `SDP`.

After enabling the DLP API, you can see the SDP console. To create the SDP template, go to the **CONFIGURATION** tab, and click the **CREATE TEMPLATE** button.

This is my configuration example:

- **Template ID** = `inspect-template-1`
- **Resource location** = `us (multi-region)`

The second section is the most important aspect of SDP, which is choosing the infoTypes. Let's do that by clicking the **MANAGE INFOTYPES** button, and you can see all the **BUILT-IN** infoTypes. You can choose up to 150 infoTypes. Even though it's tempting to do so, this may impact the performance. It's better to choose only the relevant infoTypes for your business. For this exercise, let's choose **ALL_BASIC, DOMAIN_NAME, EMAIL_ADDRESS, FIRST_NAME, GENDER**. The infoTypes choices look like the following figure:

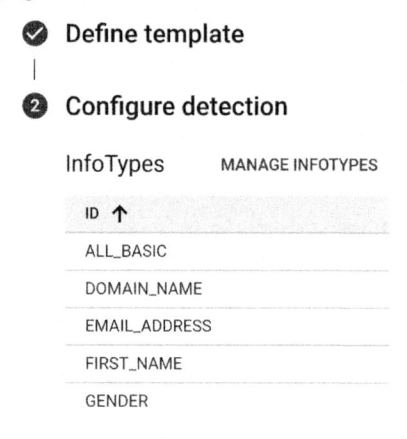

Figure 10.29 – Choosing the infoTypes

Finish the SDP template creation by clicking the **CREATE** button.

Step 3 – Create the SDP Discovery configuration

Once we have our SDP template, we can configure SDP Discovery. To do that, from the SDP console, choose the **DISCOVERY|- SCAN CONFIGURATIONS** tab and click **CREATE CONFIGURATION**.

Figure 10.30 – Select the Scan configuration

On the **Create scan configuration** page, leave everything as the default settings up until the **Select inspection template** option. Choose **Select existing inspection template** and you can input the full SDP template's full ID in the form: `projects/packt-gcp-data-eng/locations/us/inspectTemplates/inspect-template-1`

Check this figure to see what the form looks like:

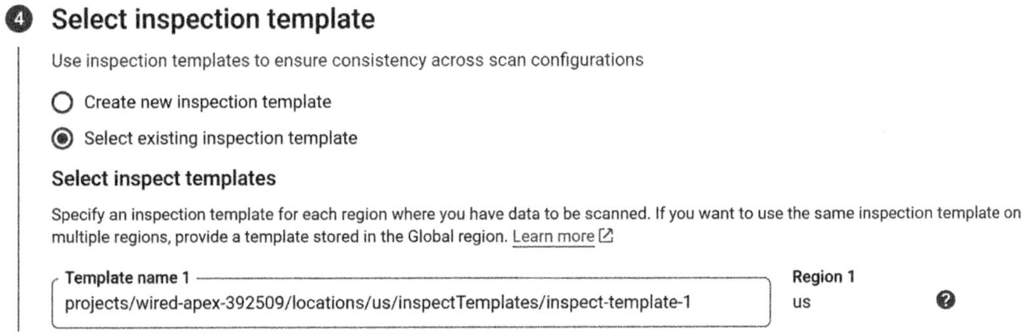

4 Select inspection template

Use inspection templates to ensure consistency across scan configurations

○ Create new inspection template
● Select existing inspection template

Select inspect templates

Specify an inspection template for each region where you have data to be scanned. If you want to use the same inspection template on multiple regions, provide a template stored in the Global region. Learn more

Template name 1: projects/wired-apex-392509/locations/us/inspectTemplates/inspect-template-1
Region 1: us

Figure 10.31 – Choose the created inspection template

Lastly, when selecting the actions for this exercise, disable all actions other than **Save data profile copies to BigQuery**. With this option, the SDP service will automatically create a new table in a BigQuery dataset to export the findings. Check out the following figure:

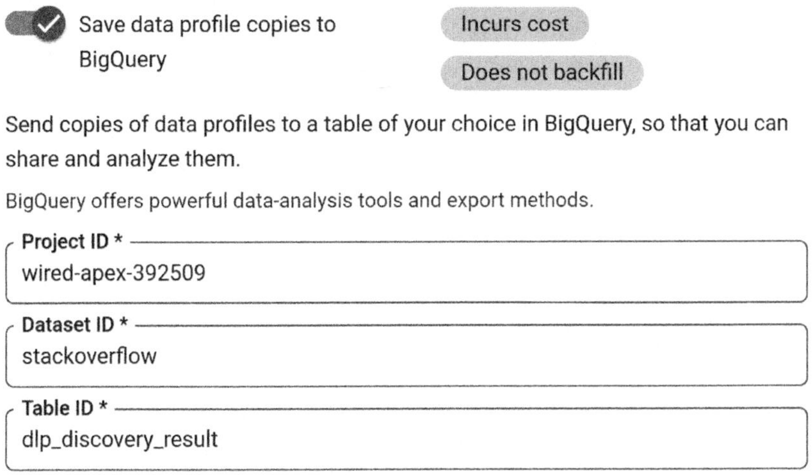

✓ Save data profile copies to BigQuery   *Incurs cost*   *Does not backfill*

Send copies of data profiles to a table of your choice in BigQuery, so that you can share and analyze them.

BigQuery offers powerful data-analysis tools and export methods.

Project ID *: wired-apex-392509
Dataset ID *: stackoverflow
Table ID *: dlp_discovery_result

Figure 10.32 – Choose the BigQuery table output

Finish the configuration by clicking the **CREATE** button. That's all we need to do to scan our entire BigQuery tables to find PII data. The SDP Discovery process will automatically run in the background after you create the scan configuration. With our current data size, the result usually will take around 5 – 30 minutes.

Understanding the SDP Discovery result

When the SDP Discovery process finishes, the result will be called SDP Data Profiles. You can access this under the SDP console on the **DISCOVERY | PROFILES** tab. Check out the following figure for the example result:

Sensitive Data Protection

OVERVIEW	DISCOVERY	INSPECTION	RISK ANALYSIS	CONFIGURATION	SUBSCRIPTIONS	COMPARE OFFER

Location *
multiple regions in United States (us)

Data Profiles for packt-gcp-data-eng

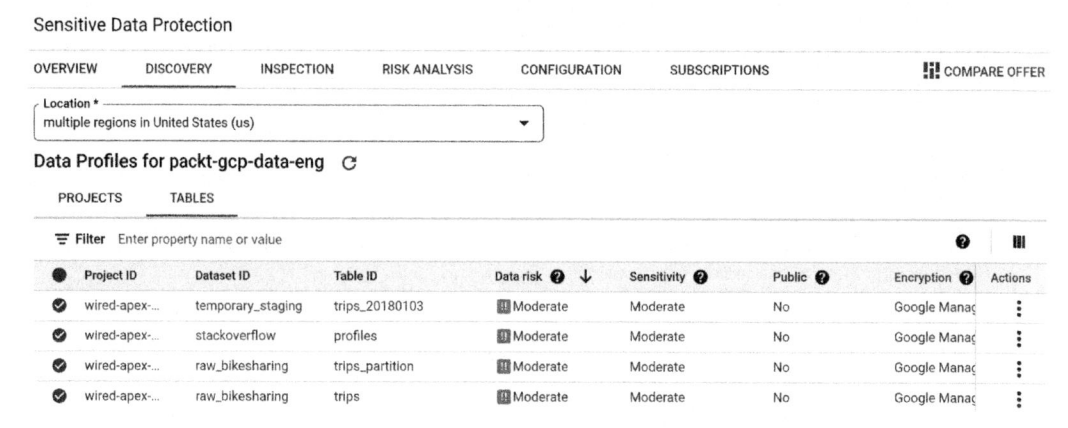

PROJECTS | TABLES

Project ID	Dataset ID	Table ID	Data risk	Sensitivity	Public	Encryption	Actions
wired-apex-...	temporary_staging	trips_20180103	Moderate	Moderate	No	Google Manag	
wired-apex-...	stackoverflow	profiles	Moderate	Moderate	No	Google Manag	
wired-apex-...	raw_bikesharing	trips_partition	Moderate	Moderate	No	Google Manag	
wired-apex-...	raw_bikesharing	trips	Moderate	Moderate	No	Google Manag	

Figure 10.33 – Discovery results at the table level

As you can see from the screenshot, it will list down all tables that may contain PII columns.

Now let's try to click the dummy table that we created named: `stackoverflow.profiles`. In the **Column Profiles for this Table** page, you can scroll down to find the predicted `infoType` for each column. Notice that those are the three fields that we created, with the prediction from SDP.

Column Profiles for this Table

Field ID	Data risk	Sensitivity	Predicted infoType	Other infoTypes (Estimated prevalence)
name	Moderate	Moderate	–	FIRST_NAME (100%)
gender	Moderate	Moderate	GENDER	
id	Low	Low	–	

Figure 10.34 – Discovery results at column level

There are two prediction fields, **Predicted infoType** and **Other infoTypes (Estimated prevalence)**. Both are equally important predictions. If there are fields that the predictions show in **Other infoTypes(Estimated prevalence)**, it simply means that there are PII detected, but possibly not in 100% of the records. Thus, the estimated prevalence in percentage is provided.

There is also data risk and sensitivity information, those values are attached from the `infoTypes` and SDP template, which is configurable. For example, if the `Predicted Infotype` is GENDER, the data risk and the sensitivity will be `moderate`. Each infoType has been pre-configured with its data risk and sensitivity values. The definition of each value can be found in the public documentation: `https://cloud.google.com/dlp/docs/sensitivity-risk-calculation`.

Next, we can go back to the SDP Profile page and choose the `stackoverflow.comments` table. If you scroll down to the **Fields prediction** section, you will find an interesting example of how SDP can find PII even in a free-text format. Please check the **text** field of the result:

Column Profiles for this Table

Field ID	Other infoTypes (Estimated prevalence)	Data type	Policy tags	Free text score
text	PERSON_NAME (12%)	TYPE_STRING	No	1
user_display_name	PERSON_NAME (6%)	TYPE_STRING	No	0.25
user_id		TYPE_INT64	No	0
score		TYPE_INT64	No	0
post_id		TYPE_INT64	No	0
creation_date	DATE (100%) TIME (100%)	TYPE_TIMESTAMP	No	0
id		TYPE_INT64	No	0

Figure 10.35 – Free text column in the column profiles

The `text` column in the BigQuery table is a free text column that contains Stack Overflow's user comments in posts. Usually without tools like SDP, it's very difficult to find if there are any PII in a free-text column.

If you open the `Other infoTypes (Estimated prevalence)` lists, here you can see SDP can predict there are around 12% person names, 9% domain names, and the `Other infoTypes (Estimated prevalence)`. Further, if you scroll to the right, you can also see the free text score information, which indicates how likely the column is a free text column. A score of 1 means 100%, which in our example SDP predicts that the text column is 100% likely to be a free text column.

There is some other information in the Profiles and the BigQuery table export. Take the time to take a look and learn what useful information you can use for your data governance. Knowing all this information, think about how you can implement or improve your Data Protection practice in a data ecosystem.

After getting a better understanding of data security, in the next section, we will move on to the data being accountable.

A deeper understanding of being accountable

The third pillar of data governance is accountability. Accountability for data is established when the processes and track records for all actions that happen in the data ecosystem are clear. In other words, data is not accountable when no one has a clear idea of why and how things happen in your data ecosystem.

The word "clear" can be expanded to some of the aspects:

- Clear traceability
- Clear data ownership
- Data lineage
- Clear data quality process

Clear traceability

Clear traceability means that for whatever event or actions occur on the data, you have a clear view of who does what and when. This is crucially important for examples such as these: events when a table that contains sensitive data is created, a list of queries that take most of the BigQuery capacity in a day, or a user that costs the most queries in a month.

Please note that the main point of this aspect of data governance is not to find who to blame when an incident happens. The main point is to make sure you have prepared a system that can track all important events, store them, and make sure you can access them anytime you need. Only when you can access this information can you increase resolution time when any unfortunate incident happens in your data ecosystem.

Fortunately, tracking user events is very easy in GCP. All GCP products' logs are tracked, stored, and accessible from a console using Cloud Logging. This applies to most of the products that we've seen, such as BigQuery, GCS, Dataproc, Cloud Composer, and Dataflow.

Optionally, you can also export any logs from Cloud Logging to BigQuery for more advanced analysis. The feature is called **Log Router**, which is accessible from the **Logging** menu, as shown in this screenshot:

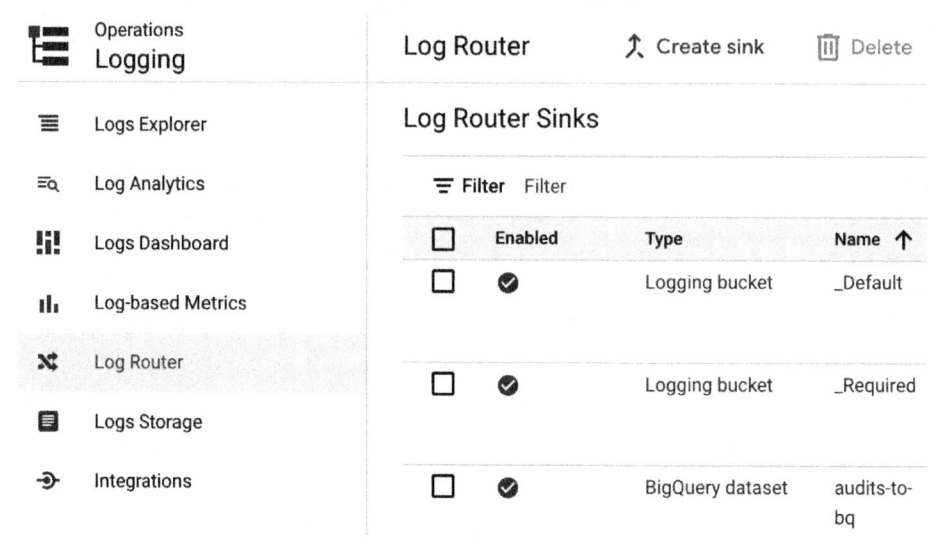

Figure 10.36 – Log Router menu in the Cloud Logging

Specifically, only to BigQuery, you can directly analyze the logs and metadata using **BigQuery Information schema**. This is a Google-managed BigQuery audit log that you can access using SQL queries. For example, you can access which user accessed BigQuery the most in the past 30 days using this SQL query:

```
SELECT
    user_email,
    COUNT(job_id) AS count_job
FROM
    `region-us`.INFORMATION_SCHEMA.JOBS
WHERE
    job_type = 'QUERY'
    AND end_time BETWEEN TIMESTAMP_SUB(CURRENT_TIMESTAMP(),
                                      INTERVAL 30 DAY)
    AND CURRENT_TIMESTAMP()
GROUP BY
    user_email
ORDER BY
    count_job DESC
LIMIT 10;
```

The preceding query will aggregate all the jobs in `region-us` by `user_email`.

There are many types of information schema tables, and they are rapidly evolving. Please check the public documentation for the full list of possibilities: https://cloud.google.com/bigquery/docs/information-schema-intro.

Understanding BigQuery information schemas is very important if you want to optimize and maintain the BigQuery environment. Make sure you spend time exploring the information schema tables and columns.

Clear data ownership

The second aspect of clear responsibilities for actions is data ownership. It's important to keep a good track of who owns the data, or in BigQuery's case, who owns the tables.

At this point, you may wonder *"Should we make any effort to know who are the data owners of each table?"* The answer is *yes*.

We should be clear that the data owners in this aspect should be the human data owners, not the GCP account. Unfortunately, we can't always track the data owners automatically using user email in the logs. Because the users that create tables most of the time would be service accounts.

For example, when we created a table in *Chapter 3, Building a Data Warehouse in BigQuery*, if we checked the logs in the BigQuery Project History, this is the log that we could see. Check out the following figure. Notice that the **User** is a service-account that we use in Cloud Composer:

Load job details

Job ID	wired-apex-392509:US.airflow_level_2_dag_load_bigquery_gcs_to_bq_example_2023_08_01T05_00_00_00_00_e0ebe65e50c3bb8f2bcbbead35c9c600
User	822672288347-compute@developer.gserviceaccount.com
Location	US
Creation time	Aug 2, 2023, 1:00:46 PM UTC+8
Start time	Aug 2, 2023, 1:00:47 PM UTC+8
End time	Aug 2, 2023, 1:00:48 PM UTC+8
Duration	1 sec
Auto-detect schema	true
Ignore unknown values	false
Source format	CSV
Max bad records	
Destination table	wired-apex-392509.raw_bikesharing.stations

Figure 10.37 – The job's user is a service account

To maintain good data ownership, you can track it using the BigQuery table's `label` or `metadata` tag, and this requires good practice. As we've discussed earlier in this chapter, good practice means the team or organization agrees and consistently follows standardized rules.

After understanding clear data ownership, let's move to data lineage in the next section.

Data lineage

Data lineage is also one of the most popular topics when people talk about data governance. The usual requirement for Data lineage is to know all the upstream dependency tables and processes to create a table in BigQuery.

There are many options that organizations can use to manage Data lineage. One of the options is to rely on ETL tools, which could be a third-party tool or GCP such as Cloud Composer, Data Fusion, or Dataprep.

The other options that are available on GCP are using Dataplex data lineage and Dataform. Dataplex data lineage is an out-of-the-box feature in BigQuery that you can access from BigQuery's table console. To use this feature, first, you need to enable the API called the **Data Lineage API**. You can find it using the GCP search box. The API screen looks like the following figure:

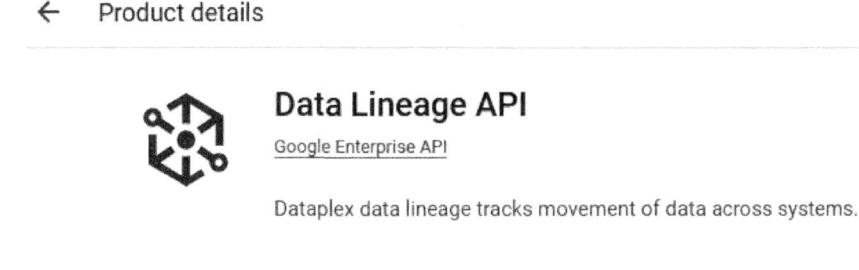

Figure 10.38 – Data Lineage API screen

After enabling the API, the Dataplex data lineage will take some time to generate the table lineage. If it's available, it will be shown under every BigQuery table or view on the **LINEAGE** tab, for example, like in the following figure:

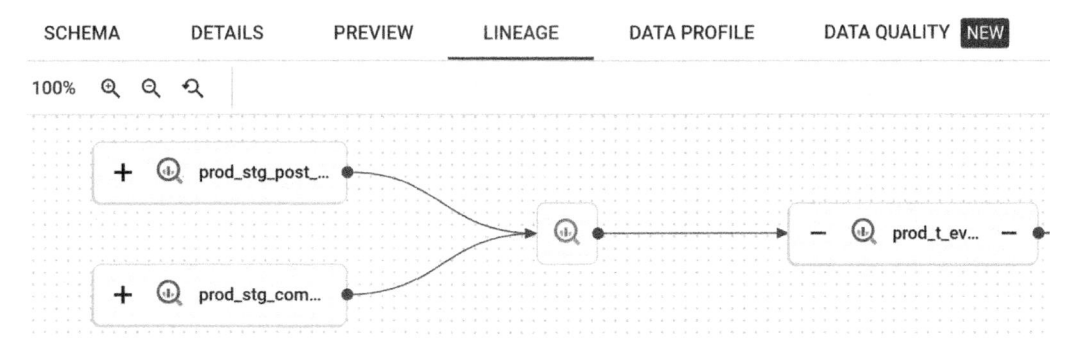

Figure 10.39 – Dataplex data lineage example

The benefit of using Dataplex data lineage is that it's automatically generated, based on queries. The downside is that because it's an automated process, sometimes it doesn't behave like what you need. To have full control of your data lineage, it's better to maintain the lineage in Dataform.

Clear data quality process

Data quality is always a hot topic of discussion in data engineering. Even though Data Quality by itself is the core of the data engineering process, it is also considered a data governance process.

To understand this aspect better, we should see the commonly mistaken perspective that an organization sees of data quality. The mistaken perspective is to see data quality from a black-and-white perspective. This means that if the users find bad-quality data, the whole data ecosystem will be labeled as bad quality. This is common because it's natural to think of it in this way. Think of a water pipeline: as the end user if we find the water that we drink is dirty, we may distrust the entire water system.

Although thinking in that manner is natural, we as the data engineer, governor, or architect, shouldn't see it in that way.

This way of thinking often leads to deciding to leave the current data system and migrate to other data technologies. The issue is when it is performed over and over again. Even though it's always easier to think in this way, this is wrong and will never end.

Managing data quality in the data ecosystem should be similar to managing bugs in software engineering. It's impossible to have no bugs in complex software, and it's impossible to have perfect data quality in a complex data ecosystem. What we should do is create a clear process and measurement.

To measure data quality on a BigQuery table, we can use Dataplex Data Quality. The process is very straightforward; please try it in your own time. You will see there are rule options that you can use to measure the table's data quality. These are the built-in rules that are available in the Dataplex Data Quality. For example, if you go to the Dataplex Data Quality menu, you will find this form to choose the columns and the standard rules to measure the data quality:

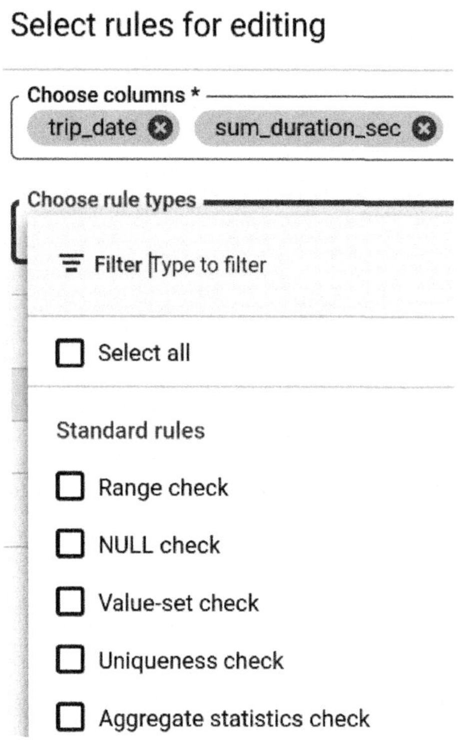

Figure 10.40 – Dataplex data Quality built-in rules

But measurement by itself is not enough, you need to have a proper testing mechanism in your data pipeline. To do this, Dataform is a great tool for enforcing and simplifying testing mechanisms. Let's understand Dataform and how it can improve the data quality process in the next exercise.

Exercise – practicing data quality using Dataform

Dataform is a platform that simplifies data transformation and management. As part of the BigQuery product family, Dataform natively supports BigQuery SQL. Dataform provides a collaborative development environment, version control, and automated orchestration to ensure data pipelines are reliable, maintainable, and scalable.

The most common question when people hear about Dataform is how it differs from Dataflow and Cloud Composer.

The positioning of Dataform is different compared to both of those tools. To understand better, let's see this ELT flow and the numbering that I will use to explain the Dataform positioning:

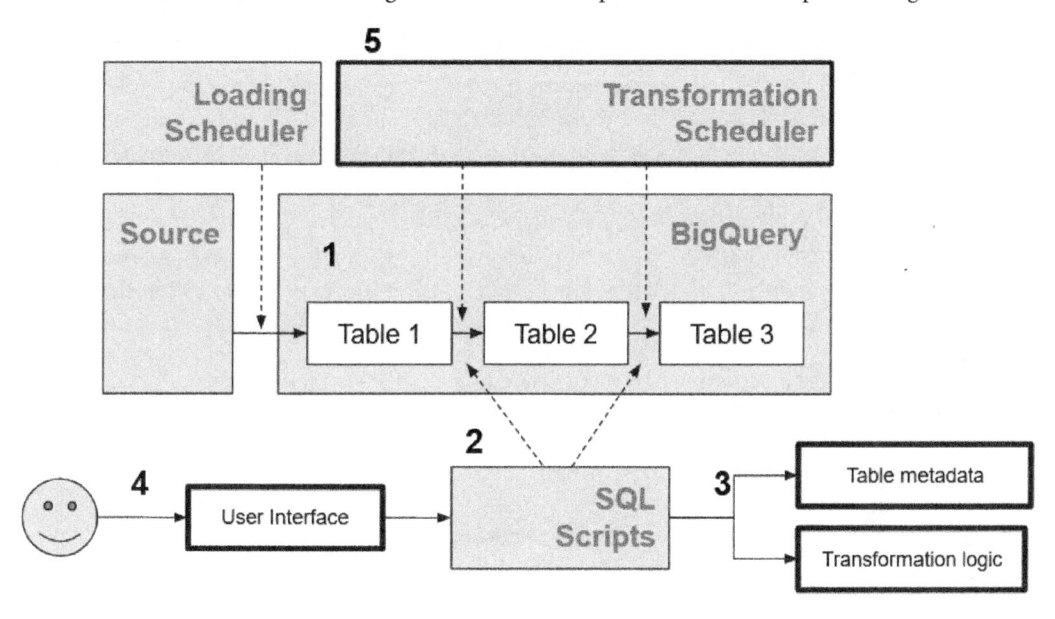

Figure 10.41 – High-level ELT flow with BigQuery

Looking at the diagram, there are five main ELT flows. I will use the flows to explain how Dataform fits in the process:

1. First, as you've learned, data in BigQuery may come from many different data sources. The process is called **data extraction** and **data loading**. After the data has been loaded into BigQuery, certain data transformations will occur.
2. The data in BigQuery tables can be transformed using Dataflow, Dataproc, or other tools, but most of the time it will be transformed using BigQuery SQL scripts.

3. The scripts contain the table's metadata and the transformation logic. This is the positioning of Dataform. Dataform helps BigQuery SQL developers manage SQL scripts. We will learn how it manages SQL scripts in the upcoming sections. But at this point, we understand that Dataform doesn't process data like Dataflow or Dataproc. The process will still happen using BigQuery computation.

4. The scripts are written by SQL developers. How do SQL developers usually write the SQL scripts? The answer is there are many different ways, they can use BigQuery console, text editor, code in Airflow format, or many other possibilities. Dataform helps standardize this by providing a specific user interface for developing SQL. The console is different from the BigQuery console, the console is equipped with many helpful features for practicing **Git operations** (**GitOps**). As you may already know, practicing GitOps is very important for managing code in a complex and big organization, for example, for version control and release management.

5. From the scheduler point of view, Dataform also has a scheduler feature to run the SQL scripts at a scheduled time. However, the Dataform scheduler won't handle the scheduling other than the SQL transformations, meaning the extraction and loading schedulers should happen outside of Dataform, which is often handled by Cloud Composer. This Dataform scheduling feature is optional. We can still use Cloud Composer to manage the Dataform run. This option is beneficial if you want to maintain the event-driven architecture using Cloud Composer as we've practiced in *Chapter 4, Building Workflows for Batch Data Loading Using Cloud Composer*. Remember from the last exercise, we don't use the scheduler to start downstream tasks but use sensors.

After understanding the positioning of Dataform and how it differs from the other services, let's drill deeper into what is inside the Dataform environment.

Understanding Dataform environment

As a Dataform user, we need to create an environment before using it for our development. The first thing that we need to understand is that Dataform is not a simple tool. It's a sophisticated platform emphasizing the GitOps practice. It usually requires proper planning between lead data engineers or DevOps or solution architect teams to agree with the sets of rules and operations.

But those roles are usually not the end users. The end users may be the data engineering team, the data analysts team, or in more modern data organizations, it's common to call them analytics engineers. If the Dataform rules and operations are configured properly, the end user will find it very easy because they only need to write common BigQuery SQL queries.

Check out this diagram to understand what is inside the Dataform illustration and how it relates to the Git environment:

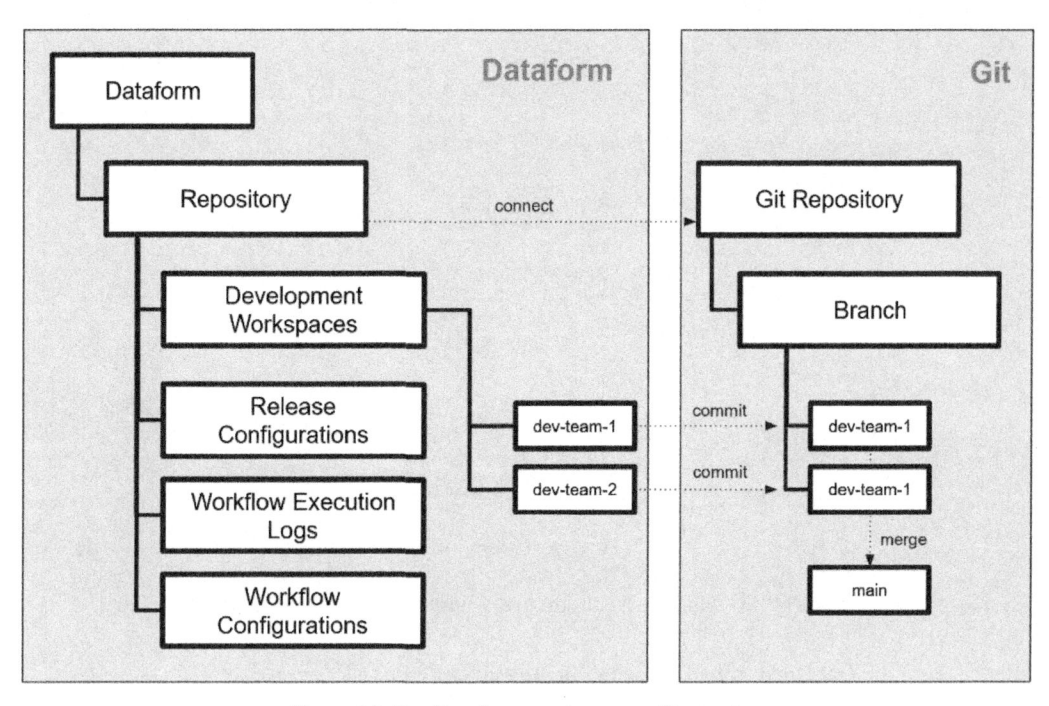

Figure 10.42 – Dataform environment illustration

Dataform has a high-level object called the repository. The Dataform repository should be connected one-to-one to a Git repository, for example, GitHub, Gitlab, or any other supported Git provider.

Inside the Dataform repository, you should create development workspaces. One development workspace is usually created for one individual team member or one development team. The workspaces will be mapped automatically one-to-one to Git branches.

When a set of SQL queries has been developed by the team, it needs to be wrapped into releases, which can be managed by release configurations. Releases can be driven by versions, tags, or in any other way. At each release, Dataform will compile the SQL code and produce the final BigQuery scripts to be run.

The final object in Dataform is the workflow. Workflows manage releases' runs. For example, you can monitor the logs under **Workflow Execution Logs**. Optionally, you can schedule the release runs using Dataform under **Workflow Configurations**.

Creating a Dataform environment

After understanding the Dataform environment, let's create the Dataform objects. You can find the Dataform console in the **BigQuery** navigation menu:

354　　Data Governance in GCP

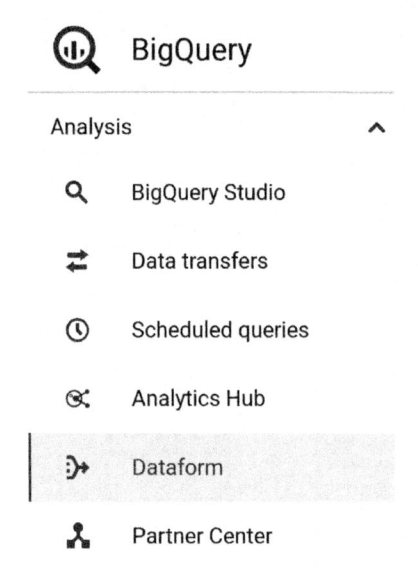

Figure 10.43 – Find the Dataform menu under the BigQuery console

After clicking the **Dataform** menu and enabling the API, please follow these steps:

1. Create a new Dataform repository.

   First, create a new Dataform repository. For this exercise, I will name our repository `dataform-repo-1` in the `us-central1` region using the default Dataform service account.

   After clicking the **CREATE** button, you will see this message:

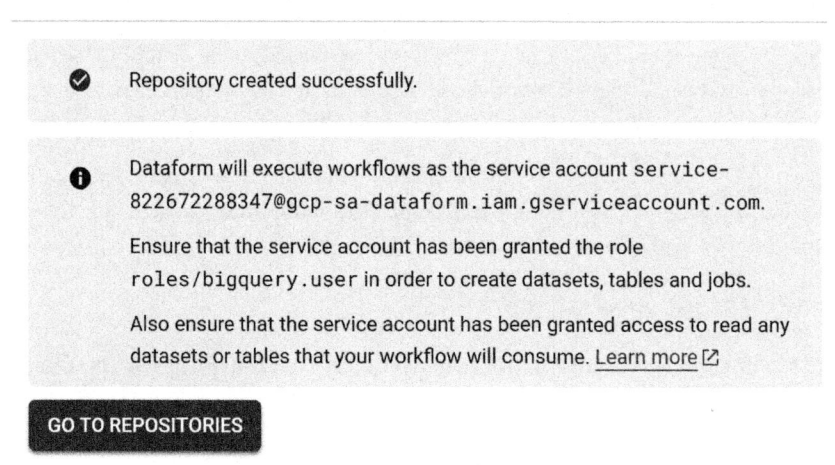

Figure 10.44 – The result after creating the Dataform Repository

Notice the service account that is shown in the message. We need to grant IAM roles to that service account.

2. Assign BigQuery roles to the Dataform service account.

   To do that, go to the IAM console from the GCP navigation menu. Assign two roles to the Dataform service account:

   - BigQuery user
   - BigQuery Data Owner

   The IAM screen looks like the following screenshot:

Add principals

Principals are users, groups, domains, or service accounts. Learn more about principals in IAM

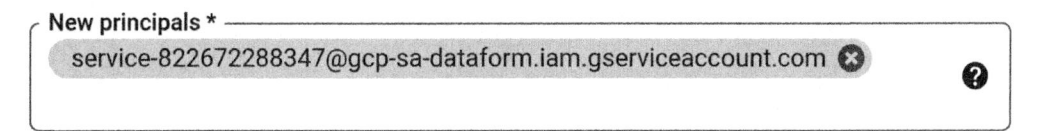

New principals *

service-822672288347@gcp-sa-dataform.iam.gserviceaccount.com

Assign roles

Roles are composed of sets of permissions and determine what the principal can do with this resource. Learn more

Role *
BigQuery User

When applied to a project, access to run queries, create datasets, read dataset metadata, and list tables. When applied to a dataset, access to read dataset metadata and list tables within the dataset.

IAM condition (optional)
+ ADD IAM CONDITION

Role
BigQuery Data Owner

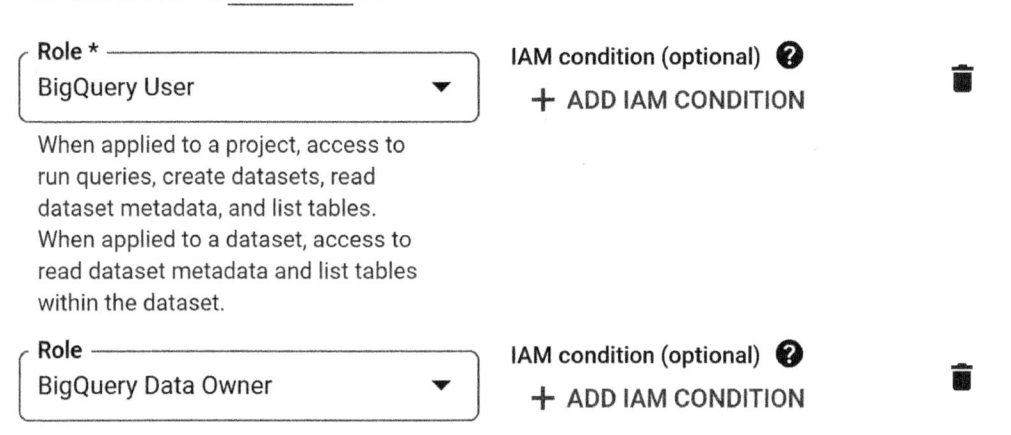

IAM condition (optional)
+ ADD IAM CONDITION

Figure 10.45 – Add the IAM roles to the Dataform service account

You need to make sure this is configured correctly before going to the next step.

3. Create a development workspace and initiate an initial Dataform project.

Now go back to the Dataform console and create a new development workspace. For example, my workspace is called `developer-1`.

If you click the workspace that you created, find the button to start initiating the Dataform project. After clicking the button, you will see the folder and files containing the Dataform files. This is what your Dataform console screen looks like:

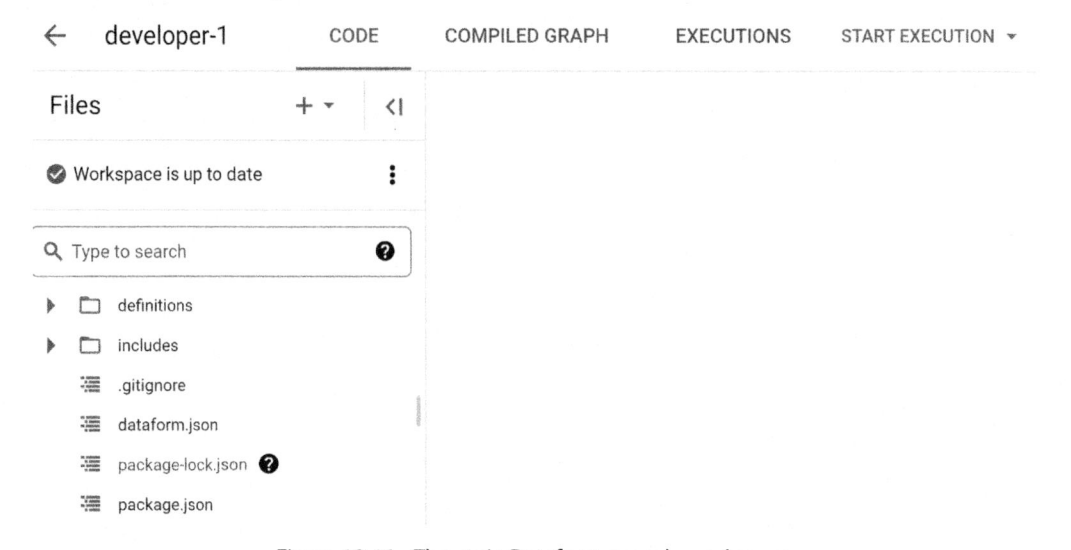

Figure 10.46 – The main Dataform console workspace

Take time to become familiar will all the menus and check the Dataform files using the `.sqlx` extension.

For example, in the initial project, you will see there are two `.sqlx` files in the `definitions` folder. Those two files will create two BigQuery views called `first_view` and `second_view`. When Dataform compiles and executes these files, it will automatically create views by using the SQL logic scripted in the files.

Now remember that Dataform is a Git tool, meaning that to start saving the entire new folder and files, we need to push the code. We will do this by clicking the **COMMIT CHANGES** button at the top of the file's directory.

You will be prompted with the **New commit** screen, check every file to add all the files:

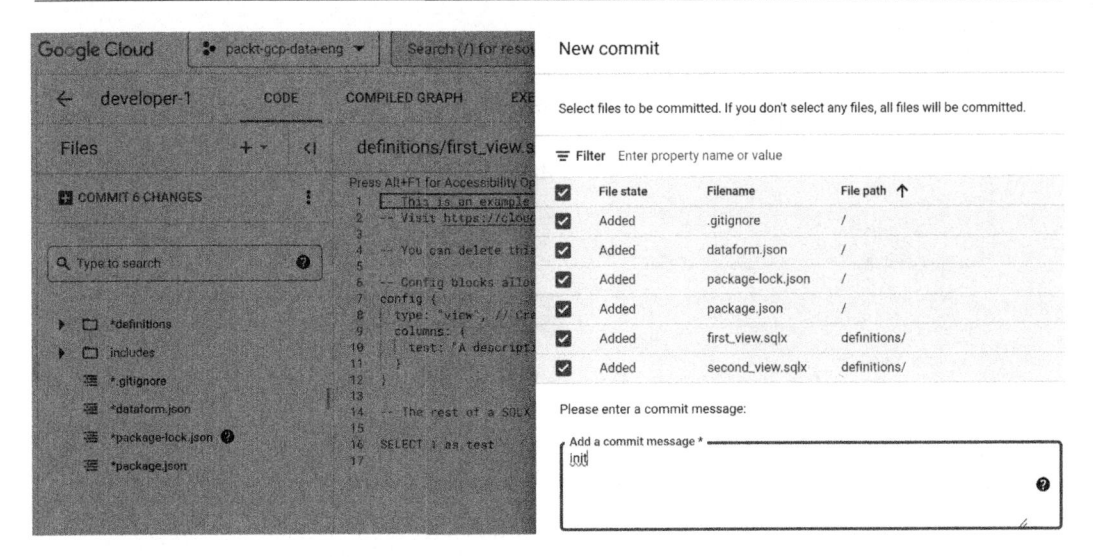

Figure 10.47 – The first Dataform commit

Complete the process by giving the commit message, clicking the **COMMIT ALL FILES** button, and clicking the **PUSH TO DEFAULT BRANCH** button.

Always remember those steps, because they are the essential steps to save and push your development files to the Git repository.

4. Create a Dataform release and compile it.

   Next, we will try to create a Dataform release. To do that, go back to the Dataform main page and click the **RELEASE CONFIGURATIONS** tab. Create a new release, and here is my configuration:

   - **Release ID**: `release-1`
   - **Frequency**: `Daily`
   - **Compilation overrides Project ID**: `wired-apex-392509`
   - **Schema suffix**: `stackoverflow`
   - **Table prefix**: `prod`

   Click **CREATE**, and after it's created, click `release-1` to go to the detail page, which looks like this:

358 Data Governance in GCP

release-1

Git commitish	main
Last compilation time	Unknown
Cron schedule	0 7 * * *
Time zone	Asia/Singapore
Compilation overrides	
Default database	wired-apex-392509
Schema suffix	stackoverflow
Table prefix	prod
Compilation variables	None

Live compilation result

8dada108-36c4-4ba4-8022-3b8ed9876a9a

Created	Unknown
Git commitish	main

↻ NEW COMPILATION

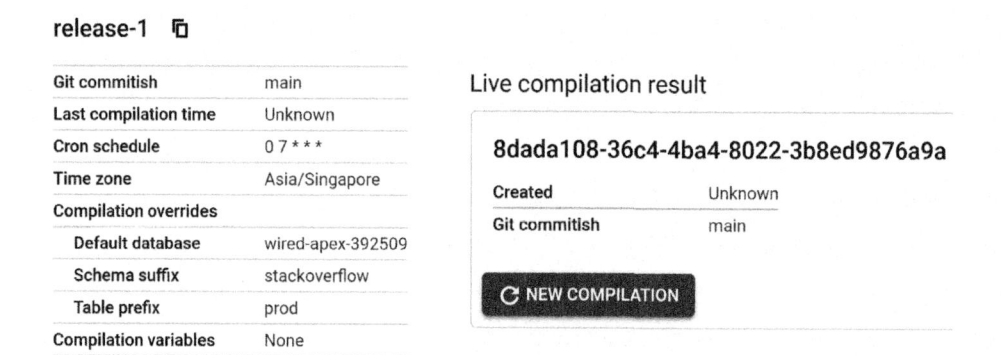

Figure 10.48 – Find the NEW COMPILATION button to compile

Notice the **NEW COMPILATION** button. This is an important button to remember.

First, let's understand what the **Frequency** in this release configuration is. The **Frequency** parameter is how many times Dataform should compile the code. Compile in Dataform means it will read our `Dataform` folder and files and if there are no code errors, Dataform will package the code as a release. This compiled release will not be executed in any way.

Now, back to the **NEW COMPILATION** button. This button is important for our development exercise because you need to click this button every time you push new development code to make sure that when we execute the code, it will execute the latest compiled release. If we don't do that, the next compilation is determined by the **Frequency** parameter.

5. Execute the Dataform release.

   To execute the release, you can go back to the **RELEASE CONFIGURATIONS** tab and click **START EXECUTION**. Choose the release that we created. The screen looks like this:

   Execute manual workflow

   Execute all actions, or select a subset of actions. Service account **service-822672288347@gcp-sa-dataform.iam.gserviceaccount.com** will be used.
   Learn more ↗

   Release configuration *
   release-1

   | ALL ACTIONS | SELECTION OF ACTIONS | SELECTION OF TAGS |

   Execution options

   ☐ Run with full refresh

   2 actions selected for execution

Destination	Type	File
wired-apex-392509.dataform_stackoverflow.prod_first_view	View	

   Figure 10.49 – Execute the release page in Dataform

Make sure you see the execution plan that says **2 actions selected for execution**. Click the **START EXECUTION** button to start the execution.

6. Check the Workflow Execution logs.

   You can check the execution logs on the **WORKFLOW EXECUTION LOGS** tab.

Status	Start time	Duration	Source Type	Source	Contents
✓	Nov 13, 2023, 3:06:51 PM	7 seconds	Release configuration		All actions

   Figure 10.50 – The execution logs under WORKFLOW EXECUTION LOGS

   If there are errors, check the error message and make sure you've followed all the steps correctly. If the execution is successful, go and check the BigQuery views that are created.

7. Check the BigQuery dataset.

   Now go back to your BigQuery console and check whether the new BigQuery dataset and views have been created according to the SQLX files that we pushed from Dataform:

   - dataform_stackoverflow
     - prod_first_view
     - prod_second_view

   Figure 10.51 – Find the views result in BigQuery

   If you have been successful, that is all that you need to understand about the end-to-end development process of Dataform.

To summarize, please remember these five steps for editing new code in Dataform:

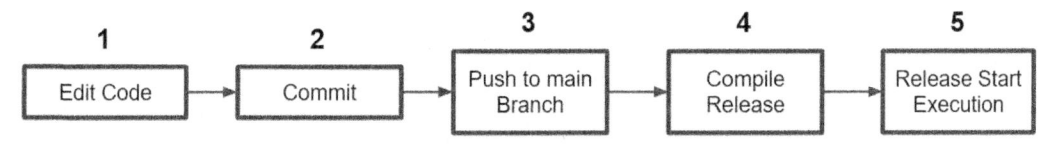

1. Edit Code → 2. Commit → 3. Push to main Branch → 4. Compile Release → 5. Release Start Execution

Figure 10.52 – The five steps to execute Dataform code

In the next scenario exercise, every time we need to add or change code, you need to remember to do all these five steps.

Create data transformation in Dataform using BigQuery public dataset

Now, let's practice developing Dataform code to create new BigQuery objects. We will use a scenario where we will transform data from two tables from a public BigQuery dataset: `stackoverflow`. Please check out the end-to-end plan:

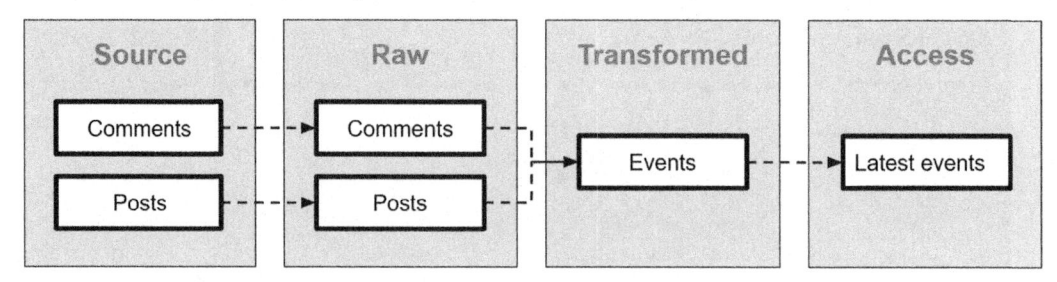

Figure 10.53 – Table flows design for the Dataform exercise

We will use the Dataform environment that we have created. You can see the final code in this repository: https://github.com/PacktPublishing/Data-Engineering-with-Google-Cloud-Platform-Second-Edition/tree/main/chapter-10. But if you want to learn the step-by-step process, please follow these steps:

1. Create a Dataform directory structure.

    Go to the workspace's folder and create the following new folders in the `definitions` folder: `stackoverflow`, `access`, `source`, `stg`, `transformed`:

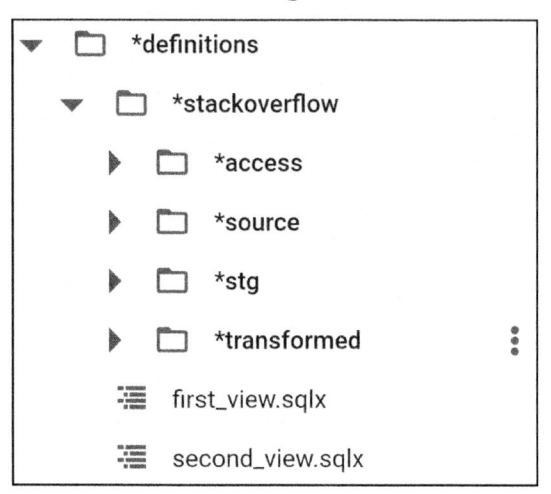

Figure 10.54 – The folder structure under definitions

The `definitions` folder is always the root folder in Dataform projects. We created new folders for our `.sqlx` files.

2. Declare the sources from the BigQuery public dataset.

   Let's declare the data sources. To do that, in the `source` folder, create a file named `comments.sqlx`.

   These are the contents of the file:

   ```
   config {
       type: "declaration",
       database: "bigquery-public-data",
       schema: "stackoverflow",
       name: "comments",
   }
   ```

   The file is a simple JSON format to declare our `stackoverflow.comments` data source. Please do the same process to create the second data source for another table from `bigquery-public-data.stackoverflow.post_history`.

3. Develop the staging layer.

   Now we will develop the staging files. To do this, create a new file named `stg_comments.sqlx` in the `stg` folder. The content looks like this:

   ```
   config {
       type: "table"
   }

   SELECT *
   FROM ${ref("comments_src")}
   LIMIT 1000
   ```

   This file tells Dataform to create a table named `stg_comments` using the SQL script that we define in the `stg_comments.sqlx` file. Notice that the table name is formatted using the `ref` function, which is the standard in Dataform. You need to always use `ref` instead of the actual BigQuery table name in Dataform. This is to make sure the integration and lineage are always maintained properly.

   After creating the file, create your own file named `stg_post_history`, follow the same process, and don't forget to set `LIMIT 1000` to make sure our exercise won't cost too much.

4. Develop the transformation layer.

   Next, we will create a new file named `t_events.sqlx` in the `transformed` folder. The logic is to combine the two tables into a single event table. The file looks like this:

   ```
   config {
       type: "table"
   }

   SELECT
     CONCAT("c_",id) as event_id,
   ```

```
      creation_date,
      "comment" as event_type,
      user_id,
      text
    FROM ${ref("stg_comments")}
    UNION ALL
    SELECT
      CONCAT("p_",id) as event_id,
      creation_date,
      "post" as event_type
      user_id,
      text
    FROM ${ref("stg_post_history")}
```

That will be all the files that we need for the transformed layer.

5. Develop the access layer.

    The last file that we will create is the access layer. Let's create a new file in the `access` folder and name it `access_latest_events.sqlx`. The content looks like this:

    ```
    config {
        type: "view"
    }
    SELECT *
    FROM ${ref("t_events")}
    ORDER BY creation_date
    LIMIT 5
    ```

6. Accessing the compiled graph feature.

    To make sure the lineage is as we expected, we can click the **COMPILED GRAPH** tab. You can see the that lineage is automatically created in the following screenshot:

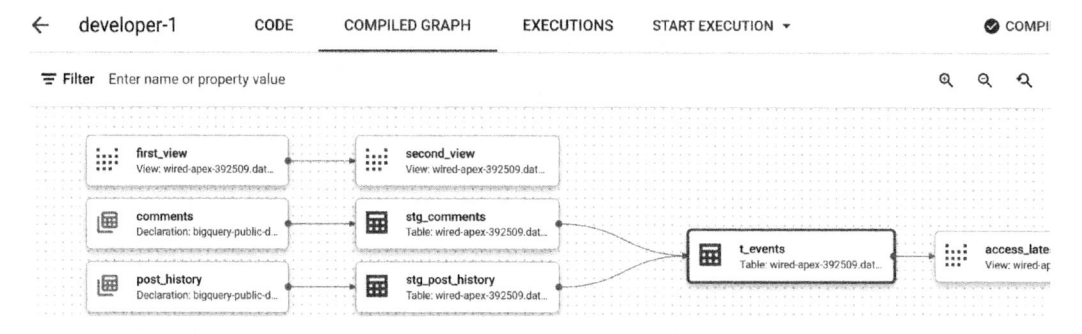

Figure 10.55 – Dataform compiled graph

At this point, you need to save and run it. To do it, don't forget the five steps to edit Dataform code.

7. Execute the new StackOverflow project code.

   If you are following the steps, to check what you have before executing the release, here are the actions to be executed:

   8 actions selected for execution

Destination	Type
bigquery-public-data.stackoverflow.comments	Declaration
bigquery-public-data.stackoverflow.post_history	Declaration
wired-apex-392509.dataform_stackoverflow.prod_access...	View
wired-apex-392509.dataform_stackoverflow.prod_first_view	View
wired-apex-392509.dataform_stackoverflow.prod_second...	View
wired-apex-392509.dataform_stackoverflow.prod_stg_co...	Table
wired-apex-392509.dataform_stackoverflow.prod_stg_pos...	Table

   START EXECUTION   CANCEL

   Figure 10.56 – Execute all the new tables and views

   There will be eight actions, including views and tables that will be created in BigQuery. Go and check your BigQuery dataset to make sure all the tables and views have been created as planned.

8. Improve the code to implement data governance practices.

   After understanding the development process, we will try to improve data governance practices using Dataform. We can do that by scripting a good quality code. For example, we will improve the `transformed.t_events.sqlx` file.

   The plan is to improve by doing the following:

   - Create the table in a specified BigQuery dataset
   - Add table and column descriptions
   - Add data owners as labels
   - Define BigQuery partition column
   - Provide data testing using assertions

   Those improvements are very simple to do in the code. You will understand this by seeing the full code here: https://github.com/PacktPublishing/Data-Engineering-with-Google-Cloud-Platform-Second-Edition/tree/main/chapter-10/code/dataform/definitions/stackoverflow/transformed/t_events.sqlx.

Try to implement it in your code, and as always, do the five steps for editing new code in Dataform, which was explained in the section *Creating a Dataform environment* to push and compile the code.

9. Execute the new code using the full refresh option.

   When you are about to execute the release, find and check the execution options for **Run with full refresh**. This option is to ask Dataform to fully recreate all tables and views. We need to do this because we want to move our table to a new dataset. The release configuration looks like the following figure:

   Figure 10.57 – Finding the full refresh checkbox when executing the job

   Finish the step by running the execution.

10. Understanding the result.

    In the BigQuery console, check if the table is now created as a partitioned table in a dedicated dataset.

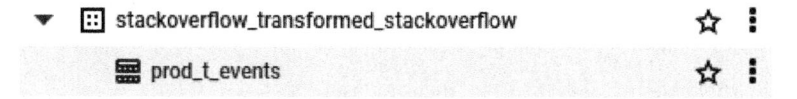

    Figure 10.58 – The table result has been recreated

    If you go to the columns, you will see all rows have a description:

A deeper understanding of being accountable 365

	Field name	Type	Mode	Key	Collation	Default Value	Policy Tags	Description
☐	event_id	STRING	NULLABLE					Unique event id
☐	creation_date	TIMESTAMP	NULLABLE					Event timestamp
☐	event_type	STRING	NULLABLE					Description of the third column
☐	user_id	INTEGER	NULLABLE					User's id
☐	text	STRING	NULLABLE					The event's full free form text

Figure 10.59 – The rows contain descriptions

If you go to the table **DETAILS**, you will also see the labels that have the data owner's information:

prod_t_events

This is a partitioned table.

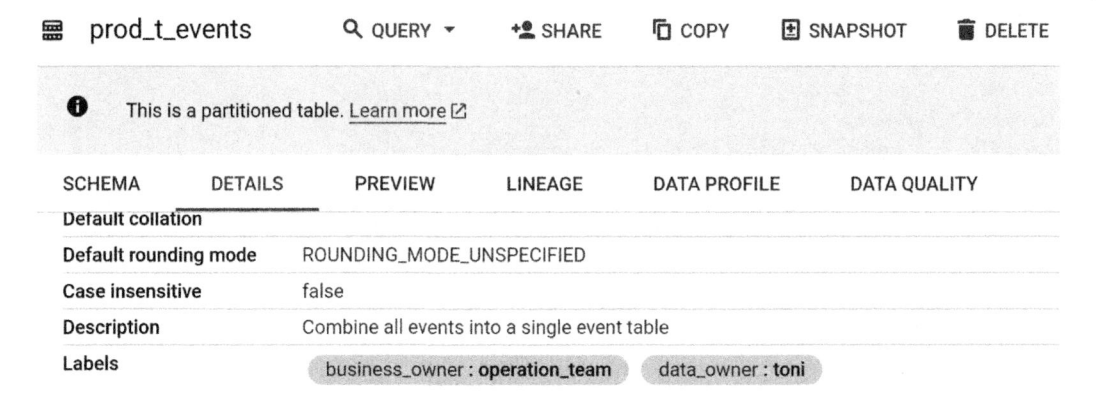

Default collation	
Default rounding mode	ROUNDING_MODE_UNSPECIFIED
Case insensitive	false
Description	Combine all events into a single event table
Labels	business_owner : operation_team data_owner : toni

Figure 10.60 – Labels have been assigned to the table

11. Testing how the unit test works.

   Lastly, let's try to intentionally change the SQL logic to make it fail the test. For example, for our `transformed.t_events.sqlx` files, we will change `event_id` to a static value, 1, in the SQL query:

   ```
   SELECT
   "1" as event_id,
   creation_date,
   "comment" as event_type,
   user_id,
   text
   FROM ${ref("stg_comments")}
   ```

If you run all the processes when you run the release execution, you will see the error logs:

Status	Start time ↑	Duration	Action	Destination	Details
✓	Nov 13, 2023, 4:00:06 PM	1 second	prod_first_view	wired-apex-392509.dataform_stackoverflow...	VIEW DETAILS
✓	Nov 13, 2023, 4:00:06 PM	2 seconds	prod_stg_post_history	wired-apex-392509.dataform_stackoverflow...	VIEW DETAILS
✓	Nov 13, 2023, 4:00:06 PM	2 seconds	prod_stg_comments	wired-apex-392509.dataform_stackoverflow...	VIEW DETAILS
✓	Nov 13, 2023, 4:00:09 PM	1 second	prod_second_view	wired-apex-392509.dataform_stackoverflow...	VIEW DETAILS
✓	Nov 13, 2023, 4:00:10 PM	6 seconds	prod_t_events	wired-apex-392509.stackoverflow_transfor...	VIEW DETAILS
❗	Nov 13, 2023, 4:00:18 PM	3 seconds	prod_stackoverflow_transformed_t_events_...	wired-apex-392509.dataform_assertions_st...	VIEW DETAILS
✓	Nov 13, 2023, 4:00:18 PM	1 second	prod_access_latest_events	wired-apex-392509.dataform_stackoverflow...	VIEW DETAILS

Figure 10.61 – The table shows the error status

If you click **VIEW DETAILS**, you can see the error message:

Nov 13, 2023, 4:00:18 PM

Status	❗ Failed
Start time	Nov 13, 2023, 4:00:18 PM
Duration	3 seconds
Executed as	service-822672288347@gcp-sa-dataform.iam.gserviceaccount.com
Failure reason	reason:"invalidQuery" location:"query" message:"Query error: Assertion failed, expected zero rows. at [27:5]": invalid argument

Figure 10.62 – The table error message

The error message says **Assertion failed, expected zero rows**. This is saying that there should be no duplicate values in the `event_id` column.

With that, we have completed our exercise using Dataform. As you can see, Dataform is a very sophisticated platform that helps enforce good practices. Enforcing good practices in our code is one of the key successes in implementing good data governance.

Summary

In this chapter, we learned about data governance. We started with a general understanding of data governance, where there are many aspects of data governance. To simplify it, we classified these aspects into three pillars: Usability, Security, and Accountability. Using these pillars, we then drill down deeper to understand the principles, the tools, and the practice of implementing them.

To better understand data usability, we learned that we need to make sure the data products that we have created are easy to use, which includes making the data easy to find and easy to understand. We then learn how to use Dataplex search and metadata tagging to support the requirements.

We then moved on to data security, which consists of two main parts, data encryption and data protection. We learned how to manage access control in BigQuery up to the column level using taxonomy and data policies. We also learned how to use SDP to find the sensitive data in our datasets.

Then we looked at a big pillar: accountability. We learned that every event and action that happens in our data ecosystem should be traceable. We learned that this is not difficult to achieve in GCP using Cloud Logging and BigQuery information schemas. Lastly, we closed the chapter by looking at an important platform, Dataform, that helps us manage data quality and enforce good practices for a successful data governance implementation.

In the upcoming chapter, we will explore a practice known as **Continuous Integration** and **Continuous Deployment (CI/CD)**. We will demonstrate its application through exercises using Cloud Composer, illustrating how to perform automated testing before deploying Airflow DAG.

11
Cost Strategy in GCP

This chapter will cover one of the most frequently asked questions from stakeholders – how much does a solution cost running in GCP? Each GCP service has different pricing mechanisms. In this chapter, we will look at what valuable information you will need to calculate the GCP costs.

On top of that, we will have a section dedicated to BigQuery. We will discuss the difference between two options for the BigQuery pricing models – on-demand and editions. Finally, we will revisit the two important features in BigQuery: partitioned tables and clustered tables. Understanding these features can optimize a lot of your future costs in BigQuery.

The following topics will be covered in this chapter:

- Estimating the cost of your end-to-end data solution in GCP
- Tips to optimize BigQuery using partitioned and clustered tables

Technical requirements

For this chapter's exercises, we will use BigQuery and GCP pricing calculators from the internet, which you can open using any browser.

Estimating the cost of your end-to-end data solution in GCP

While trying out the exercises in this book, we briefly discussed the costs that might be incurred when using various GCP services. You may have already been billed for some of the resources, so you may be wondering, *"How much will they cost in a full production system?"* This question is important and is often asked by stakeholders.

As a data engineer, it would be great if you could estimate the end-to-end data solution cost upfront. To estimate the cost in GCP, first, we need to understand that not all GCP services use the same pricing calculation.

> **Note**
> The pricing model that's described in this book is based on the latest information at the time of writing. Google Cloud can change the pricing model for any service at any time.

There are three types of pricing models:

Virtual Machine (VM)-based: There are GCP resources that are billed with the VMs. The bills that are generated by the machines have three factors:

The number of VMs

- The machine size and types (vCPU, memory, or disk)
- The total hours

For example, we used Dataproc in *Chapter 5, Building a Data Lake Using Dataproc*. Dataproc uses this pricing model. We choose the number of workers, the worker size that contributes directly to the cost per worker, and how long to use Dataproc for, from creating it to deleting it. The term *nodes* in Dataproc refers to machines or **Google Cloud Engine** (**GCE**) instances. The actual usage is not a factor in this model. So long as Dataproc is active, even if you never use it, it will still count toward the bills.

As a summary, the formula is as follows:

Cost = Number of workers x Cost per worker x Total hours

Here is the list of data-related GCP services that use this pricing calculation:

- Cloud Composer
- Dataflow
- Dataproc

Given the nature of this pricing model, some automatic optimization has been released by every different service over time. For example, Cloud Composer now has Cloud Composer 2, which introduced auto-scaling for its number of workers. This gives a lot of benefits to users who can lower the Compute Engine costs, but note that the pricing formulas are usually more complex.

- **Usage-based**: Another pricing model is the usage-based model. The factor that affects the bills is usage. The definition of *usage* differs from one service to another. For example, for **Google Cloud Storage** (**GCS**), the definition of usage is the total amount of storage that's used.

  Here is the list of data-related GCP services that use this pricing calculation:

    - GCS
    - Pub/Sub
    - BigQuery on-demand
    - BigQuery storage

- **Commitment**: Lastly, some services use a commitment model. Commitment means that you are committed to purchasing a fixed amount of resources in a fixed amount of time.

    In this book, we haven't tried this model. The main target for this model is usually an enterprise organization that requires more predictable costs for a large amount of committed resources.

    There are not many services under this model; however, it's a very important model to understand if you work with an enterprise. One of the most important examples is the BigQuery edition.

Understanding these three pricing models will give you an idea of what should be considered when estimating each of the GCP services.

Out of all these GCP services, BigQuery is unique in that you, as a user, can choose the pricing model. We will discuss this in the next section.

Comparing BigQuery on-demand and editions

BigQuery's pricing is more complicated compared to most of the other GCP services. BigQuery has two main pricing areas – compute and storage. There are also pricing areas for BigQuery complementary services – for example, ingestion, BI Engine, extraction, and BigQuery ML. Each of these areas has different terms and conditions. You can check out the full details by looking at the public documentation: https://cloud.google.com/bigquery/pricing.

I will use the next section to talk specifically about analysis pricing. Compared to the other areas, analysis pricing is usually the major cost contributor. However, at the same time, this is an area that has many optimization opportunities. Let's first take a look at BigQuery on-demand.

BigQuery on-demand

The on-demand model is based on the number of bytes that are processed for each query. For example, let's say you have a table named `transaction`, and its size is 10 GB. Now, let's say that a user runs the following query:

```
SELECT * FROM transaction;
```

This query will cost 10 GB multiplied by the BigQuery cost per TB. The BigQuery cost per TB is different for each region. For example, in the US, it costs $6.25 per TB. You can check the public documentation for the cost in other locations here: https://cloud.google.com/bigquery/pricing#on_demand_pricing.

Back to the example – if there are 100 users, where each of the users runs the same query and each of the users runs the query once a day, in a month, the cost will be as follows:

cost = (10GB / 1,000)TB x 100 users x 30 days x $6.25

The monthly cost for BigQuery on-demand, based on its usage, will be **$187.5**.

BigQuery editions

BigQuery editions were introduced by Google Cloud in early 2023. They are a replacement for the prior BigQuery pricing model called **flat-rate**. Compared to the on-demand or flat-rate pricing model, which is only for the price of BigQuery compute, editions come with bundles of features and quotas. This enables enterprise users to plan usage, features, and costs better.

Since the pricing covers BigQuery feature bundling and many other things, I'm pretty sure the editions model is evolving. It's better to check the public documentation for the detailed bundles and pricing at this link: `https://cloud.google.com/bigquery/docs/editions-intro#editions_features`.

What we want to focus on in this section is how BigQuery editions affect our data engineering works. This can be divided into the following three parts:

How will they affect the BigQuery query's performance

- Understanding the BigQuery slots autoscaling
- How much the cost of queries is

Let's start with the first part.

How will they affect the BigQuery query's performance

First, we need to understand BigQuery slots. A BigQuery slot is the smallest processing unit in BigQuery. It represents virtual CPUs and memory. Every query in BigQuery needs slots.

The number of slots that are required for each query depends on the data's size and the query's complexity. Check out the public documentation if you want to learn more about how BigQuery slots work: `https://cloud.google.com/bigquery/docs/slots`.

To simplify the understanding of slots, let me give you an example. Imagine one slot as having 1 CPU core and 1 GB of memory. For example, if a query runs for 5 seconds and needs 10 slots constantly, the total query computation requirement is 10 CPU cores and 10 GB of memory for 5 seconds. The actual number of CPU cores and memory per slot is not known, and it's not important for the users.

After understanding this example, we can now compare what the difference between BigQuery on-demand and BigQuery editions is. The BigQuery on-demand slots per project is a static number, which is 2,000 slots. This can't be changed at all.

BigQuery editions are more flexible on the total slots per project, which can range from 0 to much more than 2,000, depending on the region's quota, and they can be checked at this link: `https://cloud.google.com/bigquery/quotas#reservations`. This is usually an indicator that organizations need to switch from on-demand pricing to editions. If the query workload in BigQuery gets slower, it means it requires more than 2,000 slots. This is an indication that the organization needs to start exploring BigQuery editions.

In another case, when you are in a situation where you work for a company or a project that decides to use BigQuery editions, it is also possible that the number of slots in a GCP project is fewer than 2,000. This is important to know to understand how to improve your overall query performance in BigQuery, which oftentimes can be improved immediately just by increasing the slots in a GCP project.

At this point, you may be wondering, why do some GCP projects have fewer slots when using BigQuery editions? This can be understood by understanding one of the main features in BigQuery editions, which is slots autoscaling. Let's take a look at that in the next section.

Understanding the BigQuery slots autoscaling

To understand BigQuery slots autoscaling, let's first get familiar with the terminologies in BigQuery capacity management. You can find the BigQuery **Capacity Management** menu in the BigQuery console. Take a look at the following screenshot; the menu is located under the **Administration** section in the BigQuery console:

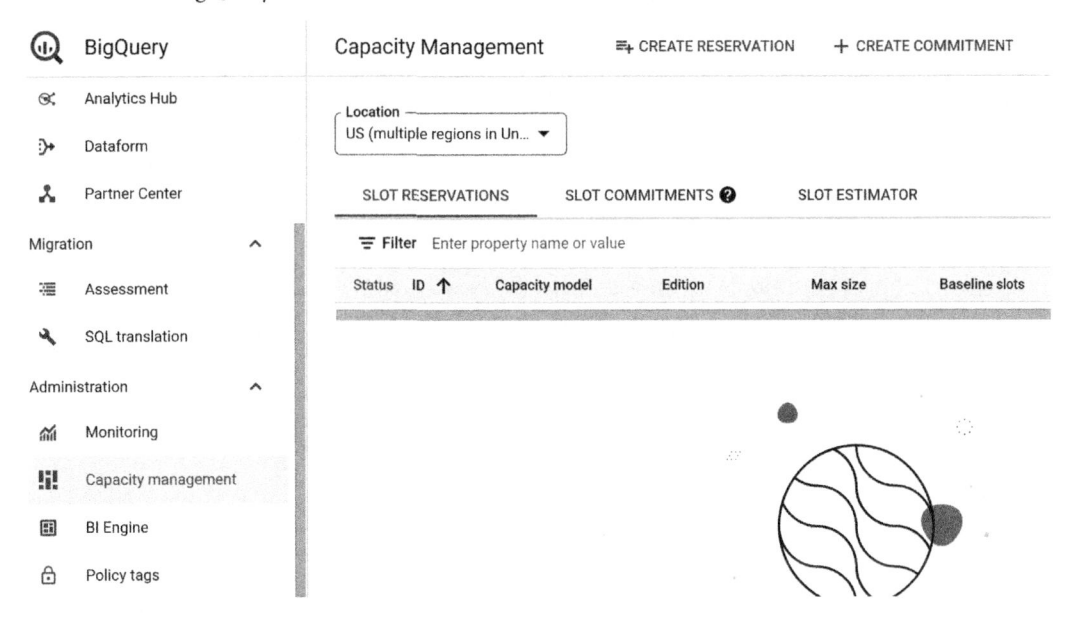

Figure 11.1 – BigQuery Capacity management menu

There are six important terminologies – **SLOTS RESERVATIONS**, **SLOT COMMITMENT**, **Slot Assignment**, **Baseline slots**, **Autoscale slots**, and **Max reservation size**.

Slots Reservations is the main object that you need to create in order to start a BigQuery edition. In the slot reservation, you can define the **Max reservation size** and **Baseline slots**, as shown in this screenshot of the **Create reservation** page:

Create reservation

Reservation settings

Reservation name *
test

Location *
us (multiple regions in United States)

Edition *
Enterprise

Max reservation size selector * | **Max reservation size**
Small (100 Slots) | 100

The reservation's maximum available slots, excluding commitments.

Baseline slots
0

Baseline is the minimum number of slots used by the reservation until this figure is changed (will not autoscale). Slots can be reserved in increments of 100, and less than max reservation size.

Additional information

Capacity summary

Edition	Max reservation size	Baseline slots
Enterprise	100	0

Cost estimate

Rate (list prices):	$0.06 slot/hour
Baseline Slots:	0
Autoscale Slots:	100
Max Slots:	100

Cost per month

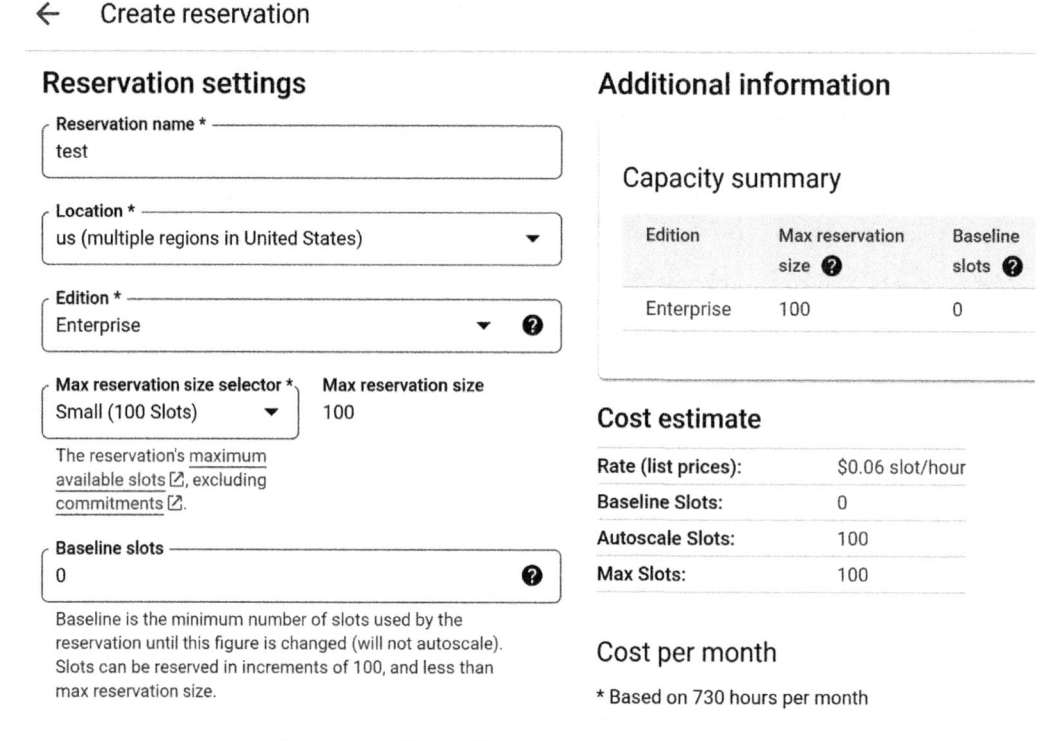

* Based on 730 hours per month

Figure 11.2 – The BigQuery Create reservation menu

Based on the **Max reservation size selector** and **Baseline slots** parameters, your number of autoscale slots will be determined automatically. As an example, take a look at the following figure:

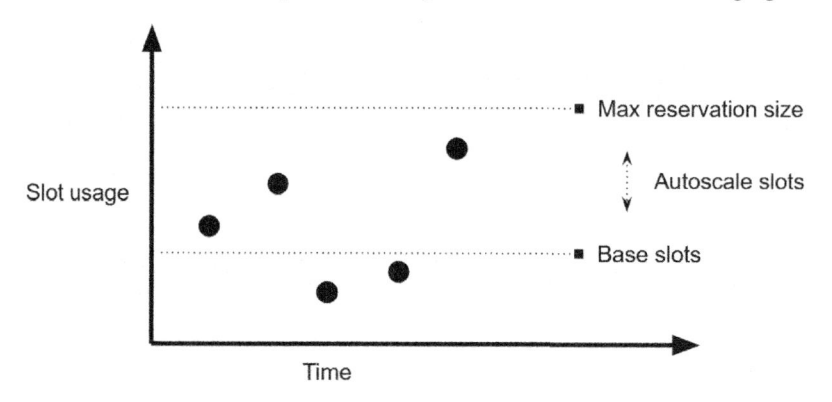

Figure 11.3 – A diagram of the different type of slots

The figure illustrates the slots that are used by the users' queries from time to time. Normally, slot usage will fluctuate depending on the user's traffic; there can be peak hours, normal hours, and also low hours.

Base slots refer to the amount of slots that you think you will always need to use. The minimum base slots can be as low as zero slots. **Max reservation size** is the number of slots that you are willing to pay for. The difference between the maximum reservation size and the base slots is the number of autoscale slots that you can use and need to pay for.

For example, if you assign 200 base slots, it means BigQuery will always reserve that amount of slots regardless of the actual usage. If you want a highly predictable cost every month and are not willing to pay more than 200 slots, you can set the max reservation size to 200 slots. This means that if all queries that run at that time require more than 200 slots, the queries will be queued.

If you can accept a more flexible cost per month and want the queries to have access to more slots, you can set the max reservation size to more than 200 – for example, 4,000. With this configuration, whenever queries need more than 200 slots, BigQuery will slowly increase the number of slots for your projects to meet the demand. The autoscale slots will add 100 slots incrementally, up to 4,000. If the slots are no longer needed, it will decrease to the base slots.

The next terminology is slot commitments; this is purely a commercial aspect and will not affect any technical aspect. Slot commitments is an option if your organization wants to get a lower price for your base slots. For example, if you purchase 1-year commitment, you will pay less but you need to utilize the slots even you don't use it.

After deciding upon and creating the slot reservation and slot commitments, you need to assign the reservations to the GCP project that you want to apply. To do this, from the **Capacity Management** menu, after the slot reservation is created, click **Actions** and choose **Create an assignment**. This launches a very simple menu that looks like this:

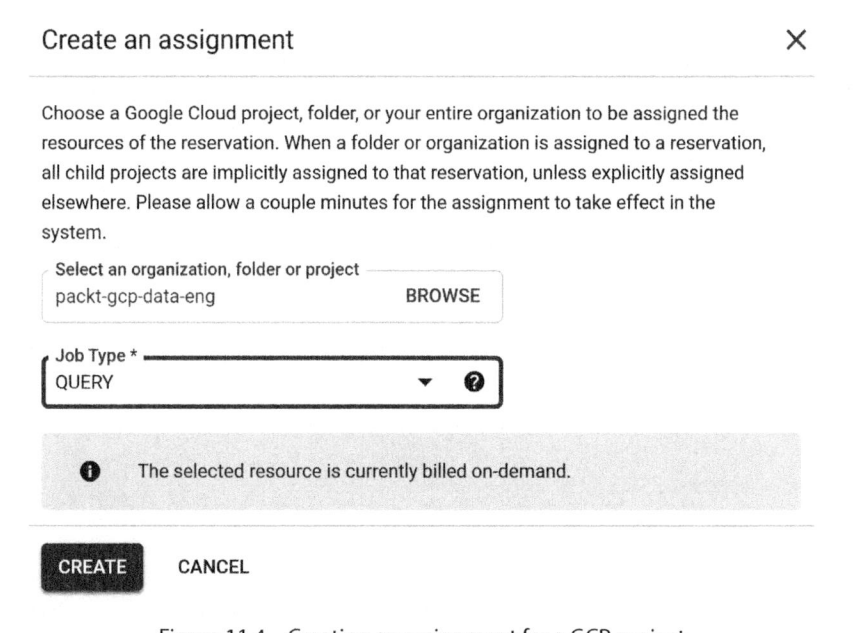

Figure 11.4 – Creating an assignment for a GCP project

Those are all the terminologies that you need to understand in order to understand BigQuery editions and the slots autoscaling feature.

How much do queries cost?

After understanding how BigQuery editions work, calculating the cost of BigQuery using BigQuery editions pricing is simpler. The total cost of your queries depends on your BigQuery reservation configuration, which consists of the price of the slots baseline plus the autoscaling slots that are used.

To wrap up this section, it's important to know that understanding BigQuery editions is not only important for cost planning but will also affect our query performance. As a data engineer, we are usually the one who needs to propose how many base slots, max reservation slots, and assignments to make to ensure the queries' performance meets expectations.

In the next section, we will move on from BigQuery pricing and start to see how we can calculate the overall GCP cost using the Google Cloud pricing calculator.

Using the Google Cloud pricing calculator

Google Cloud has a pricing calculator tool that you can access from its public page: `https://cloud.google.com/products/calculator`.

This calculator can help you estimate the cost of GCP services based on your estimated requirements. If you open the page, you will see that there are lists of GCP services. Each GCP service has input fields. Let's use BigQuery again as an example:

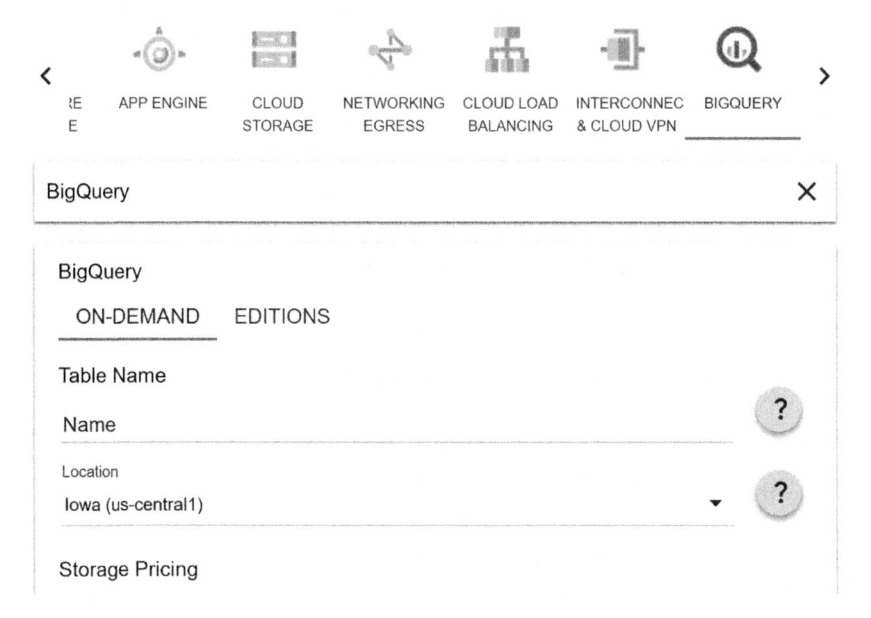

Figure 11.5 – The BigQuery ON-DEMAND cost calculator

As you can see, the calculator allows us to choose **ON-DEMAND** or **EDITIONS** pricing and all the required input fields. As another example, let's check out the other services, such as Dataproc:

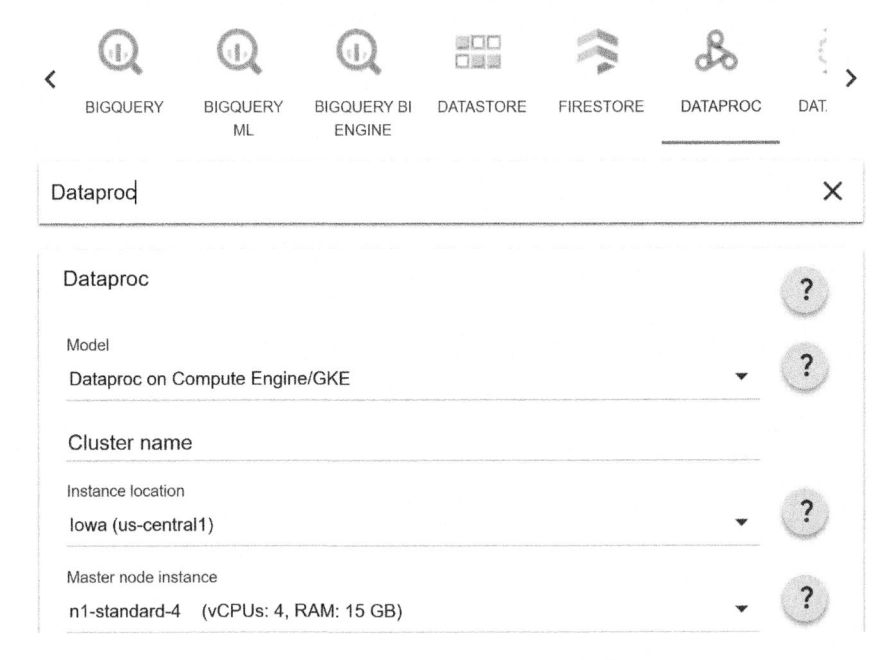

Figure 11.6 – The Dataproc cost calculator

If you choose the DATAPROC calculator, you will see the input fields as shown in the screenshot. There are many input fields in the calculator, if you scroll down you will find the inputs for the machine's sizes (node instance), the number of workers, and the estimated hours. This is what we discussed previously in the *Estimating the cost of your end-to-end data solution in GCP* section regarding the pricing model types. Dataproc service is one example that is cost based on VM-based. With this knowledge, you can fill in the input fields in the pricing calculator and get the estimated cost for your GCP services.

An example – an estimating data engineering use case

Let's try to simulate what we've learned so far by looking at an example use case. Imagine that you are a data engineer. Your organization plans to use GCP for data analytics. Your **Chief Data Officer** (**CDO**) has asked you to estimate the monthly cost, giving you these requirements:

- The source data will be stored as uncompressed CSV files in a GCS bucket. The file size is 100 GB daily.
- Some data engineers are experienced in developing ETL on Hadoop. They need a permanent Hadoop cluster with the following specifications – 3 master nodes and 10 worker nodes, where each node must have at least 4 vCPUs and 15 GB of memory, with 200 GB of SSD storage per node.

- The data warehouse should be in BigQuery. There will be 20 end users that will access the BigQuery tables. They are active users that will access the tables five days a week.
- To orchestrate the Dataproc jobs and BigQuery ELT process, Cloud Composer 2 is needed. The specification is to use the `Medium` environment size.
- There will be streaming data. The data will be ingested from one Pub/Sub topic to one subscription. The subscription's output should be processed using Dataflow. The data stream size is 2 GB per hour and doesn't need any snapshot or data retention in Pub/Sub. You should set Dataflow's maximum workers to three, using the `n1-standard-1` machine type.
- All data should be stored and processed in the US location.
- There will be only one environment for development and production. This means that you only need to calculate the estimation once, assuming you only have one environment.

How much is the monthly cost for your organization based on the given requirements?

You can use this example as an exercise. With this exercise, you can learn how to imagine an end-to-end architecture based on the requirements. Then, you can use the pricing calculator to calculate the cost of each component.

If you have finished this or just want to see the example solution, here is one solution from my calculations. First, here is the high-level architecture diagram for the data analytics environment for the organization:

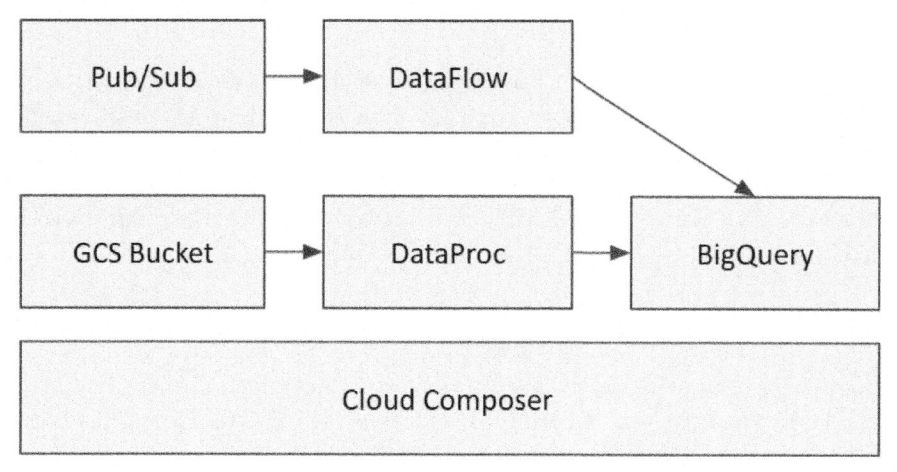

Figure 11.7 – A high-level architecture diagram

We've discussed all these components throughout this book, starting from handling streaming data using Pub/Sub, processing it using Dataflow, and storing the data in BigQuery. For the batch data, we can use a GCS bucket, process the data using Dataproc, and store the data in BigQuery. Finally, all the orchestration and scheduling processes will use Cloud Composer.

Now, let's look at the available GCP services, their cost components, their requirements, and the cost from the calculator's output. Note that there is a possibility that the cost components and the estimated cost stated here will be different compared to your calculator's output. This is because Google Cloud may update its calculator and pricing at any time. You don't need to worry much about that because what we want to focus on is how to convert requirements into cost estimation. You don't need to compare the literal cost to my example output.

The cost components can be broken down into six GCP services. Let's look at each one in detail.

Pub/Sub

For Pub/Sub, we can use the following two statements from the requirements:

- The data will be ingested from one Pub/Sub topic into one subscription
- The data stream size is 2 GB per hour and doesn't need any snapshot or data retention in Pub/Sub

In the calculator, you can use this information to calculate the volume of bytes that is published daily and set the number of subscriptions to one. You can keep the other inputs blank, since we don't need any snapshots and data retention to be performed. Take a look at the following Pub/Sub cost components table:

GCP service	Cost component	Requirements	Cost
Pub/Sub	The volume of bytes published daily	48 GB (2 GB x 24 hours)	$113.28
	The number fo subscriptions	1	

Table 11.8 – The Pub/Sub cost components table

The Pub/Sub monthly cost is estimated to be **$113.28**.

Dataflow

For Dataflow, we can use the following three statements from the requirements:

- There will be streaming data
- The data stream size is 2 GB per hour

The maximum number of Dataflow workers will be three using the n1-standard-1 machine type

In the calculator, you can use these requirements as input for the job type, the data that's been processed, the hours that the job runs per month, the number of worker nodes that are used by the job, and the worker node instance type. Take a look at the following Dataflow cost components table:

GCP service	Cost component	Requirements	Cost
Dataflow	The job type	Streaming	$189.52
	The hours the job runs per month	720 hours (24 hours x 30 days)	
	The number of worker nodes used by the job	3	
	The worker node instance type	`n1-standard-1`	

Table 11.9 – The Dataflow cost components table

The Dataflow monthly cost is estimated to be **$189.52**.

Cloud Storage

For Cloud Storage, we can use the following statement from the requirements:

- The source data will be stored as uncompressed CSV files in a GCS bucket. The file size is 100 GB daily.

In the calculator, you can use this requirement as input for the total amount of storage. Assuming that the data is stored every day for one month, we can assume that, in one month, the data size will be 3,000 GB. Take a look at the following Cloud Storage cost components table:

GCP service	Cost component	Requirements	Cost
Cloud Storage	The total amount of storage	3,000 GB (100 GB x 30 days)	$60

Table 11.10 – The Cloud Storage cost components table

The Cloud Storage monthly cost is estimated to be **$60**.

Dataproc

For Dataproc, we can use the following two statements from the requirements:

- They need a permanent Hadoop cluster with the following specification – 3 master nodes and 10 worker nodes
- Each node must have at least 4 vCPUs and 15 GB of memory, with 200 GB of SSD storage per node

In the calculator, you can check the **Enable High Availability Configuration (3 Master nodes)** checkbox to calculate the three master nodes and use the `n1-standard-4` machine type to meet the node's specifications. Take a look at the following Dataproc cost components table:

GCP service	Cost component	Requirements	Cost
Dataproc	The master node instance	`n1-standard-4`	$2,062.63
	Enable High Availability Configuration (3 master nodes)	Yes	
	The worker node instance	`n1-standard-4`	
	The number of normal worker nodes	10	
	The number of Spot worker nodes	0	
	The hours the cluster runs per month	720 hours (24 hours x 30 days)	
	Storage (per node)	PD SSD - 200 GiB	

Table 11.11 – Dataproc cost components table

If you see the preceding output in the calculator, then there will be more than one cost table. Compute Engine and storage disk costs will also be shown. You need to use the total estimated cost instead of the Dataproc cost. The total estimated cost is the result of adding Dataproc, Compute Engine, and the storage disk cost.

Looking at the total estimated cost, the Dataproc monthly cost is estimated to be $288.99 + $963.29 + $ 374.40 + $435.95 = $2,062.63.

Cloud Composer

For Cloud Composer, we can use the following statement from the requirements:

- To orchestrate the Dataproc jobs and BigQuery ELT process, Cloud Composer 2 is needed. The specification is to use the `Medium` Environment size.

In the calculator, Cloud Composer 2 is pretty simple. You just need to define the environment size. There are variables that are difficult to define initially, which are the number of days and hours that we need; for that, we can assume the Cloud Composer environment will run for 7 days a week for 24 hours a day. This means that the cost in the calculation is the maximum cost and may be less, depending on the workload.

Take a look at the following Cloud Composer cost components table:

GCP service	Cost component	Requirements	Cost
Cloud Composer	The average days per week each server is running	7	$495.33
	The environment size	Medium	

Table 11.12 – The Cloud Composer cost components table

The Cloud Composer monthly cost is estimated to be **$495.33**.

BigQuery

For BigQuery, we need to make some assumptions. The assumption won't be 100% accurate, but this is good enough for estimation purposes.

For storage calculation, let's assume that the data warehouse and data mart layers will store the same size as the data source. This means that we will have the raw data from the data source – that is, 100 GB – the data warehouse that has already transformed using the data model, which is 100 GB, and the data mart for the end user, which will be 100 GB. Thus, the total storage that's needed is 300 GB every day:

Queries = 20 end users x 5 days x 4 weeks x 100 GB

Assuming that all 20 users access the tables in the data mart once a day, the active storage becomes as follows:

Active storage = 300 GB x 30 days

With these assumptions, we can make the following calculations:

GCP service	Cost component	Requirements	Cost
BigQuery	Active logical storage	300 GB X 30 days (9,000 GB)	$444.66
	Queries	20 end users X 5 days x 4 weeks x 100 GB (40,000 GB)	

Table 11.13 – The BigQuery cost component table

After calculating all the services in the Google Cloud pricing calculator, we will get the following monthly cost estimation summary:

Service	Monthly Cost
Pub/Sub	$113.28
Dataflow	$189.52
Cloud Storage	$60
Dataproc	$2,062.63
Cloud Composer	$495.33
BigQuery	$444.66
Total	$ 3,365.42

Table 11.14 – The GCP services' monthly cost summary table

If your calculation is not exactly the same as what's shown in this book, you don't need to worry – GCP pricing can change from time to time. The important thing to take away from this section is to understand how the pricing mechanism works on GCP for data engineering services.

To conclude our simulation, remember that to estimate the end-to-end solution cost in GCP, you need to prepare three things:

- A list of GCP services
- The cost components
- How to use the cost components as input in the Google Cloud cost calculator

Of course, there must be a gap between estimation and reality. The reality can be more or less expensive – it depends on the real usage and how much our assumptions are close to reality. However, having the cost estimation table can help you and your organization make important decisions, as well as whether you want to go with the proposed solutions or make any adjustments. For example, in our results, Dataproc seems expensive compared to the other services. This can lead to a discussion with the team about whether you should substitute the component or go with the plan.

In the next section, we will revisit the two important BigQuery features – partitioned and clustered tables. In my experience, these two features play a significant role in the total cost of an entire end-to-end data solution. Understanding the implication that using these two features has on the cost is especially important.

Tips to optimize BigQuery using partitioned and clustered tables

BigQuery tables can store data from zero bytes to petabytes of data. There is no difference between creating a small-sized table or a large-sized table. To simplify the context and for illustration purposes only, let's say a small-sized table ranges from KBs to 100 GB. The large-sized tables range from 100 GB to PB of data. Technically, both tables are the same, but if you think about optimizing performance and compute cost, you can configure the tables using two features called **BigQuery partitioned tables** and **BigQuery clustered tables**.

These features are helpful for both on-demand and flat-rate pricing. In on-demand pricing, the features will cut the billed bytes and will reduce the overall cost that is calculated from the billed bytes. With flat-rate pricing, it doesn't affect the cost directly. Remember that the cost of flat-rate pricing is flat per period. However, when you're using features, it will reduce the number of slots needed for the queries. If we need fewer slots, this means we can reduce the number of purchased slots.

In this section, I will use the on-demand scenario as an example. Since BigQuery on-demand can affect costs directly, it's easier to imagine and calculate the impact. Now, let's understand both features.

Partitioned tables

We discussed and completed an exercise using partitioned tables in *Chapter 4, Building Workflows for Batch Data Loading Using Cloud Composer*, in the *Introduction to BigQuery partitioning* section.

Let's quickly refresh on the important points that we should execute in this chapter.

BigQuery partitioned tables will divide data in BigQuery tables using partitions into segments, using a key. This key can be a time-unit column, the ingestion time, or an integer column. The most common practice is using either the time-unit column or the ingestion time daily.

For an illustration of how BigQuery partitioned table works under the hood, see *Figure 11.15*. This figure shows a BigQuery table called `example_table`. The table contains three columns called `Val 1`, `Val 2`, and `Date`. Let's create this table in BigQuery *without* defining any partition column:

```
CREATE TABLE example_table
(
   val1  INT64,
   val2  STRING,
   date  DATE,
)
```

Now, we can access the table using the `SELECT` statement without any filtering:

```
SELECT *
FROM example_table;
```

By doing this, BigQuery will access all the columns and rows, as shown here:

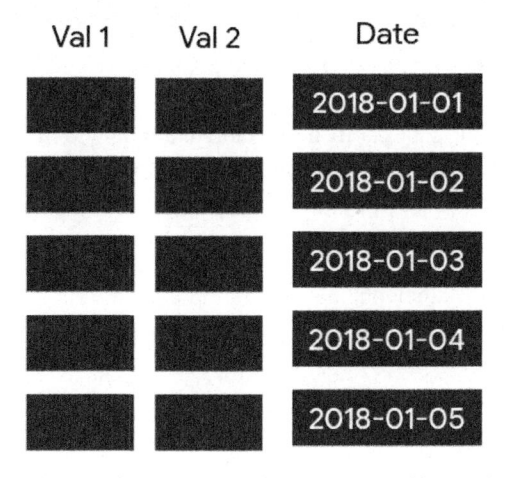

Figure 11.15 – The rows and columns accessed by BigQuery

Each dark-colored box shows that BigQuery accesses the data in those particular rows and columns. From a cost perspective, the dark-colored boxes contribute to the total billed bytes that drive the BigQuery on-demand cost.

Let's say you access the table using the query `SELECT` only to the `Val 1`s and then filter the `date` using a WHERE clause:

```
SELECT val1
FROM example_table
WHERE date = '2018-01-03';
```

BigQuery will access only the selected column and all the rows, as shown in the following diagram:

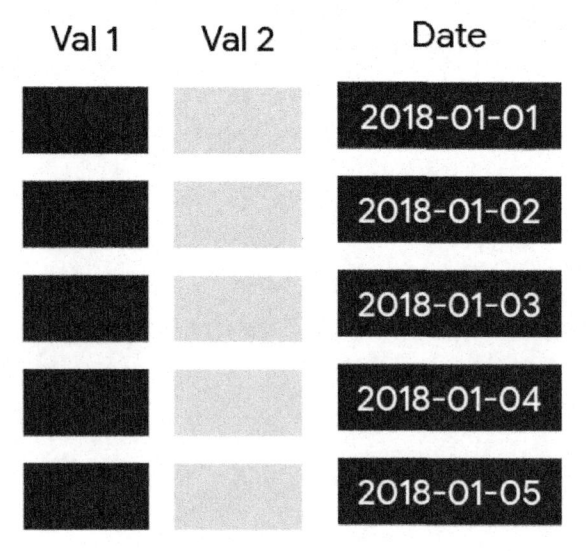

Figure 11.16 – The selected rows and columns accessed by BigQuery

Note that, in this case, the Val 2 boxes are light-colored. Jumping to the cost perspective, this means that the query cost is cheaper compared to the one shown in *Figure 11.15* because the total billed bytes are fewer:

- To improve the BigQuery cost even further, you can create a partitioned table by defining it in the CREATE TABLE statement:

    ```
    CREATE TABLE example_table
    (
        val1  INT64,
        val2  STRING,
        date  DATE,
    )
    PARTITION BY (date);
    ```

- Now, let's run a query and only select the val1 column with a filter on the partition column date:

    ```
    SELECT val1
    FROM example_table
    WHERE date = '2018-01-03';
    ```

Here, BigQuery will access the Val 1 table and the Date columns. The Date column is included because it's used in the WHERE clause. However, because we partitioned the table using the date column and used it to filter in our query, BigQuery will only access the rows in that particular partition. In our case, this is the 2018-01-03 partition. The following diagram shows this:

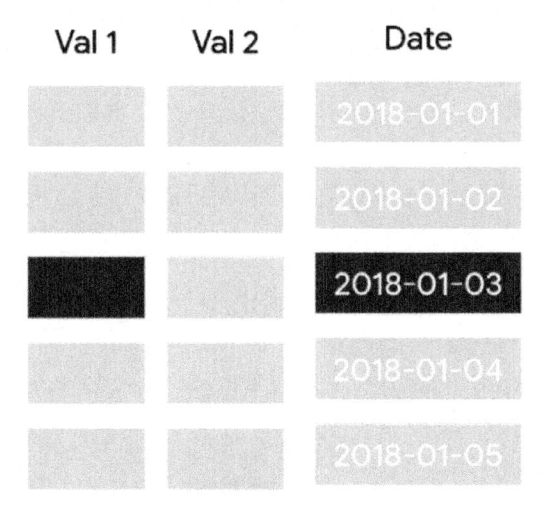

Figure 11.17 – The partitioned table

This will reduce a significant amount of cost compared to the non-partitioned table. For example, if the whole table is 1 TB and consists of five days' worth of data, then querying one single date will cost 200 GB (⅕ of the total size).

> **Note**
> One thing to remember is the partitioned table quota. The maximum number of partitions you can have in a table is 4,000. Check out the following public page to find the latest quota: https://cloud.google.com/bigquery/quotas#partitioned_tables.

If you store data daily, you will have 365 partitions each year, which means you can store around 10 years' worth of data.

Remember that you can partition your table per hour using integer columns. Always keep your quotas in mind when designing a table. For example, in the hourly partitioned table, you will have 8,760 partitions each year (365 days x 24 hours). This means that you can store only around five months' worth of data. This is useful for some use cases but not for most.

Clustered tables

You can use a clustered table in BigQuery to automatically organize tables based on one to four columns in the table's schema. By **organizing**, we mean that BigQuery sorts the storage blocks in the background using the specified columns.

Remember that BigQuery is a big data database, so it stores data in a distributed storage system. As an example, one large table that's 1 TB in size will be split and distributed into small chunks. Each chunk contains records from the table. In the data space, this chunk is called a **block**.

388 Cost Strategy in GCP

If you don't specify the clustered BigQuery table, each block will contain random sets of records. If we specify the clusters, the block will contain sorted records. Now, the question is, how can the sorted records help reduce cost?

When a table is sorted by cluster, internally, BigQuery will know which blocks it should access specifically and ignore the irrelevant blocks. Take a look at the following diagram. The query has two filters, a `date` at `2018-01-03`, and the `Val 1` column equals 'frida'. It runs on a partitioned table, but it's not clustered:

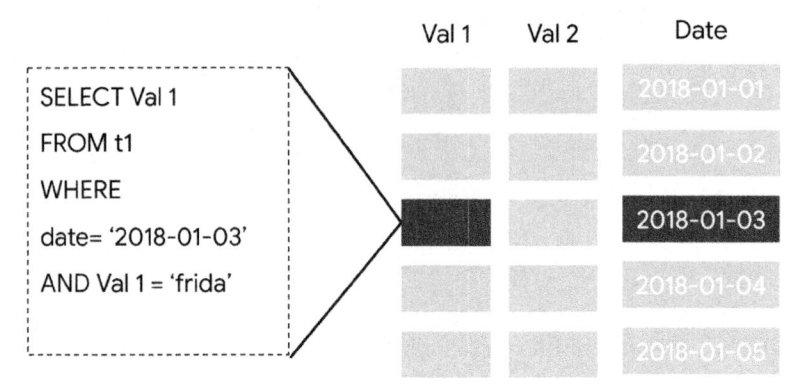

Figure 11.18 – A partitioned table without a clustered column

The query will access the whole partitioned table, as explained previously in the *Partitioned tables* section. You can improve the BigQuery cost even further by defining the clustered table in the `CREATE TABLE` statement, as follows:

```
CREATE TABLE example_table
(
   val1 INT64,
   val2  STRING,
   date DATE,
)
PARTITION BY (date)
CLUSTER BY val1;
```

The `SELECT` statement query will access a small subset in the `2018-01-03` partition, as shown in the following diagram:

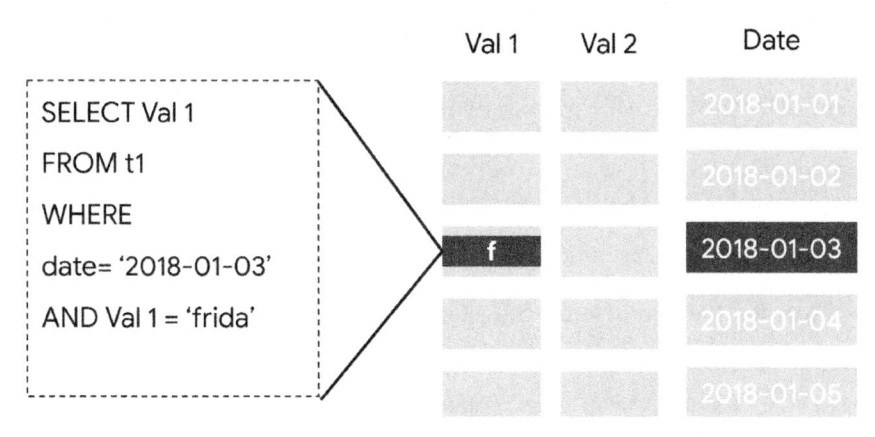

Figure 11.19 – The partitioned table with a clustered column

In this example, BigQuery will only access the f block because it's the first letter of `'frida'`. BigQuery understands where to find this specific f block because the records on each partition are already sorted, so it will skip blocks a to e and won't look at blocks g to z. From a cost perspective, using clustering , you will optimize the cost not only to the date level but also to the date and block level. This scenario will significantly reduce the total billed bytes from a large-sized table.

Note that the f block is an illustrative example. In reality, we won't know what data range is stored in a block. This is managed internally by BigQuery, and we, as BigQuery users, don't have visibility into BigQuery storage at the block level. What we need to do as a BigQuery user is make sure we define the cluster column whenever cost optimization is needed for BigQuery tables.

What we should consider when using a clustered table is which column(s) we should use for clustering:

- The first rule of thumb is choosing the column that is used the most by the user's queries. In our example, we use `Val 1` as the cluster column because the filter states `Val 1 = 'frida'`.
- The second rule of thumb is the number of columns and their order. We can use up to four columns in a clustered table. The order of the columns when we define them is important. For example, take a look at the following `CREATE TABLE` statement:

```
CREATE OR REPLACE TABLE t1
PARTITION BY DATE(date_column)
CLUSTER BY
   country, region, city, postal_code
```

We cluster the table using four columns, as this is the best practice. The best practice is to order them from the least to the most granular columns. In this example, the list of countries is less granular compared to the region. The list of regions is less granular compared to cities. Here, `postal_code` is the most granular.

An exercise – optimizing BigQuery on-demand cost

In this exercise, let's try to prove the concepts that we discussed previously as an experiment. For this experiment, we will create three tables. These three tables will be created from the BigQuery public dataset – specifically, the `stackoverflow_posts` table. We will run a query on the three tables and compare the total billed bytes. The fewer bytes that are billed, the better for us.

Follow these steps to run the experiment:

1. Open your BigQuery console and go to the SQL Editor.

    Create a standard table using the following **data description language** (**DDL**) statement:

    ```
    CREATE OR REPLACE TABLE `chapter_10_dataset.stackoverflow_posts`
    AS SELECT *
    FROM `bigquery-public-data.stackoverflow.stackoverflow_posts`
    WHERE EXTRACT(YEAR FROM creation_date) BETWEEN 2013 AND 2014;
    ```

2. Create a partitioned table using the following DDL statement:

    ```
    CREATE OR REPLACE TABLE `chapter_10_dataset.stackoverflow_posts_partitioned`
    PARTITION BY DATE(creation_date)
    AS SELECT *
    FROM `bigquery-public-data.stackoverflow.stackoverflow_posts`
    WHERE EXTRACT(YEAR FROM creation_date) BETWEEN 2013 AND 2014;
    ```

3. Create a partitioned and clustered table using the following DDL statement:

    ```
    CREATE OR REPLACE TABLE `chapter_10_dataset.stackoverflow_posts_partitioned_clustered`
    PARTITION BY DATE(creation_date)
    CLUSTER BY
      title
    AS SELECT *
    FROM `bigquery-public-data.stackoverflow.stackoverflow_posts`
    WHERE EXTRACT(YEAR FROM creation_date) BETWEEN 2013 AND 2014;
    ```

4. Run the same query for the three tables, and change the table names to the three tables from the previous steps:

    ```
    SELECT DATE(creation_date) as creation_date, count(*) as total
    FROM `chapter_10_dataset.[THE EXPERIMENT TABLES]`
    WHERE DATE(creation_date) BETWEEN '2013-01-01' AND '2013-06-01'
    AND title LIKE 'a%'
    GROUP BY creation_date;
    ```

5. To check the billed bytes, you can check the **MB processed** information under **Query results**. Take a look at the following screenshot:

Query results   ↓ SAVE RESULTS   📊 EXPLORE DATA ▼

Query complete (0.7 sec elapsed, 299.5 MB processed)

Job information   **Results**   JSON   Execution details

Row	creation_date	total
1	2013-05-17	53

Figure 11.20 – BigQuery's Query results page showing the processed bytes

In this example, the total billed bytes for this query is **299.5 MB**. Run the query for the three tables and compare that number.

Finally, let's see the results in this table:

Table	Billed Bytes
Standard table	299.5 MB
Partitioned table	60.1 MB
Partitioned + Clustered table	57.2 MB

Figure 11.21 – BigQuery table types comparison based on Billed Bytes

As expected, the standard table processes the most bytes compared to the other tables, while the partitioned and clustered table process processes slightly fewer compared to the partitioned table.

This result proves the general idea of the three approaches, using standard, partitioned, and partitioned and clustered tables. The comparison ratio must be different case by case, depending on the table size, the partition size, the key columns that have been selected for the clustered tables, and the query. You must understand these possibilities to be able to improve your BigQuery cost, both directly when using the on-demand pricing model and indirectly when using the flat-rate pricing model.

Summary

In this chapter, we learned about two different things. First, we learned about how to estimate an end-to-end data solution cost. Second, we understood how BigQuery partitioned and clustered tables play a significant role in cost.

These two topics are usually needed by data engineers in different situations. Understanding how to calculate cost will help in the early stages of GCP implementation. This is usually a particularly important step for an organization to decide its future solution as a whole.

The second topic usually occurs when you're designing BigQuery tables, and at a time when you need to evaluate the running BigQuery solution. Even though it's obvious that using partitioned and clustered tables is beneficial, it's not a surprise in a big organization, as many tables are not optimized and can be improved.

Lastly, we performed an experiment using three different tables. It proved that using partitioned and clustered tables can reduce the BigQuery cost.

In the next chapter, which will be the last technical chapter, we will discuss a practice called **continuous integration/continuous deployment** (**CI/CD**). This is a common practice for software engineers but is not that common for data people. Data engineers, partly as data people and partly as engineers, can benefit from understanding this practice to build a robust data pipeline.

12
CI/CD on GCP for Data Engineers

Continuous integration/continuous deployment (**CI/CD**) is a common concept for DevOps engineers, but most of the time, data engineers need to understand and be able to apply this practice to their development endeavors. This chapter will cover the necessary concepts of CI/CD and provide examples of how to apply CI/CD to our Cloud Composer example from *Chapter 4, Building Workflows for Batch Data Loading Using Cloud Composer*. Upon completing this chapter, you will understand what CI/CD is, why and when it's needed in data engineering, and what GCP services are needed for it.

In this chapter, we will cover the following topics:

- An introduction to CI/CD
- Understanding CI/CD components with GCP services
- Exercise – implementing CI using Cloud Build
- Exercise – deploying Cloud Composer jobs using Cloud Build

Let's look at the technical requirements for the exercises in this chapter:

Technical requirements

For this chapter's exercises, we will use the following GCP services:

- Cloud Build
- Google Cloud Repositories
- Google Container Registry
- Cloud Composer (optionally)

If you have never opened any of these services in your GCP console, open them and enable the necessary APIs. Make sure that you have your **GCP console**, **Cloud Shell**, and **Cloud Editor** ready.

You can download the example code and the dataset for this chapter here: https://github.com/PacktPublishing/Data-Engineering-with-Google-Cloud-Platform-Second-Edition/tree/main/chapter-12/code.

An introduction to CI/CD

CI/CD is an engineering practice that combines two methods – continuous integration and continuous deployment:

- **CI** is a method that's used to automatically integrate code from multiple engineers that collaborate in a repository. *Automatic integration* can be in the form of testing the code, building Docker images, integration testing, or any other steps that are required to integrate the code.

    The main benefit of CI is that you can integrate code changes from many developers as quickly as possible. With this practice, you can detect errors quickly and locate the issues more easily.

- **CD** is a method that's used to automatically deploy the final code to the production applications. *Automatic deployment* can be in the form of pushing the built software to the production server, moving the necessary files to their destination, or any other steps that are required to deploy the final application.

The main benefit of CD is that you can deploy an application version as soon as possible to a production system. With this practice, when you detect an issue, you can handle the issue automatically – for example, a rollback mechanism.

Even though both CD and CI are highly correlated, it's not mandatory to implement both. For example, it's common for an engineering team to decide to implement CI to automate a code error in their development environment. When deploying to production, they may choose to do so manually because it's too risky to automate the deployment process.

In summary, CI/CD are steps. These steps are needed to check the developer's code and deploy it to the production systems automatically.

Understanding the data engineer's relationship with CI/CD practices

Now, the question is, what does this mean for us, as data engineers? How much do we need to know about this practice? Which part of the data pipelines can use CI/CD?

First of all, I want to say that if you are already familiar and experienced with the CI/CD practice, you can focus on what tools can be used for CI/CD in GCP throughout this chapter. But if you are new to this practice, what you need to understand is the concept. In my experience, while meeting with many data people, CI/CD is not a common practice in our space. If we compare ourselves to software engineers, the CI/CD practice is more mature in the software engineering space.

To start answering the previous questions, I will continue explaining the CI/CD practice using an illustration. I will illustrate it using an analogy from the culinary business. Imagine that you are very passionate about cooking pasta. You want to start making money from your passion. In this scenario, you have two options – open a restaurant and sell your pasta, or join a big restaurant as a pasta chef.

In the first scenario, what you need to do is focus on perfecting your cooking skills and then sell them. In the second scenario, you are one of many chefs and the other staff. What you need to do other than perfect your cooking skills is understand how a big kitchen works. In a big kitchen, there are many roles, including head chef, sous chef, waiter, and others. On top of that, there are systems such as cooking stations, receiving orders, and food testing. These systems are there, and you need to follow them to deliver the pasta to customers.

Now, let's go back to our world – data engineering. What we've learned so far in this book is our process of learning how to perfect our cooking. You've learned about all the important ingredients and components and how to use them. That knowledge is the core and the most important to any data engineer – the same as learning to cook the best pasta as a pasta chef.

If you are working on your data project by yourself or in a small team, typically two to three people, and you know that your data project is a short-term project (which means it won't have many updates in the long term), you don't need CI/CD. It is great to have it, but it's not mandatory. If you have a small restaurant by yourself, implementing a big kitchen system for your work is great, but it's too much.

If you are working in a big organization that has a big and systematic engineering team, there is a higher chance that you will need to follow a system. In engineering, the system becomes CI/CD. Now, like the pasta chef in a big restaurant, what you need to do most of the time is follow the system. A data engineer rarely needs to create an end-to-end CI/CD system from scratch. It's more common for this responsibility to be taken on by the **development operations** (**DevOps**) team or, sometimes, the infrastructure team. What's important is to understand the concept, the components, and why they're there.

Let's go back to our original questions in this section. For data engineers, understanding CI/CD is not a must. It depends on where you work and what the practice is in that organization. However, if you work in an organization that uses CI/CD as a practice, you need to understand it.

In the data pipeline, any code-based application can use CI/CD. For example, data pipeline code in Dataflow, Spark Python code in Dataproc, Terraform scripts, Airflow DAG in Cloud Composer, and any other code-based data applications can use CI/CD as a practice. On the other hand, tools such as Looker Studio that use a full UI can't use CI/CD.

In the next section, we will try to understand CI/CD by looking at GCP services.

Understanding CI/CD components with GCP services

There are some steps in the CI/CD practice. Each step may involve different tools or GCP services. To understand this concept better, let's take a look at the following diagram:

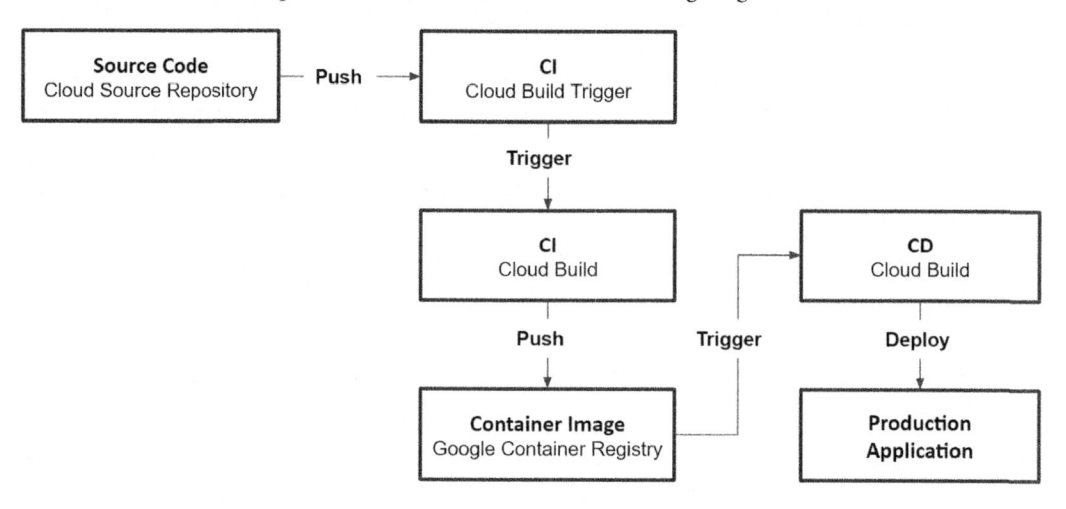

Figure 12.1 – The CI/CD steps and the GCP services involved

The diagram shows the high-level steps of a complete CI/CD. At each step, there is a corresponding GCP service that can handle that step. For example, the first step is **Source Code**. In GCP, you can create a GitHub repository using a service called a **Cloud Source Repository**. Later, in the *Exercise – implementing CI using Cloud Build* section, we will learn how to create one. For now, let's understand the steps and what GCP services are involved:

1. The CI process starts with the source code. This source code should always be managed in a GitHub repository. It can be in GitHub, GitLab, or any other Git provider. As we mentioned previously, GCP has a service called Cloud Source Repository. When a developer commits and pushes a code change to the GitHub repository, the CI process is triggered.

2. The **Push** event on GitHub can trigger **Cloud Build**. Cloud Build is a CI/CD serverless platform on GCP. You can specify the steps in Cloud Build as per your needs. We will learn about it in this chapter's exercises.

   Cloud Build has an object or feature called **Cloud Build Trigger**. We can configure Cloud Build Trigger to detect events from the Cloud Source Repository.

3. A Cloud Build run will start after being triggered by Cloud Build Trigger. The Cloud Build run will run every defined step. These are the main CI steps and can include creating a Docker image, installing packages, testing code, or any other necessary steps.

4. One option with the CI step is creating and storing the container image. The term for this is **Push**. However, instead of code being pushed, the container is pushed to a container registry. GCP has a service called **Google Container Registry** to manage containers. Again, this step is optional; not all CI needs to build and push container images.

5. Once the container image has been created, we can trigger an event to start the CD steps. There is no specific CD tool on GCP, but we can utilize Cloud Build to do this. We can define how we want to deploy the image to the production applications. This will be the final step in the whole CI/CD process.

These are the five common patterns in CI/CD at a high level. At the lower level, you need to know about the common steps inside both CI and CD, but at this point, what you must understand is the high-level concepts. In addition to that, you need to know what kind of tools are used for each step.

Using the services from GCP will give you advantages regarding serverless and seamless integration. For example, let's say you want to create a CI pipeline to handle Cloud Composer code. In that case, you know that you need to use a service account but that you also want the CI pipeline to be able to interact with Cloud Composer and GCS (remember that DAG in Cloud Composer is stored as files in a GCS bucket). With Cloud Build, you know that it can interact with both Cloud Composer and GCS using a GCP service account.

> **Important note**
> There are two services that I mentioned and will use in this chapter that are deprecating, which are the Container Registry and Cloud Source Repositories.
>
> The Container Registry will be replaced by the Artifact Registry, which mostly supports the same functionality, with additional features that we won't need in this book.
>
> Cloud Source Repositories will be replaced by **Secure Source Manager** (**SSM**), which supports more advanced Git capabilities. SSM was not yet available for public use at the time of writing.

After understanding all the concepts surrounding CI/CD and the corresponding GCP services, we will complete some exercises so that we understand each step. Note that if this is new for you, you should only focus on understanding the concept and what tools are used. You shouldn't worry too much about the details of the code. For example, if you are not familiar with Dockerfile scripts, just making them work in the exercises using the provided example is good enough. You can always expand your knowledge when you face real requirements in your real working environment. Remember the pasta chef analogy – at this point, you don't need to think too much about *how a stove can convert gas and electricity into heat*; you just need to focus on knowing that a stove is needed to cook in a big restaurant. Now, let's go to our first exercise with Cloud Build.

Exercise – implementing CI using Cloud Build

In this exercise, we will create a CI pipeline using Cloud Build. There will be four main steps, as follows:

1. Creating a GitHub repository using a Cloud Source Repository.
2. Developing the code and Cloud Build scripts.
3. Creating a Cloud Build trigger.
4. Pushing the code to the GitHub repository.

Let's get started!

Creating a GitHub repository using a Cloud Source Repository

First, let's prepare the GitHub repository. Follow these steps:

1. Go to your GCP console and find **Source Repository** from the navigation bar. It's located under the **CI/CD** section:

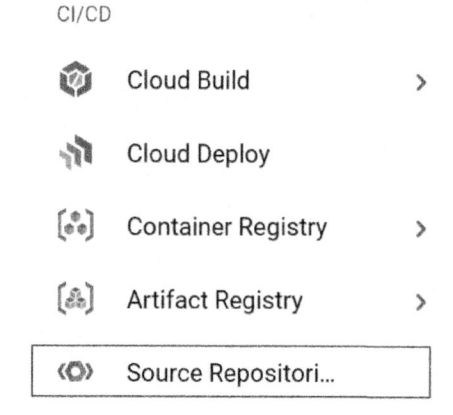

Figure 12.2 – The Source Repository option in the navigation menu

2. After clicking the menu, a new browser tab will open within the **Cloud Source Repository** console. Click the **Get started** button on this screen to create a repository:

Figure 12.3 – The Get started button

Clicking this button will give you the option to create a new repository.

3. Choose **Create new repository** and click **Continue**. You will have two inputs when creating a new repository – the repository's name and the project's name:

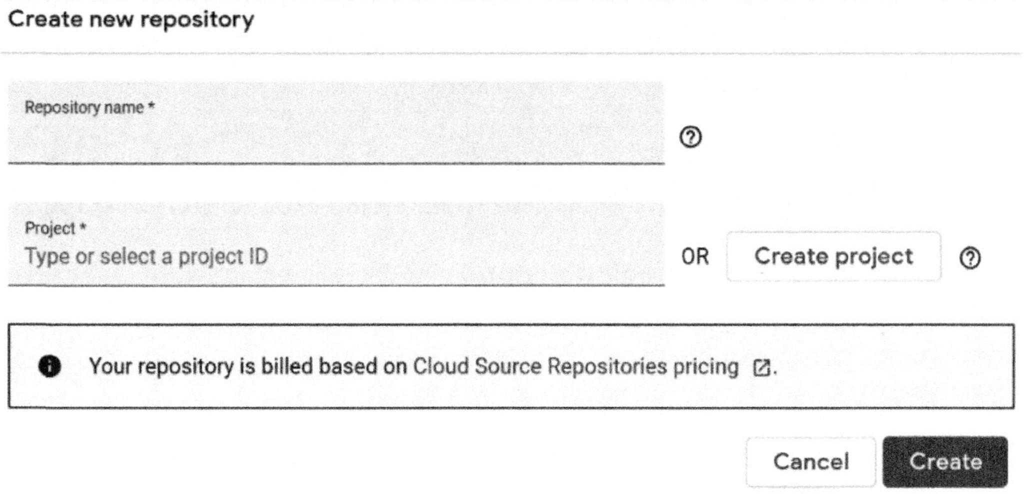

Create new repository

[Form with Repository name field, Project field (Type or select a project ID) OR Create project button, info message "Your repository is billed based on Cloud Source Repositories pricing.", Cancel and Create buttons]

Figure 12.4 – The Create new repository page

Choose a repository name. For example, mine is `packt-data-eng-on-gcp-cicd-example`. Don't use the name from my example.

For the project ID, I will use my GCP project ID, which is `packt-data-eng-on-gcp`. Make sure that you use your GCP project ID. Once you're finished, click the **Create** button.

At this point, you will have your new repository in the Cloud Source Repository for CI/CD processes.

4. Now, go back to your GCP console and open Cloud Shell.

We want to clone the empty GitHub repository that we just created to the Cloud Shell environment. To do that, call the following command from Cloud Shell under the `ci_example` folder:

```
$ mkdir ci_example
$ cd ci_example
$ gcloud source repos clone [your repository name]
--project=[your project id]
```

If this is successful, when you list the files (using the Linux `$ ls` command), you will see that the repository name is created as a folder in your Cloud Shell.

This is what it looks like in my environment:

```
adiwijaya_public@cloudshell:~ (packt-data-eng-on-gcp)$ gcloud source repos clone packt-data-eng-on-
Cloning into '/home/adiwijaya_public/packt-data-eng-on-gcp-cicd-example'...
remote: Total 171 (delta 84), reused 171 (delta 84)
Receiving objects: 100% (171/171), 16.63 KiB | 8.32 MiB/s, done.
Resolving deltas: 100% (84/84), done.
Project [packt-data-eng-on-gcp] repository [packt-data-eng-on-gcp-cicd-example] was cloned to [/hom
adiwijaya_public@cloudshell:~ (packt-data-eng-on-gcp)$ ls
dataset   hello_world.py   packt-data-eng-on-gcp-cicd-example   python_scripts   README-cloudshell.txt
adiwijaya_public@cloudshell:~ (packt-data-eng-on-gcp)$ cd packt-data-eng-on-gcp-cicd-example/
adiwijaya_public@cloudshell:~/packt-data-eng-on-gcp-cicd-example (packt-data-eng-on-gcp)$ pwd
/home/adiwijaya_public/packt-data-eng-on-gcp-cicd-example
adiwijaya_public@cloudshell:~/packt-data-eng-on-gcp-cicd-example (packt-data-eng-on-gcp)$
```

Figure 12.5 – An example of the expected commands and outputs

Now, we have a repository for our CI exercise. Let's continue to the second step.

Developing the code and Cloud Build scripts

In this step, we will use the code from Packt's GitHub example: https://github.com/PacktPublishing/Data-Engineering-with-Google-Cloud-Platform-Second-Edition/tree/main/chapter-12/code/cicd_basic.

If you check this folder, you will see that there are three files and one folder. The main Python function is in the calculate.py file; there's another file called Dockerfile, and a yaml file called cloudbuild.yaml. The tests folder contains a Python unit test script that will be used to check the function in the calculate.py file.

To clarify the repositories, I will call this GitHub repository packt github. Don't confuse this with your self-created GitHub repository in **Cloud Source Repository** (CSR), which I will call the my CSR repository.

The packt github repository refers to the github.com link that you can use to copy and paste the code for our exercise. The my CSR repository refers to the CSR repository that you created in *step 1* of this exercise.

What you need to do is copy all the files from the packt github repository to the my CSR repository. I won't give step-by-step instructions on how to do this; you can do this using any approach you like. You can copy and paste manually for each file or clone the repository and copy it, using Linux commands. Use the approach that you are most familiar with. For example, after cloning the code from the packt github repository, inside the directory, I copied the files using the following Linux command:

```
$ cp -r * ~/ci_example/packt-data-eng-on-gcp-cicd-example/
```

The expected output is that your my CSR repository will contain the following files:

```
adiwijaya_public@cloudshell:~/packt-data-eng-on-gcp-cicd-example (packt-data-eng-on-gcp)$ ls
calculate.py  cloudbuild.yaml  Dockerfile  tests
```

Figure 12.6 – Listing the files in the directory

Let's quickly look at what these files are. As a heads-up before continuing to the code explanation, you might get confused here, as mentioned previously. There are a lot of details that I chose not to explain in this book, such as containerization, Docker, and unit testing. I am not going to look at these topics in depth since they are huge topics. But that is not going to stop you from getting to the essence of this chapter about CI/CD for data engineers on GCP. Here, we will focus on understanding the high-level steps and what tools are involved. Now, let's look at the code:

1. The most important file here is the `cloudbuild.yaml` file. Pipelines in Cloud Build are defined under `steps:` in the yaml file.

    Let's take a look at the first code block:

    ```
    - name: gcr.io/cloud-builders/docker
        id: Build Image
        args: [
                'build',
                '-t', 'gcr.io/$PROJECT_ID/cicd-basic',
                '.'
             ]
    ```

    The goal of this Cloud Build step is to create a Docker image and give it a tag of `gcr.io/$PROJECT_ID/cicd-basic`. This tag will contain all the files from our my CSR repository.

    First, let's understand the `name` parameter. The `name` parameter is not just a random name for an identifier. It is used to specify which Docker image or environment you want to use to run on that particular step. In this case, we want to use the publicly available image from `gcr.io/cloud-builders` that contains Docker libraries.

    The `id` parameter is the step identifier. This value needs to be unique for each step.

    The `args` parameter represents the arguments that you can define, depending on the image that you loaded from the `name` parameter. In this case, `args` is the Linux command to call Docker pull requests. To see what's happening, we will run this step in a Linux virtual environment. The virtual environment will call the following Linux command:

    ```
    $ docker build -t gcr.io/$PROJECT_ID/cicd-basic .
    ```

Note that every value in the args parameter will be converted into Linux commands. For example, if you want to create a directory called test_directory in the environment, the args parameter will be as follows:

```
['mkdir','test_directory']
```

This will be used in every other step.

2. Now, continue to the second step. The goal of this step is to validate our Python code using the Python unittest package:

```
- name: 'gcr.io/$PROJECT_ID/cicd-basic'
    id: Validation Test
    entrypoint: python
    args: [
            '-m',
            'unittest',
            'tests/test_calculate.py'
    ]
```

Note that we set the name parameter to gcr.io/$PROJECT_ID/cicd-basic. This means we can use the Docker image from the first step and use and test the code that is already stored in that image.

There is an additional parameter here called entrypoint. The entrypoint parameter is used to change the default entry command in the environment. In this case, we are using Python. To illustrate this, we will convert the parameters we mentioned previously into this command, and it will run in a container:

```
$ python -m unittest tests/test_calculate.py
```

Note that this step can fail or succeed, depending on the unit test results. If it fails, Cloud Build will stop the process and won't continue to the next step.

3. For the final step, the main goal is to push the image to **Google Container Registry (GCR)**:

```
- name: gcr.io/cloud-builders/docker
    id: Push Image to GCR
    args: [
            'push',
            'gcr.io/$PROJECT_ID/cicd-basic:latest'
    ]
```

The last step is similar to the first step – that is, using the public Docker image from gcr.io/cloud-builders/docker. However, in this step, we will use the push command to push the image to our project container register.

To summarize this step, we need to copy all the code examples from the `packt github` repository to our repository. This step also explains the `cloudbuild.yaml` file. We've learned that to create a CI pipeline in Cloud Build, you must define the steps in the `yaml` file by configuring the necessary parameters. At this point, you don't need to change any code in this example.

Creating a Cloud Build trigger

Now, go back to your GCP console and go to the Cloud Build console. You can find it in the navigation bar, under the **CI/CD** section:

1. There are five menus in the Cloud Build console – **Dashboard**, **History**, **Repositories**, **Triggers**, and **Settings**. Let's choose **Triggers** by clicking the respective button:

   Figure 12.7 – The Cloud Build Triggers page

   Let's create a trigger by clicking the **CREATE TRIGGER** button.

2. On the **Create trigger** page, input any name as the identifier.

   Take a look at the types of events that can invoke triggers. We can push to a branch, push a new tag, or pull a request, all of which are commonly available in GitHub or GitLab. Looking at these options will give you an idea of how automation can occur. Imagine that you and your colleagues change the code in a repository; every push or pull request will trigger a Cloud Build run.

   Keep all the inputs as-is except for the source repository. If you click **Repository**, you will see your GitHub repository from *step 1*. In the **Branch** field, click the form and use .* (any branch) from the suggested input. Here is an example:

   Figure 12.8 – Configuring the Repository and Branch fields

When you're done, click the **CREATE** button.

Pushing the code to the GitHub repository

So far, we have three elements:

- A GitHub repository
- A Cloud Build trigger attached to the GitHub repository
- Code in the Cloud Shell environment

The final step is to push our code from the local Cloud Shell environment to the GitHub repository. Let's get started:

1. First, go back to your Cloud Shell.

   Inside the GitHub repository folder that you created in the second step, push the code using the following `git` commands:

   ```
   $ git add .
   $ git commit -m "initial commit"
   $ git push
   ```

   If this is the first time you are committing to using `git` from your Cloud Shell environment, you will see an error message stating **Please tell me who you are**. In this case, follow the instructions in that message by running the following two commands:

   ```
   $ git config --global user.email "[Your email address]"
   $ git config --global user.name "[Your name]"
   ```

   You will only need to do this once in every new environment.

   After running these commands, you can check the **Build history** page:

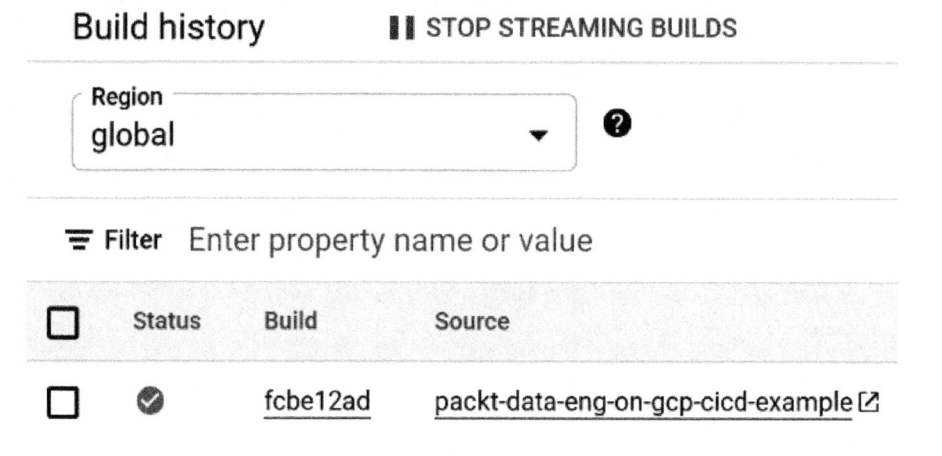

   Figure 12.9 – An example of a Cloud Build run successfully running

2. Check whether the Cloud Build run has been triggered and is running successfully. After successfully pushing it, go to your Cloud Build console and open the **History** menu. You will see the **Build history** page. If there are no issues after running these four steps, you will see that a Cloud Build run is running in the build history:

   If you click the respective build ID (`fcbe12ad`), you will also see the steps that we learned about in the *Developing the code and Cloud Build scripts* section, when we discussed the `cloudbuild.yaml` file:

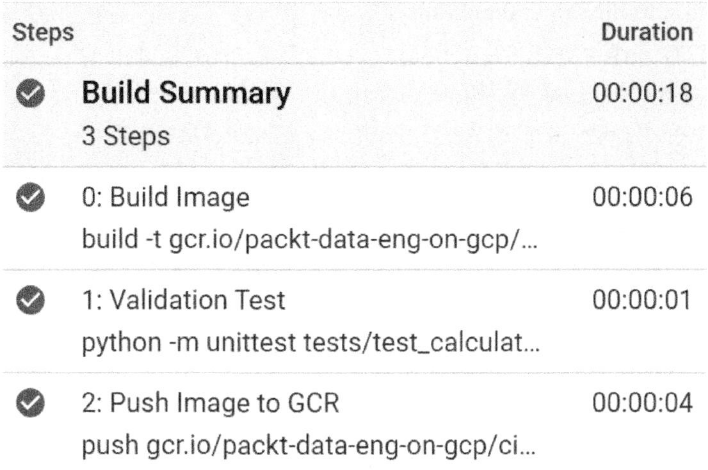

Steps	Duration
✓ **Build Summary** 3 Steps	00:00:18
✓ 0: Build Image build -t gcr.io/packt-data-eng-on-gcp/...	00:00:06
✓ 1: Validation Test python -m unittest tests/test_calculat...	00:00:01
✓ 2: Push Image to GCR push gcr.io/packt-data-eng-on-gcp/ci...	00:00:04

   Figure 12.10 – Build Summary and the respective steps

   Check whether all the steps have run successfully.

3. Finally, we want to check the stored container. To do that, in the GCP console, find **Container Registry** from the navigation menu, under the **CI/CD** section. You will see that the image is there:

   packt-data-eng-on-gcp

Name ↑	Hostname	Visibility
ci-example	gcr.io	Private

   Figure 12.11 – The Container Registry console

   `ci-example` is the Docker image that is hosted in `gcr.io`, which is managed by Google Cloud. By default, the visibility of this Docker image is **Private**, which means that only you or any other users with the right IAM permissions can access this image.

For illustration purposes, let's try to make some unit tests fail intentionally. For example, I will change the `calculate.py` file, as follows:

```
result = arg_1 + arg_2
```

The preceding line of code will make the plus (+) icon change to a multiply (*) icon:

```
result = arg_1 * arg_2
```

I will commit and push it to the GitHub repository. As expected, Cloud Build will automatically trigger and start the Cloud Build run.

The result will be **Failed**. You can check this by clicking the Cloud Build step's log. For example, you will see the following logs upon clicking the **Validation Test** step:

```
1  Already have image: gcr.io/packt-data-eng-on-gcp/cicd-basic
2  F
3  ======================================================================
4  FAIL: testValue_sum (tests.test_calculate.TestSum)
5  ----------------------------------------------------------------------
6  Traceback (most recent call last):
7    File "/workspace/tests/test_calculate.py", line 7, in testValue_sum
8      self.assertEqual(calculate.sum_two_values(1,2), 3, "Should be equal to 3")
9  AssertionError: 2 != 3 : Should be equal to 3
10
11 ----------------------------------------------------------------------
```

Figure 12.12 – An example of AssertionError in the Cloud Build logs

And that's it! The log shows you that the expected value is not correct. That's the power of CI. Imagine that there are tens of developers working in a repository and that there are hundreds of commits in a day. This automation will help your day-to-day life as an engineer.

In this exercise, I didn't mention or provide an example of CD because it only involves a few steps. You can create the CD steps in the same way that you perform CI using Cloud Build. Also, it depends on what applications you have; the CD steps might be different. For example, to productionize our `calculate.py` file, we can deploy it as a web API. Learning how to deploy a web API is outside the scope of this book, so we won't discuss it here. You can see a documentation example of how CD works with Cloud Run here: https://cloud.google.com/run/docs/continuous-deployment-with-cloud-build.

To summarize, in this exercise, you learned how to use all the GCP services to run a CI pipeline using a Cloud Source Repository, Cloud Build triggers, a Cloud Build run, and a Google Container Registry. At the end of this exercise, you learned how automation can save you a lot of time while you're testing code when many developers are collaborating. However, you also learned that the steps to create automation are not easy. We have illustrated everything we discussed regarding CI/CD considerations and the pasta chef analogy. Now, let's use Cloud Build to deploy Cloud Composer code.

Exercise – deploying Cloud Composer jobs using Cloud Build

In this section, we will continue creating a Cloud Build pipeline. This time, I will help you get an idea of how this practice can be implemented in terms of data engineering. To do that, we will try to create a CI/CD pipeline to deploy a Cloud Composer DAG.

In this exercise, we will use the DAG from *Chapter 4, Building Workflows for Batch Data Loading Using Cloud Composer*. Let's refresh ourselves a little bit on the exercises from that chapter.

In *Chapter 4, Building Workflows for Batch Data Loading Using Cloud Composer*, we learned how Cloud Composer works. We learned that in Cloud Composer, you can develop DAGs to create data pipelines. These data pipelines can use Airflow operators to manage BigQuery, CloudSQL, GCS, or simple Bash scripts. In those exercises, we practiced five levels of DAGs, with the level-one DAG being the simplest one and the level-five DAG being the most complex. To deploy a DAG, we can store the Python file containing the DAG in the Cloud Composer GCS bucket, in a specific directory named `dags`.

In this exercise, we will use the level one DAG from *Chapter 4, Building Workflows for Batch Data Loading Using Cloud Composer*. We will use level one to avoid any complexity that is not relevant to this chapter, such as preparing the Cloud SQL instances, BigQuery datasets, and the other long steps that were discussed in that chapter. However, the same technique that applies to this level-one DAG can be applied to the other DAG levels. As a high-level summary, here are the steps that we will go through:

1. Preparing the CI/CD environment.
2. Preparing the `cloudbuild.yaml` configuration file.
3. Pushing the DAG to our GitHub repository.
4. Checking the CI/CD result in the GCS bucket and Cloud Composer.

You have two options to run this exercise:

- The first option is to recreate the Cloud Composer environment and deploy the DAG in the new Cloud Composer environment. In this case, you can use the new GCS bucket that's being used by Cloud Composer as the target deployment.

- The second option is to use the GCS bucket from your Cloud Composer environment from *Chapter 4, Building Workflows for Batch Data Loading Using Cloud Composer*. Creating a Cloud Composer environment can be time-consuming (around 30 minutes) and costly. You can choose not to create the Cloud Composer environment and only use the GCS bucket as the target deployment.

Either way, what you need is a GCS bucket that you can use in the `cloudbuild.yaml` file later. Now, let's get started.

Preparing the CI/CD environment

The first step is preparing the environment, which includes doing the following:

- Creating a GitHub repository in the Cloud Source Repository
- Cloning the empty GitHub repository to Cloud Shell
- Creating a Cloud Build trigger and connecting it to the GitHub repository

I won't show you each step in this exercise. Practice going through them yourself by using your experience from the previous section, *Exercise – implementing CI using Cloud Build*.

At the end of this step, your environment will be ready. For example, here is mine:

- Cloud Source Repository name: `packt-data-eng-on-gcp-cicd-cloud-composer`
- Cloud Build trigger name: `cicd-cloud-composer-trigger`

In Cloud Shell, I have the following GitHub repository folder after using the `gcloud clone` command:

```
adiwijaya_public@cloudshell:~/packt-data-eng-on-gcp-cicd-cloud-composer
(packt-data-eng-on-gcp) $ pwd
/home/adiwijaya_public/packt-data-eng-on-gcp-cicd-cloud-composer
```

Figure 12.13 – The expected directory is inside the repository folder

Make sure you are in the right directory, which is inside the project folder. In the next section, we will prepare the `cloudbuild.yaml` file.

Preparing the cloudbuild.yaml configuration file

Now, let's prepare the `cloudbuild.yaml` file and the other necessary code. The example code for this exercise can be downloaded or git-cloned from the packt github repository: https://github.com/PacktPublishing/Data-Engineering-with-Google-Cloud-Platform-Second-Edition/tree/main/chapter-12/code/cicd_cloud_composer

Note the difference between this project compared to the previous exercise in the Python file. In the previous exercise, we had the `calculate.py` file as the main code, while this time, we have the `dags` folder containing the Airflow DAG.

The next thing you need to do is copy all the files in the example code to the GitHub repository that you created in the *Preparing the CI/CD environment* section. For example, this is what it looks like if I open the folder via Cloud Editor:

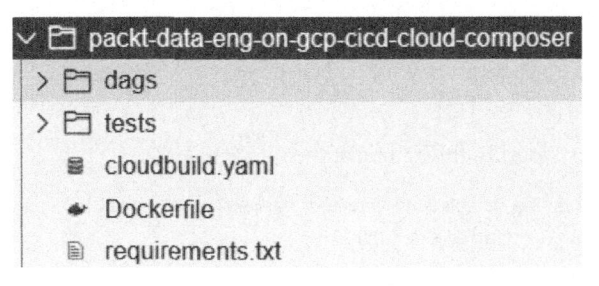

Figure 12.14 – Example code files in Cloud Editor

Now, let's look at `cloudbuild.yaml` and the necessary CI/CD steps:

1. The first step is using Docker to build the image from the Dockerfile:

   ```
   - name: gcr.io/cloud-builders/docker
       id: Build Airflow DAGs Builder
       args: [
               'build',
               '-t', 'gcr.io/$PROJECT_ID/airflow-data-pipeline',
               '--cache-from',
               'gcr.io/$PROJECT_ID/airflow-data-pipeline:latest',
               './'
       ]
   ```

   If you open the Docker file, you will see that it involves installing Airflow, as stated in the `requirements.txt` file:

   `RUN pip3 install --upgrade --no-cache-dir -r requirements.txt`

   This is important because we will need the Airflow Python package to unit-test the DAG in the next step.

2. The second step is performing unit testing:

   ```
   - name: 'gcr.io/$PROJECT_ID/airflow-data-pipeline'
       id: Validation Test
       entrypoint: python
       env:
         - AIRFLOW__CORE__DAGS_FOLDER=/workspace/dags
       args:
         - -m
         - unittest
         - tests/dag_tests.py
   ```

   We learned about all the parameters in this step in the previous exercise, except for the `env` parameter. The `env` parameter is used to set Linux environment variables. We need to specify the `AIRFLOW__CORE__DAGS_FOLDER` parameter so that Airflow knows where to find the DAG files. The `dag_tests.py` file will check your DAG and stop Cloud Build from running if there are issues in your DAG.

3. The third step in Cloud Build is to push the image to GCR:

   ```
   - name: gcr.io/cloud-builders/docker
     id: Push Image to GCR
     args: [
             'push',
             'gcr.io/$PROJECT_ID/airflow-data-pipeline:latest'
     ]
   ```

   There is nothing new in this step compared to the previous exercise. This step is straightforward. But let's discuss why we need this image to be stored in GCR.

   At this point, you know that you can deploy a DAG to Cloud Composer by uploading the Python file containing the DAG to a GCS bucket. We can't use Docker images to deploy a DAG, so this third step is optional. The main reason we are performing this step is so that we can reuse it for the next run as a cache. Note that, in the first step, when we build the Docker image, we declared the `--cache-from` parameter, like this:

   ```
   '--cache-from', 'gcr.io/$PROJECT_ID/airflow-data-pipeline:latest'
   ```

   The benefit of doing this is that we can make the Cloud Build runtime quicker.

4. Finally, we must deploy the `dag` parameter from the container to the GCS bucket using the `gsutil rsync` command:

   ```
   - name: gcr.io/cloud-builders/gsutil
     id: Deploy DAGs
     args:
       - -m
       - rsync
       - -r
       - -c
       - -x
       - .*\.pyc|airflow_monitoring.py
       - /workspace/dags
       - [GCS bucket dags path]
   ```

   Change `[GCS bucket dags path]` to your GCS path – for example, mine is `gs://us-central1-packt-composer--76564980-bucket/dags/`.

   The `gsutil rsync` command will copy the files from the `/workspace/dags` directory to the GCS bucket. If you are not familiar with `rsync`, it's similar to the command to copy files but only if the file does not exist in the destination folder.

You may also be confused about the -m, -r, -c, and -x parameters. They are all just additional parameters in `rsync` – for example, -m is used to make `rsync` be parallel or, in other words, faster. You can check all the parameter descriptions and what `gsutil rsync` is by reading the public documentation: https://cloud.google.com/storage/docs/gsutil/commands/rsync.

To summarize, in this step, you must copy all the files from the packt github example to your GitHub repository in Cloud Shell. Then, you need to change [GCS bucket dags path] to your GCS bucket path.

Now we need to use the Cloud Build file by adding it to the GitHub repository. We will do that in the next section.

Pushing the DAG to our GitHub repository

The next step is straightforward – you need to commit and push the code in your GitHub repository. For example, from inside your GitHub repository folder, use the following commands:

```
$ git add .
$ git commit -m "initial commit"
$ git push
```

These commands will push your code to the Cloud Source Repository and trigger the Cloud Build run.

Checking the CI/CD result in the GCS bucket and Cloud Composer

If everything has been successful, you will see the Cloud Build run in the CI/CD pipeline:

Steps	Duration
✓ **Build Summary** 4 Steps	00:01:31
✓ 0: Build Airflow DAGs Builder build -t gcr.io/packt-data-eng-on-gcp/...	00:01:02
✓ 1: Validation Test python -m unittest tests/dag_tests.py	00:00:01
✓ 2: Push Image to GCR push gcr.io/packt-data-eng-on-gcp/ai...	00:00:17
✓ 3: Deploy DAGs -m rsync -r -c -x .*\.pyc|airflow_monit...	00:00:03

Figure 12.15 – Cloud Build – Build Summary with four steps

The pipeline will check `level_1_dag` in the validation step, and the deployment will be done using the `gsutil rsync` command.

You can check your GCS bucket to see whether the `level_1_dag.py` file has been copied to the correct path:

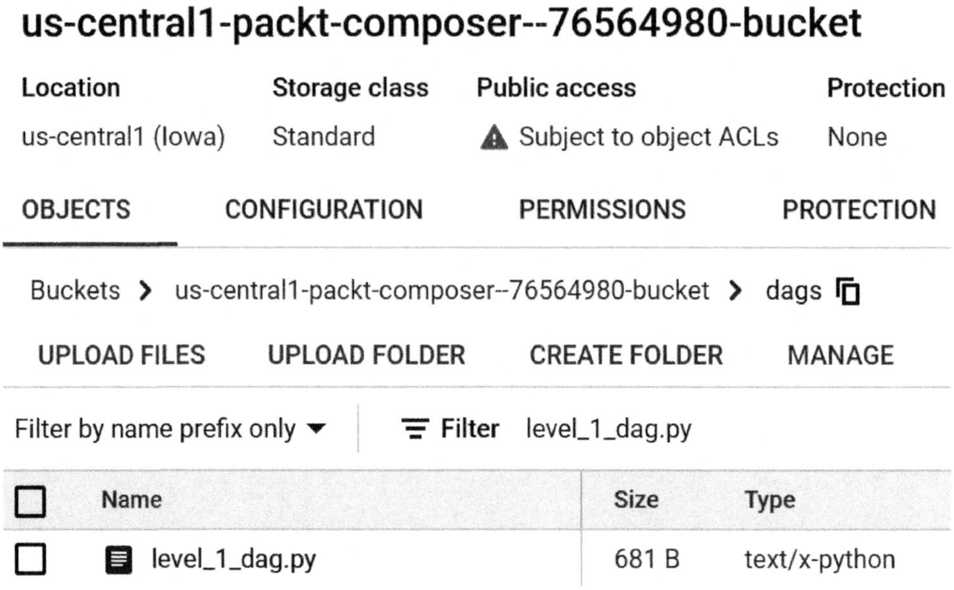

us-central1-packt-composer--76564980-bucket

Location	Storage class	Public access	Protection
us-central1 (Iowa)	Standard	⚠ Subject to object ACLs	None

OBJECTS | CONFIGURATION | PERMISSIONS | PROTECTION

Buckets > us-central1-packt-composer--76564980-bucket > dags

UPLOAD FILES   UPLOAD FOLDER   CREATE FOLDER   MANAGE

Filter by name prefix only ▼   ≡ Filter level_1_dag.py

Name	Size	Type
📄 level_1_dag.py	681 B	text/x-python

Figure 12.16 – The Cloud Composer GCS bucket contains the DAG file

If it is, then congratulations! You have just created a CI/CD pipeline that manages Cloud Composer DAGs.

If you choose to create a Cloud Composer environment to practice this exercise, you can also check the Airflow UI to see whether the DAG is running. However, if you don't have the Cloud Composer environment running, that's not an issue – whenever a Python file containing a DAG is uploaded to the `/dags` directory, it will automatically run in Airflow. If you are not sure about how DAG works in Cloud Composer and Airflow, you can always go back to *Chapter 4, Building Workflows for Batch Data Loading Using Cloud Composer*.

To test whether the validation step works, I'll try to make the DAG fail intentionally. For example, in the `dags/level_1_dag.py` DAG file, when we're defining `schedule_interval`, it should look like this:

```
schedule_interval='0 5 * * *',
```

The format for `schedule_interval` should follow `cron` expression syntax. I will change it to a normal string here, like this:

```
schedule_interval='This is wrong',
```

After pushing this change to the GitHub repository, this is what happens to the Cloud Build run:

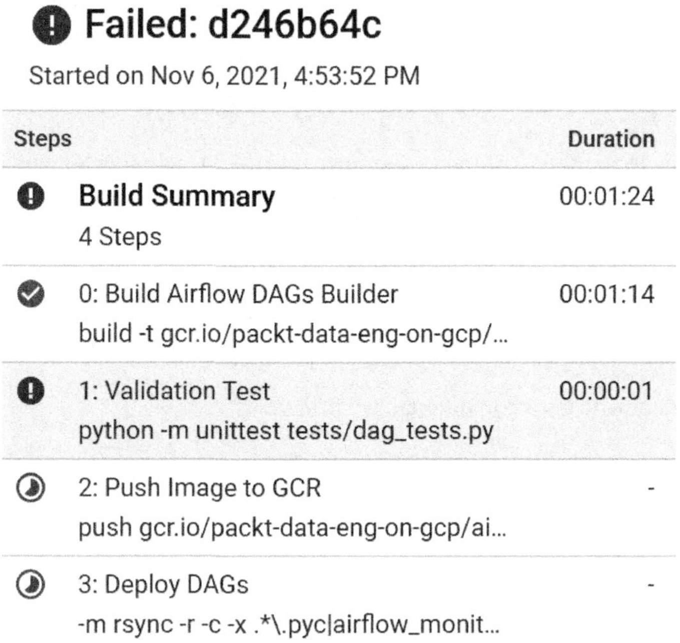

🔴 Failed: d246b64c
Started on Nov 6, 2021, 4:53:52 PM

Steps	Duration
🔴 **Build Summary** 4 Steps	00:01:24
✅ 0: Build Airflow DAGs Builder build -t gcr.io/packt-data-eng-on-gcp/...	00:01:14
🔴 1: Validation Test python -m unittest tests/dag_tests.py	00:00:01
◐ 2: Push Image to GCR push gcr.io/packt-data-eng-on-gcp/ai...	-
◐ 3: Deploy DAGs -m rsync -r -c -x .*\.pyc|airflow_monit...	-

Figure 12.17 – The Cloud Build run failed the test

The Cloud Build stops at the **Validation Test** stage. Here are the logs, explaining the error:

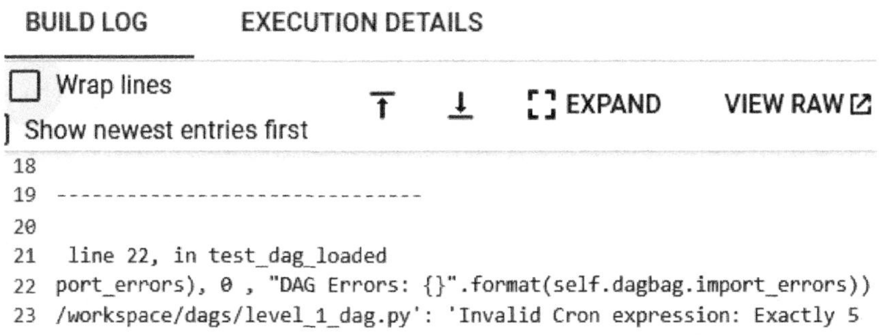

```
18
19  ------------------------------
20
21    line 22, in test_dag_loaded
22  port_errors), 0 , "DAG Errors: {}".format(self.dagbag.import_errors))
23  /workspace/dags/level_1_dag.py': 'Invalid Cron expression: Exactly 5
```

Figure 12.18 – An example DAG error message in the Cloud Build logs

It says that `/workspace/dags/level_1_dag.py : Invalid Cron expression`. This is perfect! With this mechanism, if anyone pushes a failed DAG, the DAG won't be deployed to the GCS bucket. On top of that, we can use these logs to work out which code has an issue and what it is.

With that, we've finished learning about CI/CD on GCP. Let's try to review the CI/CD as a concept, and I'll share some of my thoughts on the best practices and anti-patterns to implement CI/CD in data engineering.

CI/CD best practices in data engineering

After learning how to use the GCP tools to implement CI/CD, you now hopefully have an idea of the possibilities available to a data engineering team when implementing CI/CD on a data platform.

You may start to think of some ideas, such as the following:

- Checking how clean your code is
- Checking your data quality before going into productions
- Planning automatic testing in different environments

In data engineering specifically, after working with dozens of companies from many industries, I haven't seen any golden standard on how to implement CI/CD. It depends on the skill set of the team, the number of people in the team, the complexity of the systems, and the budget.

What makes this topic exciting is that it's still evolving. Even though there is no golden rule and almost endless possibilities, I saw some patterns. In this section, I will share my thoughts on the considerations and best practices I've seen implemented in data engineering teams:

- **Prioritize code testing over data testing**:

    Implementing CI/CD in data engineering is not always straightforward. Why? Because, often, the data engineering team's focus is to make sure the data is clean. This data team's goal is not wrong, but cleaning data is not as straightforward as cleaning code.

    For example, if you want to make sure your code works properly, it's easy to create unit test scenarios to check the input and output of functions. However, making sure a data pipeline's output is correct is never easy because data engineers rely on unknown data sources. Unknown here means there are often no guarantees from the data source providers that the data is clean.

    Because data engineers need to handle unknown data sources, they often use some data testing approaches – for example, checking null values, checking data types, checking value distribution, counting the values, and some other data testing techniques. These approaches are valid and very common to be implemented as data testing scenarios, but as you may have noticed, those approaches will never guarantee the data output is valid.

    Further, even though the team is satisfied with the data testing approaches, it may raise concerns about the cost of running all those tests on all data which is big in size.

    As you can see, implementing CI/CD from scratch that focuses on data testing is not straightforward, which is often counterproductive. My best practice is to start implementing CI/CD that focuses on code testing.

Often, implementing CI/CD that focuses on code alone in data engineering will give a lot of benefits to the entire data pipeline quality.

Before integrating data testing, it's beneficial to establish a solid CI/CD foundation focused on code. This ensures that the team is comfortable with the automation processes and has already improved code quality. With this strong base, the team can then effectively brainstorm and implement data testing within the existing CI/CD pipeline.

- **Follow the best practices from software engineering practice**:

    As I mentioned earlier in this chapter in the *Understanding the data engineer's relationship with CI/CD practices* section, CI/CD has been practiced a lot by software engineering teams. There are already a lot of best practices that are worth following. Data engineers should be aware of them and try to follow them. I will not explain them in detail in this book because it's a common topic that you can find on the internet easily. Here are some examples of great practices – maintain versioning, commit to a repository often, automate testing, and have a deployment strategy.

    What I will add here is that you need to add SQL code testing on top of other code testing. What I mean by SQL code testing here is really testing the SQL as code, not the data results, as already explained in the first point about code testing.

    For example, you can check the SQL cleanliness by using SQL linter. One of the popular ones that supports the BigQuery dialect is SQLFluff; you can check it out at this link: https://sqlfluff.com. By using SQL linter, you can set a standard on how you want data engineers to write SQL scripts.

    Other examples are to have a SQL peer reviewer mechanism and implement some unit testing, which is doable using Dataform, as explained in the *Exercise – practicing data quality using Dataform* section in *Chapter 10, Data Governance in GCP*.

    Just to be clear (and related to the first best practice point) – the primary focus of SQL testing is code quality, not data quality. When this focus is achieved, the team can start expanding the test on data quality.

- **Considering budget and data testing**:

    If the data engineering team decides to implement CI/CD for data cleanliness, they should think about how to test the data. This can be done with some approaches, as mentioned in the first point, *Prioritize code testing over data testing*.

    This topic of discussion when deciding data testing will most likely involve budget as an important aspect. The reason is that testing data needs to be done by running queries, and doing so to all data in a data platform is expensive.

    For example, it's common to have production and non-production environments, where non-production environments can be more than one environment – for example, a **user acceptance testing environment** (**UAT**), **system integration testing environment** (**SIT**), and a **development environment** (**DEV**).

While it is common to have those multiple environments for software engineering, for data engineering, it may raise a concern. For example, if a production environment has 1 PB of data, the common questions are as follows:

- Should we duplicate all the 1PB data to all the non-production environments?
- Should we run all testing queries to all the incoming data in all non-production environments?

I'm sorry that I don't have a single answer to those questions for now. The answer and the final decision often come down to the budget of an organization. Ideally, the answer is yes to all the preceding questions because the more tests we do on actual datasets, the better. However, often, the cost of implementing them is too high, so this is an area that has no single correct answer.

I often encountered data platforms that only store data in production; thus, the development and testing run in a production environment. In another case, I encountered data platforms that implement sampling and store data in non-production environments. Some others chose to replicate all the data and do the testing in multiple non-production environments.

Every data engineering team should decide together with the decision-makers, by understanding the budget constraint, to implement the best-fit data testing strategy.

- **Always try to be consistent by making it a team effort**:

    The last point I want to share is about how we should see CI/CD as a practice. *Practice* means it's something that the entire team should do together day by day. CI/CD should be practiced as a team effort and consistently. I'll explain what I mean by that.

    I often see the implementation of CI/CD that is too complicated and results in very inconsistent processes. This is a very counterproductive to what CI/CD is for, which is to fasten development and deployment iterations. The complication usually comes because there is no clear communication and documentation.

    For an individual, it's not that difficult to plan a CI/CD pipeline, but making sure all the team agrees and understands the pipeline is very important. This is often overlooked by an organization.

These best practices are the last section in this chapter. Now, let's summarize what we've learned in this chapter.

Summary

In this chapter, we learned about how CI/CD works in GCP services. More specifically, we learned about this from the perspective of a data engineer. CI/CD is a big topic by itself and is more mature in the software development practice. However, lately, it's become more and more common for data engineers to follow this practice in big organizations.

We started this chapter by talking about high-level concepts and ended it with an exercise that showed how data engineers can use CI/CD in a data project. We used Cloud Build, a Cloud Source Repository, and Google Container Registry in the exercises. Understanding these concepts and what kind of technologies are involved were the two main goals of this chapter. If you want to learn more about DevOps practices, containers, and unit testing, check out the links in the *Further reading* section.

This was the final technical chapter in this book. If you have read all the chapters in this book, then you've learned about all the core GCP services related to data engineering. At this point, I hope you've got the confidence you need to build a data project on GCP. The next chapter will be the final chapter of this book, where we will revisit the content of this book in a quiz format to boost your confidence and help you if you don't understand anything. I will also share tips on how to get the Google Cloud certification and how to follow the data engineering career path.

Further reading

To learn more about the topics that were covered in this chapter, take a look at the following resources:

- *DevOps practice*, by Google Cloud: `https://cloud.google.com/devops`
- *Containers on the cloud*, by Google Cloud: `https://cloud.google.com/containers`
- An updated blog post on software engineer testing: `https://testing.googleblog.com/`

13
Boosting Your Confidence as a Data Engineer

In this chapter, we will review and check our understanding of all the topics that have been covered throughout this book. We will do that by simulating the Google Cloud certification's question format. I'll start by talking about the Google Cloud certification so that you become familiar with it.

As the last part of this book, I will share my thoughts on what the future of data engineering is. I hope that, by reaching the final section of this book, you will have all you need to have confidence as a data engineer working with **Google Cloud Platform** (**GCP**).

In this chapter, we will cover the following topics:

- Overviewing the Google Cloud certification
- Quiz – reviewing all the concepts you've learned about
- The past, present, and future of data engineering
- Boosting your confidence and final thoughts

Let's get started!

Overviewing the Google Cloud certification

Let's start this final chapter by talking about the Google Cloud certification. In my opinion, taking the certification is important. I highly recommend that you take it – not only to get the certificate on paper but also to validate how much you know about the topics that are needed to be a Google Cloud professional. The experience that you receive while preparing for the certification is the most important part of your journey. Regardless of whether you passed or failed the exam, I believe that you will gain knowledge along the way.

Google Cloud provides a list of official certifications that you can use to validate your expertise with Google Cloud technology. There are three main categories available:

- Foundational
- Associate
- Professional

Foundational is intended for anyone with no hands-on experience with Google Cloud technology. *Associate* is recommended for anyone who has 6+ months of Google Cloud experience. Finally, *Professional* is recommended for anyone who has 1+ years of Google Cloud experience, with 3+ years of industry experience.

My suggestion is to take the certifications based on your experience. However, in terms of data engineering, there is only one certification available at this time. This is under the *Professional* category, and it's called **Google Cloud Data Engineer**. I highly recommend that you take this one. Check out the public information about the Google Cloud Data Engineer certification at `https://cloud.google.com/certification/data-engineer`.

The other relevant certifications that can support your data engineering skills are Cloud Architect, Cloud DevOps Engineer, and Machine Learning Engineer. They are not at the core of data engineering, but if you plan to expand your knowledge, they are good candidates.

In this chapter, I will focus on discussing the Professional Data Engineer certification. I will share the preparation tips, example questions, and their relevance to the content of this book. My sharing will be based on my experience passing the certifications three times, in 2019, 2021, and 2024. There might be changes in the future or when you read this book, but hopefully, there won't be many. As a disclaimer, note that everything that I have shared in this book, and especially in this chapter, is purely my personal opinion based on my own experience. For the official and most updated information from Google Cloud, you can always go to its public website.

Exam preparation tips

First, let's talk about *whether you should prepare for the certification.* My answer is, yes, you should! This doesn't only count for beginners – even if you already have enough hands-on experience with engineering data in Google Cloud, you should start preparing.

There are a lot of questions that are detailed and cover edge cases. For example, some questions might be asked about **Google Cloud Storage** (**GCS**), which you probably already have good knowledge and experience using, due to the exercises that were presented in this book. In the exam, there might be questions such as the following: *What is the best storage class in Cloud Storage if the user intends to access the data less than once every quarter?*

    A. **Standard**

    B. **Nearline**

C. **Coldline**

D. **Archive**

The answer to this question is **Coldline**. If you are not sure what this means, take a look at the following screenshot, which shows the creation of a GCS bucket:

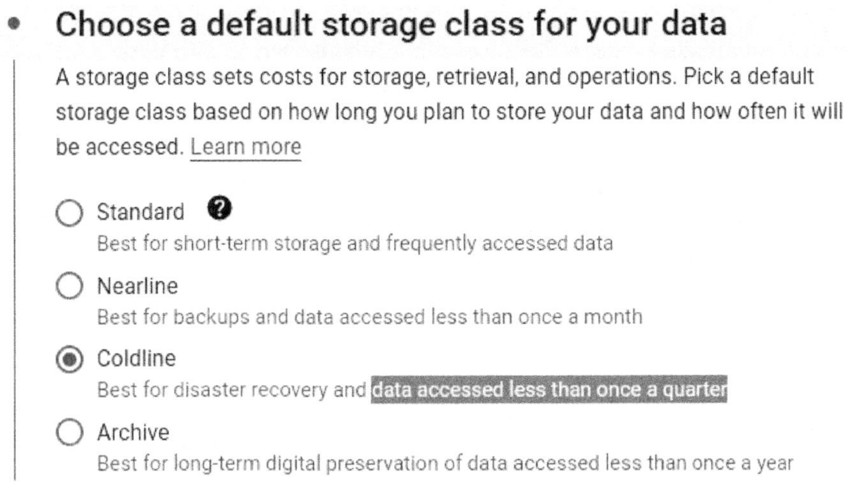

- **Choose a default storage class for your data**

  A storage class sets costs for storage, retrieval, and operations. Pick a default storage class based on how long you plan to store your data and how often it will be accessed. Learn more

  ○ Standard
    Best for short-term storage and frequently accessed data

  ○ Nearline
    Best for backups and data accessed less than once a month

  ◉ Coldline
    Best for disaster recovery and data accessed less than once a quarter

  ○ Archive
    Best for long-term digital preservation of data accessed less than once a year

Figure 13.1 – The GCS bucket storage class options

Sometimes, you need to remain aware and remember detailed information about each of the technologies, so make sure you are prepared and practice a lot.

Now, let's talk about what is covered in the exam. There are five sections in the Data Engineer exam:

- Designing data processing systems
- Ingesting and processing data
- Storing data
- Preparing and using data for analysis
- Maintaining and automating data workloads

Each section will validate your knowledge of all the GCP services related to data engineering. You can cross-reference with the Google Cloud public website to make sure the list is still the same and check the more detailed sub-topics.

Compared to what we've learned in this book, the exam topic area is broader. Remember that the goal of this book is to help you narrow down the most important knowledge that's required for you – to be a data engineer who can use GCP. On the other hand, the exam tests your knowledge very broadly. This means you need to expand a little bit from what you've learned in this book.

The GCP services that might be included in the exam are:

- BigQuery, GCS, Cloud Composer, Dataproc, Dataflow, Pub/Sub, CloudSQL, Dataplex, Dataform, Data Loss Prevention or Sensitive Data Protection, Looker Studio, Vertex AI, IAM, Looker, Cloud Data Fusion, Bigtable, Spanner, Datastore, Memorystore, Data Transfer Service, Dataprep, Cloud Logging, Cloud Monitoring, and Analytics Hub.

To compare and summarize what we've learned in this book, here is a list of the GCP services that we used in our exercises:

- BigQuery, GCS, Cloud Composer, Dataproc, Dataflow, Pub/Sub, CloudSQL, Dataplex, Dataform, Data Loss Prevention or Sensitive Data Protection, Looker Studio, Vertex AI, IAM, Cloud Shell, Cloud Editor, Cloud Build, Google Container Registry, Cloud Source Repository, and Terraform.

Based on these two lists, we've learned about almost all of the topics mentioned. However, some topics haven't been discussed in this book, including:

- Looker, Cloud Data Fusion, Bigtable, Spanner, Datastore, Memorystore, Data Transfer Service, Dataprep, Cloud Logging, Cloud Monitoring, and Analytics Hub.

These are important technologies available on GCP, but I decided not to create dedicated chapters for those technologies in this book. In the next section, I will briefly talk about them and point out the common questions that are related to those technologies.

Extra GCP service materials

In this section, I will list all the other GCP services that might be part of the Google Cloud Data Engineer certification's questions. The information that will be provided here is not the most complete resource to learn about technologies. What I will put is a very generic explanation for you to at least be familiar with the terminologies and their positioning compared to the other GCP services.

Bigtable, Spanner, and Datastore

These three services shared a common positioning in technology architecture. They are highly scalable application databases. Refer to the *Service mapping and prioritization* section in *Chapter 2, Big Data Capabilities on GCP*, for more information.

It's important to know how to choose between these three application databases. The following diagram provides an overview of them in the form of a decision tree:

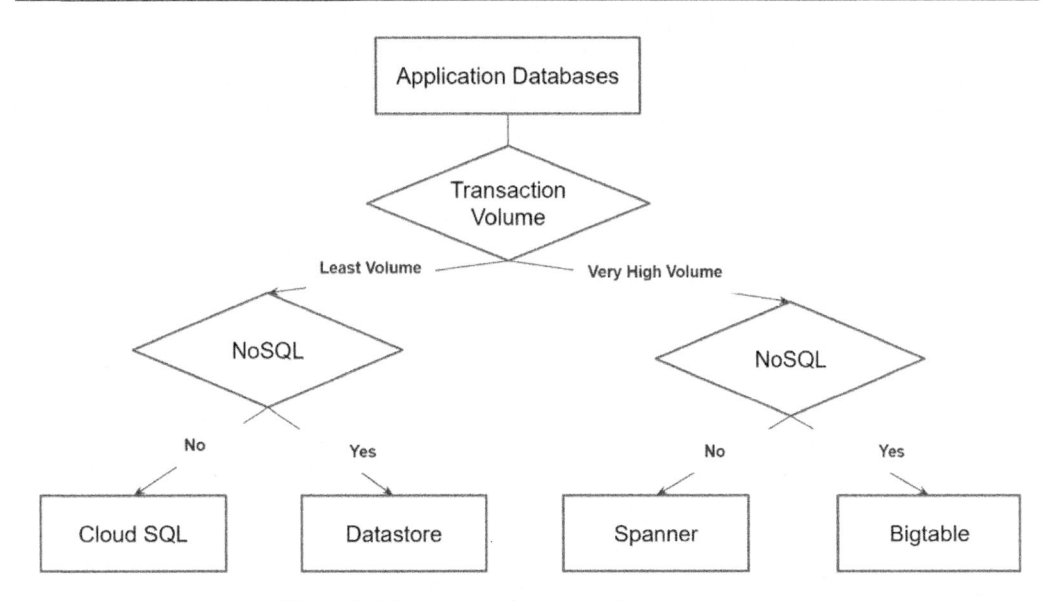

Figure 13.2 – A decision tree to choose application databases on GCP

The preceding diagram shows a highly simplified decision tree to choose between four GCP services for application databases. I added Cloud SQL here because this service is also an option for application databases. The first consideration is the data volume. If there is a requirement to handle an extremely high volume of data, such as more than 1 TB a day, that's a good indication to use either Spanner or Bigtable. On the other hand, if the data to handle is less than 1 TB a day, you should choose either Cloud SQL or Datastore.

The second consideration is whether the application database requires SQL or NoSQL databases – in other terms, a structured or unstructured database. On the left-hand side of the diagram, if the requirement is to handle structured data, choose Cloud SQL. Otherwise, you can choose Datastore. Datastore is a NoSQL database with a document data model. On the right-hand side of the diagram, for remarkably high volumes, Spanner is the best option for structured and semi-structured data. Bigtable is the best option for unstructured data, as it is a managed wide-column NoSQL database.

There are many other aspects to consider when you need to decide between these GCP services, such as high availability, the replication method, zonal regional or global replication, price, available expertise, and other aspects. However, for the certification's purposes, you need to know their high-level positioning. There might be questions such as the following: *Your company needs to choose a database to handle data that is more than 10 TB in size. The data is generated from sensors that should be handled in a NoSQL database. The end product is a real-time application that requires high throughput and low latency. Which service should you use?*

- **Cloud SQL**
- **Datastore**

- **Spanner**
- **Bigtable**

The answer is **Bigtable**. The data volume is high, so it requires a NoSQL database.

Regarding these four services, there will be more questions regarding Bigtable compared to the others. We'll talk about it in the next section.

Bigtable

As we mentioned previously, Bigtable is a Google Cloud-managed wide-column NoSQL database. Bigtable is a very scalable technology that has extremely high throughput and low latency and provides high availability.

Bigtable is highly correlated to an open-source product called Apache HBase. Bigtable supports the Apache HBase client through Java.

Bigtable works well for use cases such as storing time series data for real-time applications, transaction histories, stock price histories, and IoT. The key difference between Bigtable and BigQuery use cases is the real-time aspects. Even though BigQuery is capable of handling real-time data ingestion using streaming ingestion, it's not suitable as a database that serves real-time data for low-latency applications. On the other hand, Bigtable is not capable of handling data warehouse use cases that require a lot of `JOIN` operations.

There are many ways to optimize Bigtable. One of the easiest ways to improve performance is to switch from using an HDD as the underlying storage to SSD. Another way to make sure that performance is optimal is by choosing the right key for each table. Bigtable performance can be very severely affected by key hotspots. For example, some bad key examples are a website domain name and a timestamp. Some good key examples are random numbers, timestamps combined with other columns, and reversed domain names. Check out the public documentation from Google Cloud regarding this topic: `https://cloud.google.com/bigtable/docs/schema-design#row-keys-avoid`.

Another important aspect of Bigtable is that the service is available. If a node in a Bigtable cluster is down, you don't need to worry about the data. Data in Bigtable is separated from the compute, meaning that if one of the nodes goes down, then the data won't be lost.

Memorystore

Memorystore is a managed service for Redis and Memcached in-memory databases. Both Redis and Memcached function similarly to store cache data in memory, and both are open-source technologies. Memorystore is relevant to application development and is not for data analytics.

The common use case for Memorystore is when applications frequently access a subset of data and require an extremely high latency to read. This can be done, for example, by exporting a subset of data from Cloud SQL to Memorystore in the key-value pair format. Since the data in Cloud SQL is stored on disk and data in Memorystore is stored in memory, Memorystore will naturally improve the read latency significantly.

Dataprep

Dataprep is a tool that's used for data preparation and is developed by Trifacta. Data preparation can include analyzing data to understand its distribution, finding outliers, data cleansing, and data transformation. The difference between using Dataprep and our approach of using Cloud Composer and BigQuery operators is the expected user experience. In Dataprep, a user can do data preparation using a **Graphical User Interface** (**GUI**) and require no code. This is a good option when there is no one in an organization who can code but needs to do data analytics.

Now, let's use the knowledge we've gained in this section and all the chapters in this book for the next section's quiz.

Cloud Data Fusion

Cloud Data Fusion is an ETL tool that helps data engineers extract, transform, and load data on GCP. The technology is based on an open-source project called **CDAP**.

Compared to Cloud Composer, Data Fusion is the right option if the data engineering team prefers point-and-click GUI. It comes with many connectors to extract and load data. The transformation mainly relies on Dataproc or using push-down, for example, to BigQuery execution.

Compared to Dataprep, the positioning is similar, which allows users to use the GUI to develop an ETL pipeline. The difference is in the user experience and compatibility; Cloud Data Fusion has a user experience that is built for data engineers, with a lot more connectors and compatibility with Dataproc. Dataprep has a user experience that is built for data analysts or data scientists who need quick data cleansing, which some people call data wrangling.

Data Transfer Service

This service is required when a company migrates its data from outside to inside GCP. Many approaches can be chosen when you're moving data to GCP, and the common pattern is moving data to Cloud Storage.

One of the main considerations when moving data to Cloud Storage is the data's size. If you're transferring data that's less than 1 TB in size, you can use the `gsutil` command. We used this command in some of our exercises. However, if you need to transfer more than 1 TB of data, you can use a service called **Storage Transfer Service** on GCP. Finally, if you need to transfer data more than 100 TB of data at once, you need Transfer Appliance. Transfer Appliance is a physical appliance for moving offline data that can be used for more than 100 TB of data.

Cloud Logging and Cloud Monitoring

Cloud Logging is an out-of-the-box service on GCP that logs all of your GCP services. This is useful for checking errors, warnings, or historical usage from users. You can find Cloud Logging in the **Navigation** menu on your GCP console. What is important about Cloud Logging regarding the certification is that you know that Cloud Logging captured logs from GCP services. You can also export cloud logging to other storage options, such as Cloud Storage, BigQuery, and Pub/Sub.

Cloud Monitoring is an out-of-the-box service on GCP that can be used to monitor GCP services. Cloud Monitoring is highly configurable for each different service. You can configure your monitoring dashboards using Metrics Explorer.

Cloud Monitoring works by metrics – for example, to monitor Dataflow's current number of vcpu running, you can use the `job/current_num_vcpus` metric. There are hundreds of metrics available that you can check out at this link: `https://cloud.google.com/monitoring/api/metrics_gcp`.

For the certification, it's important to be familiar with the metrics available in the data engineer core services, such as Dataflow and BigQuery.

Analytics Hub

Analytics Hub is a data exchange service that supports BigQuery datasets. This service is useful when an organization decides to practice data sharing across business units and with external parties. The service will help simplify the IAM permission, help secure the data, and track the data published and subscriptions.

Now, let's proceed with a quiz!

Quiz – reviewing all the concepts you've learned about

In this section, I will give you examples of what the Google Cloud Data Engineer Certification questions look like. The 12 example questions are grouped into 5 categories.

I will list all the questions first; the key answers will be provided in the next section, after the 12th question.

Questions

Each question has four options, and you need to choose the correct answer.

Designing data processing systems

Choose one answer for each of the questions in this section:

1. Your company is implementing a data pipeline to load data from the source system to thousands of BigQuery tables. There is a new regulation that there can't be phone number data in any datasets. As a data engineer, you need to report how many tables in BigQuery contain phone number information. You need to do it as fast as possible with minimum effort. How are you going to find the information?

    A. Develop a Dataflow script in Java. Use regular expressions to access all BigQuery tables. Report the number of matched patterns from the Dataflow job.

    B. Create a template with the phone number **Infotype** in SDP or DLP. Run **Discovery** at the organization level to all BigQuery datasets. Use the report from the SDP console.

    C. Define `PolicyTag` in BigQuery column-level security. Make sure all columns that name phone numbers use `PolicyTag`.

    D. Access the BigQuery information schema table. Find the columns that contain the phone number. Report from the query result.

2. Your company runs a variety of Spark jobs on an on-premises cluster. You are planning to migrate to GCP quickly and easily. What kind of deployment would you recommend?

    A. Deploy a Cloud Dataproc cluster to run Spark jobs.

    B. Run Spark and Hadoop jobs in Cloud Dataflow.

    C. Migrate HDFS files to Cloud Storage. Load data from Cloud Storage into BigQuery. Convert all the Spark jobs into BigQuery SQL.

    D. Run new jobs on a custom Spark deployment in Compute Engine but run legacy jobs on a Cloud Dataproc cluster.

3. Your company implements a data and analytics ecosystem using a Cloud Storage bucket and BigQuery. There are three different types of users – data administrators, data providers, and data readers. What should you do to make sure each user gets the required permissions?

    A. Assign IAM roles for each user to Cloud Storage predefined roles and BigQuery predefined roles on both Cloud Storage and BigQuery individually.

    B. Assign a primitive Owner role to the administrator at the project level and a primitive Editor role to the data providers and the data readers.

    C. Create three custom IAM roles with the appropriate policies for the access levels needed for Cloud Storage and BigQuery. Add these users to the custom roles.

    D. Assign a primitive Owner role to the administrator at the organization level and the primitive Editor role to the data providers and the data readers.

Let's continue to the second section.

Ingesting and processing data

Choose one answer for each of the questions in this section:

4. Your company has multiple systems that all need to be notified of orders being processed. How should you configure Pub/Sub?

    A. Create a topic for orders. Create multiple subscriptions for this topic, one for each system that needs to be notified.

    B. Create a topic for orders. Create a subscription for this topic that can be shared by every system that needs to be notified.

    C. Create a new topic for each order. Create multiple subscriptions for each topic, one for every system that needs to be notified.

    D. Create a new topic for each order. Create a subscription for each topic that can be shared by every system that needs to be notified.

5. Your company has multiple MySQL databases on Cloud SQL. You need to export all the data into Cloud Storage and BigQuery for analysis. Once the data has been loaded into BigQuery, you need to apply multiple data transformations for the business users. You need to repeat all these processes every day at 5 A.M. How should you approach this?

    A. Use Pub/Sub and Dataflow to process and schedule the required transformation.

    B. Create a Cloud Composer environment. Develop DAGs that extract data from Cloud SQL and load them into Cloud Storage and BigQuery. Apply the transformation using a BigQuery operator and schedule the DAG as per the requirements.

    C. Configure a Dataproc Spark job to load the data from Cloud SQL and schedule the job using Hadoop.

    D. Configure a compute engine to create Python scripts to handle all the processes. Use crontab to schedule the script's execution daily.

6. Your company needs to be able to handle logs streaming data. The logs come from multiple devices, and you need to be able to process and store them. The final output will be used for data analytics purposes. What services should they use for this task?

    A. Cloud Logging, Cloud Dataproc, and Cloud Spanner

    B. Kubernetes Engine, Cloud Dataflow, and Cloud Datastore

    C. Cloud Pub/Sub, Cloud Dataproc, and Bigtable

    D. Cloud Pub/Sub, Cloud Dataflow, and BigQuery

Let's continue to the third section.

Storing the data

Choose one answer for each of the questions in this section:

7. Your company is planning to choose a managed database service in Google Cloud. The database will be used to serve as a web application that handles product catalogs. Your database is 500 GB in size. The data is semi-structured. Which storage option should you choose?

    A. Cloud Bigtable

    B. Cloud SQL

    C. BigQuery

    D. Cloud Datastore

8. You worked in a large organization with four different business units. All of the data teams managed their BigQuery datasets and GCS buckets in multiple projects. This resulted in an overly complex process to manage and find the data that can be used by other users. The chief data officer wants to improve the data governance issues with a minimum development effort. How will you solve this?

    A. Migrate all datasets and GCS buckets from the business units to a fresh new GCP project.

    B. Run a DLP Discovery at the organization level to find the info types of each BigQuery column.

    C. Implement Dataplex and create lakes for each business unit. Simplify the Identity and Access Management (IAM) for all BigQuery datasets and GCS buckets using Dataplex. Allow the users to search datasets using the Dataplex Catalog.

    D. Implement Data Fusion to create a visible data pipeline from a centralized GUI.

Let's continue to the fourth section.

Preparing and using data for analysis

Choose one answer for each of the questions in this section:

9. You are using Looker Studio to present a report that uses live user interaction data from BigQuery. One of the business users has found that the data in the report is not up to date. What should you recommend to them?

    A. Contact the infrastructure team to check whether there are any issues with the Looker Studio instance.

    B. Click the **Refresh Data** button on the Looker Studio report to clear the BigQuery cache.

C. Recreate the underlying BigQuery table.

D. Clear the browser cookies and reload the Looker Studio web page.

10. You are building a machine-learning model. You have found that the model performs very well on training data but very poorly on new data. What is the potential issue in this case?

   A. There is not enough data in the training set.

   B. There are insufficient infrastructure resources assigned to the model.

   C. There is not enough data in the validation set – the model has been overfitted.

   D. There is not enough data in the test set – the model has an implicit bias.

Let's continue to the last section.

Maintaining and automating data workloads

11. Your company has used BigQuery to store data for more than one year. Some queries need to access the full historical data, but most of the queries only need to access the last 10 days' worth of data. Over time, the cost of the queries keeps rising. What can you do to optimize the query's cost?

   A. Use integer range partitioned tables.

   B. Create a new table every 10 days. Use `JOIN` statements to conduct long-term analytics queries.

   C. Ensure that the BigQuery table uses date partitioned tables and the partitioned column used in the queries.

   D. Use Cloud Composer to automatically archive data that is more than 10 days old in Google Cloud Storage.

12. Your company is considering using Bigtable. What will happen to data in a Bigtable instance if one node goes down?

   A. Lost data will automatically rebuild itself from Cloud Storage backups when the node comes back online.

   B. Data will be lost, which makes regular backups to Cloud Storage necessary.

   C. Bigtable will attempt to rebuild the data from the RAID disk configuration when the node comes back online.

   D. Nothing, as the storage is separate from the node compute.

Answers

Here are the answers. Check whether you answered the questions correctly. For each answer, I have mentioned the relevant chapter from this book:

1. The correct answer is *B*. The question is about finding the phone number data in the organization. SDP or DLP is the easiest approach to get this information. Review *Chapter 10, Data Governance in GCP*.

2. The correct answer is *A*. Pay attention to keywords such as *Spark jobs* and *quickly and easily*. Dataproc is the best technology in GCP for running Spark jobs. The other options are possible, but they require a lot of unnecessary effort. Review *Chapter 2, Big Data Capabilities on GCP*.

3. The correct answer is *A*. Granting permissions to users for specific GCP services is recommended compared to doing so at the organization or project level. Also, if possible, using predefined roles is simpler compared to custom IAM roles. Review *Chapter 9, User and Project Management in GCP*.

4. The correct answer is *A*. Remember that a Pub/Sub topic can handle multiple publishers and subscribers, so you only need one topic. The multiple systems need to be notified individually so that you can create multiple subscriptions – one subscription for each downstream system. Review *Chapter 6, Processing Streaming Data with Pub/Sub and Dataflow*.

5. The correct answer is *B*. Cloud Composer is the best option for orchestrating multiple steps of tasks from multiple GCP services. Cloud Composer is also able to handle scheduling. Review *Chapter 4, Building Workflows for Batch Data Loading Using Cloud Composer*.

6. The correct answer is *D*. For streaming data, we can use Pub/Sub to handle ever-increasing amounts of telemetry data. Pub/Sub can't process data, so we need Dataflow to process it. When it comes to analyzing the data, BigQuery is the best option. Review *Chapter 6, Processing Streaming Data with Pub/Sub and Dataflow*.

7. The correct answer is *D*. There are three key points as per the requirements in the question – a database needs to serve web applications, the database's size is 500 GB, and the data is semi-structured. BigQuery won't be suitable for serving web applications. Bigtable is suitable for data above 10 TB. Cloud SQL can't handle semi-structured data, so Cloud Datastore is the best option. Review the data life cycle from *Chapter 1, Fundamentals of Data Engineering*, and *Chapter 13, Boosting Your Confidence as a Data Engineer*, in the *Extra GCP service materials* section about Datastore.

8. The correct answer is *C*. Dataplex can help BigQuery IAM by forming lakes on top of BigQuery datasets and GCS buckets. In addition, Dataplex Catalog can help data users to search for data using keywords.

9. The correct answer is *B*. There is a **Refresh Data** button in Data Studio that can be used to clear the BigQuery cache and refresh the data. No additional action is needed. Review *Chapter 7, Visualizing Data to Make Data-Driven Decisions with Looker Studio*.

10. The correct answer is C. The model has been too well trained on the training data and will fit it too closely, so it will perform badly when it's exposed to real-world data for predictions. Increasing the amount of data can help to reduce this overfitting. Review *Chapter 8, Building Machine Learning Solutions on GCP*, and additional resources from the public internet about basic machine learning models – for example, `https://towardsdatascience.com/what-are-overfitting-and-underfitting-in-machine-learning-a96b30864690`.

11. The correct answer is C. In BigQuery, using the `DATE`-partitioned tables can reduce the cost of queries based on the date filters, which in the given question is 10 days of data. Review *Chapter 3, Building a Data Warehouse in BigQuery*, and the Tips for optimizing BigQuery using partitioned and clustered tables section in *Chapter 11, Cost Strategy in GCP*.

12. The correct answer is D. In Bigtable, storage and compute are separate. This topic is not discussed in depth in any of the chapters in this book, so check out the *Extra GCP service materials* section in *Chapter 13, Boosting Your Confidence as a Data Engineer*.

I hope this gives you an illustration of what the exam questions look like and that you can summarize what you've learned in this book. Remember that this book is only one tool for you to get prepared. Check the official website and other resources to be 100% ready to take the Google Cloud Data Engineer certification.

In the next section, I will share my opinion on the future of data engineering.

The past, present, and future of data engineering

The data engineering practice has been there since the early internet era in the 1990s. Going back to *Chapter 1, Fundamentals of Data Engineering*, in the *Start with knowing the roles of a data engineer* section, in the past, data engineers were mostly ETL developers using specific tools. Most of these tools were proprietary tools and located on-premises. The term *data engineer* itself wasn't commonplace; the more common terms used to be data modelers, database admin, and *ETL* developer (*ETL* references the proprietary ETL tool's name). Each of the ETL tools had the necessary expertise and best practices surrounding them.

Now, in the present, data engineering has evolved into a more mature and singular role. This means that the practice is receiving a lot more common principles, concepts, and best practices. This is due to two reasons – the rapid improvement in the technologies supporting the practice and the fact that data engineering has become a critical and central role to organizations.

"Data engineering-specific interviews increased by 40% in the past year," according to a 2020 report from the `interviewquery.com` website. The platform analyzes 10,000 data science-related interview experiences, specifically looking at how COVID-19 changed data science interviews in 2020. Data engineering remains the top data science job, with an incredibly significant year-over-year growth. Check out the full report here: `https://www.interviewquery.com/p/data-science-interview-report`.

I have to say that the present day is the best time for anyone who wishes to become a data engineer.

The words *big data* and *the cloud* are no longer considered as the future – they are the present. If you are looking for jobs in data engineering, you must have strong knowledge of both of these. If you are a representative from a company that is looking for data engineers, you must ask the candidates about these two words. This is unavoidable and has become a new norm because they represent the present.

Now, what does the future look like?

There are two aspects of which I can think. The first is the technology aspect, while the second is the role aspect:

- From a technological perspective, now, in 2024, the adoption from on-premises to the cloud is still happening. It's still an uptrend, but it's still far from the peak. Currently, it's not a question for start-up companies to use the cloud compared to managing their on-premises systems. However, when it reaches its peak, traditional companies such as banking corporations and the government will adopt the cloud – not only in certain countries but globally.

    The advancement in data security, data governance, and multi-cloud environments is essential. As you may already know, the regulation for data has been maturing in a lot of countries in the last few years. The data and cloud technologies need to keep adapting to these regulations, especially when it comes to financial industries. On top of that, the capabilities to integrate data and technologies across cloud platforms and on-premises systems will become more mature.

    The current surge in interest surrounding generative AI is poised to have a decidedly positive impact on the data engineering ecosystem. Much like the 2014 enthusiasm for machine learning, which significantly elevated the awareness of big data, the current hype around generative AI is set to heighten awareness regarding the crucial role of data engineering. Companies will increasingly recognize and appreciate the importance of robust data engineering practice.

- The second aspect is the data engineer role. This role will go back to being a non-singular role. There will be clearer and more specific roles compared to the *data engineer* role. Companies will start to realize that the data engineer roles can be broken down into more granular roles. It will be easier for them to find good candidates for specific needs.

    One other thing about the role is about who will write SQL queries. In the past, and still in the present, data engineers are the ones who take full responsibility for writing SQL queries to transform business logic into answers. It is starting now and will occur more in the future – non-engineers will be SQL-savvy people. The non-engineers can include the marketing team, the human resources department, C-level, or any other role. They are the best at understanding the business context and gain the most benefit when they can access data directly via databases using SQL. One example is the appearance of a new popular role called *analytics engineer*, which was discussed at `getdbt.com`. Check out the blog post here: `https://www.getdbt.com/what-is-analytics-engineering`.

For data engineers, this means that the role will be more focused on shaping the data foundation, which may include data architecture, governance, and the data pipelines. In terms of ELT, the extract and load process will still be handled by data engineers, but the majority of the transformation process will probably be taken over by non-data engineers. Going back to what I mentioned previously, data engineers will need to be more focused on designing and developing data security and data governance as a foundation.

Knowing that the future of the data engineer role is very bright, now it's your turn to be one of the experts. In the last section of this book, I will share my final thoughts.

Boosting your confidence and final thoughts

One thing that I hope you get after reading this book is more confidence – the confidence to design and develop a data pipeline and, more importantly, the confidence as a data engineer to use GCP.

I will quote the definition of the word *confidence* in a physiological context by the *American Psychological Association*: "*Confidence is Self-assurance: trust in one's abilities, capacities, and judgment.*"

By following all the chapters throughout the book, you've learned about the important GCP services related to data engineering and tried them out in your environment by completing the hands-on exercises provided. You've tried 19 new technologies from GCP, including BigQuery, GCS, Cloud Composer, Dataproc, Dataflow, Pub/Sub, Cloud SQL, Dataplex, Dataform, Data Loss Prevention or Sensitive Data Protection, Looker Studio, Vertex AI, IAM, Cloud Shell, Cloud Editor, Cloud Build, Google Container Registry, Cloud Source Repository, and Terraform.

These are your new abilities, and I have to tell you that these abilities are in remarkably high demand! I suggest that you start implementing your data projects using these technologies, outside of what we've tried in the exercises.

Back to the definition of confidence – the second factor is capacities. It is correlated to your experience. Depending on how much experience you gained when reading this book, if you are someone who is just starting the journey, always remember to start small. You've learned that the topics in terms of *Data Engineering with Google Cloud Platform* are very wide. Adding those topics to the number of other materials that you need to learn for the Google Cloud Data Engineer certification might be discouraging if you are new in this space. My suggestion is, don't be!

The broad landscape of data engineering is there for many data experts to collaborate. Depending on how big an organization is, it's quite common for a data engineer to focus on one aspect of data engineering. For example, many roles in the market require you to only know about BigQuery, just Hadoop (Dataproc), or other specific tools. If you have just started, I suggest that you start with those roles as a small step, and then build and grow your capacities. Then, one day, you won't realize you know most of these things.

Finally, believing in your judgment is also part of gaining confidence. I have to say that good judgment in data engineering is highly dependent on the first two factors in the definitions of confidence – abilities and capacities. But in addition, most of the time, you need to go back to the fundamental principles. For example, in this book, we talked about some principles such as the principle of least privilege, the data modeling principle for data warehouses, and ETL versus ELT. My suggestion is to go back to the fundamental principles whenever you're in doubt.

Summary

In this chapter, we conclude everything we've learned throughout this book. We started the chapter by overviewing the certification options from Google Cloud. There, we covered most of the GCP services that are part of the certification. But for those that weren't, I suggest that you take a look at those services by looking at other resources.

In the next section, we looked at some quiz questions to help you gain a better understanding of the types of questions that will be asked and the format of the certification. I highly suggest that you review the other chapters if you missed some points from any of these questions.

Finally, I shared my thoughts on the past, present, and future of data engineering. Do remember that big data and the cloud are present concepts. You, as a data engineer, are and will be the center of it. Today is the best era for data engineering, and I'm 100% confident in this. I hope that you enjoyed reading this book and have a great data engineering journey with Google Cloud Platform.

Index

A

Access Control List (ACLs) 307, 331
accountability 345
    clear traceability 346, 347
acknowledge (ack) 200
Airflow 110
    backfilling 143
    catchup 143
    rerun 143
    used, for loading bike-sharing tables 138-142
    working 111, 112
Airflow dataset 154-157
    used, for handling DAG dependency 150-152
Airflow deferrable 155
Airflow jobs
    task idempotency for incremental load 149, 150
Airflow macro variables 137
Airflow sensor 153-155
Airflow smart sensor 155
Airflow web UI 115-118
analytics
    services 36, 37

analytics engineer 433
Analytics Hub 101, 426
Apache Beam
    used, for creating HelloWorld application 210-217
Application Default Credentials (ADCs) 274
application programming interface (API) 111, 298
artificial intelligence (AI) 4, 259
automatic deployment 394
automatic integration 394
AutoML 271
    GCP, using to train ML model 276-280

B

backfilling 143
Bash scripts 111
batch prediction
    creating, with training dataset output 266, 267
BI Engine 252, 255-258
    working 252-255
big data 4, 15, 21
    used, for storing data 16

BigQuery 23, 43, 44, 111, 233, 382-384
  column-level access control,
    setting up 331-335
  data location 45, 46
  result, checking in 231
BigQuery ACLs
  planning, on eCommerce
    organization 308-311
BigQuery clustered tables 384, 387, 389
  optimizing 384
BigQuery console 46-48
  dataset, creating 48, 49
  data types, comparing to databases 53, 54
  local CSV file, loading into
    BigQuery table 49, 51
  public data, using 51-53
  timestamp data, comparing to databases 55
BigQuery console, sub-menu options 100
  Analytics Hub 101, 102
  assessment 102
  BI Engine 102
  BigQuery routine 102
  capacity management 102
  dataform 102
  data transfers 101
  migration 102
  monitoring 102
  policy tags 102
  scheduled queries 101
  SQL translation 102
BigQuery cost
  impacting, from Looker Studio 250
BigQuery DAG
  Python configuration file, avoiding 131
BigQuery data mart
  creating 70, 71
BigQuery data masking 337-339

BigQuery dataset
  configuring, with Terraform 316, 317
  creating 228
BigQuery editions 372
  versus BigQuery on-demand 371
BigQuery features 99, 100
BigQuery ML 271
BigQuery on-demand 371
  cost optimization 390, 391
  versus BigQuery editions 371
BigQuery operator
  GCS storage, using 128, 129
  using, for data transformation 129-131
**BigQuery partitioned
  table** 103-105, 384-387
  optimizing 384
BigQuery partitioning
  concept 148
BigQuery public dataset
  machine learning (ML) dataset,
    preparing with table 262-264
  used, for creating data transformation
    in Dataform 360-366
BigQuery Python library
  avoiding 132
BigQuery query's performance 372, 373
BigQuery quotas
  reference link 39
BigQuery routine 102
  remote functions 103
  stored procedure 102
  table functions 103
  user-defined function (UDF) 103
BigQuery slots
  autoscaling 373-376
  reference link 372
Bigtable 424

Index

bike-sharing tables
  loading, with Airflow 138-142
bike-sharing tasks
  dependencies, handling 142, 143
bitshift operators 112
block 387
Business Intelligence (BI) 151
business tags 328

C

catchup 144, 145
CDAP technology 425
Change Data Capture (CDC) 36, 225
cheap storage 7
Chief Data Officer (CDO) 377
chief executive officer (CEO) 197
CI/CD
  best practices, in data engineering 414-416
CI/CD components
  with GCP services 396, 397
CI/CD environment
  preparing 408
CI/CD practices
  data engineer's relationship with 394, 395
CI/CD result
  checking, in Cloud Composer 411-414
  checking, in GCS bucket 411-414
CI pipeline, with Cloud Build
  Cloud Build trigger, creating 403
  Cloud Source Repository, used for creating GitHub repository 398-400
  code, developing 400-403
  code, pushing to GitHub repository 404-406
  scripts, developing 400-403
clear data ownership 347, 348
clear data quality process 349, 350
clear traceability 346, 347

cloud 22
  services 23
  versus non-cloud 22, 23
Cloud Build pipeline
  scripts, developing 401-403
  used, for deploying Cloud Composer jobs 407
  used, for implementing CI 398
Cloud Build trigger
  creating 403
cloudbuild.yaml configuration file
  preparing 408-411
Cloud Composer 40, 109-111, 381, 382
  bucket directories 118, 119
  CI/CD result, checking in 411-414
  DAG file, deploying 123-126
  data download, avoiding 132, 133
  Level 1 DAG 120-123
  Level 2 DAG 126, 127
  Level 3 DAG 133
  Level 4 DAG 146
  Level 5 DAG 150-152
  provisioning, in GCP project 113-115
  task idempotency 146
  used, for building data pipeline orchestration 119
  used, for building ephemeral cluster 190-192
  variable types 134-137
Cloud Composer 1 113
  versus Cloud Composer 2 113
Cloud Composer 2 113
  versus Cloud Composer 1 113
Cloud Composer Console 114, 115
Cloud Composer jobs
  deploying, with Cloud Build pipeline 407
Cloud Composer jobs, with Cloud Build
  CI/CD environment, preparing 408
  CI/CD result, checking in Cloud Composer 411-414

CI/CD result, checking in GCS bucket 411-414
cloudbuild.yaml configuration file, preparing 408-411
DAG, pushing to GitHub repository 411
cloud computing 4
Cloud Data Fusion 425
Cloud Editor 44
Cloud Logging 426
Cloud Monitoring 426
Cloud Shell 44, 171, 298
used, for running Terraform scripts 314, 315
Cloud Shell Editor 298
Cloud Source Repository (CSR) 400
used, for creating GitHub repository 398-400
Cloud SQL 43, 139
MySQL database, creating 62
Cloud SQL operator
using, to extract GCS bucket data 127, 128
Cloud Storage 380
reference link 39
code
developing 400-403
code-based approach
versus GCP console 72, 73
Colossus 45
column-level access control
setting up, in BigQuery 331-335
comma-separated values (CSV) 127
commitment model 371
Connection 228
continuous deployment (CD) 394
continuous integration (CI) 394
implementing, with Cloud Build 398
continuous integration/continuous deployment (CI/CD) 393, 394
Control-M 111

CronJob format
reference link 121
Customer Managed Encryption Key (CMEK) 330
Customer Supplied Encryption Key (CSEK) 331

D

DAG
pushing, to GitHub repository 411
DAG dependency
handling, with Airflow dataset 150-152
DAG file
deploying, into Cloud Composer 123-126
DAG Run 112
data analysis
preparing 429
using 429
data analytics 3
data architecture 3
data definition language (DDL) 63, 323
data description language (DDL) 390
data download
avoiding, to Cloud Composer 132, 133
data encryption 330
data engineering (DE) 3, 151, 432, 433
CI/CD, best practices 414-416
data life cycle flow 11-13
roles 9, 10
versus data scientist (DS) 10, 11
data engineering (DE), concepts 13
big data 15
big data, used for storing data 16
ETL 13
MapReduce 17-19

Index   441

data engineering (DE), use case 377, 378
  BigQuery 382-384
  Cloud Composer 381, 382
  Cloud Storage 380
  dataflow 379
  Dataproc 380, 381
  Pub/Sub 379
data engineer's relationship
  with CI/CD practices 394, 395
data extraction 351
Dataflow 17, 195, 200, 201, 379
  using, to stream data from Pub/
    Sub to GCS 210
Dataflow job
  running, from Dataflow template 231
Dataflow streaming job
  creating, with aggregation 222-224
  creating, without aggregation 217-222
Dataform 102, 322
  data transformation, creating with
    BigQuery public dataset 360-366
  used, for practicing data quality 351, 352
Dataform environment 352, 353
  creating 353-359
DataFrame concepts 163
data governance 320-322
data ingesting 428
data lake 5, 160, 161
  building, on Dataproc cluster 167
  versus data warehouse 6, 7
data lake, concept 164
  data loading 165, 166
  data storage 164
  distributed file process 165
data lakehouse 166
data life cycle 4, 7
  elements 8
data lineage 348, 349

Data Lineage API 348
data loading 351
Data Loss Prevention (DLP) 339
data manipulation language (DML) 323
data masking 335, 336
data modeling 85-87
  business questions result,
    storing in table 98, 99
  dimension table, creating 94, 96
  fact table, creating 94, 96
  for BigQuery 92-94
  Inmon method versus Kimball
    method 89-92
  purpose 88, 89
  with nested data types 96-98
data pipeline orchestration
  building, with Cloud Composer 119
Dataplex 323
  functionalities 323
  used, for implementing metadata tag 324
Dataprep 425
Dataproc 33, 159, 160, 380, 381
  used, for building ephemeral cluster 190-192
Dataproc cluster
  creating, on GCP 167-169
  jobs, creating 177
  jobs, running 177
  log data, preparing in GCS 178
  log data, preparing in HDFS 178
  Spark ETL job, developing from
    GCS to BigQuery 184, 185
  Spark ETL job, developing from
    GCS to GCS 182, 183
  Spark ETL job, developing from
    HDFS to HDFS 179-181
  used, for building data lake 167
data process
  avoiding, in Python 133

data processing systems 428
  designing 427
Dataproc filesystem
  Google Cloud Storage (GCS), using 169
Dataproc master node shell 171
Dataproc metastore (DPMS) 323
Dataproc positioning
  on GCP 166, 167
Dataproc Serverless 167
  Spark ETL job, submitting from GCS to BigQuery 192-194
data protection 331
  Access Control List (ACLs) 331
  column-level access control, setting up in BigQuery 331-335
data quality
  practicing, with Dataform 351, 352
data scientist (DS) 151
  versus data engineering (DE) 10, 11
data security 329
  data encryption 330
  data masking 336
  data protection 331
dataset 150
data silos 5
data storing 429
Datastream 225, 226
Datastream ETL streaming to BigQuery, best practices
  CloudSQL MySQL table, creating 226
  Dataflow job, running from Dataflow template 231
  dataset, creating 228
  GCS bucket, creating 227
  GCS notification, creating to Pub/Sub topic and subscription 227
  job, configuring 228-230

  result, checking 231
  value, inserting in MySQL 231
Datastream job
  configuring 228-230
data transfers 101
Data Transfer Service (DTS) 101, 425
data transformation
  BigQuery operator, using 129-131
  creating, in Dataform with BigQuery public dataset 360-366
data usability 322
data visualization 233
data warehouse (DWH) 43, 151
  BigQuery requirements for scenario 1 60
  BigQuery requirements for scenario 1, handling 61
  BigQuery requirements for scenario 2 72
  BigQuery requirements for scenario 2, handling 73, 74
  concept 5
  developing 59
  GCP console, versus code-based approach 72, 73
  need for 4, 5
  used, for creating Looker Studio report 241-250
  user access control 307
  versus data lake 6, 7
data warehouse (DWH), BigQuery requirements for scenario 1
  BigQuery data mart, creating 70, 71
  GCS, loading to BigQuery 69, 70
  MySQL database, creating in CloudSQL 62
  MySQL database, extracting to GCS 65-68
data warehouse (DWH), BigQuery requirements for scenario 2
  daily batch data loading handling for stations table 80- 82

daily batch data loading handling
for trips table 78, 79
data modeling designing 84, 85
regions table loading 77, 78
trips table loading 75, 76
data warehouse (DWH), prerequisites
Cloud Shell, accessing 56
current setup, checking with
command line 56
data, uploading to GCS from Git 58
example data, downloading from Git 57
gcloud init command, initializing 57
preparing 56
data workloads
automating 430
maintaining 430
decision maker 198
denormalized table 89
dependencies
handling, for bike-sharing tasks 142, 143
**development and operations
(DevOps) 317, 395**
development environment (DEV) 415
dimension table 90
directed acyclic graph (DAG) 112, 190
distributed file system (DFS) 161
Dremel SQL 45
dummy workflow
deploying, with Vertex AI Pipelines 281, 282

E

eCommerce organization
BigQuery ACLs, planning 308-311
endpoints 267
end-to-end data solution
cost estimation, in GCP 369

enterprise data warehouse 89
ephemeral cluster 23, 185, 186
advantages 185
building, with Cloud Composer 190-192
building, with Dataproc 190-192
concept 185
workflow template, practicing
on Dataproc 187-189
event streams
publishing, to Pub/Sub 201
Extract, Load, and Transform (ELT) 13
versus Extract, Transform,
and Load (ETL) 14
**Extract, Transform, and Load
(ETL) 10, 111, 332**
concept 13
versus Extract, Load, and
Transform (ELT) 14

F

fact table 90
flat-rate 372
fully managed services 33

G

GCP console 44, 298
versus code-based approach 72, 73
GCP folder 303-305
GCP model service
detect text function, creating
in Python 274, 275
image, uploading to GCS bucket 272, 273
using 272
GCP organization 303-305
IAM and GCP service requirements 305

GCP organization, projects 305
   cost tracking 306
   limits and quotas 306
GCP permission types
   access permissions 307
   job permissions 307
GCP project
   Cloud Composer, provisioning 113-115
   hierarchy 303-305
   managing, with Terraform 317
   structure, planning 301, 302
GCP resources
   managing, with Terraform 317
GCP service materials 422
   Analytics Hub 426
   Bigtable 422-424
   Cloud Data Fusion 425
   Cloud Logging 426
   Cloud Monitoring 426
   Dataprep 425
   Datastore 422-424
   Data Transfer Service 425
   Memorystore 425
   Spanner 422-424
GCS bucket
   CI/CD result, checking in 411-414
   creating 58, 227
   information, entering 58, 59
   local file, uploading with gcloud 59
GCS notification
   creating, to Pub/Sub topic and subscription 227
GCS storage
   using, for BigQuery operator 128, 129
GitHub repository
   code, pushing 404-406
   creating, with Cloud Source Repository 398-400

   DAG, pushing 411
Git operations (GitOps) 352
Google App Engine (GAE) 300
Google Cloud
   pricing calculator 376, 377
Google Cloud certification
   exam preparation tips 420-422
   overviewing 419, 420
Google Cloud Data Engineer 420
Google Cloud Engine (GCE) 370
Google Cloud Platform (GCP) 13, 21, 23, 24, 109, 159, 195, 234, 297, 319, 419
   CI/CD components 396, 397
   Cloud Shell, using 30-32
   console 25, 26
   Identity and Access Management (IAM) 298-301
   pinning services 26, 27
   project, creating 28, 29
   using, in AutoML to train ML model 276-280
Google Cloud Platform (GCP) services 269-272
   for data engineering 32
   quotas concept 38, 39
   serverless services 33-35
   service mapping and prioritization 35-38
   user account, versus service account 39, 40
Google Cloud Storage (GCS) 43, 44, 110, 111, 160, 370, 420
   data, loading to HDFS 171, 172
   file, accessing from PySpark 177
   HDFS, accessing from Hadoop node shell 170, 171
   HDFS file, accessing from PySpark 173-175
   Hive table, creating on HDFS 172
   loading, to BigQuery 69, 70
   using, as Dataproc filesystem 169

Google Cloud Vision 272
Google Colossus 45
Google Compute Engine (GCE) 33
Google Container Registry (GCR) 402
Google File System (GFS) 161
Google Kubernetes Engine (GKE) 300
Google Managed Encryption
    Key (GMEK) 330
Graphical User Interface (GUI) 425

H

Hadoop 6, 139
Hadoop cluster 162
Hadoop components 161, 162
    distributed file system (DFS) 161
    MapReduce 161
    YARN 161
Hadoop Distributed File System
    (HDFS) 23, 45, 161
Hadoop ecosystem 160, 161
Hadoop positioning
    on GCP 166, 167
Hadoop use case
    in GCP 163
HelloWorld application
    creating, with Apache Beam 210-217
high scalability 7
hyperparameter tuning 265
Hypertext Preprocessor (PHP) 199
HyperText Transfer Protocol (HTTP) 207

I

identity and access management
    (IAM) 65, 127, 297
    account 299
    in GCP 298-301
    permission 299
    role 300
identity and management tools
    services 37
Illustrative use case 235
    INFORMATION_SCHEMA 236
    INFORMATION_SCHEMA table,
        accessing with Looker Studio 237-241
    Looker Studio report, creating from
        data warehouse 241-250
Informatica 111
INFORMATION_SCHEMA table
    accessing, with Looker Studio 237-241
infoTypes 339
Infrastructure as Code (IaC) 297, 311
    concept, practicing with Terraform 311
Inmon method
    versus Kimball method 89, 91, 92
input and output (I/O) 211
integrated development
    environment (IDE) 118
Internet Protocol (IP) address 214

J

JavaScript Object Notation (JSON) 128, 204

K

Key Management Service (KMS) 330
Kimball method
    versus Inmon method 89, 91, 92

L

Level 1 DAG 120-123
Level 2 DAG 126, 127
Level 3 DAG 133

Level 4 DAG 146
Level 5 DAG 150-152
Looker 235
Looker Studio 233-235
   BigQuery cost, impacting 250
   data warehouse 251
   table access 251, 252
   used, for accessing INFORMATION_SCHEMA table 237-241
Looker Studio Pro 235
   reference link 235
Looker Studio report
   creating, from data warehouse 241-250

M

machine learning and BI tools
   services 38
machine learning (ML) 3, 46, 131, 160, 259-261, 301
   accuracy/model performance 261
   batch prediction 262
   dataset 261
   features 261
   hyperparameter 261
   online prediction 262
   target 261
machine learning (ML) code 270
   practicing, with Python 262
machine learning (ML) dataset
   preparing, with table from BigQuery public dataset 262-264
machine learning (ML) model
   training, with Random Forest in Python 264-266
managed service 33
MapReduce 17-19, 161

Materialized Views 252
   creating 252-255
Memorystore 424
metadata tag
   assigning, to BigQuery table 325, 326
   data modeling for data usability 328, 329
   implementing, with Dataplex 324
   templates, creating in Dataplex catalog 324, 325
   used, for finding tables from Dataplex Search 327, 328
minimum viable product (MVP) 305
MLOps 268
   basic principles 268, 269
   GCP services 269, 270, 272
MySQL
   value, inserting in 231
MySQL database
   CloudSQL instance, creating 62
   creating 63
   creating, in CloudSQL 62
   CSV data, importing into 63-65
   extracting, to GCS 65-68
   MySQL instance, connecting 63
   table, creating 63

N

nested data types
   used, for data modeling 96-98
non-cloud
   versus cloud 22, 23
normalized table 89

O

object storage 44
Online Transaction Processing (OLTP) 85

Index   447

operator 112
Oracle 139
orchestrator 133

P

Parallel Do (ParDo) 214
parameterized variables 133
partitioned tables 103
personally identifiable
    information (PII) 331
  dummy table, creating from
    public dataset 340, 341
  finding, with SDP 339
  SDP Discovery configuration,
    creating 342, 343
  SDP Inspect template, creating 341, 342
policy tags 102, 331
Power BI 235
pre-built model 271
pricing model
  commitment model 371
  usage-based model 370
  Virtual Machine (VM)-based model 370
principle of least privilege 300
Pub/Sub 195, 199, 200, 379
  Dataflow, using to stream data
    from to GCS 210
  event streams, publishing to 201
  terminologies and flows 199, 200
  topic, creating 202, 203
Pub/Sub publisher
  creating and running, with Python 203-206
Pub/Sub topic and subscription
  GCS notification, creating to 227

PySpark 163
  resilient distributed dataset (RDD) 176
Python 111
  data process, avoiding 133
  machine learning (ML) model, training
    with Random Forest 264-266
  subscription, creating 206-210
  used, for creating Pub/Sub
    publisher 203-206
  used, for developing Vertex AI
    Pipelines 283-285
  used, for practicing machine
    learning (ML) code 262
  used, for running Pub/Sub
    publisher 203-206
Python API 72

Q

queries cost 376
quotas 38

R

random-access memory (RAM) 164
Random Forest 261
  used, for training machine learning
    (ML) model in Python 264-266
Relational Database Management
    System (RDBMS) 14
remote functions 103
rerun 144
Resilient Distributed Dataset
    (RDD) 163, 214
  in PySpark 176

S

schedule queries 101
scikit-learn model pipeline
    deploying, with Vertex AI Pipelines 287, 288
    ML model file, creating, in GCS 288-290
    model file, using from prediction results as CSV file in GCS 292
    running, in Vertex AI Pipelines 291-293
SDP Discovery result 344, 345
Secure Source Manager (SSM) 397
security
    services 38
Sensitive Data Protection (SDP) 339
    used, for finding personally identifiable information (PII) 339
Sensitive PII (SPII) 336
sensor 153
serverless services 33
service account
    versus user account 39
Simple Mail Transfer Protocol (SMTP) 112
snapshot data 80
    used, for handling loads 82-84
Software-as-a-Service (SaaS) 32
software development kit (SDK) 201
Spark 17
Spark cluster 23
Spark DataFrame 164
Spark ETL job
    submitting, from GCS to BigQuery with Dataproc Serverless 192-194
Spark RDD 163
SQL execution engine 45
SQL interface 45
SQL translation 102
storage and database
    services 37
Storage Transfer Service 425
stored procedure 102
streaming 46
streaming data
    processing 196-199
Structured Query Language (SQL) 130, 219
system integration 112
system integration testing environment (SIT) 415

T

Tableau 235
table functions 103
Talend 111
task idempotency 145-147
taxonomy 331
technical tags 328
Terraform 298, 311
    used, for configuring BigQuery dataset 316, 317
    used, for managing GCP project 317
    used, for managing GCP resources 317
    used, for practicing Infrastructure as Code (IaC) concept 311
    variables, using 313, 314
Terraform backend
    configuring, to GCS bucket 312
Terraform scripts
    creating 311
    downloading, to Cloud Shell 312
    running 311
    running, with Cloud Shell 314, 315
Tez 17
Trifacta 37

U

Uniform Resource Locator (URL) 214
United States dollars (USD) 115
usage-based model 370
user acceptance testing
　environment (UAT) 415
user account
　versus service account 39
user-defined function (UDF) 103
user-driven mindset 94
user interface (UI) 111, 311

V

variable types
　in Cloud Composer 134-137
Vertex AI batch predictions 267
Vertex AI online prediction 267
Vertex AI Pipelines 281
　developing, on Python 283-285
　GCS bucket, creating 282
　monitoring 286, 287
　used, for deploying dummy
　　workflow 281, 282
　used, for deploying scikit-learn
　　model pipeline 287, 288
virtual environment (venv) 212
virtual machine (VM) 33, 132, 160, 221, 268
Virtual Machine (VM)-based model 370

W

worker nodes 162
workflow template
　practicing, on Dataproc 187

Y

YARN 161

‹packt›

packtpub.com

Subscribe to our online digital library for full access to over 7,000 books and videos, as well as industry leading tools to help you plan your personal development and advance your career. For more information, please visit our website.

Why subscribe?

- Spend less time learning and more time coding with practical eBooks and Videos from over 4,000 industry professionals
- Improve your learning with Skill Plans built especially for you
- Get a free eBook or video every month
- Fully searchable for easy access to vital information
- Copy and paste, print, and bookmark content

Did you know that Packt offers eBook versions of every book published, with PDF and ePub files available? You can upgrade to the eBook version at packtpub.com and as a print book customer, you are entitled to a discount on the eBook copy. Get in touch with us at customercare@packtpub.com for more details.

At www.packtpub.com, you can also read a collection of free technical articles, sign up for a range of free newsletters, and receive exclusive discounts and offers on Packt books and eBooks.

Other Books You May Enjoy

If you enjoyed this book, you may be interested in these other books by Packt:

Data Engineering with Google Cloud Platform

Adi Wijaya

ISBN: 978-1-80056-132-8

- Load data into BigQuery and materialize its output for downstream consumption
- Build data pipeline orchestration using Cloud Composer
- Develop Airflow jobs to orchestrate and automate a data warehouse
- Build a Hadoop data lake, create ephemeral clusters, and run jobs on the Dataproc cluster
- Leverage Pub/Sub for messaging and ingestion for event-driven systems
- Use Dataflow to perform ETL on streaming data
- Unlock the power of your data with Data Studio
- Calculate the GCP cost estimation for your end-to-end data solutions

Database Design and Modeling with Google Cloud

Abirami Sukumaran

ISBN: 978-1-80461-145-6

- Understand different use cases and real-world applications of data in the cloud
- Work with document and indexed NoSQL databases
- Get to grips with modeling considerations for analytics, AI, and ML
- Use real-world examples to learn about ETL services
- Design structured, semi-structured, and unstructured data for your applications and analytics
- Improve observability, performance, security, scalability, latency SLAs, SLIs, and SLOs

Packt is searching for authors like you

If you're interested in becoming an author for Packt, please visit `authors.packtpub.com` and apply today. We have worked with thousands of developers and tech professionals, just like you, to help them share their insight with the global tech community. You can make a general application, apply for a specific hot topic that we are recruiting an author for, or submit your own idea.

Share Your Thoughts

Now you've finished *Data Engineering With Google Cloud Platform*, we'd love to hear your thoughts! Scan the QR code below to go straight to the Amazon review page for this book and share your feedback or leave a review on the site that you purchased it from.

`https://packt.link/r/1-835-08011-1`

Your review is important to us and the tech community and will help us make sure we're delivering excellent quality content.

Download a free PDF copy of this book

Thanks for purchasing this book!

Do you like to read on the go but are unable to carry your print books everywhere?

Is your eBook purchase not compatible with the device of your choice?

Don't worry, now with every Packt book you get a DRM-free PDF version of that book at no cost.

Read anywhere, any place, on any device. Search, copy, and paste code from your favorite technical books directly into your application.

The perks don't stop there, you can get exclusive access to discounts, newsletters, and great free content in your inbox daily

Follow these simple steps to get the benefits:

1. Scan the QR code or visit the link below

    https://packt.link/free-ebook/9781835080115

2. Submit your proof of purchase
3. That's it! We'll send your free PDF and other benefits to your email directly

Printed in Great Britain
by Amazon